Politics and Society in the Developing World
Third Edition

Peter Calvert and Susan Calvert

University of Southampton

D1103553

PEARSON
Longman

Harlow, England • London • New York • Boston • San Francisco • Toronto
Sydney • Tokyo • Singapore • Hong Kong • Seoul • Taipei • New Delhi
Cape Town • Madrid • Mexico City • Amsterdam • Munich • Paris • Milan

Pearson Education Limited
Edinburgh Gate
Harlow
Essex CM20 2JE
England

and Associated Companies througł

Visit us on the World Wide Web a
www.pearsoned.co.uk

First published 1996 (Politics and Society in the Third World)
Second edition published 2001 (Politics and Society in the Third World)
Third edition published 2007

© Pearson Education Limited 2007

The rights of Peter Calvert and Susan Calvert to be identified as
authors of this work have been asserted by them in accordance
with the Copyright, Designs and Patents Act 1988.

ISBN-13: 978-1-4058-2440-8
ISBN-10: 1-4058-2440-9

British Library Cataloguing-in-Publication Data
A catalogue record for this book is available from the British Library

Library of Congress Cataloging-in-Publication Data
A catalog record for this book is available from the Library of Congress

10   9   8   7   6   5   4   3   2   1
11   10   09   08   07

Typeset in 10/12pt Sabon by 35
Printed and bound in Malaysia   (CTP - VVP)

The publisher's policy is to use paper manufactured from sustainable forests.

IN MEMORIAM
IRENE CALVERT
1909–2000

Contents

List of tables, figures and maps		xiii
List of plates		xv
List of abbreviations		xvii
Preface to the third edition		xxi
Acknowledgements		xxiii

Part I	The developing world	1

1	Third World or developing world?	3
	What is development?	3
	Which are the developing countries?	4
	First World and Third World	5
	South v North	5
	Survival of the term Third World	13
	Colonisation and post-colonial society	13
	Independence and the legacy of war and militarism	17
	Gender and the roles of women and men	19
	Women and development	24
	Research in the developing world	26
	Social and other indicators	27
	China: the dragon awakes?	32
	Competing ideologies and interpretations of development	36
	Strategies of industrialisation	44
	A right to development?	48
	Development in the free market	51
	Transnational corporations	53

Globalisation: what is it and what effect does it have?   57
Neo-liberalism   59
Conclusion   62
Key terms   63
Questions   64

2   The infrastructure of the developing world   65
Physical location   65
Main geographical features   66
Case study 2.1: The Asian tsunami of 2004   69
Relief and drainage   72
Boundaries and territorial disputes   75
Case study 2.2: Refugees: the case of East Timor
(Timor Leste)   80
Terrorism   81
Agricultural activity   82
Mining   86
Human settlement   88
Case study 2.3: Refugees: the case of Rwanda   91
Land reform   92
Urbanisation   95
Migrants   100
Communications   101
Small island developing states   105
The balance sheet: assets and problems   106
Key terms   108
Questions   108

3   The crisis of the developing world   109
Poverty and basic needs   109
Water   111
Food   113
Sanitation and health   120
Infant mortality and life expectancy   121
Medical services   125
Case study 3.1: Malaria   127
Case study 3.2: HIV/AIDS   130
Housing   131
Case study 3.3: Bird flu   132
Education   134
Population growth   135
Key terms   140
Questions   141

Part II	Social and economic contexts	143

4	The economic context	145
	Introduction	145
	How is economic policy made?	146
	Africa: globalisation and marginalisation	152
	Case study 4.1: Ghana	152
	Cash crops	154
	Latin America: the persistence of debt	155
	The debt boomerang	161
	The 'war on drugs'	161
	Policy choices for indebted countries	163
	The crisis of 1997	164
	Asia: the newly industrialising countries	165
	The rise of the NICs	166
	The fear of insecurity: the South-east Asia crisis and after	169
	Globalisation	171
	Transnational links	172
	Business and politics: taxation, tariffs and privatisation	174
	Bretton Woods	175
	The International Monetary Fund	176
	The World Bank	179
	The GATT and WTO	180
	Case study 4.2: Bananas	184
	Regional economic groupings	186
	Conclusion	189
	Key terms	189
	Questions	192

5	The social context	193
	Introduction	193
	Gender and society	193
	Women and work	194
	Women and children	198
	Women and political power	200
	Women and the orthodoxy of development	204
	Impact of development on other disadvantaged groups	206
	Ethnic cleavages	207
	Class and state	209
	The family	218
	Indigenous peoples	221
	Social factors favouring development	225
	Maintaining social provision in an evolving society	226

Religion, politics and society   228
The clash of cultures   230
The concept of modernity: competing cultures   233
The global network   235
Impact of transnational media   236
'McWorld?'   239
Opinion formers   240
News management and international perception
  of the developing world   241
High culture   242
Conclusion   246
Key terms   247
Questions   248

6   The international context   249
Introduction   249
Two hours that shook the world   250
George Bush and the aftermath of '9/11'   250
War in Iraq   252
The post-war situation   253
Terror and the developing world   254
The breakdown of the state   254
Intervention   256
Non-alignment   260
Developing world conflicts   264
Weapons of mass destruction in the developing world   266
The role of the United Nations   268
Regional alignments   270
The first Bush Administration and Panama   273
The rise of 'humanitarian intervention'   274
The Gulf War 1991   275
Rwanda   277
International peacemaking/peacekeeping   280
The international politics of oil   281
The oil majors as actors in South–North relations   285
Libya and the North   286
Oil in South–North relations today   288
The international politics of water   290
Conclusion   293
Key terms   294
Questions   294

Part III	Politics of the developing world	297

7	State-building	299
	Introduction	299
	Who makes the law?	302
	The problem of the weak state	303
	Constitutional government	303
	Parliamentary systems	307
	Presidential systems	308
	Interest groups	310
	Political parties and elections	311
	Organisation of political parties	314
	Rise and fall of the 'one-party state'	315
	Populism and democracy	320
	Causes of insurgency	321
	Nationalism	322
	Religion and ethnicity	323
	Case study 7.1: Sri Lanka	325
	Personalism	326
	Corruption	331
	Conclusion	333
	Key Terms	334
	Questions	335

8	Dictatorship and democratisation	337
	Introduction	337
	Authoritarianism	338
	Coercive structures	339
	Military intervention	341
	Structure and roles of armed forces	344
	Military developmentalism	347
	Case study 8.1: Democratisation in Argentina	349
	Arms procurement	351
	Regional powers	352
	Requirements for liberal democracy	357
	Democratisation in the developing world	359
	Empowerment and the growth of civil society	363
	Democracy and development	366
	Democracy promotion	369
	Case study 8.2: Democratisation in Ghana	371
	Conclusion	373
	Key terms	373
	Questions	374

Part IV	Policy issues	377

9	Policy issues	379
	Introduction	379
	Aid	380
	Trade	391
	South–South trade	392
	Tourism	394
	Case study 9.1: Goa	397
	Case study 9.2: Belize	398
	Case study 9.3: Costa Rica	398
	Case study 9.4: The Caribbean Islands	399
	Case study 9.5: Kenya	401
	Case study 9.6: The Gambia	402
	Case study 9.7: Southern Africa	402
	Environment	404
	Key terms	420
	Questions	421

10	Conclusion	422
	Modernisation in Asia	423
	The radicalisation of the Middle East	424
	The decline of Africa	425
	The de–industrialisation of Europe	426
	The future of the poorest countries	427

| | References | 428 |
| | Index | 449 |

List of tables, figures and maps

Tables

1.1	GNP per capita of selected states, 1992	7
1.2	GNP per capita of selected states, 1997	10
1.3	GDP and GNI per capita, Atlas method, selected countries, 2004	28
1.4	GDP and GNI per capita, PPP (current US$), selected countries, 2004	29
1.5	HDI index and world rankings, selected states, 2004 (data from 2002)	30
1.6	World's largest economies by 2005 rank order	33
1.7	Perspectives compared	45
2.1	Primary aluminium production, by country, 2003	87
2.2	World production of bauxite, by country, 2004	87
2.3	World's most densely populated countries, 2005	89
2.4	World's largest cities, 2005	96
3.1	Countries experiencing water scarcity in 1955, 1990 and 2025 (projected), based on availability of less than 1,000 cubic metres of renewable water per person per year	112
3.2	World's highest infant mortality rates, 2005	122
3.3	Under-five mortality rate, selected countries, 2005	123
3.4	World's lowest life expectancies, 2006 estimates	124
3.5	HIV prevalence and total number living with AIDS, 2003	129
3.6	Incidence of TB and HIV in selected countries, 2004	131
3.7	Basic needs satisfaction, 1950–95	135
4.1	Total external debt of selected states, 1992	147
4.2	Debt as percentage of GNP, selected states, 1992	157
4.3	Total identified external debt in excess of US$20 billion, 1986 and 1992	158
4.4	World's most indebted states, 1992	159

4.5   World's most indebted states, latest figures   160
5.1   World's lowest literacy rates, 2005   207
6.1   Expenditure on defence in excess of 12 per cent of budget
      in 1990 with 1992 percentage   260
6.2   Developing world conflicts 1990–2002   262
7.1   Freedom House ratings, 2005   305
7.2   World's most corrupt countries, 2005   333
8.1   Three waves of democratisation   364
9.1   OECD countries, net ODA in 2004 as percentage of GNI   381

Figure

9.1   Environment, development and democracy   415

Maps

2.1   The North–South divide according to Brandt   66
2.2   Map of countries according to the World Bank classification
      of income   67

List of plates

1 Where South meets North: Turkey 6
2 Drying fish: Sri Lanka 70
3 Vegetable cultivation: Cuba 85
4 Transport: Brazil 104
5 Hydroelectric power: Paraguay 112
6 Urban school: Brazil 137
7 Avellaneda Bridge, declining traditional industry: Argentina 148
8 Anti-capitalist, anti-American politics: Uruguay 178
9 Husking coconut: Sri Lanka 216
10 Traditional lifestyles: Iran 222
11 Globalisation: Chile 237
12 UN peacekeeping 269
13 Voters registration drive: Mexico 312
14 Street scene: Sierra Leone 380
15 Green and other politics: Uruguay 405
16 Earth Summit, 1992 420

List of abbreviations

ACS	Association of Caribbean States
AFRC	Armed Forces Ruling Council (Ghana)
AICs	advanced industrialized countries
AIDS	Acquired Immunodeficiency Syndrome or Acquired Immune Deficiency Syndrome
AFTA	ASEAN Free Trade Area
ASEAN	Association of Southeast Asian Nations
Avianca	Compañía Aerovías Nacionales de Colombia S.A.
AU	African Union
BCE	before Common Era
BHP	Broken Hill Proprietary Company Ltd., now BHP Billiton
BJP	Bharatiya Janata party (India)
CAP	Common Agricultural Policy (EU)
CARICOM	Caribbean Community and Common Market
CBI	Caribbean Basin Initiative
CERDS	Charter of Economic Rights and Duties of States
CFA	Communauté Financière Africaine
CFCs	chlorofluorocarbons
CFF	Compensatory Financial Facility (World Bank)
CIA	US Central Intelligence Agency
CIS	Commonwealth of Independent States
CITES	Convention on International Trade in Endangered Species of Wild Fauna and Flora
CNN	Cable News Network
COMESA	Common Market for Eastern and Southern Africa
CPP	Convention Peoples Party (Ghana)
CPT	Pastoral Land Commission (Brazil)
DAC	Development Assistance Committee (OECD)
DRC	Democratic Republic of Congo
ECA	UN Economic Commission for Africa
ECCAS	Economic Community of Central African States
ECLA	UN Economic Commission for Latin America

ECLAC	UN Economic Commission for Latin America and the Caribbean
ECOMOG	ECOWAS Military Observer Group
ECOWAS	Economic Community of West African States
EITI	Extractive Industries Transparency Initiative
EOI	Export-Oriented Industrialisation
EPZ	Economic Processing Zone
ESF	Economic Support Fund
EU	European Union
EZLN	Ejército Zapatista de Liberación Nacional (Zapatista National Liberation Army, Mexico)
FAO	UN Food and Agriculture Organization
FRELIMO	Ruling Front for the Independence of Mozambique
G77	the Group of 77
G8	the Group of 8
GATT	General Agreement on Tariffs and Trade
GDP	gross domestic product
GNI	gross national income
GNP	gross national product
HEP	hydroelectric power
HIPC	Heavily Indebted Poorer Countries
HIV	human immunodeficiency virus
HKSAR	Hong Kong Special Administrative Region of China
HYV	High Yield Variety
IBRD	International Bank for Reconstruction and Development ('World Bank')
ICJ	International Court of Justice ('World Court')
IDA	International Development Agency
IFC	International Finance Corporation
IFIs	international financial institutions
ILO	UN International Labour Organization
IMF	International Monetary Fund
IMR	infant mortality rate
INC	Intergovernmental Negotiating Committee on Biological Diversity
IO	international organization
IPCC	Intergovernmental Panel on Climate Change
IPKF	Indian Peace-Keeping Force (Sri Lanka)
ISI	Import-Substitution-Industrialisation
KLM	Koninklijke Luchtvaart Maatschappij (Royal Dutch Airlines)
LDCs	Less Developed Countries
LTTE	Liberation Tigers of Tamil Eelam
Mercosur	Mercado Común del Sur (Southern Common Market)
MINUGUA	UN Mission in Guatemala
MINURSO	UN Mission for the Referendum in Western Sahara

MNR	National Revolutionary Movement (Bolivia)
MST	Movimento Sem Terra (Landless Movement, Brazil)
NAFTA	North American Free Trade Agreement
NAM	Non-Aligned Movement
NDC	National Democratic Congress (Ghana)
NED	National Endowment for Democracy (US)
NGOs	non-governmental organizations
NICs	Newly Industrialized Countries
NIEO	New International Economic Order
NIEs	Newly Industrializing Economies
NPP	New Patriotic Party (Ghana)
OAS	Organization of American States
OAU	Organisation of African Unity – see African Union
ODA	official development assistance
OECD	Organization for Economic Cooperation and Development
OPEC	Organization of Petroleum Exporting Countries
OSCE	Organization for Security and Co-operation in Europe
PACD	Plan of Action to Combat Desertification
PEMEX	Petróleos Mexicanos
PJ	Partido Justicialista (Argentina)
Pluna	Líneas Uruguayas de Navegación Aérea
PNC	People's National Congress (Guyana)
PNDC	Provisional National Defence Council (Ghana)
PPP	purchasing power parity
PPP	People's Progressive Party (Guyana)
PRB	Population Reference Bureau
PRG	Provisional Revolutionary Government (Grenada)
PRI	Institutional Revolutionary Party (Mexico)
PSRPs	Poverty Reduction Strategy Papers
PT	Partido dos Trabalhadores (Brazil)
RCC	Revolutionary Command Council (Libya)
RENAMO	Mozambique National Resistance
RPF	Rwandan Patriotic Front
SAARC	South Asian Association for Regional Cooperation
SADC	Southern African Development Community
SADR	Sahrawi Arab Democratic Republic
SAPs	Structural Adjustment Programs
SLFP	Sri Lankan Freedom Party
SICA	Sistema Andina de Integración (Andean System of Integration)
SIDS	small island developing states
SLORC	State Law and Order Restoration Committee (Myanmar)
SPC	South Pacific Commission
SPF	South Pacific Forum
SPLA	Sudan People's Liberation Army (Sudan)
SSA	Africa South of the Sahara

SWAPO   South West Africa Peoples' Organisation
TNC   trans-national corporation
UAE   United Arab Emirates
UK   United Kingdom of Great Britain and Northern Ireland
UMA   Arab Maghreb Union
UNITA   União Nacional para a Independência Total de Angola
UNAMIR   United Nations Mission in Rwanda
UNCED   United Nations Conference on Environment and Development
UNCTAD   United Nations Conference on Trade, Aid and Development
UNDP   United Nations Development Programme
UNEP   United Nations Environmental Programme
UNFPA   United Nations Population Fund
UNGASS   UN General Assembly Special Session
UNHCR   United Nations High Commission on Refugees
UNICEF   United Nations International Children's Emergency Fund
UNMEE   United Nations Mission in Ethiopia and Eritrea
UNTAET   United Nations Transitional Administration in East Timor
U5MR   under-five mortality rate
US, USA   United States of America
USAID   US Agency for International Development
USSR   Union of Soviet Socialist Republics
WCED   World Commission on Environment and Development
WMD   weapons of mass destruction
WTO   World Trade Organization
WWF   World Wide Fund for Nature
YPF   Yacimientos Petrolíferos Fiscales (Argentina)

Preface to the third edition

Why are so many of our fellow citizens of this planet so poor? As we will try to show in this book, it is not for most of them because they have had opportunities and failed to take them. And it is certainly not because there are not enough resources. So what has gone wrong? Some developing countries, such as the Gulf states and some Caribbean islands, are relatively well off, the former because of oil and the latter because of tourism. Yet they are not developed countries, and as things stand they are not going to be any time soon. This sort of development is constrained, lopsided and hence vulnerable in an increasingly globalised world. Other countries have gone the other way. They are the 'failed states', the victims of war, civil war and militarism. Yet Haiti was once the richest part of the French Empire and the Democratic Republic of the Congo has failed to benefit from mineral resources almost unparalleled in the world. They are not developing in any meaningful sense that increases the well-being of their people.

But the real surprise is just how many 'developing' countries there are. Only thirty of the world's countries can really be classed as developed. So the developing world includes perhaps five-sixths of the world's countries and four-fifths of its population. This situation is obviously unstable. Unless you try to understand it, you will not be able to understand the problems of the developed world, still less put them in perspective. Three key issues recur: 'development', 'democratisation' and 'environment'. As will become clear, on all three counts, there are still some grounds for optimism, but with each passing year these diminish.

Lack of development means that most people in the developing world lead shorter and more stressful lives than they need, and many lack some or most of the basic necessities of life. This is bad not only for them but for all of us. Not only is it a waste of much of the world's most valuable resource, the talents of its people, but in addition poverty breeds global threats. 'Bird flu', for example, is the consequence of keeping chickens and people in close proximity in Vietnam and south China, a practice which has long since been effectively ended in the developed world.

Until quite recently most of the countries of the world have had authoritarian governments, many of them military dictatorships. Since 1975 this has been changing and in 2006 the majority of the world's countries are functional democracies. But already there are signs that their inhabitants are getting very impatient. Whoever they vote for, things do not seem to be getting better. And even under nominally democratic governments, the money (as after the Asian tsunami) does not seem to be getting down to the poor. Worse still, since '9/11' the attention of the United States and much of the developed world has been taken up by the military aspects of the 'war on terror', ignoring the social conditions that gave rise to terrorism in the first place. So in Iran, Iraq and the Occupied Territories some people have turned to extremists who promise simple, deadly 'solutions'.

Development comes at a cost, and it is only in recent years that the environmental costs of uncontrolled development have begun to be realised. In Nigeria the local inhabitants have long complained about the damaging effect of oil spills on their crops and water supplies. Yet at the same time the oil companies have been flaring off huge quantities of valuable and irreplaceable gas amounting, according to some estimates, to some 5 per cent of world production. Properly used, this could have brought untold benefits. Instead, corruption is rife, the rich get richer, the poor stay poor and the environment suffers.

Many remedies have been proposed for these problems but few have been adopted, let alone sustained. The reason is that their causes are not just economic, but political and social. All too often, politicians are only interested in the next election, journalists only in meeting the deadline for the next news bulletin.

The study of the politics and society of the developing world, therefore, is not only exciting and interesting in itself, it is essential to understanding why things so often go wrong. With the internet at our disposal, the issue is no longer a shortage of information, but how to make sense of the flood of fascinating and relevant knowledge that is readily available. The purpose of this book is to provide an introduction to the developing world, its political institutions and issues of social and economic development, and we hope you will find it a useful starting point for your own further study.

Chandlers Ford
April 2006

Acknowledgements

We are grateful to the following for permission to reproduce copyright material:

AFP for an extract from "China's economy likely to be in world's top 5 in 2005" 23 January 2006 © AFP; British Broadcasting Corporation for the article "The mystery of Malaysia's tsunami aid" by Jonathan Kent, 20 June 2005, published on www.news.bbc.co.uk; Telegraph Group Limited for the following extracts: "Mugabe strikes his final blow against white farmers" by Peta Thornycroft, published in *The Daily Telegraph* 22 September 2005, "Street fighting boys" by Lutz Kleveman published in *The Telegraph Magazine* 17 September 2005, "Darfur bleeds in the great scramble for Sudan's oil" by David Blair published in *The Daily Telegraph* 8 February 2006, "Flow of the Nile is cut to let Lake Victoria fill up again" by Mike Pflanz published *The Daily Telegraph* 9 March 2006, and "Peat bog burning blamed for much global warming" by Charles Clover published in *The Daily Telegraph* 3 September 2005 © Telegraph Group Limited; Guardian Newspapers Limited for the following extracts: "African migrants die in quest for new life" by Giles Tremlett published in *The Guardian* 30 September 2005, "The world pays a heavy price for our cheap Christmas miracles" by Madeleine Bunting published in *The Guardian* 19 December 2005, "Two countries, one booming, one struggling" by Larry Elliott published in *The Guardian* 12 December 2005 © Guardian Newspapers Limited 2005, "Thousands throng streets as Bolivian leader sheds tears but talks tough at inauguration" by Jonathan Rugman and Dan Glaister published in *The Guardian* 12 January 2006, "India tilts to the West as new poles emerge" by Charles Grant published in *The Guardian* 12 January 2006, © Guardian Newspapers Limited 2006, "Rwandan PM killed as troops wreak carnage" by Lindsey Hilsum published in *The Guardian* 8 April 1994 © Guardian Newspapers Limited 1994, "Killings overshadow India's general election" by Randeep Ramesh published in *The Guardian* 21 April 2004, © Guardian Newspapers Limited 2004, "Window on the world" by Murray Armstrong published in *The Guardian* 8 June 2005, "Chinese communists dash hopes of democratic reform" by Jonathan Watts published in *The Guardian* 21 October 2005, "Donkeys and camels hired to aid Afghan poll" by Declan Walsh published in *The Guardian* 16 September 2005, and "Whingeing Poms" by George Monbiot published in *The Guardian* 3 September 2005 © Guardian Newspapers Limited 2005; The Perseus Book Group for an extract from "Argentina: decline and revival" by Peter Calvert taken from *Latin America, Its Problems and Its Promise* edited by Jan Knippers Black ©Westview Press, a member of Perseus Books L.L.C.; and "Kuwaiti women seek right to vote" by Ilene R Prusher reproduced with permission from the 8 August 2000 issue of *The Christian Science Monitor* (www.csmonitor.com) © 2000 *The Christian Science Monitor* All rights reserved. Tab 2.3 from *The World Factbook, 2004– 2005*, Central Intelligence Agency; Tab 2.4 from *http://www.geohive.com/*, Geohive.com; Tab 4.5 from *http://www.cia.gov/*, Central Intelligence Agency; Tab 7.1 From *Freedom in the World, 2005*, Freedom House. Plate 12 © Reuters/CORBIS.

In some instances we have been unable to trace the owners of copyright material and we would appreciate any information that would enable us to do so.

PART I

The developing world

CHAPTER 1

Third World or developing world?

What is development?

The meaning that you attach to the term **development** depends on where you start from. It means different things to different people, even at its most mundane and practical level. For example, a resident of rural Senegal might see development as the availability of very basic services such as a reliable source of potable water; someone living in the suburbs of Greater Buenos Aires would expect rather more. Certainly both would associate the term with some sort of improvement in the quality of their lives. A concern with quality rather than quantity contrasts sharply with the traditional view of development measured simply as an increase in a country's gross domestic product (GDP), now called gross national income (GNI).

Then 'development' was seen as making economic changes which would seek to counter the problem of global poverty, which was being addressed for the first time in the post-war era. Poverty was believed to be measurable in economic terms, simply as the amount by which per capita income fell short of the US level, and so was easily solvable by economic changes. Today development is a much more complex concept, involving consideration not only of the crude increase in production, but of the nature of that production and the range of social facilities which accompany it. It is this stress on quality rather than quantity which distinguishes 'development' from 'growth'.

But this still does not answer the often-asked question of whether the concept is properly an economic or a political one. Development agendas change over time (see the discussion on poverty and basic needs in Chapter 3). A decisive response laying strong emphasis on political or economic aspects of development usually reflects strong attachment to a particular perspective. It would be hard to criticise the scope and range of the definition given by Michael Todaro:

> Development must therefore be conceived of as a multidimensional process involving major changes in social structures, popular attitudes and national institutions,

as well as the acceleration of economic growth, the reduction of inequality, and the eradication of poverty. Development, in its essence, must represent the whole gamut of change by which an entire social system, tuned to the diverse basic needs and desires of individuals and social groups within that system, moves away from a condition of life widely perceived as unsatisfactory toward a situation or condition of life regarded as materially and spiritually 'better'. (Todaro 1994: 16)

At its simplest and most cogent the term may be best expressed as in the work of Amartya Sen (Sen 1981) as a reduction in vulnerability and as increased strength to counter problems consequent upon an enhancement of the options available. For Sen, development involves the increased freedom of the population. There is in this a validity that other definitions do not so adequately express, since income as measured by purchasing power gives freedom, but the freedom it gives also includes a capacity to meet a series of needs within society, for participation, health, education, etc.

Which are the developing countries?

Like most things in the social sciences, this is not as simple as it looks. The term **developing countries** is a very general term which may be applied to all except the **advanced industrialised countries (AICs)**. That is to say, it includes countries designated by the World Bank and International Monetary Fund as low and middle-income countries (the Bank additionally divides the middle-income countries into upper and lower middle-income countries). Not the least of the problems with the term is that not all the 'developing' countries are in fact developing. We can divide them loosely into groups, though there is some overlap between these.

1. The very poorest (low income) countries, most though not all in Africa, which have failed to develop in terms of the quality of life of most of their population. Most have remained critically dependent on the export of a single raw material or crop (Ghana, Namibia). Others, like Afghanistan, the Democratic Republic of the Congo, Liberia or Sierra Leone, have been ravaged by civil war and will need massive support from abroad to rebuild their devastated infrastructure.
2. The large majority of lower and upper middle-income countries which despite their efforts remain relatively poor by world standards.
3. The oil (petroleum) producing countries which gain a high income from the depletion of their irreplaceable resources and are able to sustain a relatively high standard of living for their peoples, but which otherwise lack any of the basic requirements for sustained economic growth. Some, like the United Arab Emirates (UAE), are high-income countries.
4. The newly industrialised countries (NICs) or newly industrialising economies (NIEs), of which more later.

In recent years the term 'developing countries', fashionable in the 1950s, has been regaining popularity at the expense of its two more recent predecessors: the **Third World** and the **South**.

First World and Third World

During the Cold War the term 'Third World' gained acceptance quickly as a convenient term to denote all those countries which were neither 'Western' AICs, with well-developed free market economies, nor countries of the former Soviet bloc, with command economies.

Though Third World countries were developing countries in the economic sense, the reason was political: the three-way division of the world reflected the political dilemma facing the newly independent states in an era characterised by two power blocs. The earliest tentative moves towards the establishment of the Non-Aligned Movement (NAM), notably the Bandung Afro-Asian Solidarity Conference in 1955, included states on the basis of their independence not their ideological leanings. Cuba, despite its strong Cold War alliance with the former Soviet Union, became a leading member of the Non-Aligned Movement, as did Pakistan, despite its clear pro-Western orientation. But both could conveniently be grouped together with others as being part neither of the First World (the advanced industrial economies) nor the Second World (the command economies of the USSR, Eastern Europe and China).

During the Cold War, the 'Third World' became an arena for conflict, for two reasons. Despite the apparently overwhelming power of both the United States and the Soviet Union, each sought to influence the world balance of power by winning allies and friends among the uncommitted. Some, such as India, made a particular point of asserting their independence of either power and so made particularly desirable friends. Secondly, the nuclear stand-off made the prospect of war between the two superpowers so dangerous that the conflict between First and Second Worlds was played out by proxy in the Third – Korea, the Congo, Vietnam. Clandestine support to insurrectionary movements by both the Soviet Union and the United States added another zone of conflict.

South v North

Many developing countries resented the numerical suggestion of a 'pecking order', and for a time academic writers preferred to divide the world between the developed 'North' and the less-developed 'South'. But the term 'South'

Plate 1   Where South meets North, Istanbul, Turkey

needed to comprise the Americas as far north as Mexico (which is in North America); the whole of Africa; Asia apart from the former Soviet Union, China and Japan; and Indonesia, the Philippines and New Guinea but not Australia and New Zealand (cf. Clapham 1985: 1). This does not make for a term that is easily recognised on a map. As can be seen from the map (see Map 2.1) which illustrated the Brandt Report and which familiarised many people with a non-Mercator projection for the first time, the line which demarcated 'the South' (see also Burnell and Randall 2005) meandered across the northern hemisphere before plunging southwards to exclude Japan, Australia and New Zealand (see Table 1.1).

Hence some countries which observers would generally consider to have much in common become disconnected by the division of North and South. The geographical implications of the terms have proved rather too hard to overcome. Further, Mexico in North America, and Argentina and Brazil in South America, cannot simply be lumped together in a common 'South' grouping with countries in the Horn of Africa which are much newer, immensely poorer and altogether weaker states. And for people in English-speaking North America, the term South has long since been appropriated to designate the Southern states of the United States. There are also more specific questions that could be raised. China is not included because it was part of that Second World which was perceived to exist before the collapse of the USSR.

Table 1.1   GNP per capita of selected states, 1992

RANGE	Population 1992 (millions)	GNP per capita 1992 (US$)	Growth 1980–92 (%)	Life expectancy (years)	Adult illiteracy (%)
LOW INCOME	3,191.3	390	3.9	62	40
1 Mozambique	16.6	60	−3.6	44	67
18 India	883.6	310	3.1	61	52
21 Nigeria	101.9	320	−0.4	52	49
27 Ghana	15.8	450	−0.1	56	40
28 China	1,162.2	470	–	69	27
32 Sri Lanka	17.4	540	2.6	72	12
37 Indonesia	184.3	670	4.0	60	23
LOWER MIDDLE INCOME	1,418.7	2,490	−0.1	68	–
43 Côte d'Ivoire	12.9	670	−4.7	56	46
44 Bolivia	7.5	680	−1.5	60	23
68 Jamaica	2.4	1,340	0.2	74	2
75 Thailand	58.0	1,840	6.0	69	7
80 Turkey	58.5	1,980	2.9	67	19
85 Chile	13.6	2,730*	3.7	72	7
UPPER MIDDLE INCOME	477.7	4,020	0.8	69	15
80 S. Africa	39.8	2,670	0.1	63	–
92 Brazil	153.9	2,770	0.4	66	19
99 Mexico	85.0	3,470	−0.2	70	13
100 Trinidad & Tobago	1.3	3,940	−2.6	71	–
102 Argentina	33.1	6,050	−0.9	71	5
107 Greece	10.3	7,290	1.0	77	7
108 Portugal	9.8	7,450	3.1	74	15
109 Saudi Arabia	16.8	7,510	−3.3	69	38
HIGH INCOME	828.1	22,160	4.3	77	–
110 Ireland	3.5	12,210	3.4	75	–
112 Israel	5.1	13,220	1.9	76	–
116 Australia	17.5	17,260	1.6	77	a
117 UK	57.8	17,790	2.4	76	a
124 France	57.4	22,260	1.7	77	a
127 USA	255.4	23,240	1.7	77	a
131 Japan	124.5	28,190	3.6	79	a
132 Switzerland	6.9	36,080	1.4	78	a

a = UNESCO data, illiteracy less than 5%
* = revised upwards from 2,510
Source: World Bank (1994)

As suggested above, its size makes it virtually impossible to ignore, but its inclusion (or exclusion) may distort our view of other developing countries. (Similarly, generalisations about South Asia are distorted by the sheer human weight of India.)

NORTH AMERICA

MEXICO

Official name: The United Mexican States (Estados Unidos Mexicanos)
Type of government: Federal presidential republic
Capital: Mexico City
Area: 1,958,000 sq km
Population (2005): 106,202,903
GNI per capita (2005): $6,230 (PPP $9,600)

Evolution of government: Core of present state dominated by Aztecs before arrival of Spaniards 1519. Struggle for independence began 1810, effective 1821, federal presidential republic established 1824. In wars in 19th century lost half its national territory to the United States; the long dictatorship of Porfirio Díaz (1877–80, 1884–1911) introduced economic liberalism but demands for political reform triggered agrarian and labour unrest. The Mexican Revolution of 1910 was followed by far-reaching social reform and single-party dominance 1929–2000.

Main features of government: Constitution of 1917 established important social rights in programmatic form. Single-member single-ballot system modified to give proportional representation to opposition parties. Strong presidency increasingly restrained by bureaucratic immobility under long period of one-party dominance. Weak legal system. Thirty-two states with a common constitution each have elective governor and state legislature, contention for which paved way for breakdown of one-party rule.

SOUTH AMERICA

ARGENTINA

Official name: The Argentine Republic (Republica Argentina)
Type of government: Federal presidential republic
Capital: Buenos Aires
Area: 2,766,890 sq km
Population (2005 est.): 39,537,943
GNI per capita (2005): $3,720 (PPP $12,460)

Evolution of government: Spanish settlement began 1536 but present territory was never fully settled; autonomy proclaimed by Buenos Aires 1810 and independence for greater part of former Spanish viceroyalty 1816. Civil wars between Buenos Aires and interior temporarily arrested by dictatorship of

▶

SOUTH AMERICA continued

Juan Manuel de Rosas (1835–53). At fall of Rosas, federal presidential regime established but tension between Buenos Aires and interior ended only in 1870s with federalisation of capital. Boosted by immigration, spectacular economic growth under oligarchical regime 1876–1930 when armed forces stepped in. Politics since 1943 dominated by attitudes towards personalist regime of Juan Domingo Perón (1946–55) culminating in return of Perón and outbreak of serious unrest. Thousands died under military-led 'Process of National Reorganisation' 1976–82 when armed forces defeated in war for the Falklands/ Malvinas, and return to civilian rule 1983.

Main features of government: Constitution of 1853 survives substantially un-altered. Peronists have remained party with the majority tendency; elections by d'Hondt system produce relatively few parties and stable coalitions in Congress, which remains essentially an arena. Weak judiciary subject to executive interference. President Menem (1989–99) made extensive use of decree powers to bypass Congress and impose will on provinces but handed on a major economic crisis to his successor.

BRAZIL

Official name: The Federative Republic of Brazil (Republica Federativa do Brasil)
Type of government: Federal presidential republic
Capital: Brasília
Area: 8,512,000
Population (2005 est.): 186,112,794
GNI per capita (2005): $3,090 (PPP $8,020)

Evolution of government: Coastal Brazil settled by Portuguese from 1500; independence 1822 as Empire ruled by heir to Portuguese throne. Abolition of slavery triggered military revolt and fall of Empire 1889, when federal parliamentary republic established. Military revolt in 1930 paved way for fascistic 'New State' under Getúlio Vargas in 1930s, but Brazil's participation in the Second World War aroused armed forces to country's weakness and in 1964 the armed forces siezed and established a military developmentalist regime led by a 'modernising oligarchy'. After a long period of 'decompression' elections were conceded and civilian rule restored in 1985 under a presidential republic.

Main features of government: Executive presidency with extensive powers. A highly fragmented multi-party system results in shifting coalitions in the highly transformative Congress, which can and do frustrate executive initiatives. Though the federal government is very powerful, the size of the country has meant that the states can resist pressures for change. Immensely rich in natural resources, both agricultural and mineral. History of rapid economic growth accompanied by persistent inflation; economic liberalisation measures under the 'Washington Consensus' have failed to stabilise the economy but led to widening of the gap between rich and poor. The opening up of the Amazon has already led to serious ecological damage and seems to be running out of control.

Table 1.2   GNP per capita of selected states, 1997

RANGE	Population 1997 (millions)	GNP per capita 1997 (US$)	Growth 1996–97 (%)	Life expectancy (years)	Adult illiteracy (%)
LOW INCOME	2,036	350	3.9		
207 Mozambique	17	140	10.5	45.2	59.5
191 Nigeria	118	280	2.8	50.1	40.5
177 India	962	370	4.3	62.6	46.5
173 Ghana	18	390	1.7	60.0	33.6
154 Côte d'Ivoire	14	710	4.3	46.7	57.4
LOWER MIDDLE INCOME	2,283	1,230	6.2		–
148 Sri Lanka	19	800	5.9	73.1	9.3
145 China	1,227	860	7.4	69.8	17.1
141 Bolivia	8	970	1.4	61.4	16.4
135 Indonesia	200	1,110	2.6	65.1	15.0
119 Jamaica	3	1,550	-2.9	74.8	14.5
95 Russia	**147**	**2,680**	**0.6**	**66.6**	**a**
94 Thailand	61	2,740	-2.1	68.8	5.3
UPPER MIDDLE INCOME	574	4,540	0.6		
91 Turkey	64	3,130	6.8	69.0	16.8
89 S. Africa	41	3,210	-0.4	54.7	16.0
81 Mexico	94	3,700	6.3	72.2	9.9
76 Trinidad	1	4,250	7.0	73.8	2.2
73 Brazil	164	4,790	1.9	66.8	16.0
72 Chile	15	4,820	5.7	74.9	4.8
64 Saudi Arabia	20	7,150	-1.4	71.4	26.6
57 Argentina	36	8,950	6.7	72.9	3.5
HIGH INCOME	927	25,890	1.9		
52 Portugal	10	11,010	4.3	75.3	9.2
49 Greece	11	11,640	0.7	78.1	3.4
32 Israel	6	16,180	-0.6	77.8	4.6
28 Ireland	4	17,790	7.3	76.3	a
23 Australia	19	20,650	-0.6	78.2	a
22 UK	59	20,870	3.7	77.2	a
15 France	59	26,300	3.2	78.1	a
10 USA	268	29,080	2.8	76.7	a
4 Japan	126	38,160	1.5	80.0	a
3 Switzerland b	7	43,060	2.5	78.6	a

a = less than 1%
b no state is ranked 1 or 2!
Source: World Bank, 1999, *World Development Indicators*, Table 1.1: Size of the economy;
http://www.worldbank.org/

At the same time, with the collapse of the Soviet Union the continuing relevance of the rival concept of a Third World was called into question. Without a Second World, the term is obsolete. If it is to be retained, its use is complicated by the liberation of the former Second World states from that category and their varied and sometimes ambivalent relation to the remaining categories of First and Third Worlds. Where do the Central Asian Republics fit, the Ukraine or Russia? We need to differentiate the different parts of the former Soviet Union if trying to apply Clapham's definition: economically Estonia ranks as an upper middle-income country, Belarus, Kazakhstan, Latvia, Lithuania, the Russian Federation, Ukraine and Usbekistan rank as lower middle-income countries and Armenia, Azerbaijan, Georgia, the Kyrgyz Republic, Moldova, Tajikistan and Turkmenistan as low-income countries (World Bank 1997).

Another problem is presented by the division of Africa as between North Africa and Africa South of the Sahara. North Africa, fronting on the Mediterranean basin and historically closely linked with Europe, was colonised by the Arabs and consequently is closely linked also with the turbulent region which in Europe is known as the Middle East and in the USA is called South-West Asia. Africa South of the Sahara (many from those countries dislike the more common term 'Sub-Saharan Africa') was the subject of intense rivalry from various European states from the fifteenth to the nineteenth centuries (see Table 1.2).

NORTH AFRICA

EGYPT

Official name: Arab Republic of Egypt (Jumhuriyat Misr al-Arabiyah)
Type of government: Presidential republic
Capital: Cairo
Area: 1,001,000 sq km
Population (2003): 68,000,000
GNI per capita (2005): $1,310 (PPP $4,120)

Evolution of government: Egypt was first unified c.3200 BCE, but from 341 BCE to 1922 was ruled by foreign dynasties. In 641 it fell to the invading Arabs, who imposed the Arabic language and the Islamic religion but allowed the Coptic Christians to retain theirs. Its conquest by the Ottoman Turks in 1522 left the native slave rulers, the Mamluks, intact, until they were overthrown at the beginning of the 19th century by an Albanian adventurer, Muhammad Ali. He established a native dynasty which came under British and French control in 1882, and was nominally independent from 1922. In 1952 the monarchy and the parliamentary system which had begun to emerge were overthrown and replaced by a revolutionary government led by Muhammad Naguib and Gamal Abdel Nasser. Nasser's successors maintained a single-party system under which the president was elected or re-elected without opposition every six years. At the first multi-party election since the days of the monarchy, Muhammad Hosni Mubarak was re-elected in 2005.

▶

NORTH AMERICA continued

Main features of government: Executive presidency with extensive powers. Legislature consists of the People's Assembly, elected by popular vote for a five-year term, and an Advisory Council which has consultative powers only. Both are dominated by the ruling National Democratic Party (NDP). Trade unions, professional bodies and non-political NGOs are tolerated; political parties have to have government approval. The main opposition comes from the illegal Muslim Brotherhood, which has had a considerable influence on Islamic movements in other countries. Some 70,000 Palestinian refugees live in the country; as elsewhere in the Middle East many hold very influential positions. A rapidly growing population occupying only a very narrow strip of irrigated land implies serious poverty and breeds resentment.

ALGERIA

Official name: People's Democratic Republic of Algeria (Al Jumhuriyah al Jaza'iriyah ad Dimuqratiyah ash Sha'biyah)
Type of government: Presidential republic
Capital: Algiers
Area: 2,832,000 sq km
Population (2005 est.): 32,531,853
GNI per capita (2005): $2,280 (PPP $3,260)

Evolution of government: Part of the Roman Empire from 106 BCE, Numidia came under Arab rule in the 7th century and was incorporated in the Ottoman Empire at the beginning of the 17th century but the majority of the population, though Muslim, are Berber not Arab. From 1671 onwards the Dey of Algiers, chosen locally, was the main ruler in the region but the coast was controlled by pirates trading in slaves. In 1830 the French began the conquest of Algeria by deposing the Dey. Under French rule European immigration was promoted and Algeria was treated as part of metropolitan France. A revolt against French rule broke out in 1954. Led by the Front Nationale de Liberation (FLN), under Ben Bella, it forced the de Gaulle government to concede independence in 1962. However, growing discontent with the FLN led to the success of the Islamic Salvation Front (FIS) in elections held in December 1991. The armed forces intervened to nullify the election, triggering a revolt which over six years killed more than 100,000 people; the French-educated elite being particular targets. Militant wing of the FIS, the Islamic Salvation Army, disbanded in January 2000.

Main features of government: President Abdelaziz Bouteflika fraudulently imposed by the army in 1991; re-elected for five-year term 2004. President is chief of state; appoints prime minister, whose government is formally responsible to a bicameral parliament consisting of the National People's Assembly and the Council of Nations. Members of the Assembly are directly elected by popular vote to serve for five years.

Hydrocarbons (oil and gas) account for some 60 per cent of government revenues.

Survival of the term Third World

The term Third World has survived because it is already well known and because it has a distinct meaning. Moreover it does still have its uses:

1. In some ways the discipline of the Cold War and its alliances was a stabilising force. This now removed makes the former Third World a far more important area of study and concern, since it now constitutes in many ways a greater threat to the apparent stability of international relations.
2. The collapse of the Eastern bloc left many of its former parts having nowhere else to go. There are no alternatives to being poor in a Western-dominated global system, it seems, and, in so far as the Third World ever was polarised into two ideological camps, a division of the Third World has disappeared.
3. The term was at least in part one of self-definition for poorer states whether within the ambit of one of the main power blocs or not, and, as we have already seen, many of them are not really 'developing' at all.

Colonisation and post-colonial society

Inheriting a colonial economy determines the pattern of infrastructure available to a newly independent state. Since 1945 there has been an increase in the number of independent countries in the world from around 50 to nearly 200. Naturally this complicates the idea of a single category to embrace some two-thirds of the states, but at the same time this process has made consideration of this group of countries and their histories more vital than ever.

Nearly all developing states are former colonies. Three exceptions are China, Thailand and Iran, each of which was subject to considerable pressure from colonising powers but ultimately maintained its independence as a result of conflict between two or more potential colonisers. A fourth, Ethiopia, escaped colonisation in the 19th century only to fall briefly victim to the imperial ambitions of Mussolini in the 1930s, but was liberated as part of the campaigns of the Second World War.

However, the historical experiences of colonisation in different parts of the world are in fact very different. They vary with the stage at which colonisation took place and with the economic development of the colonial power involved, the different policies and practices of the colonial powers, and the nature of indigenous societies. It is still very much a matter for debate as to how far the subsequent experiences of post-colonial societies resulted from colonial intervention or the nature of traditional societies, and in fact there is almost certainly no clear answer to this question.

Certainly the policies and practices of the colonial powers varied greatly. The pioneering colonisers, Portugal and Spain, were responsible for the introduction of slavery to the Americas. Later colonisers maintained and extended the practice, though they did not introduce it elsewhere. French colonial rule emphasised cultural superiority while British rule stressed racial superiority. Once colonies adopted French culture they became part of France, and one in particular, Algeria, was actually incorporated as part of metropolitan France. Britain's ideology of superiority clearly would not permit such incorporation, but on the other hand made rejection by the colonies easier to take. When the French left Sekou Touré's Guinea, they smashed everything that they could not take with them.

But it would be absurd to underestimate the strength and resilience of indigenous societies. In much of Latin America there has been a far longer period of independence and there was much less traditional society to supersede and/or absorb. In Asia colonial rule was shorter, independence more recent and colonial absorption of existing political systems was much more variable and sometimes much less complete. 'Protectorates' such as Egypt, Morocco, Vietnam, and parts of Malaysia, Nigeria etc. were least affected.

WEST AFRICA

NIGERIA

Official name: Federal Republic of Nigeria
Type of government: Federal presidential republic
Capital: Abuja
Area: 924,000 sq km
Population (2005 est.): 128,771,988
GNI per capita (2005): $390 (PPP $930)

Evolution of government: British colonial control of coast region with capital at Lagos, extended to Protectorate over Muslim north in 1907 under system of dual mandate. Independent 1960; parliamentary federal republic of four states 1963 but military coup by northerners in 1966 led to attempt of Igbo (Ibo) of the coast to secede as Biafra and to civil war 1967–70. Under continuing military dominance several unsuccessful experiments in constitution-making before present return to civilian rule 1999.

Main features of government: Federal system of 36 states with state governors and legislatures. Central government a presidential republic led by former soldier and military president, General Olusegun Obasanjo, elected president 1999. Continuing strong role of the military. Serious unrest followed first introduction of Muslim Shar'ia law in northern state of Zamfara 1999. Despite being major oil producer country's economy remains in crisis and is notorious for clientelism and corruption. Society is split between the less-developed north, mainly Muslim

▶

WEST AFRICA continued

with a significant fundamentalist movement wanting to introduce Shar'ia law, and the more developed south, mainly Christian. In 2003 3.6 million Nigerians were estimated to be living with HIV/AIDS.

GHANA

Official name: Republic of Ghana
Type of government: Unitary presidential republic
Capital: Accra
Area: 240,000 sq km
Population (2005 est.): 21,029,853
GNI per capita (2005): $380 (PPP $2,280)

Evolution of government: Internal self-government established in colonial period; at independence 1957 a parliamentary republic. Prime Minister Kwame Nkrumah, however, transformed into presidential system under his own leadership with East European touches. In 1966 Nkrumah was overthrown by army and police, inaugurating long period of military dominance and intervention. Flt. Lt. Jerry Rawlings siezed power in coup 1979 and shot three of his predecessors before restoring civilian rule; in 1982 he again seized power on behalf of a Provisional National Defence Council. In 1989 a slow move back towards liberal democracy began. Rawlings was elected president in 1992 and 1996 but his designated successor failed to win in 2000, so Ghana is unusual as an example of successful democratisation in Africa.

Main features of government: Presidential republic. Strong presidency established by charismatic leader with populist appeal. Liberalisation followed by democratisation; having failed to discredit elections, opposition has now successfully contested power. Independent judiciary. Women traditionally influential. Ghana is heavily dependent on the changing world price of a single crop: cocoa.

SIERRA LEONE

Official name: Republic of Sierra Leone
Type of government: Unitary presidential republic
Capital: Freetown
Area: 72,000 sq km
Population (2005 est.): 6,017,643
GNI per capita (2005): $200 (PPP $790)

Evolution of government: Freetown and coastal settlement established by British philanthropists as settlement for freed slaves 1788; Colony established 1808 and interior proclaimed a Protectorate 1896. Independent 1961; proclaimed presidential republic under one-party rule by Siaka Stevens 1971. Role as base for regional peacekeeping mission in neighbouring Liberia precipitated an invasion

▶

WEST AFRICA continued

by insurgents sponsored by Charles Taylor. Savage civil war followed marked by mutilation of captives and civilians and impressment of child soldiers, often under the influence of drugs. By referendum 1991 officially returned to multi-party government under elected president but the civil war has been slow to die down.

Main features of government: Presidential republic with strong executive presidency. Government ineffective in hinterland, where armed bands supported by Liberia continue to dominate the diamond fields and other key areas. Tribal loyalties strong as are secret societies. Diamonds could pay for development, but government unable to control market. Country's infrastructure has been destroyed by civil conflict and there is acute poverty in both Freetown (swollen by refugees) and the countryside. In 2001 some 7.1 per cent of the population were estimated to be infected with HIV/AIDS.

SOUTHERN AFRICA

SOUTH AFRICA

Official name: Republic of South Africa
Type of government: Semi-presidential republic
Capital: Tshwane (Pretoria)
Area: 1,219,000 sq km
Population (2005 est.): 44,344,136
GNI per capita (2003): $2,750 (PPP $10,130)

Evolution of government: Dutch settlement began in the 17th century. As part of their strategy in the Napoleonic Wars, the British seized the Cape of Good Hope in 1806. Many Dutch settlers (Boers) trekked north to found their own republics. But discovery of diamonds (1867) and gold (1886) encouraged British expansion and after initial defeats they defeated the Zulu. The Boers resisted British encroachments, but although they were defeated in the Boer War (1899–1902), in 1910 Britain gave them internal self-government as part of the Union of South Africa. Elections in 1948 brought the Nationalists to power, and they used a variety of legal restrictions to impose their policy of apartheid – the 'separate development' of the races. They proclaimed a Republic in 1961 defying resistance to apartheid from the Commonwealth (which South Africa has since rejoined). The 1990s brought an end to apartheid in a negotiated transition and ushered in black majority rule.

Main features of government: Executive president, elected by the National Assembly for a five-year term, is head of state and head of government. National Assembly directly elected by proportional representation; Council of Provinces (former Senate) has reserved powers to safeguard minorities. Legal system combines Romano-Dutch and British traditions; independence of judiciary preserved

▶

SOUTHERN AFRICA continued

even under apartheid. Some 5.3 million of the population are estimated to be living with HIV/AIDS.

MOZAMBIQUE

Official name: Republic of Mozambique
Type of government: Parliamentary republic
Capital: Maputo
Area: 801,590 sq km
Population (2005 est.): 19,406,703
GNI per capita (2005): $210 (PPP $259)

Evolution of government: A Portuguese colony in south-eastern Africa until independence granted in 1975 following the revolution in Portugal. The Ruling Front for the Independence of Mozambique (FRELIMO) had to confront a well-financed terrorist movement, the Mozambique National Reistance (RENAMO), supported by South Africa, in a civil war which cost tens of thousands of lives. Peace between the warring parties was brokered by the UN in 1991. In the Assembly of the Republic elected 2004 FRELIMO holds 160 seats and RENAMO 90.

Main features of government: President head of state elected by popular vote for five-year term, appoints prime minister. Legislature unicameral Assembly of the Republic (Assembleia da Republica) directly elected for five-year term. The Supreme Court has power to review cases involving the Constitution. Mozambique is one of the world's poorest countries, with limited natural resources other than aluminium, and most of its population live by subsistence farming. Despite some relief under the IMF's Heavily Indebted Poorer Countries (HIPC) scheme the country is still suffering the legacy of the civil war. The only member of the Commonwealth not formerly a British colony.

Independence and the legacy of war and militarism

Common features of the colonial experience include:

1. The establishment of arbitrary territorial boundaries notably in the interior of Africa which was penetrated late and then not for settlement, which was mainly coastal.
2. The imposition of a political and administrative order ultimately based on force though often legitimised locally by superior technology and the mystique of power.
3. Centralised, authoritarian administrative systems. All colonial rule, even that of a democratic country like the United States, which was the colonial power in the Philippines and (briefly) Cuba, is authoritarian.

The importance of each of these varied according to how early the country was colonised and how long it remained under colonial rule. Just as it is significant when a country was colonised, so it is of great significance when it finally achieved independence. Most of Latin America became independent at the beginning of the 19th century, much earlier than the rest of the developing world. Thus Argentina was effectively independent in 1810 and formally so after 1816, though it was not recognised as such by Spain until 1853.

Independence came to the rest of the European empires much more recently. The Second World War destroyed the myth of invincibility which helped make colonial rule acceptable and it encouraged the growth of nationalism in the developing world. Invariably such nationalist movements were led by Western-educated individuals such as Kwame Nkrumah in the Gold Coast (Ghana). After 1945 the will to hold the colonies no longer existed among large sections of the elite of the exhausted Western powers: Britain, France, the Netherlands and Belgium. At this point there was much less contradiction than there had been previously between the values of the colonial power and the ideal of independence. With independence, however, these perceptions were to change rapidly, as the new state's identity was defined.

In all cases it was the institutions created by the colonial power for its own purposes on which the state at independence had to depend to govern. This made the newly independent state at once strong and weak. It was strong in so far as it was intact, functioning and usually centralised. Only Argentina, Brazil, Mexico, India and Nigeria emerged into independence as true federal states and in each case the struggle between federal and state governments has gone on ever since with varying outcomes. Even in these cases the independent state was weak in that it was inflexible and subject to nationalist criticism that its existing forms were inappropriate. It was associated with a small ruling clique and not with society as a whole, and so lacked legitimacy. This lack of legitimacy fed corruption, which in turn contributed to the lack of legitimacy.

Westernised elites, who saw themselves as heirs to colonial overlords, sought to milk the state for all it was worth. This distorted the development of the newly independent state. Government did not adequately plan for development and in any case could not pay for it. The benefits accruing from control of the state so far exceeded those available from other sources that desperation to control the state resulted in, at best, an undignified scramble which undermined its already tentative legitimacy, and, at worst, in the suppression of opposition and the use of clientelism to reward political supporters. The illegitimate state does not find it easy to rebuild that legitimacy slowly through evolution. Rather, there is a tendency to make frequent changes of constitutions, spend heavily on showy projects and make other superficial attempts to enhance the legitimacy of the state.

Internal insecurity goes hand in hand with external insecurity, which may be summarised as vulnerability due to lack of autonomy. Such weaknesses would exhibit themselves in the world market and also in the lack of power in institutions like the International Monetary Fund (IMF). US domestic policy can hit developing world states, as in the 1980s when interest rates were at historically high levels. But the same vulnerability has indirect effects too and developing world states are also much more susceptible to natural disasters, as is evident from the very different capacity to manage flooding in Bangladesh and the Netherlands, for example.

Gender and the roles of women and men

The end of colonial rule left the new states with traditional social structures. The most important among these was patriarchy.

In gender politics 'patriarchy' refers to a society stratified by gender, in which political power is monopolised by male leader figures and by men in general, with women confined to subordinate roles. In the emerging states the traditional exclusion of women from active participation in decision-making was reinforced by the image of independence as having been secured by heroic male figures brandishing weapons. There were notable exceptions where, as in Sri Lanka, independence was achieved by patient negotiation with the former colonial power or, as in India, by widespread passive resistance. It is no coincidence that in both of these countries women have been able to achieve high political office and to be respected as leaders.

The subordination of women has, however, far-reaching economic consequences. Most obvious is the pre-eminence of men in leadership roles in commerce, industry and trade unions, and the undervaluing of the female role in economic production. Women comprise half of the world's adult population and constituted in 2003 40 per cent of the world's official labour force. However, of the world's 550 million working poor – those getting less than a dollar a day – 330 million (60 per cent) were women (ILO Press Release 04/09, Friday 5 March 2004). In the widely quoted words of Barber B. Conable, Jr., president of the World Bank: 'Women do two thirds of the world's work. Yet they earn only one tenth of the world's income and own less than one per cent of the world's property. They are among the poorest of the world's poor.' This became the informal slogan of the Decade of Women (see also Robbins, 1999: 354).

Most of the world's food is produced by women, and this is especially true in developing countries. Estimates vary between 75 per cent and 90 per cent. In developing countries they are also responsible for the carrying of water and the collection of fuelwood. So those who do most of the work actually get least of the money.

Between 60 and 100 million women are missing altogether from the world's population as a result of son preference. Development is about social change and women are disproportionately subject to the effects of social change. In the distorted way development has largely been perceived, modernisation has emphasised capital accumulation. Yet the move away from artisan production tends to disadvantage women, since as employees they are not in a position to accumulate meaningful amounts of capital, and industrialising makes them part of the labour force in a way not previously the case. If they are married women their earnings essentially become the property of their husband and contribute to his standing rather than their own. Such inequitable distributions of work and benefits are obviously topics which social scientists would wish to probe.

Women in many countries are excluded from education. When families migrate to the AICs it is very noticeable that it is the women who are illiterate and have not had the opportunity to learn the language of the country to which they have come.

Men in many societies continue to justify a division between the public and private spheres which ensures that women confined to the home. This often has the sanction of organised religion, whose leadership roles are monopolised by men who preach the subordination of women. It is hardly surprising therefore that women continue to be treated as chattels for the sexual enjoyment of men. At its most extreme, this means that women who have been raped are still murdered by their families in Pakistan and Bangladesh, and women in Africa south of the Saraha (SSA) are subjected to so-called 'female circumcision' (infibulation) to ensure they are 'virgins' on their bridal night; and the widespread belief in southern Africa that sex with a virgin is a cure for HIV/AIDS and that the woman's feelings in the matter are irrelevant has helped towards that potentially rich area being filled with broken families who have lost one or more of their parents and who may well themselves be infected.

SOUTH-WEST ASIA

IRAN

Official name: Islamic Republic of Iran
Type of government: Islamic republic
Capital: Tehran
Area: 1,648,000 sq km
Population (2005): 68,017,860
GNI per capita (2005): $2,010 (PPP $2,300)

Evolution of government: Iran, known as Persia before 1935, was partially occupied by British and Russian forces in the Second World War because of its strategic location and abundant oil resources. In 1953 popular revolt brought Mohammed Mosadegh to power and the Anglo-Iranian Oil Company was nationalised, but the autocratic regime of the Shah was restored by the United States. It was overthrown in 1979 by a popular revolution capitalising on anti-US feeling, but the revolution was speedily captured by the Islamic Shi'ite leader, Ayatollah Khomeini, and an Islamic Republic proclaimed. The United

▶

SOUTH-WEST ASIA continued

States supported the aggressors, Iraq, in the Iraq-Iran War of 1980–88, which cost hundreds of thousands of lives on both sides. Since then, would-be reformists have been successfully frustrated by conservative religious elements.

Main features of government: Chief of state and Supreme Leader Ayatollah Ali Hoseini-Khamanei succeeded the late Ayatollah Khomeini in 1989 and can veto actions of government as contrary to Islamic law. President Mahmoud Ahmadinejad, head of government elected by popular vote for five-year term. Legislature (Majlis) unicameral elected by popular vote. Women are largely excluded from the **public sector** and are required to wear the all-enveloping chador outside the home; strict religious laws are policed by self-appointed militias. Iran's economy is dominated by the oil sector and attempts to industrialise and modernise under the Shah were frustrated by the endemic corruption and the inefficiency of the state sector. Unsurprisingly, given its recent history, the Islamic government has chosen to waste a great proportion of its resources on building up Iran's arms capacity, including **weapons of mass destruction**. This has, since the election of Ahmadinejad, escalated into confrontation with the United States.

IRAQ

Official name: Republic of Iraq (Al Jumhuriyah al Iraqiyah)
Type of government: Parliamentary republic
Capital: Baghdad
Area: 438,000 sq km
Population (2005 est.): 26,074,906
GNI *per capita (2004)*: PPP $2,100 est.

Evolution of government: Mesopotamia, the land between the two rivers, the Tigris and the Euphrates, was home to the world's oldest civilisation. Conquered by the Arabs in the 7th century it subsequently became part of the Ottoman Empire. Occupied by Britain during the course of the First World War, in 1920 it was declared a League of Nations mandate under British administration and attained its independence as a kingdom in 1932. The king and many of his advisers were murdered in 1958 and a republic proclaimed, which in practice meant a series of military dictators ending with Saddam Hussein. In 1980 his troops attacked Iran, leading to an eight-year war with massive losses on both sides. In 1990 he tried to annex Kuwait, but was driven out by a coalition led by the United States in the Gulf War of 1991. Finally in 2003 the US government used the pretext that there were weapons of mass destruction in Iraq to invade the country and overthrow Saddam. In June 2004 power was transferred from the interim military government to an Iraqi Interim Government which secured a majority for a new Constitution in 2005. Ironically, under the secular regime women in Iraq were subject to less serious discrimination that in many other Arab countries.

SOUTH ASIA

BANGLADESH

Official name: People's Republic of Free Bengal (Gana Prajatantri Bangladesh)
Type of government: Parliamentary republic
Capital: Dhaka
Area: 144,000 sq km
Population (2003): 138,000,000
GNI per capita (2005): $440 (PPP $1,980)

Evolution of government: As East Bengal, part of British India until 1947. Aided by India, the former East Pakistan rebelled against Pakistani rule and gained its independence in 1971. Political unrest and the assassination of its first president, Sheikh Mujibur Rahman, inaugurated a period of military intervention until civilian rule was restored in 1986. The country consists of the greater part of the delta of the Ganges and Brahmaputra so uniquely 97 per cent of the country is liable to flooding and damage from cyclones in the Bay of Bengal.

Main features of government: Presidential power reduced 1991 following unrest the previous year. Two-party system, involving persistent and at times violent confrontation between Awami League (in power from 1996) and Bangladesh National Party, in 2001 both led by women. The single-chamber parliament has 30 reserved seats for women. However, in the poorer sectors of society, traditional attitudes prevail, and women are still treated as chattels of their fathers and/or husbands, and denied education and independence.

INDIA

Official name: Republic of India
Type of government: Federal parliamentary republic
Capital: New Delhi
Area: 3,387,000 sq km
Population (2003): 1,064,000,000
GNI per capita (2005): $620 (PPP $3,100)

Evolution of government: Northern India unified in the 15th century by the Mughals, a Central Asian dynasty, but rule disintegrated after the efforts of Aurangzeb (1658–1707) to convert his Hindu subjects to Islam had led to war with the Marathas backed by Britain. British and French rivalry to control India, decisively settled in favour of Britain by 1763, followed by expansion of British East India Company. Following the 'Indian Mutiny' (now known as the First War of Independence, 1857) Mughals deposed and British India placed under direct rule from London. Some 500 princely states under varying degrees of control incorporated in Indian Empire 1877 with Queen Victoria as Empress. Limited self-government introduced by the Montagu-Chelmsford reforms 1919, but increasing pressure and resistance led by Mahatma Gandhi and the Congress Party led to promise of independence. Independent as Dominion 1947 and became Republic within the Commonwealth 1950.

▶

SOUTH ASIA continued

Main features of government: Presidential functions largely ceremonial. Parliamentary government interrupted only briefly by state of emergency under Indira Gandhi 1975–77. Subsequently voted out of office, she was re-elected in 1980 but her assault on the Golden Temple and her assassination by her Sikh bodyguard 1984 ended the unquestioned dominance of Congress Party. In recent years rise of Hindu nationalism provides main unifying factor in fragmented multi-party system. In 1966 states consolidated on linguistic lines and vestiges of old princely states swept away; now 25 states under appointed Governor-General and elected legislature. Central government has frequently used its power to place recalcitrant states under 'President's rule', but states still retain a substantial degree of autonomy. Owing to linguistic diversity, English remains a working language of government.

PAKISTAN

Official name: Islamic Republic of Pakistan (Islami Jamhuriya-e-Pakistan)
Type of government: Thinly-disguised military rule
Capital: Islamabad
Area: 803,940 sq km (*Note*: Pakistani-controlled Kashmir, known in Pakistan as Azad Kashmir, and the Northern Areas are disputed by India.)
Population (2005): 162,419,946
GNI per capita (2005): $600 (PPP $2,160)

Evolution of government: As India until 1947. The Muslim desire for a separate state led to simultaneous independence of India and Pakistan in 1947, whereupon the princely states were constrained to accede to one or the other. Pakistan (including East Pakistan, later Bangladesh) initially a parliamentary republic led by Jinnah, whose early death left his Islamic League leaderless. Patrimonial rule by large landowners terminated by military intervention, so-called 'tutelary democracy', and the overthrow and subsequent execution of the charismatic Bhutto by General Zia. Under Zia's military dictatorship 1977–88 new capital built at Islamabad and Islamic Law adopted. When Zia was killed in an air crash civilian government was restored but the vendetta of Prime Minister Nawaz Sharif against his chief rival, Benazir Bhutto, whom he forced into exile, led to unstable and unpopular government. His government's attempt to oust India from disputed territory in Kashmir, however, failed and in October 1999 General Pervez Musharraf assumed power. He proclaimed himself President in 2001, a title confirmed by referendum in 2002 for a five-year term, but his value as an ally of the United States post-'9/11' means that no serious attempt has been made to press him to restore effective representative government. In 2005 a major earthquake centered on Mushaffarabad killed tens of thousands in Pakistani-controlled Kashmir, and showed up the inefficiency of the military regime in bringing relief.

Main features of government: Federal state of four provinces and federally-administered tribal areas. Military dominance. Bitterly divided two-party system. Importance of patrimonialism in electoral politics; accusations of corruption are standard charges against politicians. Founded as an avowedly Muslim state,

▶

SOUTH ASIA continued

government is subject to strong internal pressures from Islamist radicals; violence against women is common and traditionally sanctioned.

SRI LANKA

Official name: Democratic Socialist Republic of Sri Lanka (Sri Lankā Prajathanthrika Samajavadi Janarajaya). Also known as Ceylon, Serendib, Taprobane
Type of government: Presidential republic
Capital: Colombo (Legislative: Sri Jayawardenepura at Kotte)
Area: 64,500 sq km
Population (2003): 19,000,000
GNI per capita (2005): $1,010 (PPP $4,000)

Evolution of government: Unified state under Sinhalese leadership emerged c.200 BCE. Island was part conquered in turn by Portugal (1505), the Netherlands (1658) and Britain (1796), but the Kingdom of Kandy remained independent until its voluntary cession to Britain 1825. Not part of India, Ceylon (as then known) was the second territory in the former British Empire to hold election under full adult franchise 1929. Independent as Dominion 1948. Sirimavo Bandaranaike was the world's first woman prime minister (1960–65, 1970–77) and name Sri Lanka restored for parliamentary republic 1972. Transformed into presidential republic 1982–83 under personalist leadership of Junius Jayawardene 1977–87. However, after 1983 both the unitary state and Sinhalese dominance was challenged by a civil war in north and east led by Tamil secessionist movement the Liberation Tigers of Tamil Eelam (LTTE). A ceasefire was negotiated in 2002, but following the election of a hardline president appeared on the point of breakdown early in 2006.

Main features of government: Presidential government but with strong two-party system and active parliament. President Chandrika Kumaratunga elected president 1995 reappointed her mother, Mrs Bandaranaike, prime minister, for the third time (1995–2000). President Kumaratunga survived a suicide bomber's assassination attempt in 1999, but failed to reach agreement with Tamils, who form approximately 20 per cent of the population, and the new president elected in 2005 is committed to reviewing the terms of peace. Women have a high degree of personal and political freedom and play active roles in economic activity.

Women and development

Essentially over the years in approaches to the understanding of the situation of developing world women have reflected the changing perception of the development agenda. The 'modernisation' approach of the 1950s and 1960s quite simply ignored women. It was assumed that what benefited men also benefited 'their' women. Women were not recognised as constituting a distinct – and particularly disadvantaged – group.

The 'basic needs' or anti-poverty approach to development in the early 1970s, expressed, for example, through UN Conferences on Food and Population held in 1974, for the first time drew attention to the fact that social policies, developmental or otherwise, had not been gender neutral. It was recognised that a disproportionate number of the world's poor were women and that, if considered with the dependent children for whom these poor women carried responsibility, they constituted the vast majority of the poorest people on earth. Hence their well-being was a primary ethical question for developmental schemes.

The effects of development on women and its corollary, the role of women in the development process, were therefore opened up to research and the UN declared 1975 International Women's Year, with a major conference held in Mexico City. However, in Mexico the majority of women are still poor and still work extremely hard. They may do so out of economic necessity or they may do so because of social expectation. They do not do so because of legal bonds, since although the population are nominally Catholic the majority of poor people are not formally married (Lewis 1962).

The period 1976–85 was decreed the UN Decade for the Advancement of Women. The position of women, together with that of indigenous peoples, was established as a key human rights issue for the World Conference on Human Rights (June 1993), and at the UN's Fourth World Conference on Women, in Beijing, China, in 1995 governments made solemn undertakings to protect and promote the human rights of women and girl children; promises which in many cases have yet to be fulfilled.

Apart from moral and ethical questions concerning their rights as human beings, women form a vital part of the development process and their contributions to a sustainable form of development are integral. Environmental degradation is increased by inappropriate development, which is a consequence of poverty, and it then in turn increases the poverty from which it arises. It is most painfully experienced by the poorest elements of society. These usually include women and children. More radical approaches also stress that women are a separate issue on the development agenda, but they do so for functional as well as moral reasons. They argue either:

(a) that the involvement of women is vital for the efficiency of any developmental scheme; or
(b) that the empowerment of women is the motor force for development of any meaningful kind.

Empowerment, a concept deriving from the work of Brazilian educationalist Paulo Freire, means acquiring the awareness and the skills to take charge of one's own environment. This perspective, combining as it does elements from radical and Marxist feminist thought, often also takes on board other poor sections that suffered under colonialism and now continue to do so under a form of development perceived as distorted and exploitative of both people and of nature (Shiva 1988: 2).

Research in the developing world

No study of the developing world could be complete without first noticing the very serious problems of undertaking social and political research in developing countries. Some of these problems, such as governmental secrecy, the tendency of politicians to use interviews for polemic rather than information and the high cost and limited scope of social surveys, are problems that will be encountered anywhere. But there are also some additional difficulties.

(a) Press views. Coming to a developing country, especially for the first time, it is important to remember how little real information is generally available about it abroad, and the extent to which that information is the product of transnational media agencies which have established a stereotype which they find difficult to avoid. In fact, use of the newspaper files as background will ensure that this stereotype is regularly repeated – if not always very accurately; remember reporters are by definition not experts on the countries in which they are reporting. In English, the dominant view will inevitably be that of the United States and the Washington consensus. Researchers should therefore try as far as possible to clear their minds of preconceptions and begin by observing carefully what they actually see before them.

(b) The official version. In developed countries, a variety of news media will be available and the official version of things will be contested. In many developing countries, without necessarily involving any form of censorship, the media are frequently reticent about matters which might embarrass their proprietors or even endanger individual commentators. Much easier to reprint official handouts, sometimes with only minor emendations, more often just as they are.

(c) Official statistics. Governments by definition have a monopoly over the supply of official statistics. Even where the resources exist to provide alternatives, the government is in a strong position to contest their accuracy. But it should not be taken for granted that the role of a governmental statistical service is to provide accurate information. Those who have been seconded to provide advice to developing countries can confirm that all too frequently their staff understand very well that their career depends on presenting the government in the best possible light.

(d) The Chinese jack-in-the-box. When in 2005 the World Bank announced that China had become the second largest economy in the world after the

United States, it was hard to find any commentator who expressed any doubt about this. In fact, since then, by constant repetition this assertion seems to have become accepted as fact. It is long overdue, the Chinese think, for them to be taken so seriously as a major world power. However, China, for all its capitalist enterprise, is still a Communist country, and there is a strong prima facie case for treating its statistics as of just as much (or as little) value as those of the former Soviet Union, which Russians can now confirm were largely fictitious. As for the World Bank's role, it would be reasonable to ask just how much growth they could reasonably expect of a country in a single year and why they had not noticed it happening earlier.

Social and other indicators

Since many concepts used routinely in political discussion, such as development, are very complex, social scientists are used to employing indicators of various kinds to measure them. Thus it has long been traditional to measure economic development in terms of a single indicator, per capita GNI: that is to say, the gross national income, formerly known as the gross domestic product (GDP) of a country divided by its population. In Table 1.3, selected figures for 2004 are given. They show not only how wide was the gap between the most developed nations and the rest at the end of the Cold War, but, more worryingly, how it was tending to open up, as the developing world itself was 'pulling apart'.

In 1992 there was no real difference between the highest low-income country, Indonesia, and the lowest middle-income country, Côte d'Ivoire. By 1997, however, Indonesia ($1,110) ranked as a lower middle-income country and well ahead of Côte d'Ivoire ($710). Chile ($4,820), an upper middle income country in 1992, had moved further ahead of South Africa ($3,210), while Ireland ($17,790), like Israel ($16,180) had nearly twice the GNI per capita of the lowest high-income country, Slovenia ($9,840). At the other end of the scale, the Democratic Republic of the Congo (DRC) ($110), Mozambique ($140), Sierra Leone ($160) and Rwanda ($210) remained among the poorest countries in the world (World Bank 1999).

In 2003 the upper boundary of the low-income countries was $765 but the conditions of the poorest countries were unimaginably bad. The DRC, racked by civil war, had fallen to $100 and Sierra Leone to $150; Rwanda was worse off in real terms at $220, though Mozambique, at $210, had improved its position significantly. At the upper end of the band the outbreak of civil war in Côte d'Ivoire had brought it down from $710 to $660.

Indonesia, at $810, remained a very poor lower middle-income country, ranking ahead of India ($540) but behind Sri Lanka ($930). Though one of

Table 1.3   GDP and GNI per capita, Atlas method, selected countries, 2004

COUNTRY	Total GDP (million current US$)	GNI per capita, Atlas method (current US$)
Algeria	84,649	2,280
Argentina	151,501	3,720
Bangladesh	56,844	440
Brazil	604,855	3,090
China	1,649,329	1,290
Egypt	75,148	1,310
Ghana	8,620	380
India	691,876	620
Indonesia	257,641	1,140
Iran	162,709	2,300
Iraq	–	826–2,355e
Malaysia	117,776	4,650
Mexico	676,497	6,770
Mozambique	5,548	250
Nigeria	72,106	390
Pakistan	96,115	600
Sierra Leone	1,075	200
South Africa	212,777	3,630
Sri Lanka	20,055	1,010
Thailand	163,491	2,540
UAE	70,960	over 10,066e

High income = GNI per capita $10,066 or more
Upper middle income = $3,256–$10,065
Lower middle income = $826–$3,255
Low income = less than $825
e = estimate
Source: World Bank, 2006

the richer countries in Africa, South Africa at $2,750 was still a lower middle-income country, only just ahead of Brazil, which, despite being the world's ninth-largest economy, only produced $2,720 per head.

With the boundary between lower and upper set at $3,035, Chile remained an upper middle-income country but at $4,360 was significantly worse off in real terms – and Argentina, at $3,810, had fallen even further after the crisis of 2001. But the real contrast was with the high-income countries, which, with the exception of Israel ($16,240), had improved their positions markedly. On the eve of joining the European Union (EU), Slovenia had risen to $11,240 while Ireland, an enthusiastic existing member, registered a spectacular $27,010 (World Bank 2005).

In recent years, however, there has been increasing dissatisfaction with the crudity of this measure. First, comparisons of per capita GNI were rendered very difficult indeed by wide variations and wild fluctuations in exchange rates. This was to some extent met by using calculations of purchasing power parity (PPP), as in Table 1.4. Secondly, the indicator in itself does not show

Table 1.4 GDP and GNI per capita, PPP (current US$), selected countries, 2004

COUNTRY	GDP and rank order	GNI PER CAPITA
Algeria	210,657 (39)	6,260
Argentina	486,366 (23)	12,460
Bangladesh	263,434 (32)	1,980
Brazil	1,482,959 (09)	8,020
China	7,123,712 (2)	5,530
Egypt	282,026 (30)	4,120
Ghana	48,747 (69)	2,280
India	3,362,960 (4)	3,100
Indonesia	779,719 (15)	3,460
Iran	505,019 (21)	7,550
Iraq	–	–
Malaysia	246,036 (35)	9,630
Mexico	1,014,514 (12)	9,590
Mozambique	23,583 (96)	1,160
Nigeria	155,571 (50)	930
Pakistan	336,050 (25)	2,160
Sierra Leone	4,429 (143)	790
South Africa	510,102 (20)	10,960
Sri Lanka	81,144 (57)	4,000
Thailand	510,268 (19)	8,020
UAE	–	21,000

Source: World Bank

how the economic resources generated are actually used. Unless they are being channelled back into investment or social welfare they will not necessarily generate further development. To give a clearer picture of what is going on, therefore, more indicators are required. Economic indicators include the actual purchasing power of the currency in terms of daily necessities, the rate of saving, the level of investment in industry and inequality of income and wealth. Social indicators include life expectancy, infant mortality rate (IMR, meaning the deaths of children under one year per thousand live births), the number of persons per doctor, the proportion of children in school and the percentage of adults who are able to read and write. Political indicators include governmental instability, the frequency of elections and the tendency to military intervention.

In 1990 the UN Development Programme published the *Human Development Report* which used for the first time the Human Development Index (HDI). This ranked countries by a single measure derived from a small number of carefully selected indicators. The most important difference from older measures was the rejection of the use of fluctuating and frequently misleading exchange rate conversions in favour of purchasing power parities. There are four basic indicators: life expectancy, adult literacy, mean years of schooling and average income. From 1994 the comparisons between countries formulated on the basis of the HDI are made more realistic by fixing maxima and minima for each variable range (UNDP 1994a). Adult literacy cannot exceed 100 per cent, and 98.5 per cent is probably a more realistic maximum. Life expectancy is unlikely to attain 85 years in any country in the foreseeable future, nor is it likely to fall below 25. Mean years of schooling vary between 0 and 15. Such refinements reflect the growing awareness that economic growth, changes to the productive sectors and increased per capita income do not necessarily bring benefits to whole societies (UNDP 1994).

Some general conclusions emerge very clearly from Table 1.5, which is based on figures from 2004. Comparison with Table 1.3 shows how with the effects of exchange rates taken out the differences within countries can be seen to be as important as, if not more important, than the differences between them. The percentage in poverty is highest in South Asia and Africa South of the Sahara. South Asia has 30 per cent of the world's population but nearly half the world's poor. Average life expectancy is 77.7 years in the developed world, 62.7 years in South Asia, 48.9 years in Africa south of the Sahara – a figure which has actually declined since 1988. Moreover these effects are reflected in wide disparities within developing world states – in Mexico (where the average in 1997 was 72.2 years), life expectancy for the poorest 10 per cent is 20 years less than for the richest 10 per cent (UNDP 1999).

Table 1.5   HDI index and world rankings, selected states, 2004 (data from 2002)

COUNTRY	HDI Index	World ranking	GDP per capita rank minus HDI rank
Algeria	0.704	108 Medium	−25
Argentina	0.853	34 High	14
Bangladesh	0.509	138 Medium	1
Brazil	0.775	72 Medium	−9
China	0.745	94 Medium	5
Egypt	0.653	120 Medium	−12
Ghana	0.568	131 Medium	−3
India	0.505	127 Medium	−10
Indonesia	0.692	111 Medium	2
Iran	0.732	101 Medium	−31
Iraq			
Malaysia	0.793	59 Medium	−2
Mexico	0.802	53 High	5
Mozambique	0.354	171 Low	−14
Nigeria	0.466	151 Low	15
Pakistan	0.497	142 Low	−7
Sierra Leone	0.273	177 Low	−1
South Africa	0.666	119 Medium	−66
Sri Lanka	0.740	96 Medium	16
Thailand	0.768	76 Medium	−9
UAE	0.824	49 High	−26

Source: UNDP, *Human Development Report*, 2002

Most striking, however, is the way the so-called 'Asian Tigers', in East and South-east Asia, have succeeded in maintaining high levels of growth over a long period and making the transition to developed status.

SOUTH-EAST ASIA

MALAYSIA

Official name: Federation of Malaysia
Type of government: Federal parliamentary monarchy
Capital: Kuala Lumpur
Area: 330,000 sq km
Population (2005 est.): 23,953,136
GNI per capita (2003): $4,650 (PPP $9,630)

Evolution of government: Peninsular Malaysia was formerly part of Mahadjpahit, a Hindu empire. Britain established trading posts in the Malay Straits in Malacca and Penang in 1786; later in the 19th century brought the southern Malay states under a Protectorate. Occupied by Japan 1942–45. In 1948 Federation of Malaya confronted Communist insurgents led by Chin Peng, but the insurgency was successfully defeated by Commonwealth forces. Independence was granted in 1957 and the Emergency officially ended in 1960. In 1963 the east Malaysian states of Sabah and Sarawak, together with Singapore, joined the Federation which became the Federation of Malaysia. Indonesian efforts to conquer Sarawak and Sabah (the so-called Confrontation) were successfully resisted, but Singapore, with its large ethnic Chinese majority, seceded from the Federation in 1965.

Main features of government: Elective monarchy; the Malay Rulers choose one of their number to act as king for a five-year term. Prime Minister is head of government; parliament is however dominated by the ruling coalition, now called the Barisan Nasional (BN), which has monopolised power since independence. The government retains very extensive emergency powers, though any serious threat from insurgents has long since ended.

THAILAND

Official name: Land of the Free (Muang Thai)
Type of government: Parliamentary monarchy
Capital: Bangkok (Krung Thep)
Area: 513,000 sq km
Population (2005 est.): 65,444,371
GNI per capita (2005): $2,540 (PPP $8,020)

Evolution of government: A unified Thai kingdom, known as Siam until 1940, was established in the mid-14th century. Despite pressure from France, Thailand

▶

SOUTH-EAST ASIA continued

is the only South-east Asian country never to have been colonised by a European power. A bloodless revolution in 1932 led to a constitutional monarchy. Occupied and forced into alliance with Japan during the Second World War, in the post-war period Thailand was subject from time to time to intervention by the police and the army, and is currently facing armed violence in its three south-ernmost provinces, where there is a Muslim majority.

Main features of government: The monarch has limited formal powers but very high prestige. He designates the prime minister from the majority parties in the House of Representatives (Sapha Phuthaen Ratsadon), which is chosen by universal suffrage. The party system is complex and unstable.

INDONESIA

Official name: Republic of Indonesia (Republik Indonesia)
Type of government: Presidential republic
Capital: Jakarta
Area: 1,919,440 sq km
Population (2005 est.): 241,973,879
GNI per capita (2005): $1,140 (PPP $3,460)

Evolution of government: Colonised by the Dutch in the 17th century, the islands were occupied from 1942 to 1945 by Japanese forces. After the war the Indonesians proclaimed their independence and finally obtained it by agreement in 1949. Sukarno, Indonesia's first leader, balanced pressures from the Communists and the armed forces until an outbreak of violence in 1966 led to him being deposed in 1967 by General Suharto, who held power as a military dictator with support from the United States for two decades. Following the East Asian crisis of 1997, the collapse of the Indonesian economy and the endemic corruption led to widespread riots and he resigned in 1998, following which Indonesia made a successful democratic transition.

Main features of government: President is both head of state and head of government. Unicameral House of Representatives. With military backing under Suharto, one party, Golkar, gained hegemony, and remains the largest party.

China: the dragon awakes?

China presents a genuine anomaly. First of all, its economy is so large that it is one of the largest in the world (see Table 1.6). Just how large, however, is an interesting question. At the beginning of 2004 it was ranked fifth among world economies and was expected to pass Germany by 2008. Yet in 2005 a

Table 1.6 World's largest economies by 2005 rank order

GDP (US$bn)	2001	2002	2003	2004	2005
USA	10,208	10,437	10,400	10,980	11,750
EU		–	–	–	11,650
China	1,158*	1,273	5,700	6,449	7,262
Japan	4,148	3,934	3,550	3,567	3,745
India	480	547	2,660	3,022	3,319
Germany	1,847	2,012	2,184	2,271	2,362
UK	1,424	1,513	1,520	1,664	1,782
France	1,307	1,421	1,540	1,654	1,737
Italy	1,089	1,192	1,438	1,552	1,609
Brazil	504	471	1,340	1,379	1,492
Russia	309	347	1,350	1,287	1,408
Canada	699	746	923	957	1,023

* less the HKSAR
Sources: 2001 China excluding HKSAR,
http://www.deed.state.mn.us/lmi/publications/trends/0603/backtab.htm
2002 Countrywatch, http://www.countrywatch.com/includes/grank/gdpnumericcer.asp
2003 CIA World Factbook, http://www.theodora.com/wfb2003/rankings/gdp_2003_0.html
2004 CIA World Factbook, http://www.immigration-usa.com/wfb2004/rankings/
economy/gdp_2004_0.html
2005 CIA World Factbook, http://www.photius.com/rankings/economy/gdp_2005_0.html

statistical revision by the World Bank placed it second in the world after the United States and ahead of Japan.

Secondly, moreover, China's population is also vast. Hence even on the optimistic view, it ranks very low in per capita GNI ($1,290). Though by purchasing power parity the figure of $5,530 per capita looks relatively generous, this should lead us to suspect, what most financial observers already know, that China's remarkable performance is largely the product of its being able to maintain a seriously undervalued currency. Since it is undervalued rather than overvalued China has been able to make only token attempts to revalue it. In this respect China has still far more in common with the developing world than with the advanced industrialised countries which it seeks to emulate.

Thirdly, it retains the political forms and the authoritarian style of the former Second World at a time when many developing world countries have already taken major steps along the road to democratisation. It is this centralised control that enables the Chinese authorities among other things to fix an artificially low exchange rate for their currency, the renminbi. Yet China pays lip-service at least to the principles of free trade and a free market, suggesting that its leaders see no necessary connection between the economic and the political.

It is becoming a global economic powerhouse and its almost insatiable demand has driven up the costs of the raw materials it needs, as despite its size China is not well supplied with minerals. Investors in emerging markets have tended to narrow their preferences down to what by 2005 had become known as the BRIC (Brazil, Russia, India and China) countries, of which China is generally seen as the most important.

One thing is clear: China certainly cannot yet be regarded as an advanced industrialised country and statistically it is so significant that it can hardly be categorised on its own. China, therefore, will be treated here as a developing country, although for some purposes it will be necessary to consider it separately.

The View from the Ground

By *Staff Writers*, Shanghai (AFP), 23 January 2006

China's Economy Likely to be in World's Top 5 in 2005

China's economy likely became one of the world's five biggest in 2005 as booming exports and surging investment again helped secure growth of well above nine percent, analysts said Monday.

Ahead of Wednesday's release of China's 2005 economic data, analysts expect the world fastest growing major economy to surge between 9.5 and 10.3 percent to surpass the two-trillion-dollar mark.

"It will definitely go past France, so for sure China is going to be the number five economy in the world," Chen Xingdong, an economist at BNP Paribas in Beijing, said.

France's economy posted gross domestic product (GDP) of 2.04 trillion dollars in 2004, according to World Bank figures, and economists estimate its economy was unlikely to have grown by more than two percent last year.

Given China's rate of growth – around five times faster than Europe's – the Asian juggernaut could even surpass powerhouse Britain, the world's fourth largest economy.

"It would depend on the UK's GDP (last year). Number one the nominal GDP growth and number two the exchange rate of the British pound against the US dollar," said Chen.

Only last month the Chinese economy had officially been worth 1.6 trillion dollars, a still formidable sum that placed China seventh on the list of world's largest economies.

But Beijing's announcement on December 20 that the economy had been erroneously undervalued by 284 billion suddenly lifted China past Italy into the sixth spot. Following the revaluation, the government said China's economy had expanded at an average rate of 9.9 percent between 1993 and 2004, up from 9.4 percent reported previously, with growth of 10.1 percent in 2004.

For years international economists warned that the Chinese economy was undervalued because millions of service-orientated businesses had been unaccounted for.

The adjustment led the National Development and Reform Commission, the nation's top economic planning body to overhaul its 2005 GDP growth forecast from 9.4 percent to 9.8 percent.

The tax bureau also raised its estimate to 9.8 percent.

Economists were pleased with the revaluation because it meant the economy was in better shape than previously thought.

"The details of the revisions also suggest that growth is on a more sustainable footing," Lehman Brothers economist Robert Subbaraman said in a note to clients.

The imbalances had led to fears both at home and abroad that the massive amount of fixed-asset investment, which at times neared a nerve-wracking high of 50 percent of GDP, could lead to an inflationary crisis.

But now that the economy is worth 284 billion dollars more, fixed-asset investment levels, a major barometer of how much the government is spending on major infrastructure projects, have improved.

"It is likely that the investment-to-GDP ratio for 2004 will be revised down closer to 40 percent," said Subbaraman, who expects annual GDP growth of 9.8 percent with inflation to remain under control.

Even China's consumption-to-GDP ratio, long a source of concern for a government looking to shift more of the economic burden to the consumer, has improved.

"The revised GDP data shows a less imbalanced economy: over-investment and hence concerns about a potential oversupply problem in China's economy are less severe than previously thought," said Subbaraman.

EAST ASIA

CHINA

Official name: People's Republic of China (Chi Zhonghua Renmin Gonghe Guo)
Type of government: Unitary people's republic
Capital: Beijing
Area: 9,598,000 sq km
Population (2003): 1,288,000,000
GNI per capita (2005): $1,290 (PPP $5,530)

Evolution of government: Unified government first established c.200 BCE; collapse of Ming Dynasty in 1644 coincided with early contacts with Western Europe. In the 19th century China was subject increasingly to pressure for concessions from Europe and the USA. In 1911 the Nationalists under Dr Sun Yat-sen overthrew the monarchy but were unable to establish a working republic; with much of the country under the rule of local warlords, in 1931 the Japanese invaded Manchuria. War resumed in 1937 and merged with the Second World War. Weakened by the war effort, the Nationalists were overthrown by the Communists under Mao Zedong in 1949, who established a Soviet-style regime which shed its dependence on Moscow after the death of Stalin and was increasingly characterised by a 'cult of personality' (Chapter 7). After the failure of the Great Leap Forward (1958–59) Mao launched the Great Proletarian Cultural Revolution in 1966 to destroy all vestiges of the old order but the movement got

▶

EAST ASIA continued

out of control and the army was called in to restore order. Since Mao's death in 1976 a gerontocracy.

Main features of government: Leadership in general secretary of Communist Party; administration in prime minister and 45-member State Council. 'Leading role' for Communist Party. Elected National People's Congress of 3,000 deputies rubber-stamps decrees. Harsh legal system with death penalty for numerous offences. Substantial economic liberalisation in 1990s and creation of economic development areas in e.g. Guanzhou. Hong Kong since 1997 a Special Administrative Region.

Competing ideologies and interpretations of development

1.   The conservative tradition: modernisation theory

The Cold War resulted in the United States taking a direct interest in some parts of the world almost for the first time, especially but not exclusively to fill the gap left by the dismantling of the European colonial empires. Its initial approach was based on the notion of modernisation.

The attraction of the United States for the rest of the world was that it represented modernity. There was little initial resistance, therefore, to the US belief that the rest of the world was destined in time to follow the example of the United States. Indeed, this view has, in the longer term, turned out to be at least partly true.

What was termed 'modernisation theory', though, derived from two influences: the structural-functionalism of Talcott Parsons, based on the work of Herbert Spencer and Emile Durkheim, and Max Weber's work on values and attitudes. McClelland and Inkeles concentrate on values and take up the theme of evolution in their tendency to see growth towards equilibrium. Some of the early work of the structural-functionalists now seems almost naive in its touching belief in stability and pluralist consensus. Almond's work combines elements of Parsonian social theory and David Easton's political system analysis.

The best-known example of the school is the work of the American economist W.W. Rostow (1971). Rostow's five stages of development – traditional society, preconditions for take-off, take-off, sustained growth, mass consumption – represent stages in the process of development in the United States (Rostow 1960, 1971). As with Clark Kerr et al. (1960), this was seen as a unilinear process leading to an end-state akin to that of the United States in the 1950s. For these writers, modernity implied liberal-democracy and pluralism. Hence political development was virtually synonymous with modernisation. It was a concept largely sustained by Ford Foundation finance and its dominance expired with the grant in 1971.

The early modernisation theorists saw traditionalism and modernity as two poles and in zero-sum relationship with one another, though it was recognised that there were political problems with economic development (Staley 1954). Later material acknowledges the survival of the traditional alongside the modern. The persistence of ethnic distinctions, clientelism etc. would exemplify the survival of traditional patterns, likewise the continuing importance of caste in Indian elections. Traditional, however, did not necessarily mean static. Traditional culture was not internally consistent and traditional societies were not necessarily homogeneous in social structure nor were they always in conflict with modern forms and therefore liable to be destroyed by change.

The failure of the first, optimistic modernisation theories results in more sophisticated 'modernisation revisionism'. Huntington, who coined the term (1976), stresses the importance of indigenous social structures but also the need for strong government. Unlike early modernisation theory which was optimistic in an era of assumed progress, modernisation revisionism exuded a new pessimism and saw modernisation itself as a force for the breakdown of order and the development of praetorianism. The process of development mobilises social groups previously neglected or ignored and temporary disorder must be contained until institutionalisation restores stability. South Korea, one of the few countries to achieve successful economic development under an authoritarian regime, is often taken as an example.

Ensuring order during the development process rests on strengthening the government and state. Its techniques often include repression, co-optation and ideological penetration. Huntington himself laid a strong emphasis on the value of the military as modernisers. Some modernisation revisionists, e.g. J. J. Johnson, took the role of the military one step further. They argued that the military is a substitute for an effective middle class as an agent of developmental change (Johnson 1964). However, the experience of Argentina under the so-called Argentine Revolution after 1966 suggests the exact opposite.

More recent neo-liberal interpretations of development return to the older-style optimistic approach to modernization (Sklair 1994). The benefits of development will trickle down to the less developed because the market will ensure that production relocates to where costs are cheapest and therefore advantage moves from region to region ensuring the distribution of global resources. No action is necessary. The way in which firms in the developed world have been outsourcing their call-centre and other service sector work to cheaper locations in the developing world is an example of just this process. In this respect India has enjoyed a special advantage, through the widespread use of the English language. Outsourcing has since 2000 become a key ingredient of India's economic development.

There are strong arguments that sustainable development is best achieved under a liberal democratic government. However, to assert that the liberal democratic state is the ultimate form of human social organisation (e.g.

Fukuyama 1992), is reminiscent of the unwarranted optimism of early moder-nisation theories, which were shaped on an implied long-term blueprint based on Western industrial capitalism. Today, the salvation of the developing world is too often seen as achievable through the operations of the global market-place and the benevolence of the Group of Eight (G8) nations, while experi-ence on the ground quickly suggests that matters are not so simple.

2. The social reformist tradition: developmentalism

Alternatively, there is a perspective which is broadly associated with the social reformist tradition of thought, which acknowledges the present inequity, but sees it as redeemable through First World action. Such ideas are found in the Brandt Commission Report (Brandt 1980) and are therefore sometimes called a North–South model. Benefits could and should be redistributed in favour of the developing world. This could be done through restructuring trading relationships, through aid and investment. There are, though, obstacles to its success which must be addressed; problems such as protection of First World economies, repatriation of profits and interest on debts.

In this perspective belief in the primary role of the state in economic development was supported by Alexander Gerschenkron's theory of relative economic backwardness (REB) (Gerschenkron 1962). Gerschenkron measured an economy's relative backwardness partly in terms of psychological and physical distance from Great Britain, the first industrial nation, and partly in terms of the ability and willingness of banks to mobilise risk capital and to assume an active ownership role in other firms ('universal banking'). He also advanced a number of reasons for relative economic backwardness based on historical experience in Europe, the USA and Japan. These included the role of agriculture in capital formation, the significance of mechanisms of capital accumulation (colonialism and banks), the availability of technology, market expansion and the role of the state (industrialisation imperative, protection-ism). The main examples used were for the United States: Hamilton and civil war (1791); Germany: List and Bismarck (1841); Japan: the Meiji Restoration (1880); and Russia (foreign investment in oil and manufacturing after the end of serfdom).

Gerschenkron's argument was that in each of these cases the patterns of finance of industrialisation could be understood as responses to relative eco-nomic backwardness. Retained profits and private investors would dominate in well-advanced countries. Bank finance and entrepreneurship would be import-ant in conditions of moderate backwardness. In extreme backwardness the state would be the necessary key to industrial investment (Sylla and Toniolo 1991).

Though many of Gerschenkron's arguments have not withstood criticism of their basis in European economic history, especially in terms of his key cases, Germany and Russia (Sylla and Toniolo 1991), a most useful contribution has been his concept of 'substitutes for prerequisites'. He started from the generally accepted view that backwardness entailed the absence of factors that served as preconditions for development in more advanced countries. Thus he highlighted the importance of examining the ways in which, in conditions of backwardness, substitutions for the absent factors were achieved (Gerschenkron 1962: 46). Specifically, Harley (1991) suggested that this might largely be construed as the endogenous substitution of hierarchies for markets in backward areas: that is to say, that the state or family groups take over the role of entrepreneur. This would account for the greater role of large firms and bureaucracies in those countries.

However, relying on the state to spearhead the escape from backwardness also incurs risks. State-owned enterprises are notoriously subject to agency problems which undermine productivity performance. The state itself may be predatory and unable credibly to commit itself not to expropriate the returns from private sector investment, as happened with the military developmentalists of Latin America. Where you get centralised industrial policy and protected markets, rent-seeking behaviour, and specifically corruption and **nepotism**, tend to flourish.

3. The radical tradition: dependency

An economic emphasis characterises work in the 'dependency' school, whether it be of the *'dependentista'* tradition established by workers at the UN Economic Commission for Latin America (ECLA, now UN Economic Commission for Latin America and the Caribbean – ECLAC – see Prebisch 1950) or André Gunder Frank's 'development of underdevelopment' (Frank 1966). The dependency thesis originated with the Marxist analysis of developing world economies by Paul Baran (1957). It was Baran who first distinguished Third World economies as being on the periphery of the world economic system, whose centre was in Europe and North America.

As the Spanish term *dependentista* would suggest, the dependency thesis was developed and popularised in Latin America, by a variety of writers not all of whom were Marxists (Jaguaribe 1967; Cardoso and Faletto 1979, first published 1969; Dos Santos 1969, 1970; Cardoso 1972; Furtado 1970; Sunkel 1969; Ianni 1975) and in a very similar version has since been widely adopted in other regions of the developing world (Amin 1990a, b). Cardoso made a long, slow journey rightwards. After a spell as Senator from São Paulo, he became President of Brazil for two terms 1994–2002, and has now written his memoirs (Cardoso 2006).

(a) Dependency

The term 'dependency' is derived from the view that because developing world economies are on the periphery of the world capitalist system, they have become *dependent* on the advanced industrialised countries. It rejects the developmentalist view that developing world states can in time undergo the same form of development as the existing industrialised states, for at least as long as the capitalist system exists in its present form. The reason, its adherents argue, is that the 'centre', the AICs, sets the terms on which the system operates. As a result, the terms of trade are unfavourable to developing world countries and the flow of capital is asymmetrical, tending to flow from the periphery towards the centre. This outflow is a structural constraint that ensures that the states of the 'periphery' are weak, open to penetration from the centre and with little or no scope for autonomous action (Bonilla and Girling 1973).

Most of these authors as well as the relevant international institutions and non-dependency theorists would accuse early modernisation theorists of stressing the political to the exclusion of the economic and would charge revisionists with ignoring the international dimension, and these are the key elements of dependency theory.

Dos Santos writes:

> [underdevelopment] is a conditioning situation in which the economies of one group of countries are conditioned by the development and expansion of others. A relationship between two or more economies or between such economies and the world trading system becomes a dependent relationship when some countries can expand through self-impulsion while others being in a dependent position can only expand as a reflection of the expansion of the dominant countries.' (Dos Santos 1970)

The duality of coexistent modern and traditional sectors found in modernisation revisionism made life easier for the development of dependency theory but it has its roots in two sources:

1. The non-Marxist nationalism of Latin American structuralism. This school was exemplified by ECLA, established in 1949 at the request of the Latin Americans, who wanted 'a Marshall Plan for Latin America'. Its leading representative, Raúl Prebisch (1950), criticised the theory of comparative advantage. He and other ECLA theorists were the first to divide the world into centre and periphery and to argue that the oligopoly of markets in the centre leads to a long-term tendency towards declining terms of trade and to the concentration of industrial production in the centre and, in turn, to Latin American dependence on imports. As a result, sustained development depends on the nationalist bourgeoisie promoting industrialisation – at first through **import-substitution industrialisation (ISI)**.
2. Marx's distinction between core and periphery. Although Marx saw the exploitation of the developing world as part of the inevitable development of industrial capitalism, he argued also that imperialism breaks up traditional societies and creates new markets for industrial goods. Baran, Frank, Cardoso and Faletto were all influenced to some extent by this argument, but pointed out that things did not go thereafter entirely as Marx had envisaged. The fact was that capital did not accumulate in the developing world to be invested *in situ* to the benefit of the state. Instead it was repatriated to the centre, thus accentuating the centre's dominance in terms of capital formation.

(b) The development of underdevelopment

The notion of the development of underdevelopment is associated particularly with the work of André Gunder Frank (1966, 1967, 1969). Frank argues that developed countries were formerly 'undeveloped' but they have never been 'underdeveloped'. Underdevelopment for Frank is a process of structural distortion. The economies of underdeveloped countries have been partially developed, but in a way that enhances their economic value, not to their own citizens but to the AICs. In this process, he, in common with other dependency writers, ascribes a special role to two agencies. The first is what he terms the 'lumpenbourgeoisie', otherwise generally known as the national bourgeoisie or, for the Maoists, the 'comprador' bourgeoisie (from the Portuguese word for a merchant: Frank 1970, 1974). The ruling classes in peripheral states actively encourage the outflow of wealth from their countries by using their 'control of state power to protect the interests of multinational capital' (Kitching 1982). It is they who find their economic interests best served by an alliance with the second agency, the foreign corporation, to exploit their own fellow countryfolk.

Thus, for Frank, development in metropolis and underdevelopment in its satellites are two sides of the same coin. The metropolitan centres were never *under*developed, because it is capitalist penetration which causes underdevelopment and development in the satellites is only possible when they break away from their metropolitan exploiters. This is rarely possible and only takes place in moments of major crisis, such as war or severe economic depression (see also Amin 1990b).

Hence for Frank differing levels of development are not the product of different historical stages of development but of the different functions the areas concerned perform in the international system. Production in colonies was determined not by the needs of those colonies (except colonial settlers 'needing' luxury goods) but by the needs of the colonial power. Hence unequal power relations have developed and continue to be maintained both between First and developing world countries (metropolis and periphery) and within developing world countries (city and 'camp', elite and mass). The worst off are the masses of the developing world since they suffer from 'superexploitation' by both their own elite and that of the metropolis. Such inequality is known as 'structural heterogeneity' and stems from the fact that the local political elite are the agents of the international class and the state is their instrument.

Dependent economies are subjugated to the needs of the world economy by foreign (metropolitan) control of markets and capital, as well as by ownership of concerns which have competitive advantages over local firms leading to the further continued outflow of capital. This has two causes: the need for capital-intensive foreign technology and imported capital goods on the one hand, and endemic balance-of-payments problems on the other. It is the reliance on the export of primary products hit by fluctuating prices that leads to balance of payments problems and thus to reliance on foreign direct investment and aid. The repatriation of profits, technological dependency and the dominance of multinational corporations all serve to undermine sovereignty. Tied aid and loans are examples of capitalism's need to continue its penetration of the developing world; establishing factories in developing countries enables the AICs to maintain their control of the world economic order (Froebel et al. 1980).

(c)   World systems analysis

The third subdivision usually distinguished within the dependency school – Wallerstein's world systems analysis – is subtly different. Wallerstein's world-systems model assumes that a peripheral position in the world economy by definition means a weak state whereas being part of the core means having a strong state (Wallerstein 1974). However, this is just not true. Wallerstein's argument is reversed by those who see late industrialisers as developing under the protection of a strong state. Late industrialisers such as Japan have been able to develop through the leadership of a strong state bent on the objective of economic development. The case of the NICs is still controversial and will be discussed later.

In recent years there has been a variety of criticisms made of the dependency/*dependentista* school. The most serious criticism, if one difficult for nonspecialists to assess, is that its theories do not fit the historical facts. As Laclau (1977) points out, Frank's historical analysis of the origins of capitalism is not accurate, so that Smith (1979) can describe dependency theory as 'theoretically logical but empirically unsubstantiated'. The next most important criticism is that national differences are neglected or even ignored altogether. Dependency theory does have a tendency to ignore differences between states. The global economy is the key and national characteristics such as political parties and military establishments are, if not incidental, at least very secondary. Thirdly, it was developed to 'explain' the case of Latin America, and is not really relevant elsewhere. The hegemony achieved by one country, the United States, in the western hemisphere has no parallel in any other part of the world.

If there are strong criticisms from the empirical point of view there are equally strong criticisms of the theoretical concepts employed by dependency writers. Their work fails adequately to define 'development' and their use of terms such as 'class' is inconsistent. It relies on 'latent conspiratorial assumptions' (Kamrava 1993) rather than a realistic perception of how business executives and politicians actually think. Much of the early debate within the dependency school tailed off into an internal Marxist squabble about the past which offered no hope for the future.

However, not all dependency theory is Marxist (see Chilcote 1978: 61; see also Chilcote and Edelstein 1974) and dependency theorists are no longer as simplistic or depressing as they have been in the past. They would not now accept a simple core–periphery split but would want to introduce intermediate categories such as semi-periphery (a category which would include a large and powerful state like Brazil) and sub-metropolis. Cardoso and others recognise internal forces as agents, making choices and decisions that impact on development though their options are limited by external factors: this is 'national underdevelopment' (Cardoso and Faletto 1979, p. 21). Some internal groups wish to maintain dependent relations. Others oppose them. So dependency is not simply an external variable.

These writers have moved on from the early work of André Gunder Frank in seeing some kind of development as possible within capitalism even if it is dependent development. Thus they may be seen to take some account of the emergence of the NICs.

4.   The radical tradition: Marxism and neo-Marxism

Those concerned with the role of the state in the process of development have stressed either political or economic aspects. 'Class/state politics' (for further details see Randall and Theobald 1985: 137–78) stresses both. This may occur within either:

(a) a Marxist framework, such as is to be found in the writing of Roxborough (1979). His frequent stress on 'modes of production' shows in the choice of term the Marxist base and the use of the plural indicates the importance of individual national histories and states, which are of course essentially political.

(b) a non-Marxist schema such as that found in the works of Stepan (1973, 1978), Schmitter (1979) or O'Donnell (1988).

Later neo-Marxist post-dependency explanations make class alignments within dependent states and the relative autonomy of the state central to their analysis. More emphasis is placed on examining indigenous structures. Obviously class formations are central, but so too is the political role of the state, not just as a representative of the dominant class but as a participant in its own right. Pre-existing (i.e. pre-capitalist) modes of production survive in peripheral economies subjected to the capitalist mode (this idea is found in the work of Laclau). Indeed, several modes of production may coexist and the role of the state is vital in determining the role of the national bourgeoisie (e.g. Roxborough 1979).

By comparison with old-fashioned Marxism these explanations are flexible. Maoist influence can been seen in the fact that peasants are recognised as being a potentially revolutionary force (see also Colburn 1994). However, those they seem to have in mind are not peasants in the true sense, who remain a very conservative stratum, but those who constitute a 'peasantariat' like the plantation workers for transnational corporations (TNCs) such as Del Monte.

Conversely, there is a belated recognition that far from being a powerful force for change, the industrial proletariat may constitute a small, privileged elite in the developing world, as, for example, in Mexico, where the trade union sector formed one of the three pillars maintaining the dominance of the

Institutional Revolutionary Party (PRI) until its defeat in the presidential elections of 2000. On the other hand, tin and copper miners in Bolivia and Chile were left-wing, while the urban working class in Brazil and Argentina followed Vargas, Goulart and Perón, populist figures of the centre-Left.

The view that the state is not simply part of the superstructure and an instrument of the dominant class has obvious sources within Marxist thought, especially the work of Gramsci. The state is seen as above squabbles by fractions of the ruling class pursuing their own short-term interests. There is a non-Marxist emphasis on the state from those, such as Stepan and Schmitter, who see an authoritarian stage as a historic necessity, not actually desirable but something that unfortunately cannot be avoided at a critical stage of development.

O'Donnell (1988) developed the widely-used concept of '**bureaucratic-authoritarianism**' to describe the situation when, in a post-populist society constrained by the limits of industrialisation, civil and military technocrats ally with foreign capital to demobilise or repress popular movements. However O'Donnell's model not only is not generally applicable to Latin America, but it fits very narrowly the very specific case of Argentina between 1966 and 1973. For this reason 'military developmentalism' may be a more widely acceptable term to describe the common features of the repressive military regimes of the 1960s and 1970s.

There is also a Marxist form of modernisation theory. Although most Marxists are critical of it, some think that development is possible but will be of a distorted kind. This is progress, they believe, in that it takes the developing world a stage closer to eventual socialism. These ideas are associated with Bill Warren and Nigel Harris. Warren believes Marx made it clear that capitalism is a transitional stage between feudalism and socialism which cannot be avoided. It is therefore inevitable (and even desirable) that the developing world becomes enmeshed in the capitalist system. For Warren capitalist imperialism functions to drag the developing world with it, thus promoting economic development (Warren 1977). Harris's is a globalisation model with a single interdependent global economic system with TNCs moving freely around it. The nation state is increasingly irrelevant and nationalism is destined to decline. Thus it is impossible to maintain a separate category of countries termed the developing world (Harris 1986; see below Harris on the experiences of NICs).

Strategies of industrialisation

The success of industrialisation has undoubtedly depended to a great extent on what people have chosen to make. In the early stages of industrialisation there is a strong demand for capital goods, machinery and tools that have to be imported from the AICs. Sufficient capital needs to be available, therefore, to

Table 1.7 Perspectives compared

	Liberal/neoclassical	Disadvantage	Structural/dependency	Social democratic/reformist	Ecological-green	Religious world view	Feminist
PROPONENTS	Rostow; OECD	Myrdal	Baran, Amin, various schools	Brandt; UNCTAD	Brundtland; Greenpeace	–	Shiva; Boserup, etc.
OPTIMISTIC/PESSIMISTIC	Optimistic – trickle-down	generally pessimistic	degree of pessimism varies, non-Marxist most	cautiously optimistic	generally pessimistic	millenarian	generally pessimistic
EMPHASIS ON	the operation of markets; equilibrium	development economics	world capitalist system; global class structure	North–South division; basic needs	sustainable development	personal salvation	role of women in development process
VIEW OF TNCs	transfer advantages	good for thriving region, not others	exploit developing world	advanced industrial countries need to control	destructive beyond redemption	foreign, therefore suspect	male, therefore suspect
VULNERABLE GROUPS	will eventually benefit	developing world generally	peripheries	South	ultimately all living things; immediately the world's poor	poor, meek, downtrodden	women
DEVELOPMENT SOLUTION	break-out is inevitable	possible escape with overflow from advantaged countries	structural inequality; escape only possible with a) fall of capitalism, or b) in dependent form	North–South dialogue; concerted action by UN agencies	restrict growth; control pollution; encourage return to pastoral state	–	women
ENVIRONMENTAL PROBLEMS	irrelevant – the market will resolve when the time is right	exported pollution from developed countries	byproduct of capitalism; remedy social revolution	tends to rely on technological 'fix'	supreme crisis of humanity in one lifetime	–	created by men

fund these imports until the machinery is up and running and making products that can be sold. Thereafter two forms or even stages of industrialisation as a development strategy have been identified.

Import-substitution industrialisation

Import-substitution industrialisation (ISI) generally comes first, as indeed it did in the case of Britain and France, where indigenous manufactures replaced imports of textiles from India and the Middle East and ceramics from China. But because of the limitations of an internal market, sustained development is usually held to necessitate **export-oriented industrialisation** (EOI), and that is a different matter, as the problem is to find goods to market and markets for goods.

Either way, development relies in the first instance on the availability of funds for infrastructure and setting-up costs. Developing states generally get such funds as revenues from import/export duties, fees and taxes on TNCs, profits made by state agencies for the import or export of products, foreign loans or aid and the manipulation of exchange rates. Domestic revenues are much more difficult to extract so developing regimes may be reluctant to contemplate any development strategy which hits international trade/relations. Indeed, given the strong pressure from the AICs for developing countries to **liberalise** (open up) their domestic markets, it is doubtful if today ISI is still possible other than in a few specialist areas.

ISI was the strategy proposed and associated with the Economic Commission for Latin America (ECLA), a regional economic think-tank established by the UN for Latin America, and the first of a number of UN Commissions intended to promote the development of newly emerging economies

Structuralist thought effectively began with the publication of two pamphlets: *The Economic Development of Latin America and Some of its Main Problems* (1949) and *The Economic Study of Latin America 1949* (1950). The economist behind these key publications was Raúl Prebisch (1950). These papers identified the concepts of centre and periphery but saw development on the periphery as possible if the periphery broke out of its specialisation in primary products for export. This it could do by supplying its own import needs in the short term and building up an industrial base that way. The state must afford adequate protection to infant industries which could begin to supply manufactured goods locally for the home market. This protection would involve tariffs and import quotas, along with subsidies on local products. These local products would be light industrial at first. Import reduction would conserve foreign exchange. The state would have the resources and incentive to develop infrastructure.

ISI was not generally successful, although just occasionally production originally intended to substitute for imports has been able to transform itself into a successful export industry: e.g. South Korea's Hyundai. For the most part the featherbedding of local industries meant inefficiency. The luxury goods which were produced had relatively small local markets and the high cost of importing the capital goods on which this production rested drained foreign exchange anyway. A new kind of dependency was being created. The 'Chicago Boys' (monetarist economists from the University of Chicago) were able to point up the problems and win the ideological debate without having to explore the consequences of their solutions. TNCs were ready and willing to take over many of the areas of production, indeed much of the technology needed for development, especially that needed to get beyond ISI, must come from the developed countries and often from their TNCs. The hijacking of ISI by TNCs is illustrated by the case of Brazilian pharmaceut-icals, originally developed to save the high costs of imports but now 85 per cent TNC owned.

Export-oriented industrialisation

The ideology of the free market found itself much more comfortable with the other main industrialising strategy, export-oriented industrialisation (EOI). This developed in the late 1960s and early 1970s in East Asia. It was out-standingly successful in the case of Japan (which had already established export industries in the 1920s and 1930s) and very successful in the 'Four Little Tigers' (Singapore, South Korea, Taiwan and Hong Kong) which were held up as models of what could be achieved. This strategy involved the pro-duction of light industrial goods for export. It led to an increase in the share of global manufacturing output by NICs and mid-income countries which went up from 19 per cent to 37 per cent in the years 1960–81. It was thought to reflect a value-oriented modernisation process with a stress on education and human effort.

The success of the NICs – or NIEs (preferred because of Singapore and Hong Kong) – was proposed as a model for the rest of the developing world to follow, but there are problems:

- The Cold War. Examined closely, each of the NICs developed under unique conditions which are unlikely ever to be closely replicated. South Korea and Taiwan, for example, each received massive amounts of US aid for ideolo-gical reasons and used it for infrastructural development (Calvert, 2005b).
- Economic, social and ecological costs. The present generations have made massive sacrifices and there is evidence that the young will not be pre-pared to do the same. In some cases repressive government enabled rapid development, forced savings, low wages, poor conditions of labour, loss of traditions etc. A stable system of government is vital to develop medium term (5–7 years) comprehensive development plans and/or a national development ideology. Such an ideology, for example South Korea's New Community Movement, is an assertion of government control of the eco-nomy. But a stable government does not have to be a dictatorial government

and stable government is quite compatible with changing politicians in office – as the case of France between 1944 and 1958 makes clear.

- The need for markets. The NICs and China have been and are heavily reliant on the US market. However, this reliance is meeting with increasing resistance within the USA, as the logic of free competition has been to drive down costs and hence wages in the USA itself. At the moment this is offset by heavy US borrowing funded by the developing countries, but this has its limits. Will the USA allow even greater penetration of its domestic market? China's strong export performance has reflected in part its undervalued currency relative to the dollar. As it revalues, and it is under huge international pressure to do so, its trade surplus with the USA can be expected to decline.
- The pressure on resources. The inputs required for industrial development (fuel and raw materials) have become relatively much more costly with steadily increasing demand from developing countries, especially China, which for such a large country is surprisingly lacking in natural resources.

It is possible it might all come together and the NICs could act as poles of development, encouraging and supporting the development of other neighbouring countries by acting as an example, by supplying technology and skills, by promoting a market for goods made in developing countries and by providing development capital. Or they could move on to bigger and 'better' things as manufacturing costs rise, leaving a gap for other peripheral states to move into. But the Asian crisis of 1997 and the resulting disaffection within the NICs suggests this is rather optimistic. And SSA is so far behind economically that it is hard to know where it can start in the struggle to develop.

A right to development?

The second World Conference on Human Rights (14–25 June 1993) revealed once more the extent of the North–South divide on the issue of the 'right to develop'. Altogether 160 countries accepted the United Nations invitation to participate in the Conference, held in Vienna, and it marked an important landmark in establishing the rights of women. However, it also showed that human rights are defined differently the world over. The arguments as to whether or not there is a 'right to development' can be divided into two main groups. Developing countries argue that political and civil rights are not separable from and certainly not more important than economic, social and cultural rights. The industrial West argues that political and civil liberties should come first. Some thinkers believe that economic, social and cultural rights cannot be regarded as true human rights, since they depend on the ability to make economic resources available. But this view is not really likely to be acceptable to countries most of whose inhabitants endure a very low standard of living.

A further question is whether collective (i.e. developmental) rights should outrank individual rights. The question is complicated by the fact that, as so often in international politics, countries have put their names to high-sounding statements of general principles which they are not always prepared to put into practice. But human rights, by definition, are about individual human beings. To state that something is a human right is not only to state that the individual has that right simply by virtue of being human, it also implies that the individual can as a result make a claim against all other human beings for that right to be made good. This raises some very serious problems, since the 'international community' lacks effective mechanisms to do this. So the only way individual human beings can make claims is through the state in which they live, and the problem for those who need help is that the state is not just part of the solution, it is part of the problem.

The **Vienna Declaration** did, however, embody an unequivocal commitment to development as a fundamental right, placing the 'human individual' at its centre:

8. Democracy, development and respect for human rights and fundamental freedoms are interdependent and mutually reinforcing. Democracy is based on the freely expressed will of the people to determine their own political, economic, social and cultural systems and their full participation in all aspects of their lives. In the context of the above, the promotion and protection of human rights and fundamental freedoms at the national and international levels should be universal and conducted without conditions attached. The international community should support the strengthening and promoting of democracy, development and respect for human rights and fundamental freedoms in the entire world.

9. The World Conference on Human Rights reaffirms that least developed countries committed to the process of democratization and economic reforms, many of which are in Africa, should be supported by the international community in order to succeed in their transition to democracy and economic development.

10. The World Conference on Human Rights reaffirms the right to development, as established in the Declaration on the Right to Development, as a universal and inalienable right and an integral part of fundamental human rights.

(http://www.unhchr.ch/huridocda/huridoca.nsf/(Symbol)/
A.CONF.157.23.En?OpenDocument)

But just how significant was this? After all, as early as 1948 the UN confirmed development as a right in Article 28 of the Universal Declaration of Human Rights. This commitment had been reiterated and deepened on many subsequent occasions. The 1960s were proclaimed as the UN 'Decade of Development'. Yet the results for many developing countries were so disappointing that a second Decade was proclaimed for the 1970s. Any hope that this might be more successful was to be abruptly cut short by the first 'oil shock' of 1973.

This was enormously ironic since the oil crises of the 1970s were initially seen by both oil-rich and oil-poor states as an opportunity to redress the balance between the developed and the developing worlds. However in practice it was the developing countries that did not have access to their own oil reserves and lacked the leverage to gain preferential access on the world market that came off worst. In 1979 the Brandt Commission proposed a formal redistribution of wealth from the developed to the developing states by way of a 'global income tax' (Brandt 1980). However, the 1980s were a decade of neo-liberal 'solutions' and high interest rates. The Brandt recommendations were ignored and by 1990 most developing countries were actually worse off than they had been in 1979, though this was less obvious than it should have been because of the exceptional performance of a few states in Asia.

Already with the enlargement of the United Nations there had come in 1964 a response to Western domination of trade in the holding of the United Nations Conference on Trade, Aid and Development (UNCTAD). That first meeting of UNCTAD, UNCTAD I, stressed the need for structural reforms in world trade if rapid development was to be achieved by the South. But although UNCTAD became a permanent organisation, holding a sequence of major conferences, it had no real power, and the northern states were unwilling to consider more than minor tinkering with the existing system.

At UNCTAD III at Santiago de Chile, the President of Mexico, Luis Echeverría Alvarez, called for the creation of a **New International Economic Order (NIEO)**. The Mexicans voiced the feelings of most developing world governments when they criticised the prevailing terms of trade. They saw themselves as being condemned by the existing system to export large quantities of primary products at low prices, and to import the manufactured goods they needed at very high ones; hence the demand for an arrangement that would link producer prices to changes in the price of manufactured goods. They were backed by the President of Venezuela, Carlos Andrés Pérez, and by most of the other OPEC states. In April 1974 the UN General Assembly, which was then heavily dominated by developing world states, endorsed the idea of the NIEO.

This resulted in the adoption by the UN General Assembly in December 1974 of the **Charter of Economic Rights and Duties of States (CERDS)**. Its main planks were:

- fair terms of trade for developing countries;
- a new world currency linked to the price of primary materials; and
- the abolition of IMF conditionality as a requirement for new loans.

Although the resolution to adopt CERDS was carried by 120 votes to six with ten abstentions, the programme it represented was in fact totally, though largely secretly, opposed by the governments of the United States and most of the other AICs, and so was effectively a dead letter (Thomas 1985: 65–6). CERDS might, on paper, have been agreed but, not surprisingly, it was never implemented. For example, it was intended that prices of primary products would be pegged to prices of manufactured goods, but this proved to be unrealistic. Manufacturers were unwilling to pay more, and competition between developing world suppliers kept prices down. It was true that OPEC had for a time been successful in driving up the price of crude petroleum, but similar cartels for other products failed for a variety of reasons and during the 1980s they were systematically dismantled. The UN called the Cancun Conference of 1981 to promote global negotiations on the NIEO but it came to nothing.

The problem was not just economic but political. In general the United States does not feel itself bound by UN decisions with which it does not agree. The fact that it foots 25 per cent of the bill for the UN is the most powerful argument for this. The agreement by Japan in September 1994 to become the UN's second-largest supporter and pay 15 per cent of the costs of maintaining the organisation gave Japan a great deal of leverage if it chooses to use it but in practice on most issues it had consistently sided with the United States. Not only did the United States under Ronald Reagan withdraw from UNESCO and constantly chivvy other agencies into accepting its wishes, but on the first occasion when it was confronted with a legal challenge before the World Court to its clandestine war on Nicaragua it refused to accept that body's jurisdiction. At the same time by choosing to work through other groupings such as the G7 it was able to bypass many of the constraints that the developing world domination of the UN General Assembly would otherwise impose on its freedom of action.

An NIEO would depend on stability. To achieve this, the Brundtland Report argued that what first would be needed is a democratisation of international relations, just as democracy and participation must accompany development at a local or national level (see WCED 1987: 297). The restoration of superpower hegemony could restore stability, but that state of affairs would be unlikely to meet the *economic* aspirations of developing world countries.

Development in the free market

Different developing world states have devised their own strategies for development. These routes have varied with starting point, location, tradition and ideology. For example, while some states such as Zambia have continued to rely on exporting primary products and some, such as Cuba, have been forced to do so, others have chosen (or perhaps 'chosen' is too strong, given the constraints) more unusual directions like India's quest for self-sufficiency or Singapore's investment in technology and education. Some have favoured export-led growth as in Taiwan or South Korea, taking advantage of, if not actively embracing, a free market ideology premised on the assumption that benefits will trickle down to the poorest sectors. This latter strategy is also illustrated by the cases of Brazil, Chile and other countries of Latin America.

For most of the countries which have sought to emulate the NICs, an easier and more acceptable means of doing so in a dominant neo-liberal ideological climate has been to allow foreign investors to provide infrastructure and employ cheap local labour. Thus the tendency for both models of industrialisation has been replacement of indigenous industrial activity by the role of TNCs.

In some cases there may be a conflict between a developing state's development strategy and the interests of TNCs. Although a state must be fairly small for TNCs to still have a great degree of national power, a number of them, particularly in SSA, are still very weak, and some TNCs, like the oil majors, are very strong. Generally speaking the two parties, the state and the corporations, need each other, but the relationship is often unequal and the increasing globalisation of the world economy and deregulation of transnational activities are enhancing linkages between TNCs and thus increasingly marginalising the weaker developing countries.

Development relies on availability of funds for infrastructural and other capital investment. Developing states generally get such funds as revenues from import/export duties, fees and taxes on TNCs, the profits made by state agencies for the import or export of products, foreign loans or aid and manipulation of exchange rates. Domestic revenues are much more difficult to extract, since local elites resist often successfully any attempt of the state to set realistic levels of personal taxation. Hence developing world regimes must necessarily be reluctant to contemplate any development strategy which hits international trade relations, and certainly their relatively small size in the main precludes the realistic possibility of economic autarky.

Development directions may be influenced either externally or internally or both. Externally they are shaped by advice and pressure from the **US Agency for International Development (USAID)**, the World Bank, the IMF etc. The combined effect of these powerful bodies is striking, and the examples of the **Caribbean Basin Initiative (CBI)** is instructive. During the 1980s, when the United States moved from being the world's largest creditor to being the world's largest debtor, its economy was booming as a result and the CBI was supposed to enable it to benefit its smallest neighbours, allowing them preferential access to the US market for selected products. But at the same time the small nations of the Caribbean, which faced a declining price for their few commodities, were being told by the international lending agencies to stop 'living beyond their means'. The combined effect of structural adjustment on their economies was to export capital to the advanced industrial economies, a situation made much worse by prevailing high dollar interest rates, which had increased so much that they significantly worsened the terms of borrowing and so the debts that the countries concerned had been forced to assume.

In 1987, the Caribbean as a whole paid out US$207 million more to the foreign governments, banks and multilateral agencies that are 'aiding' the region than it received from all of them combined in the same year. This net outflow of funds was mainly in the form of interest and principal payments on the region's foreign debt, which totalled US$20.9 billion in 1988. The removal of funds from the Caribbean would have been even greater had not a major portion of official debt bills been repeatedly postponed; Jamaica's debt payments, for example, have been rescheduled every year since 1979. The consequence is accumulation of arrears and even higher bills to be paid in the future. (McAfee 1991: 13)

However, no less significant are internal political considerations such as who must be consulted and who must be bought off. Vested interests are just one indigenous obstacle to development. Others may include a lack of industry and infrastructure at independence, especially in Africa; low literacy, poor education, low school enrolment; rapid population growth and urbanisation; little administrative capacity; poor financial institutions; archaic social structures; and internal conflicts. External assistance is important but the key requirement is for self-directed development using human and material resources to satisfy local needs.

Transnational corporations

Because the majority of TNCs are small companies with headquarters in one country and often only one other branch abroad, the term 'transnational corporation' is preferred both here and by the World Bank, rather than 'multinational' corporation which implies a large enterprise with regional or even worldwide reach and many foreign subsidiaries.

Transnational corporations are responsible for 40 per cent of world trade, 90 per cent of world trade in commodities and 30 per cent of world food production. The largest TNCs are responsible for most of the world's foreign investment. The United States provides most such investment, with the UK second and Japan third. The largest firms are household names like IBM, Exxon, General Electric and General Motors.

Although more than three-quarters of TNCs are based in the United States or in Europe, there are TNCs based in developing countries also and hence some developing country transnational corporation involvement in other developing countries. Brazilian companies are involved in West Africa, Indian companies in Indonesia and Malaysia and the Argentine corporation Bunge y Born in Brazil and Uruguay. The UN estimates that TNCs employ more than 60 million people worldwide. The figures are sobering. The annual turnover of Nestlé is more than seven times the GNP of Ghana. In 1984 no African state had an annual turnover as big as Exxon. Only South Africa, Nigeria, Egypt, Morocco and Côte d'Ivoire had GNPs big enough to get them places amongst the top 100 corporations. Transnational corporations now control more than 40 per cent of world output and as much as 30 per cent of world trade takes place not between but within large corporations (Thrift 1986).

Why is this so? A major reason is the number of states and the relatively limited number of major corporations. There is keen rivalry between developing countries to attract TNCs. Once they have chosen to set up operations, the governments concerned find that they cannot effectively regulate them as it is so easy for large corporations to switch production to another developing world state. Sometimes TNCs transfer dangerous or polluting operations to the South. But there are always countries available to allow them to do so, in view of the very large legal and illegal returns that they expect to obtain.

In some states there have been attempts to develop different development strategies and eliminate the involvement of TNCs. The Bolsheviks in Russia seized their oil fields in 1917. The oil companies were slow to realise that the change was permanent, but by 1924 they were ready to compete both openly and secretly with one another to market Soviet oil abroad. However as Stalin consolidated his grip foreign participation in the Russian economy was ended and did not return until after the collapse of the Soviet Union in 1991. Later TNCs were squeezed out of the oil industry in the 1930s in Bolivia and Mexico, in the 1940s in Romania, in the 1950s in Brazil, in the 1960s in Peru and in the 1970s in Algeria, Libya, Iraq and Venezuela. However, the key to the oil industry, as John D. Rockefeller, Sr., was the first to realise, is not production but distribution and marketing, and by 2000 the 'Seven Sisters' (Sampson 1975) who for so long dominated the industry were only five: BP-Amoco, Chevron, Exxon-Mobil, Gulf, Texaco, and Royal Dutch-Shell.

By the 1970s most developing countries were finding that nationalisation was a strategy fraught with dangers. In Jamaica the ownership of sugar production was taken out of the hands of Tate & Lyle and the plantations nationalised. Twenty-three cooperatives were established from 1976 on by the People's National Party led by Michael Manley. With the plantation workers in charge of production they succeeded in producing one-half of the country's sugar. However, several factors worked against them: plant diseases, the hostility of the USA and the IMF and a drop in sugar prices. In 1980 the PNP lost the elections, the cooperatives were shut down and Tate & Lyle was invited back in.

Supporters of TNCs use arguments associated with free market economic theories. They claim that TNCs fill gaps of various kinds which exist in local economies. Such corporations, they argue, enhance the earning capacity of host states and generate foreign exchange. They see them as risk-takers, that are exceptionally dynamic in promoting growth. They argue that TNC investment may reduce the need of a host country to borrow abroad or may fill a need not met by borrowing. Notably, when bank lending declined during the debt crisis of the 1980s TNC investment became still more important. Company investment not only supplements local savings but also increases saving by increasing local income and stimulating domestic investment to provide inputs for TNCs.

Manufacturing output is seen as the motor of development and some 30 per cent of developing country manufacturing output comes from TNCs. Some of the most successful emerging economies are to be found in the regions that have been most penetrated by transnationals; in Singapore more than 60 per cent of manufacturing output is generated by TNCs. Such organisations enhance the earning capacity of host states and generate foreign exchange. Local individuals and companies are paid for their part in production. While some profits are repatriated, some are reinvested in local plant and supplies and much flows into the local economy by way of wages and salaries. Transnationals are also responsible for generating substantial additional tax revenues.

Several other aspects of TNC activity can be seen as positive. Some technical knowledge is transmitted to local employees and contractors along with managerial skills, resulting in new products becoming available locally and a more efficient use of local labour. In particular TNCs are often seen as a major force in modernising agriculture, the sector traditionally most resistant to change.

Transnational corporations frequently pay well above the going market rate in salaries and wages. Additionally they often provide social services for their workforces, contributing to local health and education and minimising any drain on local provision.

Some even argue that they act as buffers insulating the host economy from the full harshness of the international system. There is widespread agreement that they tend to have a generally liberalising effect in the developed economies in which they are based. One of the results is that they have a strong incentive to lobby against quotas and tariffs which would limit entry of their developing world products to the AICs.

Critics of TNCs take a very different view of both the economic and political processes involved.

They note that most TNC investment occurs in countries which have been in a position to promote export-led growth, such as Brazil and Malaysia. Transnational corporations are conspicuously absent from many parts of Africa South of the Sahara (SSA). Zambia's economy, 70 per cent controlled by transnationals, has collapsed since 1991 as a result of a combination of structural adjustment and trade liberalisation. The critics cast doubt on the real rate of return a country can expect from attracting TNCs. The inducements offered, such as tax concessions and stable exchange rates, can be very expensive to the host government and in business terms hardly justify their use.

Far from adding to local capital resources, critics argue, transnationals consume them. Through their presence, foreign investment is made easy for the local foreign-oriented elite. They do not promote domestic development but seek only to invest where they can maximise their profits. Agricultural TNCs do even more harm by buying up high-quality land which could be better used for domestic food production, and so indirectly increase the need to import food. Such corporations hit local economies by repatriating an excessive level of profit, at the same time minimising their real rate of return to local economies through devices such as transfer pricing. Transfer pricing involves the undervaluing of transnational products in the host country, but their revaluing by the time they have reached the home base of the corporation by being sold on through the company's subsidiaries. As with transfer pricing, the high cost of imported inputs, whether real or as an exercise in accounting, reduces the profits which can be locally taxed.

Transnational corporations go abroad to find new sources of inputs which are declining or becoming more expensive at home. This includes labour. Skilled labour is to be found in middle-income rather than poor developing world states, so the more technical operations are located there.

Transnationals use the protection of developing country import-substitution industrialisation strategies but tend to go where new markets open up in order to exploit those temporary advantages.

As for their transferring technology to the local economy, they do often use superior technology, but this can be quite inappropriate to local conditions and invariably much more capital-intensive. Developing country TNCs are often thought to provide more labour-intensive technologies and therefore to be more acceptable. However, in both cases the sharp end of advanced technology may be kept under wraps at home to prevent transfer, in order to preserve the corporation's competitive advantage.

Lastly, wherever they operate, transnationals may enhance the unevenness of development. Manufacturing companies charge the local population premium prices for local products carrying popular brand names. They may displace local firms. They often produce inappropriate products intended originally for the First World and stimulate local consumption of products such as cigarettes, baby milk formula and brand-name drugs. This is the technique of 'coca-colonisation'. On the other hand, mining companies and plantations worsen the rural/urban imbalance, use up natural resources much faster than otherwise would be the case and bring about environmental degradation.

An open question following the Bhopal disaster has been that of safety. Certainly in that case the standards maintained by a local subsidiary of a TNC were found to be very inadequate, and there are serious doubts as to whether such a dangerous process should have been located so close to a centre of population. However, in their defence it can be argued that generally TNC standards of environmental protection and safety are higher than those of small local companies which can afford less.

The prejudice against TNCs in many developing world countries is very great. Times of crisis weaken developing world states in the face of TNCs and the debt crisis of the 1980s made TNCs more vital to developing world states and enabled them to rebuild their position. On the other hand, TNCs are mainly involved in the more autarkic sections of the developing world, because middle-income countries offer them diversified economic structures, sophisticated and substantial markets and the skilled labour these corporations most often need. The 1960s and 1970s saw the development of a variety of controls on their activities. States prescribed the degree of local investment required, the maximum length of time an activity could be left under TNC control before transfer to local interests, etc. Such restraints on freedom of manoeuvre caused IBM and Coca-Cola to leave India in the 1970s. The ultimate weapon was expropriation, but this has been very rare outside the oil industry. There was some use of nationalisation in emerging states in the 1960s and 1970s, but the number of countries prepared to confront transnationals was always small and among the most notable were Chile, Cuba, Uganda, Zaire and Zambia. Generally, where nationalisation has taken place, output has fallen and the expected benefits have not been for the most part realised. Most such developing world's weapons against the power of TNCs have disappeared under the new World Trade Organization (WTO) regime.

Globalisation: what is it and what effect does it have?

It is widely believed that established ideas about the differences between developed and developing countries are outdated because the whole world is now influenced by the process of **globalisation**.

Globalisation has been defined by Giddens as:

Intensification of world-wide social relations which link distant locations in such a way that local happenings are shaped by events happening many miles away and vice versa. (Giddens 1990: 64)

There are four main themes in the globalisation debate:

- the integration of peoples;
- the speeding up of communications;
- the blurring of national boundaries;
- the steady rise of technocratic dominance.

(a) There has been and is a steady integration of peoples. As people move from place to place in search of work, to get away from conflict or simply in search of new experiences the cultural differences between societies have been eroded.

The cultural effects of globalisation are obvious. The USA has been the main source of influences in the twentieth century through the invention of the cinema and the desire to emulate the lifestyle of Hollywood, USA, which was uniquely well placed to develop the new medium. Viewers sought to buy the clothes, furniture, cars and other products typical of at least a modified version of the Hollywood lifestyle. Blue jeans, baseball caps, trainers, Coca-Cola, McDonald's, horror movies, pop music and many other staples of everyday life have been internationalised. The products themselves, however, are increasingly made in the developing world.

Obviously for the vast majority of people in the developing countries their ability to share this style is constrained by cost. This accounts for one of the few exceptions to the cultural dominance of the USA: the popularity in the developing countries of football (soccer), for which the only real requirement is the ball itself. The USA itself is very resistant to globalisation and though in recent years soccer has gained some popularity there its spread has been slow.

(b) Communications and travel have been speeded up. The farthest points of the planet can be reached by air in less than 24 hours. Electronic communications transmit text, pictures and sound all but instantaneously. The inhabitants of developing countries are now much more aware than they used to be of the lifestyle available in the developed countries, and many are determined to try to achieve it for themselves and their families. In 2005 the Disney Corporation opened its eleventh theme park in Hong Kong and is said to be pursuing plans to build an even bigger one in Shanghai.

It is the zeal to consume that sustains the worldwide economic system, within which it is not just the products that matter, but the way in which they are sold. Fast-food outlets and supermarkets have broken the traditional link between seller and buyer. No less importantly they have broken the link between the production of food and its consumption, creating a world in which what you buy is a matter of what you are prepared to pay. In 2005 in British supermarkets the diligent shopper could choose between Israeli oranges, Brazilian mangoes, Chilean onions and Kenyan sweet potatoes. Those items which are locally produced tend to be those which have a much lower unit price, for example potatoes, cabbages and cauliflowers.

(c) Boundaries between states have become blurred. For some purposes, especially the spreading of rumours and the movement of money, boundaries have practically ceased to exist. This has all sorts of practical consequences. Wealthy countries find it easier than ever to subsidise organisations or political parties in developing countries. This may be for benign purposes, such as the promotion of democracy, but it may be simply to buy political support. The Japanese, in face of world opinion, want to go on eating whale meat. Because there is strong resistance to this, they have paid for a number of small island states to become members of the International Whaling Commission, and vote for the resumption of commercial whaling. Other countries which lack other resources have been able to reinvent themselves as offshore financial centres, enabling the wealthy to avoid tax and criminals and terrorists to move money without detection.

There are important macropolitical consequences, which have a crucial significance for the relationships between the developed and the developing countries. In the 'shrinking world' it is no longer possible to say something in one place and assume that it will not be heard in another. However, politicians have been slow to realise this, or perhaps the desire to secure votes from their electorates overrides all other considerations. The more they talk the more they give offence. At the same time, they are continually at the call of a globalised press, dominated in news management by the largely US-owned press agencies, and satellite television, dominated by the News Corporation-owned Sky. US cartoonists, and columnists, are syndicated throughout the world. News of what is happening in countries such as Afghanistan or Iraq is presented first by American agencies and interpreted according to the current view in Washington or New York, not Baghdad or Kabul. The modern media transcend boundaries. In the age of satellite television, Sky broadcasts to China but only at the price of self-censorship, by ensuring that its channels do not carry news about, for example, the Chinese conquest of Tibet. However US dominance does not go unchallenged. The Chinese news agency itself is widely quoted. Al-Jazeera (which is based in Qatar) broadcasts to the entire Middle East, including both Israel and the Occupied Territories (also known as the West Bank and the Gaza Strip).

(d) Worldwide there has been an increasing tendency to accept such technological developments at face value and to see the 'technological fix' as the solution to all problems, including social and political ones. The claim of experts to know better than others has resulted in the steady rise of technocratic dominance not just in scientific matters, such as computer science or medicine, but social scientific areas such as economics and psychology. The accepted wisdom of the AICs, and, among those, the United States, has gained a global authority. Since its inception, the so-called Nobel Prize in Economics (actually a separate memorial prize in honour of Alfred Nobel) has been consistently awarded to US economists – 31 to date. Only once, so far, has it gone to an economist from a developing country, Amartya Sen (India).

Satellite television offers the world a choice of sensation and package tourism enables people for the first time to encounter cultures very different from their own and to do so in numbers sufficiently large significantly to affect the economies of many smaller countries (see Chapter 9). Most recently, the internet affords the opportunity to select for oneself from an unparalleled range of information and, with the linking up of the internet and television, also entertainment.

Neo-liberalism

Neo-liberalism has very little to do with classical liberalism, which is a predominantly *political* doctrine prioritising individual freedom above all other values. As such, political liberalism has been a major force in creating the postcolonial world through the assertion of independence and the disintegration of empires.

Neo-liberalism, by contrast, is a primarily *economic* doctrine. It revives nineteenth-century ideas of a free market, free trade and the absence of state 'interference'. It had its origins in the USA and Western Europe in the 1970s. Its early advocates included Hayek (1960) and Friedman (1962), but it was converted into political action by Margaret Thatcher in the UK (and especially after the adoption of privatisation in 1983) and Ronald Reagan in the USA and his so-called 'Reaganomics'. Its supporters argue a political as well as economic case for neo-liberalism: they associate any form of state intervention with 'socialism', and do not recognise the social-reformist position which achieved hegemony during the Second World War and was implemented to a greater or lesser extent throughout Europe as well as in many developing countries in the period after 1945. Moreover, it is a doctrine for rich countries, hence for the developing world it:

- authorises greed and self-interest;
- further weakens the structure of the state; and
- weakens and attempts to remove altogether the only protection a developing country has against unequal competition from developed countries. Such measures include US farm subsidies, its use of grain exports under PL540 to reduce surpluses, the Common Agricultural Policy (CAP) of the European Union and China's manipulation of its currency.

The world capitalist system, governed (if at all) through the Bretton Woods institutions (see below), has been revitalised and has established an effective hegemony worldwide. After 1992 developing countries accepted the neo-liberal model of capitalism as embodied in the so-called 'Washington consensus'; they had no alternative model to propose. By the phrase, the Washington consensus, its inventor, John Williamson, of the Institute for International Economics, meant in 1989 simply a list of policies that the Bank thought were desirable for implementation in Latin America. Only subsequently did it come to mean a set of economic policies advocated for developing countries in general by official Washington, comprising both international organisations, such as the IMF and World Bank, and US government, specifically the Treasury Department. These policies augmented the original policies advocated by Williamson, and emphasised institutional reforms. These policies and these reforms formed a model of development which claimed that there is only one road to prosperity, that it is to be achieved by the operation of the free market impeded as little as possible by national boundaries, and this view was generally accepted.

As Thomas (1999) points out, this last point was the most important – the extent to which the liberalisation of trade and the free market had become, in Gramscian terms, hegemonic values not just for US (or British, French or other European) policy-makers but also for international institutions, including financial institutions, thus transmitting those values to the rest of the world. Stanislaw and Yergin, however, suggest that it has become an excuse for the failures of developing world governments themselves (Stanislaw and Yergin 2002; Santiso 2004) and it must be said that this is now Williamson's own view (Williamson 1999).

A further consequence is that any distinction between centre and periphery is blurred (for neo-liberalism encourages the emergence of multiple centres and peripheries). New regional economic groupings have emerged strengthening regional hegemons, for example China, South Africa and Brazil. And the periphery itself is differentiated, especially by the spread of dependent development, in which developing countries provide cheap labour and an almost total absence of regulation, and the profits are remitted to the AICs.

The main consequence, however, is that the most important centres of economic power now lie outside the developing state and in most cases lie beyond its control. Neo-structuralism argues that as a result the state can no longer control its own economy, and is subject to the unpredictable play of market forces. It is therefore restricted in what it can do and interest groups, political parties and legislatures have to come to terms with but seek to avoid the consequences of their own powerlessness. The keenest advocates of the globalisation thesis argue that the process goes much further than this, that national boundaries are disappearing and for the first time in human history there has emerged a truly global economic system. This system is subject only to global market forces and individual states no longer have the capacity to govern the transnational companies which are its main actors (Ohmae 1990). This may be economically desirable but it is not democratic. Democracy, previously challenged by the Cold War, superpower dominance and the national security state, has achieved a new level of acceptance, only (paradoxically) to have to meet the new threat posed by the neo-liberal paradigm.

Furthermore there has been a new assertiveness in the world capitalist system since the collapse of communism in 1991. This world system is governed (if at all) through the Bretton Woods institutions, the International Monetary Fund (IMF), the World Bank and the World Trade Organization (WTO). The first two of these international organisations have the power to control national spending by setting terms for treasuries and central banks (conditionality). The third has the power to regulate trade in goods and services and to punish countries which breach its rules by authorising other countries to inflict financial harm on their manufactures. Yet even the countries which suffer from this process do not challenge the legitimacy of the system under which they deprived themselves of the possibility of making decisions. Because, in Gramscian terms, the Washington consensus has achieved **hegemony**, governments in Europe have voluntarily embarked on a process of economic liberalisation: deregulating economic activity, privatising state industries, weakening trade unions and cutting down on social security provision.

External agencies (especially TNCs) dispose of huge resources. They are able to make use of the structural weaknesses of the domestic economy to their own purposes, including (if they feel like it) bribing potential purchasers, cabinet ministers, media entrepreneurs etc. Hence the terms of trade are stacked against the developing countries and the markets on which they depend offer them only a limited range of opportunities. The belief that fairer terms (and perhaps some aid) from the AICs can enable countries to overcome these problems, therefore, has not been realised. Instead AICs have taken the lead in the Uruguay Round in enforcing neo-liberal ideas on developing countries and enforcing them through a new regulatory organisation, the WTO. This is discussed in more detail in Chapter 4.

However, there are arguments on the other side. Hirst and Thompson draw a sharp distinction between a truly globalised economy and one that is merely 'internationalised'. Transnational corporations are indeed powerful and we would be wise to remember that. But they are not 'stateless'; they trade from a base in a national economy and their national identity continues to be important to them, providing a structure of law which regulates their actions, a common culture which gives them their competitive edge over less integrated companies and the backing of a powerful patron which can afford a variety of forms of concealed support. Europe, Japan and North America remain the main providers of direct foreign investment. Together they exercise a considerable degree of control over world financial markets, though for ideological reasons they may well not choose to exercise the power they have (Hirst and Thompson 1999: 2–3).

Secondly, the developing world is by no means uniform. Three areas or regions have distinctive economic advantages and/or disadvantages: (1) the oil-rich Middle East (Saudi Arabia, Iran, Iraq, Bahrain, the UAE); (2) the 'Asian Tigers' and their imitators (South Korea, Taiwan, Singapore, Malaysia); and (3) small island developing states (SIDS) such as St Vincent and St Lucia in the Caribbean, the Maldives in the Indian Ocean and Kiribati in the Pacific. These are a reminder that the world is a much more complex place than it may look from an air-conditioned office in Washington or New York.

Conclusion

Some of the reasons for the underdevelopment of the developing world are quite obvious; others less so.

Natural resources are very unequally distributed. For example, Cuba failed to industrialise and returned to growing one crop, sugar. The smaller Caribbean islands are under threat from US banana interests. But even where resources exist they may not be used for development. Inflows to help develop them are unreliable.

Capital movements are short term and unpredictable. Investors have had their fingers burnt by the 'tequila' crisis of 1994 and the East Asia crisis of 1997 and they have taken a long time to get over these crises (Krugman 1995).

Governments take easy options. Brazil has abundant resources but they are wastefully exploited by foreign corporations. It has very unequal land distribution, but turned settlers loose on Amazonia rather than risk their social basis of power by letting them loose in the big cities. Desperation provided the force for the industrialisation of Japan, Korea and Israel; without it their histories might have been very different.

When scarce financial resources have to be shared out in a largely poor country governments (especially post-colonial governments) easily succumb to personalism, patrimonialism and clientelism (see Chapter 7). All of these lead to corruption, which distorts economic performance and results in the chronic waste of already scarce resources.

Key terms

advanced industrialised countries (AICs) – those countries which were industrialised before the Second World War, including the United States and Canada, Western Europe, Japan, Russia and Australia

bureaucratic authoritarianism – for O'Donnell, the situation when in a post-populist society constrained by the limits of industrialisation civil and military technocrats ally with foreign capital to demobilise or repress popular movements

Caribbean Basin Initiative (CBI) – US initiative launched in 1984 and still current providing for tariff exemptions or reductions for most products from 24 participating countries in Central America and the Caribbean region

Charter of Economic Rights and Duties of States (CERDS) – declaration of the UN General Assembly (A/RES/39/163 of 17 December 1984) advocating a New International Economic Order more favourable to developing countries

development – economic growth, especially in terms of raised GNI and/or the enhancement of living conditions; by extension, increases in social resources

developing countries – residual category of all but the advanced industrialised countries

empowerment – for Paulo Freire, acquiring the awareness and the skills to take charge of one's own environment

export-oriented industrialisation – industrialisation geared to competition in world markets, based on advantages such as cheap labour and the absence of regulation

globalisation – for Giddens "Intensification of world-wide social relations which link distant locations in such a way that local happenings are shaped by events happening many miles away and vice versa"

hegemony – for Gramsci, when an ideology secures the people's assent to its continued control

import-substitution industrialisation (ISI) – the first stage of industrialisation, based on the manufacture of substitutes for commodities previously imported, e.g. paper, textiles, ceramics

liberalisation – in economic terms, deregulating economic activity, privatising state industries, opening trade and commerce up to competition

nepotism – the employment of or granting of favours to relatives

New International Economic Order (NIEO) – see CERDS

public sector – the portion of the economy administered by all levels of government and excluding households and businesses

South – alternative term for what was formerly known as the Third World

Third World – all other countries other than the AICs (First World) and the countries of the former Soviet Bloc plus China (Second World)

US Agency for International Development (USAID) – the principal US agency to extend assistance to countries recovering from disaster, trying to escape poverty, and engaging in democratic reforms

Vienna Declaration – a common plan for the strengthening of human rights work around the world adopted by the World Conference on Human Rights at Vienna, Austria, 25 June 1993

weapons of mass destruction – weapons capable of destroying large areas of territory and/or killing larges numbers of people

Questions

1. What characteristics, if any, do the developing countries have in common?

2. Why, to understand development, is it necessary to understand the special position of women?

3. What problems might you expect to encounter while conducting research in the developing world?

4. With the second largest economy in the world, why might we continue to regard China as a developing country?

5. Is development a fundamental human right?

The infrastructure of the developing world

CHAPTER 2

Physical location

The nature of the developing world is significantly influenced by geography, something that is so obvious that it is often dismissed as trivial by experts in other fields. And the way in which the developing world is perceived by the developed world is partly conditioned by the fact that our global home has to be mapped on a flat surface. Mercator's map projection, used in Europe since the sixteenth century is still the most popular and indeed the most useful for finding one's way over moderate distances. But it has one great disadvantage: it exaggerates the relative size and hence the visual impact of northern states, and hence of Europe, Canada, the United States and Russia. Only at the equator is latitude correct in relation to longitude. The distortion becomes infinite at the poles, turning the Antarctic into a white smudge round the bottom of the map. The effect is even more dramatic with a polar projection such as that on the flag of the United Nations. Exaggeration has its value – a circular map of the world centred on New Zealand places Antarctica in the near foreground, which says much about the relationship between the two territories. But it transforms Spain and Portugal into a thin brown line round the edge. The currently favoured Peters Projection (used by Brandt), which distributes the distortions between the equator and the poles, renders more accurately the proportions between the more and less densely inhabited parts of the earth. It is more appropriate than older projections, therefore, to enable the viewer to understand the relative importance both of the developing world as a whole and of individual countries within it. Unfortunately it would be of little or no use in helping you to get from one part of the developing world to another, unless you wanted to go due North–South or East–West (see Map 2.1).

Redrawing the map of the world to reflect in terms of relative area non-geographical variables such as wealth or political power, is, unfortunately, impossible without distorting spatial relationships to a point at which they

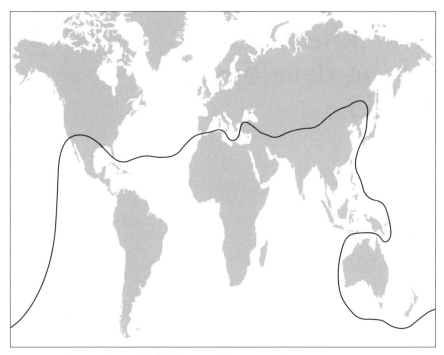

Map 2.1 The North–South divide according to Brandt

become completely unrecognisable. However, any map of the world that differentiates countries by, say, their place in the World Bank classification by per capita income, is a useful corrective to the simple North–South model (see Map 2.2). Sadly, many of the oil-rich countries of the Middle East are very small, or the map would show up very clearly the secondary concentration of wealth in the region (World Bank 1999).

Main geographical features

The term 'South' does not imply it, but most developing countries do lie in the tropical and/or subtropical zones. However, both Chile and Argentina, which are truly southern, span the entire range of climates from subtropical to sub-Antarctic. Mongolia, Kazakhstan and much of China fall within the northern temperate zone.

In tropical countries there is little division between hot and cool seasons, but there are other very important climatic differences between countries and between regions. For example, West/Central Africa has a hot wet equatorial climate, very heavy rainfall and a rapid rate of evaporation. East Africa has

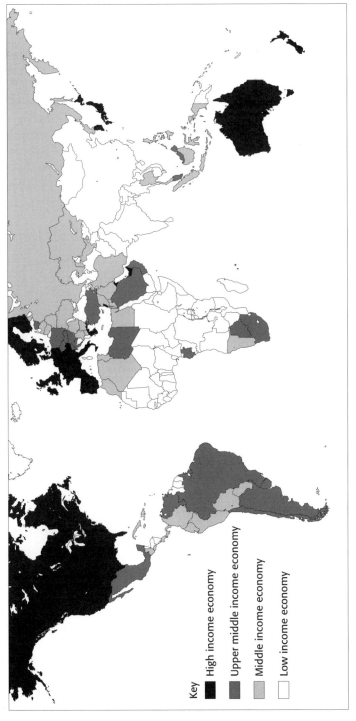

Map 2.2 Map of countries according to the World Bank classification of income (1999)

Key
High income economy
Upper middle income economy
Middle income economy
Low income economy

both a wet tropical and a dry savannah climate owing to its mountain and plateau features. The Horn of Africa is arid, though many of its problems are exacerbated by human action (or inaction).

The fact is that a vertical separation of climate zones is often more import-ant for most purposes than a horizontal one. In Latin America, whether in Mexico, in Central America, or the Andean countries, the traditional division is made between the *tierra caliente*, below 1,000 m, which is low-lying, hot and humid; the *tierra templada*, lying at a moderate altitude, between 1,000 and 2,000 m, which is cooler and so capable of growing temperate zone crops; and the *tierra fría*, the zone that lies between 2,000–3,000 m and which is mountainous, cold and subject to frost. Above that lies an alpine zone stretching from 3,000 m to the snowline over 4,500 m. In both Mexico and Colombia snow remains on the highest peaks all the year round.

Altitude is the key to the nature of human settlement in such regions. It is essential to the growing of cash crops such as tea and coffee. Not only do these crops need cooler conditions but the height – preferably with forest cover – is required for reliable precipitation. This is just one of the ways in which mainland Central and South America gains geographically over the Caribbean islands, where production of almost anything is more difficult and thus expensive. Of course, if cost is of no object, production at the margin is often considered to be of the highest quality. This is said of Caribbean bananas; it is indisputably true of Jamaican Blue Mountain coffee. Low-lying Caribbean islands lack moisture and many of the smaller ones are uninhabited in conse-quence. The Bahamas rely on imported water.

Within the tropical zone, the shifts in prevailing winds bring the monsoon, seasonal winds that carry large quantities of moisture with them; hence local reliance, as in the Western Ghats of India or in Sri Lanka, on the storage of water from the monsoon in 'tanks' (reservoirs) to use during the dry season. The complexity of the patterns involved even in a small area like Sri Lanka, is shown by the fact that the north-east (mid-October to mid-February) and south-west (April to June) monsoons affect different parts of the island; part of the island, notably the main city Colombo, gets both, and other parts get neither and are arid.

If a country uses less than 10 per cent of its annual renewable water resources it is unlikely to experience shortages of water. China and most of southern Asia use more than this, but not more than 20 per cent, so shortages, when they do occur, happen on a regional rather than a national basis. However, in the North China Plain there are already acute water shortages, as demand outstrips supply. By 1990 twenty countries were already 'water scarce', that is to say, they had less than 1,000 cubic metres of renewable fresh water per person per year (National Council for Science and the Environ-ment 2000). By 2000 nearly 508 million people in 31 countries were facing a serious shortage of clean water, the principal areas affected being the Mediterranean basin, India, parts of China, most of Africa south of the Sahara and the western United States. UNFPA has calculated that by 2025 those numbers will rise to 3 billion people in 48 countries (UNFPA 1992; IDRC/ CRDI 2006). Access to water resources is likely to become more problematic and more subject to international disputes in the very near future (Thomas and Howlett 1992; see also Chapter 6).

Case study 2.1   **The Asian tsunami of 2004**

At 07:58 local time on 26 December 2004 an undersea earthquake occurred off the west coast of Sumatra. In Sumatra itself a large number of casualties resulted from the direct effects of the earthquake, which at magnitude 9.15 was the second most severe shock ever recorded. But the shift in the fault line underwater generated a tsunami, which US Geological Survey figures estimate killed 283,100 people around the shores of the Indian Ocean. In addition 14,100 have been recorded as missing and some 1,126,900 lost their homes and livelihoods. The majority of the known deaths occurred in Indonesia, Thailand, India, Sri Lanka and Somalia, but a casualty was recorded in Port Elizabeth, South Africa, some 8,000 km from the epicentre of the earthquake.

The shock had been registered even further away at the Pacific Tsunami Warning Center at Ewa Beach, Hawaii. Tsunamis are a frequent occurrence in the vast Pacific; there were, for example, 17 between 1992 and 1996. Despite the existence of an early warning system they resulted in nearly 1700 deaths. However, there was no early warning system in place for the Indian Ocean area and when the staff of the Pacific Center saw what had happened and tried to alert surrounding countries they were unable to find official telephone numbers to contact. Yet, interestingly enough, on the Indonesian island of Simulue, so close to the epicentre that the earthquake itself would have been their only warning, many were saved because the island had been devastated in 1907 by a similar event and people recognised the signs.

The poorest people, perhaps inevitably, suffered most from the disaster itself. Living often on marginal land by the sea, their boats were smashed and their shelters swept away. There were less obvious consequences. Women were four times as likely to be killed as men, as they were home at the time. Fishermen who were actually out in their boats at the time were likely to survive and many did not even know that the wave had passed underneath them until they returned to shore. And one-third of all fatalities were children, who lacked the physical strength to cling on until the wave had receded. The destruction of whole communities deprived the survivors of the traditional support mechanisms available in more routine disasters, and the fact that transport links had been washed away meant delay in bringing in help from outside.

Partly because there were a great many Western tourists in the area at the time, the disaster received extensive publicity worldwide, and the response came in an outpouring of public generosity and donations and pledges of help totalling more than $3 billion. However, six months later, Oxfam reported that the poorest victims had benefited least from the relief effort. In Sri Lanka, which was particularly hard hit, more than 30,000 had died and half a million were homeless. But only about half of the homeless had temporary homes and work had hardly begun on the 90,000 permanent dwellings which would be required.

Plate 2 Drying fish, Sri Lanka

The View from the Ground

By *Jonathan Kent*, BBC News, Kuala Lumpur

The mystery of Malaysia's tsunami aid

When the 26 December tsunami struck countries around the Indian Ocean rim, Malaysia escaped largely unscathed.

Protected from the main waves by the Indonesian island of Sumatra, the country's death toll reached only 68.

Yet six months on, some Malaysian villages hit by the tsunami are still struggling to get back on their feet.

Some villagers say help has been slow in coming, others say they have yet to receive any aid at all. And in some cases, aid appears to have simply disappeared into a black hole.

Kampung Sungai Muda, in the state of Kedah, was one of the worst affected villages. Twelve people died there.

'The village was celebrating a festival when the waves came,' said fisherman Badaruddin bin Hamid, in the once modestly prosperous settlement that now lies in ruins.

The people ran, but some were trapped in their houses and drowned. Malaysia was not overwhelmed by the scale of the disaster. Fewer than 10,000 people are believed to have been affected.

And by the standards of the region, Malaysia is well off. Its income per capita is almost five times that of Indonesia, and four times that of Sri Lanka.

'They promised me just over $6,000 to help put things right, but that's a loan. I don't know how much of it I'm going to have to pay back and it hasn't even all reached me yet.' (Abu Hassan, fisherman, Penang)

Yet many are still waiting for help.

'The government promised us two things,' said Badaruddin: '$6,500 for those who lost fibreglass boats, and $18,000 for those who lost wooden ones.

'But all we've been given is $250 for fibreglass boats, and $800 for wooden boats.'

Many of the villagers have left, moved 1–2 km inland to temporary accommodation provided by the government.

At the new settlement in Kota Kuala Muda, gratitude is mixed with frustration. Village headman Yusof Awang said that many of the 600 people now living in the white painted plywood dwellings had been worried the buildings might fall down.

'I'm glad to have a home but there have been some structural problems and we were worried that it wasn't safe. After we told the government, they did send some people to inspect the building and they made some repairs – so we're feeling a bit happier now.'

To be fair, to Acehnese or Sri Lankan eyes, these temporary homes – with power, water and telephones – might appear to be the answer to a prayer.

But the inhabitants want to know when work on permanent housing will start, and there is no sign of it yet.

Just the other side of the Muda Estuary, over the state boundary in Penang, there are more fishermen waiting for help.

Two hundred petitioned the state government for aid, but according to their representatives, were told to apologise for their temerity. For its part the state says it investigated the claims and found that some had already received help.

Abu Hassan gets by mending nets. When the tsunami swept up the Muda River it smashed his boat and left him on crutches.

But despite the generosity of ordinary Malaysians who rushed to donate money, Abu Hassan said none had been given to him. He has only been offered a loan, and he has not even received all of that.

'I have already lost my boat and the engine is under repair,' he said. 'They promised me just over $6,000 to help put things right, but that's a loan. I don't know how much of it I'm going to have to pay back and it hasn't even all reached me yet.'

GS Soma, who operates a local legal advice centre and who has been giving support to fishermen still seeking help, said the authorities simply have not been taking charge of the situation.

'The government thinks it's already helped the people adequately as far as the tsunami disaster is concerned,' he said.

'But the problem is the people who have been affected are not getting the aid. Somebody along the middle line is not able to make that aid reach them.'

Lost in the system

That hints at what people privately tell visitors over and over again, that somewhere along the line middlemen are helping themselves to money meant for tsunami victims. The BBC put these complaints to the man in charge of Malaysia's tsunami relief operation, Deputy Prime Minister Najib Razak. However, he remains confident the relief effort is largely going well.

'Generally we have been very pleased of the outcome of all the efforts we have undertaken to help the tsunami victims,' he said. 'But I do accept that there could be individuals who have not been able to get the kind of help that they're supposed to get.'

Mr Najib explained that it was not always an easy process to identify genuine claimants, and to underscore the government's good work he pointed to new houses already built for those who lost their homes on Malaysia's showcase holiday island of Langkawi.

> We know full well that when we took along gifts donated by viewers and readers to the villages, very often they went no further than the headman. But what can you do? (Media executive)

Questions, though, remain about what has happened to the fruits of Malaysia's generosity.

Where it was given by one person to another the impact is obvious – as on Penang Island. In the village of Pulau Betong life is already almost back to normal. Zainun Jainul, a Muslim, said she got help direct from charities and even from Buddhist and Taoist groups.

'I'm very proud of everyone because they came so fast and helped everyone regardless of their race or religion,' she said. 'They were here much faster than the government and they really made a difference.'

But it is less clear how the millions of dollars raised by media and entertainment campaigns – money handed over to the government to distribute – has been spent.

One media executive told the BBC: 'We know full well that when we took along gifts donated by viewers and readers to the villages, very often they went no further than the headman. But what can you do?'

The tsunami clearly brought out the best in millions of Malaysians, but it also brought out the worst in a few. But few in authority seem to want to confront the issue.

Source: BBC News
http://news.bbc.co.uk/go/pr/fr/-/1/hi/world/asia-pacific/4100030.stm
Published: 2005/06/20 14:47:06 GMT
© BBC MMV

Relief and drainage

Of course, nowhere in the world is totally free from the effects of the continual shifts on the plates in which the continents rest. There are major geological fault lines under both developed countries (Japan, the western United States, Iceland, Greece, New Zealand) and developing countries (Iran, Indonesia, Philippines, Peru, Colombia, Mexico, Turkey). The relative geological stability of much of the United States, Canada, northern Europe and northern Asia is undoubtedly an asset to economic and social development. On the other hand, Japan, a model of successful economic development for much of today's world, is spectacularly unstable and experiences on average 700 earthquakes a year. However, as we shall see later, where the incidence of natural disasters is the same, the impact of them is generally very much less in developed states than in developing ones.

The massive block of the Himalayas determines much of the geography as it does much of the climate of a sizeable section of the developing world. The range is high enough to interrupt the circulation of winds in the Indian Ocean such as takes place in the Pacific, and the result is the **monsoon,** the periodic rains which make cultivation possible. In South America, the Andes, the highest and longest major cordillera of young fold mountains, are geologically extremely active. Extensive trough faulting gives stepwise topography, and volcanoes and earthquakes attest to continuing upward movement of strata. The Andes, like the Himalayas, are a major climatic barrier, and it is now thought that the formation of both ranges was responsible for ending the relative warmth of the Tertiary era and bringing about the onset of the Ice Ages.

Today, mountains still have a great importance for human beings. They establish political boundaries, structure communications, source major rivers, yield important minerals, and provide temperate foothills and low uplands where human settlement is safer and more comfortable than on the plains. Even smaller mountain ranges have a regional/local significance. The only frontier between the First and Third Worlds that consists of no more than a line on a map is that between the United States and Mexico. Otherwise the Mediterranean, the Dardanelles, the Caucasus Mountains and other features act as natural barriers.

As the case of the Asian tsunami shows, orogenic (mountain-building) processes continue under water. A celebrated underwater fault line encloses the Caribbean, stretching from the Virgin Islands by way of Puerto Rico to the Dominican Republic, where west of the Cordillera de Cibao it forks, giving to the north the northern peninsula of Haiti, the Sierra Maestra of Cuba and the Cayman Islands, and to the south the southern peninsula of Haiti and Jamaica. Though relatively quiet at present, the volcanic origin of the Lesser Antilles has been accompanied by dramatic evidence of its continuing importance, notably the eruption on Montserrat beginning in 1997, which rendered four-fifths of the island uninhabitable for years. But fewer than might have been expected were prepared for the dramatic revival of vulcanism in Indonesia, although the eruptions of Tambora in 1815 and Krakatoa in 1889 both generated massive tsunamis and are well known to have changed not only regional but global weather patterns owing to the vast amount of volcanic ash they ejected.

Great **river basins** have everywhere been the seat of the earliest known human civilisations, both in the Middle East (the Nile and the Tigris–Euphrates) and in East Asia (Yangtze, Hoang Ho, Mekong). Great rivers have formed the major routes both into and out of new areas in Europe and North America (St Lawrence, Mississippi–Missouri, Rhine, Danube) in the era before wheeled land travel became a reasonably convenient alternative to transport by water. The celebrated amber route from the Baltic to Byzantium ('Middlegarth' to the northerners) followed the rivers. In Asia, the Jordan, Tigris–Euphrates, Indus, Ganges–Brahmaputra, Irrawaddy, Salween, Mekong, Hoang Ho and Yangtze, have all helped shape the distribution of human settlement.

In North America, the two great navigable river systems account for the growth of and still serve Canada and the United States. Mexico has to share the waters of the Colorado and the Rio Grande with the United States. Neither is navigable and heavy use has split the Rio Grande into two muddy parts. Most of Mexico's rivers flow directly but seasonally from the Sierra Madre to the sea.

In South America, on the other hand, the situation is very different. The Magdalena, Orinoco, Amazon, and the Parana, which with its tributaries and the Uruguay flows into the estuary called the Rio de la Plata, are all navigable, while others, the Tocantins and São Francisco in Brazil, and the Colorado, Negro and Chubut in Argentina, fulfil other important local needs.

In Africa, apart from the Nile, the Zambesi, Orange, Congo, Niger and Senegal rivers have similarly acted as traffic routes since well before the age of colonial penetration. Of all the major regions of the world, only Oceania fairly obviously lacks major river systems, with the rather doubtful exception, perhaps, of the Murray River in Australia.

The value of navigable river systems lies, above all, in their connection with the sea. However, the sea not only links navigable rivers, but coastal and island civilisations, e.g. Japan, China, Korea, Taiwan. The sea has the distinctive property of joining all coastal points on the globe with one another, without the need for the navigator to go through territory controlled by others.

The sea is the great motor of climate. Now that they can be measured more accurately and over the entire world's surface, changes in sea temperature are known to have massive effects on regional climates. It had long been known that 'El Niño' affected the flow of the cold Humboldt Current northwards along the west coast of South America, causing the fish harvest to fail. Only at the end of the last century did it become clear that the shift in this current, which has its beginning in the positioning of some relatively small islands some 3,000 km out in the Pacific, has much wider implications. The episode which began in February 1997 brought torrential rain to Peru and Ecuador and exceptional heat in North America in 1998. It was also associated with heavy storms in China, hurricanes of record strength in the Pacific and a delayed onset for the monsoon in India (National Council for Science and the Environment 2000).

The question of whether the increasing frequency of El Niño is a natural variation or an aspect of the process of **human-induced climate change** is disputed. The present authors accept the weight of evidence in favour of the latter view (see Chapter 9). Certainly, despite statements to the contrary by a small number of lobbyists for the oil industry, there is no doubt at all that global warming is taking place, and even if human-induced climate change merely adds to natural changes the important thing to remember is that it is the bit that at least we can do something about. Global warming poses a serious threat to the developing world, especially where, as we shall see, the effects of drought are amplified by the degradation of the land through overuse.

Drought in turn causes changes in river use. The controversial Sardar Sarovar dam on the Narmada River in India was designed to cope with the droughts in Gujarat occasioned by the failure of the monsoon (Vajpeyi 1994, 1998). But human action also has great impacts on river systems, especially where it involves the generation of hydroelectric power. This is quite possible even where rivers are not navigable, as in the case of the Bumbuna Falls project in Sierra Leone, but it permanently alters their flow and hence relationship to the surrounding countryside.

Boundaries and territorial disputes

Frontiers are influenced by and in turn influence geography. In some parts of the world, notably in Europe, international boundaries have not only been agreed, but are formally demarcated by the placing of posts, fences or checkpoints. In the case of developing countries, this is often not the case.

The major influence on present-day international boundaries in the developing world has been colonial expansion. Time and again the frontiers between colonial empires were settled by diplomatic conferences by people who had no first-hand knowledge of the areas and features to which they were referring. In addition, only occasionally were they formally demarcated. Hence unless they follow the lines of rivers, they often cut across the territories of indigenous peoples or tribes. A classic example of this is in West Africa, where British settlements in The Gambia, Sierra Leone, Ghana and Nigeria adjoin and are surrounded by states that were formerly part of French West Africa. Prescott quotes a Yoruba chief in Dahomey (now Benin), separated by the colonial frontier from the majority of his tribe in Nigeria, as saying: 'We regard the boundary as separating the French and the English, not the Yoruba' (Prescott 1965: 63). The same may be said of East Africa, where Uganda exemplifies the arbitrary nature of colonial boundaries. An even odder example is to be found in Southern Africa, where Namibia's boundaries are extended eastwards into the narrow Caprivi Strip running between Angola and Botswana to Barotseland in what is now Zambia. This illogical feature was originally intended to allow the former colonial power, Germany, to build a railway to link its East and West African territories.

The potential for boundary disputes is great and is not helped by the fact that many treaties of the colonial period did not refer to identifiable physical features but assumed the existence of a boundary that was well known to all concerned at the time. However, the fact is that, newly independent or not, the successor states have proved to be every bit as imperialistic as the European empires in their day, as the following examples show (Calvert 2004: 18–22, 64–74, 184–197).

Ethiopia–Eritrea

Between 1998 and 2000, two of the poorest countries in the world fought a bitter war. It resulted in the death of more than 70,000 people and displaced hundreds of thousands from their homes. The origins of the dispute go back to the nineteenth century, when the newly united kingdom of Italy tried to carve out for itself an empire in Ethiopia, the one part of the continent that had not already been claimed by a European power. The Ethiopians, under Emperor Menelik, defeated the Italian forces at the battle of Adowa (1896), and complelled them to recognise Ethiopian independence, but did not succeed in wresting back control of the coastal province of Eritrea. In 1935 Italy occupied Ethiopia again, but was met with fierce resistance, and in 1942 the country regained its independence with the aid of Commonwealth forces. Eritrea, however, remained for the duration of the war under British protection, until the newly-formed UN could decide what to do with it. In 1952 it was decided to federate it with Ethiopia as an autonomous region and the US government acquired a 25-year lease on a communications base at Asmara. Meanwhile the Ethiopian government had suspended the Eritrean constitution and in 1962 Eritrea was annexed. Neither the USA nor the Soviet Union objected.

However, with Arab support and Soviet weapons the Eritrean Liberation Front (ELF) began a campaign against Ethiopian domination which among other things forced Ethiopia to close the US base at Asmara.

The fall of Emperor Haile Selassie in 1974 briefly checked the conflict. However, the new revolutionary government, the Derg, soon made its intentions clear by sending some 5,000 more troops into Eritrea. Despite Soviet support, however, the Derg were unable to reconquer the territory, and in 1991, following the collapse of the Soviet Union, the government of Haile Mengistu also fell. In April 1993 a UN-sponsored referendum in Eritrea opted overwhelmingly for independence. With both sides under new leadership, relations were apparently friendly right up to the sudden outbreak of hostilities on 6 May 1998, when Eritrean troops occupied the town of Badme near Asmara, claimed by both sides.

With both sides under relatively democratic governments the urge to war proved irresistible, made worse by the fact that landlocked Ethiopia had until 1997 relied on Eritrea for its outlet to the sea, until the introduction of a new currency in Eritrea had greatly increased the costs of cross-border trade. In June 2000 both sides agreed a ceasefire and in September 2000 a UN peace-keeping force, the UN Mission in Ethiopia and Eritrea (UNMEE) took up position in a 25 km-wide Temporary Security Zone separating the two countries. Though a formal settlement was also agreed in Algiers in 2000, it has at the time of writing proved impossible to implement it.

Western Sahara

Until 1975 Spain retained a number of colonial possessions in North Africa, though the area now known internationally as the Western Sahara had only been under Spanish rule since the 19th century. Although the International Court of Justice (ICJ) held that the inhabitants were entitled to self-determination, Spain, then still under the rule of General Franco, agreed to allow Morocco to the north and Mauritania to the south to partition the territory between them. The Polisario Front, however, refused to accept this and in 1976 proclaimed the independence of the area as the Sarahan Arab Democratic Republic (SADR), which was immediately recognised by Algeria and later by many Arab and African states. The strain of the conflict was too much for sparsely populated and impoverished Mauritania, which had had to devote some 60 per cent of its budget to defence. In 1979 it concluded an agreement with the Polisario and withdrew from the southern sector, Tiris el Gharbia, which was immediately occupied by Morocco, which soon found itself spending a quarter of its annual budget on war with the Polisario.

At the 1980 summit of the Organization of African Unity (OAU) in Freetown, Sierra Leone, 26 of the 50 member states supported the application of the SADR for membership. However, after Morocco had threatened to leave the Organization the application failed to gain the necessary two-thirds majority, and Morocco went ahead with building a defensive wall around the disputed territory which eventually was to isolate it completely. In 1981 King Hassan of Morocco said that he would be bound by the outcome of a referendum in the territory but as the Polisario suffered a series of reverses, nothing was done. In 1985 the UN took over the task of mediating the dispute and in January 1989 agreement was formally reached on a peace plan, but it was two more years before a ceasefire came into effect in January 1991 and armed UN troops took up their positions along the so-called defensive wall. At this stage King Hassan raised objections to the UN list of 74,000 Sahrawis entitled to vote and demanded the inclusion of 120,000 'refugees'. Since then the referendum has been repeatedly postponed and the mandate of the UN Mission for the Referendum in Western Sahara (MINURSO) has been repeatedly extended, but the issue remains unresolved.

Kashmir

Kashmir at the time of the partition of India was a princely state, or, strictly speaking, two princely states under the same ruler, the Maharaja of Jammu and Kashmir. The Maharaja was a Hindu, but the majority of his subjects (77.1 per cent at the 1941 census) were Muslim, though Hindus predominated in the northern territory of Jammu. It was assumed that on partition the territory would accede to Pakistan, to which it was linked geographically by its river system. Unfortunately the then Maharaja hesitated, and before he could make up his mind a revolt had broken out among the Muslim community, supported by Pakistan.

The Maharaja thereupon decided to accede to India, and this was accepted, but on behalf of the Indian government the then Governor-General, Lord Mountbatten, made it a condition that as soon as peace was restored the people should have the right to decide by referendum. Unfortunately the government of Pakistan refused to accept these assurances, or to prevent tribesmen from entering the disputed area from Pakistan, and indeed by the beginning of 1948 it had become clear that the insurgency was receiving the wholehearted support of Pakistan, where a further 100,000 troops were being trained for the insurrection. At first Indian forces were successful in driving the insurgents out of the Kashmir Valley, but in December 1947 fighting broke out in south-west Kashmir. The insurgents there were reinforced by regular Pakistani forces in May 1948 and heavy fighting followed. When a ceasefire brokered by the UN came into effect on 1 January 1949, the territory was divided in two, the northern part under Pakistani control, known in Pakistan as Azad Kashmir (Free Kashmir), and the southern part, under Indian control, known in India under the old name of Jammu and Kashmir. Both sides agreed to introduce no further forces into the region, but neither by this time was prepared to withdraw, and in September 1954 the question was left to the UN Security Council for resolution.

Meanwhile the new Administration of General Eisenhower in the United States had in February 1954 been approached by the Pakistani government for military aid. This was granted, and although Eisenhower assured the Indian government that the decision was not aimed at India, the Indian government refused to accept further US mediation and proceeded to integrate Jammu and Kashmir into the Indian Union, moves which aroused corresponding hostility in Pakistan. On 5 August 1965 armed infiltrators from Azad Kashmir entered Indian Kashmir to stir up revolt. In response India deployed troops across the ceasefire line and for a second time full-scale war broke out between it and Pakistan. In the Tashkent Declaration of January 1966 the two countries agreed to withdraw their forces to the positions occupied before the war and to settle all their disputes by peaceful means.

After a long series of unsuccessful negotiations, the possibility of partitioning the territory permanently was discussed in 1962–63. When these talks failed the Indian government continued to maintain its position that the whole territory was rightfully part of India. But the Indo-Pakistan War in December 1971, the third to occur between India and Pakistan since 1947, did not arise directly out of the Kashmir question, but as a result of civil war in East Pakistan, which seceded from Pakistan (with Indian support) to form Bangladesh (Free Bengal). Inevitably, though, there was also fighting along the de facto frontier in Kashmir, which was significantly altered as a result. The new line of control was agreed at Simla after the ceasefire on 17 December, and the Prime Minister of India, Indira Gandhi, went so far as to say that her government was now prepared to consider proposals for converting the line into a permanent frontier. However, instead she later asked for the UN observers to be withdrawn, on the grounds that the former line no longer existed, while in 1982 President Zia of Pakistan radically altered the situation by his claim that the northern territories of Gilgit, Hunza and Shardu were not part of Azad Kashmir, but an integral part of Pakistan.

The Soviet intervention in Afghanistan brought a momentary thaw in the relations between India and Pakistan and in November 1981 President Zia formally suggested talks with a view to concluding a non-aggression pact and as a first step a joint commission was formed. However, by 1984 Indian suspicions that Pakistan was actively fomenting Sikh unrest in the Punjab led to the joint commission being suspended, and at the same time fighting broke out for the first time in Kashmir in the area of the Siachen Glacier. This had been agreed by China in 1963 to be on the Pakistani side of their common frontier, but in the 1970s Indian mountain troops were sent into the region and the Pakistani forces had failed to dislodge them. The fighting in early 1987, however, broke out as a result of tension following military exercises in the Punjab. It was followed by unrest in Indian-controlled Kashmir, which aroused a dangerous level of tension among nationalists on both sides and continued despite a ban on the Kashmiri Liberation Front and other pro-Pakistan insurgent groups. A series of attempts to reach some kind of settlement were made throughout the 1990s but despite repeated declarations on both sides that talks would be welcomed, in practice so many conditions were placed on them that they inevitably failed.

The conflict assumed a new significance when in May 1998 both India and Pakistan carried out nuclear tests and admitted that they were potential, if not actual, nuclear powers. Within days India had publicly restated what had become its position on Kashmir, that it was not prepared to allow an international settlement of the dispute. Then in June 1999 militants from Pakistan again crossed the Line of Control into Indian-occupied Kashmir, and serious fighting in the Kargil area ensued. The insurgents agreed to withdraw rather than face defeat, but Pakistan was widely blamed and in October 1999 its elected government was overthrown by General Pervez Musharraf, who became head of government and later, after a plebiscite, President.

After US intervention in Afghanistan in October 2001, General Musharraf declared unequivocal support for the allies, raising tension in India. On 13 December a separatist attack on the Indian Parliament building in Delhi, which left 14 dead, was interpreted by India as a hostile act, however. Diplomatic relations and transport links were severed and within days nearly a million troops were deployed by both sides along the Line of Control. Although by October 2002 both sides backed down and diplomatic relations were restored, it was estimated that at the end of the year between 40,000 and 60,000 people had been killed in Kashmir since 1989, and an official ceasefire between the two countries was not achieved until 25 November 2003.

Case study 2.2 **Refugees: the case of East Timor (Timor Leste)**

At the collapse of the Portuguese empire in 1975, Indonesia sent troops into the territory of East Timor, the larger West Timor already being an acknowledged part of Indonesia. The world community did not accept Indonesian occupation of East Timor, but despite the fact that 200,000 Timorese died under Indonesian military rule between 1975 and 1999, it did not organise any effective opposition to it. Worse still, successive Australian governments consistently supported Indonesian annexation and in 1989 even signed a treaty with the government of General Suharto, to exploit offshore oil resources in the Timor Gap. Oil production began there in July 1998 and was expected to yield 29 million barrels of light, low-sulphur crude in only four years (Australian Broadcasting Company 1998).

Resistance to the occupation continued, however, and with the fall of General Suharto, in 1999 his successor, President Habibie, agreed to release East Timor's leader, Xanana Guzmão, to permit a referendum on the future of the territory and to abide by the result. Unfortunately only a small group of UN observers was sent to oversee the referendum and the security of the poll was left to the Indonesian army. Once the votes had been counted and it had become evident that the result had been heavily in favour of independence, local commanders conspired with so-called 'militias' to sack the towns and villages and to drive the bulk of the population out of the territory into Indonesian West Timor. There, inevitably, many continued to live in fear, concerned that if they expressed a wish to return home they might be killed before they could get there. The World Bank estimate was that 75 per cent of the population (now only 900,000) had been displaced and nearly 70 per cent of all houses and public buildings had been systematically destroyed. International pressure resulted in the territory being placed under international trusteeship and in May 2002 it gained its independence. However under the new Timor Gap Treaty signed between Australia and the UN Transitional Administration (UNTAET) in February 2000, a large part of the new state's potential oil and gas revenue continues to go to Australia's BHP and its partners, Santos, Petroz and Inpex Sahu.

OCEANIA

TIMOR-LESTE

Official name: Democratic Republic of Timor-Leste (Republika Demokratika Timor Lorosa'e)
Type of government: Parliamentary republic
Capital: Dili
Area: 15,007 sq km
Population (2005 official est.): 1,080,880
GNI per capita (2005): $550 (PPP $400)

Evolution of government: Timor was colonised by the Portuguese in the mid-16th century but in 1859 Portugal ceded the western portion of the island to the

OCEANIA continued

Netherlands, and it became part of Indonesia in 1949. East Timor declared itself independent on 28 November 1975 after the Portuguese Revolution. It was invaded and occupied by Indonesian forces, however, and forcibly incorporated into Indonesia in 1976 as the province of East Timor. Subsequent 'pacification' cost an estimated 100,000 to 250,000 Timorese lives. On 30 August 1999, in a UN-supervised referendum, an overwhelming majority voted for independence, but before the Australian-led multinational peacekeeping force arrived in late September 1999, West Timorese militias killed some 1,300 Timorese, drove 300,000 people into West Timor as refugees, and destroyed homes, irrigation systems, water supply systems, schools and nearly all the country's electrical grid. On 20 May 2002, East Timor was internationally recognised as an independent state.

Main features of government: Currently the newest of the world's independent countries. President's role is largely symbolic. Prime Minister is leader of largest party in unicameral parliament. Supreme Court still to be established. During the period of Indonesian occupation Australia signed an agreement for joint exploitation of the oil resources of the Timor Gap, and retains a substantial interest there.

Terrorism

The rise of al-Qaeda under the leadership of Osama bin Laden (Ushama bin Ladin, or 'UBL' in the USA), has caused special concern both in the USA and in Europe because of its ability to strike across international boundaries. However there is nothing new in this, and in fact the problem is much more serious for countries in the developing world than it is for the AICs.

To start off with, frontiers in the developing world are often poorly defined and hence porous. The most striking example is the longest undemarcated border in the world, the border between Pakistan and Afghanistan, which also runs across some of the world's most difficult terrain. At the end of 2005 it was thought that after the US-led attacks on Tora Bora in Afghanistan, where he was then believed to be hiding, Osama bin Laden escaped across this frontier into Wazirstan in neighbouring Pakistan.

Secondly, countries in the developing world lack both the resources and the sophisticated equipment to patrol a frontier and the internal organisation to pick up infiltrators once they have succeeded in getting in – after all, even the AICs have been unable to do either of these things with any degree of reliability, and despite repeated attempts to tighten security on the southern frontier of the USA with Mexico, with all the technological skill at the command of the US government, the number of illegal immigrants to the USA continues to rise.

Thirdly, in the case both of the destruction of the World Trade Center and the death of many of its innocent workers on 9/11, and the bombs which killed so many Londoners on 7 July 2005 ('7/7'), the perpetrators were already in the countries attacked, and in the latter case had lived there for many years. In developing countries, the situation is further complicated by the close relationships that exist between members of the same tribe, where as so frequently is the case, tribes have been split by artificial colonial boundaries. Indeed, such artificial boundaries actually serve to intensify communal identities and grievances.

As we can see, particularly in the case of Kashmir, a well-established boundary dispute is, if carefully exploited, a most useful vehicle for nationalist politicians to seek or to maintain power. Again, rulers invariably try to portray secessionist movements as terrorist, despite the fact that without such movements much of the modern world would not exist in its present form. After the Great War, the principle of self-determination was accepted as a fundamental addition to international law. However, in 1923 the Kurds were denied their own state, and they remain the largest national group in the world not to have one. Again in 1967 the coastal region inhabited primarily by the Igbo tried to secede from Nigeria under the name of Biafra; once more the international community closed ranks against them and after a prolonged war Nigeria was reunified.

Agricultural activity

Inequality in land ownership is not confined to the developing world. Australia, an advanced industrial country, has one of the most unequal land distribution ratios in the world as measured by the Gini index, the standard measure of land inequality. However, the developing world is distinguished by the survival of traditional cultivation, even if this is now often under threat. It is important to distinguish between peasants, cultivators who have traditional rights to land, and plantation workers on large estates, who work for wages.

Peasants have (a) access to land, (b) family labour, (c) small-scale technology and (d) the ability to generate surplus in a cash economy. Even small-scale technology requires cash for purchase and maintenance. Peasants make up some 80 per cent of farm workers in the developing world.

Traditional peasant cultivation was balanced between the need to produce for subsistence and exchange and the need to conserve. The key requirement is production for subsistence. This is conditioned by the nature of the crops available: there are three major variants based on:

- wheat (subtropical, temperate): Europe, North-West Africa, Middle East, 'Southern Cone' of South America;
- rice (tropical, humid): South, South-east and East Asia, West Africa;
- maize (subtropical, dry): the Americas, East Africa.

Production for subsistence is based on traditional knowledge and under-standing of the needs of the soil. It is therefore resilient and because of its varied nature and limited expectations forms the best possible protection for the poor against the possibility of famine. The big problem with it is that as population expands the land areas cultivated are subdivided until production is often barely adequate, implying that large sectors of the population must be malnourished. Because peasants are producing large-bulk low-value crops in the main they are also not very productive in monetary terms, which leads their contribution to be underestimated by those in the so-called 'modern' sector of the economy.

With rising population too many people in the developing world are work-ing too little land. There are two possible 'solutions': land reform by redistri-bution, which is politically difficult with the vested interests involved, and land colonisation. The latter is, of course, only possible where land is available. Increases in the 1970s in the land area cultivated in Latin America, China, South and South-East Asia have been considerable though at the cost of dam-age to marginal land and its fragile ecosystems. The 'carrying capacity' of the land, that is to say, the number of people a given area can support, has also been increased at least temporarily, as a result of the so-called 'green revolu-tion', involving the use of high-yielding strains and chemical fertilisers. On the other hand there has been a marked decline in the production of both wheat and maize in Africa, despite (or because of) the increase in production of **cash crops** for export, such as tobacco, cotton and even roses.

Estates vary a great deal. They have existed in their present form in Latin America since the sixteenth century, and Brazil has experienced three succes-sive 'boom' periods in sugar, rubber and coffee respectively. In South Asia, plantations have been established since the 19th century, producing tea and cotton. In tropical Africa plantation agriculture dates often only from the beginning of the twentieth century, and crops produced include cocoa, peanuts and palm oil. Of course a considerable part of plantation production is con-sumed within the developing world itself; for example, before the Gulf War Iraq was the major consumer of Ceylon (Sri Lankan) tea. Nor are all planta-tion crops necessarily in direct competition with local food production. Tree and shrub crops such as tea and coffee usually occupy a relatively small part of a country's cultivated land. Even bananas, which as a cultivated crop are very wasteful of land, are largely grown for consumption within the develop-ing world.

Land colonisation has a detrimental effect on the land where, as it usually does, it results in permanent land clearance. Initially the methods are very similar to that of traditional **'slash-and-burn' agriculture**. This is still practised, usually in tropical rainforest, sometimes in savannah. The main locations which have been significant in recent years have been: Central America, Western Amazonia, West/Central/East Africa, Philippines, Malaysia, Indonesia. A fresh site is selected, trees are cut down, larger tree stumps left in place and then branches, twigs and bushes are burnt, leaving the charred landscape covered with a layer of wood ash, which acts as a fertiliser. Intercropping of species is normal and the system, which was devised for local crops, such as manioc and cassava, has successfully assimilated crops introduced from elsewhere.

However, when intensively practised the results are very different. 'Slash-and-burn' cultivation can be used successfully over very long periods provided not too much is asked of the land. But the fertility of the thin forest soils falls off rapidly and yields in the third year are normally only half these of the first. The success of the method therefore depends on cultivation of relatively small patches which are shifted every 2–3 years. One or two years of crops in Brazilian/West African/South-east Asian rainforest are followed by periods of fallow varying between 8 and 15 years during which secondary vegetation is re-established and the forest begins to regenerate. It is impossible to accelerate this cycle without damage, but this is in effect what the new settlers are trying to do. Land clearance opens up areas to permanent settlement. Population growth leads to reduction in fallow periods. Global demand leads to the sale (or usurpation) of the land by large landowners or corporations, followed by intensive cultivation by mechanical and chemical means, and attempts to realise increased profit, in particular by the introduction of ranching after the initial decline in fertility. The result is the permanent degradation of the land, leading over time to a general decline of its carrying capacity in face of rising demand. The UN Food and Agriculture Organization (FAO) has identified a number of 'critical zones' where land resources were already inadequate to feed their 1975 populations. Most of these were areas subject to severe land degradation, where the natural carrying capacity of the land was already seriously impaired, and their total population was in excess of a billion (Higgins et al. 1982). In 1998 thirty developing countries were facing food emergencies (Oneworld 1998); in December 2005 the number of those facing serious emergencies in Africa alone, according to the FAO, had risen to 28: Angola, Burkina Faso, Burundi, Central African Republic, Chad, Democratic Republic of Congo, Republic of Congo, Côte d'Ivoire, Eritrea, Ethiopia, Guinea, Kenya, Lesotho, Liberia, Malawi, Mali, Mauritania, Mozambique, Niger, Rwanda, Sierra Leone, Somalia, Sudan, Swaziland, Tanzania, Uganda, Zambia and Zimbabwe.

Marketing and supply

The development of towns was initially the result of grain cultivation and the need for protected storage. Towns soon found themselves forced into alliance or conflict with local big landowners for political power. Towns need a rural hinterland to ensure their feeding. The long-term trend everywhere has been first the expansion of towns and then the urbanisation of the countryside. The concentration of wealth in the towns made them a tempting target, and an alliance with local landowners offered them necessary protection for their markets, in return for a considerable profit for the landowners. The growth of

Plate 3   Vegetable cultivation, Cuba

populations was accelerated by irrigation and the development of wet rice farming where this was possible.

Getting products to market, however, implies some element of food preservation. The traditional methods developed in the neolithic era were drying (pulses, tubers, meat), smoking (meat, fish) and the use of salt or brine (fish, meat). Canning uses more modern technology, but still does not rely on the availability of a power supply for storage. Refrigeration, first developed in the mid-ninteenth century but much extended in the past forty years, opened up the possibility of marketing high quality products. The success of the application of preservation and marketing techniques to agriculture, or 'agribusiness' as it is now often known, is that it creates added value in the end product and ensures its marketability. Bananas and other soft fruit depend for almost all their very high value in the shops on the measures that have been taken to get them there.

Speeding up transport makes the preservation and marketing of food much easier. Since the traditional overland routes from Europe to the east were blocked by Turkish expansion, first the Portuguese and then the Spaniards sought the way to the east by water. The Portuguese empire was built on the spice trade, and though later disputed by Dutch and English traders, it had, when Macao reverted to China in 1999, lasted just over 500 years. Fast clipper ships brought tea to Britain in the nineteenth century; in the twentieth century the steamship made tropical produce available widely for the first time. In recent years it has become possible for developing world produce to be sold in the AICs competitively even at the time of year at which local produce is in season, while even a slight variation of the harvest season enables Mexican fruit to be sold in the United States when direct competition with Florida and California might make this seem impossible. Many developing countries' dependence on an external market is reflected in the nature and orientation of their communication links, by land or water.

Mining

If the Portuguese empire was built on the spice trade, the main motivating factor in Spanish colonial expansion was the search for gold and silver. However, by the end of the 1980s the major producers of gold were two oddly matched but relatively developed states, South Africa and the former Soviet Union. In the meanwhile developing states had been the scene of colonial and post-colonial rivalries over access to a whole variety of mineral deposits, and the latest gold rush has been taking place in the northern part of Brazilian Amazonia.

As in the development of the Soviet Union under Stalin, but with less drastic methods, early attempts to industrialise developing countries were based on the traditional 'smokestack' industries of coal and steel. Hence in Brazil primacy in the 1930s went to the creation of an indigenous steel industry, centred on the massive Volta Redonda project. In China during the 'Great Leap Forward' an attempt was made to substitute labour for investment by encouraging the creation of 'backyard' blast furnaces. What metal these succeeded in producing, however, proved to be of such poor quality that the experiment was allowed to lapse, though not, unfortunately, before it had created considerable environmental damage. More recently, competition from the NICs and from Japan has driven down the world price of steel to the point at which there is now a substantial oversupply of basic steel products.

Although there is much less demand for steel as such than there was, it still remains central to successful industrialisation. In the developed world, for a variety of uses it has been superseded by aluminium. Aluminium is one of the commonest elements in the earth's crust and in the form of bauxite is found throughout the world. However, it is such an active chemical element that its separation from the ore involves a very high input of electrical power. Hence only where there is a very considerable surplus of power available at low cost, as in developed countries such as Canada which have considerable quantities of bauxite, is aluminium production economic (see Table 2.1). An additional problem is that the fabrication of aluminium alloys involves relatively expensive techniques if it is to be successful, thus limiting the spread of technology from the AICs into the developing world.

The result is that only a quarter of world production comes from the developing world, from Guyana, Jamaica and Suriname (see Table 2.2). In the case

Table 2.1 Primary aluminium production, by country, 2003

Country	000 tonnes
China	5,450
Russia	3,474
Canada	2,792
USA	2,703
Australia	1,857
Brazil	1,381
Norway	1,150
India	790
Germany	650
France	450
Mozambique	408
Bahrain	525
South Africa	385
New Zealand	340
Netherlands	300

Source: US Geological Survey

Table 2.2 World production of bauxite, by country, 2004

Country	000 tonnes
Australia	55,602
Guinea	15,500
Jamaica	13,444
Brazil	13,148
China	12,400
India	10,002
Venezuela	5,200
Kazakhstan	4,737
Suriname	4,215
Russia	4,000
Greece	2,418
Guyana	1,590
Indonesia	1,094

Source: US Geological Survey

of Jamaica, bauxite is the island's sole mineral resource and in 1980 Jamaica was still forced to sell most of its unprocessed bauxite for a relatively meagre return (Dickenson et al. 1983: 136–7). In Sierra Leone bauxite has been mined for decades by Sieromco, part of Alusuisse of Switzerland. The high bulk and low value of most minerals exported in this way means that some of the abundant mineral resources of the developing world have not been exploited at all. Those deposits most readily accessible by river or sea have, generally speaking, been opened up first and certainly remain most competitive on the world market; for example the copper of Chile or Peru, or alluvial tin in Malaysia and Indonesia. However, world economic conditions can change rapidly as mining from a country like Chile demonstrates and the ability of TNCs to switch production from one part of the world to another makes the negotiating strength of developing world governments much weaker than their nominal sovereignties would suggest. The collapse of the world price of copper has dealt a severe blow to the economies of Zaire (now Democratic Republic of the Congo) and Zambia.

The fate of Guatemala's dealings with International Nickel over its subsidiary Exploraciones y Explotaciones Minerías Izabal (Exmibal) is instructive. No sooner had the government of the day realised that the nickel ore was there than it hastened to 'renegotiate' Exmibal's 1968 contract, giving the government a 30 per cent share in the proceeds. However, with oil accounting for one-third of the cost of production, Exmibal's nickel plant at Chulac-El Estor in Guatemala did not begin operations until 1977 and never worked at more than 20 per cent of capacity until production was suspended in 1981 in adverse world economic conditions (Calvert 1985: 150–2).

The situation does not seem to be much better for a small developing country that happens to have a really unusual resource. Sierra Leone is not just a producer of bauxite, it is also one of the few places in the world where there are substantial deposits of rutile, the black sand from which the space-age metal titanium is extracted. Each year since 1983 Sierra Rutile Ltd, a subsidiary of the US TNC Nord Resources Corporation, has extracted 150,000 tons of rutile worth more than $80 million. Sierra Rutile is the country's largest employer, but wages are still meagre. Conditions are even worse than before the transnational moved in. The effect of mineral extraction there has been to create huge areas of devastation. Often mining gives rise to other infrastructural developments. This has not been the case for Sierra Leone. Representatives of the mining companies blame the corruption of the Sierra Leone government and the people, and not the terms of trade which they have had to accept. Successive IMF structural adjustment packages (SAPs) have failed. The government agreed to float the Leone, which devalued 25,000 per cent against the dollar, and to cut subsidies on fuel and food. Sierra Leone was virtually bankrupt, even before half its national territory was occupied by rebel forces from Liberia.

Human settlement

Population

One person in four in the world lives in China. Three out of four live in the developing world. Over the past 40 years the population of the developing world has grown exponentially, leading some (including, notably, the Chinese

Table 2.3 World's most densely populated countries, 2005

Country	Area (km²)	Population	Population per km²
1. Bangladesh	144,000	144,319,628	1,002
2. Taiwan	35,980	22,894,384	636
3. Occupied Palestine Territories	6,220	3,761,904	605
4. Korea, South	98,480	48,422,644	492
5. Puerto Rico	9,104	3,916,632	430
6. Netherlands	41,526	16,407,491	395
7. Lebanon	10,400	3,826,018	368
8. Belgium	30,510	10,364,388	340
9. Japan	377,835	127,417,244	337
10. India	3,287,590	1,080,264,388	333
11. Rwanda	26,338	8,440,820	320
12. El Salvador	21,040	6,704,932	319
13. Sri Lanka	65,610	20,064,776	306
14. Israel	20,770	6,276,883	302
15. Philippines	300,000	87,857,473	293
16. Haiti	27,750	8,121,622	293
17. Vietnam	329,560	83,535,576	253
18. Jamaica	10,991	2,731,832	249
19. United Kingdom	244,820	60,441,457	247
20. Germany	357,021	82,431,390	231

Source: *The World Factbook 2004–2005*, CIA

and Indian governments) to place control of population at the centre of their strategy to achieve a reasonable standard of living for their people. The 1992 *State of World Population Report* (UNFPA 1992) called for 'immediate and determined action to balance population, consumption and development patterns: to put an end to absolute poverty, provide for human needs and yet protect the environment'. Certainly many states in the developing world have very high population densities by world standards (see Table 2.3).

But what is a balanced population? First of all, a note of caution. Censuses even in the AICs can be incomplete and therefore unreliable. Accurate information about the size of families and the ages of family members may be even harder to obtain elsewhere, especially where the majority of the population is illiterate.

According to the *Report*, world population in mid-1992 was 5.48 billion. It would reach 6 billion by 1998, by annual increments of just under 100 million. Nearly all of this growth would be in Africa, Asia and Latin America. Over half would be in Africa and South Asia. In the event, these figures proved to be somewhat pessimistic, and the population of the world reached 6 billion officially in October 1999. In July 2005 it was estimated by the Population Reference Bureau to be 6.477 billion (PRB 2005).

Only 1.211 billion lived in the more developed countries. Excluding China, 3.963 billion lived in less developed countries.

Asia is more than four times as heavily populated as any other part of the developing world. With a population of 3.921 billion in 2005, its density of population (320/sq mile) is eight times that of Northern America excluding Mexico: 329 million (43/sq mile). It also includes seven of the ten largest countries by population: the largest, China (1,304 million), the second-largest, India (1,104 million), Indonesia (222 million), Pakistan (162 million), Japan (128 million) and Bangladesh (144 million). Of these only Japan is an AIC.

Latin America is relatively sparsely populated. With a total population in 2005 of 559 million, it includes two countries that have a population of more than 100 million, Brazil with 184.2 million in 2005 and Mexico which had risen from 91.1 million in mid-1995 to 107 million in 2005. But although it is the fifth largest country in area in the world (after Russia, Canada, China and the United States), Brazil is not at all densely populated (56/sq mile), and the only country on mainland America that approaches European standards in terms of population density is tiny El Salvador, in Central America (with a population of 5 million or 847/sq mile). Many Latin Americans quite reasonably regard their countries as being underpopulated. Argentine public policy, for example, still favours 'peopling the pampas'.

Africa, too, is sparsely populated (77/sq mile). However, though population statistics for its poorest countries are notoriously unreliable and overall estimates therefore have to be approached with care, its estimated 906 million population is growing at an average rate of 2.3 per cent a year. This has fallen slightly since the early 1990s and may not seem much, but it would lead to the population of the continent being nearly three times as great by 2025. The second largest country by area in Africa, Nigeria, has the largest population. This is currently estimated at 131.5 million (2005). However, as the results of the 1962, 1963 and 1973 censuses had to be set aside owing to political unrest, there is still some doubt as to whether these more recent figures are in fact correct.

Oceania, by contrast, has accurate statistics but is the most sparsely populated region. Including developed Australia (20.4 million) and New Zealand (4.1 million), only some 33 million people are scattered over its vast area. Many of them live on very small island states where the distinctions we make elsewhere between town and countryside are of relatively little use (see also UNDP 1998).

As a result of population pressure in the developing world increasing numbers of migrants are crossing national boundaries in search of work. In the 1980s, an average of 603,000 immigrants entered the United States legally every year, and an equivalent number went to Canada and Australia. In Europe, politicians played on the fears of voters to push through legislation restricting legal immigration, and the former British colonial government of Hong Kong forcibly repatriated Vietnamese who were described as 'economic migrants' not political refugees.

Of the 57 countries in the world which by 1990 had passed laws to reduce immigration, no less than 43 were themselves developing countries. Until 1982

Nigeria, the largest country in Africa, enjoying a oil boom, welcomed migrant labourers. With the recession in 1983, its military government summarily expelled a million Ghanaians, who were left to make their way back to their own country on foot, by bus or by car, as best as they could.

Case study 2.3   Refugees: the case of Rwanda

In 1994 the world was shocked by news of the large-scale massacres in the tiny Central African state of Rwanda. Before April 1994 Rwanda was the most densely populated country in Africa with more than 6 million people farming the fertile land. But the country was divided between two antagonistic groups: the Tutsi, traditionally the warrior class, and the Hutu, traditionally the labourers, and many Tutsi had been forced out of the country soon after independence in the 1960s. In 1979 they formed the Rwandan Patriotic Front (RPF) in exile in Uganda and in 1993 at Arusha, Tanzania, a peace agreement was signed. Meanwhile resentment grew at the continuing poverty of the population, exacerbated, as many saw it, by the need to conform to the requirements of the IMF and World Bank (Chossudovsky 1995).

The spark that ignited the new conflict was the death of the country's Hutu President Habyarimana (1973–94) when his aircraft was shot down as it was landing at Kigali. Within hours government forces and accompanying militias had begun to slaughter Tutsis. The RPF retaliated, but by deliberate state policy the slaughter continued, leaving half a million people dead, and up to a million Hutu and Tutsi languishing in refugee camps in Burundi, Tanzania and Zaire (now the Democratic Republic of Congo). The French government, which had its own agenda, sent in troops two months after the start of the slaughter and tried to establish a safe area within the country and deliver humanitarian aid, but soon withdrew. By the end of August Rwanda was looted and large areas deserted.

Having failed as a peacekeeper, the UN faced formidable difficulties in mounting a successful relief effort; in the end most of the work was done by non-governmental organisations (NGOs) under the general direction of the United Nations High Commission on Refugees (UNHCR). The refugee camps were hardly able to cope with such a massive displacement of humanity: in Zaire the water supply was polluted by corpses and the volcanic ground was too hard to dig graves, while in Tanzania refugees deforested the landscape in search of fuel and the resentment of the local population was only just kept under control (Toma 1999).

Traditional rural settlement

Despite urbanisation, traditional rural society remains and is indeed essential to the survival of the developing world. The duality of many developing economies is well recognised. The modern formal sector can be contrasted with the traditional informal sector, and the urban with the rural. However, the distinctions are neither clear nor separate. The one depends on the other.

Standard poverty measures ignore subsistence production. It is therefore very difficult to determine accurately levels of poverty in rural areas, though it is clear that they are generally poorer than urban areas – hence the direction of migration. Lower levels of participation in the economy, whether as producer or as consumer, are found among the poor in all parts of society, but especially among the rural poor.

It is said that the degree of rural inequality in India is declining. This is questionable although evidence from Indian government surveys does show increasing diversification of the rural economy. India's overall economic growth is impressive (predicted to be 7–8 per cent a year between 2005 and 2010) and by 2003 it was already the twelfth largest economy in the world. (*Financial Review*, 7 January 2003). However, its growth is mainly urban and is severely constrained by weaknesses in the country's infrastructure. It consists largely of the secondary production of consumer durables for the urban elite. There is, though, one major achievement in rural development: self-sufficiency in cereal production was achieved during the 1980s. Nevertheless, at the same time, in many rural areas, population is growing rapidly, agricultural production is stagnant, unemployment is high and consumption is down. Inequality in land-holding, as measured by the Gini index, has increased and, more critically, so has the proportion of holdings that are too small to be viable.

Among regional variations, it is in the South and East that there has been the slowest growth in agricultural output. The Central, South and East regions also record the highest proportions of rural poor, and the highest mortality rates are to be found in the Central region and the East. By contrast, urban poverty has been declining as a proportion in urban areas, though it is still growing in absolute terms (Ghosh and Bharadwaj 1992: 140–6).

The survival of the traditional rural sector was seen in the nineteenth century by classical liberals as an obstacle to development. It is still seen as such by neo-liberals today, though at the same time the greens offer a sharply contrasting interpretation, arguing that traditional rural lifestyles are the way forward to sustainable development.

Land reform

Land reform is one means by which the state can act to help the poorest sectors of society by the redistribution of property. It can take various forms. The three most common are:

1. the distribution of publicly owned land to the landless poor;
2. legislation limiting the size of estates, forcing the sale of 'surplus holdings';
3. rent control.

In the state of Kerala in South India, because of the second form of land reform, there is a much greater degree of equality in landholding than there is in, for example, semi-feudal Pakistan, and production levels are high.

However, land reform is far from easy to carry out. Land reform is often opposed on the grounds that it will lead to a fall in production. Although this argument is particularly popular with landowners, that does not mean that it is not true, and in fact most land reform programmes, however successful in the long term, have led to an immediate drop in production – the most notorious in recent times being the collapse of agriculture in Zimbabwe following a politically motivated and hence badly executed land reform programme.

The power of existing landowners to resist any serious land reform by political pressure and legal obstruction is of course a major consideration. Moreover, their resistance is frequently reinforced by the inclusion within their ranks of senior army officers. In Latin America major land reform programmes have either followed or been accompanied by high levels of violence. In Mexico land reform was made possible by the alliance forged between rural interests and the leaders of the Mexican Revolution (1910–40). In Bolivia it followed the revolution of 1952 which placed the National Revolutionary Movement (MNR) in power, and in Cuba it was a consequence of the Cuban Revolution of 1959. But in Chile between 1970 and 1973 the government of Salvador Allende was unable to overcome a strong alliance between the local landowners and the armed forces, supported by the United States. Later land reform in the Dominican Republic, though pressed by the Carter Administration in an attempt to avert revolution, was successfully killed by military opposition.

Even where a government has the strength to carry out land reform, the technical problems are immense. First, land is by no means a homogeneous commodity that can be shared out at will. Its varying quality, the availability of water and transport and its nearness or otherwise to the market, all affect its utility. Secondly, it is not always easy to agree who should get access to land. Those who already work it regard themselves as having a prior claim. But what of the needs of the landless? Should those who have worked the land be made to share their good fortune with strangers? In the Mexican case serious conflict between the competing claimants played into the hands of the traditional owners.

Collectivisation seems at first sight to be an ideal solution. In Latin America, where land had been traditionally regarded as the property of the state, the pioneering experiment was that of Mexico, where limits were placed on the size of estates that could be held, and in the 1930s cooperatives (*ejidos*) were endowed with the land that had been expropriated, which was declared inalienable. Working practices varied, the earlier *ejidos*, broadly speaking, being divided into equal sized plots worked by separate families and the later worked in common by all the families settled on them. These *ejidos* were strongly criticised by their political opponents as inefficient and unproductive, but the evidence is that, having regard to the nature of the land in each case, they were as efficient as privately owned land. Not until 1992 did a Mexican government actually challenge the nature of the land reform carried out by its predecessors.

Communists and some socialists regard such measures as half-hearted. Disputes over ownership, for them, can be simply resolved by the state assuming ownership of all land. It is then for the state to create collective institutions by which individual farms can be managed by those who work them. However, after the initial impetus given by mechanisation, and despite the social benefits of community centres, health clinics and the rest, Soviet collective farms proved to be unable to meet their country's needs for basic foodstuffs, while in the developing world the record has been similarly ambiguous. In China, collectivisation after 1949 led to a level of production sufficiently high to reduce hunger but it failed to provide additional funds for industrialisation. In Cuba, attempts at diversification and industrialisation failed and after 1970 the country returned to its traditional dependence on the large-scale production of sugar, though for the Soviet rather than the American market.

In Africa, land has not normally been expropriated as private holdings. Tanzania from the beginning saw collective ownership as traditionally African as well as socialist. Critics of the Tanzanian experience, however, remark that after some 30 years of a socialist economy it remains one of the poorest countries in the world. A different problem, however, has arisen in Zimbabwe, where the independence settlement guaranteed the rights of existing white settlers to much of the best land in the country. In 2000 President Mugabe, finding himself increasingly unpopular, tried to divert hostility towards the former colonial power. When the ruling Zanu-PF sponsored occupations of white-owned land he refused to enforce a legal decision ruling the occupations unlawful. His supporters then succeeded in mustering a majority in Parliament to amend the Constitution to allow expropriation of the lands without compensation while systematic attacks were launched on white farmers to force them to yield (Dorman 2000; *Financial Times*, 8/9 April 2000). By 2005 the economy of Zimbabwe had shrunk by 30 per cent and the country was experiencing severe food shortages, alleviated only by foreign aid, much of it funded by the very countries President Mugabe tried to blame for his plight.

The View from the Ground

Peta Thornycroft, The Daily Telegraph, Thursday, 22 September 2005

Mugabe strikes his final blow against white farmers

About 3,500, or 90 per cent, of white commercial farmers have been forced out by Mr Mugabe and his cronies since 2000. Irrigation systems are broken, cattle have been eaten and hundreds of thousands of Africa's most skilled farm workers have fled abroad or are unemployed.

Zimbabwe was a net exporter of food but now depends on imports and the United Nations says up to four million people, or a third of the population, need emergency feeding.

The economy shrank by a third in five years and inflation will reach at least 400 per cent by the year's end, according to government statistics. There has been no hard currency for fuel for the past month.

The government admitted this week that it has no foreign currency to import seed or fertiliser for the summer season, which began on September 1, and expects the worst harvests in living memory.

Mr Mugabe refused a South African offer of a $500 million (£276 million) loan last month because it contained conditions for political and economic reform. Foreign banks in Harare say that instead he raided exporters' foreign currency accounts to pay the International Monetary Fund $120 million (£66.2 million) to avoid Zimbabwe's immediate expulsion.

The best white-owned farms have been taken by Mr Mugabe's cronies and most of the landless people he claimed would be beneficiaries of the land grabs live in acute poverty and are among those in urgent need of food aid.

Urbanisation

The most striking feature of developing countries is rapid urbanisation. In 1950 only 29 per cent of the world's peoples lived in cities; in 1990 three times as many people did so, and the proportion had risen to 43 per cent. But, more strikingly, in 1950 only about half the world's urban population was in developing cities. By the year 2000 the population of cities in the developing world was expected to outnumber that in the rest of the world by more than two to one: 2,251.4 million to 946.2 million (Hardoy et al. 1992: 29). By 2007 UN projections show that for the first time more than half the world's population will live in cities (Earth Policy Institute 2004).

However, Hardoy et al. identify three inaccurate assumptions about urbanisation in the developing world which tend to be repeated: namely that 'most of the problems (and much of the urban population) are in huge 'megacities', that 'the high concentration of population and production is a major cause of environmental problems' and that these problems are accurately documented in the existing literature (Hardoy et al. 1992: 31).

It is hardly surprising that in the developed world people tend to think of urban areas in the developing world as megacities (see Table 2.4). In 1950 there were only two cities, London and New York, with a population of more than 8 million. Already by 1990 there were 20 such giant cities, and 14 of them were in the developing world (UNFPA 1992: 16). By 2015 the UN expects there to be 21 megacities. However, it is also true that in 1990 only a third of the urban population of the developing world lived in cities with more than 1 million inhabitants. In fact, in many of the smaller and/or less populous countries, half the urban population lived in cities with populations of less than 100,000.

Table 2.4 World's largest cities, 2005

City, country	Population	Latest information
1. Mumbai (Bombay), India	11,914,398	2001c
2. Shanghai, China	10,996,500	2003e
3. São Paulo, Brazil	10,927,985	2005e
4. Seoul, South Korea	10,207,296	2002e
5. Moscow, Russia	10,101,500	2001c
6. Delhi, India	9,817,439	2001c
7. Karachi, Pakistan	9,339,023	1998c
8. Istanbul, Turkey	8,831,805	2000c
9. Beijing, China	8,689,000	2001e
10. Mexico City, Mexico	8,591,309	2000c
11. Jakarta, Indonesia	8,389,443	2000c
12. Tokyo, Japan	8,340,000	2003e
13. New York City, USA	8,085,742	2003e
14. Tehran, Iran	7,796,257	2004e
15. Cairo, Egypt	7,629,866	2004e
16. London, UK	7,172,036	2001c
17. Lima, Peru	7,029,928	2004e
18. Bogotá, Colombia	6,712,247	2001e
19. Bangkok, Thailand	6,320,174	2000c
20. Rio de Janeiro, Brazil	6,094,183	2005e

Notes: City (as opposed to agglomeration) means within city limits
'c' = census figures
'e' = estimated
Source: GeoHive (2006) Cities: largest (without surrounding urban areas),
www.geohive.com/charts/city_notagg.php

Such smaller cities have also grown very rapidly in recent years, and it is this rapid growth, rather than the overall size of the cities, that is associated with the problems of urbanisation. The problems which urbanisation brings do not stem solely from its overall level, which varies a great deal from one region to another.

In 1994 the most urbanised part of the developing world was Latin America (73.7 per cent), which was comparable with Europe (73.3 per cent) but had some way to go before overall it reached the level of North America (76.1 per cent). Other parts of the developing world were much more rural: East Asia was only 36.1 per cent urban, Africa 33.8 per cent, and South Asia 28.4 per cent, but this was not likely to last long (UNDP 1994b).

Bangladesh is rural and has only 17.7 per cent of its population living in cities. But it has in fact a higher population density ($935/km^2$) than the Netherlands ($457/km^2$), the most densely populated country in Europe, which has 88.9 per cent of its population living in cities (World Bank 1999). What is most worrying, undoubtedly, is that countries that have the fastest rate of population growth overall also tend to have the fastest rates of growth of urban populations.

The main feature of developing world cities are:

1. One large 'primate' city, which is usually but not necessarily both the capital and the main commercial centre, predominates, containing anything up to a quarter of the entire population. The disproportion can be striking. The extreme case is the city-state of Singapore (100 per cent urban). But Montevideo, capital of Uruguay, contains half the country's people; Buenos Aires, capital of Argentina, some 23 per cent. The feature is equally marked in Africa, where it is often attributed to colonialism, but this can hardly be the case in Latin American states that have been independent for a century and a half. Dependency theorists would argue that the size of cities is linked to their role as a point of contact with the world economic system, but this seems rather to understate the role of government. Occasionally there are two large cities, such as Rio de Janeiro and São Paulo in Brazil, Ankara and Istanbul in Turkey, Cape Town and Johannesburg in South Africa, Beijing and Shanghai in China. Where this happens usually one either is or has been the capital, the other the major commercial centre (Gamer 1976: 131–9). Two major exceptions to the primate city model exist: China and India.

2. The dominance of 'primate cities' and the 'view from the capital' that they encourage is compounded by the fact that other cities are surprisingly small in comparison. In Mexico, Mexico City is some ten times as big as the next largest city, Guadalajara. Traditionally migration has taken place over relatively short distances, owing to the difficulty of transport, though disentangling these flows is not easy because in the developing world, as in the industralised countries, there is of course also a substantial amount of movement from one city to another in search of work. Hence these smaller, regional centres act as 'way stations' for migration to the capital/largest city, and indeed at one time this may have been the case everywhere. However, in modern times evidence is that in Latin America at least the main migration flows are direct from the countryside to the largest city.

   The BBC reported in 2004: 'The biggest mass migration in the history of the world is under way in China, and it is creating what some are calling the second industrial revolution' (BBC News, 11 May 2004, *http://news.bbc.co.uk/1/hi/world/asia-pacific/3701581.stm*). The scale of this migration could be gauged from the fact that in 2003 half of all the concrete used in the world was poured in China's cities, most of them on the eastern seaboard of the country.

3. Developing world cities are characteristically swollen by heavy recent immigration. China until recently was an exception, only because until the 1990s movement from place to place had been rigorously controlled by the authorities and very little development had in fact taken place. In Africa and Asia the cities attract an excess of young men in search of work, while women often stay in their villages and keep their farms or plots going for subsistence. In Latin America and the Caribbean young women predominate

in the burgeoning cities and towns. In both cases many migrate as part of an existing family unit.

4. Migration places the maximum strain on the infrastructure (roads, transport, housing, utilities, education, health, other public services). However, city governments tend to spend very little on housing or other services for the poor, partly because they do not want them to come in the first place, partly because they do not get much from them in the way of taxes. In all but the most favourable times, much of the urban area of developing world cities consists of shanty towns.

5. **Shanty towns**, perhaps unexpectedly, are not always very densely populated, and many of the worst urban conditions develop in older-type properties which have been allowed to fall into disrepair and are then subdivided. In Brazil these overcrowded tenement slums are called 'beehives' (*colmeias*). Living in them consumes the greater part of a new immigrant's resources and offers little in the way of services. It is not very surprising therefore that people soon move out into the shanty towns (called in Brazil *favelas*). By definition shanty towns seldom, if ever, have reasonable mains services, though some Brazilian *favelas* have been established for so long that they have some mains services laid on. The notorious shanty-town of Rocinha, high in the hills above Rio de Janeiro, is in many respects quite a pleasant place to live, with well-built homes, electricity and running water, and a fine view over Copacabana beach. The inhabitants are generally well dressed and carry expensive mobile phones. The area has 'shops and restaurants, several gyms, a bank, a post office – and even two police stations' (Kleveman 2005: 30). But the favela is subject to policing only in so far as it suits the gang bosses who are the real local authority there.

The absence of piped water and sanitation (World Bank 1992) for urban areas would be a dangerous combination in any circumstances. But shanty towns tend to congregate in the least favoured areas, and there are more immediate dangers when a shanty town locates close to factories or other sources of employment. Hundreds died in February 1984 when petrol (gasoline) leaking out of a fractured pipe exploded under a shanty town at Cubatão in Brazil but this was only the most spectacular evidence of an environment so heavily polluted by unchecked industrial development that children had to go to hospital daily to breathe unpolluted air (Hardoy et al. 1992: 85–7). Although some effort has been made to clean up Cubatão since this incident, more recently a similar leak into another city's sewers destroyed several blocks in Mexico's second city, Guadalajara, in a series of explosions over three days. Three thousand were killed or permanently disabled by toxic gas and 200,000 were evacuated following a release of methyl iso-cyanate from a chemical plant at Bhopal in India on 3 December 1984 (Hardoy et al. 1992: 92). Despite such hazards, and the routine ones of pollution and disease, cities are, by contrast with the countryside, seen as favoured places to live, especially by young people.

The View from the Ground

Lutz Kleveman, Telegraph Magazine, 17 September 2005: 30

Street-fighting boys

Somewhere between 150,000 and 250,000 people are estimated to live in Rocinha, though no one really knows how many. Their homes are a chaotic jumble of ramshackle brown huts and concrete blocks clinging precariously to the steep slope. It is overshadowed by a giant cliff of gloomy granite rock which now, with dusk advancing, reflects the deep red light of the setting sun, while the strip of tropical forest beneath it already lies in the dark, looking like giant broccoli heads. It smells of the day's rain, the smoke of meat being fried and cheap fuel.

Favelas have been described as tumours, disfiguring blemishes on a city where the wealthy live by the beach and the poor hang on to the hills above. But Rocinha is more like a glacier, sliding slowly but relentlessly downwards to the main road. Often the armed gangs have taken their battles down to the city below. Tourists have been caught in the line of fire. Recently, the highway to the airport had to be closed as gangs waged shoot-outs right across it.

6. Above all, in developing world cities, industrial activity is unable to provide jobs for all the immigrants. Production is dominated by TNCs who by the standards of the society are capital-intensive and employ relatively few people. The main job opportunities come in the disproportionately large services sector, in which government employment predominates. Much of the population as a result is unemployed or underemployed. Links with the home village are maintained therefore as much out of economic necessity as out of family loyalty. This is quite the opposite of what is usually intended, as, for example, in Africa, where tribal identity is very strong and urban workers send remittances to their families, expecting in due time to return to the village.

Provided that urban areas are well governed, they have important advantages. It is much easier and cheaper to deliver efficient public services where distances are short and costs relatively low. Properly planned transport systems can not only make it easy for citizens to get to work, but also to enjoy a good range of recreational and other facilities – the rich have always liked to live in cities. Policy-makers are urban dwellers and in their decisions they tend to favour what they know best. It is, of course, in the city that democratic politics originally evolved and there is widespread agreement that a satisfactory environment can only be attained in developing world cities by the empowerment of those directly affected.

Migrants

Naturally many people who are unable to find work, or simply wish to better themselves, try to leave the developing world altogether and to see a better life in an advanced industrial country. However, ever since the United States imposed a quota system on immigrants in 1924, they have found themselves facing increasing difficulties in doing so. There are two areas in which the pressure is now so great that it has become a major political issue: on the long frontier between Mexico and the United States, and along the land and sea routes that lead into the European Union.

The View from the Ground

Giles Tremlett in Ceuta, The Guardian, Friday, 30 September 2005

African migrants die in quest for new life

Spanish border police armed with riot gear and rubber bullets faced hundreds of sub-Saharan Africans prepared to risk their lives yesterday to get across the razorwire-topped perimeter fence around a Spanish enclave in north Africa in an attempt to claim immigrant status.

Two would-be immigrants died on the Spanish side of Ceuta's frontier and the bodies of three more were found on the Moroccan side after they tried to storm over the border shortly before dawn.

One bled to death after his neck was caught on the razorwire and another was trampled and suffocated during the stampede, Spanish media reports said.

According to unconfirmed reports, Moroccan police fired into a crowd of 500 people trying to scale the double, three-metre (10ft) high fence using scaling ladders made from branches and string. One of the three victims on the Moroccan side was reportedly a baby.

Spain then ordered troops to patrol the frontiers around its two enclaves in north Africa to reinforce the border police.

The deaths brought to at least eight the number of people killed over the past month in the increasingly desperate attempts by crowds of young Africans to break their way through the only land frontier between them and the EU.

More than 100 Africans were believed to have made it into Ceuta yesterday, just as several hundred had got into Spain's other north African enclave, Melilla, during similar raids on Monday and Tuesday.

Some 200 people were detained by Moroccan police when they charged the fence at Melilla yesterday morning, Spanish authorities said.

Those who make it in are generally allowed to stay because Spanish immigration laws do not allow police to expel people whose identity and nationality they are unable to prove within 40 days.

Television pictures showed newly arrived immigrants yesterday looking for a Spanish police station so that their 40-day period could start as soon as possible. Other pictures showed injured immigrants screaming in pain or crying from hunger and exhaustion.

Some of the several hundred people arriving in immigrant centres in Melilla over the past week were being shipped to mainland Spain yesterday, from where they will be allowed to travel into other countries in the EU's Schengen zone.

Armed members of the Spanish Legion were patrolling the fence at Melilla yesterday as the defence minister, José Bono, promised to send 480 soldiers to back the hundreds of frontier police stationed in the two enclaves. 'The prime minister has given me the order that as of today the civil guard [frontier police] should be reinforced by the army,' he said.

Andres Carrera, the head of the Ceuta branch of Spain's police trade union, said: 'There are said to be more than 1,000 more people waiting outside Ceuta who are planning to try to get in. I am not sure that sending the army in will help, as they are not trained for this. The soldiers are there to fight wars.'

He added: 'Police pressure alone will not work either. It is hunger that pushes so hard. To them, this is paradise.'

Ceuta's hospitals were yesterday flooded with immigrants who had been injured crossing the wire before dawn. At least 50 immigrants with broken or twisted limbs and deep cuts were treated, according to the medical staff.

'I have mopped up a lot of blood this morning. It took several hours,' said a municipal workman, Felipe Sánchez, who was sent to help clean up the section of the frontier fence where yesterday's mass crossing took place.

Abdul Loum, 30, from Guinea-Conakry, rested at an immigrants' shelter run by Salesian monks after getting across the fence yesterday. 'I tried to get in to Melilla four times and this was my third try at getting across the fence into Ceuta,' he said.

'I set out from Conakry two years ago. I have been through Senegal, Mali, Algeria and Morocco. The Moroccan police expelled me over the border into Algeria twice, but I just walked back.'

Spanish authorities are in the process of doubling the height of the frontier fences, which stretch for seven miles around Melilla and five miles around Ceuta. The president of Ceuta's council, Juan Vivas, called for all immigrants to be automatically expelled, and Spanish opposition parties blamed Morocco for allowing the immigrants to plan the raids on the enclaves, which are claimed by Morocco.

Communications

The impact of air travel

In some ways, the new ease of air travel in the age of the jumbo jet, which has compressed space and time, has helped widen, not close, the gap between the AICs and the developing world and perhaps more importantly between the more developed countries of the developing world where infrastructure is sophisticated and the poorer countries where it is often virtually non-existent.

Because of the special conditions of Latin America – its size and the obstacles to travel by land – air travel was taken up with particular interest and enthusiasm. Avianca, Colombia's flag carrier, is the second-oldest in the world after KLM – this is no coincidence. Owing to the incredibly broken terrain, Colombia's surface transport network remains fragmented and inadequate. Air freight has played and continues to play a significant role in its economic development, particularly in the export of cut flowers to the USA and Europe (Hilling 1978: 91). Air travel has also helped make possible a degree of unity between East and West Malaysia, and between the thousands of islands of Indonesia and the Philippines. Otherwise it is an expensive luxury for a developing world country to have its own airline. It is a legend in Latin America that Pluna in Uruguay at one time had 4,000 employees and only one aircraft. But there are not many ruling elites who have been able to resist the temptation. In recent years some have been seeking to divest themselves of the expense through privatisation, only to find that there are relatively few players willing to buy. Such is the internationalisation of the air industry that in the holiday season you can easily find yourself travelling from Buenos Aires to Montevideo on an aircraft chartered from Royal Jordanian Airlines.

Railways

Transport systems developed during the colonial period (or in Latin America during the early national period) were very basic. Given the limits of technology, there was little difference between those for local use and those oriented towards export. It was the application of steam power to locomotive propulsion that enabled railways to become both a practical means of transport and an instrument of colonial expansion, particularly in its last phase, the scramble for Africa. Cecil Rhodes's dream of a 'Cape to Cairo' railway was never realised, but an African transcontinental railway was eventually completed, although the engineers who surveyed it were lucky enough to arrive on the scene only a few days after the end of the Ashanti Wars. It was the railway which made a united India possible. Railways remain a significant means of transport in East, South-east and South Asia.

Once the infrastructure is in place, railways are easy to maintain: even if a bridge is washed away by floods, it is much easier to replace it for a train than for road transport. Against this, of course, there is the problem of inflexibility: goods have to be transhipped to train or lorry for eventual delivery to their destination. Such inflexibility often reflects the purpose for which developing countries were originally linked into the global economy. Railways built to serve the transport needs of colonial or semi-dependent production are quite often no longer in the right place for modern centres of population. Examples of this can be found in the radial pattern of the railways on the pampas of Argentina and in the short railways feeding the hinterland from a variety of ports in West Africa. Many of these have proved useless for modern conditions and have been closed.

More generally, from the 1960s onwards, rail has had to contend with an unfavourable political climate. Increasingly for long distance passenger travel, not least by politicians and the staffs of development agencies, trains have been superseded by aircraft. Cheap motor vehicles became available in large numbers, and for people in the developing world offered a freedom of movement they had never previously enjoyed. Four-track vehicles offered a reasonable ride on the worst of surfaces. The high cost of building and maintaining roads was borne, not by the passenger, but by the state. So rail networks were run down and in some countries disappeared altogether.

This had significant social consequences, as an example will show. Some colonial railways did come to benefit the independent nations. Though built originally with strategic defence of the Protectorate in mind, the Sierra Leone Government Railway had since its opening become a major factor in knitting together the country's many tribes and providing employment. Its closure was the price paid by the Siaka Stevens government for IMF support. Today few signs of it remain and at Magaburaka, once an important centre but now lying off the main road, it is almost impossible to trace the outlines of what was once the station yard. The only railway in the country now is a recently constructed mineral line carrying iron ore from the mines down to the harbour at Port Loko. Being electrified (in a country where parts of the capital only get four hours electricity a day!) it employs very few people and having no other function it makes no useful impact on the surrounding countryside. Instead both passengers and freight have to contend for space on the country's few roads, even fewer of which have anything which might be termed an all-weather surface. Not surprisingly, anyone who can afford it, or can get someone else to pay for it, drives a Mitsubishi Pajero (Shogun).

Road

Much of the traffic of West Africa is still carried by the so-called **mammy lorry**, an improvised bus on a truck chassis. Many if not most of these are brightly painted with surprising but sometimes all too appropriate slogans, often with a religious flavour. Similar improvisations, notably the ubiquitous 'jeepney' in the Philippines, are to be found with local variations in many other developing countries. However, the enthusiasm for these picturesque vehicles often shown by visitors from wealthier countries should be tempered with a greater realisation of their environmental disadvantages. In the countryside these may not be so apparent. But badly tuned diesel engines are one of the biggest problems of developing world cities, pumping out vast quantities of toxic fumes which constitute the major element in polluting the atmosphere in cities as far removed as Calcutta, Cairo, Lagos and Mexico City, and overall increase the concentration of greenhouse gases and contribute to global warming.

Roads of a sort are not hard to build and they have the great advantage that improvements can be phased in as funds or labour become available. In addition road building is labour-intensive and requires relatively simple skills. It makes therefore an important input into a developing economy. However, good roads are expensive to build and difficult to maintain. In West Africa heavy rains can bring flash floods that can wash away whole sections of surfaced road. Not surprisingly Africa is very short of surfaced roads; in fact Africa and Latin America together have only 7 per cent of the world's surfaced road. At least a third of all World Bank loans have consistently been for road projects and in June 1971 the UN Economic Commission for Africa took the initiative to set up a permanent bureau to construct a Trans-African Highway, to stretch 6,393 km from Mombasa to Lagos, linking a number of existing 'growth areas' and using for the most part existing roads which were to be upgraded to an approved standard by their respective national governments (Hilling 1978: 88–9). Tragically, the constuction of this highway has had the unpredicted (and unpredictable) effect of encouraging the spread of HIV/AIDS from one side of the continent to the other, as truckers seek consolation for lonely evenings away from home.

The military government of Brazil (1964–85) placed the building of access roads at the centre of its strategy to open up Amazonia. The move of the capital to Brasília in 1960 had been accompanied by the building of an access road from Belem to Imperatriz and thereafter up the valley of the Tocantins, opening up a large sector of Eastern Amazonia. In the mid-1960s Rondônia was opened up by a new road from Cuiabá to Pórto Velho, again linking with the highway from Brasília via Goiana. But the centrepiece of its

Plate 4   Transport, Brazil

National Integration Programme of 1970 was the Transamazonian (Rodovia Transamazônica), a massive project to connect the coast to Humaita and thence to Pórto Velho, while at the same time facilitating land colonisation along a 10 km strip on either side of the proposed route (Hilling 1978: 90).

The work of 'opening up' Amazonia was to be continued subsequently by the building of an even longer strategic road, the Rodovia Perimetral Norte, round Brazil's northern frontier, connecting up with feeder roads into all the neighbouring countries of the Amazon basin. Such alarm has been created at the environmental implications of effectively unrestrained logging and the impact this has had on Brazil's Indian communities and the wildlife of the area, that most of the original plan remains on the drawing board. However, the northern section has been constructed to link up with the road northward from Manaus and eventually with Georgetown in Guyana. In 2006 a road already existed but was unpaved and the journey from Lethem on the border to Georgetown could take several days.

Small island developing states

While transport across the enormous distances of the continental developing world remains a central problem, some parts of the developing world exhibit very different needs. The global problems of climate change and the potential rise of mean sea level has, at least for the moment, called attention to the special problems faced by **small island developing states**.

There are two major areas in which such states are to be found: in the Caribbean, in close proximity to larger mainland states, from which they owe their independence to the accidents of colonial rivalry, and in the Pacific, where their isolation gives them a natural geographical identity. At Barbados in 1994 an organisation was formed under UN auspices to defend their common interests.

1. SIDS are particularly vulnerable, owing to their small size and frequent dependence on a single export crop, to natural and environmental disasters. In the long term, their extremely limited supplies of land are easily exhausted. In what is now the Republic of Nauru, mining for phosphate in the colonial period had left one-third of the small island state a waste of dead coral, with its 5,000 population crowded into the part that remains. Biological diversity on the remaining land is minimal. Although as points of access to our maritime environment the islands offer particular advantages, their capacity to absorb significant increases in tourism, their only obvious source of additional revenue, is very limited. As a result of the need to import food etc. for tourist consumption, the island state of St Vincent in the Caribbean actually loses money on its tourist industry.

2. Many of them are low lying and depend on infrequent rains for freshwater supplies. Hence over-rapid development can easily exhaust what limited sources of water they have. Fortunately, given that most if not all of these states lie in the tropics, the use of solar power for desalination is a realistic option. However, the problem of the disposal of waste is not so easily solved.

3. Dependence on fishing makes their immediate maritime environment particularly sensitive to disturbance. Their traditional habit of discharging wastes into the sea therefore has to be superseded as a matter of urgency by effective management of wastes and care of irreplaceable coastal and marine resources. This is at once a threat from the tourist influx and a threat to the attractions that bring them. Chief among these are the living corals of which many of the Pacific islands are composed, and which now face an immediate threat from rising sea temperatures and increased acidity.

4. Their geological structure, rising from the deep sea bed, means that for energy resources they are for the present extremely dependent on the import of fossil fuels. Although again the harnessing of solar, wave and wind power are all practical 'renewable' alternatives, the cheapness and availability of petrol and diesel engines means that they have often been preferred, despite the long-term consequences of dependence. Needless to say these countries are high on the list of those affected by the soaring price of crude oil and its derivatives since 1999.

5. Some of them are so remote that their dependence on the outside world for transport and communication is total. This brings its own problems. An island community which has only intermittent contact with the outside world is alarmingly vulnerable to many of the germs common in other parts of the world and to which they have no natural resistance (Diamond 1998).

The balance sheet: assets and problems

To sum up, therefore, developing countries other than the SIDS mostly have a complex balance of assets and problems. To consider their assets first.

On either side of the tropics, there is plenty of sunshine and a generally reliable and predictable climate pattern, though in the tropics themselves mist and haze can persist well into the morning, lowering the overall temperature but raising humidity. In the subtropical zones, there is generally a considerable annual surplus of rainfall. In conjunction with the great rivers as sources of irrigation this has enabled these regions, through the wet cultivation of rice, to develop some of the world's largest concentrations of population. While there is considerable argument about how far the earth's capacity to produce food can be extended, some expansion at least does appear to be a reasonable possibility, although in the case of rice by extending the area cultivated and not by increased productivity.

The tropical rainforest offers the most spectacular possibilities for the development of new and valuable products from its rich biodiversity. But the amount of information that has to be gained first is so great that conservation is of vital significance if this asset is ever to be realised.

Many developing states have significant mineral deposits, some of which are still unexploited. Yet owing to the development of satellite sensors, the location of key minerals can now be made by those having access to space technology, which means, in practice, a small handful of AICs and the TNCs they shelter. Developing world governments that can get access to this information and can bargain effectively, could, if the companies are willing to let them, plough back the proceeds of these irreplaceable resources as Venezuela initially did and Kuwait (until the Gulf War) continued to do with their oil, either into infrastructure or long-term investment, or both. With their large populations, developing world states also have vast human resources. Many of their citizens have already to be very resourceful simply to survive. Some countries, such as the **Asian Tigers**, or what has been termed the East Asian 'powerhouse' (see Chapter 4), set out systematically to unlock the potential of their citizens by promoting education, particularly for women (see Chapter 5). They have found, as others are likely to find, that their investment is very well spent in terms of the general betterment of society.

On the other side, however, there are also deep-rooted and persistent problems.

Poverty is the root of many of the most persistent problems of the developing world. Floods, drought and hurricanes all threaten human life and pose serious challenges to governments. However, people are much more vulnerable to these emergencies if they live in inadequate shelter and lack the economic resources to protect themselves against them.

Population growth may not of itself be a problem, but population growth coupled with the compelling pressure to achieve First World standards of living undoubtedly is. A child born today in an AIC will, it is estimated, consume around 40 times the natural resources that a developing world child will consume before it reaches adulthood. This contrast is not only unethical but also unstable. Not surprisingly, many of those who live in the developing world, but who can see on films or television what they assume are the affluent conditions awaiting them in the developed world, will take almost any steps they can to realise their dream.

The pessimists who have warned of the coming exhaustion of land and mineral resources have so far generally been shown to be wrong. However, even the largest mineral deposits can and do run out and the dire state of Bolivia's tin industry is there to prove it (Crabtree 1987). Similarly, agricultural land once lost, whether to neglect, to urbanisation or otherwise, cannot easily be replaced, if indeed it can be replaced at all. So it would be prudent to assume that at some stage shortages will act, in a way not at present predictable, to check development in some if not all developing countries.

Key terms

Asian Tigers – countries which have been particularly successful in promoting economic growth, especially South Korea, Taiwan, Hong Kong and Singapore

cash crops – crops grown not for immediate local consumption but for export, such as tobacco and cotton

human-induced climate change – that part of the current rise in the average temperature of the Earth caused by raised levels of CO^2 in the atmosphere as a result of deforestation and the burning of fossil fuels (e.g. coal, oil)

mammy lorry – in West Africa, an improvised bus on a truck chassis

monsoon – periodic rains in South Asia generated by warm air from the Equatorial regions being blocked by the Himalayan range

river basin – all that area drained by a river and its tributaries, divided from adjacent basins by a watershed

shanty towns – clusters of improvised housing, often in very poor quality materials, built by private enterprise on unoccupied or underexploited land on the edge of existing urban settlements

'slash-and-burn' agriculture – clearance of land by part felling and setting fire to forest in order to grow crops

small island developing states (SIDS) – small island states, particularly in the Caribbean and the Pacific, especially vulnerable to world economic conditions

tsunami – massive destructive wave generated by underwater earthquake or volcanic eruption

Questions

1. How far, if at all, are geographical factors relevant to the problems of the developing world?

2. Why is urbanisation seen as a major problem for the developing world?

3. What connection, if any, is there between the problems of the developing world and the rise of immigration as a political issue in developed states?

4. What are the special problems of small island developing states?

5. How far are the transport systems of developing countries able to fulfil their tasks?

6. How far is it possible for a developing country to find replacements for (a) exhausted mineral deposits, or (b) degraded agricultural land?

CHAPTER 3

The crisis of the developing world

Poverty and basic needs

One billion people in developing countries – or one in five of the world's population – live in **poverty**. In other words they either cannot meet their **basic needs** or have so few resources that they cannot count on being able to meet them in the future. While the manner of organising to meet them varies with circumstances, basic human needs are universal:

- clean water
- good food
- proper sanitation and health facilities
- reasonable housing
- education.

Generally speaking, where population is high relative to the resources available to sustain it, the basic needs are most difficult to meet and the most marked forms of poverty and vulnerability are likely to occur. Aspects of material poverty as experienced in the developing world include undernutrition, malnutrition, ill health and low levels of education. However, a complicating factor is that poverty is not experienced by whole countries. Even in very poor countries (as measured by GDP/GNI per capita) there is a relatively wealthy elite, though elite lifestyles vary also. Moreover, the relative importance of the different factors making for poverty (physical, national past and present, international past and present) varies over time and from place to place.

Stressing the need to meet basic needs as the primary driving force towards development, sometimes imaginatively termed the 'basic needs approach', emphasises that health and education are motors for productivity and that the basic needs of all sectors must be met. This approach was expressed in the ideological framework of UN conferences in the early 1970s, when they confronted the older belief in the eventual 'trickling down' of the benefits of development and the 1960s' development agenda stressing employment and income distribution. In other words, this new approach saw qualitative change as the vital first step, not as something achievable through initial quantitative change. Such an approach was not then and is not now universally accepted.

In First World countries the 1970s saw the emergence of ideas associated with neo-liberalism (see Chapter 1) and in the 1980s these have been adopted in most parts of the developing world. Neo-liberals have argued that, for example, emphasising the meeting of basic needs slowed down growth in Sri Lanka in the 1960s and 1970s, impeded the development of Jamaica in the 1970s, as witness the fiasco of the sugar industry there, and proved detrimental to that of Tanzania, still after several decades one of the poorest countries in Africa. They argue that using capital to alleviate hardship forestalls its reinvestment in productive enterprises which will in the long run result in better conditions for all. However, as one of President Roosevelt's advisers pointed out in the 1930s, people don't eat 'in the long run' – they eat every day.

Despite this neo-liberal ideology of non-intervention, the fact remains that the meeting of basic needs depends for many on the continued provision of funding, and that the only way this can be done with certainty is by a system of financial transfers from the better-off to the poor at international, national and sub-national levels. Developing world countries, however, tend to lack internal transfers as safety nets for the poorest sectors. Shifting resources to the poor is a cost to the non-poor, and it is they who are likely – all other things being equal – to have a greater say in political and economic decision-making. In an extreme case, the wealthy backed by the armed forces were able to prevent the introduction of income tax in Guatemala until the early 1970s. When, finally, it was introduced, the top rate was only 4 per cent.

On the other hand, it is always difficult to target benefits to the poor. First of all, the poor often have an all too well-founded suspicion of government. Censuses do not count, or even identify, all of the poor. Officials are always suspect and census enumerators are no exception. Non-governmental organisations are better at targeting aid to the poor than are governments, but they often lack the resources. Most effective may be a process of self-selection, that is to say making available benefits that have no interest for those that are not poor, such as low-paid public-sector employment. However, economic orthodoxy frowns on creating employment in this way, no matter how socially desirable it might be, and governments that have got into financial difficulties may find themselves compelled to cut the size of the public sector regardless of the inevitable social consequences.

Water

Basic needs are, of course, interrelated, but the most important of all is clean water. Four-fifths of the globe are covered with water. However, fresh water is less than 3 per cent of the world's water, it is not evenly distributed and it is not necessarily clean. The majority of developing world populations live in rural areas where only some 15 per cent have access to clean water. Even in urban areas of the developing world most households do not have clean running water. In India, for example, it is estimated that as much as 70 per cent of all surface water is polluted.

The *World Development Report* (World Bank 1992) suggested that globally 1 billion (a thousand million) people were without access to clean water and 1.7 billion did not have proper sanitation. By 2005 the number without access to clean water had risen to 1.2 billion while 2.6 billion lacked sanitation. The situation is very different from the developed world. 'Just one flush of a toilet in the West uses more water than most Africans have to perform an entire day's washing, cleaning, cooking and drinking' (Prins 2000). The situation briefly created in New Orleans in 2005 by Hurricane Katrina is one in which many of the inhabitants of the developing world are condemned to live out their entire lives.

If action is not taken now, 135 million people could die of water-related diseases by the year 2020. That is a larger number than those expected to fall victim to the HIV/AIDS pandemic, a catastrophe that has already killed 23 million people worldwide. Furthermore, water plays a critical role in this disease since many deaths from AIDS are linked to illnesses resulting from dehydration and diarrhoea caused by unsafe water (Eliasson and Blumenthal 2005).

The problem is not just one of inadequate water supply. The combination of inadequate water for washing and cleaning and no sanitation is a guaranteed recipe for the rapid spread of water-borne illnesses. The World Health Organization (WHO 1993, 2005) says that the number of water taps per thousand population is a better indicator of health than the number of hospital beds (WHO 1993).

Not only is clean water scarce in the developing world but it is getting scarcer (see Table 3.1). Growing population, increasing urbanisation (which lowers quality through sanitation problems as well as increasing demand), rapidly rising demands from industry and the increasing pollution of watercourses by both solid and liquid wastes (Postel 1989), all combine to make potable water a rarer and therefore more valuable resource. Indeed water is also required for a variety of purposes other than drinking: washing and cleaning, irrigation for crops and, in more recent years, the generation of hydroelectric power (HEP). Seventy per cent of the world's available fresh water, it has been estimated, is used in agriculture.

The problem is at its most acute in the world's most populous country, China. China's total annual run-off of water amounts to some 2.6 trillion m^3.

Table 3.1   Countries experiencing water scarcity in 1955, 1990 and 2025 (projected), based on availability of less than 1,000 cubic metres of renewable water per person per year

A	Water-scarce countries in 1955
B	Countries added to scarcity category by 1990
C	Countries added to scarcity category by 2025 under all UN population growth projections
D	Countries added to scarcity category by 2025 only if they follow UN medium or high projections

A	B	C	D
Malta	Qatar	Libya	Cyprus
Djibouti	Saudi Arabia	Oman	Zimbabwe
Barbados	UAE	Morocco	Tanzania
Singapore	Yemen	Egypt	Peru
Bahrain	Israel	Comoros	
Kuwait	Tunisia	South Africa	
Jordan	Cape Verde	Syria	
	Kenya	Iran	
	Burundi	Ethiopia	
	Algeria	Haiti	
	Rwanda		
	Malawi		
	Somalia		

Source: Sustaining water: population and the future of renewable water supplies, Washington, DC, Population Action International, 2000, www.cnie.org/pop/pai/water-14.html

Plate 5   Hydroelectric power, Paraguay

But even with underground resources this is equivalent to only some 2,400 m³ per person per year, and in practice even this figure is quite unattainable. China uses only one-sixth of the amount of fresh water used by the United States, and even of this a very large amount is devoted to irrigation and much of that wasted by evaporation and leakage (Kang and Yong 1998).

Given the immense size and solidity of dams and irrigation works, it is easy to assume that they are permanent. Unfortunately this is not the case. The impoundment behind a dam fills up with sediment more or less rapidly depending on how turbid the river was in the first place. Where there has been extensive deforestation, the run-off from the denuded slopes brings down immense quantities of mud, which will remain in suspension only so long as the river continues to flow quickly.

All water used for irrigation contains minuscule quantities of common salt and various other minerals. This is left behind in the irrigated land and results in the steady **salination** of the soil. In principle, the salt could be washed away, but if there was enough water to do this the irrigation works would not have been needed in the first place. And excess water brings its own problems: too much can result in the **waterlogging** of the soil, and crops rot in the wet ground. The result is that every year 1.5 million ha of agricultural land become unusable and have to be taken out of production. One of the more celebrated examples is the land between the Tigris and the Euphrates in what is now Iraq, where the Marsh Arabs used to live before they were driven out by Saddam Hussein and to which they are returning now that his dams and dykes have broken down. But salination is a problem also in large parts of China and south Asia.

At the other end of the scale there are countries which suffer from an over-abundance of water. The north of Mexico is arid, but south of the Isthmus **tropical storms** falling short of a hurricane can lead to sudden floods, such as those that devastated Guatemala and El Salvador in 2005.

Food

In the 1930s developing countries collectively exported some 12 million tons of grain. By the late 1970s they were importing some 80 million tons.

The world's food production must double over the next 40 years if it is to keep up with population growth. There is no realistic way this can be achieved except by continuing to expand the wet cultivation of rice. Wet cultivation of rice, originally discovered in China, involves flooding the rice (paddy) fields and planting the new crop in the water. It enables as many as three crops a year to be grown. But UN Food and Agriculture Organization (FAO) statistics show that wet cultivation of rice consumes between 900 mm and 2,250 mm of water per day in optimum conditions, and twice that in the less than ideal conditions normally encountered (UNFAO 2004).

However, these figures conceal two paradoxes. World food production overall was sufficient even in the 1990s to feed all the people in the world to a reasonable standard. The Indian government estimates that the average person needs a minimum of 1,200 calories of nutritious food per day (Government of India 2006) and on FAO projections 3,600 calories per person is practicable (see also FAO 1999). Despite global needs, however, in 1972 the US government paid farmers $3 billion to take 50 million ha out of production and under the EU's Common Agricultural Policy (CAP) land has been 'set aside' from arable cultivation since 1988 to keep prices up and is still being kept out of production today. Land set aside can, however, be used for industrial oilseeds and energy crops. Meanwhile millions have starved over these years in the Sahel for want of a harvest (Bradley 1986) and in 2006 thousands are still dying of hunger in Sudan.

Further, grain shortages in the developing world have become increasingly severe since 1964, when for the first time grain grown for animal feed exceeded grain grown for direct consumption, and ever since then a growing proportion of world cereal production has been diverted to animal feed. Already by the end of the 1970s, in Mexico more basic grains were eaten by animals than by 20 million peasants (*International Herald Tribune*, 9 March 1978, quoted in Frank 1981). Yet a given quantity of grain will feed five times as many people if consumed as bread or porridge than if fed to cattle.

About 30 per cent of the world's land is potentially arable. About a half of this is under cultivation. Half of the land under cultivation is in the developing world but it is inhabited by three-quarters of the world's population, and the disproportion is even more marked in individual countries. Inequality of land distribution contributes to over-farming and underproduction. Some 80 per cent of the land in Latin America is held by less than 10 per cent of the population.

The environmentalist George Monbiot (*Oxfam/Guardian Supplement*, June 1992) cites the case of Brazil where farmland extending to the size of India lies uncultivated because it is held by its owners as an investment. Brazil's richest 1 per cent own 15 times as much land as the poorest 56 per cent. Under Brazilian law, land idle for more than five years may be legally occupied by any of Brazil's 10 million landless peasants. Landowners, not surprisingly, have a variety of means to resist such occupations. They are quite prepared to use violence if necessary. In Brazil's ranching country, the landless peasants' movement, the Movimento Sem Terra (MST), first occupied land in the Pantanal in 1990, as a means of dramatising its need. It has since built up a formidable presence which helped to elect 'Lula' Da Silva as president in October 2002. But Brazil's land reform provisions, enacted as part of the new Constitution in 1988, have since encountered stiff resistance both at home and abroad (see below).

At present one-quarter of the earth's population is not getting enough food. More than 500 million people are seriously malnourished. **Malnutrition** is not just an evil in itself. It lowers resistance and so exacerbates the problem of disease. These problems begin before birth: poor nutrition in mothers causes underweight babies and the incidence of low birth weight is increasing in some areas. Some 60 per cent of children in rural Bangladesh are underweight. Low birth weight is the factor most strongly correlated with later health problems. Directly or indirectly malnutrition causes the death of 40,000 children under five every day. In Africa South of the Sahara deaths of the under-fives contribute between 50 and 80 per cent to the total mortality of the population, compared with 3 per cent in Europe.

Malnutrition has been exacerbated by the tendency of some developing world countries to cease to be self-sufficient in staples and to become importers of food they used to produce. In 2005 the Malawi grain agency was forced to ration supplies of maize (UNFAO 2005). In Zimbabwe, once one of the most successful agricultural countries in the whole of Africa, hundreds of thousands were at the point of starvation. Yet Africa South of the Sahara was a food exporter until 1960. According to Shiva (1988) the region was still feeding itself as late as 1970. But by 1984, 140 million out of 531 million Africans were already dependent on being fed with grain from abroad and in 2005 more than 30 African countries faced a serious food crisis (see Chapter 2). There are, of course, causes other than persistent drought and environmental degradation; they include urbanisation, changing consumption and production patterns and the 'demonstration effect' fostered by the mass media. Even Mexico, where maize probably originated, is no longer self-sufficient in the basic staple of its diet. In fact it now exports fruit and vegetables to the United States and imports wheat in return. When developing world countries get into financial difficulties their plight is often because of the need to maintain a high – some would say excessive – level of imports of grain and other basic foodstuffs. Importing food and food products increases developing world vulnerability anyway, because of the need to deal in scarce convertible currency, but the imposition of austerity measures, along with currency devaluation, hits imports of all kinds, food included (Bernstein 1990).

Much was made at the time of the so-called **Green Revolution** which from 1940 onwards did so much to increase world food production by promoting the development of new varieties. But the 'miracle' seeds of the Green Revolution (financed by the Rockefeller Foundation in the 1940s and the Ford Foundation in the 1960s) were high yield varieties (HYVs) which, as they were intended to, produced massive increases in marketable surpluses, especially of wheat and rice. There were two problems for developing world farmers. The new seeds were hybrid. Thus they did not breed true and instead of farmers saving a proportion of their yield to plant for next season (as has happened since the first emergence of settled agriculture some 10,000 years ago) new supplies had to be bought each year. This made farmers dependent on cash sales to purchase seeds. The new varieties also needed huge volumes of water and high levels of chemical fertilisers, pesticides and fungicides. These things consumed scarce foreign exchange, increasing the national debt in the process and adversely affecting water supplies. Hence the benefits of the Green

Revolution, and there were many, were in practice skewed to the wealthier sectors because they were only easily available to larger landowners. They therefore inadvertently helped increase the serious disproportion in access to land and wealth in developing world societies.

There are important domestic consequences too. **Agribusiness** is 'modern'; it seeks to gain efficiency by mechanisation and it is the best arable land that is easiest to subject to mechanisation. The occupation or purchase of these lands displaces settlers onto marginal lands. Hence it is, ironically, often the free market in land rather than population pressure that creates refugees and/or hunger. In the case of the Philippines, marginal workers have been driven into the forests, where they in turn displace indigenous peoples, with disastrous consequences for the environment and lost lifestyles.

The most severe form of food deficit is **famine**, which differs from malnutrition in its acuteness and in the accompanying increase in deaths associated with the crisis. Famine is high profile through First World television appeals but it should not be forgotten that the greatest achievements in surviving famines are local, the result of community and family efforts in the affected areas. Famine is not simply a natural disaster and it is no accident that it is currently associated with Africa South of the Sahara and especially with the Sahel region and the Horn.

Famine was also commonplace in India historically (Weiner 1962). However, the most recent famine in India was the Bengal Famine of 1943, during the Second World War, when both government and the transportation network were strained to the limit. There has been no famine of this magnitude in India itself (as opposed to neighbouring Bangladesh) since Independence in 1947, thanks to a public food distribution system, although chronic hunger persists in India and claims many lives as a matter of course. On the other hand, China has since the Revolution greatly reduced chronic hunger as a routine condition of the population, but has nevertheless suffered famine, most notably at the end of the 1950s during and largely as a result of the turmoil of the so-called Great Leap Forward. The fact is that the cause of famine is not usually a lack of food, but rather whether food gets to those who need it – the question of the difference between availability and 'entitlement'.

As Dreze and Sen point out: 'it has to be recognized that even when the prime mover in a famine is a natural occurrence such as a flood or a drought, what its impact will be on the population depends on how society is organised' (1989: 46). Even in a country stricken with famine, most sectors do not suffer famine as such: Sen estimates only 2–3 per cent do. Most sectors have entitlement based on their capacity to produce their own food, to trade some other product for food or to earn a wage with which to buy food. The rich do not go hungry even in famine. Urban areas tend to draw resources from marginal areas, as was the case in Ethiopia, where government food purchases for the cities contributed to rural famine. In 1988 it was a time of reasonable food availability in Somalia, and the famine that shocked the world was the result of human agency. In the civil war, crops had been burnt, resulting in a flood of refugees without reserves or mutual support networks and no 'entitlement' to food. In 1994 in Rwanda the flood of refugees was so massive that in only three weeks a major disaster was created (see also Wijkman and Timberlake 1984).

Climatic factors are not the causes of famine in any real sense, therefore. Rather, like wars and political crises they are trigger factors. Droughts have occurred year after year in Africa South of the Sahara in the past but have not necessarily been accompanied by famine (see Schmandt 1994). Much of the United States is arid but it does not suffer from famine, as it has the complex infrastructure to ensure that in emergencies resources are more equitably distributed. This infrastructure is vital to reduce vulnerability. But in their former colonies traditional defence mechanisms were often dismantled by European colonisers, as Gita Mehta describes in *Raj* (Mehta 1990). Famine therefore emerged as an unintended consequence of the ways in which local economies were restructured to meet the needs of the colonial powers. The most productive land was taken for settlement or plantations, reducing land available for production to meet local needs. Competition frequently destroyed local artisan production which could have earned funds for times of food shortage. It is also true, however, that colonial powers sought to counter famine by funding and building large-scale irrigation works, and without the roads and railways which they built no one outside the famine areas might have known that anything was happening.

Food aid can make things worse. Critics have particularly targeted the sending of infant feeding formula as part of aid packages, as there is some evidence that both this and the aggressive marketing, (by companies run by men) of artificial baby milk powder to mothers in the developing world is resulting in many unnecessary deaths; this has led in some quarters to attempts to boycott the products of companies like Nestlé. The formula itself is not the problem, but it has to be made up with clean water in sterile equipment, and, even where mothers understand the need for hygiene, the facilities are often inadequate or non-existent. More often the formula is made up with dirty water and diluted to make it go further, so that even if the child fails to contract gastroenteritis or dysentery, it is of low body weight and so less well equipped to resist other challenges to its immune system. Breastfeeding is by far the safest method for developing world babies, particularly as it also conveys a degree of immunity against local diseases. In Sierra Leone, where in 1999 170 children per thousand died before the age of one and a quarter (males 277 per thousand, females 248) of all children died under the age of five, babies often thrive until weaned. Among the many adverse effects of chronic food shortage (or lack of entitlement), however, is that women usually have to do without. As a result nursing mothers may well not be able to produce the milk their infant children so desperately need (Whitehead 1990).

Unhappily, food aid, though an essential humanitarian response to short-term crisis, can very easily be exploited as a political weapon. In 1974, for example, US government disagreements with Bangladesh led to a reluctance to release food aid in a time of famine. Even when food aid arrives at its intended destination, as in Somalia in 1993, it may be hijacked by local warlords or power blocs and used by them to reward their own political supporters. In 2005–6 there has been criticism of the Islamic government of Sudan, which is blocking urgently needed relief supplies to the Christian south. Lastly, the availability of free food drives down the price of staples on the local market. If the supply of aid goes on too long, therefore, the incentive to plant for the new season is eliminated and the cycle of deprivation is set to continue. In this way food aid has ironically and tragically acted to prolong the effects of drought in Ethiopia.

The View from the Ground

By *David Kane*

Land Reform and Poverty Alleviation Project (Cedula da Terra)

Antonio da Silva came to João Pessoa eleven years ago after he was forced off the land he had been planting by the owner of the land. He worked a short time cutting sugar cane, but didn't make enough to even feed himself sometimes. He came to the city desperate for work and a better life. Here he found little relief. He only found sporadic jobs, none lasting more than three months. After two years of this, he swallowed his pride and started living and working in the city dump. A couple years later he met a woman from his home town and they married. In his years at the dump, Antonio did all that he could to help people in difficult situations, helping buy medicines, helping new families build their shacks on top of the dump, etc. But all this time, Antonio dreamed of returning to the land and working on his own piece of land.

Now, Antonio, his wife Maria, and their 6 year old son, Bilu, are joining up with other families in similar desperate situations to live as farmers on their own land. They have become part of the

landless movement in Brazil struggling for a better life. Unfortunately, their chances of improving their lives has been made even more difficult by changes in Brazil's land reform laws.

Until this year, Brazil's land reform law, which was created as part of the 1988 Constitution, was one of the most progressive in the world. The law worked like this: If a landowner had a piece of land larger than approximately 500 acres that was not being used, the government was to confiscate the land, pay the owner the market value for the land and then redistribute the land to landless families. As with most laws in Brazil, the government had difficulties or a lack of interest in actually enforcing the law. But landless families helped the government in fulfilling its duty.

These families, often with help from the Catholic church's Pastoral Land Commission (CPT) or the national Landless Movement (MST), identified pieces of land that should have been confiscated by the government and occupied them. Usually the landowners would fight back to not lose their land, many times violently by employing hitmen to intimidate and/or attack the landless families. But almost always, after a long, difficult struggle, the landless families won the title to the land and began their lives as farmers again. In addition to giving the land, the government helped the families by providing food while they were camped out waiting for the land to be confiscated as well as providing them with low or no interest loans to buy seeds and equipment to start up their farms after they had title to the land. The Brazilian land reform, at least on paper, has been a stellar example for all the world.

All of this will end, however, if President Fernando Henrique Cardoso and the World Bank have their way. They are trying to start a new way of doing land reform called the Land Reform and Poverty Alleviation Pilot Project, or Cedula da Terra here in Brazil. This project will de facto put an end to land reform in Brazil. The project creates a 'land bank' of money from the World Bank to be used by landless families to buy land from landowners. The families would then have to pay back the loan within 20 years. But there are a number of problems with this project.

First, it relieves the government of its responsibility to implement land reform and forces landless families to take out high interest loans which will be extremely difficult or impossible to pay back. Currently, with fees and taxes included, the loan has a 19 per cent interest rate, lower than the current market rate of 27 per cent, but far too high for a poor Brazilian to pay.

Second, landowners will only sell if they want to sell and will only sell the parts of land that they choose. Thus, landowners will sell the worst pieces of land to the landless who will not be able to pay back their debts to the bank. This project also increases Brazil's already staggering external debt of US$270 billion with the bulk of the money coming from the World Bank.

The project was designed to only complement already existing agrarian reform by allowing landless families access to land that is smaller than 500 acres or is somewhat productive and thus not appropriate for confiscation. But the government is using it instead to dismantle its agrarian reform and cut its budget in order to comply with International Monetary Fund requirements of social spending reductions. According to Roberto Araujo of the CPT, there are already a number of cases where land that is appropriate to be confiscated by the government, has been declared inappropriate in order to avoid having to pay the owner with government money. In these cases, landless families were forced to buy the land with money from the land bank. At the same time the government has cut 38 per cent from its agrarian reform budget.

The World Bank has a reputation for planning projects without any input from the people directly affected or social organisations. The Cedula da Terra is no exception. The planning meetings included only people from the government and the World Bank. No other input was solicited even though the MST is arguably the most organised landless movement in the world and has published a number of feasible projects that would truly improve Brazil's agrarian reform. This lack of input from people who are most directly affected will always result in projects with questionable benefit for the people they are designed to help.

Source: NEWS FROM BRAZIL supplied by SEJUP (Serviço Brasileiro de Justiça e Paz). Number 355, June 18, 1999. http://www.oneworld.org/sejup/ http://www.converge.org.nz/lac/articles/news990623d.htm

Sanitation and health

Clean water and sanitation are vital. From 1992, beginning with Peru, South America experienced its first cholera epidemic for more than 100 years. The cost of the Peruvian cholera epidemic in terms of lost tourism and agricultural exports exceeded by far what it would have cost to avoid the problem.

The estimate of the number of cholera infections each year is enormous, some 6 million. Cholera breeds in the gut and is spread by contaminated food and water. It hits hardest at the weak, the old and the young. Convulsions, vomiting and diarrhoea produce dehydration which can kill in 4 hours. Yet years of neglect made Peru highly susceptible to this disease. For Peru it is a man-made disaster. Cholera was brought by boat to Chimbote in 1990–91, where the Peruvian preference for raw fish and the absence of simple sanitation (communal latrines and contaminated water supplies) combined to pave the way for an epidemic. Chimbote should be a prosperous place with an adequate infrastructure for the general health of its population. It is the world's largest fishmeal producer. But the European-descended elite who control the profits from fishmeal do not get cholera. They do not invest in infrastructure, arguing that this is the government's job and its absence the government's failure. Like their counterparts in other Latin American countries, the Peruvian elite prefers to keep its money abroad in more stable countries.

Within weeks the epidemic had spread to five neighbouring states and it is now again endemic in South America. Mountain villages have been hit by cholera too, although they might have been assumed to be healthier places, because their rivers which are their main source of water are also their sewers. The main exception was in areas controlled by the guerrilla movement Sendero Luminoso. Where the building of latrines was ordered by Sendero, and those who did not use them were threatened with death, there was no cholera (*Assignment*: 'Peru in the Time of the Cholera', BBC Television, 1993).

One good thing has come out of this: schools are now teaching basic hygiene for the first time, but most such education and other assistance has been left to the aid agencies – Peru's hospitals were totally overwhelmed. But it does not take an epidemic to overwhelm developing world hospitals. Poverty has the same effect, if more slowly. Poverty is the main reason for poor health.

Where basic needs are not met, the effects can be devastating. For example, a major world effort is needed to break into the cycle of infection and reinfection which in recent years has led to millions of deaths in countries in Africa South of the Sahara. In 1995 an outbreak of the Ebola virus in Zaire led to headlines throughout the developed world featuring its terrifying consequence, acute haemorrhagic fever leading in over 80 per cent of cases to death through the dissolution of the victim's internal organs.

Health improved dramatically in Europe in the nineteenth century with the provision of public water supply and sewerage, and this long before there were significant advances in the ability of medicine to cure illness. Many diseases in the developing world today were once as common in the now developed world but public expenditure solved the problems that gave rise to them. Economic development in its fullest sense, therefore, is the quickest and surest way to better health for all.

However, aid agencies have continued in recent years to seek to increase economic growth through large-scale industry and agribusiness knowing full well that this would primarily benefit the health of the already fairly healthy higher income sectors. The touching belief remained that the benefits of this development would in time 'trickle down' to the poorer sectors of society. But in practice the health gap between rich and poor continued to widen. In 1978, therefore, the 134 countries which attended the WHO conference of that year agreed on behalf of their peoples to seek as a conscious goal the target of 'Health for All'. In 1981 health was identified by WHO as a fundamental human right and the year 2000 was set as the target date for 'Health for All' (Thomas 1987: 106).

Primary health care was identified as the main means through which the target could be met. Social indicators were to be used for monitoring the success of health programmes, which would stress accessibility, participation and health education in their design. The main policy initiatives were to be in the areas of adequate food, safe water, family planning, immunisation, the provision of essential drugs and the treatment of common injuries and illnesses.

By 1985 it was clear that the achievements in health care varied enormously and the early optimism had waned. At this point the Rockefeller Foundation published *Good Health at Low Cost*, an investigation into the successes of China, Sri Lanka, Costa Rica and, perhaps most notably, the state of Kerala in south-western India. In all of these areas, residents all had life expectancies of more than 65 despite the fact that, as their low per capita GDPs demonstrated, these areas were all very poor indeed by world standards. Four factors were found which reduced the infant mortality rate sufficiently to raise life expectancies to developed country levels:

1. an ideological commitment to equity in social matters;
2. equitable access to and distribution of public health care provision;
3. equitable access to and distribution of public education;
4. adequate nutrition at all levels of society.

Infant mortality and life expectancy

The logic is clear. Malnutrition aggravated by infectious diseases spread by poor sanitation and polluted water supplies causes the bulk of developing world mortality, especially in children under five. Of the 15 million unnecessary infant deaths each year 4 million are from one or more of six cheaply immunisable diseases and a further 5 million result from diarrhoea preventable by

Table 3.2 World's highest infant mortality rates, 2005

Country	Deaths under 1 (per 000 live births)
1. Western Sahara	191.2
2. Angola	163.1
3. Afghanistan	143.6
4. Sierra Leone	130.8
5. Mozambique	128.9
6. Liberia	121.7
7. Niger	116.8
8. Mali	116.7
9. Somalia	110.8
10. Tajikistan	107.2

Source: Information Please® Database, © 2005 Pearson Education, Inc. All rights reserved

oral rehydration therapy, the salts for which cost next to nothing. The cost of just three weeks of what the world's governments spend on arms would pay for primary health care for all developing world children, including ensuring access to safe water and immunisation against the six most common infectious diseases.

Infant mortality rate (IMR), defined as the number of children per thousand who die in the first year of life, varies strikingly between the major regions of the world (see Table 3.2). The world average in 1998 was 57 per thousand. This compared with, on the one hand, Europe, where the average was 21 (a figure that had actually risen from 16 in 1988), and Africa, where it was 91. These figures also conceal striking variations within regions. Likewise IMRs are always higher in rural areas which are less likely to have the same levels of access to medical services, female education, potable water and proper sanitation or indeed the incomes necessary to achieve adequate levels of nutrition.

Where urban conditions are grimmest and overcrowding most marked the differences between urban and rural IMRs still exist but they are less pronounced. At the beginning of the 1990s the world's highest IMR was for Sierra Leone, at 180 deaths per thousand, but the rate for Equatorial Guinea was almost as bad. In 2000 Western Sahara was believed to have the world's highest IMR (191.2 per thousand). Another African country, Angola, ranked second highest with 163.1 deaths per thousand, but it was Afghanistan, after three decades of war, invasion, insurgency, civil war and systematic destruction of its infrastructure that came third, with 143.6 deaths, and Sierra Leone, also ravaged by civil war, fourth with 130.8. On the other hand one of Africa's richer countries, Zimbabwe, had an IMR of 86 in 1970 but by 2005 it had only improved to 52, while neighbouring Zambia, 109 in 1970 had fallen to 88 in 2005 (US CIA World Factbook 2006). www.cia.org/cia/publications/factbook/rankorder/2091rank/html and UNDP 2005.

Since, sadly, many more small children die after the age of one, there is an increasing tendency amongst agencies involved in development to prefer

Table 3.3   Under-five mortality rate, selected countries, 2005

Country	U5MR (per 000 live births)
Algeria	41
Argentina	20
Bangladesh	69
Brazil	35
China	37
Egypt	39
Ghana	95
India	87
Indonesia	41
Iran	39
Iraq	125
Malaysia	7
Mexico	28
Mozambique	147
Nigeria	198
Pakistan	98
Sierra Leone	284
South Africa	66
Sri Lanka	15
Thailand	26
UAE	8

Source: UNICEF (2006), *The State of the World's Children*, UN Department of Social and Economic Affairs, millenniumindicators.un.org/unsd/mi_series_xnxx.asp?row_id=561

under-five mortality rates (U5MRs) to IMRs as indicators (see Table 3.3). Using these rates UN International Children's Emergency Fund's (UNICEF's) 2006 figures suggest that Sierra Leone has the worst rate: 284, well ahead of Niger (198) and Iraq (125). Such statistics are not surprising for the poorest countries of Africa, but what is perhaps most interesting and hopeful is the significantly lower rates now being achieved by some still very poor countries. India has a U5MR of 87, China 37 and Sri Lanka 15, while Malaysia, at 7, has achieved First World standards of care (e.g. the USA's is 8).

A high IMR is the main reason for low **life expectancy** at birth. In most parts of the developing world, if you survive childhood, you have a fair chance of living almost as long as people do in Europe or the United States, but in Sierra Leone life expectancy at birth in 2005 was only 38 and in Afghanistan 42. Again, because of the high IMR, many of the worst life expectancies are to be found in Africa South of the Sahara – as a result of the HIV epidemic in Swaziland life expectancy in 2003 was only 35. Life expectancy is not directly linked to a country's available resources: it all depends how they are spent. China (life expectancy at birth 71) and Cuba (77) are both relatively poor, but have excellent rates of life expectancy. Nigeria has a very high national income, but a surprisingly low rate of life expectancy (45). Of the major countries, Japan has the highest life expectancy in 2005, though it is exceeded by the tiny state of Andorra in the Pyrenees.

The figures for life expectancy are usually broken down by gender, since almost invariably women live longer than men, and in some societies, Japan being the most obvious example, there is such a wide gap that it calls for explanation. Male/female life expectancy gaps do tend to be smaller in poorer countries, though, and the gap is non-existent in Bangladesh, for a variety of reasons which are dealt with later in Chapter 5. Today only the Maldives (female 64, male 66) has a lower expectancy of life for women than for men.

For Africa some representative figures for 2006 were:

Angola, 40: female 42, male 38
Chad, 46: female 47, male 44
Guinea, 52: female 53, male 51
Malawi, 42: female 42, male 41.

In Sierra Leone, devastated by civil war, the 1998 figures were again the worst in the world: 37.2 overall (female 39, male 36). In 2003 they had improved only marginally, to 38 overall (female 39, male 37). It is true that not all very low life expectancies are to be found in Africa, but the exceptions are few. Afghanistan was the lowest in Asia even before the Taliban took over in 1996. But a more representative figure for Asia is that for India, which in 1998 had a life expectancy of 63 years for women and 62 years for men compared with 53 and 53 years respectively in 1988 (UNDP 1999; WHO 1999), though this has not improved since the later figures (see Table 3.4).

Table 3.4 World's lowest life expectancies, 2006 estimates

Country	Life expectancy (in years at birth)
1. Swaziland	32.62
2. Botswana	33.74
3. Lesotho	34.40
4. Angola	38.62
5. Zimbabwe	39.29
6. Liberia	39.65
7. Mozambique	39.62
8. Zambia	40.03
9. Sierra Leone	40.22
10. Malawi	41.70
11. South Africa	42.73
12. Djibouti	43.17
13. Afghanistan	43.34
14. Namibia	43.39
15. Central African Rep.	43.54

Source: US CIA, The World Factbook, 2006,
www.cia.gov/cia/publications/factbook/rankorder/2102rank.html

Medical services

Although when things go wrong there is no substitute for good medical help, the least important factor in general good health is the provision of good medical services. Medical solutions tend to be rich-world solutions, they are generally expensive and involve technology. However, they do include vaccination, which is relatively cheap and simple to administer, and, while poverty may be the factor most intimately bound to the health of the population, levels of immunity to infectious diseases are important to public health also. Although in the UK 95 per cent of one-year-olds are fully immunised against measles and 99 per cent of school-age children against tuberculosis, the corresponding figures for Zambia are 69 per cent and 81 per cent. Hence Zambia had 481.8 cases per 100,000 of tuberculosis in 1996 compared with 10.3 for the UK (UNDP 1999).

Paradoxically, one of the growing problems of the developing world is not that drugs are not available, but that there are too many of the wrong kind. Some 30 major companies control some 50 per cent of the world pharmaceutical trade. External regulation of them by developing world countries is often weak, since they lack both the resources and the expertise to control what is sold. Pharmaceutical companies are big foreign exchange earners so restrictions in their home countries in the developed world may not be too tight either. The market is very competitive – the merger of Glaxo Wellcome with SmithKline Beecham in the UK in January 2000 created the then world's largest drug company, but it still accounted for only 9 per cent of the world market. The WHO itself is only an advisory body and its advice is not always followed. Frequently drugs banned in the developed countries are either tested in developing countries or left on sale in developing countries long after they have been withdrawn from sale elsewhere.

Drug companies need to make money to recoup development costs as well as to keep shareholders happy. To do this, they want to sell, not generic drugs from which the returns are relatively low, but specific branded products over which they can claim right of 'intellectual property'. Through heavy advertising they promote the sale of branded drugs where generics would do. Prices are high and developing world health budgets low but what is purchased may have virtually no additional therapeutic value, except possibly to the elite in the main urban centres. WHO has identified 200 cost-effective tried and tested drugs seen as basic and indispensable to any country's health needs, but in the name of free trade the developed countries can offer strong and successful resistance to any attempts to limit provision in this way.

However, drug regulation legislation has been proved to decrease reliance on expensive imported drugs. Sri Lanka established a National Formulary as early as 1959 and in 1972 the government of Mrs Sirima Bandaranaike established the Sri Lanka Pharmaceutical Corporation to produce generic drugs at low prices. Following independence in 1975 Mozambique established a central purchasing organisation and an effective national formulary, though the circumstances of the country did not allow it to establish its own national drugs industry, as had been hoped. In 1982 Bangladesh replaced its 1940 Drugs Act with a detailed National Drug Policy, banning many branded drugs altogether and establishing tight controls over the activities of TNCs in the country. Although this policy had strong support in the region, the US government threatened reprisals on grounds of free trade regardless of the ethical implications of forcing high cost products on the population of one of the poorest countries in the world (Thomas 1987: 106–14).

At best, the power of the international drug companies can mean that developing world markets are flooded with branded cough medicine but penicillin and other key drugs are unobtainable. Generally, it can mean the widespread availability of suspect products banned in the USA and Japan. At worst it means that a flourishing black market in prescription drugs grows up and, through their overuse, valuable antibiotics and anti-malarial drugs cease to be effective because germs and parasites develop resistance to them.

Health care in the developing world is often disproportionately used by the wealthy. As elsewhere, the rural poor are the group least likely to have access to it. Not only is it more difficult for logistical reasons to provide reliable health care in rural areas, but developing world governments, in health as in other aspects of provision, often prefer to put their limited resources into large visible expenditures on urban hospitals, rather than devote it to primary health care, still less to essential health education.

While circulatory diseases are the main killers in the First World, infectious gastroenteric and respiratory diseases are more important in the developing world. It is, however, the rural populations who still suffer disproportionately from largely preventable infectious diseases (Danida 1989). For example:

- Tuberculosis is still widespread in the developing world.
- Over 400 million people in the world suffer from malaria.
- At least 225 million have hookworm (infestation by parasitic roundworms of any of several species of the genus Nematoda).
- Some 200 million are sick with schistosomiasis (infestation by blood flukes).
- Twenty million suffer from trypanosomiasis, an endemic disease formerly known as 'sleeping sickness' (caused by a protozoan parasite or *trypanosome* carried by the tsetse fly).
- Twenty million are afflicted onchocerciasis (better known as 'river blindness'), prevalent in West Africa. In this case a water-borne filiaral (thread-like) parasite enters the skin, usually in the lower body. It migrates through the body to the eyes, and if untreated ultimately destroys the optic nerve, resulting in irretrievable loss of sight.
- Other preventable causes of blindness in tropical countries include trachoma, chronic infection of the conjunctiva by the bacterium *Chalmydia trachomatis*, and xeropthalmia, loss of sight through a simple deficiency of Vitamin A.

- Worldwide between 30 and 40 million children each year contract measles. A condition which is rarely fatal in the developed world, it can and occasionally does lead to serious complications even there, and in many parts of the developing world children lack resistance to the virus and many die. There is an extremely effective vaccine, and a joint programme by WHO and UNICEF helped bring global deaths from the disease down from 873,000 in 1999 to 530,000 in 2003.

Case study 3.1 **Malaria**

On 28 February 2005 Lomana LuaLua, who normally plays as a striker for Portsmouth Football Club in England, was reported to be suffering from malaria, which he had contacted while captaining his country, the Democratic Republic of the Congo, against neighbouring Cape Verde. The strain he had contracted was said to be particularly virulent, and even with the very best medical care he was out of action for six weeks, though happily he seems to have made a full recovery. Malaria is one of the worst of the world's scourges. It is not only a life-threatening disease, but it is quite difficult to treat and many people who recover from it experience regular recurrences of fever. It is also a disease that could be relatively easily addressed, if sufficient resources could only be delivered to the task on a coordinated basis.

The figures speak for themselves, though reporting is patchy among the poorer countries and of the countries discussed here neither The Gambia nor Cambodia reported in the latest year available. In 1995 there were 15,594 cases per 100,000 people in Kenya, 21,054 in Papua New Guinea (PNG), 30,030 in the Comoros, 30,269 in the Solomon Islands and 32,867 in Zambia. Of these, both Kenya and the Comoros are popular long-haul holiday destinations for Europeans and PNG and the Solomon Islands for Australians.

Malaria is a parasitic disease characterised by a high fever, alternate sweating and shaking chills, extreme exhaustion and anaemia. It was once thought that the disease came from vapours rising from marshes, hence the name *mal aria* (bad air). In 1880, scientists discovered the real cause of malaria: a single-cell parasite called *Plasmodium*. Later they discovered that the parasite is transmitted from person to person through the bite of a female Anopheles mosquito, which requires blood to nurture her eggs. Unfortunately because the cause is a parasite and not a bacterium, it has not proved possible so far to devise a vaccine against malaria. The first effective treatment for malaria was quinine, derived from the bark of a Paraguayan tree. More recently, similar drugs were developed artificially, which were more effective and could prevent the disease developing by stopping any parasites from reproducing. Used in conjunction with other preventative measures to minimise the risk of insect bites, chloroquine and other drugs have given effective protection for years. Now, however, malaria parasites are developing unacceptable levels of resistance to one drug after another and many insecticides are no longer useful against mosquitoes transmitting the disease. Years of vaccine research have produced few hopeful candidates and although scientists are redoubling the search, an effective vaccine is at best years away. That malaria may soon become virtually untreatable is a real prospect in the year 2006. New, at present untreatable, forms are appearing in places as far apart as The Gambia in West Africa and Cambodia in South-east Asia, and new drugs are not being developed as quickly as they were.

▶

Case study 3.1 continued

The disease was once more widespread but it was successfully eliminated from many countries with temperate climates during the mid twentieth century. Early work by the WHO in the 1950s was mainly an attack on the carriers, the mosquitoes. Attacking the vector itself rather than trying to immunise or cure people is cheap and effective. DDT was extensively used until it was banned, but it turned out to be unnecessary. Simply covering stagnant water with a thin film of paraffin was enough to deter the mosquito from breeding. The campaign therefore was very successful. For example, the number of cases in Sri Lanka was reduced from thousands to an average of only 12 a year by 1998. Sadly, the campaign was not carried through to its logical conclusion. Residual cases remained and from these malaria parasites were transmitted again with greater frequency once the mosquitoes had become immune to the pesticides being used against them and resources were no longer devoted to spraying the ponds and lakes. Today Sri Lanka again spends some 60 per cent of its public health budget on malaria control.

In fact in 2006 malaria is common throughout the tropical zone and approximately 40 per cent of the world's population, mostly those living in the world's poorest countries, is at risk. Currently malaria causes more than 300 million acute illnesses and at least one million deaths annually. Together with HIV/AIDS and TB, it is one of the major public health challenges undermining development in the poorest countries in the world.

The tiny West African state of The Gambia was until the 1994 coup an increasingly popular 'long-haul' tourist resort. However, it was long known to sailors as the Graveyard Coast, and with good reason. In their villages Gambians can expect an average of three bites per night from malaria-bearing mosquitoes. The Gambia has one of the strongest malaria control programmes in West Africa, but only just over 40 per cent of households have mosquito nets, as they would be considered an expensive luxury by most Gambians. Nor can most Gambians afford imported malaria preventatives; if they reach adulthood they build up resistance. Hence malaria is a serious risk, especially to children, who have not yet had time to develop resistance. Just over 50 per cent of Gambian children under five receive anti-malarials. But *P. falciparum*, the kind found in The Gambia, can and often does cause cerebral malaria in young children. This attacks and destroys the brain, hence those who do not die may still suffer irreversible mental impairment.

Ninety per cent of malaria cases today occur in Africa where over 200 million people get it each year; many, as in The Gambia, in a drug-resistant form. But it is not only in Africa that drug-resistant forms are re-emerging and presenting a formidable challenge to the resources of the major drug companies. Along the Thai/Cambodia border among prospectors the strains are virtually untreatable. The Thai operate mobile clinics along the border, but parasite resistance is encouraged by the abuse of anti-malarial drugs. The problem is the availability of drugs in Thailand, where malaria is under control, and their use as prophylaxis in Cambodia, a country which had been dislocated by 20 years of war, where they promote resistance. Already the effects of the cheapest and most widely available drug, chloroquine, are diminishing worldwide and in this part of the world it is now ineffective. Aid workers have been seriously concerned at the absence of medical advice when Cambodians buy malarial treatments. As a result this area now has the most virulent form of malaria in the world.

►

Case study 3.1 continued

The problems presented by malaria are not only medical but social. People move much further than mosquitoes, and in great numbers too in an area with refugees such as Thailand/Cambodia. The dispersal to the rest of the world of the 22,000 UN troops formerly in Cambodia, many of whom will have been sent from malarial areas, has not helped either as they have taken resistant strains home with them. But after 1989 US military interest in developing malaria prevention diminished since it was now much less likely that US troops will be put in large numbers into South-east Asia. Instead malaria is losing out in the competition for funds. Since the victims of malaria are generally from poor countries, there is no money in tropical medicine. Reports say that the big drug companies do not even bother to send their represent-atives to international conferences on tropical diseases – WHO does all the cajoling, but often to little effect (*Assignment*: 'Fatal Latitudes', BBC Television, 1993).

Three out of five developing world governments spend more on arms than they do on health. Although there are marked variations, the *World Development Reports* suggest that this tendency is actually stronger in the low-income developing countries than it is in others. Two-and-a-half hours is all the time it takes for world military spending to consume the equivalent of the entire annual budget of the WHO. The cost of eradicating smallpox worldwide was only $83 million, the same as the cost of just one strategic bomber. But work against malaria was delayed due to 'shortage of funds' and the outlook does not look too good for the new target date for worldwide eradication: 2010.

Table 3.5 HIV prevalence and total number living with AIDS, 2003

Country	Est. HIV prevalence rate, adults (per 100, 000)	Total number living with AIDS
Algeria	<1	<10,000
Argentina	<1	100,000–<500,000
Bangladesh	–	–
Brazil	<1	500,000–1m
China	<1	500,000–1m
Egypt	<1	10,000–100,000
Ghana	1–<5	100,000–500,000
India	<1	>2m
Indonesia	<1	100,000–<500,000
Iran	<1	10,000–<100,000
Iraq	<1	<10,000
Malaysia	<1	10,000–<100,000
Mexico	<1	100,000–<500,000
Mozambique	10–<25	1m–<2m
Pakistan	<1	10,000–<100,000
Sierra Leone	–	–
South Africa	10–<25	100,000–<500,000
Sri Lanka	<1	<10,000
Thailand	1–<5	500,000–1m
UAE	–	–

Source: WHO, http://www.who.int/globalatlas/dataQuery/reportData.asp?rptType=1

Case study 3.2 **HIV/AIDS**

The toll of lives from malaria is more than 20 times greater than deaths from AIDS. AIDS or, in full, Acquired Immuno-Deficiency Syndrome, is the acute form of a viral infection caused by the Human Immunodeficiency Virus (HIV), a retro-virus which attacks the human immune system. The virus is spread by sexual contact or the interchange of body fluids, for example by intravenous drug abuse using shared needles. It can also be transmitted *in utero* from mother to child. The virus steadily weakens the body's immune system until it can no longer fight off infections which can lead to gastroenteritis, pneumonia, tumours and other illnesses, all of which can be part of AIDS. Unable to fight back, most people die within three years of the first signs of AIDS appearing.

There is as yet no cure for AIDS once it has developed but the development of HIV infection in the body can be arrested by therapy with a combination of anti-retroviral drugs. Timely use of these has been successful in stopping children from inheriting the disease, but so far this is the only stage at which it seems possible to speak of a cure.

The problem for people in developing countries is that they cannot afford even to be tested for HIV let alone treated with the expensive 'cocktail' of drugs used to arrest the development of the virus in patients in the AICs. Since no conventional cure is so far available the position has been worsened by resort to a variety of dubious treatments at the hands of traditional curers. Hence the disease has shown an alarmingly rapid spread in developing world countries and that is now where the main concern is. Of the 6.5 million people known to need anti-retroviral treatment in developing and transitional countries, less than 1 million are in fact receiving them (see Table 3.6).

In 1997 Japan had 1.2 cases of AIDS per 100,000 people, the UK 25.9, Canada 50.4 and the USA, where the first case of AIDS was reported in 1981, 225.3 cases per 100,000. But Zimbabwe had 564.4, Zambia 530.1 and Malawi 505.4 (UNDP 1999). These figures, unlike those for other diseases, are cumulative. Worldwide 33.4 million people were believed to be infected with HIV at the beginning of the century (*The Guardian*, 1 January 2000). At the end of 2004 the mid-range estimate by Avert-org, the AIDS charity, was 39.4 million, with a range of 25.9 to 44.3 million. However, in 2004 some 4.9 million had been newly infected with HIV while some 3.1 million had died of AIDS. As a sexually transmitted disease, HIV particularly threatens the young, some 6,000 of whom contract the virus every day.

Proportionate to their population, the individual countries most severely affected are Barbados and the Bahamas, which may come as a nasty surprise to holidaymakers. Africa south of the Sahara, however, had in 2005 most of the world's known cases of HIV infection: 25.8 million, and more than 12 million AIDS orphans. In fact it is not too much to state that the incidence of HIV/AIDS in Africa South of the Sahara is so great that the actual survival of societies such as those of Zimbabwe, Zambia, Malawi, Swaziland and Lesotho is threatened. Moreover AIDS is already out of control in Eastern and Central Africa, nurtured and spreading northward and westward across the continent as the result of a deadly combination of migrant work patterns, macho attitudes towards sex and unwitting spread by truckers and the prostitutes who service them. As one would expect, women account for just under a half of all HIV victims worldwide; in Africa South of the Sahara, however, women account for 57 per cent. For an excellent collection of material on the scale of the problem see also Poku 2006 (see Table 3.6).

Table 3.6 Incidence of TB and HIV in selected countries, 2004

Country	TB cases per 100,000 2004	Estimated adults and children living with HIV 2003
Algeria	53.9	9,100
Argentina	53.0	130,000
Bangladesh	435.4	[2,500–25,000]*
Brazil	76.7	660,000
China	221.1	840,000
Egypt	34.9	12,000
Ghana	376.1	350,000
India	312.2	5,100,000
Indonesia	275.2	110,000
Iran	35.3	31,000
Iraq	199.5	<500*
Malaysia	132.7	52,000
Mozambique	635.1	1,300,000
Nigeria	531.3	3,600,000
Pakistan	328.7	74,000
Sierra Leone	847.3	NA
South Africa	669.9	5,300,000
Sri Lanka	90.9	3,500
Thailand	207.7	570,000
UAE	25.9	NA

* range only available
Sources: World Health Organization (2006), Core Health Indicators, www.who.int;
Report on the global AIDS epidemic – tables (2004), www.unaids.org/bangkok2004/
GAR2004 htm/GAR2004 32 en.htm; Avert (2006), *World HIV and AIDS Statistics*,
September 2005, 5http://www.avert.org/worldstats.htm

Housing

Two main aspects of this problem are important: the quality of housing and its location. For the first 100 million people have no shelter at all and a further 1 billion are inadequately housed. For the second, most of the world's population still live in rural areas. However, many of them are landless, or nearly so, and hence have little to hold them there. Their natural course is to migrate to the big cities.

In 1950 only New York had more than 10 million inhabitants; by 1970 two Asian cities, Tokyo and Shanghai, had grown that large. Two decades later, in 1990, 13 urban agglomerations had at least 10 million residents, and that number is projected to double by 2010, to 26. All but one of the new cities are in the less developed regions. Nine of the 13 largest urban agglomerations in 1990 were in the less developed regions; the proportion is expected to increase to 21 of 26 in 2010 (UNDP 2000).

It is already difficult adequately to describe the extent of the pollution in downtown Mexico City. The air is thick with photochemical smog generated by cars, diesel engines and industrial machinery. Since the city was built on a dried-up lake bed the city centre has sunk by some 5 m and sewage has to be pumped uphill to get it out of the way. With such serious problems of pollution the future could be horrendous. It is even possible to contract hepatitis 'A' in Mexico City from the windblown faecal dust from the city's sewage farms. As noted above, overcrowding, most likely in urban areas, enormously increases the spread of air-borne diseases such as TB and diphtheria.

In rural areas, on the other hand, poverty and the poor standard of housing facilitate the spread of sicknesses often unknown to the urban dweller. Thus in rural Argentina dirt floors allow the spread of Chagas disease, a tick-borne parasitic illness. An additional hazard is that in many parts of the world humans have traditionally shared their homes with other animals, including pigs and chickens. All three of the major influenza pandemics of the twentieth century are now known to have originated in China, when a disease common among poultry successfully crossed the species barrier and spread rapidly among human populations across the globe. Pure self-interest, therefore, should have required the AICs to spend some of their wealth on combating poverty in the developing world. Otherwise the crisis of the developing world can all too easily become the crisis of civilisation as a whole.

Case study 3.3   **Bird flu**

Bird flu is an infection caused by avian (bird) influenza (flu) viruses. These viruses occur naturally among birds. Wild birds worldwide carry the viruses in their intestines, and may not contract the disease themselves. However, bird flu is very contagious among birds. Hence it can and does spread to domesticated birds, including chickens, ducks and turkeys. The result is that the birds become very sick and often die.

There are many different subtypes of bird flu viruses known. These sub-types differ because of certain proteins on the surface of the flu A virus called hemagglutinin (HA) and neuraminidase (NA). All sub-types of flu A viruses can be found in birds. However, when we talk about 'bird flu' viruses, we are referring to those flu A sub-types that continue to occur mainly in birds. They do not usually infect humans, even though we know they can do so. When we talk about 'human flu viruses' we are referring to those sub-types that occur widely in humans. There are currently only three known sub-types of human flu viruses (H1N1, H1N2, and H3N2 – the H2 type that caused the 1957 outbreak now exists only in laboratories). However, it is now generally believed that some genetic parts of current human flu viruses came from birds originally.

The risk from bird flu is normally low to most people because the bird viruses do not usually cross the species barrier to infect humans. However, during an outbreak of bird flu among poultry (domesticated chicken, ducks, turkeys), there is a possible risk to people. Two classes of people are at special risk: those who have contact with infected birds or surfaces that have been contaminated with excretions from infected birds, and those who live in close proximity to infected livestock, as is particularly the case in developing countries. This raises an additional danger, that of transmission ▶

Case study 3.3 continued

between humans. Flu viruses are constantly changing, and so bird viruses could adapt not just to infect individuals but also to spread among humans. As the mortality rate among victims of bird flu has been very high, infection itself is bad enough. There is particular risk if an individual who contracts bird flu is already carrying human flu viruses, as the viruses are then able to exchange genetic material creating a new strain to which humans do not have immunity, and there is strong evidence that this is what happened with each of the great influenza pandemics of the twentieth century.

The oldest record of a bird flu outbreak having an impact on human health was the 1918 human flu pandemic. This is believed to have originated in China as the result of a bird flu virus combining its genetic material with a human flu virus, thus becoming very infectious to humans. Its effects in Europe and the United States were devastating because of the aftermath of the Great War; however it also killed a great many people in China and India. After 1918, H1 flu evolved into an 'ordinary' flu, and continued to circulate.

The 1957 pandemic started in China before spreading worldwide, killing an estimated 2 million or more people. It was triggered by the hybridisation of human H1 flu with flu viruses from birds which carried another surface protein, H2. It was more lethal than the then-circulating H1 strains because no human had ever encountered the H2 protein before, and so lacked any immunity to the new strain. Furthermore, travel had become much easier, enabling the virus to spread over large distances undetected. After 1957, all traces of H1 flu in humans disappeared and were replaced by H2 strains, to which, however, again most people had developed a degree of immunity.

A similar process occurred again in 1968, when another hybrid virus emerged in China carrying a third haemagglutinin, H3. This caused the 'Hong Kong flu' pandemic, which killed an estimated one million people worldwide. But in turn, after 1968, H2 flu disappeared – so anyone born after this year will have no immunity to H2 flu in the event of a future outbreak.

The H5N1 virus does not usually infect humans. In 1997, however, the first case of spread from a bird to a human was seen during an outbreak of bird flu in poultry in Hong Kong. The virus caused severe respiratory illness in 18 people, six of whom died. The authorities responded with a mass cull of all poultry which most experts agree was successful in averting a new pandemic. However, new outbreaks of H5N1 occurred among poultry in eight countries in Asia (Cambodia, China, Indonesia, Japan, Laos, South Korea, Thailand, and Vietnam) during late 2003 and early 2004. At that time, more than 100 million birds in the affected countries either died from the disease or were killed in order to try to control the outbreak. By March 2004, the outbreak was reported to be under control. But during this wave 35 human cases were confirmed in Vietnam, Thailand and Cambodia, of whom 24 died.

Beginning in late June 2004, however, new deadly outbreaks of H5N1 among poultry were reported by several countries in Asia (Cambodia, China, Indonesia, Malaysia, Thailand, and Vietnam). During August to October 2004, sporadic human cases of H5N1 were reported in Vietnam and Thailand. Of particular note is one isolated instance of probable limited human-to-human transmission occurring in Thailand in September 2004. However at this stage there were only nine new human cases reported, of whom eight died.

▶

Case study 3.3 continued

Since December 2004, a resurgence of poultry outbreaks and human cases have been reported in Vietnam. On 2 February 2005, the first human case of avian influenza A (H5N1) infection from Cambodia was reported. In late March 2005, state media in the Democratic People's Republic of Korea (North Korea) officially reported the country's first outbreak of avian influenza A H7 in poultry. On 21 July 2005, the first laboratory-confirmed human case of avian influenza A (H5N1) in Indonesia was reported. Between 16 December 2004 and August 2005 the WHO recorded 68 new human cases, of whom 25 died, giving an overall mortality rate of some 50 per cent. By February 2006 the first cases in domesticated poultry had been reported from France.

Because of the instability of flu viruses, prevention is very difficult. Culling has a very high political and economic cost, and is in any case very difficult to enforce in developing countries: the case of Hong Kong was unique. With small numbers of birds widely owned enforcing a quarantine is very problematic, and reports from Russia in September 2005 suggest that the virus may have spread westwards carried by migratory wild birds. To vaccinate those at highest risk, those doing the culling, with human flu vaccine may have little effect on them but at least it could avert the danger of exchange of genetic material. Vaccinating the birds themselves against the bird flu virus remains controversial as an effective means of controlling the disease since there are so many varieties of bird flu. In 1997, the Chinese government decided to vaccinate poultry in order to limit the spread of the disease. However, in retrospect it appears this decision may have in fact contributed to the spread of the disease, since an ineffective vaccine can allow a virus to replicate without birds or animals showing any symptoms, a phenomenon known as a 'silent epidemic'. Lastly, H5N1, the bird flu virus responsible for the recent outbreaks in Asia, has been found to be resistant to the two oldest and cheapest flu drugs available, namely rimantidine and amantidine. Researchers with Australia's Commonwealth Scientific and Industrial Research Organization claim that flu drugs Relenza (zanamivir) and Tamiflu (oseltamivir) are effective treatments against the disease. But there is a worry that anti-viral drugs are expensive and in limited supply, and in any case may not work.

Education

At first sight, education might not appear to be as essential a need as water, food or shelter – or medical care. However, education plays a vital role in enabling human beings to become part of and work within modern society. It is of course inseparable from health issues, in particular family planning and thus population growth. As the British trade union slogan has it: 'If you think education is expensive, try ignorance.'

The availability of education is measured in various ways: by the percentage of children who attend school, by the mean number of years of schooling they receive, by the proportion of government expenditure devoted to education

Table 3.7   Basic needs satisfaction, 1950–95

Life expectancy up generally by over 50 per cent
- but in 70s in Argentina, Cuba, Sri Lanka;
- in 40s in SSA (less in Afghanistan);
- variations within countries, e.g. Mexico, poor live 20 years less than rich.

Food production has exceeded population growth, except in SSA
- food availability per head up from 1,957 to 2,480 calories;
- but 20 per cent of the world's population remains undernourished;
- perhaps 40 per cent (2 billion people) suffer from serious deficiencies.

Infant mortality (U5) down from world average 295 to 100
- but Cuba 17, Jamaica 18 – Sierra Leone 284, Niger 320.

Literacy has doubled since 1950
- two-thirds of all adults now literate;
- but regional and gender inequalities remain;
- doubling of women in secondary education achieved in Thailand, Malaysia, Singapore, South Korea – but what about costs?

and, above all, by **literacy** – the percentage of the population that can read and write, though this is not an easy figure to determine accurately.

In the developing world, 30 per cent of children aged 6–11 and 60 per cent of youngsters aged 12–17 do not attend school. However, much depends on the policies pursued by national and state governments. Thus in the State of Kerala in India there is 87 per cent adult female literacy, compared with only 29 per cent for India generally, and 94 per cent adult male literacy, which is much higher than in any other low-income region or country. In middle-income Brazil, where only 3 per cent of government expenditure goes on education, less than a quarter of primary school entrants successfully complete their courses. This compares very unfavourably with a much poorer country such as Sri Lanka which spends a far greater proportion on educating its children and where nearly 9 out of 10 successfully complete their primary school courses. Hence in Sri Lanka, literacy rates are much higher than they are in Brazil and this is reflected in Sri Lanka's far better performance on all the social indicators (see Table 3.7).

Population growth

In April 1992 a UN Report saw population growth as the greatest threat to humanity. This view was shared by many of the world's leaders, notably the Prince of Wales, who said that same month: 'we will not slow the birth rate much until we find ways of addressing poverty; and we will not protect the environment until we address the issues of population growth and poverty in the same breath'.

However, leaders from the First World were unsuccessful in their efforts to make population control a central theme of the Earth Summit. Their argument stemmed from the Malthusian view, which had become received wisdom in the Western industrial nations, that increased population will at some stage confront finite world resources. It was publicly resented by much of the developing world, and a great deal of time was wasted on a sterile debate about whether developing world population or First World consumption was a more serious threat. Since the two are not mutually exclusive, the debate as such cannot have an outcome.

Population growth is highest in the countries of the developing world as the figures for average population growth 1995–2000 by continents shows: Africa 2.37 per cent per year, North America 0.79 per cent, South America 1.5 per cent, Asia 1.38 per cent, Europe 0.03 per cent (UNDP 2006). Average population growth 2000–5 by continent was: Africa 2.21 per cent per year, North America 0.71 per cent, South America 1.5 per cent, Asia 1.26 per cent, Europe –0.08 per cent, world 1.27 per cent. Population growth places serious strains on the ability of developing world countries to feed, clothe and house their populations. But population is also a resource: where capital is scarce, labour is cheap (Boserup 1981). So the balance from a purely economic point of view is not clear-cut. But two much more immediate reasons for population control that are usually cited in Malthusian lines of argument are harder to dispute. Population control directly acts to raise the quality of women's lives. By facilitating the spacing out of families it indirectly contributes to the better health of children also.

Population growth in the South is an issue in the North because it threatens northern lifestyles through environmental pressures. Perhaps more seriously, it promotes a fortress mentality in response to refugees' desire to escape, whether from persecution or from poverty.

There has in recent years been a vigorous debate as to whether poverty stimulates population growth. However, recent evidence is that, although birth rate drops dramatically once IMR is reduced, it is not poverty as such but the availability at a reasonable cost of means of artificial birth control that has the most immediate relevance to population growth. Thirteen (rich) nations have already achieved zero population growth. But 4.3 billion people or 78 per cent of the world's population were already living in developing countries in 1995, and on current trends there will be 5.9 billion or 82 per cent by 2015 (UNDP 1998). The developing world has 90 per cent of the world's population growth. Hence the world population, growing by 100 million people a year at present, is expected to rise by 2050 to around 9 billion. Without natural disaster or human intervention or both it will probably not level off until it reaches 14 billion, nearly three times today's level.

Interpreting the consequences of this growth, however, is more problematic. The present rate of population growth in the developing world alone would mean a 75 per cent increase in developing world energy consumption by 2025, even at present inadequate per capita levels. It is also possible to argue that

Plate 6   Urban school: Brazil

population is only a problem in relation to use of the world's resources. Since the developing world currently only uses about 20 per cent of the world's resources, it is if anything underpopulated, so population is not an issue. The population of the developing world is not expected to grow enough to consume as much as the North in the foreseeable future. Hence population will probably never have the equivalent environmental impact of northern consumption as the South's consumption is not increasing at a sufficient rate to do so.

If we look at contribution to global toxicity, then we find that the population of rich countries is contributing some ten times the per capita municipal/ industrial waste of those of the developing countries. It has been suggested that if I = impact on the environment, P = population, A = affluence, T = technology, then I = P × A × T (*New Internationalist*, September 1992: 8). Although the linear equation may seem simplistic at first glance, it does seem reasonable to suppose that affluence and technology operate as multipliers, because consumption increases with affluence and because increased access to advanced technology increases the use of natural resources.

On the other hand, up to a point, affluence can increase the carrying capacity of land: that is to say, the numbers which can be supported without threatening an area's capacity to do so in the future. So its absence exacerbates the problems of population increase to much of the developing world. Population increase is a problem in Africa south of the Sahara (SSA) because the carrying capacity of its land is low, not because population density is particularly high – there population density is less than 20 persons per km², while that of The Netherlands is more than 400 persons per km². However, the case of SSA is illuminating also because it demonstrates that the question of population distribution is vital to any consideration of the matter. SSA has overpopulated regions where carrying capacity is less than the population seeking a living there, especially in its vast and growing cities, in crowded coastal areas and in the most marginal highland ecosystems. At the same time there are enormous uncultivated and underpopulated fertile tropical areas with as yet underutilised carrying capacities. Despite this Africa has long been the most deprived area of the world (Thrift 1986; Timberlake 1985) and all the signs are that matters are going to get much worse.

There are a number of factors that can be shown to reduce population growth:

- urbanisation, which raises the cost of child-rearing at the same time as reducing the pressure for child labour;
- a reduced infant mortality rate, especially when resulting from better access to clean water;
- improved health care, which reduces fear of destitution in old age etc. and includes family planning, which enables parents to space out their families with resulting improvement in maternal health;
- female literacy, which gives more earning opportunities for women, tending to delay marriage as well as giving incentives to have smaller families.

Only 30 per cent of couples in the developing world outside China who wish to use artificial methods of birth control have access to contraceptives. In China the regime has tried in urban areas to enforce a single child policy, with various sanctions against couples who produce two children. However, this has created a new social problem, that of over-cosseted offspring and the potential problem of later dependency ratios.

The View from the Ground

By *Madeleine Bunting, The Guardian*, Monday, 19 December 2005: 23

The World Pays a Heavy Price for our Cheap Christmas Miracles

For frazzled parents, shops such as Primark offer a bonanza of spectacularly cheap clothing. You can do a bulk-buy of presents for a brood of children in one trip and still have change from a £50 note. Those seams might unravel before too long, but it looks glam enough to last the Christmas holidays. The details – the stitching and embroidery – come at ridiculously low prices. Never mind the babe in the manger; this is the kind of Christmas miracle that means glad tidings of great joy for shoppers.

Now fast forward to next Christmas or the one after. By then the chances are that a huge proportion of these Christmas presents will already have been thrown out. The worst possible scenario is that some of this mountain of clothing will be rotting in landfill sites. The British throw about a million tonnes of clothing straight into the dustbin every year, and only 10 per cent of our discarded clothing is reused here. Some will go into car-seat filling, but it is more likely to be shipped by the tonne to developing countries, many in Africa, as part of a huge global trade in second-hand clothes.

The roads through the barrios – shanty towns – of Maputo, Mozambique, are lined with stalls selling second-hand clothes. In one area carts are lined up alongside each other full of trainers. A bit further along there are racks of jeans, and beyond, more racks of shirts and T-shirts. It goes on for mile after mile like some sort of drive-through open-air shopping mall. Curtains, pillowcases, duvet covers, towels – you name it, every kind of textile and footwear is on sale here. All around is the deafening hubbub of radios blaring and traders bargaining with their customers in this second-hand clothes trade, which is central to the street economy of many developing countries.

Put aside the qualms about Africa dressing itself in western castoffs and what's the problem, some ask. On the positive side, a lot of people in Asia get jobs making the clothes; westerners get a few months or a year of the novelty of a new style and then pass it on; a Mozambican gets a still-decent piece of clothing at a cost she can afford.

But there is a problem, argues the American economist Juliet Schor in new research in which she coins the phrase the 'imperial consumer'. She claims that rising living standards in the west are increasingly dependent on cheap goods that do not pay their ecological and social costs. Because the goods are so cheap, consumers buy more of them, which is driving up the ecological costs. She points to the fact that the cost of clothing fell in the US in the 90s as huge quantities of cheap – often Chinese–made – goods were imported. As a result, hyper-consumption boomed, so that by 2002 the US was importing 48.3 pieces of clothing per person per year. (The trend for toys was similar, so that each child had 69 new toys each year by 2001.) At the same time, the bottom fell out of the US second-hand clothing market as the volume of dumped US clothes soared.

There are high ecological costs to this accelerating global cycle of new and discarded clothes. One doesn't usually see cotton as a 'dirty' product like plastics, but in fact cultivation involves high concentrations of fertiliser, herbicide and pesticide. Cotton accounts for only 2.5 per cent of all agricultural land use, but for 22.5 per cent of all insecticides applied in agriculture. During the processing many more chemicals are used in the bleaching and dyeing. Finally, every stage of cotton agriculture and processing is water-intensive – often in areas of the globe where water is not in plentiful supply. If the T-shirt is going to end up in a landfill after a couple of outings, it represents a spectacular waste of environmental resources of soil and water.

* * * * * * * * *

Meanwhile, at the other end of the global cycle, the second-hand clothes swamping developing countries kill off the chance of any indigenous clothing industry. In Maputo there are very few new clothes shops and little hope of setting up an indigenous textile industry as part of Mozambique's post-civil-war economic rehabilitation. Textile production has always been a vital stepping stone in industrialisation (it was for us) because it's low-skill and requires only a low capital investment, but the vibrant trade in second-hand clothes will ensure that it's not one Mozambique will be able to use.

At each point in the global clothing trade the room for manoeuvre has been cut, locking manufacturers and their employees into a system from which they extract a precarious living, and locking millions of Africans into wearing western hand-me-downs.

Sitting in prime position at the top of the system is the west, greedily consuming two-thirds of the annual $1 trillion of clothing produced globally. This is the reason why Schor talks of the 'imperial consumer'. She argues that it is only maintained through the exercise of economic and political power such as we have seen in evidence at the World Trade Organization summit in Hong Kong. There, US and EU intransigence produced little to benefit Africa's farmers. While US cotton farmers receive more than $4bn a year in subsidies, at Hong Kong all their government offered were empty gestures that one African representative described as 'like sticking a Band-Aid on a wooden leg'. A global trade is rigged to provide us with Christmas miracles.

See also: Schor (1998)

Key terms

agribusiness – term used to describe the relationship between intensive agriculture and the large corporations who develop and market new seed varieties etc. and/or buy up the crop for onward sale

basic needs – requirements for a reasonable existence: clean water, good food, proper sanitation and health facilities, reasonable housing, education

demonstration effect – changes in the behaviour of individuals or groups caused solely by observing the actions of others and their consequences

famine – widespread sickness and death as a result of food scarcity

Green Revolution – the transformation in agriculture brought about by the development and marketing of new crop varieties

infant mortality rate (IMR) – the number of children per 1,000 who die in the first year of life

internal transfers – payments from public funds intended to improve the condition of the poor

life expectancy – at a given age (usually birth), the number of years the average person may be expected to live

literacy – the percentage of a population that can read and write by a specified age

malnutrition – chronic ill health caused by persistent lack of food or of the balanced diet needed to sustain growth and development

poverty – lack of the money or resources needed to meet basic needs

salination – build-up of salts in the soil as a result of inefficient drainage or excessive dependence on irrigation

tropical storms – storms of great force arising in the equatorial regions which may evolve into hurricanes, cyclones or typhoons

waterlogging – excess stagnant water in the soil which prevents most crops from germinating or rots their roots if they have already grown

Questions

1. Why are so many developing states poor?

2. What do we mean by 'basic needs' and why are they often lacking in developing countries?

3. Does the developing world's desire for a better life threaten world stability?

4. What can be done to promote human security in a global economy?

5. Is 'health for all' a realistic target?

6. Why has HIV/AIDS proved to be such a danger to developing countries?

PART II

Social and economic contexts

The economic context

CHAPTER 4

Introduction

Developing countries generally made social and economic progress relative to developed countries between 1945 and 1975. Then there was a decline, followed by a world **recession** lasting from 1980 to 1983, after which the developed countries have been pulling away again, despite a further decline and plunge into another recession, led by the United Kingdom in 1989 (see also Hayter 1983; Adams 1993). Recovery in the early 1990s was accompanied by accelerating liberalisation of economies, which further advantaged the already strong.

The impressive growth in almost all developing world countries between the 1950s and the late 1970s was accompanied by a decline in the proportion, though not the numbers, of developing world populations living in absolute poverty. Agriculture was modernised to some extent almost everywhere by the so-called 'Green Revolution'. Public health and educational provision improved.

However the boom ended as dramatically as it had begun. The trigger was the first **oil shock** of 1973–74. The sudden increase in the price of oil hit developing world countries as well as the advanced industrialised countries (AICs). Unlike the latter, the former were in a weak position to meet the challenge. By the early 1970s private capital flows had far outstripped aid to the developing world and amounted to nearly 70 per cent of the net bilateral flows from industrialised to developing countries. This reflects the growth of **transnational corporations (TNCs)** as well as the involvement in the process of recycling the oil revenues of more than 500 private banks including the very largest in the United States, Japan, Germany, France and the UK. As a result, the 1980s saw net debt transfers of some $40 billion per year from developing to developed countries, a figure in excess of colonial repatriation and more than developing world spending on health and education (Adams 1991).

Foreign investment did encourage some modernisation which was sometimes extended through linkages to the rest of the economy – though it more often promoted the development of 'enclaves' of advanced technology. These limited gains had to be set against outflows in the form of profits, fees and royalties, payments for imported inputs and losses due to transfer pricing by TNCs.

Geographical catastrophes added to economic crisis for some of the developing world. There was drought in Africa and wars in the Congo (now the DRC), the Horn (Somalia and Ethiopia), Angola and Mozambique, fuelled and prolonged by the rivalries of the Cold War. First World greed and incompetence certainly helped cause the devastating impact of the 1980s downturn on the developing world and especially on Africa. But so too did unrealistic hopes and expectations as well as greed and incompetence in the developing world itself. The main problem was that even those rulers of newly independent Africa who wanted economic development (and not all did, for example traditionalists like Dr Hastings Banda of Malawi), believed that all they had to do was to imitate what had been done in Europe and the United States. They were soon to find that the world was a much more complicated place than they had thought.

How is economic policy made?

Many a developing country labours under two great disadvantages from the economic point of view. It is heavily dependent on the export of primary raw materials and has a very weak currency, the value of which is disproportionately affected by changes in the world environment and particularly by changes in world commodity prices (especially the cost of oil). The finance/economy ministry is constantly under attack for the prevailing poverty and has little or no alternative but to do what it is told by the IMF, World Bank, banks etc. If it does, however, there will be riots in the streets and the government may fall. Consequently states are mostly heavily indebted; if they devalue their problems are increased by having to pay back loans, not in their own currency, but in dollars which have just become more expensive (see Table 4.1). Some of the consequences are:

(a) Their presidents serve for a limited period of office and if permitted re-election this tends to be a dominant consideration in their tactics. If dependent on popular choice, they will take great care not to alienate potentially powerful support groups.
(b) Ministers are vulnerable to political unpopularity and no one wants to raise taxes (even if the army will let them . . .).
(c) To get elected politicians in the past encouraged the electorate to look to the state for help; once in power they find that there is no help they can give.

Table 4.1   Total external debt of selected states, 1992

RANGE	External debt ($m)	Debt per capita ($)
LOW INCOME		
1 Mozambique	4,929	298
18 India	76,983	303
21 Nigeria	30,959	270
27 Ghana	4,275	59
28 China	69,321	367
32 Sri Lanka	6,401	457
37 Indonesia	84,385	87
LOWER MIDDLE INCOME		
43 Côte d'Ivoire	17,997	1,395
44 Bolivia	4,243	565
68 Jamaica	4,303	1,792
75 Thailand	14,727	253
80 Turkey	54,772	936
85 Chile	19,360	1,423
UPPER MIDDLE INCOME		
80 S. Africa	–	–
92 Brazil	121,110	786
99 Mexico	113,378	1,333
100 Trinidad & Tobago	2,262	1,740
102 Argentina	67,569	2,401
107 Greece	–	–
108 Portugal	32,046	3,270
109 Saudi Arabia	–	–
HIGH INCOME		
110 Ireland		
112 Israel		
116 Australia		
117 UK		
124 France		
127 USA		
131 Japan		
132 Switzerland		

Source: World Bank (1994)

(d) **Privatisation** is no longer a solution. Many state resources were sold off at knockdown prices in the 1980s and 1990s; there is now little or nothing left to sell.

(e) In the rare event of a discovery of important new resources this encourages a bonanza mentality. Governments easily persuade themselves that 'with one bound they will be free'. Important historical examples are the discovery of new oilfields in Mexico in the 1970s, and the collapse of the economy of Sierra Leone with the **deregulation** of the diamond industry.

Plate 7 Avellaneda Bridge: declining traditional industry, Argentina

Hence policy is basically about the avoidance of decisions; any decision is as likely to be wrong as it is right. To do nothing will not incur blame; to make the wrong decision is to court political oblivion.

In the study of Argentina that follows, it should be borne in mind that this is not a typical developing country, even if there were such a thing, since according to the World Bank Argentina is one of the few Latin American states classified as an upper middle-income country. But the fact that its experience has more in common with poverty-stricken Bolivia next door than with that of an AIC such as Britain or France make its experience particularly interesting.

The View from the Ground

The Argentine Problem

Argentina, the eighth largest country in the world, presents many paradoxes. With an area of some 2,767,000 km^2 it had a population of only 38 million in 2003. It is incredibly rich in agricultural land: the vast pampa, stretching westward between Buenos Aires and the Andes, makes Argentina one of the world's few grain-exporting nations and the only one in the Southern Hemisphere. Yet some three-fifths of the population live and work in the sophisticated urban environment of Greater Buenos Aires. Argentina is also self-sufficient in oil and natural gas and wealthy in mineral resources. Although comparable in size with Australia, however, it has not only failed to develop along the same lines but in 1930 entered on a long period of decline. In 1930 Argentina was the seventh richest country in the world. By 1980 it was seventy-seventh, and its rulers, it seemed, were resigned to permanent membership of the Third World. A literate and sophisticated people had been subjected to an exceptionally brutal military dictatorship. 'Argentina,' people said, 'is the land of the future, always has been and always will be.'

The jury is still out on whether the transformation of its economic prospects brought about since the return of demo- *cracy in 1983 can be maintained. Though democracy itself has survived more successfully than anyone expected, the Radical (UCR) government of Raúl Alfonsín was quite unable to grapple successfully with its economic problems, and in 1989 resigned five months early having notched up a record 640,000% inflation in five-and-a-half years.*

Power passed to the charismatic Carlos Menem of the rival Peronist party (PJ). For two years Menem continued a policy of muddling through. But in January 1991 he made a series of ministerial changes which were to transform the country's economic prospects. The new minister of the economy, Domingo Cavallo, proceeded to implement his so-called Convertibility Plan. This had three main planks. The first was the so-called dollarization of the economy, whereby the Argentine economy was linked to the U.S. economy by the establishment of a fixed exchange rate of 10,000 australes (or one new peso) to the U.S. dollar. This brought inflation down into low single figures in a few weeks and some US$20 billion of 'hot money' back into the country. The second was a program of privatization that would reverse forty years of Peronist policy and buy time to fulfil the third, a plan to improve government finances by raising revenue by collecting taxes that were widely evaded. By the time of Menem's first state visit to the United States in November, he was celebrated as Latin America's leading free-market reformer and U.S. ally. As a result, in March 1992 Menem secured a promise of debt reduction under the Brady Initiative. Argentina's accumulated debt was reduced from over US$60 billion to some $48 billion.

In the event, the presidential elections of 1995 were overshadowed by the impact on the economy of the Mexican economic crisis (the 'tequila effect'). Unemployment, which rose between April and July from 12.5% to 18.6% of the economically active population, was the subject of a $1.5 billion initiative. Yet it was not the opposition Radical candidate who made the running but a dissident Peronist, who took support from both Radicals and [other] dissident Peronists. So President Menem won re-election decisively, gaining 49.8% of the votes cast in the only round of balloting. The president had carried every province, and his party, the PJ, gained an overall majority of three seats in the 257-seat Chamber of Deputies.

In the aftermath of his victory, President Menem confirmed his intention to retain Cavallo as economy minister. But later in the year tension grew between the two as Cavallo complained publicly of resistance to free-market reform among entrenched interests in government. Eventually, in 1996, Cavallo was dismissed – as Menem said: 'ministers are like fuses, they are replaced when worn out'. But his Plan had been so successful, that, even after recession set in in 1997, the government was reluctant to contemplate devaluation. At the same time falling revenues, and the inability to control expenditure by the provincial governments, created a widening fiscal gap, which could only be filled by increasing borrowing. Meanwhile though Menem was able to see out his second term, his efforts to prevent Governor Duhalde from succeeding him

further split the Peronists, while Cavallo formed a new party, Action for the Republic, and attracted some support. Hence at the 1999 elections, the conservative UCR Mayor of Buenos Aires, Fernando De la Rúa Bruno, heading an Alliance between UCR and the dissident former Peronists (Frepaso), won the presidency decisively. The PJ lost control of the Chamber of Deputies, but retained its majority in the Senate.

Unfortunately by the time that De la Rúa took office the country was already deep in recession. Unemployment was reaching record levels. In March 2001, therefore, he brought Cavallo back for a second spell as Economy Minister. This appointment stabilised the situation briefly. However the government was so weak that when Cavallo announced his plan to reduce the budget deficit in 2001 by $3 billion it was to be achieved by tax increases rather than by spending cuts, which would have involved dismissing public sector workers, cutting their salaries or reducing state retirement benefits. Confidence was further undermined by Cavallo's frenetic activity, constantly unveiling new measures and holding press conferences three times a day. After a deal with 14 powerful provincial governors, in July the Senate was finally persuaded to pass a 'zero deficit' law which was unlikely to have any practical effect. With this as an excuse, in August the IMF reluctantly agreed to disburse $1.2 billion due in September and even lend a further $8 billion, despite clear signs that the situation was already out of control and in the face of strong reservations of the Bush Administration in the USA, who wanted to make an example of Argentina to other states to pay their debts.

At the mid-term elections on 14 October the electorate showed their anger in the most unmistakable way, by giving the opposition Peronists a majority in both houses of Congress. From there they watched as Cavallo made a desperate effort to avoid default. In response to a massive run on the banks, on 30 November the government imposed limits both on cash withdrawals (the *corralito*) and on capital movements, effectively ending convertibility. Throwing gasoline on the flames, the IMF in response held back the $1.3 billion due to be paid in December. At the weekend of 15/16 December public order began to break down as desperate people started to loot supermarkets. Others banged empty pots (*cacerolazo*) and hammered on the shutters of the banks in frustration. Huge crowds collected in front of the presidential palace in the Plaza de Mayo shouting for the government to go. Heavy-handed police intervention claimed 25 lives, injured hundreds and led to thousands of arrests but only made matters worse. Finally on 20 December President de la Rúa asked the Peronists to join a government of national unity. They prudently refused. He resigned and was lifted off the roof of the Casa Rosada and into safety by helicopter while Cavallo, in fear of his life, fled to Patagonia.

Over the next two weeks, five different people served as interim president. When on 1 January 2002 the Peronist-dominated Congress chose Eduardo Duhalde to serve out De la Rúa's term, therefore, the country had already gone into default on its debt. Congress granted the new President emergency powers and the peso was devalued on 7 January. But the peso's value could not be sustained; the stock market re-opened on 17 January to a sharp fall and violent demonstrations continued across the country at the shortage of cash brought about by the corralito. When on 9 February the government unveiled plans to cut the already spartan federal budget by $370 million some 3,000 demonstrators again filled the Plaza de Mayo for a new cacerolazo. In response the government restored convertibility, and agreed to allow people at least to cash their pay checks in full.

Fresh rioting followed. Yet at the beginning of April Argentina was given the uncompromising message by the IMF that no further help would be available unless even more drastic cuts were forthcoming. On Monday, 22 April, therefore, the banks were all closed again by government decree. The following day the Economy Minister resigned together with most of the rest of the Cabinet after failing to win support for an emergency plan to switch frozen bank deposits for government bonds. At that point the peso had fallen from par to 3.50 pesos to the US dollar, having lost approximately a further 69% of its value since the beginning of the year. The rate of inflation had risen to 2% p.a., millions had effectively lost their savings, public sector workers were rioting, and half the population was said to be living below the national poverty line. In consequence there had been a steep rise in robberies, kidnappings and other crimes which the underpaid police were either unable or unwilling to combat. Thieves who stole nearly 3,000 miles of copper wire between January and September seriously disrupted the telephone service and utility workers were physically attacked when they tried to carry out repairs.

To his credit, President Duhalde remained calm and avoided inflammatory language and throughout constitutional processes were maintained. By the time elections came round in March 2003 the economy had fallen so far that it was already beginning to pick up. With Duhalde himself ruled out, the PJ chose Néstor Kirchner, the charismatic and financially successful Governor of Santa Cruz, as their presidential candidate. Menem, who had been scheming for re-election, ungraciously withdrew. But Kirchner's victory gave Argentina a promising start in trying to rebuild on more realistic lines.

Source: Calvert (2005a)

Africa: globalisation and marginalisation

The **decolonisation** of Africa began in 1957 with the independence of the British West African territory of the Gold Coast, which assumed the name Ghana. In the following year Guinea, which had been the only French territory not to vote for the new French constitution, was summarily ejected from the French community. However even the independence of the much larger federal state of Nigeria in 1960 was overshadowed by the decision of President Charles de Gaulle to grant independence to all the remaining French territories in Africa south of the Sahara, a move which it was hoped would enable France more easily to maintain its position in Algeria. In expectation of this, the boundaries were first adjusted so that the French government could retain control of the oilfields.

It was not at all surprising that the European colonial powers would wish to continue to maintain profitable commercial relations with their former colonies even after independence. The profits made by their firms trading in those colonies had been considerable and this led the rulers to make two incorrect assumptions. On the one hand they assumed that the wealth of the trading companies could after independence simply be diverted into investment in growth in other areas. On the other they assumed that once deprived of their special position, the companies would want to go on trading with them no matter what.

In 1957 the prevailing view among economists was that state investment in basic industries could lead to successful industrialisation and, beyond a certain point, to self-sustaining economic growth. The early history of independent Ghana illustrates the hopes and failures associated with the **'take-off' model of development** popularised by W.W. Rostow.

Case study 4.1   **Ghana**

Ghana's future leader, Kwame Nkrumah, returned in 1947 to the Gold Coast, as it was then known, from the USA where he had been a postgraduate student and had taken his doctorate. By 1949 he had formed his own political party (CPP) seeking immediate independence from Britain which had been the colonial power for more than a century. In 1951 the Gold Coast held its first elections. Nearly a million people voted. Although Nkrumah himself was still in gaol, his party swept to power and he became prime minister in an elected government which had full internal self-government although Britain still controlled foreign and defence policy. In 1957 he became the first leader of a newly independent Black African state and set out to turn Ghana into a modern industrial utopia.

The British had planned the Volta dam to provide hydro-electric power to smelt aluminium, but in 1956 cancelled the project, saying it was too expensive. Nkrumah saw the Volta dam as a means to the power needed to fuel the modernisation of Ghana. It would be a source of power for comprehensive development as well as the means to irrigate the Accra plains. Eisenhower, anxious that Ghana should be

▶

Case study 4.1 continued

pro-United States in the Cold War, suggested that US aluminium manufacturers might be interested in supporting the Volta scheme. In 1958 Kaiser Industries agreed to build a smelter in Ghana and to buy the electricity generated by the scheme. Nkrumah asked the World Bank for £30 million, the largest loan ever requested down to that time.

In accordance with the 'take-off' model, power on a massive scale was just what was needed to bring about industrialisation and therefore development. In 1960 the World Bank approved the scheme in principle but expressed some reservations about the prices Kaiser had agreed to pay to Ghana for energy to run the smelter. The World Bank took the view that these prices must be higher if Ghana was to have a chance of realising the development plans which were an integral part of the Volta River scheme. Kaiser were determined not to pay more than the lowest rates available anywhere in the world. Nkrumah had little option but to agree to Kaiser's price or Kaiser would pull out and the dam would not be built.

Nkrumah wanted to keep Ghana out of the Cold War tensions, but the United States saw the dam and his developmental aspirations as the means to win him over. The US had agreed to lend millions to the scheme and used these loans to pressure Nkrumah into accepting US policies. Hence the Volta River scheme was shaped by political and economic pressures, not by Nkrumah's idealism. As an investment, Ghana was initially seen as an excellent prospect. The colonial power, Britain, had left it a good infrastructure and an educated population. Thus the dam got built.

Construction of the Volta dam took four years. The process came to illustrate the high levels of corruption in Ghana. It was not just that there were corrupt government officials, but also corrupt foreign suppliers who would do anything to make a sale. European industrialists seeking to sell their products in Ghana found that the easy way was to offer a bribe and bribery soon became the business culture of Accra. One result was a rush to sell Ghana anything no matter how inappropriate. The most grandiose development schemes were encouraged by foreign suppliers and domestic vested interests and taken up by local politicians eager to win popular support. Most proved expensive and some unviable.

The key to Ghana's strong economic position was cocoa. However, in 1964 cocoa prices collapsed and since cocoa was Ghana's main source of foreign exchange, Ghana, which had been one of the richest countries in Africa, slid into debt. Nkrumah's vision was now beginning to be seen as megalomania. Only one month after the dam was finished in 1966 the armed forces took over the government while Nkrumah was abroad. Nkrumah took refuge in Guinea where he died in 1972.

Significantly, therefore, the post-Nkrumah years were also a period of economic failure. The Kaiser aluminium plant flourished and the World Bank loan was paid off with the money paid for power, but as electricity prices rose everywhere in the 1970s Kaiser still paid very little. In 1979 it looked as if things might change. Flt Lt Jerry Rawlings took power in the seventh coup since Nkrumah and he was determined to get more from the Kaiser smelter. In 1983 the Ghanaian government tried to get Kaiser to renegotiate prices by allowing rumours of nationalisation to circulate and by keeping the dam shut down until Kaiser agreed, and two years later, in 1985, a new agreement was signed which raised prices threefold (*Assignment*: 'Pandora's Box', BBC Television, 1993).

Cash crops

The idea of using the profits from a successful agricultural economy to fund industrialisation was neither odd nor eccentric. It was the wealth generated by the **agricultural revolution** of the early eighteenth century that enabled Britain to begin its path towards industrialisation. The difference was that in the case of the newly independent countries they had lost the protected market they had previously enjoyed and were now forced to compete in the world export market. Starting in the 1930s, exporting countries had been able to arrange cartels to stabilise the export prices of some of their commodities. Sugar and coffee were examples, but not cocoa. After 1945 world cocoa prices rose steadily until 1953–54 and then fell back as new planting came into production. But when prices suddenly doubled in 1958 it was all too easily assumed that this state of affairs would last, while in fact a steady fall followed into the early 1960s (Weymar 1968).

It was not until 1973 that the International Cocoa Organization (ICCO) was established in order to administer the first International Cocoa Agreement, that of 1972. The agreements were concluded among the governments of cocoa-producing and cocoa-consuming countries, under the auspices of the UN, and the most important provision was the maintenance of buffer stocks to try to even out fluctuations in prices. Exporting members of the ICCO in mid-2005 were Brazil, Cameroon, Côte d'Ivoire, Dominican Republic, Ecuador, Gabon, Ghana, Malaysia, Nigeria, Papua New Guinea, Togo, Trinidad & Tobago and Venezuela (ICCO 2005). However, the idea of maintaining steady prices is contrary to the more recent economic orthodoxy of the Washington consensus. The buffer stock provisions were dropped from the 1993 agreement and were absent from the most recent one, which was concluded in 2001 and came into force in 2003. The lesson is that with advancing globalisation the interests of the producers of primary commodities and the countries in which they live have been increasingly marginalised in favour of the short-term interests of the AICs who call the shots.

Ghana illustrates the problem that the persistence of poverty in Africa is largely the consequence of the persistence of the export-oriented economies established under colonial rule and the resulting dependence on single commodity production of **cash crops**. Other African states particularly dependent on the export of cocoa are Côte d'Ivoire, which is by far the world's largest exporter of cocoa, and Cameroon, the world's fifth largest producer, where cocoa, coffee and cotton account for 40 per cent of export earnings. Nigeria, also a considerable cocoa producer, was historically a major producer of rubber and of palm oil, used in the manufacture of soap and cosmetics as well as for cooking. However, it has been either fortunate or unfortunate to emerge as Africa's biggest producer of petroleum and petroleum products, which in 2004 accounted for 95 per cent of its exports. Rwanda remains dependent on agriculture which accounted for some 70 per cent of export earnings, with tea as the major crop, followed by coffee. Burundi relies on coffee for 50 per cent of export earnings and Ethiopia for 60 per cent. Benin depends on cotton, The Gambia on groundnuts (though tourism is of growing importance). These countries not only rely for their foreign trade on a very narrow productive base, they also do not have the power to make the rules of the global system and must accept what have generally proved to be declining terms of trade. Ghana's economic power does not match that of Nestlé, the company that buys Ghana's cocoa. It is therefore very difficult for it, or for most other African countries, to earn the foreign exchange necessary to provide for the imports its people need and want.

However, it would be a mistake to continue to ascribe this situation, as some do, solely to colonial rule. Independence is now a long time ago, and, as the above examples show, Ethiopia (which was not effectively colonised) suffers from the same problems as other African countries. Before colonisation, settled agriculture had not developed in Africa South of the Sahara owing to a combination of climate and a scarcity of suitable indigenous crops. Millet has a poor yield compared with wheat and especially compared with rice, but the dry cultivation of rice in West Africa gives a much lower yield than wet cultivation in Asia. Consequently cereal production per hectare in Africa is only just over half the world average (Diamond 1998). Of course, much of the better land in countries such as Kenya and Zimbabwe has long been used for cash-cropping for export and this makes the problem worse, by encouraging overproduction on marginal lands with fragile soils and unreliable rainfall and thus accelerating the processes of desertification.

Latin America: the persistence of debt

Dollar surpluses from oil had been loaned to the developing world. They were all too often spent either, as in the case of Mexico or Venezuela, on producing a glut of oil the price of which then collapsed or, as in the case of Argentina or Nigeria, on arms. Between 1975 and 1985 military expenditures accounted for 40 per cent of the increase in debt. By the end of the 1980s annual world military expenditure was of the order of $1,000 billion. Of this 15 per cent was being spent in the developing world where average military spending was 30 per cent more than expenditure on health and education. Often these massive expenditures were being incurred by military governments which had never been elected by their people. For many people this raises an important ethical question. It is hard to see why the mass of the civilian population should later have to pay back the debts contracted by military governments.

In 1981–82 Argentina's military government postponed its **debt service**. However debt did not really become a big issue and the term **debt crisis** did not appear until in August 1982 the two biggest debtors (Brazil and Mexico) suspended interest payments with the risk that in time they might actually default. It was this possibility that shook the stability of the world economy. In 1982, within two days of Mexico's announcement that it could not service its debt, the US government was already putting in place emergency measures. The government of Mexico almost at once agreed to terms that enabled it to reschedule. Financial support came through the IMF with the backing of the US government, worried about the political and financial stability of its southern neighbour. IMF support however was supposed to be backed by long-term adjustment through 'reforms' proposed by IMF technical advisers in consultation with the Mexican government of President Miguel de la Madrid.

These measures included the devaluation of the peso, import liberalisation to force local prices down and 'stabilisation', that is to say, cutting the endemic budget deficit which had led to printing money and therefore to inflation. As in other cases, the IMF recommended that the government balance its books more by reducing expenditure than by increasing revenue, with the rationale that tax rates had to be kept low to encourage compliance and reduce the burden on the most 'dynamic' sectors. However, the Mexican government for political reasons baulked at the advice that because subsidies (on water and electricity) were not targeted they could therefore be safely reduced with a more limited safety net put in place to support the very poorest sectors. Nor initially did they welcome the advice to embark on a far-reaching programme of privatisation, starting with the most obvious assets, the state airlines.

This package became the model for dealing with subsequent cases, in most of which, as in Mexico, governments found themselves able to comply with only part of the strict conditions laid upon them. However, the anxiety of the world financial community was such that when this happened, further adjustments were made and new packages agreed, though inevitably with further costs. Some 25 countries were in arrears a year later but through the cooperation of the debtor nations the creditors had already achieved 15 renegotiations. The process did not always go easily. The new civilian government in Argentina signed a deal with the IMF in 1984 but proved quite unable to meet its targets. In 1985 the incoming government of Alan García in Peru refused to pay more than 10 per cent of its export earnings. Brazil for a time suspended payment to force debt relief but did not get it. And given the weakness of many developing world economies, it was often unrealistic to expect them to pay off their debts without help (see Table 4.2).

On the other hand, this case-by-case handling prevented the debtor countries cooperating with one another, still less, as the banks feared, forming a 'debtors' cartel' (Roett 1985). The fact is that debt empowers creditors and does not empower debtors – unless they are very large debtors and act in concert (see Table 4.3). In practice, the desire to secure a more favourable deal for themselves, the Prisoners' Dilemma, stops them from doing so. Individual debtor countries did call for debt relief, but did not combine to challenge creditors as they wanted to keep contacts with the world financial system in order to be able to arrange new loans. Most of all, they did not want to be

Table 4.2   Debt as percentage of GNP, selected states, 1992

RANGE	External debt ($m)	Debt as % GNP
LOW INCOME		
1 Mozambique	4,929	494.8
18 India	76,983	25.9
21 Nigeria	30,959	108.4
27 Ghana	4,275	39.1
28 China	69,321	12.8
32 Sri Lanka	6,401	41.0
37 Indonesia	84,385	61.9
LOWER MIDDLE INCOME		
43 Côte d'Ivoire	17,997	191.0
44 Bolivia	4,243	61.2
68 Jamaica	4,303	131.7
75 Thailand	14,727	35.2
80 Turkey	54,772	47.8
85 Chile	19,360	48.9
UPPER MIDDLE INCOME		
80 S. Africa	–	–
92 Brazil	121,110	31.2
99 Mexico	113,378	34.1
100 Trinidad & Tobago	2,262	45.7
102 Argentina	67,569	30.3
107 Greece	–	–
108 Portugal	32,046	39.0
109 Saudi Arabia	–	–
HIGH INCOME		
110 Ireland		
112 Israel		
116 Australia		
117 UK		
124 France		
127 USA		
131 Japan		
132 Switzerland		

Source: World Bank (1994)

pariah states denied all access to outside funds and so forced to borrow internally in their own currency. (The only country that has an advantage in this respect is the United States itself. From 1986 on, net US debt was the largest in the world, but this debt was in its own currency, so overseas creditors did not have same power to ensure that it could be repaid, and in fact as of 2006 it has been remorselessly rising.)

Weaknesses in commodity markets coincided with the effects of tight monetarist policies in the industrialised countries and net resource flows were reversed. Africa South of the Sahara was most heavily indebted and hardest hit

Table 4.3 Total identified external debt in excess of US$20 billion, 1986 and 1992

Country	1986	1992
Mexico	108.3	113.1
Brazil	106.3	121.1
South Korea	57.7	43.0
Argentina	49.9	67.6
Indonesia	37.2	84.4
Egypt	37.0	40.0
India	36.4	77.0
Venezuela	29.3	37.2
Israel	*28.8*	*N/A*
Philippines	28.6	32.5
Greece	24.9	N/A
Turkey	23.8	54.7
Chile	22.3	19.4
Portugal	21.6	32.0
Algeria	21.8	26.3
Malaysia	21.5	19.8

Note: High income countries in italics
Source: World Bank, *World Debt Tables* (March 1987), and World Bank (1994)

by interest rate rises. Most of the 26 most severely indebted nations were in that region. The **Group of Seven (G7)** Toronto Protocol allowed rescheduling for these countries and the IMF has similar arrangements, but repayments were still massive in proportion to resources. To make matters worse, half of them were the francophone countries hit by French withdrawal of financial support and consequent forced devaluations in January 1994.

The consequences were drastic. Africa may have lost as much as 30 years of development. For Latin America the 1980s were a 'lost decade'. Net transfers had been positive for Latin America (that is to say, new funds borrowed exceeded debt repayments) until 1983, but the 1980s saw inflation without growth in most of the region. South Asia had borrowed heavily but repayments were more manageable in proportion to their growing economies. Some East Asian countries, on the other hand, enjoyed favourable balance of payments situations, and were largely unaffected by the crisis until the mid-1990s. The debts remain. In 1997 the external debt of countries with a per capita income of $1,500 or less was $2 trillion or $400 per head (*New Internationalist*, 312, May 1999: 18). Servicing them continued to place an immense burden on many of the states of the developing world. In six of the eight years 1990–1997 inclusive, external debt payments (servicing and capital receipts) exceeded receipts from new loans. It is not surprising that the UN Conference on Trade and Development (UNCTAD), NGOs and other groups sought to mark the new millennium with a debt moratorium for the most heavily indebted nations (see Table 4.4).

Table 4.4 World's most indebted states, 1992

Country	Total external debt as % exports	Total external debt as % GNP
22 Nicaragua	3,161.7	750.3
1 Mozambique	994.5	494.8
12 Guinea-Bissau	6,414.2	200.5
43 Côte d'Ivoire	473.7	191.0
3 Tanzania	784.4	177.7
56 Congo	327.6	166.0
60 Jordan	203.1	163.2
31 Mauritania	342.4	158.4
4 Sierra Leone	574.0	158.3
68 Jamaica	148.9	131.7
66 Bulgaria	202.6	124.5
13 Madagascar	649.4	116.8
21 Nigeria	232.5	108.4

Source: World Bank (1994)

Debt has many adverse consequences. It contributes to the pulling apart of the developing world, focuses attention on big debtors to the exclusion of small ones (Costa Rica was unable to get rescheduling on its small debts and was summarily ordered to pay up or face the consequences), and results in a vast increase in poverty. Other factors acting against a satisfactory resolution of the debt problem as far as the developing world is concerned include the policies of TNCs, the growing cost-effectiveness of labour-saving manufacturing technology, the bias of the world trading system against primary products, protectionist measures by developed countries and the policies of the IMF and World Bank through whom creditor countries may intervene in debtor economies to ensure debts are serviced. The IMF's **Heavily Indebted Poorer Countries Initiative**, begun in 1976, required the 40 countries identified as in need of debt relief to meet all the IMF's requirements for six years before any relief would be granted. Since 1996 the debts of HIPCs have increased and by 2000 only one of them had received relief (see Table 4.5).

The ultimate irony was that private banks boosted profits for several years in the mid-1980s and have already been repaid many times over, not least because the money loaned often returned to the lending banks on deposit from the developing world elites to whom it had been lent. Their lending was irresponsible as borrowers were not necessarily elected by their people but the money was loaned to a country with the assumed security that implied, and much of the money was squandered or purloined by the borrowers. It is morally wrong to ask people who had nothing to do with the contracting of the debts to repay them – debt is not a national problem for debtor countries, but rather a burden which falls disproportionately on the poorest and weakest sections of developing societies (see below and Chapter 9).

Table 4.5   World's most indebted states, latest figures

Country	Size of debt (US$)	Latest figures
OVERSEAS DEBT OVER US$ 50 BILLION		
1 **World**	2,000,000,000,000	2002 est.
2 United States	862,000,000,000	1995 est.
3 Brazil	222,400,000,000	2002
4 Australia	176,800,000,000	ye 2002 est.
5 Argentina	155,000,000,000	2001 est.
6 Russia	153,500,000,000	ye 2002
7 Mexico	150,000,000,000	2000 est.
8 China	149,400,000,000	2002 est.
9 Korea, South	135,200,000,000	ye 2002 est.
10 Indonesia	131,000,000,000	2002 est.
11 Iraq	120,000,000,000	2002 est.
12 Turkey	118,300,000,000	ye 2001
13 India	100,600,000,000	2001 est.
14 Spain	90,000,000,000	1993 est.
15 Sweden	66,500,000,000	1994
16 Poland	64,000,000,000	2002
17 Greece	63,400,000,000	2002 est.
18 Thailand	62,500,000,000	2002 est.
19 Philippines	60,300,000,000	2002
OVERSEAS DEBT US$ 20–50 BILLION		
20 HKSAR China	49,500,000,000	2002 est.
21 Malaysia	47,500,000,000	2002 est.
22 Israel	42,800,000,000	2001 est.
23 Chile	40,400,000,000	2002
24 Colombia	38,400,000,000	2002 est.
25 Venezuela	38,200,000,000	2000
26 New Zealand	33,000,000,000	2002 est.
27 Pakistan	32,300,000,000	2002 est.
28 Hungary	31,500,000,000	2002 est.
29 Egypt	30,500,000,000	2002 est.
30 Finland	30,000,000,000	1993 Dec.
31 Nigeria	29,700,000,000	2002 est.
32 Peru	29,200,000,000	2002 est.
33 Belgium	28,300,000,000	1999 est.
34 Saudi Arabia	25,900,000,000	2003 est.
35 South Africa	24,700,000,000	2002 est.
36 Taiwan	24,700,000,000	2002
37 Czech Republic	23,800,000,000	2002
38 Syria	22,000,000,000	2002 est.
39 Denmark	21,700,000,000	2000
40 Algeria	21,600,000,000	2002 est.

Notes: Latest available information
Omits states on which information not available
ye = year end
Source: US Central Intelligence Agency

The debt boomerang

As Susan George (1993) points out, debt is also 'bad news' for all but a few people living in the creditor countries. The general population of the creditor countries gives tax relief to private banks on their bad debts and finances tax concessions when they write off debts. A further economic cost to the North is the unemployment consequent upon the loss of sales to developing world countries which cannot afford to buy so many First World products. There are social costs too. Notably, drugs are a major foreign exchange earner for heavily indebted countries and not only does this have serious social consequences for the developed countries, but in financial terms this again hits the developed country taxpayer. George leaves us with the sobering thought that since 1982 the North has received the cheapest ever raw materials from the South. Who then is the real debtor?

Debt is not about being weak and vulnerable because you owe money to someone else: it reflects the underlying power structure. The US debt is largest in the world, but because that debt is in its own currency, as noted above, its creditors do not have the same power. In any case, as Susan George points out, debt has repercussions everywhere (the **debt boomerang**) but it is everywhere the least powerful sectors who bear the brunt. The 'debt boomerang' constitutes the South's best argument for better treatment:

1. Environment – debt-induced poverty encourages damaging exploitation of natural resources.
2. Unemployment – exports to developing countries would be much greater if they were not constrained by debt.
3. Immigration – many go to richer countries to escape poverty and the effects of IMF-imposed restructuring.
4. Drugs – illegal drugs offer many the only plausible possibility of making money for heavily indebted countries.
5. Taxes – northern governments subsidise the bad debts of their banks; cost is borne by the northern taxpayer.
6. Conflict – debt causes social unrest and war.

The 'war on drugs'

If the northern countries really believed in the virtues of free trade, they could find in them a compelling reason for allowing free trade in **narcotic drugs**. Such drugs are, of course, at best harmful and at worst deadly. But in the nineteenth century Britain waged war on China (twice) to obtain the right to sell opium (the raw form of heroin) to the Chinese, so there is a precedent for legalising the drug trade; in fact, it was only after the First World War that it became illegal. A few economists have argued that the drug trade is only a problem because it is illegal; if drugs were legally traded there would be much less point in trading them illegally as the price would drop to the point at which other activities would be of more interest. It is also true that in countries in which drugs are actually produced, the local inhabitants generally do not consume them in their refined form. However, drugs are a subject so emotive that no politician in the developed world is prepared to consider such a radical solution.

The US role in the continuing war on drugs in the Andean region, the centre of the cocaine trade, is of interest also to students of US intervention in Afghanistan, the world's major producer of heroin. Since Nancy Reagan ('just say no'), successive Administrations have focused instead on ill-judged plans to avoid hard domestic choices by trying to choke off the supply of drugs at source. The problem is that the USA has to rely on weak governments in southern states to do this, e.g. Afghanistan, Bolivia, Colombia, Pakistan. They are under pressure from their own people, and the fact that the USA has increasingly tended to intervene directly with military means has helped con-solidate hostility to the whole project and to the US government.

Anti-Americanism was previously almost unknown in Bolivia; it is now widespread as a result of the indiscriminate effects of the US-sponsored coca eradication programme. Worst of all, as was disclosed after the death of President Banzer in 1998, claims that the programme is working are simply not true. And the main reason why it is not working is that there is no other profitable crop that people living at such high altitudes can grow. Coca (not cocaine) is part of the traditional way of life at the high altitudes of the Andes and sadly is a necessity, not an optional extra, for the bulk of their population who are required to perform hard manual labour in the thin air of the alti-plano. In 2006 the leader of the coca growers union, Evo Morales, took office as the first elected indigenous president of Bolivia, with a mandate to legitimise all coca growing.

The civil war in Colombia ended in 2002; it was in its 42nd year. It was fuelled by the drug trade, which has made the Revolutionary Armed Forces of Colombia (FARC) the world's richest terrorist movement and one of the least radical. Again the coca eradication programme is not working. The area planted to coca went up from 140,000 ha in 2000 to 170,000 ha in 2002. This would not have happened had the 'war on drugs' not driven up the value of cocaine on the US market to the point at which the illegal trade became so profitable that the desire to make money outweighed the risks. Despite the aerial spraying of some 130,000 hectares in 2004, in March 2005 it was estimated that there were still some 114,000 ha planted to coca, although as much of this was new planting it was less productive than the old (US Office of National Drug Control Policy 2005).

In post-war Afghanistan the opium poppies are flourishing and very little else is. The only Afghan government successfully to suppress poppy growing was the Taliban; the success of the Northern Alliance opened the way again to the 'golden triangle' and very large profits. The need at the same time to keep Pakistani support means that the United States ignores the importance of smuggling in the undefined border regions. At the end of the 2004 crop season the US government estimated that 206,700 ha had been cultivated, equivalent to 4,950 tonnes of opium, the equivalent of approximately 582 tonnes of potential heroin production. This represented an increase of 239 per cent in the poppy crop and 73 per cent in potential opium production over 2003, the comparable figures for poppy cultivation being 61,000 ha in 2003; 30,750 in 2002; 1,685 in 2001; 64,510 in 2000; and 51,500 in 1999 (US Office of National Drug Control Policy 2004).

Policy choices for indebted countries

Countries that are indebted and face problems with their creditors (and who does not?) have four choices:

- earn more;
- spend less;
- sell off assets;
- get foreign aid.

None of this is as easy as it looks.

Earn more. This depends on the resources available. Among Commonwealth countries in the Caribbean, Grenada was punished for its independence by being cut off from credit after 1979 when the Provisional Revolutionary Government (PRG) sought help in Cuba and Eastern Europe. This in turn promoted a desire to encourage tourism in order to break out of dependence on nutmeg. But this meant building an international airport with a runway long enough to take direct flights from the USA and Europe, which in turn aroused fears in US government circles that Grenada might be used as a Soviet base. After 1983 the new government received considerable aid from the USA, but unfortunately the Americans do not eat nutmeg so production was slow to recover.

In 2005 the entire island was devastated by Hurricane Ivan, a rare event so far south in the Caribbean. It killed 39 people, left 90 per cent of the nation's 28,000 houses in ruins, and destroyed 80 per cent of the nutmeg, mace, cinnamon, ginger and clove plantations. Briefly, tourism too came to a complete halt. The world responded generously for three months, but then came the Asian tsunami and the centre of interest shifted again. Fortunately by then most of the schools had been reopened, but only 33 new houses had been built by the end of 2005.

Spend less. After 20 years of the Washington consensus, governments have long since cut non-essential expenditure (except on themselves). They face the dilemma of cutting essential expenditure or denying themselves. So they do nothing.

Sell off assets. The ability to raise funds quickly accounts for much of the popularity of privatisation, adopted first in Europe in 1983 by the Thatcher government. However, much of the capital raised from privatisation sales was frittered away, as in Britain, on short-term expenditure to enable the government to retain power. Once the main assets have been sold off, the remainder is unlikely to be of much interest to overseas investors.

Get foreign aid. For many developing states, an increase in poverty was accompanied by the surrender of economic sovereignty by encouraging investment from TNCs. This accounted for more than the entire value of foreign aid during the same period. The 1980s saw net debt transfers of around $40 billion per year from developing to developed countries.

Jamaica's dependence on sugar has declined but it still needs markets for its bauxite. It shares with other countries in the region its relative weakness compared with large US corporations and their interconnection with local political interests. Jamaica's Edward Seaga made sure that he was the first state visitor to the White House after the inauguration of Ronald Reagan in 1981 and got extensive aid from his Administration. By contrast the situation of Jamaica under the first Manley government had been made much worse by his decision to confront the IMF when his government could get no more credit and had failed all its performance indicators. His policy in his second term was much more cautious.

The crisis of 1997

The Heavily Indebted Poorer Countries (HIPCs) Initiative was intended to wipe the slate clean for the very poorest countries. It was taken up in the millennium initiative, but it proved surprisingly difficult to get an agreement on how and where it was actually to be applied. The main problem was that the very poorest countries had very little political leverage, so they were treated throughout as the objects rather than the initiators of action (or inaction).

In the meanwhile, two crises reminded the world economic community that their investments could go down as well as up. The East Asian crisis of 1997 was sparked off by the overheating of the Thai economy and the consequent decision to devalue the baht. Just as Japanese banks had earlier invested well rather than wisely in South Korea, so in turn Korean banks had lent heavily to the smaller, tiger, economies: Thailand, Singapore, Malaysia, Indonesia. The crisis in Thailand, coinciding as it did with the fall of Suharto in Indonesia and the consequent uncertainties this generated, therefore triggered economic crisis throughout much of East and South-east Asia.

Just as stability seemed to have returned to Asia, a new crisis in Russia in 1999 was followed by the resignation of President Yeltsin and the emergence of a new and untrained leadership. At the same time the 'dot.com' bubble, which had swelled prodigiously in the USA and Europe in 1999, finally burst. On the major markets shares peaked in the last week of 1999 and then collapsed. It was some three years before the confidence that was lost then began to return.

Asia: the newly industrialising countries

The possibility of a successful late start to development was exemplified in the period before 1945 by Japan, Germany and the former Soviet Union. In the period since 1945 the further dramatic growth of these economies and, more recently, the rise of the newly industrialising countries (NICs) has certainly exacerbated the many problems of conceptualising the developing world (Dicken 1986; cf. Dickenson et al. 1983). The problem of developing world variety requires us to take account of the varying degrees of economic autonomy that may be possible within the global economy.

South Korea, Taiwan and Singapore are perceived as having already 'made it' from the developing world to fully industrialised status and along with Hong Kong they constitute what was initially termed the 'Gang of Four' or the 'Asian Tigers'. Thailand, Indonesia, Malaysia, Argentina, Brazil and Mexico have been seen as on the same track, possibly to be followed by the Philippines and Mauritius. However, there is less agreement on which other countries should be included in this category. Different institutions and different authors express different opinions about what constitutes an NIC. Further, the East Asian crisis of 1997 clearly illustrates the vulnerability of many of these emergent economies, though there is a case for arguing that in a globalised world the vulnerability does not stop there, as the ten-year recession in Japan has shown.

Specifically the question arises whether the NICs are a symptom of the changing order which signifies what Harris has called 'the end of the Third World'. As Harris points out (Harris 1986: 102), as recently as 1960 North America and Western Europe had 78 per cent of the world's manufacturing output. By 1981 their share had fallen to only 59 per cent. At the same time, manufacturing output of the NICs and other middle-income countries had risen from 19 per cent to 37 per cent, while that of low-income countries, including Africa South of the Sahara, had remained virtually the same. Meanwhile, from 1979 to 2004 Chinese economic growth averaged 8 per cent a year, with exports growing at 15 per cent per annum.

However, the impact of development is sometimes glaringly obvious even on the simplest of indicators. For example, in 1967 Indonesia was much poorer than India in terms of per capita income. In 1970 60 per cent of the population of this vast, sprawling archipelago lived in what the World Bank defined as 'poverty'. By 1990 this figure had dropped to 15 per cent. Asia is the most significant area when it comes to dramatic economic growth precisely because of the huge numbers of human beings involved. Between 1970 and 1990 the number in absolute poverty more than halved despite rapid population growth. There can be no clearer evidence of the massive market expansion in that region, which has accompanied its rapid industrialisation.

It is hardly surprising that the relatively advantaged and diversified middle-income countries should seek to increase their share of global markets but only a small proportion of them have done so. The NICs represent the most important blurring of the developed/developing world division to date, as they have set out successfully to challenge the developed nations, both on their own traditional bases of industrialisation, e.g. iron, steel and heavy industry, and also in the new consumer markets.

The rise of the NICs

This can be seen by closer examination of the recent economic histories of the 'core' NICs – those on which there will be general agreement. South Korea and Taiwan will be taken as examples.

South Korea was hard hit by the Second World War and the division of the peninsula between East and West. Korea had developed a significant manufacturing sector before the First World War but most of its industry was located in the North. Hence despite the flight of many North Korean entrepreneurs to the South, South Korean industry had to establish itself with few resources and a dense population dependent on what it could produce. However, although manufacturing in 1945 constituted less than 10 per cent of the South's output, and exports and the savings rate were both low, native enterprise initially benefited from the distribution of confiscated Japanese property. Then came a major setback, the Korean War (1950–53), which devastated the country and caused major hardship. The war, however, marked a turning point, since US aid, given to maintain a strategic ally in the Cold War, was used to pay for infrastructure and spent on roads, railways, ports, communications, power supplies etc.

South Korea met the first oil shock by borrowing oil surpluses from private commercial banks. Its overall borrowing in the 1970s and 1980s was already high. However, this borrowing was not wasted, as so often occurs, but was put to work for developmental purposes. There was a strong emphasis on education. There were strict if not harsh labour laws, but popular disaffection with growth at the cost of poor conditions and low pay did not really surface until the military lost control in the wake of President Park's assassination in October 1979. The land reform which was part of liberation had led to the emergence of much small-scale rural enterprise. The period from the late 1960s to the end of the 1980s was a time of high real per capita growth, averaging more than 6 per cent per annum. This period, initially characterised by high savings and investment rates, gave way to a period of artificially suppressed interest rates which attracted low domestic savings. This further stimulated borrowing abroad. Debt prompted the seeking of a World Bank structural adjustment loan and IMF encouragement along with US pressure based on the US desire for reciprocity of markets led to liberalisation.

Everywhere the role of the state was apparent at least until this liberalisation in the 1980s, and the interplay of government policy along with a culture of work and saving is often seen as the source of South Korean development. Equally important was the concentration of economic activity in 18 large conglomerates, the *chaebol*, who competed, not with one another, but with the outside world. Initially export-led development of labour-intensive manufactures was given every possible assistance, with exports from the new industries protected by subsidies, use of selective tariffs and protective quotas against imports to develop a home market for indigenous goods. Foreign exchange manipulation was employed to retain an export advantage. It is true that the 1970s saw the beginning of the liberalization of the South Korean economy. However, far from this process liberating hitherto unrecognised potential, it is in fact not yet complete. The South Korean economy still exhibits many of the features of its early origins. Wages are still low, hours long, working conditions poor and strikes are common. Structural weaknesses are its overdependence on a few products and especially on the US market for them, the dominance of the powerful *chaebol* and the reliance on internal borrowing both between these powerful corporations and from Japanese banks which in 1997 proved themselves to be dangerously overextended.

Harris points out that neoclassical explanations will not do for South Korea. The importance of the role of the state is far too clear. But nor will explanations based on the massive civil and military aid from the USA. Accelerated growth came after the period of high inputs of aid and was in part the result of attempting to compensate for its loss. Foreign investment tended to concentrate in certain sectors only, to follow rather than precede growth and was in any case less than that enjoyed by many other places which did not experience comparable levels of growth (Harris 1986: 44–5).

Taiwan had been colonised by Japan from 1895 to 1945, a much longer period than South Korea. It was densely populated and to this it added in the 1950s émigré Chinese nationalists, many of them entrepreneurial in ideology, who ruled it virtually as a colony in the name of the government of nationalist China. In 1949 it was poorer than the mainland, though it did have a small established industrial base dating from the 1930s. Between 1949 and 1955 land reform limited size of individual holdings though generous compensation was given to the larger landowners who used the funds to start their own businesses. High interest rates encouraged high domestic savings and foreign borrowing was unnecessary.

However, because of its strategic location Taiwan did get an enormous amount of US aid, which again was used for infrastructural development and education. Given its military orientation, Taiwan came naturally to adopt a model of state-led economic growth. The authoritarian and effectively colonial government undertook the largest industrial enterprises and used high levels of tariff protection for its infant industries (though this was being reduced by the 1980s). It also controlled exchange rates.

Taiwan, having been less indebted, was in some respects more successful than South Korea. Exports showed massive growth to some 60 per cent of GNP and much of that was heavy industrial. However, there was a downside. Despite egalitarian income distribution, conditions for labour remained poor and Taiwan's overreliance on the US market made it vulnerable to shifts in US policy. Again Harris is clear that neoclassical explanations fail in the case of Taiwan's accelerated growth, government action, especially in keeping down labour costs, is seen as too important to the process. For Taiwan: 'The invisible hand was more of an iron fist' (Harris 1986: 53).

What both South Korea and Taiwan along with the other Asian Tigers have achieved is a specialised role in the world economy. They have done so from different starting points with different resources available to them and by way of different policy decisions (*The Economist*, 30 October 1993).

It can be seen that, unlike Japan, many NICs were originally penetrated economies. There are therefore four ways NICs could encourage development in the wider developing world:

- as an example to others;
- as suppliers of technology and skills;
- as a market for developing world goods; and
- as providers of development capital.

The NICs are seen by some as indicative of a genuine shift of economic power away from the First World. They are the first developing world countries to make the transition to fully developed status. China, what the World Bank has recently begun to call the eight 'high performing economies' Japan, Taiwan, Hong Kong, South Korea, Singapore, Malaysia, Indonesia and Thailand and possibly Vietnam, have now developed to the point at which they are no longer strongly affected by fluctuations in the US economy though they do remain vulnerable to the decisions of other global economic players such as financial speculators. In the recession of 1991–93, when most of the Organization for Economic Cooperation and Development (OECD) economies were static, the economies of all the NICs continued to grow strongly.

Certainly the OECD countries (less Turkey) are no longer overwhelmingly dominant in the world economy. By local exchange rates they still account for

73 per cent of world output, as against less than 18 per cent for the developing countries and only 2 per cent for China. But by assessing the relative strength of economies by purchasing power parities, the IMF has placed the relative strength of the OECD and the 'Tigers' in a very different perspective. By this measure the OECD countries (less Turkey) account for only 54 per cent of world output as against 34 per cent for the developing countries and 6 per cent for China, making the Chinese economy in absolute terms the third largest in the world after the United States and Japan, and even those figures have since been revised upwards.

But there are many questions still to be answered. Having 'made it', will the NICs be more sympathetic to their former companions of the developing world or will they simply join the rich world clubs (OECD, **World Trade Organization (WTO)**, IMF, World Bank) in accepting the burdens they lay on the less fortunate? Moreover, they made the transition under specific circumstances, with in each case a good balance of payments situation at a crucial moment, with closed markets and (often though not always) authoritarian regimes. Nor can independent states hope to replicate the unique circumstances of the former British colony of Hong Kong.

The fear of insecurity: the South-east Asia crisis and after

By joining the rich world the NICs accepted – at least on paper – the prevailing ideology of market liberalism. However, their reactions to the 1997 East Asian crisis suggest that they may now be having second thoughts. The crisis was precipitated by heavy speculation against the Thai baht, but in fact the Thai economy had been overheating for some time and no action had been taken to counter it. In the case of Hong Kong, the government of the Special Autonomous Region (HKSAR) took immediate action to prop up the stock market. Malaysia went further still. Blaming the crisis on a Western conspiracy, the government of Dr Mahathir effectively suspended the convertibility of the ringgit and forced investors wishing to repatriate their profits to accept government bonds in lieu of cash – usually the last resort of a desperate government.

The effects of the Asian economic meltdown were felt in a variety of ways. *New Internationalist* (320, January–February 2000: 25) cites higher school drop-out rates owing to rises in fees in Thailand, declining real wages and rising unemployment in South Korea, an accelerating bankruptcy rate in Malaysia and a massive increase in poverty in Indonesia, where subsidised food had to be distributed in a vain attempt to stave off political unrest. Moreover, under the WTO, all these countries will be expected to comply with the terms of the Uruguay Round by ending systems of export incentives, upholding intellectual property rights protection, guaranteeing foreign investment, eliminating tariffs and non-tariff barriers to trade and liberalising government procurement policies, services and exchange rates. It remains to be seen how far in practice they will comply with these standards and, if they do, what effect it will have on their ability to compete. For, up to now, the most striking thing about them is what the World Bank terms 'pragmatic flexibility', combining government support for infrastructure and heavy industry, directed credit for specific industries especially in the field of new technologies, free enterprise in manufacturing and distribution and (contrary to prevailing models in the developed countries) a policy of promoting rapid wage growth to create a strong internal market as a basis for export success.

Existing NICs had advantages of cheap labour giving a potential for surplus, but not too many other costs to prevent such a surplus being accumulated and therefore to dissuade investors. It is precisely the advanced nature of many NICs and the size of their internal markets, especially in Latin America, which has attracted investment from the outside world, including the NICs themselves. However, the Mexican peso crisis of 1994–95 demonstrated that despite the advantage of cheap labour, capital could equally as well flow out again should there be any loss of confidence in the strength of the existing order.

Other less developed countries (LDCs) hope that manufacturing costs will now rise for NICs as they get richer and that others will be able to take their places at the top of the developing world pile. They expect that their capital accumulation will, as with the industrialised countries, be limited by their need to distribute to a more demanding labour force with raised expectations. The present NICs would then become the markets for the kind of LDC product which they grew rich on while moving on to more high-tech capital-intensive production themselves.

Others think that the NICs' export success is unlikely to become much more general in the developing world. Moreover, if it did, the response of the developed countries might be protectionism. Who would buy the quantity of manufactured products produced by all the other countries of the developing world if they were in a position to export at the rate of the existing NICs? The price in terms of environmental degradation could also be unsustainable. As noted above, the sort of free trade envisaged by the makers of the WTO would work against the kind of advantages existing NICs enjoyed during their period of most rapid growth. Circumstances today are not only different, but they are very different for different regions. The ability to generate manufactured exports seems to have been vital to the success of all the NICs. Yet less than 10 per cent of all LDC manufactured exports come from Africa South of the Sahara. Where will Africa begin to find the money to fund the levels of infrastructural investment it needs?

Again there are consequences which AICs would do well to heed. On paper, thanks to the use of flags of convenience, Liberia is one of the great maritime nations of the world. In practice, it is an extremely backward country devastated by civil war. Nobody is going to invest in Liberia after its recent dismal history. It will take too many years for malnourished ill-educated generations to be replaced by healthy and bright successors. Neither the ruling military elite nor the weak civilian governments they uphold have either the ability or the means to achieve these changes. So who, therefore, in the meanwhile, is going to ensure that the notionally Liberian tanker and container fleet is soundly built, properly maintained and directed by crews who are able to tackle both the everyday and the unexpected hazards that the world's oceans can present?

The ageing tanker *Prestige*, which ran aground off the coast of Galicia, Spain, in November 2002, was carrying some 70,000 tonnes of industrial oil. When it split in two and sank in the middle of one of Europe's most important fishing zones, it covered some 300 km of the coastline with toxic sludge, illustrating perfectly the way in which exploiting the weaknesses of developing countries enables both governments and corporations of developed countries to avoid responsibility in such cases. The ship was built in Japan. But it was owned by a Liberian company, registered in the Bahamas and managed by a Greek shipping cartel. The oil, which was being taken from Latvia to Singapore, was owned by a Gibraltar-based subsidiary of a Russian company which had its headquarters in Switzerland. The ship's captain was Greek, but his crew were Filipino. And the decision of the Spanish government to order the Dutch salvage company to tow the hull clear of Spanish waters appears in retrospect instead to have hastened the final disaster (*Financial Times*, 20 November 2002).

Globalisation

For the past century and more we have been witnessing a process of globalisation, 'the process by which events, decisions, and activities in one part of the world can come to have significant consequences for individuals and communities in quite distant parts of the globe' (McGrew et al. 1992: 23). Globalisation is the key characteristic of the modern economic system and even, it has been argued, of modernity itself (Giddens 1990). As a result, theorists of international relations have come increasingly to emphasise the systemic factors affecting state behaviour rather than the individual decisions of states themselves.

The notion of systemic factors, however, implies the existence of an international system. By system we mean an enduring set of interactions between individuals, or, in this case, states (Nye and Keohane 1971; Keohane and Nye 1977). States are in themselves functional systems, and can be viewed either as such or as subsystems within the larger international context. Despite the formal absence of authority in the world system, states have in general behaved in an orderly way which presupposes some notion of international order (Bull 1977). The world is a very complex place and with the speeding up of communications during the present century we have all come to interact with one another, across national boundaries, to a much greater extent than was ever before possible. Hence despite the formal absence of global political authority, states do cooperate, with each other and with a whole variety of non-governmental organisations (NGOs) and international organisations (IOs), to make decisions that for the most part are effective. Indeed, in some areas, such as television broadcasting or air traffic control, they have no practical alternative.

The concept of system, though, is inappropriate to the developing world as such. Indeed, it is not always of much use in a regional context. There is one obvious exception: the western hemisphere. Not only is it isolated by water from the main arena of world politics (Calvert 1988), but it is even conceptualised by those who live there in system terms, and the notion of an 'inter-American system' has, as noted above, actually been embodied in a regional international organisation. But few would concede the same degree of identity, for example, to South Asia. Differences of perception are easily illustrated:

> The open invitation in the early 1950s by Pakistan to 'foreign powers' to support it against India led to an Indian condemnation that has never really stopped. Yet Pakistan has argued that India's subsequent policy of non-alignment, and the need for Cold War rivalry to be kept out of the South Asia region, was a rather purple Indian version of simple power politics, a cunning disguise of Indian expansionist interests dressed up in the language of moral virtues. This belief is still held to this day. A well-known Pakistani commentator has pointed out that: 'It is significant that many Indians, when they speak of the *Indian* land mass cannot refrain from making it clear that what they are really talking about is the entire South Asian region'. (Hewitt 1992: 27)

Otherwise we are left with the rather vague concept of a world system, and the problem with this is that while it may in some sense be true that everything and everyone in the world influences to some degree everyone else, in practice we have to establish some sorts of limits on our enquiry if we are to make any sort of sense of it. What then are the sort of transnational links that transcend the nation state? How far are they actually able to avoid the power of the national state to regulate and to control them?

Transnational links

Theorists of international relations no longer accept the classical view of their discipline as being concerned only with relations between states – the so-called **'billiard ball'** model. However many other links there are between people and organisations, though, the fact remains that the state system, originally evolved in Europe at the Treaty of Westphalia (1648), continues and is likely to continue to structure all such relationships.

The first problem begins with the notion of citizenship and the requirement of an individual to have a passport and permission to enter another country. Citizens of developing world states, unless they are very wealthy, do not enjoy the same freedom of movement as citizens of the AICs, and their governments are unable to give them even the same limited degree of protection that most of the industrialised countries can arrange. If they have to flee from persecution, in theory they have to be received wherever they go. In practice the industrialised countries have made matters very difficult for refugees, and by classifying all other potential immigrants as 'economic migrants' they have absolved themselves from any obligation to receive them. Only the universal human institution of the family, to a limited extent, transcends these barriers: in some, but not all, cases successful immigrants are allowed to sponsor their relatives as immigrants also.

The second problem comes from the multiplicity of currencies and the lack of an agreed world standard of value. It is true that this has in recent years been supplied to some extent by the US dollar. However, since the devaluation of the dollar by the Nixon Administration in 1971 its pre-eminence has no longer been taken for granted, although it is still more widely available and more widely accepted than any other currency. In recent years a growing difficulty has been the growth of global currency dealing on a scale which makes even the currencies of the AICs vulnerable to sudden attack on the financial markets. The fact that billions can be moved in seconds renders the currencies of smaller states even more vulnerable than those of larger ones. And the global market is all too prone to sudden alarms. The devaluation of the Mexican peso in December 1994 not only smashed the illusion of financial stability Mexico had cultivated since 1987, but immediately threatened the stability of the financial systems of other Latin American states, especially Brazil and Argentina, and the governments of those countries found it very difficult indeed to counter the impression that they too were in some way affected. The private citizen of a developing world state lives with this perpetual instability, which gets greater the more open his or her country is to the world market.

The third problem concerns the availability of information. As we have already noted, the provision of world news has long been dominated by the AICs and their news organisations. Only in the last 15 years has the spread of the internet, which celebrated its 30th anniversary in 1999, begun to erode this control. The irony is that although the computers that have made this possible are actually manufactured and assembled in the developing world, it is the inhabitants of the developed countries who benefit from the new freedom of communication.

Similarly, it is they who have benefited most from the rapid decline of sea travel in favour of air, and of rail travel in favour of the private car. The explosion in long-haul holidays has turned Thailand into a major tourist destination for Europeans and is in the process of doing the same to the Indian state of Goa. The policy implications of tourism and its impact on developing countries will be covered in detail in Chapter 9.

Business and politics: taxation, tariffs and privatisation

The problem for developing states of the links between TNCs and local interests have already been mentioned. The main relationships between such corporations and governments concern three prime issues: taxation, tariffs and privatisation.

International law accepts that companies are subject to local taxation wherever they operate. However it is quite a different matter for a weak developing world government actually to obtain the revenues to which it feels entitled. The fact that the country needs the company more than the company needs the country weakens its bargaining position. The practice of 'transfer pricing', by which goods are sold internally by one branch of a company to another can, if judiciously employed, result in a much reduced tax bill. In extreme cases a company can, if it has sufficient resources, simply buy the outcome that it wants, preferably in a weak, undervalued local currency.

One thing at least has changed. It is no longer acceptable for a company that feels hard-done-by to appeal to its home government for military force to be used in its defence. It is also true that they would seldom need to do so.

Much economic growth in the developing world has taken place behind protective tariff barriers. The conclusion of the Uruguay Round, and the creation of the WTO, if taken literally, rules out such a strategy and leaves developing world countries vulnerable to strong selling pressures from the AICs. However common sense suggests that both tariff barriers and non-tariff barriers will be employed for some time yet. The fact is that for major TNCs they have always been manipulable by a variety of devices, even if the country concerned has not, as in many cases it has, been so keen to invite in foreign investment that it has been prepared to waive all tariffs on imported capital goods for a substantial period, typically ten years.

In the current economic climate, the nationalisation of foreign-owned enterprises is unlikely to be an issue in the immediate future. Its place as a problem area has been taken by privatisation.

'Privatisation' now generally refers to the process by which state assets are transferred to private ownership. In this sense it is a new term, originally popularised in Britain when, following its successful re-election in 1983, the Thatcher government embarked on a crusade to divest the state of its ownership of profit-making enterprises. The sale of public enterprises has however gone on for many years – as long, perhaps, as public enterprises have existed. In Argentina, for example, a report by Raúl Prebisch for the interim military government of 1955–58 recommended the sale of all state enterprises except the railways and the oil industry, but no action was taken (Di Tella and Rodríguez Braun 1990: 7). Under President Frondizi, however, in order to reduce public expenditure the government sold off 40 companies previously German-owned which had been expropriated at the end of the Second World War and privatised the urban bus transport network in Buenos Aires, with, the then Minister of the Economy claimed, 'excellent results' (Roberto T. Alemann, in di Tella and Rodríguez Braun 1990, 69). At the same time, private participation was invited both by Argentina's state oil corporation Yacimientos Petrolíferos Fiscales (YPF) and by Petróleos Mexicanos (PEMEX) in Mexico, where, in an act widely hailed at the time as a declaration of economic independence, British and American oil companies had been nationalised in 1938.

Despite vigorous US propaganda for private enterprise, the real shift towards privatisation in Latin America did not get under way until the 1970s, when it was associated with the policies of the 'Chicago boys' in Chile. It is only since the early 1980s that it has become a major theme of Latin American economic policies (Glade 1991: 2). Its spread to the rest of the developing world has been slower, the obvious reason being that many of the poorer developing world countries have few if any major assets which a buyer would find attractive. Additionally, it is one of the ironies of privatisation programmes that, by the law of supply and demand, a government keen to privatise national assets can be expected to receive the *lowest* possible price for them, and many developing world governments that were originally keen to sell, have at least hesitated when they found that they might end up paying out more in inducements than they were going to receive from the sale.

Were the choice of either nationalisation or privatisation purely a matter of economics the question of which to adopt would be a purely technical one. Unfortunately, however, both the acts themselves, and the way in which they are executed, involve significant and complex ethical questions. For a developing world state a major problem is presented by potential foreign-owned monopolies. The desire of foreign corporations to bid for former public enterprises is much enhanced when a successful bid will give them exclusive economic control. However, turning state monopolies into private monopolies is likely at the least to breed nationalist resentment. Alternatively, where two or more companies are bidding for a key asset, the question of which bid to choose may well be determined as much by political (or even personal) considerations as by economic ones.

Bretton Woods

Rightly or wrongly, many attributed the failure of peace in the inter-war years to the defects of the world financial system. **Hyperinflation** in Germany, Austria and Hungary destroyed middle-class savings and made the victims eager recruits for fascism.

In 1944 the UN established what became known as the Bretton Woods system. The two key institutions of the new order were the International Monetary Fund (IMF) and the International Bank for Reconstruction and

Development (IBRD – now commonly known as the World Bank). The timing of its creation reflected the perception that among the causes of the war was economic nationalism. Hence the free market principles that from the beginning underlay the work of the IMF.

Today even many free marketeers would argue that markets operate less efficiently in conditions of poverty and that theories of markets and movements to equilibrium are not entirely appropriate for application to the developing world. However, in 1944 the majority of the present-day developing world states did not exist as sovereign entities and had to fit in later with a system not designed for their benefit. It was a system essentially designed to help the industrialised countries avoid the problems they had faced before the war.

The main objectives of the Bretton Woods system therefore were:

- to promote stable exchange rates;
- to encourage the growth of world trade;
- to facilitate international movements of capital.

As far as the developed countries were concerned, it has long been generally believed that it was successful. However, this view has been rejected by Sir Alec Cairncross, who has written:

The popular idea that Bretton Woods accounted for the prosperity of the post-war years has little substance. Throughout its first 10 years the International Monetary Fund did very little and the World Bank contributed only a small part of the total flow of capital into international investment. The international monetary system was managed, not by the IMF, as was envisaged at Bretton Woods, but by the United States. (Cairncross 1994)

The fact was that most of the so-called evils of the pre-war system – devaluations, inconvertible currencies, exchange controls, trade restrictions – proved very resilient and lingered throughout the classical period of the Bretton Woods system which ended with the devaluation of the dollar in 1971.

The International Monetary Fund

The purpose of the IMF is to assist countries in maintaining stable exchange rates – it is not primarily intended to promote economic growth and in practice it often does not do so. It is particularly important to the very poorest countries in the same way that the World Bank extends most of its loans to those countries which do not receive commercial bank loans.

The IMF began with 29 members, but by 2000 had 182. It is a mutual assistance society or club. The amount paid in by members is determined by a formula which broadly reflects their relative positions in the world economy.

These quotas also determine the number of votes the country concerned can exercise and its maximum potential borrowing. The US, UK, Germany, France, and Japan together have 41 per cent of the votes. With the other two members, Italy and Canada, thrown in the G7 countries control over 50 per cent. Although the US quota is now down to 20 per cent, this is enough (given the large sums that it pays in) to ensure that the US Government always has considerable influence. It is the only country that commands enough votes to be able to veto the key decisions that require 85 per cent majorities.

The theory behind the IMF – and in particular its Compensatory Financial Facility (CFF), which was set up in 1963 to give support during foreign exchange crises – is that borrowing temporarily can help a government to resolve the problems of deficits, by giving it a breathing space in which to carry out adjustments to its economy. If this were the case, it would be very convenient for developing world states, as it would enable them to make adjustments without surrendering their control over their economies.

Unfortunately, in practice developing world relations with the IMF have not been happy ones. The Fund, rightly or wrongly, is not perceived as enhancing developing world security. Developing world states see themselves as lacking influence within the IMF. At the same time the IMF is seen as imposing on them an economic orthodoxy which is against their interests and indeed violates their sovereignty through the conditions it attaches to loans ('conditionality'). In 1980 African states meeting at Arusha in Tanzania expressed their frustration and called in the **Arusha Declaration** for the creation of a new system.

The problem is that the ideology of the IMF favours orthodox economic explanations of the need for stabilisation. Those who work for the Fund think of it as an organisation which is concerned only with the technicalities of maintaining that system. Consequently, to borrow from the IMF, countries have to take measures which will as far as possible free up world trade regardless of the consequences for themselves. They will be faced with the following specific requirements:

- to reduce budget deficits through an immediate reduction in public expenditure;
- to eliminate all forms of price and wage control including the removal of subsidies on basic foodstuffs;
- to control the money supply to meet certain benchmarks;
- to devalue the currency in order to promote exports and reduce imports;
- to remove the tariffs and quotas which are needed to protect infant industries in the developing world.

These requirements were initially collectively referred to as structural adjustment packages and later as **Structural Adjustment Programmes (SAPs)**. The term 'Structural Adjustment Programme' had by the end of the twentieth century gained such a negative connotation that the World Bank and IMF have now dropped it. They launched a new initiative, the Poverty Reduction Strategy Initiative, under which countries are required to develop **Poverty Reduction Strategy Papers (PRSPs)** to access it. While the name has changed, with PRSPs, the World Bank is still forcing countries to adopt the same types of policies as SAPs.

The shared resources of the Fund are in theory available to all members but with increasingly stringent conditions. The first and second tranches (part-payments) are available unconditionally but amount only to taking out again some of the membership fee paid in. For many developing world countries it is the subsequent loans which are paid out in hard currency, and therefore have to be repaid usually over a period of 3–5 years in the same form, which are the ones on which they have come to rely. The IMF sees its role as technical (relating to short-term non-structural economic problems) and argues that where the effects of structural adjustment fall is an internal political decision. What it has only recently come to recognise, at least in part, is that its 'free market' orientation is political too.

The **austerity** measures, which are an inevitable requirement of loans in excess of 50 per cent of quotas, are supposed to boost exports, reduce imports, usually through devaluation, and lower government expenditure by constraining wages and welfare. Thus they tend to increase unemployment and to make the domestic working class pay for what is often a problem deriving from changes in world terms of trade. Such international fluctuations in any

Plate 8   Anti-capitalist, anti-American politics, Uruguay

case hit the poorest sectors and disadvantaged groups hardest (see Chapter 5). Primary producers are more at the mercy of the international system than those who produce exportable manufactured goods, so countries that rely heavily on primary exports are most likely to get into balance of payments difficulties and therefore have to resort to IMF help. But at the same time those are the countries least likely to have the resources to be able to meet the welfare needs of their people.

Conditionality is part of the ideology of stabilisation. But the IMF resists rescheduling of debts for the same reason, that its system of loans is supposed to be short term and repayments need to be available to be reloaned elsewhere. Developing countries wanted IMF principles to stress development specifically. However, the USA and the UK argued that this was role of the World Bank and not the IMF, and hence development in all member states was given equal consideration. They were of course right that this was the original objective, but even for the World Bank the reconstruction of Europe and Japan came first. With the IMF in its present form short-term loans simply to rectify balance of payments problems and the equal treatment of unequal members simply combine to produce circumstances which favour industrialised nations.

The IMF will help fund debt purchase by developing world countries. However, if those countries have already accepted SAPs and then defaulted, their past default will give them little prospect of future loans. Worst of all, the IMF's position as banker of last resort means that if the IMF will not lend to them, then no one else will do so either.

The effects of the debt crisis, in fact, were eventually to lead to some enhancement of the role of the IMF. The first response was the development of special facilities requiring detailed programmes of reform. These were rejected by India and China, and almost all the SSA countries, where the drying up of funds resulted in increased austerity. There were riots at the proposed restrictions in Bolivia, Brazil, Egypt, Venezuela and Zambia and governments ousted partly for dealing with the IMF included those of both Ghana and Nigeria. On the other hand the failure to deal with the IMF or to meet its conditions were to lead to defaults by the governments of Liberia, Somalia, Peru, Sierra Leone and Zambia, among others.

The World Bank

The World Bank has since its foundation been seen as the main source of multilateral lending to countries for individual capital projects. Its initial mandate was to fund the revival of post-war European economies but its role was later extended to the developing countries. It established the International Development Association (IDA) in 1960 to give soft loans (loans on easy terms) to the poorest countries, and certainly since 1973 the World Bank has distinguished between relative and absolute forms of poverty at personal and national levels, has stressed investment in the poor and funded projects concerned with small-scale production.

However, in the same year that the then President of the World Bank, Robert McNamara, said 'it is clear that too much confidence was placed on the belief that rapid economic growth would automatically result in the reduction of poverty', the 1977 World Bank (IBRD) Report on Africa said that aid should only be given where subsidies were abandoned even if this meant food riots.

The evident failure of the IMF to deal with the problems of developing world debt has led the World Bank, too, to offer structural adjustment packages to specified countries. One of their attractions originally was that there was no cross-conditionality. For example, a World Bank loan to Argentina has been unsuccessfully opposed by the IMF. But during the 1980s an informal or tacit 'cross-conditionality' became increasingly evident.

The GATT and the WTO

The General Agreement on Tariffs and Trade (GATT) was never intended to be permanent. It was an interim measure proposed by the AICs in 1947 at the First (Geneva) Round of trade talks, to fill the gap left in the Bretton Woods system when the US Congress refused to ratify the Havana Charter. The original idea had been to establish an International Trade Organization, with the goal ultimately of securing universal free trade and to end **protectionism**, which was believed to have materially contributed to the Great Depression of 1929. However owing to the onset of the Cold War the United States finally abandoned the idea in 1950. The GATT remained, extending its scope through a series of **Rounds**. These took longer and longer to complete, and it was only after five years of negotiating at the Eighth Round which began in Punta del Este, Uruguay, in 1986 that a Draft Act was agreed and three more years before it was signed (15 April 1994). Hence it was not until 1 January 1995 that the World Trade Organization (WTO) finally came into existence, and then without agreement between the 81 (now 134) member states on a Secretary-General.

The GATT was not designed to deal with developing world countries' problems. For example, balance of payments disequilibria were to be dealt with by pressure to adjust on the countries that are in deficit not those that are in surplus. The outcome of such adjustments would appear to favour the countries of the North and their TNCs. Where they have not liked GATT principles the developed countries have simply established trade barriers against them. Such groups as textile manufacturers, industrialists and farmers are well organised and powerful in the developed countries. Whatever they profess to believe, they resist trade liberalisation which could favour less developed countries.

The GATT (like the WTO) was based on three assumptions:

- trading results in higher living standards;
- free markets as the basis of international trade promote the greatest benefits;
- the distribution of such benefits is of secondary importance. It is a technical issue and is for the market to decide rather than for political solution.

Pessimists have taken the view that, on the contrary, there can be only limited growth in world demand for primary products, that less developed countries therefore have inherent balance of payments problems because imports are more elastic than exports, and hence that their fragile economies need protection in a way that stronger ones do not. Optimists reply that the less developed countries have comparative advantage in cheap labour and thus low unit costs. They will benefit from the opening up of their economies to world trade as this will result in diversification, which in turn will protect them from reliance on primary products and food crops which can fail.

Overall the optimists got their way in the last GATT negotiations, the Uruguay Round. This was to be expected as the Round responded in large measure to growing protectionism and bloc-building in the developed world. But though the developed world liberalised and dismantled barriers to some degree, the developing world lost protection which it needed much more. The GATT Rounds of the 1950s and 1960s had opened up new markets and thus facilitated the growth of TNCs to the advantage of the developed nations on whose territory these companies are located (and taxed). But some semblance of balance was maintained: the GATT rules allowed less developed countries to use quotas to defend themselves against balance of payments problems. Up to the Seventh (Tokyo) Round (1979), the industrialised countries were not permitted to subsidise manufactured goods or minerals, though limited subsidies to agricultural products remained. Less developed countries were allowed to continue to use export subsidies in the short term but with the rather open-ended proviso that these must not do any damage to any other signatory. Some less developed countries approaching the Uruguay Round thought that industrialised countries should deliver on agreements from previous Rounds before embarking on more negotiations.

This Eighth (Uruguay) Round brought new areas under international jurisdiction: agriculture, services (such as telecommunications, banking and transport through the General Agreement on Trade in Services – GATS), intellectual property rights (TRIPS) and investment measures (TRIMS) being the most important.

The OECD estimated that the conclusion of the Uruguay Round would add $270 billion to world output by 2002. However, this was equivalent to an increase in global GDP of only $40 per capita. Moreover, it was clear that the benefits, such as they were, would not be evenly distributed. Some two-thirds would accrue to the developed world, and especially to the European Union. The effects on the developing world would broadly be:

- South America would gain $8 billion, of which Brazil alone would gain $3.4 billion.
- India would gain $4.6 billion, as much as the whole of South America less Brazil.
- The Asian 'Tigers' would gain $7.1 billion between them.
- Africa would lose some $2.6 billion with Nigeria bearing the brunt of the loss, to the tune of $1 billion.

The astonishingly negative impact the new WTO regime was expected to have on Africa was due to the loss of trade preferences in the European market and in particular the consequences of the dismantling of the **Lomé Convention,** and its replacement by the much less favourable **Cotonou Agreement.** SSA in particular simply does not have any alternative products with which it could take advantage of the liberalisation in world trade. In summary, the outcome would contribute to the 'drawing apart' of the developing world as one-third of benefits expected to go to the developing world would go to the wealthier parts of it and to China.

Pessimists argue that the Uruguay Round deal did not address the problems of debt and low commodity prices; that it served the interests only of some sections of the industrialised countries and more particularly of TNCs. Deregulation of trade is seen as enhancing the power of international capital and giving active encouragement to the global search for cheaper labour. Thus pessimists expect negative impacts on the standard and quality of life in the developing world and for poorer sections of the First World. The environment is also threatened as investment and jobs move to areas offering the lowest production costs. Low costs often reflect the lack of environmental protection legislation in such areas with serious consequences for especially fragile ecosystems. Not surprisingly, proposals to start a new 'Round' in Seattle met with such concentrated hostility from demonstrators that the meeting had to be abandoned.

In addition, less developed countries must now deregulate, and this means removing restraints on TNCs such as the existing limits imposed on profit repatriation. Services which constitute some 20 per cent of world trade – including transport, tourism and construction – are brought under the ambit of the GATT for the first time. This is thought to present another problem for the developing world, in that it undermines the indigenous development of services without advantaging those less developed countries which do not export services. As regards financial services, less developed countries which are members of the GATT must now open their markets up to US banks and insurance companies. The predictable consequence is that nascent financial services sectors in less developed countries will be destroyed as they face unconstrained competition from northern TNCs such as American Express. A third consequence is that they must implement patent protection laws which will hit indigenous industries and in particular make the production of vital drugs in a generic form problematic. They will have to pay royalties on such developmental necessities as seeds and technology. Non-compliance can mean retaliatory action under the rules of the WTO, the new trade body which now has the power (which did not previously exist) to police and regulate international trade in the same way as the IMF regulates international borrowing.

Optimists argue that the South will get much more in return. They claim that northern markets will be opened up to less developed countries and that more investment will flow South. They also take the view that the alternative was far worse. To save their advantages the northern states could have imposed high tariffs and other protectionist measures which would have hit the developing world particularly hard. However, the WTO had hardly come into existence when after this abortive attempt to start a new Round at Seattle, negotiations were resumed in 2002 at **Doha**, where demonstrations could be much more easily controlled.

The View from the Ground

By *Larry Elliott, economics editor*, *The Guardian*, Monday, 12 December 2005: 23

Two Countries, One Booming, One Struggling: Which One Followed the Free-Trade Route?

The Harvard economist Dani Rodrik is one trade sceptic. Take Mexico and Vietnam, he says. One has a long border with the richest country in the world and has had a free-trade agreement with its neighbour across the Rio Grande. It receives oodles of inward investment and sends its workers across the border in droves. It is fully plugged in to the global economy. The other was the subject of a US trade embargo until 1994 and suffered from trade restrictions for years after that. Unlike Mexico, Vietnam is not even a member of the WTO.

So which of the two has the better recent economic record? The question should be a no-brainer if all the free-trade theories are right – Mexico should be streets ahead of Vietnam. In fact, the opposite is true. Since Mexico signed the 'Nafta' (North American Free Trade Agreement) deal with the US and Canada in 1992, its annual per capita growth rate has barely been above 1%. Vietnam has grown by around 5% a year for the past two decades. Poverty in Vietnam has come down dramatically: real wages in Mexico have fallen.

Rodrik doesn't buy the argument that the key to rapid development for poor countries is their willingness to liberalise trade. Nor, for that matter, does he think boosting aid makes much difference either. Looking around the world, he looks in vain for the success stories of three decades of neo-liberal orthodoxy: nations that have really made it after taking the advice – willingly or not – of the IMF and the World Bank.

Rather, the countries that have achieved rapid economic take-off in the past 50 years have done so as a result of policies tailored to their own domestic needs. Vietnam shows that what you do at home is far more important than access to foreign markets. There is little evidence that trade barriers are an impediment to growth for those countries following the right domestic policies.

Those policies have often been the diametric opposite of the orthodoxy. South Korea and Taiwan focused their economies on exports, but combined that outward orientation with high levels of tariffs and other forms of protection, state ownership, domestic-content requirements for industry, directed credit and limits to capital flows. Rodrik says: 'Since the late 1970s, China also followed a highly unorthodox two-track strategy, violating practically every rule in the guidebook. Conversely, countries that adhered more strictly to the orthodox structural reform agenda – most notably Latin America – have fared less well. Since the mid-1980s, virtually all Latin American countries opened up their economies, privatised their public enterprises, allowed unrestricted access for foreign capital and deregulated their economies. Yet they have grown at a fraction of the pace of the heterodox reformers, while also being buffeted more strongly by macroeconomic instability.'

This is an argument taken up by Ha Joon Chang in a recent paper for the South Centre, the developing countries' intergovernmental forum. Chang argues that 'there is a respectable historical case for tariff protection for industries that are not yet profitable, especially in developing countries. By contrast, free trade works well only in the fantasy theoretical world of perfect competition.'

Going right back to the mid-18th century, Chang says Pitt the Elder's view was that the American colonists were not to be allowed to manufacture so much as a horseshoe nail. Adam Smith agreed. It would be better all round if the Americans concentrated on agricultural goods and left manufacturing to Britain.

Alexander Hamilton, the first US Treasury secretary, dissented from this view. In a package presented to Congress in 1791, he proposed measures to protect America's infant industries. America went with Hamilton rather than Smith. For the next century and a half, the US economy grew behind high tariff walls, with an industrial tariff that tended to be above 40 per cent and rarely slipped below 25 per cent. This level of support is far higher than the US is prepared to tolerate in the trade negotiations now under way.

The lesson is clear, Chang says. South Korea would still be exporting wigs made from human hair if it had liberalised its trade in line with current thinking. Those countries that did liberalise prematurely under international pressure – Senegal, for example – saw their manufacturing firms wiped out by foreign competition.

See also: Ha Joon Chang (2005)

Case study 4.2   **Bananas**

Small producers on their family-run farms in the Windward Islands, Jamaica and Belize could not compete without some form of protection. They could not produce bananas as cheaply as the low-paid workers on the plantations of Central and South America. In fact 'dollar bananas' cost only half as much to produce and one Central American plantation can grow as many bananas as 20,000 growers in the Caribbean island states. The problem is an historical one. Although the islands were not very suitable for banana cultivation Britain encouraged the growing of bananas in its Caribbean dependencies because it wanted guaranteed prices in the financially

▶

Case study 4.2 continued

problematic post-war years and the islands' sugar production was in decline. There is little scope for diversification in the islands. Tourism is growing but some form of agricultural production is vital and whatever is grown will cost more to produce than elsewhere (see also Grugel 1995).

Bananas and other soft fruit depend for almost all their very high value in the shops on the measures that have been taken to get them there. In other words, the economic value of a product like a banana comes almost entirely from the situation of the producing country within the world market, and this means the ability of large TNCs to control the infrastructure within which bananas are marketed.

The producers of so-called 'dollar bananas', especially the three big US TNCs, Del Monte, Chiquita and Dole, wanted to increase their sales to Europe, where they already had 60 per cent of the market. These transnational corporations had established themselves throughout Central America by the 1920s. Refrigeration gave them the technology they needed and they soon had turnovers bigger than the countries in which they were operating. They were notorious for their interference in local politics. The involvement of the banana companies in local politics has many unsavoury aspects, ranging from unsecured personal 'loans' to dictators (such as the $1 million paid to Jorge Ubico in Guatemala to get a reduction in corporation taxes) to the fact that in all countries they held much land idle to prevent competition developing while they paid minimal taxes and export duties.

Honduras is the archetypical 'banana republic'. The United Fruit Company (UFCo), now Chiquita, cynically exploited the unlimited access its weak government allowed it. The banana plantations form a vast enclave in the North-East of the country, on the shore of the Caribbean and well away from the centres of Honduras's small population. There whole towns were built by the company, linked to each other and to the company ports by company-owned railways. Both workers and other local inhabitants use company stores, company hospitals and company schools.

By contrast, Costa Rica, the second largest banana producer in the Caribbean, has avoided becoming a 'banana republic' and is a democratic and politically sophisticated country. However, its prospects confront the interests of its banana growers. Eco-tourism is very important to Costa Rica, but the country has doubled the acreage given over to bananas. A chemical-free banana production system is possible, but agribusiness 'needs' take precedence over the environment. Conservation groups are very concerned. Pesticides seep into drainage systems and are threatening Costa Rica's national parks. The coral reef is dying. In addition, Costa Rica has the highest rate of deforestation in Latin America (*Assignment*: 'Banana Wars', BBC Television, 1993).

However, the WTO had hardly been established when agitation began for the US Government to use it to end the preferential treatment of bananas sold by the Caribbean island states in the EU. This was resisted fiercely by the leaders of the smaller island states, and in a meeting in Washington 13 September 1995, the Prime Minister of Jamaica, Percival J. Patterson, sought and received assurances that the US government would not pursue its case against the EU.

Despite this, on 28 September 1995, the US government went ahead and filed a complaint against the EU's banana regime on behalf of Chiquita Brands. It claimed that the Lomé system favoured imports from African, Caribbean and Pacific states over those from Central America and that in consequence Central American

▶

Case study 4.2 continued

exports had suffered. Shortly afterwards, on 6 October, the European Commission decided to permit the importation of an additional 98,800 tonnes of bananas from Latin America on the grounds that Hurricane Luis between 5 and 7 September had damaged crops in the Leeward Islands and so reduced supplies. The WTO ruled in favour of the United States and the EU modified the banana regime to comply with the ruling. However, on 7 April 1999 a WTO arbitration panel held that the EU's banana import policy, which had come into effect on 1 January, still failed to comply with earlier WTO judgments, and authorised the imposition on EU countries of unilateral US sanctions. With the banana dispute still unresolved, efforts continued in Belize to expand citrus production and shrimp farming was developing rapidly, but the situation on the islands of Dominica and St Lucia looked bleak.

Regional economic groupings

If trade is a good thing, then developing countries should find advantages in encouraging trade with other developing countries, rather than with the AICs against which they are always going to feel at a disadvantage.

Advantages

• opening up new markets;
• reciprocal advantages;
• fewer currency problems.

Disadvantages

• not always possible to source needed products (especially capital goods)
• supply may be interrupted because of difficulties with the other country's economy.

ASEAN

Most Asian countries were unwilling to be drawn into the Cold War and resisted the creation of a regional organisation for political cooperation such as the Organization of American States (OAS) or Organization of African Unity (OAU). At first they did not see any advantages in promoting intra-regional economic cooperation, as they were in competition with one another in trade with the AICs. The Association of South-east Asian Nations or ASEAN, however, was an indigenous development deriving from the common concern of the South-east Asian countries on security matters and the promotion of intra-regional cooperation on trade and economic cooperation followed.

ASEAN was established on 8 August 1967 in Bangkok by the five original member countries, namely, Indonesia, Malaysia, Philippines, Singapore and Thailand. Brunei Darussalam joined on 8 January 1984, Vietnam on 28 July 1995, Laos and Myanmar on 23 July 1997, and Cambodia on 30 April 1999. The ten countries now making up the region have a population of about 500 million and by 2004 their combined GDP was approximately equal to that of China. When ASEAN was established, trade among the member countries was insignificant, amounting to only 12 per cent and 15 per cent of regional trade. In 1993 proposals for a Free Trade Area (AFTA) were adopted and the Fifth ASEAN Summit held in Bangkok in 1995 adopted the Agenda for Greater Economic Integration, which included the acceleration of the timetable for the realisation of full free trade from the original 15-year timeframe to ten years. Within three years from the launching of AFTA, exports among ASEAN countries grew from $43.26 billion in 1993 to almost $80 billion in 1996, an average yearly growth rate of 28.3 per cent. In the process, the share of intra-regional trade from ASEAN's total trade rose from 20 per cent to almost 25 per cent. Harmonisation of communication links followed, and plans are afoot to create a common electricity grid and gas pipeline network to link the ten member countries.

Andean Community

Under the Cartagena Agreement (Acuerdo de Cartagena) signed in Bogotá, Colombia, on 26 May 1969, the governments of Bolivia, Chile, Colombia, Ecuador and Peru sought to set up an Andean Common Market, known as the Andean Pact or Group (Grupo Andino), or, more commonly, simply as the Acuerdo de Cartagena, in which all internal customs tariffs between the five member countries were to be abolished by 1980. This agreement came into force on 24 November 1969. Venezuela joined in 1973, increasing the economic weight of the organisation considerably, owing to Venezuela's role as a relatively wealthy oil exporting nation. Chile, however, withdrew in 1976, for political reasons. On 10 March 1996, the presidents of Bolivia, Colombia, Ecuador, Peru and Venezuela, meeting at Trujillo (Peru), adopted the Protocol of Trujillo, which set up the Andean System of Integration (Sistemo Andina de Integración, SICA) and renamed the Group the Andean Community (Comunidad Andina).

The Declaration of Caracas, providing a framework for the creation by January 1992 of a free trade zone between the five Andean Pact member countries (Bolivia, Colombia, Ecuador, Peru and Venezuela), was signed by the presidents of these five countries on 18 May 1991, at an Andean Pact summit meeting in Caracas, the Venezuelan capital.

The Declaration envisaged the abolition of all tariffs within the zone, although Ecuador was to be permitted to dismantle its strongly protectionist system in two stages: 50 per cent of its tariffs would be lifted by the end of 1991, and the remainder by 30 June 1992. During 1992 the Andean Pact countries would adopt a joint tariff policy for trade with the rest of the world, and subsequent measures of integration would include joint export promotion, equal commercial aviation rights and access to airport facilities, reforms of state administration and the encouragement of foreign investment. By 1995 the zone was expected to be operating as a fully integrated common market of 90 million people but in practice Peru was not fully integrated until 2005.

Mercosur

Mercosur constituted a natural development from a series of bilateral accords between Argentina and Brazil and their neighbouring countries and was formally inaugurated on 1 January 1995. Mercosur has, however, from the outset been affected by disputes between its member states, especially Brazil and Argentina, its two major members. A presidential summit, held in São Paulo (Brazil) on 19–20 June 1995, was dominated by an angry dispute between Argentina and Brazil following a Brazilian decision the previous week to reduce the quota of Argentine cars to be imported in 1996 from 70,000 to 35,000. The Brazilians claimed that they were not required to end quotas on cars until 1997 and were thus within their rights. However, on 12 July they agreed not to impose the quotas. On 22 January 1996, Argentina and Brazil signed a transitional accord intended to settle this dispute. The agreement substantially increased the quota of Argentine vehicles that could be imported into Brazil before 1999.

A joint declaration on 6 June 1999 by their two presidents that Argentina and Brazil would adopt roughly comparable mechanisms of financial restraint was presented as a step towards enhanced unity within Mercosur. On 26 July, however, Argentina tried unilaterally to impose measures against excessive imports from any country, including its Mercosur partners. Brazil immediately broke off all negotiations with Argentina, which was forced to withdraw the decree three days later, though restrictions on the import of Brazilian textiles, imposed earlier, remained in place. Later member states endorsed common standards for financial restraint and agreed to harmonise their national statistics, but failed to agree a new regime for motor vehicles, which made up 30 per cent of intra-regional trade. In mid-March 2000 Argentina and Brazil reached agreement on a transitional regime for intra-regional trade in motor vehicles. They also agreed to shelve long-standing disputes over footwear, pigs, poultry, steel, sugar and textiles. At the eighteenth presidential summit held in Buenos Aires on 30 June 2000, however, Paraguay and Uruguay rejected the agreement, although they joined the others in reaffirming their willingness to enhance integration and improve macroeconomic coordination.

Caricom

The Caribbean Community and Common Market was established in 1973 but despite encouragement from Britain and other Commonwealth countries made little progress until the 1990s. It includes some of the smallest and most vulnerable economies in the world: Antigua and Barbuda, Bahamas, Barbados, Belize, Dominica, Grenada, Guyana, Jamaica, Montserrat, St Kitts and Nevis, St Lucia, St Vincent and the Grenadines, Suriname, Trinidad and Tobago. The Bahamas are a member of the Community but not of the Common Market. The attempt to foster intra-regional commerce through the creation of a free trade area was repeatedly hampered by political disputes and by the maintenance of import restrictions in an effort to protect the domestic economies of individual island countries. In the 1990s, however, Caribbean leaders became increasingly concerned about the impact on their small and often fragile economies of developments such as the consolidation of powerful regional trading blocs through the single European market and the North American Free Trade Agreement. They also saw as a particular threat to their vulnerable economies globalisation and trade liberalisation implemented through the WTO. As a result they eventually linked up with the Central American countries under an umbrella organisation, the Association of Caribbean States (ACS). Caricom's intra-regional imports grew only marginally from 10 per cent in 1996 to 10.8 per cent in 2001, but intra-regional exports grew from 16.8 per cent of total exports in 1996 to 20.4 per cent in 2001.

Conclusion

In economic terms what developing world countries have in common is a tendency to be exploitable and thus exploited, though the extent to which this actually happens varies a great deal. Interpretations of why this is and how it might be changed have dominated theories of development. The changing position of the NICs and the extent (and impact) of developing world indebtedness remain key issues in the current debates about the economic prospects for developing countries.

Key terms

agricultural revolution – the process of developing agricultural productivity through systematic crop rotation and livestock breeding begun in Britain in the early eighteenth century; by extension a similar process in other countries

Arusha Declaration – call by the African states meeting in Tanzania in 1980 for a new international economic order

austerity – programme of restrictions on government spending involving sacrifices on the part of the population at large

'billiard ball' model – model of international relations which assumes that they are concerned only with interactions between states

conditionality – the requirement that countries agree to implement certain economic policy reforms, as a condition of receiving financial assistance

Cotonou Agreement – agreement between the EU and the ACP countries, signed on 23 June 2000, for a period of 20 years, establishing a new framework for cooperation that is consistent with WTO rules

debt boomerang – term originated by the economist Susan George to denote the harmful consequences of developing world debt for the lending countries

debt crisis – economic crisis first identified in Latin America in 1982 when Brazil and Mexico had to stop paying interest on their debts; also felt by African and some Asian countries

debt service – payment due of interest on public debt, including overseas debt

'debtors' cartel' – theoretical possibility that indebted countries might be able to drive down the cost of borrowing by concerted action

decolonisation – the deliberate policy of preparing colonies for independence

deregulation – removal of controls on the participation of private interests in the supply of public services, e.g. transport

Doha Round – round of multilateral trade negotiations begun at Doha in January 2002, focusing on two areas of contention: agricultural subsidies and trade in services

Group of Seven (G7) – term used for series of meetings of the world's leading economic powers, starting in 1973, concerned increasingly with political rather than economic issues. With the inclusion of Russia, not one of the world's largest economies, now (2006) the Group of Eight (G8)

Heavily Indebted Poorer Countries Initiative – policy launched by the IMF in 1976, which identified 40 countries, mainly in Africa, as impoverished and in need of debt relief

hyperinflation – term conventionally given to any rate of inflation exceeding 50 per cent per month; a period of inflation which leaves a country's currency essentially worthless

Lomé Convention – a comprehensive agreement regulating trade and providing for economic assistance, concluded at Lomé Togo, in 1975 between the European Union states and developing countries in Africa, the Caribbean and the Pacific (ACP countries), extended several times and succeeded by the Cotonou Agreement, signed in Cotonou in Benin in June 2000

narcotic drugs – term favoured in the USA for specific substances such as cocaine and heroin illegally used for personal pleasure

oil shock – sudden increase in the world price of oil, in 1973–74 as a result of a deliberate series of decisions by OPEC; in 1979 as a result of alarm at the Iranian Revolution

Poverty Reduction Strategy Papers (PRSPs) – documents prepared by governments in low income countries through a participatory process involving domestic stakeholders and external development partners, as a requirement of seeking support from the IMF and the World Bank. They describe the macroeconomic, structural and social policies and programmes that the country intends to pursue over several years to promote broad-based growth and reduce poverty, its external financing needs and any associated sources of funding

Prisoners' Dilemma – model of a zero-sum game in which whatever the other does, each of two prisoners is better off confessing than remaining silent. But the outcome obtained when both confess is worse for each than the outcome they would have obtained had both remained silent

privatisation – selling off government-owned assets

protectionism – policy of protecting chosen sectors of a domestic economy by putting up barriers to the importation of goods such as tariffs (taxes on imports) and import quotas (restricting the volume of goods that can be imported)

recession – negative economic growth for a short period, conventionally two successive quarters; a longer period is a depression

Rounds – series of negotiations leading to further expansion of the General Agreement on Tariffs and Trade (GATT)

Structural Adjustment Programmes (SAPs) – term formerly used for the set of economic policies required by the IMF and World Bank for governments seeking loans and debt relief – now called Poverty Reduction Strategy Papers (PRSPs)

'take-off' model of development – model proposed by the economist W.W. Rostow arguing that once development reached a certain level it would become self-sustaining

transnational corporations (TNCs) – large corporations which, though necessarily having their headquarters in one country, are staffed by personnel from many countries and do business in many parts of the world. Also known as multinational corporations (MNCs)

World Trade Organization (WTO) – organisation established in 1995 to regulate trade between the signatory countries

Questions

1. Assess the success of the Millennium initiative on debt reduction.

2. Evaluate the success of structural adjustment policies in developing countries.

3. How can the AICs best help developing countries overcome the 'crisis of development'?

4. Does the experience of developing countries support the widely-held view that the Washington consensus offers the only practicable road to economic development?

5. Assess the impact of the WTO on economic conditions in developing countries.

6. How far and in what way can regional economic groupings help developing states' economies?

CHAPTER 5

The social context

Introduction

Development implies substantial changes to social structures and practices. There are two ways of looking at this: that social change is a necessary pre-condition for development, or that development will necessarily bring about social change. Either way, one of the main problems is the law of unintended consequences. The difficulty is not that political choices, legislation, and even constitutional amendment, may be necessary to bring about desirable changes – that is inevitable. The problem is that there is virtually no legislation or political choice that does not involve unintended consequences, some of which may be undesirable.

Gender and society

Women constitute a majority in most societies. Yet **stratification** by **gender** is to be found in most developing world societies and separate organisations for men and women exist in most, if not all, of them. There are two main reasons for this. First, stratification by gender occurs in the first instance within the family and involves personal relationships between individuals not groups; it is therefore resistant not only to change but even to study and research. Secondly, because of the central importance of personal relationships, women are often seen as collaborating in their own **exploitation**.

Although in some societies there are tighter and more formal groupings, in Africa secret societies play a major role in gender differentiation. In Sierra Leone, where male secret societies were the dominant organisations before colonisation, the Poro still operates and retains considerable power today, especially among the Mende tribe, where it originated, and the Sherbro Bullom and the Temne, to which it later spread. Significantly, female secret societies also exist, and are known to be central to training girls in the social roles they are to assume as women.

Many religious traditions, too, separate men and women from one another. This is frequently defended as being both divinely ordained and socially necessary if public morality is to be maintained. Where women have been admitted, either in the past or as a result of recent changes, to the priesthood, men continue to hold the key posts and interpret religious teaching in a fashion that both requires women to accept male dominance in their daily lives and encourages them to believe that it is right that they should do so.

In Papua New Guinea women are subordinated in public affairs through the clan system and may be excluded from public discussion entirely. Clans are male dominant; their leadership is exercised by a chief (*bigman*), who presides over village meetings and as such has the power to interpret the law. Among the rights commonly assumed by men is that of wife beating. Ironically, before colonisation, women did have control over their own earnings and autonomy in economic affairs, but this has been lost as European influence reinforced male dominance (Black 1999: 232).

In modern societies, however, the most common factor placing women at a disadvantage to men in making their views felt and sharing their skills is lack of formal education. There are estimated to be a billion adult illiterates in the world, of which 60 per cent are women. The education of women, their capacity to control their fertility and their economic independence are not just concessions to a disadvantaged group – the developing world cannot afford sops. Women are functional parts of the process of development that the developing world cannot afford not to encourage. Women must play a fuller part in development in this generation and in future through their care and education of their children. Their lack of education damages their capacities as primary health carers and educators. Education for women has invariably been shown, moreover, to be the single major factor leading to limitation on family size and a fall in the otherwise inexorable rate of population growth.

Women and work

The tradition of **bride price** in Africa reflects the traditional attitude of male society to women as a commodity – though a commodity which does retain some rights and in some tribes can attain positions of considerable power. It is part of the role of women in rural society to cultivate land to provide food, and this tradition survives, modified, in the urban context. Andreski noted that in urban Ghana an artisan will typically provide his wife with capital to trade on her own account, and, while not expecting her to feed him, does expect her

to feed herself and her children (Andreski 1968: 50–1). Two traditional occupations for urban women are market trading and prostitution, though the
latter did not originally carry the social stigma it does in Europe and often
does not do so today, despite the efforts of both Christian and Muslim
missionaries to change this perception.

Colonisation in West Africa as in other places distorted the traditional role
of women. Colonialism brought foreign-owned large estates growing cash
crops for an external market. Women's labour remained important, indeed
essential to the large-scale production of cotton and tea, but the land was
owned by men who received the profits from it and imports hit craft production. Hence development brought new forms of exploitation. There were
benefits, for example, education, but in Muslim areas women were often
excluded from the benefits colonialism brought and cultural norms have been
powerful enough to resist legal changes for the benefit of women. This was
the case, for example, when after the end of the colonial period 'female
circumcision' (genital mutilation) was officially banned in Sierra Leone by
the government of Milton Margai.

The post-colonial era has brought jobs in electronics and other skilled
assembly work, where some 80–90 per cent of workers are women. Women
form the bulk of the labour force in the *maquiladoras* of Mexico and Central
America (see e.g. Petersen 1992). They work long hours for very low wages
and return to families where they are still expected to do all the housework.
In China male dominance continues in some key urban aspects, especially
in heavy industry, skilled trades, management and secondary education. It is
largely unquestioned in traditional rural areas where women's activities are
generally restricted to the household and that household is that of the husband's family anyway. Despite legal rights the real situation is that many
Chinese women do not have property, and lack the resources for independence. However, the situation had greatly improved since 1949, when 90 per
cent of women were illiterate; by 1982 the figure had fallen to 70 per cent
and by 1995 it was down to 35 per cent. During the 1980s high unemployment rates gave employers more choice in selecting workers and women were
perceived as more expensive owing to the requirement to provide for childcare, maternity leave and earlier retirement. Employers were only required to
make the rather cheaper provision of accommodation to male employees. But
since then the principle of equal pay has been established, even if it is not
always enforced.

In the Asian 'Tigers' women make up the bulk of the workforce in the
so-called Economic Processing Zones (EPZs):

The EPZ economy is based on employing cheap labour for the assembly of high-
volume standardised components. Such work is seen as particularly suited to
women. Since the 1960s young women have been employed in EPZ factories on a
large scale. They comprise the majority of child labour, often spending most of their
teenage years in sweatshops making plastic toys or garments. By the 1970s they had

moved onto the more sophisticated assembly lines – particularly electronics and pharmaceuticals. By 1982, of the 62,617 workers employed in EPZs in Taiwan 85 per cent were women. (*New Internationalist*, 263, January 1995)

Such workers are recruited in the countryside under false promises, often that they will gain valuable education as well as make a useful contribution to the marginal existence of the family group. While in work they live in dormitories under strict control and supervision. However, safety at work is not much of a consideration – in South Korea, for example, 10 or 12 hours' work a day is still normal and the country has one of the highest rates of industrial accidents in the world. If recession comes the women workers are often unaware of any rights they may possess under employment legislation and can be speedily laid off.

Such occupations, even at the beginning of the twenty-first century, are not, however, typical. Some 90 per cent of the developing world's women still depend directly on the land for survival. In fact, women produce most of the food in developing countries, and between 60–80 per cent in Africa south of the Sahara (SSA). They work longer hours and do heavier work than men. Ester Boserup popularised the view 'that African agriculture exhibited a dualism based on gender: a cash crops sector in which *men* grow highly productive income-earning export crops, and a food crop sector in which *women* use traditional methods to produce food for their families to consume' (Boserup 1981 and 1989). This view has now been shown to be wrong, as it understates the involvement of women in the modern sector of the economy and ignores the fact that food crops are also grown as cash crops (Whitehead 1990: 55). But it still leaves women responsible for the bulk of food production.

The reasons why women's productivity is so often underestimated are:

- The assumption that they are less strong and their work is therefore in some sense 'light'. This clearly is not the case. If they are less strong their work must be proportionately harder, and in any case they usually work far longer hours than men.
- The fact that domestic labour is not accorded its proper value. Domestic labour is still not counted in the calculation of GNP, although common sense suggests that it must account for a very high proportion of it in less developed countries.
- The fact that local economies are largely ignored in favour of urban and export markets and it is men who own the land on which cash crops are grown or who manage the factories in which women work.

Though women's roles are often marginal, not to say invisible, women, like men, are basic economic units. They are often wrongly perceived as dependants when in reality they are producers. Much of their time and energies have been squandered on the least productive domestic concerns from which it should have been possible to begin liberating them. In China, on marriage a woman ceases to be part of her birth family, symbolised by the physical removal of herself and her possessions to her husband's home, but she does not cease to work. In rural areas the planting and cultivation of wet rice is regarded as women's work and on any building site in China and Vietnam the bulk of the unskilled labour is provided by women.

It is also assumed that work done in or about the home and not for pay can be disregarded. Domestic labour, even if on the farm, is not accorded its proper value; production for subsistence or of chickens, ducks and vegetables for the local market, does not have the same status as the production of cash crops. Further, women have not received support for their agricultural production in the form of loans, technology or training. They have not had a say in the decision-making that affects them, so irrigation is not available for subsistence farming, only for cash crops. This is a major contributory factor to the decline of food for local consumption in most developing world countries. In the Amazon basin women who for whatever reason find themselves without male partners or mature sons cannot, according to colonization agencies, constitute 'families', so they lose their right to land. The widespread rural poverty of women has led to their out-migration as agricultural labourers in plantations, as export workers in entrepôt enclaves or as domestic help at home or abroad. Policy-makers (who are usually male) often perceive women as burdens and do not take their needs on board. Women are also responsible for overseeing the considerable additional contribution that children make to the domestic economy. Women and the children under their direction are usually exclusively responsible for domestic access to water.

Energy in the rural developing world is mainly **biomass** (fuelwood, crop residues and manure), which is collected by women and children. Biomass accounts for 75 per cent of fuel used in the developing world generally and 90 per cent of fuel consumed in SSA. Fuelwood collection is often blamed for deforestation. However rural women traditionally use fallen dead wood. Fuelwood from cut trees is usually for commercial sale to urban areas. Burning dung is, of course, a contribution to agricultural underproduction, but not a very great one. Women have well-developed skills in managing resources and, as **Agenda** 21 (see Chapter 9) specifically recognised, probably know more about sustainable development than men as they live it more directly. But while women look after their men and the environment, they pay a price. The burning of biomass in the cooking process in rural dwellings, for example, has now been recognised as having devastating effects on female and child health. It is the major, but most forgotten form of air pollution, because it occurs out of sight in the home where it causes all manner of respiratory ailments. It is hard not to conclude that it is a problem overlooked because it almost invariably affects only women.

Women's participation in development requires that they receive increased access to land, credit, skills, primary health care, water, sanitation and education. There is, of course, also an ethical question as well as practical ones. It must be clear that, if development is a right, equal opportunities to achieve development should be available to all nations and also to all individuals (Chapter 1). Without full participation in the development process, as recommended by the Brundtland Report (WCED 1987), there cannot be the peace and stability in which development can occur.

Women and children

Even within the developing world there are very considerable differences in the standard causes of death. The main avoidable risk is specific to women and is pregnancy. Half a million women still die in childbirth each year, but African women are 200 times as likely to die from pregnancy-related causes as women in industrialised countries, where perinatal mortality is now very low owing to professional attendants, good hospital resources and advanced medical techniques. In the developing world, pregnancy still carries a significant hazard of potentially fatal infection for the mother. WHO figures for 2000 showed that of 529,000 maternal deaths each year (deaths during or within 42 days of pregnancy from causes specific to the pregnancy), only 2,500 occurred in the industrialised countries. As with other diseases, the prevalence of neonatal diseases is now greater in the developing world than it was a century ago. The avoidance of pregnancy through birth control is therefore an important factor in enabling women to live longer, while by reducing the burdens of looking after large families it has important additional social benefit, especially for the children of the smaller families.

In China the establishment of the Republic in 1911 meant the end of the appalling abuse of footbinding, which was, in any case, a Manchurian custom introduced by the Qing Dynasty. After 1949 equality was a prime goal of the new Communist regime and many improvements were made in the position of women, such as the introduction of a 48-hour week, maternity leave and childcare. However, after Mao Zedong's death in 1976, there was a tendency for pragmatic economic goals to push out ideological political goals. Officially the one-child policy stresses child health, good parenting and care for the elderly. The policy has been very successful in urban areas where the vast majority of children under 12 are the only child of their family. However, in rural areas where the first child is female there are reports of high levels of female infanticide, and a second or even third child may be permitted ostensibly to help provide labour on the homestead. This may be seen as official government endorsement of traditional assumptions of male superiority. In urban areas a second child may lead to loss of benefits including the advantage of nursery care for the first child. A subsequent illegal child may mean compulsory sterilisation for the woman, not for the man.

Mahatma Gandhi said that to understand India one should study its villages and its women. The respect Gandhi accorded Indian women is not necessarily echoed in Indian society as a whole. Since 1911 there has been a steady decline in the ratio of women to men with the steepest fall since ultrasound scanning became available in India in 1979, enabling parents to determine the sex of their child before birth. Sex detection before birth was made illegal by the Indian government in 1994, but there is no doubt that it continues and in March 2006, for the first time, a doctor was sentenced to two years in prison for revealing the sex of a female foetus and agreeing to abort it. For every 1,000 boys up to the age of six, there were 962 girls in India in 1981, 945 in 1991 and only 927 in 2001 (*The Guardian*, 30 March 2006). In the UK and other developed countries, by comparison, the ratio is 1060 girls : 1000 boys.

In India baby girls used to be killed after birth. In Rajasthan female infanticide was a military custom; only boys could become warriors so girls were often killed as a ritual sacrifice to get a son (*devdasis*). Female infanticide was outlawed in India more than a century ago by the British Raj, but there, as elsewhere, laws do not necessarily change social customs and in recent years there have been reports of the continuance of the practice in rural communities in South India, where it is usually carried out by the grandmother, with the collusion of the local authorities. It is not possible not to notice that up to four out of ten baby girls are being killed soon after birth; it shows up in the sex ratio of the children in the village schools.

Women go on bearing children in the hope of having a son who will bring a dowry to the family, look after his parents in their old age, preserve the family name, keep the family property intact, attend to his parents' funeral rites and light their funeral pyre. Cradle schemes now exist so that 'unwanted' girl babies may be deposited and cared for, but they are not really unwanted in this sense and fatalism about death means that many mothers prefer to kill their girl babies and such schemes have few takers. Girls who are not killed at birth sometimes die of neglect while their brothers thrive – it is often boys who are taken to hospital when ill, girls are in some areas considered to be very lucky if they receive any medical treatment at all. Girls suffer a 30–60 per cent higher rate of mortality simply because they less often receive medical treatment when sick.

The main problem is the rising cost of dowries, or rather the high costs of 'gifts' on marriage, since there is now much less restraint on the parties involved. Dowries were made illegal in India in 1961. Then they were in any case largely confined to the upper castes, but, despite that, the institution has now spread to the poorest villages. Girls are a very expensive liability for their parents and to have even one in a family can mean financial ruin in the future. In Tamil Nadu, where expensive rituals accompany the growing up of girls, a 'dowry' can cost as much as 15 years' income and the daughter of parents who cannot pay may be outcast. With the demonstration effect of Western television programmes, families are making demands for still bigger dowries to meet their aspirations to Western luxuries. Where marriages are arranged dowries often represent a simple transfer of capital from one family to another. Or the dowry may be used as an ongoing form of blackmail and daughters may be returned unwanted to their parents when their husband's further financial demands are not met. Worst of all, some women are extremely cruelly treated for not bringing larger dowries, or to extort more money from their families, and in many cases their families refuse to take them back. The ultimate consequence is bride burning, where the bride is set on fire with paraffin to simulate an accidental fire in the cooking area. Officially bride burning claimed 2,449 women's lives in 1991, but the real figure was undoubtedly much higher (*Assignment*: 'Let Her Die', BBC Television, 1993), and awareness of the problem has become much greater in recent years. In 1994 the National Crimes Bureau estimated the number of dowry deaths at 5,119. Some ten years later, in 2003, reported dowry deaths totalled 6,208 (http://ncrb.nic.in/crime2003/cii.html). The custom of paying dowry is also found in non-Hindu communities, as are the consequences. In parts of Muslim Bangladesh, young women have been disfigured and even blinded in acid attacks after they had rejected suitors or were the innocent victims of dowry disputes with their former families (McKean 2000). Three hundred Pakistani women are burned to death each year because their husbands no longer want them (BBC News, 27 August 1999).

Deliberate cruelty of this kind is, of course, relatively rare. Much more common is the impact of cultural norms promoting inequality. These norms are sustained as much by the women who are disadvantaged by them as by the men who might be perceived as benefiting. It is women who struggle to feed their families, even actually eating afterwards in many cultures. As it is women who generally organise food in any household it seems natural to them to feed their families first and more adequately than they do themselves. Seventy per cent of pregnant women suffer anaemia caused by malnutrition. This is not really surprising as even early studies (e.g. Sinha 1976: 13) show the extent of inequality – in Hyderabad the calorie intake for pregnant and lactating women was only 1,400 per day against the average Indian requirement of 2,200 calories per day.

Women and political power

It was through her membership of the Sande (*bundu*) society that Madam Yoko (c.1850–1906), later to be chief of Moyamba and ally of the British in the Hut Tax War in Sierra Leone, acquired her initial fame which led to an influential marriage (Foray 1977). As this example shows, in pre-colonial times women could and did hold political power in West Africa, and indeed were to take an important role in asserting the right to retain African dress and their African identity, but marriage formed an important key to their possibility of social advancement. In post-independence Africa, however, few women have yet reached the highest political positions, and this, ironically, despite the survival of traditional matriarchal features in some societies. The best-known example is Swaziland, where on the death of the king, until a new king is formally selected, the queen mother acts as regent with the title of 'Great She-Elephant'. Africa's first woman president, Ellen Johnson-Sirleaf, was elected in Liberia in late 2005, and took office in January 2006 prepared to confront the warlords her predecessors had failed to subdue (Reuters, 6 January 2006).

In Asia the political position of women varies greatly. In China women notionally have complete equality, but in practice the ageing government of the People's Republic is unusual today for the almost total absence of women in high office. In South Asia, Mrs Sirimavo Bandaranaike became the world's first woman prime minister in Sri Lanka in 1960, and was again to hold that office when her daughter, Chandrika Kumaratunga, was elected President in 1994. Meanwhile, India, Pakistan and Bangladesh have all had women leaders. In South-east Asia, Gloria Macapagal Arroyo was elected president of the Philippines in 2001, the second member of her family to hold that office. In Myanmar (formerly known in the West as Burma), Aung San Suu Kyi has for more than a decade been denied by the armed forces the position of leadership to which she had been elected. Awarded the Nobel Peace Prize, for her refusal to contemplate civil violence, she was not even allowed out of house arrest to say goodbye to her dying husband.

In other parts of the developing world the situation is more mixed. In Latin America only one woman held political office in some 300 years of colonial rule and that for only three days. Nevertheless since women obtained the franchise, beginning in Ecuador in 1929, the situation in the region has steadily improved. In Mexico and Chile today the status of middle-class women can be very high. In Argentina María Estela (Isabel) Martínez de Perón became the world's first woman executive president in succession to her husband in 1974. Since then Lidia Gueiler Tejada has served as interim President of Bolivia (1979–80), and Violeta Barrios de Chamorro, Janet Jagan and Mireya Elisa Moscoso de Gruber have been elected president of Nicaragua (1990), Guyana (1998–99) and Panama (1999) respectively.

In the Caribbean, Eugenia Charles, Jennifer Smith and Suzy Camelia Römer have been prime minister of Dominica (1980), the Bahamas (1998) and Curaçao respectively. In 1999, it was Panama's first woman president, Mireya Elisa Moscoso de Gruber, who received the Panama Canal from former US President Jimmy Carter, representing the United States (which has yet to have a woman as president).

Research by UNICEF, however, shows that women's representation in national assemblies is still small. Only in a few AICs does it exceed 25 per cent, and the world average actually fell from 15 per cent to 9 per cent in the ten years from 1985 to 1995 (*The Guardian*, 9 June 1995). According to the *Human Development Report* only 10 per cent of seats in the world's legislatures were held by women and only 6 per cent of the posts in national executives (UNDP 1995). By November 2005 the situation had improved noticeably, but still fell very far short of equality. The world average had risen again to

16.1 per cent (16.3 per cent when only the sole or lower house was taken into account). In the Organisation for Security and Cooperation in Europe (OSCE) the average was 19.1 per cent. In the rest of the world the average was: Americas 18.3 per cent, Africa South of the Sahara 16.1 per cent, Asia 16.1 per cent, the Pacific 12 per cent and the Arab states only 8.7 per cent (Inter-Parliamentary Union 2006). Women are much more effective in local and grassroots organisations, but in a still state-centric world women are missing out at the levels that count. Policy-makers often perceive women as burdens and do not take their needs on board even when asked to do so.

An exception is where women band together in organisations to run base communities. For example, Tamil Nadu in India had 25,000 registered grass-roots organizations in 1993, and is believed to have at least as many today, and women play a major role in the administration and running of such organisations. And in Brazil women have been able to overcome some of the misconceptions which govern official dealings with them, because their contribution as an organised group requires a political response from elected officials and civil servants.

The View from the Ground

By *Ilene R. Prusher*, Staff writer of *The Christian Science Monitor*
Kuwait City, Kuwait (published 8 August 2000)

Kuwaiti Women Seek Right to Vote

Fatima al-Abdali and scores of other Kuwaiti women – most covered from head to toe in black – have been marching into the offices of their *mukhtars*, local leaders, to register to vote.

But the *mukhtars* are under government orders to send the women directly to the police. There, the officers record their complaints, serve them tea, then send them home.

Just getting it on paper makes it 'mission accomplished' for these women, who helped their leaders fight Iraqi occupation a decade ago. These women – as well as many Kuwaiti men – say denials of their voting rights violate the country's 1961 Constitution, which promises not to discriminate on the basis of gender.

Here in Kuwait and in several quarters of the Arab world, societies are reconsidering women's roles in politics and public life in general. While women in the far more liberal Lebanon ask why so few of them are prevalent in politics despite their longstanding rights to vote and run for office, much more conservative Kuwaitis are deciding whether women should enjoy those rights at all.

The ruler of Kuwait, Sheikh Jaber al-Sabah issued a royal decree in June 1999 that stated women should be allowed to vote and run for office in the next election. But a measure to put his will into law was defeated, 32 to 30, by legislators last November.

The problem here, and in many other Arab countries where new young leaders are promoting progressive rights, is that top-down directed change won't take, because it doesn't have widespread, grass-roots support.

'The way this issue came to the public agenda was not healthy,' says Dr. al-Abdali, senior environmental engineer with the Kuwait Oil Company. 'Women were saying they think things are fine as they are, without the vote, and that allowed legislators to say the timing is not right.'

So al-Abdali, and the scores of other women marching on the *mukhtars*, are taking what they learned as anti-Iraq protesters to demand the right to vote and an opportunity to run for office.

Constitutional basis

The country's Constitution promises not to discriminate on the basis of gender. So, in their latest step to fight city hall, Al-Abdali, the head of the Women's Issues Committee, has filed a case in Kuwait's highest court, charging that the prohibition against women voting is unconstitutional.

The case was thrown out of the Supreme Court last month, when judges ruled they had not followed court procedures. But they can file the case again next year – when they say they'll demand again to register to vote. Moreover, the Kuwaiti parliament may take up the issue again when it reconvenes this fall.

Islamic concept

At the center of the debate is an Islamic concept known as '*willaya umma*,' meaning leadership of the Muslim community. The Koran, say Islamic conservatives here, forbids women to be in such authoritative positions.

'It is in the sayings of the Prophet that people will not succeed if they allow

women to be their commanders,' says Walid al-Tubatabai, an Islamist member of parliament who led the drive to defeat the voting rights bill. 'Besides that, the entry of women into politics will cause social and political problems.'

Dr. al-Tubatabai's outlook, echoed by many men and women alike here, views this not as the suppression of women's rights, but as something akin to a democratic oligarchy in which families express political preferences through their fathers' and husbands' votes. And he argues that the nature of campaigning in Kuwait, which requires nightly visits to salon gatherings and publishing details of a candidate's history, puts politicking off-limits to a proper Muslim woman.

But others argue the term is open to interpretation, and shouldn't apply to parliamentary representation. They point to other Islamic nations that interpret the term as referring only to leadership bodies representing Muslims across the world. Women have already served as leaders in non-Arab Muslim nations such as Turkey and Pakistan, while women in the Near Eastern and North African Arab countries have voting rights.

Women in other Arab countries have enjoyed voting rights for decades: Syria and Lebanon since the 1950s, Yemen in 1967, Jordan since 1974.

In non-Arab Muslim countries such as Turkey and Pakistan, women have even served as prime ministers.

But other Arab countries grant rights

Several other Arab Gulf countries, while still lacking many basic democratic freedoms, have been taking steps to include women in the decision making arena. In Qatar, women were allowed to vote and run for office in the country's first municipal elections last March. Oman's emir last year allowed two women to sit on the Consultative Council, while Bahrain selected its first woman ambassador. And Saudi Arabia began allowing women to watch proceedings of its Advisory Council from a separate viewer's gallery.

But women are so untested in politics in the Arab world that they often don't vote for each other when they are able, such as in the Qatar election last year. Women were permitted to vote and run for office for the first time.

Several ran, but other women didn't vote for them.

'Even women do not elect women,' says Amal Khoury, a research assistant with the Lebanese Center for Policy Studies. 'There is no trust in women that they are capable of doing the job. There is still a mentality that as long as a husband is working, she should stay home and take care of the children.'

Source: http://www.csmonitor.com/atcsmonitor/specials/women/rights/rights080800.html

Women and the orthodoxy of development

International relations have until recently not paid any special attention to the position of women. There are three reasons for this. Relations between states have traditionally been seen as primarily concerned with military security, a reserve area for men. The clannish nature of foreign services has ensured that senior diplomats and policy-makers have also been mostly male. The language of international relations itself is gendered, with Darwinian overtones of the survival of the fittest.

However, 'international policies and processes, far from being gender-neutral, in practice play an important role in determining women's place in society and in structuring economic, political and social relations between the sexes' (Halliday 1994: 153). In the event of war, women may be and frequently are called on to do 'men's' jobs, but when peace comes they are again excluded. While the war lasts, they are the prime victims of war, not just as civilians, but as objects of rape, which in ethnic wars has been repeatedly employed to enforce, in the most brutal fashion imaginable, the dominance of one ethnic group over another.

In peacetime it is the economic consequences of international decisions that bear most heavily on women. As the IMF sought to maintain stable exchange rates in the 1980s, in a world afflicted by rising oil prices and accelerating inflation, structural adjustment programmes were oriented to markets and in particular to the removal of what was considered to be distortions in them. This had a detrimental effect on the standing of women. Women were largely excluded from national markets and the food subsidies and other support for the poorest sectors from which they might hope to benefit were precisely the 'distortions' to development identified by the markets liberal approach to development, and their removal the main target of such adjustments. In addition, when SAPs required cuts in developing world expenditure, (male) vested interests and (male) national pride ensured that swollen military budgets were protected. In turn, since protection for military personnel is built into those budgets, social services were hit hardest. There are a few exceptions, e.g. Uruguay, but in general a reluctance to cut social services is seen by international lending agencies as unwillingness to comply with the terms of loans and can lead to serious consequences for the credit rating of the governments that try to evade this requirement.

Women are an 'adjustment variable' on whom SAPs impact particularly hard. The problem is that austerity measures intensify as they pass down social structures. The semi-autonomous and wholly privately funded UN agency with responsibility for the children of the world, UNICEF, estimates that a 2–3 per cent decline in national income in developing countries hits the poorest sections to the tune of 10–15 per cent (UNICEF 1990). At the same time SAPs hit the public sector and women are disproportionately likely to be employed as teachers, nurses etc. This was especially true of Nigeria in the 1980s. In Nigeria women had moved into a rapidly expanding public sector during the petroleum bonanza of the late 1960s and the early 1970s. When negotiations with the IMF broke down a World Bank-backed indigenous SAP was devised. This aimed, among other things, to reduce the public sector, and the immediate result was the loss of many of these new public sector jobs.

SAPs raise food costs, also. Between 1980 and 1983 76 per cent of IMF-supported programmes included increased indirect taxation, 46 per cent increased tariffs and only 13 per cent involved increases in direct personal or corporation taxes, the least regressive of the alternatives available.

SAPs have diverted women from their families to marginal economic activities and thus have contributed to social problems such as child abandonment and delinquency, as in Brazil and some Caribbean states. Both directly and indirectly, therefore, they have lowered standards of health care and nutrition for mothers and children, causing lower birth weights, poorer child health and lower intelligence, building up problems for the future. In Chile child mortality was increased by cutbacks in the child-feeding programme in 1983, though these have since been reversed. And the long-term effects are also significant: SAPs hit education budgets and girls' secondary education is generally seen as the area most easily sacrificed.

The sad thing is that it would not cost much to protect the living standards of the poorest sectors from the impact of economic fashions. They have so little to protect. But they do not make the decisions. Because of the impact of SAPs on most disadvantaged groups, UNICEF recommended changes: more medium-term financial support and less shock, the encouragement of policies that do not hit vulnerable groups, sectoral policies confining adjustment to the productive sectors, policies to enhance efficiency and equity of the social sector, compensatory programmes and the monitoring of living standards. The World Bank is now well aware of the impact of SAPs on women and other vulnerable groups. In April 1987 it issued *Protecting the Poor during Periods of Adjustment*, but argued for compensatory measures to be added on rather than changing the basic nature of SAPs.

Impact of development on other disadvantaged groups

Development, suggesting as it does social aspects such as increasing welfare provision and decreased inequality, should be expected to have a particular and positive impact on groups such as children, the aged and indigenous peoples. Goldthorpe (1975: 23) notes, however, that there have been considerable differences between actual societies.

Development should lead to increased possibilities of education and the opening up of a greater variety of life chances. However, there are problems. In the first phase of development, rapid population growth means a greatly increased burden on the financial resources available for education, particularly in rural areas, and the urban–rural divide in provision widens. There can be considerable resentment in rural communities at state educational provision being directed towards the concerns of the town and thus remote from the needs and interests of the rural sector.

Inequalities between the rich minority and the poor majority are, of course, much more marked. Only 11 per cent of global educational spending goes on the 75 per cent of the world's children who live in developing countries. Twenty-three per cent of them do not attend school at all, compared to less than 1 per cent in the developed world. But, as ever, there are glaring disparities within the developing world, resulting in the most massive wastage of talent where it is most needed, in the very poorest countries. In 1990 the world's governments promised 'education for all' by 2015. Yet in 2005 more than 100 million primary school-age children worldwide did not attend school, 60 per cent of them girls. As most of these were in South Asia and SSA, these regions were not expected to reach the 'education for all' goal. East Asia, Latin America and the Caribbean, on the other hand, were expected to do so much sooner (World Bank press release No. : 2005/431/S, 17 April 2005).

Lack of education is 'bad news' for individuals, their families and their societies. At the individual level, most of the countries of SSA and several elsewhere in the developing world, have literacy rates below 50 per cent (see Table 5.1). This denies them access to social, economic and political power. The empowering quality of education is illustrated by the fact that women with secondary education in Bangladesh are three times more likely to take collective political action than those without. At the family level, lack of education is associated with poverty. In countries as far apart as Peru and Vietnam, for example, two-thirds of families living in extreme poverty are headed by an adult with no education. At the societal level, it is estimated that raising the average time in school by only one year adds 23 per cent growth to the GDP/GNI of developing countries.

In 1990, the world's governments promised 'education for all' by the year 2000. It would have cost some $6 billion to put every child in the world in school, less than 1 per cent of global military spending. Worse still, the continuing repatriation of debt service charges has in some cases hit domestic

Table 5.1   World's lowest literacy rates, 2005

Country	Percentage of population over 16
1. Burkina Faso	18
2. Eritrea 1	20
3. Sierra Leone	21
4. Benin	23
5. Guinea	24
5. Somalia	24
7. Sudan	27
7. Gambia	27
9. Ethiopia	28
9. Niger	28

Source: Information Please® Database, © 2005 Pearson Education, Inc. All rights reserved

resources otherwise available for the provision of services such as education. In Tanzania in 1997–98, for example, debt repayments were four times the investment in primary education (*Guardian Education*, 11 April 2000).

Development also presents different opportunities to those who might in First World countries be in secondary or tertiary education. Integration into the world culture of film and television has presented developing world societies with an almost unattainable image of the good life, as lived in penthouse apartments in Los Angeles or New York. Young people are likely to feel most keenly the disparity between their ideal and their actual circumstances. This and the pressure of population drives youngsters to seek work in the town, joining the tide of migration.

For the aged, development also offers the possibility of better medical care, access to wider horizons through public transport, radio and television and some labour-saving devices. Migration to towns and splitting up of families, however, either takes the elderly away from their village community where their skills are of use or leaves the elderly a charge on rural relatives who by definition are less likely to be able to carry the burden.

Indigenous peoples are most vulnerable to the impact of development, not least because many governments intent on rapid development see their traditional lifestyles as a drag on progress and modernity.

Ethnic cleavages

All societies are stratified, though in the most homogenous societies divisions remain those of gender and age sets, membership of the latter often being determined by the particular batch of initiates into adulthood with which a young man or woman shared the appropriate tribal rituals. Stratification implies a horizontal division, which is registered in the power structure in the form of superordination versus subordination. However, one can differentiate between horizontal and vertical systems of stratification. In the former other characteristics are spread across each band in a way that cuts across the main axis of stratification; in the latter they tend to form the basis of stratification (Horowitz 1971). These are ideal types: in practice several different criteria usually work together. Hence we must also differentiate between *rigid* and flexible systems of stratification.

Ethnic differences are usually thought of as being obvious and clear-cut. However, this is not always the case: where physical differences are not evident they may well be expressed in terms of religion, language or shared common culture. Most areas subject to colonisation were in fact already inhabited. Hence from first encounter, there arose a sense of ethnic differences. The annexation of land created new class structures. Local inhabitants were used to work the land, and where they were insufficient or failed to survive the rigours of forced labour, new workers were brought in. Slavery made a deep impact both in Africa and after 1517 in the Americas, but a century after emancipation both in Brazil and Cuba the experience has become historical and old divisions have had time to be eroded. It is worth remembering that slavery was not formally abolished in Mauritania until 1980 and that involuntary servitude in various forms is still prevalent in the Middle East and is believed to have been on the increase throughout the 1990s.

Wherever ethnic differences are conspicuous the tensions generated by them do remain socially significant and where they are of more recent origin conflict can be considerable. In a number of territories once part of the British Empire such tensions have been generated by the importation of Indian contract labourers, whose descendants today constitute a significant minority. In 1968 the government of Kenya deported the Asian minority who had contributed a disproportionate share to the government and entrepreneurial skills of the country. In 1972 President Idi Amin of Uganda did the same, attracting much international criticism. Their absence has had such negative economic effects that by the end of the 1990s their return was being actively sought.

Fijians today still share their island with the descendants of Indian indentured labourers, a minority which is almost as big as the majority. But they do so on their own terms since they bitterly resent pressure for equal access to power. When an Indian-backed party won political power it was excluded by force and Fiji withdrew from the Commonwealth rather than accept the right of the descendants of immigrants to take power.

In Guyana the descendants of Indian labourers form about 50 per cent of the population. Those of African descent account for a further 30 per cent and the division between these groups is the major social cleavage. From 1957 the country's first ruling party, the People's Progressive Party (PPP) has been dominated by the Indo-Guyanese. But serious communal violence in 1963–64 led to the adoption of the proportional representation system which had the effect of transferring power to non-Indians in the form of the People's National

Congress (PNC), led first by Forbes Burnham and subsequently by Desmond Hoyte. When Hoyte lost the presidential election of 1997 the PNC continued to exploit racial feelings among the one-third of the country's population of Afro-Guyanese origin and to do everything they could to reverse the verdict of the electorate. It took a great deal of pressure from the United States and other neighbouring states to get Hoyte to accept even a restricted term for his elected successor, President Janet Jagan, who was forced to resign in 1999 because of illness.

The existence of a substantial minority, however, does not of itself mean that they will be politically, as opposed to socially, significant and not all importations of indentured labour have led to conflict. One such exception is the island state of Mauritius. Another is Sri Lanka, where the so-called 'Indian Tamils' form an encapsulated society in the tea-growing central highlands and remain largely apart from the struggle between the Tamil separatist movement, the Liberation Tigers of Tamil Eelam (LTTE), and the Sinhalese-majority government. The Tamil Tigers, as they are generally known, represent the aspirations of elements among the so-called 'Sri Lankan Tamils', who have lived in the Jaffna Peninsula and in other parts of the north and east of the island since at least the eleventh century.

Similar hostilities have been directed at the Chinese minority, descendants of traders and settlers who can be found throughout South-east Asia, notably in Myanmar, Indonesia and the Philippines, and against the Vietnamese in Thailand. In the former British colony of Singapore, founded in 1824, they form a majority. Tension between this Chinese majority in Singapore and the Malay ruling establishment of Malaysia led to Singapore's peaceful secession from the federation.

Most developing world countries contain significant ethnic minorities of indigenous origin. In some countries, e.g. Myanmar, they are so numerous as seriously to call into question the central government's ability to control outlying areas. In others, ethnic differences have been fanned by populist leaders and the result has been large-scale social conflict and open civil war. Examples in Africa have included Burundi (1966–72 and 1994), Chad (1966–84), Nigeria (1967–70), Angola (1975–84) and Rwanda (1990–92, April–July 1994). In yet others, such as Laos and Vietnam, ethnic differences have been targeted by external powers as a way of influencing national politics.

Class and state

The colonial state maintained the structure of class dominance/subordination. Significantly, pre-revolutionary Ethiopia, which was not effectively colonised, retained the indigenous semi-feudal structure that elsewhere had to a greater or lesser degree been modified by the colonial experience. However it is important not to see the concept of class in the developing world through the prism of Marxist concepts, which were based on Europe at a particular stage of historical development. Class structures are endogenous – they arise from the particular nature and circumstances of the country concerned. And in developing world states they remain largely traditional, with the impact of industrialisation etc. being in the main accommodated to existing patterns of dominance and subordination. Thus in post-colonial Senegal politics continued to be dominated by noble and free-born families, while the descendants of slaves continued to be effectively excluded from power (Crowder 1967: 110). Although in India the former ruling families have been deprived of their traditional powers, both there and in Pakistan, Bangladesh and Sri Lanka they have used their social standing to pursue the democratic route to power as a very successful alternative.

There are instances where the colonial experience exacerbated and distorted traditional relationships in a way that would prove disastrous later. The Rwandan case (discussed in Chapter 2, p. 91) illustrates this. The Belgian colonial administration played on ethnic rivalries in asserting its political control, making the Tutsi dynastic aristocracy the tax collectors and administrators of justice. The obvious tensions in such a situation were exacerbated by demographic pressures. They exploded in the most brutal fashion following the collapse of the coffee market in 1993, reliance on which was the legacy of the colonial export economy, and the subsequent macro-economic return required by the IMF (Chossudovsky 1995).

The impact of settlement varied a great deal and it is difficult to generalise about it. Countries where settlement supplanted almost all traces of the indigenous populations include Argentina and Uruguay as well as First World countries like Australia, Canada and the USA. Countries where settlement incorporated substantial indigenous populations without exterminating them but at the cost of indigenous cultural traits include Mexico, Peru and South Africa from the developing world, and New Zealand from the developed.

Invariably where there was substantial settlement the settlers displaced the ruling class and established cultural hegemony. However, there was most often some form of alliance between settlers and the colonial authorities, not a simple forced identity of views. Settlers could come to resent colonial dominance, and in time they would seek independence, as in the United States, most of Latin America, South Africa and Zimbabwe (then Southern Rhodesia). The most important legacy has been the plantation economy. There are essential differences between the farm and the plantation as a basis of economic organisation, and this is reflected in the social structures that accompany each. Where the plantation has predominated, there has been a strong tendency to horizontal stratification of ethnic groups.

The post-colonial state has often incompletely adjusted. In Kenya the settlers and/or their naturalised descendants keep their lands and have adjusted to the new post-colonial order; in South Africa, so far, the intention seems to be to take the same course. In Sri Lanka tea plantations were nationalised and the planters allowed to repatriate only part of their compensation; in Indonesia summary nationalisation took place, but was followed by extensive corruption (Myrdal 1968). In West Africa plantations were corporately owned and there were few settlers. Only in northern Nigeria and Senegal did traditional rulers retain their powers, in both cases because the colonial powers did not seek to control the production of peanuts, and in the case of Senegal the right of eminent domain was abolished in 1964 (O'Brien 1971: 201–2; see also O'Brien 1978). Traditional rulers retained their powers in Lesotho (formerly Bechuanaland) and Swaziland, and in South Africa under apartheid in the case of the Zulu and Xhosa, some limited autonomy within the homeland system as the notional 'states' of KwaZulu and Ciskei (Suzman 1993).

The Oligarchy

In place of settlers in Africa, as earlier in Latin America, there has arisen an indigenous oligarchy. However, in Africa only in the case of Côte d'Ivoire has a local oligarchy emerged which is based on landholding. Elsewhere the new basis for power has been *political office*, which gives access to valuable economic returns. In Asia, where settlers were few and indigenous societies complex, no single oligarchy has emerged: though the dynastic basis of power is often very clear, different elites control the basis of economic wealth.

In Africa, the alliance between state functionaries and the propertied classes has taken different forms in different countries. Dr Jomo Kenyatta established himself as a chief of chiefs and made fellow Africans socially dominant within independent Kenya, allowing free rein (on conditions) to private entrepreneurs. In neighbouring Tanzania, Dr Julius Nyerere established a system in which state enterprise was dominant. Dr Kwame Nkrumah failed to do the same in Ghana and ultimately was unable to retain his power. In Uganda the government of Milton Obote drove out the Kabaka of Buganda, burnt his palace and suspended the Lukiko (traditional assembly), only to be displaced in turn by a military coup led by Idi Amin. In the 1990s the powers of the traditional rulers were partly restored.

The oligarchy has preponderant economic power, generally enhanced by its alliance with key foreign interests. It is the dominant patron–client network, to which all subordinate patron–client networks are attached. Ethnic cleavages, if they exist, are only one among a number of ways in which society can be stratified in the interests of maintaining dominance. Wealth can give access to the highest levels in most societies, enabling its holders to exercise influence if not power. Religion and education form alternative axes of stratification. Ethnic allegiances can cut across class differentiation by wealth or power. Hence in Nigeria no single ruling class emerged. Power passed into the hands of the armed forces, whose representatives have continued, despite lip-service to the ideals of democracy, to retain as tight a control over the country as they can.

In Latin America the term 'oligarchy' has strong emotive meaning as a key term in the populist/leftist critique of the landowning elite. Nevertheless the term fits very well the situation that was general in Latin America until the twentieth century, and which continues to some extent in Peru and Colombia. Landowners remain an important element in this section of Latin American society, an element which is so wealthy that it remains undisturbed by domestic economic dislocation and/or political unrest (see Peasantry below).

The bureaucracy

The higher ranks of the civil service form a key part of this elite. They are very well paid indeed compared with both lower civil servants and the general run of the population, especially when other privileges are taken into account. In Nigeria, indeed, a new upper stratum of top civil servants, the 'Perm Secs' (Permanent Secretaries), emerged as a key part of the ruling elite. In Africa generally university teachers and doctors are also very highly regarded and although their advantages have declined with time they can still be regarded as members of the upper class rather than of an intermediate middle class, with the small size of the elite giving them incomes in the top 1 per cent of the population. The importance of a university degree itself has declined with time, but is still disproportionate. In an extreme case, in the former Belgian Congo, now Zaire, there were only a handful of graduates at independence in a population of over 13 million, and no strong landowning elite to form the core of an indigenous ruling class. In the 1990s, South Africa has suffered from the consequences of the apartheid system, which by the Extension of University Education Act (1959) deliberately condemned black South Africans to a separate and second-class university education so that they would not challenge white dominance (Sampson 1999: 100).

But in Ghana, as in many other African states, a significant number of senior civil servants who had served the colonial government continued to work for the Nkrumah regime, and, on his fall, were retained by the successor governments for precisely the same reason: their specialised knowledge. In addition to senior civil servants, a considerable number of expatriate advisers and technicians continued to hold important positions in the former British colonies well after independence; in 1966, for example, 4,668 expatriates still worked in the civil service in Zambia. In the former French colonies French *assistants techniques* continued to manage key branches of the economy, justice, interior, agriculture, transport and public works and public health ministries, to say nothing of defence and internal security (Bretton 1973: 189).

Inevitably there are close links between the government of the day and the entrepreneurial or business class. As Bretton emphasises, the economies of African states are so fragile that the public sector elite, both politicians and civil servants, cannot exist independently of their outside earnings.

For a few among the higher echelons, the payoff from rule or from public office below the level of rule may be satisfaction of lust for power; for the majority, the payoff is personal wealth and economic security or both. Satisfaction of lust for power without substantial material benefit accruing to the powerful is an improbability in the real world. (Bretton 1973: 176)

The National Reformation Council report in 1968 on the assets of former government ministers in Sierra Leone is one of a number of such documents produced by successor regimes in Africa which give chapter and verse (Sierra Leone NRC 1968). Such problems continue and under the National Provisional Ruling Council (NPRC) government led by Captain Valentine Strasser considerable publicity has been given to the results of investigations into the financial affairs of high-ranking civil servants and other functionaries who had served under the Momoh regime. *West Africa* (27 September– 3 October 1993) reported that the Justice Laura Marcus-Jones Commission of Inquiry had found that the former president himself had acquired 'a sizeable collection of real property' and 'was in control of pecuniary resources and property disproportionate to his past official emoluments'. The NPRC therefore ordered these to be forfeited to the state.

Entrepreneurial/business class

At independence, many (though clearly not all) of the colonial civil servants went home. Their business and financial counterparts stayed on, and their role became more important. At the same time, with varying degrees of success, a new indigenous business class began to emerge. The new entrepreneurs, however, are often incomers. In South-east Asia it is the Chinese who perform the role of entrepreneurs; also Indians in the case of Malaysia and Singapore. The emergence of a new Malay business elite has been the objective of the Malaysian government's *bumiputra* policy – a policy of favouritism to the 'native people' or indigenous population, which has proved successful.

In Africa, other than in Zanzibar, where they formed the ruling elite, Arabs formed a similar entrepreneurial group, linking Africa north and south of the Sahara. In keeping with this tradition in West Africa a new group has emerged, the Lebanese, to perform the role of traders and entrepreneurs and to be presented as scapegoats for economic failure. In Ghana business partnerships outside the tribe have often tended to founder on mutual suspicions. There too Lebanese and Indian entrepreneurs have come virtually to monopolise medium-scale trade. In Kenya and Uganda the dominance of trade by Indian immigrants was so much resented that they were summarily expelled by post-independence governments. Friction between traders and government has, however, been commonplace in African states, although until recently it has not taken a markedly ideological form.

In Latin America the traditional structure of a family-owned conglomerate is slowly yielding to a new business elite, among whom recent immigrants, including Italians in Argentina, Germans in Brazil, Japanese in Peru and Lebanese in Ecuador, are prominent. The inability until recently to engage in almost any kind of trade without a multiplicity of forms and permissions has, as ever, ensured that close links with government were essential and has afforded a fertile field for corruption.

Peasantry

In 1970 the majority of inhabitants of the new states were still peasants. The attention of the world at the time was grabbed by occasional insurrection and civil warfare and many in the industrialised world came to regard the peasantry as a revolutionary force (e.g. Wolf 1969; cf. Scutz and O'Slater 1990; Kamrava 1992; Colburn 1994; Calvert 1990a). However, as Marx recognised, the main characteristic of peasants as a class is their extreme conservatism. This is understandable when it is remembered that, living on the margin of subsistence, their entire being is taken up by the need to earn a living (Scott 1976; Bernstein et al. 1992). Foster (1976) calls the cultural expression of this the model of limited good. Peasants, he says, see their environment as a closed system, with insufficient resources. They are aware that there are more resources outside their immediate environment, but they do not see these resources as being normally available to them.

> To guard against being a loser, peasants in traditional communities have developed an egalitarian, shared-poverty, equilibrium, status-quo style of life, in which by means of overt behavior and symbolic action people are discouraged from attempting major change in their economic and other statuses. (Foster 1976: 35–6)

It is in Latin America that there is the longest tradition of study of the peasantry in developing world states. The most celebrated example is that of the Cornell Peru Project, which was organised in 1951 at Hacienda Vicos, Department of Ancash. The purpose was to engineer rapid social change among indigenous inhabitants by altering the local power structure. Based on the social theories of Harold D. Lasswell and colleagues (Lasswell and Kaplan 1950; Lasswell and Holmberg 1966) it sought to create change through 'participant intervention'. A forerunner of modern efforts to bring about the social empowerment of deprived groups, the project replaced external supervision of work by outside employees by that of indigenous leaders, abolished free services (labour tax) in favour of paid labour, invested the returns from peasant labour in improved agricultural practices, encouraged the setting up of a body of elected leaders to plan further changes, and initiated weekly meetings of the whole labour force to review progress (Holmberg 1971). It is therefore not only one of the most striking examples of the use of the experimental method in the social sciences, but a pathfinder for 1990s notions of *empowerment* (see Chapter 8).

The major characteristic of Peruvian peasants was powerlessness, and this was not only a characteristic of the group but because of their position at the bottom of the Peruvian social hierarchy a determining characteristic of Peruvian society as a whole, although they constituted over 50 per cent of the population. Hence changes on the local and national levels (and indeed on the international level) were interlinked. 'The Vicosinos were not only part of the national society in 1951, they were in their condition essential to it – a necessary subordinated complement to the dominant oligarchy' (Dobyns et al. 1971: 17).

The Vicos peasants wanted one thing above all: land reform. Conservatives blocked local expropriation of land as well as national plans to take over lands of the Cerro de Pasco Corporation, but the elected government of Manuel Prado Ugarteche (1956–61) approved direct sale before being overthrown by a military coup. The Vicos project led to emulation by peasant movements elsewhere in the country, and the government of Fernando Belaúnde Terry (1963–68), under pressure from peasant occupations of land, was able to secure passage of agrarian reform legislation, which was not implemented. The military government of General Juan Velasco Alvarado (1968–75), how-ever, instituted 'Peasant Day' on 24 June 1969 and subsequently expropriated the large coastal estates from which the former oligarchy drew much of their wealth (Stepan 1978).

In Peru, as elsewhere in Latin America, however, lineages remain strong. Old families have found new outlets for their wealth, and have successfully incorporated newcomers. Whether in Mexico, Costa Rica or Colombia, a striking proportion of those holding political power will be descended from or incorporated by marriage into one or other of the ancient lineages, although at the same time showing a pronounced tendency to marry among themselves. Meanwhile, in the 1980s, in opposition to the intransigence of the old fam-ilies, many Peruvian peasants took to various forms of action on their own behalf. The Marxist rural insurgent movement *Sendero Luminoso* (Shining Path) sought to capitalise on this unrest, but resorted to coercion when they found that only a minority of peasants were willing to take up arms and sub-ject themselves to outsiders (Palmer 1992; Poole and Rénique 1991, 1992; Taylor 1987, 1998). In Ecuador in January 2000, however, peasant demon-strations in Quito forced the army to topple the government of Jamil Mahuad Witt after it had conspicuously failed to tackle the country's serious economic crisis (*Sunday Telegraph*, 23 January 2000).

In Africa, on the other hand, a striking consequence of the fluidity of the class structure is that many members of the upper and middle classes come from peasant families or themselves started life as peasants (Andreski 1968: 168). The peasantry remain the largest single class in many countries but the African peasantry has been generally passive. Since independence, peasant organisations have been generally weak. Only in the Portuguese African territ-ories (and, perhaps, in the disputable case of the MauMau in Kenya) did peas-ants play a major role in movements of national liberation and then under the leadership of middle-class intellectuals such as Holden Roberto and Eduardo

Mondlane. Although Nelson Mandela correctly described himself as 'a country boy', he came from a chiefly family and received a chief's education (Sampson 1999).

Various factors appear to account for the relative powerlessness of the African peasantry. Given strong tribal and kinship ties, it has been difficult for a sense of class identity to develop, and the absence of a traditional landowning elite means that there is not an easy focus for their hostility. Africa is relatively sparsely populated compared to other parts of the developing world, hence the struggle for land has not reached the degree of intensity that it has in say Guatemala or Peru. Linguistic divisions and low levels of literacy are also cited as reasons why peasant organisation in Africa has failed to develop. Such divisions make it relatively easy for the elite to divide and rule, by buying off incipient leaders.

Lacking organisation, peasants have tended to resist impositions upon them either passively or in rare instances by a form of *jacquerie* – a spontaneous, localised revolt against intolerable conditions. Maladministration and tax increases led to such a revolt in Chad in 1965 (Decalo 1980) and similar causes could be seen to lie at the root of the unrest in Kenya in 1998 ('Moi-butu must go!') or Zimbabwe in 2000. Occasionally such revolts have been more organised, but they have similarly been directed towards and focused on local grievances. Peasant revolt has been a repeated feature of life

Plate 9   Husking coconut, Sri Lanka

in Congo/Zaire since the outbreak in Kwilu province in 1964. Other African examples range from the Agbekoya rebellion in Nigeria in 1968 (Beer and Williams 1975) to the war between the Sudan People's Liberation Army (SPLA) and the government in southern Sudan or the so-called 'Ninja militias' in Congo-Brazzaville (*Annual Register 1998*).

Urban workers

Latin America became independent and was urbanised before industrial development arrived. New railways, notably in Argentina, offered a strong base for labour organisation. But movements in Peru, Chile and above all Bolivia centred on mines and so were extremely vulnerable to military repression, leaving the scattered remainder to be subjected to various forms of restriction on their joint action. In practice, therefore, urban workers in Latin America have generally been targeted by populist leaders as one of the main elements in a multi-class alliance (see Chapter 7).

African states, on the other hand, generally had some industry at independence. Although African cities have grown considerably since 1950, however, the working class remains only a small fraction of the total population. The strength of state power, moreover, has led to incipient trade union movements being either captured by the ruling elite or suppressed by authoritarian governments. In a number of single-party states, unions soon became active partners with government in seeking to increase work rates and hold down pay claims and this pattern has been repeated up to the present. However, this has not always been successful. As early as 1961 a major strike broke out among the railway and port workers at Sekondi-Takoradi in Ghana, protesting at the corruption of the elite and the increasing authoritarianism of the Nkrumah government. In 1971 a series of strikes in Dar es Salaam showed similar discontent with the authoritarian tendencies of the Tanzanian government. In Nigeria, the imposition of military government was strongly resented and in 1971 there was a series of strikes in Lagos and Kano, then the main centres of industrialisation (Williams and Turner, Dunn 1978: 165).

In several former French African colonies, notably Congo (Brazzaville) and Dahomey in 1963 and Upper Volta in 1966, strikes helped to bring about the fall of an unpopular government at the hands of the armed forces. In Senegal, by contrast, external support in the form of French military personnel helped keep Senghor's government in power despite intermittent labour unrest (O'Brien 1978: 180). The devaluation of the CFA franc in 1994 took trade unions completely by surprise. 'There were initial protest strikes and demonstrations in Benin, Burkina [Faso], Gabon and Niger. Other unions held meetings and demands for wage increases ranging from 35 per cent in Chad and 50 per cent in Burkina, Mali, Senegal and Togo, to 100 per cent in Gabon' (Percival 1996).

In states already under military government, strikes have been firmly discouraged, but workers have responded by a variety of covert means of resistance, including absenteeism, going slow, sabotage and theft, and sometimes by open rebellion, as in Ghana where the mining industry was in continuous turmoil from 1968 to 1970.

The family

Family, marriage and kinship are basic and universal, though the forms they take vary. The economic basis of marriage, for example, is usually clear, but society specific. Within marriage, the division of labour is normally clearly marked. In traditional as opposed to modern societies, the central role in social provision falls to the family.

What counts as a family is a difficult and important question. The nuclear family of northern and western Europe is distinctive and rather unusual. It is bilateral and hence forms a rather weak basis for larger structures such as clans and lineages. It is monogamous, so related households do not regard themselves in the main as having any special claim to the resources of each other. This pattern is also characteristic of Japan.

The pattern much more characteristic of the developing world is that of the **extended family**. This is usually unilateral. In India, as in China, a bride makes the physical journey to her husband's house and ceases on marriage to be regarded as a member of her former family. (This can have consequences much more significant than for a family alone: in Pakistan, for example, her mother attempted to shunt aside Benazir Bhutto from her leadership role in favour of her brother, saying that, after all, she is no longer a Bhutto.) It can be characterised by both forms of polygamy, either polygyny (as in some Arab countries) or polyandry (as in Nepal); neither of which works to the advantage of women. Even where the extended family does not coexist in one household, several generations can live together in the same complex and a very carefully graded system of relationships is recognised.

The family is not only the basic organising unit of society, it acts as a basis for all social provision. Mutual obligation in traditional communities is particularly characteristic of the extended family group. A member of the family who acquires wealth is obligated to provide for other family members. Other family members can require support. Obviously the effect of this system, as it is among the Gilbertese (now part of the Pacific state of Kiribati), is to prevent any tendency towards hoarding or conspicuous consumption. Among the Tonga of Malawi the family could be relied upon to provide for the wives and children of those seeking contract work in South Africa, and they in turn benefited from the remittances the workers sent home.

Both individuals and families are similarly linked by patterns of two-way or **dyadic exchange**. In many cases these obligations are so well developed that they form a very satisfactory way of structuring time and so are not easily surrendered. Brown found that both Samoans and the Hehe of Tanzania placed

such a high value on performing a wide range of social and political obligations, that they had a strong resistance to working for money (Brown 1957).
However, a strong solvent of these traditional relationships is to be found in
the urban market for cash crops and media images of other consumer goods.

Sociologists have paid particular attention to the tendency of the extended
family to break down in the face of modernisation (Goode 1970). Here the
dominant influence has been that of the social theorist Talcott Parsons
(Parsons 1964), who argued that what he termed the 'isolated nuclear family'
was the typical form in modern industrial society because modernisation
implied a process of 'structural differentiation'. By this he meant a tendency
for institutions progressively to shed functions, so that in the case of the family its economic, political and religious functions have long since to a greater
or lesser extent been assumed by specialised agencies and latterly the job of
caring for the old, the young and the unfit has also been assumed by the state
or by commercial enterprises. At the same time the **ascribed status** derived
from the traditional family structure is replaced by **achieved status** based on
one's own efforts and/or achievement.

Modernisation in the developing world means above all that the family
ceases to be the main economic unit of production and is replaced by the
workshop or factory. Parsons argued that the demands of factories for labour
called for the mobility and flexibility associated with the nuclear family; however, in the case of migrant workers into, for example, South Africa, the family unit itself seems in many cases to have disintegrated, the workforce being
largely composed of individual young males living together in hostels. Goode
(1970) argued that the disintegration of the extended family had in fact been
more rapid than could have been expected were Parsonian assumptions correct. He suggested that the spread of the nuclear family had been accelerated
by the image presented by the advanced countries which was attractive in
developing world countries because of the freedom it appeared to offer. In
Africa migrants from the countryside may even have welcomed town life
because of the fact that it freed them from the obligations of the extended
family (Little 1965).

It has also been suggested that it was not industrialisation in northern Europe
that brought about the decline of the extended family, it was the decline of the
extended family that facilitated industrialisation. If this is the case, this decline
in the developing world might be expected to have a similar effect.

On the other hand, the extended family remains very much part of Indian
society and Somjee (1991) argues that the economic success of local elites such
as the Patidars of Anand in the State of Gujarat owed much to it. While they
were barred by the Indian Land Tenancy Acts from increasing the size of their
landholding, they were able to gain an increased return from it by growing
cash crops such as sugar cane, bananas, cotton and later edible oilseeds, and
benefited from the absence of tax on agricultural income. However, while
retaining his interest in agriculture, it was also open to a Patidar to leave the
cultivation of the land to a brother or cousin and move into Anand itself, to

seek work in commerce or industry. The availability of this work came, of course, from other factors stimulating the growth of Anand, especially the rapid development of the transport system which brought into the town a wave of new educational, government and other institutions, and with them a wave of professionals wanting new products and services.

> While in undertaking such ventures a Patidar no doubt took some risk, nevertheless he also had his land to fall back upon just in case the commercial or industrial venture did not succeed. The closely knit extended family, together with the facility for absentee agriculture, provided the Patidars with a sense of security for new ventures. (Somjee 1991: 94–5)

The View from the Ground

By *Jonathan Rugman in La Paz and Dan Glaister, The Guardian,*
Monday, 23 January 2006

Thousands Throng Streets as Bolivian Leader Sheds Tears but Talks Tough at Inauguration

Bolivia installed its first indigenous president yesterday, Evo Morales, who insisted he would stick by radical drugs and energy policies regardless of US consternation at another South American country turning to the left.

In a pre-inauguration interview, Mr Morales vowed that he would not destroy his country's rapidly expanding coca crop, and threatened to turn to China as a partner if western multinationals refused to cooperate with his plans to nationalise vast gas reserves. "We will fight the drugs traffickers, but there's going to be no coca eradication," said Mr Morales, an Aymara Indian who easily won December presidential elections. "Zero coca programmes haven't solved the drugs problem and they've hurt Bolivia."

His accession to power was celebrated this weekend. A spiritual ceremony at ancient pre-Inca ruins on Saturday gave way to the inauguration during which Mr Morales, 46, raised his fist in a salute, and wept as he was presented with the yellow, red and green presidential sash.

He asked the audience in the Palacio Quemado, seat of the government in La Paz, to observe a minute's silence in honour of the fallen heroes of the social movements, including Che Guevara. "Glory to the martyrs of the liberation," he declared at the end of the minute, as shouts of "Evo, Evo" rang around the chamber where an emerging crop of left-wing leaders were in attendance, led by Hugo Chávez of Venezuela and Brazil's Luiz Inacio Lula da Silva.

Visiting dignitaries looked on, but senators from opposition parties mostly sat with arms folded, observing an event that they could not have envisaged: the inauguration of an uneducated Indian as president of Latin America's poorest population and its second-largest reserves of natural gas.

In his first speech, Mr Morales called his election "the end of the colonial and neo-liberal era". He promised an inclusive government, and called on all parties to join him in reform. "The 500 years of Indian resistance have not been in vain," he said. "From 500 years of resistance we pass to another 500 years in power."

The US state department says it is withholding judgement but at the Pentagon Mr Morales' ideas on tackling the cocaine trade – catching the traffickers but growing coca leaves all the same – have raised concerns. After Colombia and Peru, Bolivia is South America's third biggest cocaine supplier. A former coca farmer himself, Mr Morales is wary of alienating his rural power base. Yet unless Bolivia joins the war against drugs, it risks losing the US as its biggest foreign donor with $600m (£340m) in aid on the table. "That's America's problem, not my problem," an apparently unconcerned president told Channel 4 News. "Fighting the drugs trade is an excuse for the US to increase its control over Latin America."

With foreign investment dwindling in the face of Bolivia's lurch leftwards, Mr Morales has been under pressure from the business elite – many of them descendants of the colonial Spanish – to reassure multinationals including BP and British Gas their money is safe. Several firms threaten to sue Bolivia in the face of a big rise in gas extraction fees imposed by the last government. President Morales says he "guarantees investors will recoup their money and make a profit" but will not back down on his pledge to renationalise gas reserves worth a potential $250bn.

His first foreign tour steered clear of Britain and United States but notably took in China. "We are going to guarantee Chinese investment. What's better than state investment? We should have a petro-Americas, a partnership between state enterprise and business. Our land has been looted for 500 years and we are going to assert our right of ownership."

It is an approach that strikes a chord with the millions in Bolivia, where three-quarters of the 8.5-million population are Indian and two-thirds survive on less than $2 a day. Many see in Mr Morales a leader in the mould of Mr Chávez. The Bolivian president has signalled that the Chávez model of tapping energy wealth to fund public spending is one he will follow. Yet despite formidable gas reserves Bolivia's revenue does not compare with Venezuela's oil wealth and the moderating influence of President da Silva of Brazil – a major trading partner – may instil a willingness to compromise.

Pragmatism was in evidence during the interview with Mr Morales. At one point the president tried to terminate our interview early, incensed by questions about Bolivia's cocaine trade. But his desire to be accommodating eventually got the better of him and he carried on talking. America's diplomats must be hoping the same proves true for them.

Indigenous peoples

In 1992 the UN responded to the growing indigenous movement by establishing the Working Group on Indigenous Populations and declaring 1993 the International Year of Indigenous People. The end of that year saw the UN launch the Decade of the World's Indigenous People.

Plate 10 Traditional lifestyles, Iran

It is hard to define **indigenous peoples** as such, since from earliest times human beings have been moving about the planet. However, where such groups are clearly recognised to exist

- they tend to have a timeless relationship with their lands;
- they are descendants of the original inhabitants of the specific lands in which they live although many will not now be living on their original land;
- they share a common culture, language and ancestry.

Perhaps the simplest definition would stress cultural distinctiveness and suggest that indigenous peoples exist wherever traditional, sustainable lifestyles survive in continued opposition to the encroaching power of the modern, internationalised state. It is precisely this confrontation that brings indigenous peoples to the attention of the outside world. In extreme cases, it takes the form of physical conflict.

Indigenous people are thought to comprise some 4 per cent of the world's population, an estimated 300 million people in 70 countries, but they are very loosely defined and there is much variety. On the broadest definitions, in the Americas Amerindians still comprise some 70 per cent of the population of Bolivia, 45 per cent in Peru, 40 per cent in Ecuador, 30 per cent in Mexico. However, even where, as in Guatemala, they are substantially in a majority, they are noticeably worse off than the rest of the population. In Guatemala

Indian life expectancy is 11 years less than for ladinos (people of part European descent). Even in Paraguay the infant mortality rate in Guaraní communities is as high as 50 per cent compared with 10 per cent amongst criollos and mestizos (people of whole or part European descent).

The entry of Mexico into the North American Free Trade Agreement (NAFTA) on 1 January 1994 was accompanied by an unwelcome reminder of Mexico's indigenous past, an uprising by the self-styled Zapatista National Liberation Army (EZLN) in the State of Chiapas. Chiapas, in the extreme south of Mexico on the border with Guatemala beyond the Isthmus of Tehuantepec, is Mexico's poorest state, as was noted by the UNDP *Human Development Report* (UNDP 1994a). It had an infant mortality rate of 94. Sixty per cent of its population was living below the official poverty line and half the population had no access either to drinking water or to electricity.

The problems of Chiapas stemmed from two causes: existing inequality and the impact of recent programmes for rapid development. The land reforms of President Lázaro Cárdenas in the 1930s might have had some impact on the traditional pattern of land tenure but the quasi-feudal oligarchy resisted successfully, aided by the local bishop. Since then peasants of Mayan descent who have sought title to their lands have been forced off the land, faced violence, disappearances and killings at the hands of the local bosses or their *pistoleros* (strong-arm men). Many have been displaced and some 200,000 landless families now work on the coffee and cocoa plantations. In the 1960s the State was linked for the first time to the rest of the country by good roads (Vogt 1969), and settlers began to pour in for land colonisation and tensions rose. The PRI government installed corrupt generals to control the province and built an enormous army base in the town of San Cristóbal. Much development funding was given to Chiapas but the oligarchy and the new settlers benefited and in 1994 the former inhabitants were still deprived.

In Asia, too, indigenous peoples are disadvantaged. The Papuan people of Irian Jaya, the eastern province of Indonesia, are being forced to use violence to defend their tribal identities. They confront a well-equipped army only as a simple people with home-made weapons. Their land is the western half of the island of New Guinea (Rappaport 1968), seized in 1963 by Indonesia against the wishes of the native Papuans, who are seen as primitives in Jakarta. Their lifestyles have been marginalised by imported Javanese whom the authorities hoped would speed up the process of change.

Malaysia exemplifies many of the various pressures threatening indigenous peoples. Paul Harrison cites the case of the Semai of Musoh whose population density is already beyond what is sustainable by hunter-gathering alone. Despite this, they still operate a relatively eco-friendly lifestyle, supplementing hunting and gathering with the keeping of chickens and goats. Traditionally the Semai make use of slash-and-burn techniques to grow hill rice and cassava and then shrub crops. The land is then left for 10–20 years before being brought back into cultivation. 'Such forest peoples tread lightly on the earth. They impoverish no soils, destroy no ecosystems. Their survival does not demand the destruction of any other species' (Harrison 1993: 3). But this delicate balance is threatened now. The tribal lands are already surrounded by encroaching Malay and Chinese agriculture. Meanwhile the Semai naturally want the trappings of modern life such as bicycles and radios and to buy them they take (or allow others to take) more from the forest than they need. Semai children supply butterflies for sale in the tourist shops of the nearby Cameron Highlands. Their parents are beginning market gardens to supply urban Malaysia and logging is starting up too (Harrison 1993: 1–6). The former Malaysian Minister of Finance, Anwar Ibrahim, was quite blunt about his attitude towards indigenous peoples: 'the best course for indigenous peoples is to accelerate their integration into the global society' (Anwar Ibrahim 1993).

The Pergau Dam project on the Pergau River in peninsular Malaysia near the Thai border, begun in 1991, flooded some 73,000 hectares of prime forest and displaced 6,000 tribal people. Needless to say they were not invited to take part in the Malaysian government's International Seminar on Indigenous Peoples. But the dam has never justified expectations, as the flow of water is such that it is only economic at peak times.

However, the Penan hunter-gatherer tribespeople of the Sarawak rainforest of East Malaysia, who still shoot monkeys and birds with blowpipes, did not accept that they should yield to 'progress'. They sought to stop foreign logging companies ending their way of life through their so-called policy of 'clear felling' the mountain forest and have met violence and tear gas for their trouble. The Bakun Dam project in Sarawak approved in 1994 would flood an area the size of Singapore and displace 5,000 people who are expected to be relocated to the oil palm plantations in other parts of Sarawak. The local community were not expected to benefit from the electricity produced by the planned 2,400 MW power station. Abandoned in 1997 as a result of the East Asian Crisis, it was revived in 2001 as elections approached, but is not expected to come on stream until 2009, when it will power vast aluminium smelters relocated from the AICs.

In Tripura in India secessionist feeling grew as Bengali settlers fleeing the anti-secessionist violence of the Bangladeshi security forces who drove them from their homes in the Chittagong Hills were encouraged to settle in tribal areas to the detriment of the identity and culture of the tribal peoples.

In 1979 it was ruled that resettlement and rehabilitation of the 'tribals' displaced by the Narmada River Project must keep in step with the other two aspects: environmental protection and construction. It has not done so and the scheme is being delayed, but for the most part the land titles of lands occupied for centuries by the ancestors of those displaced have simply been ignored. Protesting tribals have been fired on by police.

Indigenous peoples' calls for rights are often interpreted as secessionist movements and therefore resisted. Also indigenous people often occupy resource-rich regions and therefore there is intense outside interest in exploitation of their homelands. However, they are also often world's most fragile environments.

The preservation of indigenous peoples with their way of life intact presents the rest of the world with a moral dilemma. Not everything traditional is desirable. Some elements of modernity, e.g. an expanded trade and protection against imported diseases, may be vital to preserve the traditional. Perhaps the only way forward is some blending together of past and present. Demonstration effects will in any case ensure that indigenous peoples (or at least the youngsters) will crave the trappings of development: the radios, television sets, CD players, bicycles, cars etc. Those who enjoy such things, or who have experienced them and rejected them, are hardly in a position to argue that such experience should not in principle be available to all who want it. It may be possible to feed that demand in some way that minimises damage to local tradition and cultures, as well as to sensitive environments. Blending of the traditional with the modern is certainly possible, as is shown by the locally produced 'Inka Kola' licensed by the Peruvian government. This yellow bubble-gum flavoured drink has become so much part of Peruvians' cultural identity that it continues to sell in massive quantities without government help or promotion.

Social factors favouring development

The early modernisers thought in traditional terms, in terms of piecemeal change over long periods of time. They recognised that the same land would have to provide food for their children and grandchildren, and they acted accordingly. By contrast, the late modernisers have been driven by the urge to create visible results during the brief period of a political mandate. Many developing countries have significantly changed their economic structures since independence, especially in the cases of Latin America, where independence came early, and Asia, where governmental responses have been particularly flexible. However, agriculture is a complex process and it takes a long time for the full consequences of changes to be either felt or understood.

The structure of developing economies often exhibits glaring divisions, especially those between urban and rural, or between the formal and the informal sectors. The main cause of this has been rapid urbanisation. Urbanisation may either precede or follow rapid industrial development. Hence urbanisation levels vary a great deal. As noted in Chapter 1, they are high in the Caribbean and Latin America (74 per cent), especially in the Southern Cone. This is in part the result of Latin America's colonial history, where the creation of towns was the key element in the success of Spanish settlement. Many of the world's largest cities are in Latin America – the 22.4 million who live in metropolitan Mexico City, the world's second-largest city (after Tokyo) formed some 21 per cent of Mexico's total population of 106,202,903 in 2005. Urbanisation, on the other hand, is relatively low in Africa South of the Sahara (32 per cent in 1997) but is expected to grow rapidly to 54 per cent in 2025.

There is, however, a strong urban bias among most developing world policy-makers, in Africa as elsewhere (Lipton 1977). Coming as they do from urban or would-be urban backgrounds, they equate urban with modern and prefer urban to rural, favouring strategies of industrial development which result in further urbanisation. Urbanisation hitherto has been seen as essential for rapid economic growth and certainly has always accompanied it, as witness the striking growth of big cities in the NICs and in China. However large cities have to be fed. Bread riots were a feature of life in Mexico City and Lima as early as the colonial period, when the local hinterland was no longer able to supply the needs of a rising population.

Urbanisation has profound social consequences. Public services tend to be concentrated in urban areas, thus making them even more attractive to rural dwellers. The most able and the most mobile (that is to say, young unmarried adults) migrate to the towns, in the process further disadvantaging the rural areas. But towns are not well adapted to receiving them. Squatter settlements are found on all continents.

In-migration to the big cities has even wider implications, bringing in its wake an awareness of social change. Social change gives rise to cultural confusion. Uncertainty gives rise to new tensions while reinforcing existing ones. Informality gives way to formality. A relatively static existence is changed by transport. Extended kinship, as Parsons noted, is replaced by the nuclear family. Social complexity increases, and there is an association between social change and political instability. The problem of unproductive urbanisation arises, and when in-migrants compete for scarce resources and temporary or part-time jobs, friction and scarcity lead to 'unregulated petty strife'.

At the same time, the other side of the coin is rural poverty. Poverty in the countryside is not a new phenomenon, and it could almost be expected in drought-prone and degraded environments such as those of the Sahel or of the Horn of Africa. In fact, as Redclift points out, the problem in both these areas owes much to the structure of land-ownership. The rich soil of Bangladesh in South Asia is not a degraded environment. However Bangladesh also has an exceedingly unequal distribution of land, such that one-third of the people of this heavily populated country are poor peasants cultivating less than 1 ha of land or share-croppers dependent on others for work (Redclift 1984: 74–5).

Maintaining social provision in an evolving society

With rapid social change come also a whole range of problems associated with the provision of housing, health and other social services. Gaps in social provision in the growing towns can be filled in a variety of ways, by (a) a church or sect; (b) other voluntary organisations; (c) occupational provision; or (d) the state.

The effects of migration are felt very differently in town and country. Typically in a plantation economy the main basis for housing provision other than the individual has been occupational: housing for the workforce. The relatively high standard of housing provided by the banana corporations in Honduras, for example, is a significant deterrent to unrest. However, such provision is relatively rare in towns, the assumption being that the cost will be picked up by the worker or by the state. In the town the major problems concern housing for young adults and these can be and are met in a variety of ways by the individuals themselves. But unless an agency such as the state steps in to ensure provision there are costs. The need to work impedes both education and training, tending to reinforce low expectations and to create a large semi-skilled labour force. For the individual it results in an unfamiliar (significant word) need to rely on groups other than the family.

For those in towns, occupational provision may or may not be made for crèche facilities, education and training schemes. Even if legally required, it may well not effectively exist or be capable of being enforced. For those left behind in the country, the remoteness of the young adults results in additional problems in the care of both the very young and the aged, which has traditionally devolved on the youngest unmarried daughters of the family, thus reinforcing their dependence on the family unit and leading to very marked differences in the experience of education between men and women. In rural areas provision of schools is much more basic, too, and once children are of an age to work they will be in demand in the fields. Their school attendance becomes spasmodic and soon ends altogether.

Authorities on Japan, the most successful non-Western society to achieve advanced industrialisation, lay particular emphasis on the distinctive role of education in its economic development. By the end of the First World War Japan had already achieved near universal literacy – something that is still far from being achieved in Central America, South Africa or Bangladesh, and is already on the decline in Britain and the United States (see above, p. 135).

Workers in modern companies often enjoy access to up-to-date health provision, and large cities in the developing world can boast medical facilities that are as good as anything in the world. However, in rural areas many peasants and their families still depend on traditional healers, whose services are not only well known and trusted, but who also have the great merit of being relatively cheap. Obviously they cannot cure everything and the reputation of modern medicine for miracle cures has created a demand worldwide for access to modern treatments. But assumptions of health in the developing world can be very different from those in developed societies. Just as the overall figures for the number of people served by each doctor do not reveal the sharp contrast between town and country, they also do not reveal the lack of access among the poorest sectors who cannot afford the services provided.

The need to get **social services** to those who require them explains why workers in the field of development have been taking increasing interest in the idea of 'empowerment' of local communities. Put simply, empowerment means making it possible for people to take their destinies into their own hands, and this in the developing world means community action. The formation of base communities (*comunidades de base*) within the Catholic Church in Brazil, and the growing impact of the evangelical movement there, has gone along with the rise of a much more active political participation among the poor, both in the countryside and in the shanty towns. These organisations are not simply religious, although Bible readings and public worship are both central aspects of their activities. They also often establish production cooperatives in the *favelas* and classes to teach basic literacy. They often have close connections with trade unions and with the Workers' Party (PT), and this ensures that, despite their religious origins and orientation, they are in conflict with the Catholic Church establishment, which sees them as Marxist.

In India, disillusion with the failure of the initial model of state-led economic growth based on the Western concept of the individual helped encourage a new emphasis on Gandhian ideas and fresh encouragement for the *panchayat* movement. Obviously there are limits to what such action can achieve unless new resources can be made available, and empowerment is of no value if it simply enables the poor to manage their own poverty.

The international media tend to give a very misleading impression of the reasons for social exclusion in the developing world. Throughout the developing world, many sectors of the population are excluded from full participation in national life on account of poverty, **ethnicity**, gender etc. Social exclusion is the process by which an individual finds him/herself excluded from opportunities for rewarding work, good housing, important educational opportunities, adequate health care or equality before the law. In fact, the law, through bias, delay and high cost, often acts to reinforce the very inequalities which legislators may seek to remove.

The media, dominated by large US corporations, portrays Colombia as a country dominated by drug barons seeking to undermine US society by smuggling drugs to be sold to American teenagers. They do not emphasise the dire poverty which makes so many Colombian youths desperate to escape by the only means that is available to them. Of the Afro-Colombian population, who live in the lowlands bordering the Caribbean ports, four-fifths live on an income less than a third of the national average.

Religion, politics and society

We have already noted that the Arab world has the lowest average number of women who become legislators. This is hardly surprising, when in many Middle Eastern countries either no legislature existed, or women were barred from standing for it. An important exception is Lebanon, where women obtained the vote in 1953, but the rigid constitutional structure designed to maintain peace between the 17 different religious or ethnic groups in the country has acted to exclude them from effective power.

However, at least in Lebanon women have been fully accepted as having the right to work. In 1998 the UNDP confirmed that for female participation in the labour force Lebanon was the highest in the Arab world with 28 per cent, followed by Yemen 27 per cent, Syria 25 per cent and Jordan with 21 per cent (UNDP 1998). And women's groups in Lebanon have been able to go further, to fight for equal pay, maternity leave and childcare at the office, and to try to deal with the difficult question of sexual harassment – difficult because there is no law against it and the courts are not sympathetic. This is hardly surprising, since even in Lebanon 50 per cent of men are opposed to allowing women to take part in politics and 30 per cent believe they should not even be allowed to drive a car.

In Saudi Arabia women are not allowed to drive cars. They are not allowed to go out on the street on their own, or with a male who is not their husband or other close relative. If they do they are liable to be arrested by the Religious Police (*mutawa'een*) on suspicion of prostitution, the punishment for which will include a severe flogging (50–100 lashes, administered by a man). In theory the male is also guilty, but in practice he is not very likely to be punished; the woman will be blamed for 'inciting' him. In public women must be veiled from head to foot, lest they incite the passions of passing men. Strict segregation of the sexes deprives Saudi women of opportunities which much of the Arab world already takes for granted and restricts them to a very limited range of occupations. They may not even escape by travel abroad without the written permission of a male relative, usually their father or husband. Needless to say, all these restrictions put an immense power in the hands of men with authority, and especially the Religious Police, which are free to use, and in some cases abuse, that power without any fear of being held to account. However, there are also positive trends. Between 1970 and 1990, Saudi Arabia raised its female literacy rate from 2 to 48 per cent By 2005 over 80 per cent were literate and increasingly finding suitably segregated employment in a country in critical need of their skills.

Following the Gulf War of 1991, some 5,000 United States troops remained in the kingdom to protect it from the ambitions of Saddam Hussein. Most were withdrawn in 2003, leaving only some 500 training personnel (BBC News, 29 April 2003). As with other foreigners, provided they stay in their compounds they have a certain degree of freedom from the restrictions outside – they may, for example, conduct Christian services, which are strictly illegal elsewhere, as the Saudi government does not tolerate other religions. The significance of this is lost unless it is understood that Saudi Arabia, with a population of some 17 million indigenous inhabitants, exploits a workforce of no fewer than 8.8 million foreign nationals, the vast majority from much poorer countries. In 2005 there were 1–1.5 million from each of Bangladesh, India and Pakistan, 900,000 each from Egypt, Sudan and the Philippines, 500,000 from Indonesia and 350,000 from Sri Lanka. The number of British or American expatriates, most of them working in the oil industry, is insignificant in comparison, but still amounts to some 25,000. Resentments fanned by al-Qaeda led to a series of violent attacks on foreign nationals in June 2004 in which 22 foreigners were killed by militants (*The Guardian*, 2 June 2004).

Iran is not an Arab country, and its inhabitants belong to a different Islamic sect from most Arabs. However, the influence of religion on social conditions looks at first sight very similar, especially so in respect of the status of women. Following the Islamic Revolution in 1979, compulsory veiling was introduced, co-education was banned and segregation was imposed in many public areas. Women were restricted from certain professions, such as law (so that women could not serve as judges), and women university students were not allowed into programmes such as agricultural engineering and veterinary sciences. Women's voices were banned from radio and female singers barred from television. Most importantly, the 1967 Family Protection Law (amended in 1974), was abrogated, re-establishing men's unlimited right of divorce and effectively denying women any right to divorce.

However, Iran's ambitions to resume the economic development achieved under the last Shah have led the Republic to modify many of these restrictions in practice. Definitions of gender are often central to social and political change (Kandiyoti 1991). And the new Constitution of the Islamic Republic maintained the right of women to vote and to be elected to all political posts except that of president. The consequences of the Iraq–Iran War (1980–88) led to the modification of the law relating to the guardianship of children and the rights of women in relation to divorce. And after 1990 barriers on study and employment were lifted piecemeal, as the country's need for a substantial, well-educated workforce was better appreciated – it was belatedly realized, for example, that some 40 per cent of farm work was done by women (Farhi 2005).

The clash of cultures

In the early 1990s, the American political scientist Samuel P. Huntington published an article (and subsequently a book, Huntington 1997) in which he argued that with the end of the Cold War, the fundamental source of conflict in the world would no longer be primarily ideological or primarily economic. The great divisions among humankind and the dominating source of conflict would be cultural. Nation states would remain the most powerful actors in world affairs, but the principal conflicts of global politics will occur between nations and groups of different civilisations. The clash of civilisations would dominate global politics and the 'fault lines between civilizations' would be 'the battle lines of the future' (Huntington 1993a).

This thesis was not universally accepted, until the events of '9/11' forced a rethink and made the 'clash of civilisations' thesis seem horribly plausible.

Huntington identifies seven or eight major civilisations, which he terms Western, Confucian, Japanese, Islamic, Hindu, Slavic-Orthodox, Latin American and possibly (sic) African:

> Civilizations are differentiated from each other by history, language, culture, tradition and, most important, religion. The people of different civilizations have different views on the relations between God and man, the individual and the group, the citizen and the state, parents and children, husband and wife, as well as differing views of the relative importance of rights and responsibilities, liberty and authority, equality and hierarchy. These differences are the product of centuries. They will not soon disappear. They are far more fundamental than differences among political ideologies and political regimes. (Huntington 1993a: 22–8)

However, sociologists do not find the concept of 'civilisations' a useful way of organising the many different cultures to be found throughout the developing world. The term 'culture' has many meanings. For the sociologist, the important thing is that it is the way in which group life is realised. As Hall and Jefferson put it:

> We understand the word 'culture' to refer to that level at which social groups develop distinct patterns of life, and give *expressive form* to their social and material life-experience. Culture is the way, the forms, in which groups 'handle' the raw material of their social and material existence. (Hall and Jefferson 1976: 10)

As a concept, it has been used to try to determine the relationships between 'culture', social structure and other aspects of society. However, ironically, there has until recently been no clearly defined 'sociology of culture' and many of the most important contributions to the literature on culture and society have been made by people who did not regard themselves as sociologists. The main debate arises between those who regard culture as the medium within which other developments take place and those who regard it as a residual category in which to group all other aspects of society that are not otherwise accounted for.

Some, with Durkheim, see culture as the method by which social relations are produced and transmitted. The role of ritual and symbols in dramatising and so reinforcing the social order has been a major preoccupation of anthropologists. However, Mary Douglas rejects the sharp division Durkheim (in common with many of his age) drew between the primitive and the modern, the former in Durkheim's view being characterised by mechanical solidarity and the latter by organic solidarity. Douglas also rejects the structuralist belief that human thought must necessarily be couched in pairs of opposites. The belief that the anthropologist can confidently determine a single true meaning for any given symbol flies in the face of evidence that symbols are almost always complex and multifaceted. Hence in any society the reinforcing effect of symbols is felt by their constancy, repetition and familiarity, rather than their precision (Wuthnow et al. 1984).

Some Marxists have in the past argued for a rather simple economic determinism, in which culture forms only part of the superstructure of society resting upon the dominant economic base. However, most modern Marxists now accept, and even argue, that the culture of a society (in the sociological sense) also affects and shapes its capacity for economic production, an idea which has antecedents also in the work of the Italian Marxist Antonio Gramsci. They therefore stress the power of ideas to shape events and the way in which some cultures come to dominate others. As Hall and Jefferson put it:

> Groups which exist within the same society and share some of the same material and historical conditions no doubt also understand, and to a certain extent share each other's 'culture'. But just as different groups and classes are unequally ranked in relation to one another, in terms of their productive relations, wealth and power, so *cultures* are differently ranked, and stand in opposition to one another, in relations of domination and subordination, along the scale of 'cultural power'. (Hall and Jefferson 1976: 11)

Certainly comparison of, say, the economic history of Argentina with the comparable instances of Australia and Canada, suggests that a mechanistic economic explanation is inadequate and that cultural differences, in the sociological sense, have to be taken into account if the differences in outcomes are to be adequately explained (Duncan and Fogarty 1986).

Anthropologists generally follow Durkheim in seeking to explain societies in their own terms. To an anthropologist, culture refers to the entire pattern of behaviour of a society. Anthropologists therefore tend to use a very loose definition of the term, following Tylor in defining culture as:

> that complex whole which includes knowledge, belief, art, morals, law, custom and any other capabilities and habits acquired by man [sic] as a member of society. (Tylor 1891: 2)

The development of anthropology as a serious academic discipline in the nineteenth century accompanied the involuntary process of encounter with new cultures brought about by colonisation. In one sense this was helpful, since it meant that much was studied and recorded that might otherwise have been lost. In another sense it was not, because the basic assumption behind colonisation – that the culture of the colonisers was in some or all senses 'superior' to that of the colonised – was seldom successfully challenged. Following the path laid down by Lamartine, the French in particular adopted the notion of the *mission civilisatrice*. The justification of colonisation lay in the opportunity it afforded for the colonised to gain access to the dominant culture of France and because of the superior advantages of that culture the French had a right, and indeed a duty, to spread it.

Here we are concerned with the impact of change on culture, 'the common, learned way of life shared by the members of a society, consisting of the totality of tools, techniques, social institutions, attitudes, beliefs, motivations, and systems of value known to the group' (Foster 1973: 11). Colonisation is a drastic change in culture. So too is decolonisation, industrialisation and, for that matter, *globalisation*. Foster notes six characteristics of cultures which are crucial to the understanding of the process of change:

1. Sociocultural forms are learned.
2. A sociocultural system is a logically integrated, functional, sense-making whole.
3. All sociocultural systems are constantly changing: none is completely static.
4. Every culture has a value system.
5. Cultural forms, and the behaviour of individual members of a society, stem from, or are functions of cognitive orientations, of deep-seated premises.
6. A common culture makes possible the reasonably efficient, largely automatic interaction between members of a society that is a prerequisite to social life (extracted from Foster 1973: 12–24).

The problem is complicated by the fact that there is a third, very common way in which the term 'culture' is used, and indeed much more commonly and widely used. This is to designate the evidences of specialised forms of self-expression such as art, music, literature etc. Culture in this sense, sometimes termed 'high culture', is generally seen as being the particular province of intellectuals, who designate what is to be regarded as 'good' or 'bad' within this specialised cultural inheritance. Thus since French culture was admired and copied by other European peoples, it seemed obvious both to them and to others that it also ought to be copied by the colonised. Time has shown how successful the policy was.

High culture, therefore, forms part (but only part) of the dominant culture in the sociological sense. But it is a particularly important part, since it embodies in the highest degree the characteristics that differentiate that culture from all other cultures (or subcultures) within that society, and so forms the core of its 'entitlement' to cultural power. This entitlement of the ruling class, and its unconscious recognition by the masses, was called 'hegemony' by Gramsci. It is the distinctive property of culture that the values and norms it conveys are internalised by members of the society in general, enabling the rulers the more easily to exercise power over them.

The concept of modernity: competing cultures

In the nineteenth century the development of industrialised society in Europe was increasingly accompanied by a belief in the 'evolution' of cultures – the survival of the fittest. Imperial powers, such as Spain, Portugal, France, Britain, the Netherlands, Belgium, the United States and Russia, saw it as their 'duty' to 'civilise' subject peoples and to impose their cultural norms on them.

The main vehicle of transmission was the education system. Utilising both the pedagogy and curriculum of the dominant culture, it subordinated indigenous values by offering those who could take advantage of the system the opportunity to share in the task of government and administration.

Critics call the policy of deliberately propagating a culture of self-defined modernity 'cultural imperialism'. They argue that although formal imperialism, in the old sense of political and military domination, has ended, informal imperialism continues. Imperialism always involved a combination of strategies: it was never simply a matter of superior force, as the history of British involvement in South Africa makes very clear. Obviously the two are closely linked, as Hoogvelt argues:

> No society can successfully dominate another without the diffusion of its cultural patterns and social institutions, nor can any society successfully diffuse all or most of its cultural patterns and institutions without some degree of domination. (Hoogvelt 1978: 109)

This process of diffusion could be highly effective. Anthropologists, often inadvertently, helped the process by designating residual indigenous cultures as 'primitive' and so by implication inferior to their own. Even when they did not, there were problems. As a social scientist, Malinowski recognised and was concerned about the risk of contaminating of cultures by observation (Malinowski 1961). However more recently anthropologists have been criticised for paternalism when they have argued that indigenous peoples should be left alone to evolve at their own rate.

Mere contact with a more powerful culture can certainly be highly traumatic. The impact of an externally-driven rapid process of change on whole societies not used to it is potentially even more devastating, since in those circumstances there is no way back to the familiar certainties of the past.

However, rapid adaptation to technological change is likely to be much easier for a society which is already faced with the prospect of rapid change and which has already come to the end of its capacity to adapt than it is for societies which have not been forced to abandon old ways. In *New Lives for Old*, a study of the island of Manus to the north of New Guinea, Margaret Mead argued that it was far more difficult for people to adopt fragments of a culture than to take on board a whole new culture. Toffler quotes her verdict approvingly, but with reservations about the limits to adaptation – beyond a certain point, he argues, peoples succumb to **culture shock** (Mead 1956; also cited in Toffler 1970: 329). Defeat in war afforded Japan and Korea the opportunity to compete on the basis of new technology. Already people are arguing that the collapse of Communism may enable large parts of Eastern Europe to do the same. But in many developing world states the problem is rather for the future of indigenous cultures surrounded by the modern state.

Certainly various cultures can coexist – if enough space separates them. The Yanomami in Brazil were largely insulated from the outside world until the arrival of the *garimpieros* (gold miners). But cultures are permeable and absorption of new elements is usual. India was simply too large and too complex for its cultures to be swept away. British culture was incorporated but did not supersede indigenous patterns, and in fact with few exceptions (e.g. the self-immolation of widows) the Raj did not seek to end traditional Indian practices. One of these practices, indeed, was the salt tax, the very tax that Mahatma Gandhi was to use as his target for anti-colonial agitation. Given the small numbers of the colonisers and the practice of indirect rule Indians had to collaborate actively in their own domination for the process to work at all. British culture was admired for its association with power, wealth and modernity. When these values ceased to be unconditionally admired, and Indian values came to the fore, the end of the Raj was at hand. Today the survival of the traditional lifestyle of 'tribals' (as indigenous people are known in India) is now threatened most by the aspirations of other Indians and the quest for 'modernity' or development.

Relationships established with colonisation do not end at independence. In his well-known attack on French policy in Algeria, Frantz Fanon (1967) argued that the psyche of black peoples in Africa had been damaged by colonisation – they had been taught to regard their 'own' culture as inferior. Time has shown this to be too pessimistic a view, based, no doubt, on his own individual experience. Fanon himself was born in the French Antilles and brought up in Martinique but his argument does not appear to have the same resonance in Africa South of the Sahara as it did in North Africa. Others have yet to explore fully the impact of the experience of empire on the colonisers themselves.

The global network

The first truly global network was established in the nineteenth century. However, although its cables crossed the seas the electric telegraph operated only on land and its impact was limited. It did, however, enable newspapers throughout the world to carry some international news and, by the beginning of the twentieth century, pictures.

Radio removed the limitation of space. Incredibly, it was first seen merely as a form of communication between individuals, and it was not until 1920 that its most obvious defect, the fact that anyone within range could hear it, was turned into an advantage and the idea of 'broadcasting' became a reality. By then the cinema had already added the visual element. Together they made a global culture possible, but not yet a reality, since despite the early lead gained by Hollywood, language differences and entrenched nationalist attitudes remained a significant barrier. But there was a foretaste of what was to come in the role played by All-India Radio in unifying the subcontinent.

Television combined all these experiences in a single medium. It was, how-ever, initially a very expensive one, limited in its coverage by the need to trans-mit along the line of sight. But by the 1960s space technology had advanced far enough for Arthur C. Clarke's proposal for a network of earth satellites to begin to become reality (Clarke 1945). Even then there were continuing prob-lems with nationalism and security issues and the first media event to achieve anything approaching worldwide coverage on television was probably the World Cup of 1986. In 1982 the Falklands War took place under a strict security blanket on both sides; by 1990 satellite uplinks enabled Cable News Network (CNN) to carry live transmissions during the Gulf War from Baghdad under bombardment and even from allied troops in the desert.

The internet grew out of links established between computers in California in the late-1960s as a means of communication between government, defence establishments and university researchers. Unlike earlier media, it was decen-tralised and so could not be disabled in the event of war. Its capacity was enormously enhanced in 1989 with the adoption of the universal protocols proposed by Timothy Berners-Lee enabling anyone with access to the system to transmit text, pictures and sound across the World Wide Web. It is this abil-ity for anyone to make use of the net that is its most interesting feature. However even it has taken time to spread. According to the Internet Society in 1996 only 134 countries had full internet access though a further 52 had limited access, as, for example, to email. In 1996 of the 50 million people who had access, 40 million spoke English. By 2000 391 million had access, of whom only 192 million spoke English. In 2005 these figures had risen to 1,100 million and 300 million (Global Reach 2006). But of the 220 million who spoke Chinese, none of those who lived in the People's Republic of China enjoyed full access, partly as a result of Chinese government action and partly because of voluntary restrictions in the content provided to China by outside ISPs, notably Google.cn.

Impact of transnational media

To the developed world, the ready availability of many channels of informa-tion seems a most desirable state of affairs. However, there are problems seen from a developing world perspective:

The need to use existing networks of communication

Cables and satellites are very expensive and use of them is controlled by the AICs – though Indonesia and the Philippines have both sought to enter the world of satellite broadcasting by commissioning their own communications satellites. The world's press is largely fed both text and pictures by the US

Plate 11 Globalisation: Chile

agencies Associated Press and United Press International; the view of the rest of the world is systematically affected by the pro-US bias of agency reporters and editors. British (Reuters), French (Agence France-Presse) and, in the past, Soviet agencies (Tass) have similarly played their part in defining the news agenda. But developing world agencies, with the rather limited exception, for brief periods, of the Cuban Prensa Latina, have not.

The problem of finding a common language

The effort to impose Hindi in India, initiated by Nehru, was only partially successful. Nehru had, after all, to make his independence speech in English. The attempt of S.W.R.D. Bandaranaike in 1956 to impose Sinhala instead of English as the sole official language of Sri Lanka backfired by alienating the large Tamil minority who had previously made use of English to gain access to the higher ranks of the civil service and other important jobs. His assassination at the hands of a Buddhist extremist was followed within a few years by riots in which Sinhalese sacked and looted the Tamil district of Colombo. Equal status for Tamil was conceded and English continues to be a working language of government, as it is in India and Pakistan.

In North Africa, ironically, Arabic is already available as a common language. Yet unity is elusive and attempts to unite existing states such as Egypt and Syria or Iraq and Kuwait have all failed. Although notions of self-interest are obviously at work here, so too has been that elusive perception of difference conveyed by dialect and idiom. Over most of Latin America Spanish serves as a common tongue, though it is resented also for the very fact that makes it universal: the fact that it was imposed from above. The Portuguese speakers of Brazil can understand Spanish, even if they do not speak it. In Africa both Nigeria and South Africa lack a common language and continue to find English invaluable as a working language of communication, though in East Africa Swahili was established as a universal language before the onset of colonisation.

The need for a common language is powerfully reinforced by the universality of radio in the developing world. Radio speaks directly to people over long distances. It is cheap and the modern transistor does not require mains electricity. In Latin America, apart from Cuba, the pattern is one of competing commercial stations. In Africa the service is generally state run. With the gradual economic decline of Sierra Leone the state-owned television transmitter in Freetown broke down and was not repaired; radio, however, continued to function even in the most remote areas.

At the moment, the universal language of the internet is English. Translation programs are already up and running which enable machine translation from one language to another. However, ambiguity and the use of idiom render many such translations at best ungrammatical and at worst absurd. Besides, the expense of devising such programs mean that at present they are available in only a few languages; inevitably the less common developing world languages are not available.

The problem of competing with systems of mass cultural production

Television is the most effective of mass media, since it does not require literacy and, though a low content medium in terms of information, it does have a strong emotive impact through use of visual images. But it is also very expensive. So the very high cost of television production means that all but the basics of news, weather and talk programmes have until recently been very expensive by developing world standards. Only now have small, lightweight cameras become sufficiently sophisticated to enable companies to compete with imports, especially in the field of drama and serials, or, as they are commonly known, 'soap operas' or '*telenovelas*'.

'McWorld'?

The United States sets television production standards – viewers come to expect a sophisticated product, even if the content is bland – as well as standards for structure, through the need in products intended originally for the US market to incorporate breaks for advertising. US productions build on the success and reputation of Hollywood and its experience of film. As with films, which have had a much longer history of exposure in the developing world, television productions propagate key images of life in America. These include:

1. Universal affluence, which creates a demand for Western products, which in turn increases dependence on imports and distorts local consumption patterns. This sometimes has specific serious effects, as in the case of the use of infant milk formula, though more usually it works in a more generalised and insidious fashion, propagating the vision of consumerism 'borne in on us by the onrush of economic and ecological forces that demand integration and uniformity and that mesmerize the world with fast music, fast computers, and fast food' (Barber 1992), dubbed by Ben Barber 'McWorld'.
2. Easy violence, from cartoons and the traditional Westerns to *Robocop* and *Terminator III*. Such images may imply that low local standards in this regard are satisfactory because they also exist in the United States, despite the fact that standards in most developed countries, and especially in Japan, are very much higher. Hong Kong is a major producer of films based on proficiency in various spectacular and undoubtedly threatening martial arts, and these are clearly very popular among young viewers. Who is to doubt that they play at least some part in the 'retribalization of large swaths of humankind by war and bloodshed' (Barber 1992)?

Major exporters of film up to the present include, as well as the USA and France, Hong Kong, India and Italy. Among developing world states, India and Brazil stand out as major producers of television. Here there have been very marked improvements. Ten years ago little of their product reached screens in the AICs, except on cable. Even then, the Mahabarat had a major impact in Britain in reawakening pride in Hinduism; in India it is believed to have contributed significantly to the rise of Hindu nationalism. Now 'Bollywood' productions are regularly available on satellite television together with news, current affairs and features in a variety of languages.

Mexico's state-owned Televisa dominates Mexican programming, but is becoming increasingly important (as is Spain) in productions for the Hispanic-American market, and Brazil's O Globo has grown from a newspaper into the largest television network in Brazil and the fourth largest in the world.

In the USA and Europe the aftermath of '9/11' propelled the Arabic language channel, al-Jazeera, into the spotlight. Based in the Gulf State of Qatar, it was formed in 1996 after Saudi Arabia had forced the closure of the BBC's Arabic service and is staffed by many of its ex-employees. It represents the nearest thing available to a well-informed, moderate Arabic viewpoint and claims to have an audience in excess of 50 million; not that this has stopped it from being denounced in the USA as a propagandist for al-Qaeda and harassed by other vested interests. In September 2004, the US-backed interim government of Iraq banned the Arabic television station from broadcasting in the country and its security officers stormed al-Jazeera's Baghdad offices and sealed the newsroom with red wax (*The Guardian*, 6 September 2004). In April 2005 the Iranian authorities shut down the Tehran offices of al-Jazeera, accusing the broadcaster of inflaming ethnic riots in the south of the country (*The Guardian*, 19 April 2005).

Rather more worryingly, on more than one occasion, its offices seem to have been the target of US fire. On 13 November 2001 during the US invasion of Afghanistan, US forces launched a missile attack on al-Jazeera's office in Kabul, after being informed of its location. During the Iraqi invasion, on 8 April 2003 al-Jazeera's office in Baghdad was again attacked by US forces, despite the United States being informed of the office's precise coordinates beforehand. Reporter Tareq Ayyoub was killed and a colleague wounded. Few in the Middle East thought that the action was accidental.

Opinion formers

Perspectives on the world propagated by media etc. are mediated through 'opinion formers', who reinforce stereotypical images. The question of where these 'opinion formers' come from and how they come to perceive the world as they do is an interesting one. Broadly, centre influences periphery, though there remains a special role for churches and sects, teachers, doctors and local government officials in the local context.

Education in India is dominated by Brahmins. Though the Western-educated elite help shape opinion in towns, in the countryside the traditional elites still hold sway. In Latin America education is skewed by cost towards the well-to-do; the wealthy in turn have traditionally owned/edited newspapers and increasingly dominate radio and television.

Ideas are carried by people as well as by the media, so travel, for whatever reason, is important in enabling ideas to pass from one place to another. War has a most dramatic influence on all societies, both because it forces people to travel and because of the challenge it presents to traditional notions of leadership and competence. Soldiers returning to Africa (Lloyd 1971) and to India after the Second World War carried with them ideas of independence and possibly even a copy of the **Atlantic Charter**. When, as in the case of Burma or Indonesia, a country was actually invaded and occupied, the effects were even more powerful. Throughout South-east Asia the Japanese invaders transmitted the electrifying message that colonial rule was not inevitable and that the former colonial powers could in favourable circumstances be challenged and even defeated.

However, the transmission of ideas works all the time in urbanising societies in a much less spectacular but probably no less efficient fashion. Those who work in towns return to the country with news and gossip about events in the wider world but also with a certain prestige which makes their ideas more weighty.

In Islamic countries the revival of Islamic **fundamentalism** has demonstrated both the power of opinion formers and the ability in certain circumstances to bypass them. The power of the mullahs in generating hatred of the Shah in Iran was clearly important. But it was following the Revolution that those pressing for the adoption of an Islamic Republic were able to use the traditional sermon at Friday prayers to great effect. On the other hand, direct criticism of the ruling elite in Saudi Arabia was not possible in this way. Clandestine sermons have therefore been circulated on audiotape and have found a ready market, thus circumventing the ban on public criticism. In both Egypt and Algeria, countries which have been much more directly exposed in the past to influences from Western Europe, a similar revival is also very evident, despite strong attempts by their governments to prevent it, particularly in the case of Algeria, where the Islamist FIS was prevented from taking power and was then banned from overt activity.

News management and international perception of the developing world

News management, the way in which news organisations seek to control the flow of news and to set the agenda for political discourse, does not just affect what is seen in the developing world. It also affects international perception of the developing world. Press agencies, television news and features all combine to present a very selective view.

It is of course natural that people all over the world are concerned with their own local needs and issues. It is also understandable that bad news tends to have a much bigger impact than good. As a result many parts of the developing world get only selective and spasmodic attention from the rest of the world, and then all too often only when some 'natural' disaster hits the headlines. Even the world's first television station with pretensions of universality, CNN, which has its base in Atlanta, Georgia, is strongly biased towards news from the United States itself.

In 1984 famine in Ethiopia seized public attention in Britain when a BBC news report showed moving pictures of starving children. In fact, the famine had already lasted more than three months, but had not previously caught the public imagination. Government aid (as usual) was slow to emerge; in the meanwhile, led by a rock star, the public spontaneously put their hands in their pockets to subscribe and increased government aid resulted. However, in some ways the manner in which the issue emerged did Ethiopia a disservice. The news coverage was inevitably ethnocentric. Ethiopians were under-represented in such broadcasts, since few spoke English, and their own relief efforts were correspondingly minimised, although they were by far the more important. Thus were the traditional stereotypes of helpless Africans and capable and benevolent foreigners confirmed in the public imagination in the AICs. In 1999 the situation was not as much improved as AICs' television neglect would suggest. Much imported food was still needed, though the rains had come and starvation was much more localised. The government of the Derg had fallen and been replaced by a weak democratic government, hardly able to tackle the country's fundamental problems.

In Somalia in 1989 the main problem was the breakdown of public order. Emphasis on this fact ultimately led to US intervention in 1992–93 and a futile attempt to oust one of the local warlords, General Aideed. Aideed proclaimed himself president in July 1995 but was not recognised by other clan leaders and died in a street battle a year later. His son succeeded him, but repeated efforts to call a conference to restore order had no success. Meanwhile heavy flooding in southern Somalia in 1998 destroyed crops and renewed the threat of famine, though in a large part of the country, former British Somaliland, without publicity, order had successfully been restored and famine was not a problem. Neglected by the outside world, by 2006 most of Somalia had fallen under Islamic fundamentalist control.

High culture

A distinctive feature of Europe has been the special role ascribed to the arts and the artist. Each of the arts has defined rules (up to a point) of appreciation, but they vary very much between one art form and another. These rules are established by an elite and subject to the whims of fashion. Breaking the rules may lead to innovation but it can also lead to the artist losing credibility.

Relationships between developed and developing world elites are complex, and this is reflected in art as in all else. Although Europe initially provided the first global culture, in the twentieth century the United States came to provide a powerful rival and mass substitute. In the plastic arts the obvious consequence has been a clear trend towards the extension and ultimately globalisation of high culture made possible by technology. Since the Middle Ages 'European' culture has incorporated many significant elements from countries that are now relatively underdeveloped – steel from what is now Iraq, carpets from Turkey and Iran, porcelain and stoneware from China, textiles from India, bronze from Thailand. Such objects were first imported and admired, then, more or less successfully, copied, and finally displaced by mass products retaining an eclectic mixture of European and overseas design. In Victorian Britain the severe Gothic architecture of the mid-century contrasts sharply with the riot of interior colour and the use of a spectacular range of elements from (among others) the Indian, Turkish, Arab and Chinese decorative arts.

In recent years there have been other influences. The tomb of Tutankhamun led to a second rediscovery of Ancient Egypt in the United Kingdom and the United States, where its spectacular quality had a powerful influence on Hollywood. The impact of African art on France in the age of Art Deco is also significant. Pablo Picasso studied African art and fused elements drawn from it into a powerful new synthesis which had a great impact on the future of Western art. And if the archaising tendencies in inter-war Mexican art were often awkward, the naive images associated with Diego Rivera, José Clemente Orozco, David Siquieros and others of the Mexican school of muralists spoke far more eloquently of exploitation and suffering and the need for revolutionary unity than did the Mexican politicians of the generation of the Revolution.

It is, of course, the capitalist West that established the idea of an art market, creating a demand for products of the traditions not only of the developed countries but of the developing world also. Art has become an international commodity. As a commodity, though, it has rather unusual rules, since its value varies very much with the degree of authenticity attributed to it, and this is in most cases much a matter of opinion. In fact, Chinese culture does not have a concept of 'authenticity' in the Western sense. The export of large numbers of objects from China and Russia since the fall of the Soviet Union has upset the market, but with the increasing globalisation of trade, other traditions have increasingly attracted the attention of collectors.

Music too requires neither language nor literacy for comprehension, but here the power of modern mass culture, spread by radio, television, the vinyl disc, audiotape and CD has been overwhelming. African rhythms reappeared at the turn of the twentieth century in American jazz; they have since been re-introduced to Africa along with (disconcertingly) another popular US musical export: country and western.

However, literature is not so easily transmitted, and here the relationship between the developed and developing worlds is often confused. Austin writes of the problem confronting the present-day African writer:

> Whereas African artists can draw on tradition in sculpture or dancing or music, it seems doubtful whether a novelist or poet can write in his mother tongue out of a background of general illiteracy. Where would his audience be? . . . There is said to be a continuing tradition of poetry in the Somali language, and Hausa epics are still recited in northern Nigeria. There have also been local attempts to recast village ceremonies in modern dramatic form, as in the Ogun plays among the Yoruba in Nigeria, or as Efua Sutherland has tried to do in village theaters among the Akan in Ghana. At every turn, however, the African writer is confronted not simply with illiteracy but with the prevalence of English or French or Portuguese. (Austin 1978: 137)

There is a problem of the 'cultural hegemony' of the former colonial language which has to be addressed by African writers who do use English or French. They gain access to a wider readership but there is a price to be paid. The first generation of post-independence writers found the transition particularly difficult, as they moved from rejection of colonialism and enthusiastic support for independence leaders to disillusion with and contempt for corrupt and dictatorial regimes. The influence of Marxism on the extent to which writers felt violence was needed for successful liberation is evident throughout; its most famous exponent and advocate, Frantz Fanon, has already been mentioned.

A distinctive feature of the francophone, as opposed to the anglophone, writers has been the positive emphasis on Africanness, first termed **négritude** in a poem by the Martiniquais poet Aimé Césaire in 1939. The concept was elaborated in the post-war period by Léopold S. Senghor, former deputy in the French National Assembly under the Fourth Republic and later president of Senegal. There is no exact equivalent of *négritude* in English.

By contrast the notion of **pan-Africanism**, which originated with Marcus Garvey and W.E.B. DuBois in the United States, had in a relatively short time to yield to the political realities of a divided continent. It led to a new emphasis on African identity in the anglophone territories, which was taken up by Nnamdi Azikiwe and Jomo Kenyatta among others, but expressed in political form by Kwame Nkrumah of Ghana, almost alone among African leaders of the independence generation.

By the end of the decade the first glow of independence was already fading. Wole Soyinka expressed disillusion with new governments: what choice was there but revolution on the one hand or a comfortable symbolic position with the UN or UNESCO on the other? Chinua Achebe of Nigeria denounced the system of corruption he saw there and foresaw the military coup that was to come. James Ngugi of Kenya Africanised his name to Ngugi wa Thi'ongo and called for revolution. Ironically white South Africa formed the one cause that united a continent.

In the nineteenth century the small elite of Latin American authors similarly rejected their Spanish heritage; in fact the first novel published in Latin America, Fernández de Lizardi's *El periquillo sarniento* ('The itching parrot'), published in Mexico in 1816, was a violent condemnation of Spanish colonial rule in all its manifestations. Uniquely at that stage, in Mexico in the latter part of the century Ignacio Altamirano (1834–93) went one stage further. Casting the invading Spaniards as the real savages, he glorified the conquered native peoples as wise and noble. Elsewhere, however, writers ignored both, and, despite the advice of Andrés Bello, rejected the challenge to establish a new and typically 'American' literature, choosing instead to try to emulate the highly artificial forms then fashionable in Europe.

This choice reflected both the contemporary cultural dominance of France among a cosmopolitan elite and growing disillusion with the actual progress of events in the Americas since independence. The theme of the struggle of human beings against hostile nature came to the fore and has remained a key theme in Latin American writing. Parallel with it was a deep disillusion with human beings and their political achievements. In the age of the dictators the novel was one method by which coded criticism could be made of the established order, and even then such critics often found it necessary to live abroad. One of the earliest and best known examples of this genre, *Facundo*, was published in 1845 in exile by Domingo Faustino Sarmiento as an attack on the rule of Rosas in Argentina. More recent examples have included the Venezuelan Rómulo Gallegos' *Doña Bárbara* (1919), the Guatemalan Miguel Angel Asturias' *El señor presidente* (1946) and the Argentine Manuel Puig's *Kiss of the Spider Woman* (*El beso de la mujer araña*, 1976). Better known outside the Spanish-speaking world is the Mexican Carlos Fuentes, who denounced the betrayal of the Mexican Revolution in *La región más transparente* (1958). This feeling of betrayal of the promise of the region was, however, expressed even more strongly by Alejo Carpentier, who in *El siglo de luces* (1962) rejected the French Revolution itself and all that stemmed from it (by implication including the very existence of Latin America).

However, whereas in the early twentieth century regionalism was the other key feature of a realistic attempt to portray the continent as it was, in the years since 1945 the major trend was away from harsh realism towards fantasy. Yet it is within the strange and exotic rules of what has been termed 'magical realism' that a generation of readers outside Latin America has first perceived and then tried to come to terms with the real social processes at work in its cities and countryside. The Colombia of Gabriel García Márquez is fiction, a product of the imagination of an outstanding writer of world stature. Yet precisely because of that, his major work, *Cien años de soledad* (1967) has an aura of reality that still today sends people in search of the 'real' Macondo.

Asia is too big and too diverse for generalisations. In South Asia, the use of English as a medium of communication by Indian writers makes their works available to the outside world without translation and they are increasingly attracting a huge and very appreciative readership in the AICs. Examples include Vikram Seth's immense epic *A Suitable Boy* (1993) and Arundhati Roy's Booker Prize-winning *The God of Small Things* (1997). Books by Sri Lankan writers, too, have received widespread critical acclaim in Britain, though many of the successful such writers deal with controversial matters at home and some may have preferred to live in self-imposed exile at least until the return of the SLFP in 1994.

However, the implied criticism of the Muslim attitude towards women in Bangladesh in Taslima Nasreen's novel, *Shame*, led to such a hostile reaction that fundamentalists held an open meeting, wrongly quoted her as condemning the Koran and pronounced a *fatwa* against her.

> The usual punishment for my so-called crime – blasphemy – is hanging. The threat makes me more determined to fight oppression. I nearly went crazy when I was in hiding after the fatwa was pronounced. There are 14 people living in our house in Bangladesh, and only one of them knew I was sheltered there. I wasn't allowed to make a sound, not even a rustle. I didn't know if it was day or night and I couldn't get food regularly. I forgot how to eat and I didn't know when I was hungry. I could only go outside at midnight, as if I was a stray cat. I didn't sleep from worry. (Taslima Nasreen, interview by Marcelle Katz, *The Sunday Times Magazine*, 22 January 1995: 54)

In August 1994 Nazreen had to leave her native Bangladesh and to seek exile abroad. The hazards facing a creative writer in the developing world are many, since the difference between fact and fiction, though it may be understood, is not always accepted as legitimate.

Conclusion

There are so many things that could be said about the social context of the developing world that any selection will be, to some extent, arbitrary. Stratification systems and institutional structures are the most vital underlying features of society in the developing world as in the AICs. However, a consistent pattern is the great gulf that separates the rich from the poor, and the central role of the state in articulating the relationship between them.

Again it is next to impossible to know how to attempt to do justice in outline to the rich cultural variety of the developing world. While a brief summary of the literature of Latin America may serve to illuminate its main themes, because its distinctive characteristic is its common inheritance from Spain from which it has grown, no such summary could ever do more than hint at the diversity of Africa, let alone Asia. Yet there is one thing that all this cultural diversity has in common: an underlying fear that it is threatened by the powerful forces of the North's 'cultural imperialism'. This populist leaders have quite understandably sought to resist. However in their attempt to appropriate cultural symbols for their own personal advantage they have also run the grave risk of stirring up sleeping resentments in the form of nationalism (as will be seen in the next chapter) in a way that can in the end prove politically unmanageable.

Key terms

achieved status – social status and prestige attributed to an individual according to achievements or skills rather than inherited social position

Agenda 21 – programme for environmental protection and recovery approved by the UN Conference on Environment and Development in 1992

ascribed status – social standing or prestige resulting from inheritance or hereditary factors

Atlantic Charter – declaration of war aims, 1941, issued by President Franklin D. Roosevelt of the USA and Prime Minister Winston S. Churchill, representing His Majesty's Government in the UK, stating 'the right of all peoples to choose the form of government under which they will live' and their 'wish to see sovereign rights and self-government restored to those who have been forcibly deprived of them'

biomass – organic matter available on a renewable basis which can be burnt or fermented to produce energy

bride price – payment made by a man to the family from whom he takes a daughter in marriage

culture shock – adverse effect of over-rapid social change resulting from individual inability to cope

dyadic exchange – relationship characterised by mutual economic payments

ethnicity – social construction of society based on perceived differences between groups based on nationality, language or religion; identification of oneself with one of those groups

exploitation – in social relationships, use or abuse of someone for one's own advantage

extended family – family group consisting of more than two generations of the same kinship line living in the same household

fundamentalism – religious movement believing in the infallibility of their sacred texts and requiring adherence to a strictly-defined set of laws or practices set out in them

gender – an individual's status as male or female and the conventions roles and behaviour ascribed to that status

indigenous peoples – descendants of the original inhabitants of an area which maintain traditional, sustainable lifestyles in continued opposition to the encroaching power of the modern, internationalised state and share a common culture, language and ancestry

négritude – French term for positive emphasis on Africanness, first used in a poem by the Martiniquais poet Aimé Césaire in 1939

news management – the way in which news organisations seek to control the flow of news and to set the agenda for political discourse

pan-Africanism – movement calling for the unification of Africa under a common government

social services – services generally provided by government that help improve people's standard of living

stratification – in social relationships, division of society into horizontal layers

Questions

1. What are the principal problems of maintaining social provision in a rapidly evolving society?

2. What role does the family play as an institution in economic development?

3. Why has the empowerment of women been so much less successful in some countries than others?

4. Do developed countries face a choice between 'jihad' and 'McWorld'?

5. How far do the transnational media shape our perceptions of the developing world?

6. What are indigenous peoples and what measures can or should be taken to preserve their way of life?

CHAPTER 6

The international context

Introduction

Until 1991 the **Cold War** was the main factor affecting relations between the developing world and the **superpowers**. Not only did the superpowers themselves evaluate everything that happened in the developing world in terms of how it would affect the global **balance of power**, but the developing world states themselves entered actively into the game of winning superpower support. In the process a great many people were to get hurt, but it could be argued that a certain element of discipline was thus imposed on the international community.

Whatever the Cold War may have meant for Europe or for the United States, for the developing world it meant one thing: foreign **intervention**. The forms of intervention varied from place to place and from time to time: sometimes overt, as in Lebanon in 1958 or the Dominican Republic in 1965; sometimes covert, as in Iran in 1953 or in Nicaragua after 1981; sometimes formal, as in Vietnam in the 1960s, sometimes informal, as in Honduras in the 1980s.

Between 1991 and 2001 the main theme in relations between the AICs and the developing world was that of 'humanitarian intervention' – to arrest some of the many local conflicts which had broken out in the wake of the collapse of the Soviet Union. Insurgency was seen as merely the temporary result of the new uncertainties, and the idea of the 'democratic peace' was widely advocated. This was the idea that armed conflict would not take place between two democratic countries. The kindest thing that can be said about this is that the jury is still out. Even in 1989, there was at least one very important historical example to the contrary, the American Civil War, and many observers think that the only reason why more democratic countries have not gone to war with one another is that until recently there have been too few of them to make this a likely possibility. The recent war between Ethiopia and Eritrea, however, involved two countries in the developing world that were at least nominally democratic, and both Venezuela and Colombia have been known to deploy troops and warships along their common frontier.

Two hours that shook the world

On 11 September 2001, four aircraft were hijacked on the East Coast of the USA with the objective of blowing up strategically important sites within the country. Fully fuelled, two were crashed into the twin towers of the World Trade Center, New York, which collapsed within an hour, and a third into the Pentagon; a fourth, probably intended for the White House, crash-landed in a field in Pennsylvania after its passengers realised what had happened and tried to regain control. More than 2,500 people, all but the terrorists themselves innocent civilians, perished, many in full view of television cameras.

No secret was made of the fact that the attacks had been launched by a network of al-Qaeda terrorists, operating from within the United States. Al-Qaeda was founded in 1989 shortly after the withdrawal from Afghanistan of the Soviet forces that had occupied it since Christmas 1979. In 1993, when it first attempted to blow up the World Trade Center, it was based in Sudan, then as now under an Islamic fundamentalist regime. In 1996 its leader, Osama bin Laden, was driven out of Sudan and returned to Afghanistan, then under the control of the Taliban. In 1998 attacks on US embassies in Kenya and Tanzania killed 224 and injured 4,500, mostly passing Africans. In 2000 an attack on the USS *Cole* in Yemen inflicted serious damage but resulted in relatively few casualties.

The rise of al-Qaeda represents a major shift in North–South relations for three reasons. Osama bin Laden and his followers were prepared not only to target attacks on US assets, but to do so in a context that would bring the greatest result in terms of shock. And their choice of terrorist methods was unusual in the extent to which they were prepared to treat civilian lives as unimportant and some of those civilians were Muslims. What shocked people in the AICs was the brutality and destruction as a means to the end of scoring a propaganda victory. In statements since, bin Laden has used two themes to whip up support in the Islamic world: US support for Israel and the presence of US troops in Saudi Arabia (Halliday 2001).

George W. Bush and the aftermath of '9/11'

The election of George W. Bush, in 2000, had already left the way open for those in the USA who wished to dismantle the structure of international co-operation that had been so painstakingly constructed, often in the interests of the USA itself, over the years since 1941. Headed by Vice President Dick Cheney, many of the key players in the new Administration, such as Defense Secretary Donald Rumsfeld and Deputy Secretary of Defense Paul Wolfowitz were conservatives and unilateralists by instinct. They were also keenly aware that, despite the quest for a **peace dividend**, the end of the Cold War had left the United States better armed than the next 15 countries in the world put together. And the new president was ready to listen to them, since he had no personal experience of war, having avoided Vietnam by joining the Texas Air National Guard.

The new Administration immediately showed its determination to ignore opinion abroad when it did not suit its interests. It made it clear that it would not sign up to the treaty creating an International Court of Justice to try individuals accused of war crimes. It went further, by concluding and signing a series of **bilateral treaties** by which states wanting US help had to agree to forgo the right to sue US citizens before the tribunal. On the environmental front, though the Clinton Administration had already ensured that treaties to curb global warming were so attenuated as to be virtually useless, the new Administration refused to accept even the much-weakened Kyoto protocol and the Ottawa Convention. On the economic front, it was soon at loggerheads with the European Union over the content of a new round of trade negotiations and the abolition of subsidies, especially in agriculture.

Armed forces exist to fight wars, and the powerful emotional upswell after the atrocity of the destruction of the World Trade Center in September 2001 led President George W. Bush to respond to this unexpected threat by proclaiming a 'war on terror'. This was in due course to lead Congress to pass the Patriot Act, which stretched the powers of the US Government at home far beyond those that the courts had previously held constitutional. The immediate, concrete response was to send troops to Afghanistan, where al-Qaeda was based, to capture the leaders of al-Qaeda by overthrowing their backers, the Taliban regime. The campaign was to be a test of the ability of the United States to wage war with the minimum of US casualties. The pretext was an ultimatum to the Taliban government to hand over bin Laden. When this was refused hostilities commenced on 8 October 2001 with a massive aerial bombardment of Taliban forces, followed up by the selective use of US Special Forces to try to capture bin Laden himself.

But Afghanistan offered extremely unfavourable terrain even for US forces. The Taliban regime soon fell to troops of the Northern Alliance backed by the USA. With fall of Kabul, the Administration was able to claim credit for overthrowing the fundamentalist regime of the Taliban, which had very little international support anyway, but they failed to capture either Osama bin Laden or any significant number of his associates. Yet the Administration was quick to claim victory, though the country was far from pacified. This task was delegated to 5,000 NATO troops. Fighting continued in a number of places.

Since September 2001 there has been a clear tendency for politicians in the United States and its allies to regard all forms of insurgency (though with certain actual exceptions) as manifestation of what President Bush has claimed is a global war on terror. The most obvious example has been the way in which the United States has supported Russia in its war against separatist Chechen rebels, despite previous doubts about the nature and effectiveness of the methods employed by the Russians.

War in Iraq

Meanwhile President Bush, in his State of the Union address in January 2002, referred ominously to an 'axis of evil', consisting of three developing states: Iraq, Iran and North Korea. Of these three unlikely associates, it was soon clear that hardliners in the Administration had chosen to settle accounts with Iraq (it is now known that in November 2001 Bush had already ordered the preparation of a plan to invade Iraq, and had received assurances, afterwards shown to be incorrect, that Iraq could be successfully taken by fewer than 100,000 troops). No attempt was made to seek confrontation with North Korea, and when that state responded by declaring its intention to acquire nuclear weapons, the US government simply tried to dissuade it through negotiation. But both the UN and US allies generally, with the sole exceptions of Britain and Australia, were satisfied that there was no justification for an attack at that time on Iraq. Iraq under Saddam Hussein had been a secular regime, which had previously been actively supported by the US government against the theocratic regime in Iran. There was no evidence of links between his regime and al-Qaeda and the efforts to prove that there were such links were embarrassingly unsuccessful.

Justification for the coming conflict shifted to the supposed presence of weapons of mass destruction (WMD) in Iraq and the threat that these posed to the United States. However, after a short break, UN weapons' inspectors had gone back into Iraq and had not so far been able to find any evidence of WMD. So apart from the United Kingdom and Australia the allies were not convinced. Security Council Resolution 1441, passed on 8 November 2002, though it referred back to Security Council Resolution 678/1990, supported the continuation of inspection and still fell short of the clear authority to use military force which the USA had demanded. It was clear, months afterwards, that there were no WMD in Iraq, they were not used in the conflict and posed no threat to the USA or to Europe. But there was real anger in the USA at the successful attempt of President Chirac of France and his ally the German Chancellor to forestall a new resolution in the Security Council before the weapons' inspectors could finish their work. Muslim states were uniformly hostile, while the most secular of them, Turkey, a NATO ally, refused to allow US troops to cross its territory to reinforce Kurdish resistance in northern Iraq.

On 16 March 2003, of the large coalition that had originally been hoped for, only the prime ministers of Britain and Spain met with President Bush in the Azores and announced that the 'only effective way of supporting peace and security' was to attack Iraq and depose Saddam Hussein. Though troops were already in place, the fighting itself began unexpectedly on 20 March 2003 with a pre-emptive strike designed to kill Saddam Hussein and decapitate the regime. It continued with a massive invasion by 140,000 US forces from Kuwait, while 18,000 British forces sought to stabilise the area around Basra and the port of Umm Qasr. The forces advanced quickly, meeting very limited resistance, and Baghdad was soon captured. On 1 May President Bush flew to the middle of the Indian Ocean and from the deck of the aircraft carrier USS *Abraham Lincoln* proclaimed active hostilities at an end.

The post-war situation

After that, unfortunately, Iraqi resistance began to grow, to the point at which divisions emerged within the US Administration as to what to do next. The planning for the new kind of limited war, economical in US casualties, had not allowed for the need to organise the peace and assume the responsibility of maintaining order. Reluctance to spend the vast sums needed to restore a country devastated by decades of war and UN sanctions impeded the effort to assume the burdens of military occupation and restore order (Shearer 2000). And with increasing unrest in Iraq there has been a slow realisation that although the USA has tried to take over the UN role as international peace-keeper, the UN is far from obsolete. In September 2003 the Administration finally turned to its allies to invite them to share the burdens of occupation. It was hardly surprising that they made it clear that they would not even begin to think of doing so unless the task was placed under the authority of the UN, and in April 2004 President Bush invited the UN to undertake the task.

The terrorist attack on Madrid on 11 March 2004, however, had already opened up the danger of division between the USA and its closest allies. Bombs had been planted in commuter trains to explode simultaneously as they entered Atocha station. Though the timing was inaccurate, 191 people were killed and 1,460 injured. The conservative Spanish government, in the middle of an election campaign, tried to pretend that the attack was the work of Basque separatists. The electorate punished them by voting heavily for the opposition Socialists, who immediately carried out their campaign pledge to withdraw Spanish troops from Iraq. Although the new Spanish government remained strongly committed to the alliance (thought not to keeping troops in Iraq) and was apparently highly successful in rounding up the members of the Moroccan cell which actually launched the attack, they were vilified in the United States and by conservatives across Europe.

On 7 July 2005 ('7/7') it was the turn of the UK to come under attack, when suicide bombers exploded three devices on underground trains and a fourth on the top deck of a London bus. Fifty-six people were killed (including the four bombers) and more than 700 injured. Two weeks later a second, similar, attack was aborted when the bombs failed to explode, and all four suspected bombers were arrested.

Terror and the developing world

The '9/11' attack showed all too clearly just how difficult terrorism might be to counter. No sophisticated weapons were used, only small knives and box cutters, and although there were many hints that something very big was in the offing, there was no specific information on which the US government could act. The spectacular result was out of all proportion to the means used.

However, a sense of proportion is required; the United States is still very much more powerful than the next 11 states in the world. Its main weakness has been (a) its openness to the rest of the world, and (b) the tendency of its armed forces to try to turn the war into a conventional conflict against a visible enemy – hence Iraq. Al-Qaeda has also been alarmingly successful in provoking the United States and Britain to suspend human rights guarantees and adopt a range of authoritarian methods which up to now they have rightly criticised in developing countries. The war in Iraq has been conspicuously unsuccessful in preventing further terrorist attacks. In fact, even some former supporters of the war believe that it was a disastrous diversion which, with its revelations of torture and the sexual abuse of inmates detained by US troops in Baghdad, has done untold damage to the image of the United States and its allies in the eyes of the developing world.

The breakdown of the state

The way for the so-called humanitarian intervention of the 1990s and the unilateralism of the early twenty-first century was paved, for the United States, by the *new interventionism in Latin America*. The United States has always reserved the 'right' to intervene in Latin America in defence of its own interests (the Monroe Doctrine), and although the Latin American states had persuaded the Roosevelt Administration to renounce the practice in 1936 (the 'Good Neighbor policy'), it was revived as early as 1954, in the age of the Cold War.

When Ronald Reagan was elected president of the United States in 1980, the military elites of Guatemala and El Salvador were both challenged by leftist insurgent movements. They welcomed Reagan because he rejected the

Carter policy of trying to encourage the growth of democracy and human rights in these small Southern states in favour of a more traditional policy of shoring up dictatorships. For President Reagan both Nicaragua and Grenada (where Maurice Bishop's New Jewel Movement had seized power in 1979, and the new People's Revolutionary Government had adopted a non-aligned socialist policy) were proxies for Cuba, which, in turn, was acting as the agent of the USSR. It was assumed in Washington that the insurrection in El Salvador was planned and supported from Nicaragua, despite the evidence of European reporters that the arms carried by the Salvadorean guerrillas were of Western origin. The Soviet presence in Nicaragua was minimal, although Cuban advisers gave assistance in training both the Sandinista People's Army and a large militia force prepared to meet the US invasion the Sandinistas believed would soon come. When, instead, in 1982 regular attacks began by former Somoza supporters operating across the frontier from Honduras, it took some time to become clear that these 'freedom fighters' (as President Reagan called them) or 'Contras' were clandestinely sponsored and supported by the United States.

In October 1983, Bishop was overthrown and summarily shot following an internal coup backed by the left. The United States, which had just withdrawn marines from Lebanon, sent troops instead (with the support of some of the Caribbean countries) to Grenada and established a pro-US administration. At the same time the flow of US arms and aid to El Salvador was increased, leading to an impasse in the civil war, which by early 1984 had been in a hiatus for some months. Then, as presidential elections approached in the United States, pressure on Nicaragua was also increased. Harbours were mined and the economic blockade intensified. In Honduras a series of military exercises, which began in 1983, established a virtually continuous US presence, in a clear attempt to influence the Sandinista regime. Opposition parties in Nicaragua itself first tried to postpone and then boycotted the presidential elections held in November, which, outside the United States, were regarded as generally fair and gave a substantial victory both to the Sandinistas and to their leader, Daniel Ortega Saavedra.

The re-election of President Reagan in 1984 brought a major change of style in foreign affairs. The illusion that the Contras were Nicaraguan 'freedom fighters' gave way to the frank admission of US desire to put pressure on the Nicaraguan government. The prospect of a full-scale war in Central America, however, since 1982 had been a cause of considerable concern to the Contadora group of states (so called because their representatives, from Colombia, Mexico, Panama and Venezuela, had first met to discuss the initiative on the Panamanian island of Contadora). Their efforts resulted in a draft treaty, accepted by Nicaragua, in August 1984, by which all foreign forces and military advisers would be withdrawn from the region. The peace process languished, however, as, under US pressure, the other Central American states decided that the treaty did not go far enough and made no move to sign it. At the general assembly of the OAS in November 1986 the Contadora initiative effectively came to an end. Subsequently, it was resumed by the newly elected president of Costa Rica, Oscar Arias Sánchez, whose peace plan for the region, dubbed the Arias Plan or, from the place of its origin, Esquipulas II, was belatedly accepted by all five Central American states in August 1989. However, in 1990 the Sandinista government in Nicaragua was defeated in a free election and the Contras were subsequently demobilised under UN oversight (Calvert 1994).

Intervention

Intervention means coming between contending parties in such a way as to alter the balance between them (Little 1975). Hence the usual meaning in international relations is support for opposition movements or insurgents or even the direct use of armed force to overthrow an existing government or regime. Strictly speaking, support for an incumbent government which has been formally recognised by the international community is not only not intervention but is something that every friendly government should be prepared to give. However, support for an unpopular government to protect it against the anger of its own people does constitute intervention in the eyes of many developing world countries. In addition, there can be a number of ways in which indirect pressure can be exerted to affect the political, economic or social stability of a target state.

We must therefore distinguish between different modes of intervention:

- Military intervention. When other forms of intervention are not specified, use of the term 'intervention' will be understood as meaning military intervention. Sending troops to support an incumbent government is legitimate in international law if their presence is requested and hence is not strictly speaking intervention. Direct military intervention against a government, on the other hand, is an act of war unless sanctioned by UN or regional bodies, and possibly then also. Invasion, bombardment or armed blockade of a country's ports are all acts of war and may invite retaliation as well as criticism by third parties. Since the 1950s therefore both the United States and the former Soviet Union have used indirect military intervention, including support to insurgents, military training for friendly personnel and support for military governments.
- Economic intervention. This can be carried out through a variety of institutional devices. Pressure can be brought to bear either directly through increasing or decreasing bilateral aid, or indirectly (in the case of the United States, which has a preponderant say) though international lending bodies such as the IMF. Pressure can be exercised less effectively though trade restrictions such as blockades, sanctions or the imposition of tariffs, since

the ideal of free trade is embodied in a series of international agreements. It is difficult in many cases to determine how far a national agenda is pursued by TNCs or whether they follow their own. The US corporation ITT was eager for US intervention in Chile in 1970 but the Administration response was limited.

- Diplomatic (psychological) intervention. Major powers can influence events by suggesting action rather than by direct intervention. They do this by developing contacts and building friendships which enable them to discourage or to encourage specific political outcomes.
- Cultural intervention. It is doubtful whether this constitutes intervention at all, since cultural influences are so slow and it is often impossible to point to any one moment at which they take effect. However, since aid and trade distribute the culture of industrialised nations (see Chapter 5) along with its products they also assists the far more pervasive force of ideological penetration by CNN and the major news agencies.

Sensitive as they inevitably were to any violation of their newly won **sovereignty** (the traditional right of independent states to do what they liked within their own borders), developing world states have generally regarded all forms of intervention as illegitimate and were inclined to extend the meaning of the term to include all actions of which they disapproved. They pressed for the norm of non-intervention enshrined in the Charter of the United Nations to be taken literally. In practice, the question of how far (if at all) intervention was legitimate was determined not by the developing world state but by external powers such as the United States, the Soviet Union, Britain, France or Israel.

For the developing world, the problem of the Cold War was that it complicated their desire for independence by presenting them with the need to choose a position in the international arena for reasons that they felt were not of their making. In Asia independence was substantially complete by the 1970s and by 1975 the United States had withdrawn from direct involvement. In Latin America the experience of Cuba meant that with the rather idiosyncratic exception of Grenada between 1979 and 1983 there was no serious attempt after 1962 for an American state to choose the Soviet Union as a partner.

In Africa all internal crises of independence, however, were externalised when states called on the outside world for help. The UN operation in the Congo/Zaire in 1960 was complicated by US and French intervention and before the decade was out the French, Russians, Americans and Chinese were all involved in various ways. In 1963 the French intervened in Gabon to reverse a military coup and to restore the government of President M'ba. In 1964 Britain sent help when the armies of Kenya, Uganda and Tanzania mutinied. It was reluctant to do the same when in the following year the European settlers of Rhodesia made a unilateral declaration of independence. Soon it became clear that the new government was receiving the tacit support of both Britain and the United States, to say nothing of South Africa. The British, French and Soviets all became involved in the Nigerian civil war after

1967. In 1975 under Operación Carlota Cuban troops arrived to support the Marxist government of Angola just as large consignments of weapons began arriving from Eastern Europe, and later the same year more Cuban troops were flown into Ethiopia to support the Ethiopians against the US-backed Communist (sic) government of Somalia.

Such unity as there was resulted from the fact of Western tolerance of, and covert support for the white South African regime. Protected as it was behind the UN mandate territory of Namibia (former German South-West Africa, administered by South Africa as an integral part of its territory) and a screen of what were later to become the 'front-line states', namely Angola, Botswana, Mozambique, Tanzania, Zambia and Rhodesia (until 1980, now Zimbabwe), the apartheid regime proved very difficult indeed to dislodge. Then revolution in Portugal in 1974 broke up the Portuguese Empire from within, much as the invasion of Spain in 1808 had led ultimately to the independence of Spanish America. Marxist governments obtained international recognition in Angola, Mozambique, Guinea-Bissau and Cape Verde. This sudden unexpected 'success' of Marxist liberation movements and the subsequent revolution in Ethiopia led to a dramatic transformation of the scene in Africa. It was followed by Soviet interventions in Angola, Mozambique and Ethiopia, seeking to support friendly governments and extend their influence in a region where the Soviet Union previously had had rather limited success in winning friends.

A number of armed conflicts were soon in progress. The Soviet Union, finding itself faced with confrontation between its former ally Somalia and the Derg in Ethiopia, had no hesitation about supporting Ethiopia, which was seen as strategically far more important. Cuban troops, serving under Soviet command, successfully recovered the Ogaden for Ethiopia, while the Somali government turned to its former antagonist the United States for help. Meanwhile the United States, hesitant about direct intervention after the fiasco of Vietnam, countered the threat of a Communist takeover in Southern Africa by enlisting African groups to help undermine the Soviet-sponsored states of Angola and Mozambique, and offered indirect support to South Africa's intervention in Angola through the organisation, training and supply of Jonas Savimbi and the National Union for the Total Independence of Angola (UNITA). Proxy conflicts provided an outlet for hostilities and ideological revitalisation.

American politicians of all parties had been wary of intervention ever since the hurried end of the Vietnam War. Direct intervention in Africa was unthinkable. However, quite legally in terms of international law, the United States propped up pro-Western states such as Kenya and Zaire. Here as elsewhere the value of development aid was far exceeded by military assistance. Arms exports were seen by some as the chief instrument of US and Soviet foreign policy towards Africa in the 1970s and 1980s.

Ronald Reagan, President of the United States 1981–89, saw all crises in the South as the product of East–West divisions. The radicalisation of much of the developing world and US failure to penetrate ideologically many former

European colonies was taken hard by the New Right. Reagan's State of the Union message in December 1985, with an eye specifically on Nicaragua and El Salvador, pledged US support for developing world anti-communist guerrillas. This policy became known as the Reagan Doctrine. A major consequence was that economic aid was withdrawn and/or replaced to some extent by military aid. However, both the burden of military spending and Reaganite free market economic policy, with the accompanying interest rate rises necessary to counteract US overspending, contributed to the debt crisis which broke at the beginning of the 1980s and continued to be a problem for developing states throughout the decade.

Despite its rhetoric, by the late 1980s the Reagan Administration, fragmented and discredited by the Iran-Contra scandal, had rediscovered the necessity of superpower cooperation. Bilateral talks at all levels focused on the twin problems of stopping the growth of nuclear arsenals and limiting the spread of nuclear weapons. At the same time the superpowers increasingly found themselves with a common interest in joint diplomatic action to resolve developing world crisis points. In Washington observers began to talk about the emergence of a superpower condominium.

After the high human, financial and diplomatic costs of the invasion of Afghanistan in 1979 and the consequent loss of developing world support, the 1980s saw the rethinking of Soviet policy towards the developing world. The high cost of intervention did not sit well with the economic problems facing the USSR at home. There was a movement away from support for 'wars of national liberation' and the maintenance of client states to the tacit acceptance of diplomatic and economic expediency. Soviet aid was in any case very limited compared with that of the United States and larger OECD nations owing to the inconvertibility of the Soviet currency and its lack of leverage on the world economic system. Soviet weapons sold freely and circulated widely but the USSR's own military capacity was very limited at levels 'useful' in the developing world. For example, when the USSR sent humanitarian aid to Peru following the earthquake of 1970, the mission had to be cut short when one of the Antonov AN-25 transports was lost in the sea off Iceland.

In addition, Soviet allies in the developing world were often ideologically untrained and not very reliable. Allende, who was never a Communist, was overthrown in Chile in 1973 and Guinea began to move away from association with the USSR after the death of Sekou Touré in 1984. With three heads of government in four years, the USSR itself had also become very unpredictable. The Gorbachev government, even more than its predecessors, made good relations with the United States its top priority in foreign affairs. Faced with gathering crises at home, it withdrew from Afghanistan, yielded to the pressure for change in Eastern Europe (which had repercussions in Central Asia) and limited its intervention. It did not seek to stop the US-led UN response to the Gulf Crisis in 1990.

With both North–East (Russia) and North–West (USA and Europe) seeking to resolve developing world conflicts and limit arms supplies to the developing

Table 6.1 Expenditure on defence in excess of 12 per cent of budget in 1990 with 1992 percentage

Country	1990	1992
United Arab Emirates	41.9	N/A
Oman	41.0	35.8
Syria	40.7	42.3
Pakistan	30.9	27.9
South Korea	25.8	22.1
Israel	25.4	22.1
Burma (Myanmar)	24.7	22.0
El Salvador	24.5	16.0
Jordan	23.1	26.7
United States	22.6	20.6
Kuwait	19.9	N/A
Thailand	17.3	17.2
India	17.0	15.0
Zimbabwe	16.5	N/A
Bolivia	14.1	9.8
Iran	13.6	10.3
Guatemala	13.3	N/A
Paraguay	13.3	13.3
Ecuador	12.9	12.9
Egypt	12.7	N/A
United Kingdom	12.2	11.3

Note: High income countries in italics
Source: World Bank (1992)

world (at least in public), both sides came to recognise the value of the UN as a potential peacekeeper. However, in the meanwhile developing as well as developed countries had in most cases begun to commit very large proportions of their national budgets to the purchase of weapons and the maintenance of armed forces. The consequences for their future development were inevitably extremely harmful, and the governments of the developed countries bear a large share of the responsibility for the waste of human resources and the resulting misery.

Non-alignment

The Non-Aligned Movement (NAM) had its origins in the Afro-Asian Conference at Bandung in 1955 and has met triennially since 1961 (with the exception of 1967). It included all the African states, which belonged automatically as members of the OAU, most of the Asian countries and some of the Latin American republics. The original thinking behind non-alignment was to create an association sufficiently strong to avoid association with either of the two blocs. However, from the beginning the concept was regarded with great suspicion by both sides, and this suspicion was at times well justified, as, in particular, when Fidel Castro as president of the Non-Aligned Movement abused his position to call on the non-aligned at the Havana Summit of 1979 to align themselves with the Soviet Union as their natural ally. The invitation was not well received and the Soviet invasion of Afghanistan later the same year put an abrupt stop to any further moves to revive it.

The collapse of Communism ended the moral justification for much US intervention. The change was not immediate: the new public vocabulary included phrases such as 'ensuring international stability' or 'the worldwide crusade for democracy'. But the new US Administration of George Bush did not show much respect either for national sovereignty or for democracy. Its intervention in Panama in December 1989, claimed to be enhancing the cause of democracy, was carried out in breach of the charters of both the UN and the OAS, and was censured by the OAS. Then in 1991, the decision after a long period of delay to launch Operation Desert Storm on Iraq was justified as defending what Bush claimed was 'the legitimate government' of Kuwait. Though Saddam Hussein had few friends even among Arab states, and his own government had formally recognised that Kuwait was not the nineteenth province of Iraq, the Emir's government was certainly not democratic. In fact, the decision to go to war had much less to do with defending democracy than with ensuring that the combined oil output of Iraq and Kuwait did not pass out of Western control, while the unilateral US decision to end the war after only 100 hours has had long-lasting consequences for the stability of other smaller oil-producing states in this key region.

The United States had become a 'lonely superpower' (Huntington 1999). However, it did not turn out to be, as Huntington forecast, constrained by its own internal divisions to tread a much more cautious course, and in 2001 lost little time in creating a new enemy to confront. In proclaiming its 'war on terror' it took no account of Huntington's warning that, however powerful, it could not act alone. Other countries have different agendas and in groups could be powerful, but Russia too is torn by internal dissension and the decision of Chancellor Kohl to recognise Bosnia split the European Union (EU) and left the way open for the United States to ignore its pleas for caution. China is still preoccupied with economic growth. The end of the Cold War may well mean that in the future there will be no superpowers there to restrain their former client states when local conflicts threaten to get out of hand. In a bipolar world in a sense every conflict matters to the two camps as victory for one is defeat for the other. In an era of multipolarity most developing world conflicts will not matter to the First World at all. If regional leaders do not intervene no-one may do so, and this may be even more undesirable.

Table 6.2   Developing world conflicts 1990–2002

Country	Dates	Cause
Afghanistan	1979–92	War of *mujahedin* guerrillas against Soviet-backed government
	1992–	Fighting between rival groups continues
Algeria	1992–	Coordinated anti-government activity
Angola	1975–91	South African backed insurrection (UNITA)
Azerbaijan	1991–94	Armenian secessionist movement in Nagorny Karabakh
Burma	1989–	Armed ethnic opposition
Burundi	1993–94	Ethnic violence
Cambodia	1978–91	Civil war
Chad	1975–93	Insurrection
	1971–94	Part occupied by Libya
Congo, Democratic Republic	1998–	Second Congo War
Djibouti	1991–94	Afar insurrection
Ecuador	1995	War with Peru over boundary delimitation
Egypt	1992–	Coordinated anti-government activity
El Salvador	1979–91	Civil war; government backed by USA
Eritrea	1994–98	Insurrection backed by Sudan
Eritrea	1998–2000	War with Ethiopia
Gambia	1994	Coup and counter-coup
Georgia	1991–94	Secessionist movement in Abkhasia
Ghana	1994	Insurrection in Northern Region
Guatemala	1960–94	Guerrilla operations
Guinea	1994	Armed clashes with opposition forces
Haiti	1994	US intervention to restore President Aristide
India	1947–	Armed Kashmiri resistance
Indonesia	1976–99	Resistance to annexation of East Timor
Iraq	1990–91	Invasion of Kuwait
	1991	Gulf War
Kenya	1994	Ethnic violence
Kuwait	1990–91	Occupied by Iraq
	1991	Gulf War
Lebanon	1982–2000	Part occupied by Israel and allies
Lesotho	1993–94	Fighting between rival army factions
Liberia	1989–96, 1999–2003	Civil war
Libya	1973–94	Occupation of disputed territory in Chad
Mali	1992–	Continued clashes with Tuaregs
Mexico	1994–	Agrarian insurrection in Chiapas
Morocco	1976–	War against Polisario Front of Western Sahara
Mozambique	1986–94	South African-backed insurrection (RENAMO)
Nicaragua	1981–91	US-backed insurrection (Contras)
Peru	1995	War with Ecuador over boundary delimitation
Rwanda	1990–	Insurrection by Rwandan Patriotic Front (FPR)
	1994	Ethnic violence following death of president
Sierra Leone	1991–2000	Insurrection backed by National Patriotic Front of Liberia (NPFL)
Somalia	1991–	Ousting of Siad Barre followed by civil war
South Africa	1990–94	Inkatha/ANC clashes
Sri Lanka	1983–2002	Separatist war led by Liberation Tigers of Tamil Eelam (LTTE)
Sudan	1983–	Separatist guerrillas in South
Togo	1994	Insurrection against President Eyadema
Uganda	1987–	Lord's Resistance Army insurrection

Sources: Third World Guide 93/94; Keesing's Record of World Events

The View from the Ground

By *Charles Grant, The Guardian*, Thursday, 12 January 2006

India Tilts to the West as the World's New Poles Emerge

But while China is a pole that seems destined to oppose the US, India is experiencing a tectonic shift in the opposite direction. For most of the half-century that followed independence, India kept its distance from the US. Jawaharlal Nehru, India's first prime minister, helped to found the non-aligned movement, which was defined by opposition to American foreign policy. Nehru also built an alliance with the Soviet Union that survived his death; India supported the invasion of Afghanistan in 1979.

Although broadly democratic for most of that half-century, India closed its economy to global capitalism and saw no reason to ally with other democracies. But over the past 15 years, while India has slowly opened its economy to the rest of the world, its foreign policy has shifted from non-alignment towards cooperation with the west. One sign of this shift – which shocked many developing countries – came last October when, at the International Atomic Energy Agency, India voted with the US and EU to condemn Iran's nuclear programme. China and Russia abstained.

One force driving this realignment is India's desire to break out of the international isolation that followed its nuclear tests in 1998. The Nuclear Suppliers Group – the club for countries with nuclear power industries – imposed sanctions on India. This hurt: India lacks sufficient nuclear fuel for its power stations. So last July the prime minister, Manmohan Singh, struck a deal with the Bush administration. India promised to separate its civilian and military nuclear facilities, and to put the former under international inspection. In return the US would pass legislation to ease the export of sensitive technologies to India, and urge the group to lift the sanctions.

The implementation of this deal would amount to India being forgiven for building atomic bombs. India would join the big league of nuclear nations, alongside the US, Russia, China, France and Britain. But the deal is controversial. Any reward for a country that builds nuclear weapons undermines the non-proliferation regime – and makes it harder to dissuade Iran, North Korea and others from making their own bombs.

The deal could yet unravel. The US, Russia, Britain and France want the suppliers group to lift the sanctions. But other members of the group, such as South Africa and Brazil (which gave up their own nuclear weapons programmes) and the Nordic countries, disagree. India will need a lot of American help to get the July bargain implemented. It therefore has strong reasons for staying close to the US.

Another reason is the rise of China, which mesmerises India. Like a lot of Americans, Indians want to engage with China, but at the same time they fear it.

Many Indians are quite relaxed about China's economic might, because trade between the two countries is booming in both directions. But they worry about being surrounded by unstable countries that are allied to China. The Chinese helped the Pakistanis to build their bomb, and the two countries are still close.

China supplies arms to Nepal's mad and autocratic king. In Burma it dominates the eastern provinces and is the junta's best friend. China is also a big influence in war-torn Sri Lanka and in increasingly unstable Bangladesh.

India frets that China may use these troublesome neighbours to put pressure on it. And it is concerned that China's superior financial clout enables it to win friends, and contracts for natural resources, in other parts of Asia. Recently, for example, Chinese companies outbid their Indian rivals in a competition for Kazakh oil. China has thus become the dominant power in much of central Asia and south-east Asia, while Indians note that China is doing nothing to help them fulfil their ambition of gaining a permanent seat on the United Nations security council, or to get the nuclear sanctions against India lifted.

How permanent is this Indian tilt to the west? Indian public opinion remains quite hostile to America. And, formally at least, India is keeping its options open. Its foreign minister meets regularly with his opposite numbers from Russia and China. India has also just become an observer at the Shanghai Cooperation Organisation, the security club led by Russia and China that includes most of the central Asian states.

However, India's participation in such clubs is not significant. As senior figures in the government put it, India needs to turn up so that it knows what is going on. Among India's elite – the leaders of the governing Congress and opposition BJP parties, as well as officials and business chiefs – there is a growing consensus that India's long-term interests require warm ties with America. They know that India's IT and service industries are booming thanks to American investment. India's leaders, unlike those in China, know they want to join the west.

Developing world conflicts

Among the developing world 'hot spots' where intervention has continued into the post-Cold War era, are Cambodia, Cuba, Angola, Ethiopia, Liberia and Somalia.

The withdrawal of the United States from Cambodia in 1975 left the country to the Communist Party of Cambodia, generally known by its French nickname 'Khmer Rouge' ('Red Khmer'). Hardened by their long and bitter struggle, the guerrillas marched into Phnom Penh and immediately instituted a reign of terror against the town-dwellers, and especially the intellectuals, whom they detested as having 'collaborated', first with the French and later with the Americans. Some 1.7 million of their fellow countrymen are estimated to have died as a result of execution, forced labour and starvation, and tens of thousands of skulls testify still to the ruthlessness with which the process was carried out. However, when in 1979 reunified Vietnam sent troops into Cambodia to remove the Khmer Rouge and institute a Soviet-style government, the Western powers, with breathtaking cynicism, switched their support to any group that could get rid of the Vietnamese, including the

Khmer Rouge, which was formally dissolved in 1982. Later, with the changing world balance the Vietnamese, seeking to better relations with the USA, decided to withdraw from Cambodia and the successful UN supervision of elections in 1993 paved the way for a coalition government to assume power under the nominal authority of King Norodom Sihanouk, deposed in a US-backed military coup in 1970.

Another casualty of changing international alignments has been the significance of the Soviet-backed regime in Cuba. Since the end of the Cold War the government of President Fidel Castro has lost its superpower patron and come under much external pressure from the United States, which has tightened its embargo on trade with the beleaguered island. The most serious blow was the withdrawal in 1991 of its guaranteed supply of Russian oil, which had not only fuelled its agriculture and industry but provided a considerable surplus that could be sold abroad for hard currency. However, despite increasing diplomatic isolation and a serious economic crisis, the Cuban government survives and the US government has so far not risked direct intervention.

Even before the crisis in Eastern Europe in 1989, Soviet military support for the Popular Movement for the Liberation of Angola (MPLA) had dried up and the Cuban troops that had been supporting the internationally recognised government of the country were withdrawn. Meanwhile, US material and strategic support to the South African sponsored UNITA continued unabated, and Zairian troops arrived to lend them material support. Early in 1993, UNITA held some two-thirds of the country. Although the US Ambassador to the UN, Margaret Anstee, described the situation in Angola as full-scale civil war, she still argued that there was nothing the UN could do. Nevertheless by the end of the year the UN was sponsoring peace talks.

Ethiopia received the most military aid of all the African states from both the United States and the Soviet Union. However, despite all their efforts, the government of Gen. Mengistu Haile Mariam was unable to suppress the secessionist movements in Tigray and Eritrea. When Soviet and Cuban support for him became too embarrassing, it was withdrawn and Mengistu was overthrown and forced to seek political asylum in Zimbabwe in May 1991.

It was noted earlier that for a century Liberia, a state for freed slaves on the West Coast of Africa, had been dominated by the settler elite at the expense of the tribes of the interior. In September 1990 the government of Samuel Doe was ousted by a military coup and the deposed president and much of the political elite hacked to death. The United States, which had sponsored the formation of Liberia, and which benefited from the rubber produced there for the Firestone Tire Co., refused to intervene, though President Bush did send a small team of marines to rescue US citizens. The civil war which followed led to a joint military intervention by the Economic Community of West African States (ECOWAS), and was apparently ended by a peace agreement signed in Benin in July 1993. However, the UN remains concerned that the armed forces appear to be still out of control and it continues to receive reports of refugees being murdered.

Weapons of mass destruction in the developing world

The idea of deterrence due to the threat of mutual annihilation is really a product of a bipolar world and relies on the rationality and stability of the actors concerned. But as Keith Colquhoun has put it (1993: 210): 'The problem of North Korea is that the government is widely perceived to be insane.' Yet it is only one of the developing countries seeking to develop weapons of mass destruction in the post-Cold War era.

Since 1989 there has been a sharp change away from bipolar confrontation but the world is still littered with the debris of Cold War; literally so in the case of the conventional and nuclear weapons of the former Soviet Union. Week by week the news of the interception of smuggled uranium consignments compounds the uncertainty about the future intentions of middle-range states, especially Iran. The US post-Cold War strategy is to keep enough nuclear weapons to confront 'any possible adversary' and this continued nuclear hegemony is thought by some to be a means to prevent proliferation. However, the current non-proliferation regime rests on a crucial misconception, that a small group of nuclear states can retain nuclear weapons while denying them to others. The assumption is that we have moved into an era of an interdependent world military order which is both established and hierarchical. The problem, it has often been suggested from the perspective of the AICs, is that nuclear capacity does not necessarily follow this hierarchy. The emergence of a Hindu nationalist coalition with a different agenda in India in 1997 has shown the fallacy of these assumptions both in India itself and in neighbouring Pakistan; both powers have now 'gone nuclear'.

In 1945 only the US had nuclear weapons. During much of the Cold War era the nuclear 'club' remained limited to the USA, USSR, UK, France and China. Moreover, the power blocs gave rise to an ideological line-up and only China could be said to have an independent nuclear capability. However the West not only gave significant help to enable France to develop its 'independent' deterrent but connived secretly at Israel's nuclear programme and ignored South Africa's first (and only) nuclear test. By the end of the Cold War a further six countries, including Pakistan, were on the verge of acquiring nuclear weapons and 10 more, including India, Brazil and South Africa had the capacity to do so.

It is clear that the original US strategy of non-proliferation has failed. This is not surprising, since successive summits were aimed primarily at reducing the inherent risks of superpower confrontation and the United States felt it necessary to connive at the acquisition of nuclear capability by friendly countries such as Britain, France and Israel, rather than risk its overall strategic dominance. The Non-Proliferation Treaty was negotiated to try to limit superpower activity and was not really aimed at the developing world.

The spread of nuclear weapons to more countries is generally termed horizontal proliferation and was inherent in the nuclear game from the outset owing to the diffusion of knowledge about nuclear processes. The spread of civil nuclear technology cannot be stopped and indeed was actively encouraged by the capitalist countries as a way of building up their own nuclear capability. The inherent tendency for scientific knowledge to diffuse did the rest (with a little bit of unofficial help in the case of France). Hence Argentina and Pakistan both have uranium enrichment plants which could produce nuclear weapons material rather than reactor fuel, but they have developed these capabilities themselves despite having been unable to purchase such sensitive technology on the world market, and Pakistan has therefore been in a position to match India's decision to 'go nuclear'. In 1981 Israel forestalled any attempt by Iraq to develop nuclear weapons by launching a pre-emptive air strike on its nuclear facility at Osiriak near Baghdad. As US aircraft were used, it must be assumed that this public breach of the UN Charter was approved by the US government. In September 2004 the US was reported to have given, or be in the process of giving, to Israel its latest technology, several 'bunker busting' bombs,

The whole world is now a single strategic arena, and military deployment of nuclear weapons in any future confrontation would be global. However, this does not mean that horizontal proliferation does in fact present serious dangers. Happily Argentina and Brazil have been able to forge a new relationship and to move decisively away from confrontation. It is not clear what the use of nuclear weapons could achieve for a developing state that happened to possess them given their likely political objectives. The obvious reason would be to enhance their power in relation to surrounding states. For this purpose a mere bluff may suffice and some argue that this is so in the case of North Korea. Secondly, the normal response to fear of a nuclear attack seems to be to respond in kind, as in the case of India and Pakistan, whose relative position has not changed as a result. Thirdly, the acquisition of nuclear weapons might be sought to empower a southern state in face of a threat from the North. It has been argued that customers always have some leverage against their suppliers so that they can gain a degree of empowerment through purchase. On the other hand, a more realistic perception is that any advantage gained is offset by the weakness of needing spare parts, and support services in the form of technological advice and periodic updates. It would also be extremely expensive. If new standards are set by technology, striving to achieve them is a treadmill, and certainly does not constitute empowerment.

Chemical weapons are sometimes called 'poor man's atom bombs'. They are much cheaper, they use much more readily available and more easily disguised technology, and the major powers (officially at least) have chosen not to have them. They are for these reasons the WMD most obviously inclined to proliferation in the developing world. In view of the rapidly blurring boundaries between the destructiveness and grossness of nuclear and conventional weapons, the distinction no longer really makes sense.

The manufacture of chemical weapons is an offshoot of the civil chemical industry and therefore the potential exists in many moderately industrialised countries in the developing world. The most notorious example was Iraq under Saddam Hussein, who used them against his own citizens at Halabjah and so breached what had been becoming an unwritten norm of international conduct unbroken since Mussolini's Italy used mustard gas in Ethiopia in 1935–36.

Chemical weapons exist in countries other than Iraq. They are known to exist in the United States, France and the former USSR. But more worrying is the extent of their probable existence in the developing world. Argentina, Chile, Cuba, Guatemala, Peru, Angola, Chad, Ethiopia, Libya, South Africa, Afghanistan, China, India, Myanmar, Pakistan, Thailand and Vietnam are all believed to have a chemical capability. Perhaps Iran does also – it is believed to have been very active in seeking supplies in 1993–94 and is unlikely to have ceased trying to do so. The biggest concern since 9/11 for the United States and its allies, however, is the possible use of chemical weapons by terrorists, on the model of the release of the nerve gas Sarin by the Japanese sect Aum Shinrikyo in the Tokyo underground on 20 March 1995. Twelve people died and some 3,800 people were injured, a small number permanently,

The problem in dealing with chemical weapons as WMD is that the manufacturing processes involved are relatively simple, so that a plant could be easily disguised as a factory producing infant milk formula, for example. The basic chemicals required are those which are needed for almost any industrial process. Detecting breaches of international agreements is therefore much more difficult than with nuclear weapons, where the tell-tale signs of reprocessing and storage facilities are hard to conceal from the circling spy satellites. However, it is also true that nerve agents and other chemical agents are difficult to deploy successfully, their effectiveness varies considerably with the nature of the environment in a way that is difficult to predict, and that in consequence they present much greater dangers to those who seek to use them than to those against whom they are to be used.

The role of the United Nations

After the end of the Cold War the United States reverted for a time to its 1945 policy of supporting the UN. During the Cold War the UN's capacity for action was little used, but in the 1990s it became the northern-dominated instrument of intervention. Vetoes of substantive issues in the Security Council all but ceased, the United States and other major powers acted together and their actions were legitimised as they were UN-sponsored. Since only the decisions of the Security Council are binding on member states, this means that in practice the organisation continued to be dominated by the AICs. Since 2001 this too has changed. The unconcealed contempt for the organisation shown by the neo-conservatives in Washington has created a new polarity between

Plate 12 UN peacekeeping © Reuters/CORBIS

the United States and the developing world, for many of whom the UN is their only hope of being able to influence events rather than being influenced by them.

The UN is an **international**, not a **supranational** organisation. 'International' means between nations, with the implication of theoretical if not actual equality, while 'supranational' means something above nations which in some way limits sovereignty. However, in reality international, supranational and transnational links all act to reduce not only sovereignty (which is an old-fashioned, impractical and now largely meaningless concept anyway) but also the autonomy of all but (or perhaps even) the largest states.

The UN represents states not non-governmental organisations (NGOs). Though the latter may be bigger and of more service to the UN they have no votes, although they may be represented and speak at major international conferences. The member countries of the UN are organised politically into groups which frequently take up common positions to increase their influence. Organisations of this kind, other than regional conferences, include the Non-Aligned Movement (NAM) and the Group of 77 (G77). The so-called 'Group of 77' is an economic grouping actually made up of 132 members. It is a lobby group within the UN, established on 15 June 1964 by 77 developing countries signatories of the Joint Declaration of the Seventy-Seven Countries issued at the end of the first session of the United Nations Conference on Trade and Development (UNCTAD) in Geneva. All developing countries are members except China.

The most striking feature of UN activity since 1989 has been the dramatic extension of UN peacekeeping. More UN intervention has taken place since 1989 than in the whole of the previous 44 years of the organisation's history. Since UN peacekeeping operations are not funded out of the UN budget, but from precepts on member states, the situation has been viewed with increasing concern by both supporters and opponents of the UN role.

Regional alignments

One obvious way to avoid excessive dependence on or influence by great powers was to create regional organisations. However the oldest such organisation, the Organization of American States (OAS), founded in 1948 as a regional organisation within the UN system, is not clearly a developing world organization. Since its foundation, as a development of the old Pan-American Union, it has been dominated by the regional and world superpower, the United States, and the parallel military alliance, the Inter-American Treaty of Reciprocal Assistance (commonly known in English as the Rio Pact) was specifically created in 1947 to form one of a network of alliances supporting the United States against the Soviet Union.

The OAS was largely bypassed in the confrontation between the United States and Cuba which led to the exclusion of the latter from the working of the organisation in 1962. In the 1960s and 1970s its numbers were swollen by the accession of Suriname and the former British colonies in the region. Two others, Belize and Guyana, were still excluded because they had frontier disputes with existing members. However, both were admitted at the beginning of the 1990s, together with Canada which had previously chosen to stand aloof. Hence the organisation, which was reorganised along UN lines by the Protocol of Buenos Aires in 1970, reproduces many of the conflicts which characterise the working of the UN itself.

The African Union (AU) comprises 53 states in Africa and the Indian Ocean. It replaced in 2002 the Organisation of African Unity (OAU), which was formed in 1963 in the first flush of independence. Despite the hopes expressed at the time by Kwame Nkrumah of Ghana, it did not aim so high as to create some form of pan-African superstate. Its three main aims were the eradication of colonialism, the promotion of economic cooperation and the resolution of disputes among member states. Originally annual meetings were held in different capitals, which nearly bankrupted the host government; since 1970 there has been an established permanent centre in Addis Ababa.

At its inception the organisation created an African Liberation Committee to channel aid to liberation movements. However, most African governments have given little and in the major case, that of South Africa, the strategy of armed confrontation destabilised the so-called 'front-line' states without any obvious effect on apartheid. The Lusaka Declaration of 1970 was a belated admission that negotiation might be a more effective way to secure the desired objection of decolonisation. The collapse of Portuguese colonial rule in 1974 was followed by the alliance of the 'front-line' states to give support to the liberation of Rhodesia/Zimbabwe, but in the years that followed the South African government successfully organised guerrilla forces to destabilise both Angola and Mozambique. In its major confrontation with South Africa the main instruments of the OAU were a combination of sanctions and economic boycotts, but once again a significant number of African states failed effectively to implement sanctions. A few, notably Malawi under Dr Hastings Banda, openly rejected them, and Dr Kenneth Kaunda of Zambia, who consistently pressed for a peaceful transition of power in Rhodesia/Zimbabwe, was prepared to meet South African leaders and even to support their action in intervening against the Marxist government of Angola (Tangri 1985: 142).

The AU recognises the right to independence of Western Sahara, which is a member under the name of the Sahrawi Arab Democratic Republic. Consequently Morocco is not a member.

The OAU's Economic and Social Council was set up to promote economic collaboration, but with a few small exceptions it has been notably unsuccessful. Most African states have only slowly lost their trade and other economic links with their former colonial powers. Instead a number of sub-regional organisations were formed. They are the Economic Community of West African States (ECOWAS) founded in 1975, the Southern African Development Community (SADC) formed in 1980, the Economic Community of Central African States (ECCAS/CEEAC) established in 1985 and the Common Market for Eastern and Southern Africa (COMESA) created in 1994, which includes many of the members of SADC. By the Treaty of Abuja, 1991, the African states agreed to form an African Economic Union of which the regional organisations would be 'pillars' and in 2005 most had agreed, with the exception of members of the North African Arab Maghreb Union (UMA) and the Sahrawi Republic (which was occupied by Morocco).

It is as a political organisation seeking to maintain the defence of the sovereignty of existing national territories that the OAU was most successful. An early and important decision was to recognise the existing colonial boundaries of member states. Since then it has had to deal with conflicts of three main kinds:

- challenges to state integrity;
- challenges to regime integrity;
- ideological/personality disputes.

The three great achievements of the OAU were the settlement of the 1967 frontier dispute between Kenya and Somalia, the independence of Zimbabwe (formerly Rhodesia) and the collapse of apartheid in South Africa. However, on most of the major post-colonial issues it has shown itself weak and divided, failing to contribute effectively to the settlement of the Congo/Zaire crisis, the Nigerian civil war, the Angolan crisis and the dispute between Morocco and Mauritania over the Western Sahara. In 1982 the member states were so divided that it was unable initially to obtain a quorum to hold its annual summit.

Meanwhile a steady build-up of arms in the region led to an increasing willingness among African states to use force. Significantly this tended to be on an individual state or sub-regional level. Armed support for incumbents was given when Guinean troops were sent to support Siaka Stevens in Sierra Leone in 1971 and Senegalese forces to The Gambia in 1981. Armed intervention to end a state of anarchy and civil war included Tanzania's intervention in Uganda in 1979 to expel Idi Amin and the ECOWAS intervention in Liberia in 1989, which unexpectedly led to the destabilisation of Sierra Leone itself, the fall of President Momoh and civil war (Francis 2001). Armed aggression to obtain additional territory has been rarer. Libya's intervention in Chad in 1983, which led to the virtual annexation of one-third of its territory, was countered, ultimately successfully, by US and French intervention. Only in this last case did the OAU act to set up a peacekeeping force (largely Nigerian) which was withdrawn after a few weeks for lack of support (Francis 2006).

The main weaknesses of the African Union as an organisation it has inherited from the OAU. They are: nationalism, the difficulty of getting member states to pay their contributions and the fears of African heads of state and heads of government that they will be deposed while they are out of country at conferences. The end of apartheid in South Africa has taken away the one cause that motivated the desire for unity. The replacement of the OAU by the AU has not changed this.

Other sub-regional organisations

Asia is too big to have a clear existence as a continent so there is no regional equivalent to the OAU or the OAS. Western attempts in the 1950s and 1960s to set up regional alliances in the Middle East and South-east Asia foundered on the realities of local politics. Sub-regional organisations in the 1990s include:

- The Commonwealth of Independent States (CIS – *Sodruzhestvo Nezavisimykh Gosudarstv*), founded in 1991, the ghost of the former Soviet Union hovering over the oil wells of the Caspian basin. It consists of 11 former Soviet Republics, and includes two different but overlapping economic unions. Although rivalry between Russian Federation and the Ukraine over the Crimea and the Black Sea fleet seems to have died down, regional rivalries are for the time being sufficiently strong to forestall any greater degree of unity.
- The Arab League, correctly The League of Arab States, founded in 1945 under British auspices, which is effectively a regional organisation for

South-west Asia and North Africa. The League, whose original seven members have now grown to 22, displays vast political differences between member states despite their religious and ethnic bonds. However, its members dominate the more recently formed Islamic Conference, which with 41 members is now the most powerful regional bloc in UN politics.

- The Association of South-East Asian Nations (ASEAN), founded in 1967, which currently has ten members: Brunei Darussalam, Cambodia, Indonesia, Laos, Malaysia, Myanmar, the Philippines, Singapore, Thailand and Vietnam.
- The South Asian Association for Regional Cooperation (SAARC), founded in 1985, with eight member states: Afghanistan, Bangladesh, Bhutan, India, the Maldives, Nepal, Pakistan and Sri Lanka.
- The South Pacific Forum (SPF), founded in 1971 as an association of the self-governing states in the Pacific, which meets annually. It has gradually superseded the older (1948) South Pacific Commission (SPC), consisting of representatives of the non-self-governing Pacific territories and their administering Powers.
- The Commonwealth. The, to some, extraordinary survival of the Commonwealth owes much to the relatively peaceful transition to independence of many of its members and to the informality of its organisation. With the return to membership of South Africa, the accession of Namibia and Mozambique and the resignation of Zimbabwe after its membership was suspended in 2003, it now has 53 members; Fiji was self-excluded by its refusal to accord equal treatment to its citizens of Indian origin but rejoined in 1997. Hence despite the inclusion in its membership of two of the G8 nations (Canada and the UK) as well as Australia, New Zealand and South Africa, the Commonwealth is very much an organisation in which the developing world can speak informally to the developed world, which helps account for the fact that both the former British Prime Minister Margaret Thatcher and the present British Prime Minister Tony Blair, so obviously had or have little or no time for it. The Commonwealth, however, is not a federation but a club. Its effectiveness, which is greatly underrated, lies precisely in the fact that it operates through informal meetings and relies on a shared language and shared understandings which do not have to be put into words.

The first Bush Administration and Panama

With the Administration of President George Bush (1989–93), the focus of US interest in the western hemisphere shifted once more to Panama, and to General Manuel Antonio Noriega, Commander of its Defence Forces. General Noriega, who had been a CIA informant and contact for many years, had recently been indicted for drugs-related offences by US federal grand juries in Miami and Tampa (Florida). Following this, on 25 February 1988, the Panamanian president, Eric Delvalle, unsuccessfully attempted to dismiss him.

On 4 March the USA 'froze' all Panamanian assets, but, while the pressure intensified, a coup attempt failed to dislodge General Noriega, who proceeded to try to consolidate his position in elections scheduled for 7 May 1989.

When, however, serious irregularities were confirmed by the Inter-American Commission on Human Rights, the government cancelled the election and countered with charges that the US authorities were planning intervention. Thereupon, the Bush Administration intensified economic sanctions against Panama and dispatched a brigade-sized force to the Canal Zone in reassertion of US rights there. Then, in December 1989 the new national assembly named General Noriega head of government and proclaimed Panama to be in a 'state of war' with the USA. An alleged attack by Panamanian troops on US personnel became the pretext for President Bush to order armed intervention in Panama early on 20 December.

Intervention in Panama was not supported by the UN, and was specifically censured by the OAS. Possibly by coincidence, it averted a potentially embarrassing situation for the USA. Ten days later, on 31 December 1989, under the 1977 treaties, a Panamanian was due to take over as chairman of the Panama Canal Commission. Despite a lack of sympathy with General Noriega, who surrendered to US forces only to be tried and imprisoned in the USA, the fact that he was captured and tried for actions which were not performed within US territory marked a significant extension of US claims to act unilaterally anywhere in the world, and as such marked a step towards intervention in Afghanistan and Iraq. Armed intervention was greeted with widespread hostility in Panama and the new government was not popular.

The following are the reasons given by President Bush for ordering the intervention in Panama (Calvert 1990b).

1. To safeguard US lives.
2. To ensure traffic through the Canal.
3. To interdict drug trafficking.
4. To capture General Noriega.

The rise of 'humanitarian intervention'

At the same time, many key decision-makers in the USA had already been alienated, both from its allies and from the UN, when the fall of the Berlin Wall and the subsequent dissolution of the Soviet Union seemed to herald a new era of peace. During the Cold War the UN's capacity for action was little used. However, with the disappearance of the traditional division between East and West, the long-standing division between North and South (developed and developing countries, respectively) became more prominent. Even the People's Republic of China, the only major power likely to disturb the consensus, chose to act indirectly, withholding its consent altogether only in cases directly affecting its own interests. Since only the decisions of the Security Council were binding on member states, this meant that, in practice, the organisation continued to be dominated by AICs and, among them, by the USA.

The first case of **humanitarian intervention** – intervention designed to promote human rights and/or to alleviate suffering – backfired. A military revolt in Somalia in January 1991 had deposed the tyrannical regime of President Mohammed Siad Barre and was almost universally welcomed. However, as time progressed no new government was able to gain power and the country relapsed into tribal conflict between factions led by contending warlords. Then at the end of 1992, after his defeat in the US presidential elections, President Bush sent US Marines to Mogadishu, the Somali capital, nominally to protect food aid to the starving people. Soon they were embroiled instead in a futile attempt to eliminate one of the war-lords, Gen. Mohammed Farah Aideed, whom the USA accused of interfering with the aid convoys. In October 1993 both US and UN policy changed away from seeking to oust General Aideed to seeking a peaceful settlement with some new government which could obtain control. The UN halved its troops in the country to 15,000 and President Clinton eventually pulled US troops out of Somalia in March 1994, after US troops had been slaughtered and their mutilated bodies paraded through the streets of Mogadishu (Bowden 2001).

The significance of this rather tangled story is that UN Resolution 794 of December 1992, which authorised intervention in Somalia, made no pretence that UN forces had been invited into Somalia, since they had not. Its justification for intervention is that its objectives were reconstruction and disarmament and not just peacekeeping. The problem was that in active pursuit of these objectives subsequent resolutions reconfirmed both the objectives and the role of UN troops. The conclusion is that UN intentions may have been worthy enough but the extension of its powers that this implied conflicted with the norm of non-intervention and was bound to raise doubts. Additionally, the fact that the Somalis soon started complaining of human rights abuses did the UN no credit and set back the cause of so-called humanitarian intervention. The abrupt withdrawal of US forces made the lone super-power look weak. Early in 1995 the new Republican majority in the US House of Representatives passed legislation which was intended to end UN intervention, since it required the president to subtract from the cost of any contribution to UN peacekeeping budgets the cost of UN forces and would effectively transform the US contribution into a negative balance.

The Gulf War 1991

The first successful test of the 'New World Order' was the Gulf War in 1991 (Freedman and Karsh 1993). This was to set the scene both for 9/11 and for its aftermath. In August 1990, with international attention focused on events in Europe and the disintegrating USSR, and Iraq in financial crisis following the long war with Iran in which it had been armed and funded by the United States, its leader, Saddam Hussein, ordered his forces to invade and occupy Kuwait. Before doing so, he was careful to sound out the opinion of the American Ambassador in Baghdad, April Glaspie. Her reply, that the United States had 'no view' on the Kuwait question, was taken as official confirmation that the United States would not intervene. The small country on the Persian (Arabian) Gulf was quickly seized and incorporated into Iraq as its nineteenth province, although President Saddam Hussain's government had previously renounced any claim to sovereignty over the petroleum-rich emirate. When US Defense Secretary Dick Cheney announced that the United States would respond by sending troops to Saudi Arabia it was initially thought that they were only there to reassure the Saudis.

In view of later criticism of the UN, it should be noted that in this case the UN response was unequivocal. The Security Council unanimously adopted Resolution 660, demanding that Iraq withdraw unconditionally and authorising further action under the UN Charter. President Bush next took the lead in forming an international coalition of 28 powers, actively including Saudi Arabia and the other Gulf states, and persuading the Israeli government to keep out in order not to offend critically-needed Islamic allies. On 16 January 1991, after Iraq had failed to respond both to threats and to offers of mediation, air and land forces struck into Kuwait and, within 100 hours, had cleared it of Iraqi troops. At that point, acting unilaterally, President Bush declared the war at an end. Meanwhile Security Council Resolution 678 had authorised the coalition to use 'all necessary means' (a diplomatic euphemism for force) to ensure that was cleansed of WMD. A team of UN weapons inspectors was subsequently sent in to locate all such weapons and to destroy them and sanctions – a trade embargo – imposed on the country to ensure its government complied. Over the next ten years Saddam Hussein was able to ensure that, although the majority of the population suffered grievously as a result, he and his clique did not.

The official view was that the operations had been highly successful. Kuwait was freed and the Iraqis punished. The war had taken place with UN authority and this had been upheld. Saddam Hussein had lost his capacity to harm his neighbours. Aggression was shown not to pay. Others were not so sure. They argued that, as on some previous occasions, the UN had been used as a cover for war rather than an instrument for peace: intervention was a failure of diplomacy. Some 100,000 Iraqis had been killed, but Saddam Hussein retained his best troops and remained fully in control. In the months immediately afterwards the United States failed to support the rising of the Shi'a Muslims and the Marsh Arabs of southern Iraq. Both were suppressed with horrific brutality and the survivors remain sceptical of US motives to this day. US troops remained in Saudi Arabia, their presence an embarrassment to the Wahabi rulers of that country and a constant source of anger to fundamentalist Muslims elsewhere. It was to drive them out that the Saudi dissident, Osama bin Laden (known in the USA as Ushama Bin Ladin, or 'UBL') began to put together the network of terrorists later known as al-Qaeda. Meanwhile

US military action paid dividends in political support back home and support for it and for the president ran at record levels, though by November 1992 it had already ebbed and Clinton won.

The new Administration was careful in most cases to act, if at all, within a multilateral framework. It avoided unilateral intervention and gave strong backing to the Oslo Accords which were intended to settle the problem of the Occupied Territories and guarantee peace for Israel within a two-state solution. The result was the emergence of a new entity, the Palestine Authority (PA), which has been widely recognised as the legitimate government of Palestine. But implementation was both partial and tardy and Palestinian anger erupted into violence. By 1996, the first *intifada* seemed to have run its course, but the consequence was to strengthen those elements in Israel (strongly supported by recent immigrants from Russia and Ethiopia) who wanted to retain control of the Occupied Territories.

UN mediation in the 1990s was also successful in bringing to an end conflict in places as far apart as El Salvador, Guatemala, the Western Sahara and East Timor. However the collapse of former Yugoslavia was to have negative implications for the future of peacekeeping in the developing world. Three bad precedents were set for the future:

1. The task of intervention was given to a military alliance, NATO, which was not equipped for the task of peacekeeping.
2. Intervention was so slow and diplomacy so hesitant that a great deal of **ethnic cleansing** – the practice of creating ethnically homogenous territories by murdering or displacing members of rival ethnic groups – proved irreversible.
3. The Bosniaks were never treated as a nation in their own right, but consistently referred to as 'Bosnian Muslims'. Failure to support them effectively therefore had implications outside Europe, as it turned out, in the Muslim world.

Rwanda

Rwanda, a small landlocked state in the centre of Africa, had been traditionally dominated by the Belgian-favoured Tutsi. The Belgians regarded the Tutsi and the Hutu as different ethnic groups; this view is now strongly disputed, as there are good arguments that on the contrary they merely reflect the economic division of resources in Rwanda (and neighbouring Burundi) before the Belgians arrived. Be that as it may, after independence there was a rising desire for equality from many of the more numerous Hutu who in time were able to elect one of their number as president: Juvenal Habyarimana. The Tutsi disputed the validity of his election, but in August 1993 Habyarimana signed the Arusha Agreement with insurgent Tutsi forces closing in on Kigali. This provided for 2,500 UN forces to oversee the agreement and in October 1993 UN Mission in Rwanda (UNAMIR) was created for this purpose.

In January 1994, however, the UN was warned for the first time of plans for an organised massacre of Tutsi by the Hutu. On 6 April President Habyarimana was killed when his plane was shot down near Kigali. At the news, the Hutu militia, the Interhamwe, begin the organised slaughter of Tutsis. The UN was powerless to intervene. Although 11 Belgian peacekeepers had already been killed, the massacre spread rapidly and the only other country with troops nearby and able to intervene in time was France. However, although the French government did send in forces it did so only to rescue own citizens. The UN observers withdrew under fire leaving the Tutsi to their fate. Within days half a million men, women and children had been speared or clubbed to death. Yet on 20 April the Security Council, in a resolution to condemn the killings, would not use the word 'genocide' which would have required action by member states. The following day, 21 April, it actually voted to reduce its peacekeeping force, and began the process of withdrawal (Kuperman 2001).

Even before 2001 there was increasing doubt about both the legitimacy and the practicality of humanitarian intervention. In the words of James Mayall:

> It is now widely accepted that the major threat to international peace and security stems from civil conflicts that overflow state boundaries and are accompanied by the massive abuse of human rights. So why has humanitarian intervention proved so problematic? The answer to this question is partly a reflection of the negative experience of such interventions in the 1990s. But it is also a consequence of the philosophical foundations of international society, which appear to rule it out. Despite the record of the past decade, it remains in doubt whether humanitarian intervention is consistent with the prevailing norms of international relations. (Mayall 2000)

The View from the Ground

By *Lindsey Hilsum in Kigali, The Guardian*, Friday, 8 April 1994

Rwandan PM Killed as Troops Wreak Carnage

The Rwandan capital of Kigali descended into chaos yesterday as troops, presidential guards and gendarmes swept through the suburbs killing the prime minister, United Nations peacekeepers and scores of civilians.

Gangs of soldiers and youths kidnapped opposition politicians, and killed members of the minority Tutsi tribe, clubbing them to death with batons, hacking them with machetes and knives, or shooting them.

"It is becoming messier and messier. There are a lot of people with a lot of guns taking different orders and shooting and detaining people," said a Western diplomat. "A casualty toll is impossible."

"Various clans are murdering others. There is a general score settling going on in Kigali," one diplomat said.

Late last night several thousand soldiers of the rebel Rwandan Patriotic Front were moving from camps near the Ugandan border to seize power in Kigali, according to UN officials. The Front has promised to co-operate with the UN in restoring order from today.

All day the sound of gunfire, grenades and mortars resounded through Kigali and plumes of smoke rose from the hills where most of the people live.

The violence followed the death of the presidents of Rwanda and neighbouring Burundi in a plane crash on Wednesday night. The Rwandan ministry of defence says the aeroplane was brought down by a rocket as it began its descent to Kigali airport.

Troops of the Rwandan presidential guard surrounded the wreckage and disarmed and detained 13 Belgian UN observers who tried to investigate the cause of the crash.

The bodies of 11 of the Belgians were later found. 'They were dead from bullet wounds. You can call it an execution,' the UN spokesman, Mukhtar Gueye, said. Two remain unaccounted for.

The 2,500-strong UN peacekeeping force in Rwanda, which is supposed to monitor the ceasefire between government troops and Front rebels agreed last August, was powerless to stop the slaughter.

"The gendarmes are preventing us from crossing into certain parts of the town," Mr Gueye said. "Those may be the areas where there are most casualties."

The fighting was so heavy that International Red Cross officials were unable to venture out to rescue the wounded. Dozens of bodies are thought to be lying about in the town.

The soldiers belong to the late President Juvenal Habyarimana's majority Hutu tribe.

"There is shooting, people are being terrorised, people are inside their homes lying on the floor. We are suffering the consequences of the death of the head of state," the prime minister, Agatha Uwilingiyimana, told Radio France Internationale shortly before she was herself murdered.

UN officials in New York said peacekeepers guarding her had been disarmed and she had been taken by armed men from a UN aid compound where she had sought refuge.

According to the UN spokesman, in the morning soldiers kidnapped three government ministers and their families. The ministers are now feared dead. Soldiers also killed 17 Jesuit priests at a religious centre, French radio reported.

In the middle of the afternoon heavy fighting erupted around the parliament building, where under the terms of the peace agreement a 600-strong Front force is based, guarded by UN peacekeepers. It seems that some Front troops tried to leave the building under UN protection but government soldiers fired on them. The fighting continued for about two hours and there were reports of a Front attack on the headquarters of the presidential guard.

The Front says it is not a tribal force but it is dominated by the Tutsis. Although the Front denies it shot down the aeroplane carrying the presidents, forces loyal to Habyarimana's memory blame the Front, its sympathisers and Tutsis in general for the death of their leader.

Potentially the most dangerous development is the reported advance on the capital by the rest of the Front's force from its base at Mulindi near the Ugandan border. The move could restart the three-year civil war which displaced nearly a million Rwandans and devastated the economy.

Most people in Kigali were too frightened to leave their homes yesterday. But hundreds of terrified Tutsis searched for safe houses and some took refuge in the national stadium, where the UN peacekeeping force is based.

International peacemaking/peacekeeping

There are numerous problems of international peacekeeping/peacemaking:

1. Where do the troops come from? In Liberia they were drawn from the countries round about, the grouping of ECOMOG. The result was that the troops themselves were drawn into the conflict, which soon spread to neighbouring Sierra Leone, with appalling consequences.
2. How will they get there and be maintained? The attraction of neighbouring states is that the logistics of intervention are relatively straightforward; exotic transport such as heavy-lift helicopters and Galaxy transports are not required. Only the United States has the logistical ability to deploy forces worldwide, though a number of the AICs can deploy smaller expeditionary forces if required.
3. Who will pay? In recent years the US Congress has been reluctant to fund effective action. It was, however, easily persuaded to fund what has turned out to be an extremely expensive operation in Iraq.
4. What will they do? External powers are most effective if they provide observers. Direct intervention to bring about a negotiated peace is unrealistic; that task is best left to diplomacy. UK and Argentine troops jointly patrol the 'green line' in Cyprus, but the island remains divided.

There is certainly a valuable role for international organisations in the **implementation** of deals already arrived at on a bilateral basis. However, without the element of trust it seldom succeeds (look at Northern Ireland).

Guatemala in Central America had by the 1990s had some 30 years of civil war. With intense repression backed by successive US governments, it is estimated that more than 50,000 and probably nearer 100,000 were killed. A deal was brokered by the UN in 1990; providing for **decommissioning** of weapons etc. to be overseen by a UN observer group: MINUGUA. However delays on the government side meant that it was not effective until 1997 and even then the government failed to carry out many of the provisions of the the the original agreement.

In Sri Lanka an Indian military presence, the Indian Peacekeeping Force (IPKF), had some success in stemming the conflict between the government and the separatist Tamil Tigers, who had previously had considerable support in Tamil Nadu in South India. In Sri Lanka the IPKF was seen as partisan and cordially loathed by the majority Sinhalese and it was eventually withdrawn in 1990 at the request of President Ranasinghe Premadasa, who had been elected the previous year. Premadasa himself was assassinated in 1993 by the Tamil Tigers. Rajiv Gandhi, who as Indian prime minister had made the agreement to deploy troops, had been killed two years earlier by a suicide bomber while campaigning in Tamil Nadu.

The international politics of oil

Background

Oil was first discovered in Pennsylvania, USA, in 1857. It was then used mainly for lighting. John D. Rockefeller, Sr., never found any oil, but became rich controlling the transport of oil. It was he who founded Standard Oil, the world's first great oil company. Standard Oil was broken up in 1911, but its main offshoot became Exxon (Esso in UK). Britain, having no oil of its own, looked for oil in Mexico (El Aguila, which sold out to Royal Dutch-Shell in 1917) and in the Middle East. There the result was the growth of Anglo-Persian in what is now Iran, in what was then a British sphere of influence in the south of the country, and the Anglo-Dutch consortium Royal Dutch-Shell in Iraq, which was ruled by the British under a League of Nations mandate from 1920 to 1932 when it became nominally independent.

However, in the 1920s the USA, through the US-owned consortium Aramco, established control of the output of what was to become Saudi Arabia. Middle Eastern oil was abundant and cheap and it could be sold in the USA for the same price as oil from the USA or Venezuela and make much more money. In July 1928, BP, Shell, Standard Oil, Mobil and Compagnie Française des Pétroles (now Total) signed what later became known as the 'Red Line Agreements'. This was an agreement to pool their prospecting facilities and to share by mutual agreement all the oil resources found in old provinces of the Ottoman Empire including the whole of the Arabian Peninsula, and among its consequences was that the USA consolidated its control of Saudi output and Britain that of Iraq and Iran.

Allied strategic interests in Second World War led to a new British intervention in Iraq in 1941 and the deposition of the Shah of Iran in 1941. Traditional rulers controlled the whole of the Middle East until the Libyan revolution of 1969. In the post-war period the oil industry was dominated by the oil majors (nicknamed the 'Seven Sisters' although they then numbered eight) and the price of oil at the well-head steadily fell until 1973. There were two sorts of response from developing countries to the emergence of the oil majors: nationalisation (Russia 1917, Mexico 1938, Iran 1951, Libya 1971, Venezuela 1975) or renegotiation (Venezuela in 1945 was the first country to achieve a 50:50 split of profits).

The Mossadegh government in Iran in 1950 had first asked for 50:50 which now looks quite moderate. When this was refused it nationalised Anglo-Iranian, provoking an international crisis and the flight of the Shah. The Shah's restoration by the US Central Intelligence Agency in 1953 was to prove a costly mistake. In September 1960 five large petroleum producing countries (Iran, Iraq, Kuwait, Saudi Arabia and Venezuela) had reacted to pressure from the oil majors to drive down prices by forming the Organization of Petroleum Exporting Countries (OPEC). Qatar joined in 1961, and

Indonesia and Libya in 1962. The Shah later repaid the USA by his strong support for OPEC in 1973, when they took action to support Egypt against Israel and its Western backers. Concerted action by OPEC members drove the price of oil at the well-head up five-fold between October and December – the 'first oil shock'.

The 'second oil shock', though much briefer, came on top of the first when the Shah fell in 1979 and was replaced by an anti-Western regime in Iran. The oil price doubled again. But by that time three important developments were already coming on stream: new discoveries in the North Sea (1973), the Gulf of Mexico (1975) and the Alaskan North Slope (1968, effective 1977 with the completion of the trans-Alaska pipeline to Valdez), had given the AICs access to vast quantities of oil which OPEC could not control. The oil price then fell steadily in real terms until 1998 when it was actually lower (in real terms) than it was at the beginning of 1973.

A third jump in oil prices did occur in 1990 as a result of the Iraqi invasion of Kuwait, forming a short spike before and during the Gulf War in 1991, but it was not sustained.

Since the end of 1999 the AICs and the non-oil states have found themselves in a fourth period of rising oil prices. Driven up by OPEC and drawn up by falling production elsewhere, the oil price has become even more volatile and has risen to new heights. A combination of increased demand from China and India, poor production and sabotage in Iraq, and the alienation of Iran by Western pressure not to seek nuclear arms combine to mean that a third oil shock is quite possible, if indeed it has not already happened.

First oil shock 1973

1. Why did it happen?
The immediate cause was the war by Egypt, Jordan and Syria against Israel. The oil market was already tense and OPEC had asked its members for a significant increase in price. In the last three months of 1973 Saudi Arabia, Kuwait and UAE reduced volumes by about 15 per cent. Iran took no action, and Iraq reduced volumes in October, then increased production again to take advantage of the rising price! The action was called off in February 1974 after the Israeli withdrawal from the Sinai peninsula but the oil price stayed up.

2. Why was it successful?
The USA had allowed domestic production to fall; the low price at the pumps left US corporations only a small incentive for exploration. Following the release of an oil slick in the Santa Barbara channel, on 28 January 1969, President Nixon's Interior Secretary Walter Hickel had closed down 67 of 71 leases. Offshore development was stalled for 12 years, during which time the USA had become dependent on imported oil from the Middle East.

3. What were the consequences?

In the North there was economic recession, rapid inflation and political crisis, though it should be noted that inflationary pressures and currency instability were already building up at the end of 30 years of post-war growth. In 1971 Nixon broke the link between the dollar and gold, effectively devaluing the dollar. Casualties of the economic crisis in the AICs were Edward Heath in the UK in 1974, and Gerald Ford in the USA in 1976.

In the developing areas the effect was more complex: countries with oil initially did very well. Abu Dhabi, Algeria, Kuwait, Qatar, Saudi Arabia and Venezuela all nationalised their oil industries. But all were to some degree tempted into excessive spending: notably the government of José López Portillo (1976–82) in Mexico, where no new oil was actually flowing until 1979. And the oil price remained at a new level but the demand for oil fell, so even the oil-rich countries were not as much better off as they had hoped, while the AICs successfully blocked their calls for a more equitable New International Economic Order.

The problem of countries without oil was typified by Brazil. The combination of the military commitment to a growth model after 1964 and the lack of known indigenous oil resources left it extremely vulnerable both to the oil shocks of the 1970s and the collapse of foreign trade in the early 1980s. Various remedies were tried, some successfully: continued search for sales abroad; energy substitution (especially the Proalcool programme for the distillation of industrial alcohol from sugar cane), a constant insistence that the banks must negotiate a reduction of interest payments due, and delays in payment. But the moratorium of 1987–88 is believed to have cost Brazil some $1.5 billion of much-needed capital while its government absorbed 80 per cent of the credit available, leaving only a small amount for industry.

Second oil shock 1979

1. Why did it happen?

The political cause was the fall of the Shah of Iran, resulting in immediate concern about security of supply. The economic cause was that Saudi Arabia, dismayed by the Camp David Agreement between Israel and the Palestinians, refused to intervene to stabilise the market. Kuwait and the UAE cut production volumes to take advantage of the crisis, so adding upward pressure on prices.

2. What were the consequences?

For the AICs, the consequences were an immediate sharp recession. Political leaders not re-elected were Jimmy Carter in 1980, Valéry Giscard d'Estaing of France in 1981 and Helmut Schmidt of Germany in 1982. The political fallout was immense. After US hostages had been taken and held by the Revolutionary Guard in Iran for 444 days, the United States supported Saddam Hussein of

Iraq in his futile eight-year war against Iran (1980–88). The economic crisis triggered a major restructuring of Western economies along the free-market lines recommended by the 'Chicago Boys'.

For the non-oil states the main effect was historically very high interest rates, which acted as the final catalyst for the debt crisis.

For the oil states the consequences took longer. The price of crude slowly fell until in 1985 the price of $27–28/bbl was about half that in 1979 in real terms. Saudi Arabia and Kuwait, losing market share, however, raised production from 1986 onwards, driving prices down faster.

Since then the United States has remained implacably opposed to dealings with Iran, largely for political reasons (the hostage crisis of 1979–81), though it needed Iran's neutrality in both wars in Iraq. Iran joined Libya on the US blacklist when Congress in 1996 passed The Iran and Libya Sanctions Act, which was renewed in summer 2001. But from 1980 Iran's new regime would not work with other OPEC states, breaking their unified front. As a result the Middle East began a slow loss of market share lasting into the new century.

The United States, however, remained surprisingly vulnerable to pressure, repeating many of the mistakes of the past. Congress insisted that oil from Alaska could only be sold in the United States. Until the late 1990s this meant only the West Coast, as there was no transcontinental oil pipeline and it took a long time to conclude a deal with Canada to bring supplies into the eastern United States from the north. Meanwhile low petroleum prices meant that continental US oilfields (Texas, Louisiana) were neglected and the United States went back to being dependent on imported oil from the Middle East.

Iraq and Kuwait

1. Why did it happen?

Saddam Hussein was desperate for money after eight years of war against Iran. Although he had personally signed a treaty renouncing Iraq's old claim on Kuwait, he decided to ignore it. The United States (Ambassador April Glaspie) failed to warn him that there were limits to what it would be prepared to tolerate.

2. What were the consequences?

For the AICs: the United States was already in recession in the summer of 1990. Germany had reunified and was facing the consequences of paying for the reconstruction of the East. The United States sent troops to protect Saudi Arabia and persuaded them (and other oil states) to pay for the Gulf War. The main political casualties were Margaret Thatcher in the UK and George Bush, Sr., in the United States.

For the oil states: Iraq was subject to sanctions which had the perverse effect of strengthening the Iraqi elite on whom Saddam depended, who were able to trade oil even under sanctions, against the masses who were suffering under his rule. Saudi Arabia remained the balancing power in the oil market. 'The interests of the major powers in relation to Middle Eastern oil are as acute as ever. The 1990–91 Gulf conflict was over oil, not democracy in Kuwait' (Noreng 2002: 5).

For other states: the United States once more became engaged in the Middle East peace process culminating in the Oslo Accords of 1992, but neither side in the conflict tried to implement them, each preferring for political reasons to blame the other. This was to prove a very costly mistake indeed.

The oil majors as actors in South–North relations

The economic power of the oil majors is obvious. However, the production and distribution of oil is a very complicated business, and given that the commodity in which they deal is highly inflammable, the majors have a very strong interest in avoiding any kind of armed conflict.

Rhodesia/Zimbabwe

At former Rhodesia's unilateral declaration of independence (UDI) in 1965, the UN imposed an embargo on oil supplies; the Royal Navy established the Beira patrol to intercept smugglers; supplies dried up. However, all was not as it seemed.

(a) Oil continued to be landed instead in Lourenço Marques (now Maputo), capital of Mozambique. From there it travelled in unmarked tank wagons up the railway to Rhodesia, payment being handled through a South African company called Freight Services in which Harry Oppenheimer, the diamond magnate, had a part share.

(b) South Africa had no crude of its own. But oil majors made it clear they would continue to supply whatever South Africa wanted, knowing perfectly well that it was not going to stop there. Since South Africa did not send crude, but refined products, they could affirm confidently that they were not sending crude to Rhodesia. So the Smith regime did not collapse, and African states were convinced of northern perfidy.

Cuba

After 1964 the United States maintained an embargo on trade with Cuba, which still continues. There was particular anger in Washington that Cuba had nationalised US oil companies in 1960 when they refused to refine Soviet oil. The Soviet oil continued to reach Cuba, however, until the oil companies realised they could save money on transport costs. After that Cuba was supplied from Venezuela, while the Soviet oil was taken to Franco's Spain instead. And until 1991 Cuba never ran short of oil; indeed the Soviets supplied more than enough, so that they could sell the surplus on the world market.

Iraq

The Iraqi government tried to increase port fees at Basra. The oil companies paid the fees, but halved production, claiming that the higher cost made Basra uncompetitive. Alternative outlets were developed through Turkey and Saudi Arabia but this made Iraq more dependent on the goodwill of these neighbouring states. However, Iraq failed to make use of its vast resources of gas; in 1987 of the 7 million cubic metres produced, 5 million were simply flared off at the well-head. This reflected a general decay of Iraq's facilities until at the time of the Iraq War they were already seriously depleted and unable to respond to the call to produce more. The Basra refinery had been put out of action during the war with Iran and remained closed until after its end.

OPEC and Israel

In 1973 OPEC countries were angry about Western support for Israel in the 1973 war, and, having agreed to put the price up, the companies cut production and tried to ensure that specific countries should not get any. This was frustrated by the oil companies who insisted that what there was would be shared equally among their customers. But they were unable to maintain a common front to stop the panic buying which ratcheted up the price five-fold in three months.

Libya and the North

Under King Idris, Libyans sought to avoid outside dominance by leasing out their oilfields to a relatively large number of companies. Independents were responsible for half of all Libyan production by 1979 – Arco, Occidental, Continental, Marathon, Amerada Hess, Grace Petroleum, Bunker Hunt, Geisenberg. Oil had been found in 1956, and the first big strike made in 1959 by Standard Oil of New Jersey (now Exxon). Libya had become a major producer by 1966. Not only was its oil of high quality, but as Libya lies west of Suez, oil from it would not be affected by a possible closure of the Suez Canal in the event of a new war in the Middle East.

The September 1969 revolution in Libya established Muammar Qaddafi and the Revolutionary Command Council (RCC). Both were ignored by United

States even when it was told to shut Wheelus Air Force Base. The Libyan strategy was simple but effective: it was to target Exxon and Armand Hammer's Occidental for 44 cent/bbl, and a 50 to 58 per cent share of the profit. Then the RCC slowly squeezed Occidental production, until the independent, unpopular with others for undercutting, could not meet its contracts, and caved in. Meanwhile Venezuela raised its share of the take to 60 per cent, so other Arab states rejected 55 per cent and the scene was set for confrontation.

In January 1971 Libya asked for more again. This time the oil companies formed a common front, with clearance from the US State Department, but in the event failed to hold to it. By 1972 Libya, Iraq, and others found that even with sharp cutbacks they could not sell the oil they were producing. Saudi Arabia made up production and displaced Libya as a major oil exporter. The 1973 war between Israel and its neighbours triggered general OPEC action, as noted above. But by 1975 production in Libya was only 60 per cent of that of 1970 and although there was another small peak in 1979, production fell back after that. Libya never became the major oil producer that had been expected, although its oil continued to be desirable because it lay relatively close to Europe.

From the beginning the RCC was Islamist and anti-Western. Jews and Italians were expelled, for as with other Middle Eastern states at the time Libya under the new government was keen to take a lead in opposing Israel. However, hostility between Libya and the United States dates only from May 1978, when the United States identified Libya as supporting international terrorism, and banned military exports to Libya. In March 1982 the United States banned the import of Libyan oil and increased controls on exports to Libya, citing its alleged support for international terrorism and subversion. After PC Yvonne Fletcher was killed in 1984 by a shot from Libya's London Embassy ('People's Bureau') relations with the UK were also severed.

Then in 1986 the US government banned all trade with Libya, and blocked funds as far as it could, claiming Libyan complicity in the December 1985 attacks on Rome and Vienna airports. At the beginning of April 1986 a bomb in a Berlin nightclub claimed the lives of three and injured no less than 230 US soldiers. This was said to be retaliation by Libya for the sinking of two Libyan vessels in international waters in the Gulf of Sirte in March. On 15–16 April 1986, in a remarkable breach of international law, without warning the United States launched air raids on Tripoli and Benghazi, killing a number of people, including Qaddafi's daughter, in what was clearly intended to be a targeted assassination of Qaddafi himself (though in those days such an act was generally believed to be contrary to international law). However, not until June 1986 were US oil companies ordered by the State Department to leave Libya, and the ban on trade with Libya tightened.

In 1988 Pan-American Airways (PanAm) flight 103 from London to New York exploded in the air over Lockerbie, in Dumfries and Galloway, Scotland. Two hundred and seventy people were killed, including eleven who happened to be on the ground underneath, and 189 of them were Americans. The incident was regarded as an attack on the United States. Painstaking forensic examination led to the indictment of two Libyan nationals who were eventually, in 1999, handed over to Scottish police in the Netherlands where they were tried and one convicted. In September 1989 a French aircraft exploded over Niger; in 1991 a French magistrate indicted several Libyans. Finally in 1991 the UN Security Council took action for the first time; SC Resolution 833 of November 1993 embargoed the supply of key oil and refining equipment to Libya. But this did not satisfy hardliners in the United States. In 1996 the US Congress passed the Iran and Libya Sanctions Act, which introduced a 'secondary boycott' of companies doing business with Libya, even if they belonged to US allies.

The United States was clearly suspicious when in 2004 Britain announced that it was re-establishing diplomatic relations with Libya; when Libya unexpectedly announced, however, that it had abandoned earlier hopes of building WMD the way was clear for a general normalisation of relations.

Oil in South–North relations today

At the end of 1998, crude prices were even lower in real terms than they had been at the beginning of 1973, before the first oil shock. But surprisingly, at least to those who believe that the oil industry is a shining example of global free enterprise, nothing could be further from the truth. By 2001 national or nationalised oil corporations were supplying approximately three-quarters of all the world's oil. They were Aramco (Saudi Arabia), KPC (Kuwait), NIOC (Iran) and PdVSA (Venezuela). However, they could still only market their oil with the cooperation of the Seven Sisters – which as a result of mergers and acquisitions now number only five. They are Exxon Mobil (US), BP (UK), Royal Dutch-Shell (Anglo-Dutch), Total (French) and Chevron-Texaco (US).

In Venezuela, the United States is universally believed to have been behind the abortive coup to overthrow President Hugo Chávez in April 2002. Certainly the coup was not condemned by the US Administration, which immediately welcomed the new government, though the coup was condemned by the Organization of American States (OAS) as a clear breach of democratic legitimacy. An economic motive here would have been the role of Chávez in helping reactivate OPEC and its subsequent successful attempt drive up crude petroleum prices to over $20/bbl. Venezuela itself wished to double its royalties charged to the US-owned TNC Exxon-Mobil.

Chávez also earned political distrust in Washington in his role as president of OPEC in trying to build bridges with two of Washington's chosen enemies, Cuba and Saddam Hussein's Iraq (the latter because of its important role in the petroleum price calculations). By 2000, the world oil price seemed to have settled down at $22–28/bbl. However, northern demand has continued to climb and the anti-environmental stance of the Bush administration means that there is no immediate prospect of it falling, so rising price pressure is hardly a surprise. Brent crude's price on 5 April 2004 was $30.40/bbl (*Financial Times*, 21–22 April 2004); by September it was nearly $70/bbl before falling back in October to around $65/bbl; in March 2006 this new level seemed to have been generally accepted and in June 2006 Brent Crude was over $70/bbl.

Although US intervention in Iraq was probably not motivated solely by desire to get control of Iraq's oil production, this is what in fact has happened. Some expected this would help drive down prices; hence the fall in oil shares. But a decade of sanctions meant that Iraq's production and refining facilities were in poor shape. There was no sudden gush of Iraqi oil on to the world market and indeed not enough to satisfy Iraq's internal demand (like the inhabitants of other oil-producing countries, the Iraqis have got used to having very cheap fuel).

The View from the Ground

Worldstage

By *David Blair, The Daily Telegraph*, Wednesday, 8 February 2006

Darfur Bleeds in the Great Scramble for Sudan's Oil

There are 1.8 million refugees in Darfur and another 200,000 in neighbouring Chad. The unpalatable truth is that they have fallen victim to unscrupulous regimes around the world. During the Cold War, they would have been caught between the two superpowers. Today, China, Russia and a host of African countries are the authors of this tragedy – though primary responsibility must rest with Sudan's regime.

When rebels from the so-called Sudan Liberation Army launched the war in 2003, the government recruited the Arab Janjaweed militias and gave them carte blanche to loot, murder and rape. Because the rebels were mainly black Africans from the Zaghawa, Fur and Masalit tribes, these ethnic groups were written off as enemies.

But how did Sudan get away with this? The United Nations Security Council has passed 10 resolutions on Darfur since July 2004, five of them under Chapter Seven of the UN Charter, lending the strongest possible legal authority.

The first resolution, 1556, set a deadline of August 30 2004 for Sudan to disarm the Janjaweed. Those aid workers and myself who saw the aftermath of a Janjaweed raid that displaced 55,000 people a fortnight ago may be forgiven a hollow laugh.

The next resolution, 1564, in September 2004, is the most revealing. This declared that Sudan had ignored its obligation to disarm the Janjaweed and proceeded to do, well, nothing actually. The Security Council declared it would 'consider' imposing sanctions on Sudan's burgeoning oil industry.

Why only 'consider'? Well, because China pledged to veto any UN embargo. China's economic boom means that the quest for overseas oil is a central goal of its foreign policy. Sudan has 6.3 billion barrels of proved reserves which Beijing has begun exploiting on a grand scale. The China National Petroleum Company, a state-owned behemoth, has invested £8 billion in Sudan's oil. The country exports 500,000 barrels a day through a Chinese-built pipeline. Most goes to China, which depends on Sudan for about seven per cent of its oil imports.

This has given Sudan's regime a windfall. Oil revenues last year were at least £1 billion, enough to pay for war in Darfur and withstand international pressure. China has become Sudan's chief protector.

So Beijing is a key villain in Darfur's tragedy. Russia is also to blame. Land at any airport in Darfur and you see rows of Russian helicopter gunships, bristling with rockets and cannon, ready to raid villages in coordination with the Janjaweed.

Both Russia and China have supplied tanks, heavy artillery and fighter aircraft. America and the European Union have unilateral arms embargoes on Khartoum. But, astonishingly, there is no UN embargo on Sudan. Why? Because Russia and China would veto one.

Amid all the justified outrage over the Janjaweed, Darfur's rebels have escaped much of the blame they deserve. They are just as brutal as the Arab militias. Wrecked villages, all destroyed by the rebels, litter parts of Darfur.

The insurgents get their guns from Chad, Libya and Eritrea, which have long-standing grievances against Khartoum. They arm Darfur's rebels as a convenient means of retaliation. This cynical game keeps the insurgency alive and fuels the war.

Darfur's six million people – 300,000 have died in this conflict – are the helpless victims of this array of amoral governments.

So what can be done? First, we must give more aid. Aid agencies are scaling down operations because donations are drying up. Secondly, we must send a fully fledged UN peacekeeping force, with a robust mandate and proper logistical support.

But these are only palliatives. We must also face our own moral responsibility. Every time the Janjaweed destroy a village, they shame Britain, America and every country that sat in the council chamber and voted for all those UN resolutions without any apparent intention of enforcing their grand phrases.

The international politics of water

When the first oil well was drilled in 1857, its owner, Mr Drake, was looking for water. There is nothing new about a shortage of freshwater; the problem for the developing world today is that the scale is so much larger. Inevitably this has meant that in some parts of the world disputes have arisen over water resources. Where, as is frequently the case, a river flows through or around a number of countries, or acts as an international boundary between two states, then states can be found competing for the water it carries, and there are increasing fears that this competition may in some cases break into open conflict.

International law relating to rivers has in the past been concerned primarily with rights to navigation. However, since 1945 there have been important attempts to extend international law to ensure that a state upstream of a river ('the upstream riparian') has an obligation neither to stop nor divert its waters and must avoid actions or discharges which may prevent its downstream neighbours from making proper use of the water both traditionally enjoyed.

Africa is drying up. Trees have been felled and rain no longer falls in Ethiopia as it did in historical times. The competition in many parts of the continent for scarce resources is getting worse, but the effect of this scarcity on the Nile Valley is of particular interest. Since the completion of the Aswan High Dam in Egypt in 1958 the river now loses one-fifth of its water to evaporation from Lake Nasser, equivalent to all the water annually consumed in the entire continent of Africa. However, drought in Ethiopia where the Blue Nile rises, and in Uganda, which controls the outlet of the White Nile from Lake Victoria, is creating dissension between the states dependent on its flow (see below).

Most of the Middle East is arid, and not surprisingly some of the world's most intractable disputes over water are to be found there, as developing countries compete for the limited resources. The Jordan River Basin is bordered by Israel, Jordan, Lebanon and Syria. However, less than 3 per cent of the flow originates within (pre-1967) Israel, and 23 per cent from the Occupied Territories, while two of the three main tributaries, one nominally in Lebanon and the other in Syria, rise in the Golan Heights, currently also occupied by Israel. Of this flow, some 40 per cent has been diverted by Israel from the Sea of Galilee into its National Water Carrier, a canal and pipeline system supplying Israel's coastal cities and farms.

The Tigris and the Euphrates are both fed from sources in Turkey, which is one of the few countries in the region to have adequate supplies of water. The Tigris flows through Iraq to meet up with the Euphrates, which flows first through Syria and then through Iraq, into the Shatt-al-Arab. Problems began to develop when the Euphrates Dam was completed and Syria began to use a much larger proportion of its waters. As a result, in 1975 the Iraqi rice crop failed for a lack of adequate water, but relations between the three countries involved were so bad that no water-sharing agreement was discussed, let alone concluded. After the outbreak of war between Iraq and Iran in 1980 a new problem arose, as the tributaries of the Tigris which rise in the mountains of Iran flow through Iraqi Kurdistan. But in 1990 the completion of the Ataturk Dam by Turkey further reduced Iraq's choices. Not only did this mean even more water would be diverted for irrigation purposes in Turkey, but it raised the additional problem of run-off from the fields with potentially serious consequences for downstream water quality (Joffé 1993: 68–76).

The international sensitivity of water is also shown in South Asia. The Ganges (Ganga) rises in the Himalayas and flows 2,240 km southwards to form a vast delta on the Bay of Bengal. For India it is a sacred river, intensively used for drinking, washing and ritual purposes. The Indian government has objected to use of its waters by Nepal before they cross the frontier and there has been hot debate in India about the alleged effects of deforestation in Nepal. The latest evidence, however, suggests that deforestation peaked in Nepal between 1890 and 1930 and that other factors are to blame for the increasing instability of the river. India itself has contributed to its problems by failing to control deforestation, much of it generated by the need for fuel-wood and/or the need to house India's growing population (the value of fuel-wood increased dramatically as a result of the 1973 oil crisis, accelerating pressure on dwindling stocks). Urbanisation has been an important factor increasing floodwater run-off and the risk of flooding. The flow of these rivers is normally so great that in the event of a cyclone in the Bay of Bengal most of Bangladesh is liable to be flooded. Hence it relies upon early warning from its upstream neighbours to alert it to the risks. However, large-scale flooding in Bangladesh in 1985 and 1988, or the floods that killed 237 people in India in 1985, could not have been prevented even if the original forest cover had been intact (Mannion 1992: 254; see also Brammer 1990).

Plans for large-scale inter-basin transfer within India to the Narmada and other rivers remain speculative. However, conflict has already also arisen over both the quality and quantity of the water shared between India and Bangladesh in the dry season. Bangladesh accuses India of diverting more water from the river than it should. In fact the dispute began in 1951, when Bangladesh was still part of Pakistan, when India decided to construct a barrage on the Ganges at Farakka to divert some of its waters into the Bhagirathi-Hooghly River. The purpose was to reduce silting in the Indian port of Calcutta. By the time Bangladesh became independent in 1971 the Farakka Dam had already been completed and it was agreed to study the situation and decide on a joint use policy. It became a crisis in the dry season of 1976 when the main tributary of the Ganges dried up and Bangladesh was receiving only a third of the normal flow. The first agreement expired in 1984; it was renewed in the following year, but this agreement ran out in 1988 (Saravanamuttu 1993: 122). At the third attempt an interim agreement was reached and signed on 12 December 1996, but a permanent settlement of the problem was still awaited ten years later.

The View from the Ground

By *Mike Pflanz in Nairobi*, *The Daily Telegraph*, Thursday, 9 March 2006

Flow of the Nile is Cut to Let Lake Victoria Fill up Again

Drought in East Africa has caused Lake Victoria to drop to its lowest level in 80 years and forced Uganda to reduce the flow of water to the Nile.

Output into Africa's longest river from the huge Owen Falls Dam, 50 miles east of Kampala, will be cut by a third to allow the lake to refill, said Uganda's water minister, Maria Mutagamba.

Dismal rainfall has reduced water levels by 18in or more, driving fishermen further from shore, stopping ferries from docking at shallow jetties and causing power cuts at hydroelectric plants.

Reservoirs around the dam must be allowed to fill up again, Mrs Mutagamba said, by cutting the flow from 242,000 gallons per day to 76,000 gallons.

Uganda's move is likely to anger Egypt, which claims 82 per cent of the 819 million gallons shed by the Nile every second under the contentious 1929 Nile Waters Treaty, updated in 1959 to give Sudan most of what was left.

The colonial-era agreements, masterminded by Britain, limited the other countries of the Nile basin – Kenya, Tanzania, Eritrea, Ethiopia, Burundi, Rwanda, and the Democratic Republic of Congo – from interfering with the flow of the 4,200-mile river.

Tensions between the Nile basin nations have been rising as countries such as Kenya and Ethiopia, struggling with poor rainfall, have called for greater access to the water for irrigation and hydroelectric schemes.

In February, a report by Daniel Kull, a United Nations hydrologist, accused Uganda of secretly draining water from Lake Victoria to generate electricity.

However, the current drought, brought on by persistent poor rain across parts of Kenya, Ethiopia, Somalia, Eritrea and Djibouti, has also caused water levels to sink.

More than 11 million people across East Africa and the Horn of Africa are at risk of starvation, the World Food Programme has warned, due to drought that has left areas without water or pasture.

While drought is a natural occurrence, it is happening more frequently due to global warming and environmental destruction, scientists say.

Kenya's meteorological department warned yesterday that rainfall anticipated between March and May is this year likely to be below average in the country's north, where the drought is hitting hardest.

"We used to see these conditions every five or six years, but now they are coming every one, two or three years," said Daniele Donati, emergency co-ordinator for Africa for the UN Food and Agriculture Organisation.

"These people have developed the most sophisticated mechanisms for survival, but even they cannot cope with repeated droughts coming ever more often, making them progressively more vulnerable."

Conclusion

Economic weakness makes developing world countries politically powerless. Opening up their economies to investment and trade promises wealth, but brings with it a greater openness to outside influences.

Because of this, purely developing world organisations have not been particularly successful at influencing world affairs, while regional organisations incorporating a substantial power are inclined to come under the influence of that power. The OAS has not for long been able to avoid the influence of the United States, and through the francophone states France has exercised and continues to exercise a disproportionate influence within the OAU.

Though interactions between the citizens of different countries are becoming technically easier, money and political influence combine to ensure that the globalisation of world politics tends to strengthen the power of the major states and/or the AICs, and not of the developing world.

Key terms

balance of power – in international relations, multipolar system characterised by shifting alliances to stop any one country becoming too powerful

bilateral treaties – formal agreements between two countries, the basis of all international law

Cold War – period of tension between the United States and the Soviet Union beginning in 1947 and ending in 1989

decommissioning – giving up, destroying or surrendering arms

ethnic cleansing – term originating in former Yugoslavia but now used generally for the practice of creating ethnically homogenous territories by murdering or displacing members of rival ethnic groups

humanitarian intervention – intervention designed to promote human rights and/or to alleviate suffering

implementation – carrying out decisions according to agreements already made

international – concerned with relations between independent states

intervention – interference by a state in the domestic affairs of another state by diplomatic, military or other means

'peace dividend' – money expected to be saved by the end of the Cold War and the subsequent reduction of forces

sovereignty – in legal and political theory, the right of a state to do what it likes within its own borders, unaffected by any outside power

superpowers – during the Cold War, the USA and the Soviet Union

supranational – organization having authority over otherwise independent states

Questions

1. When and how should the international community intervene in internal conflict in developing countries?

2. Has '9/11' changed the nature of North–South relations? What special measures, if any, are needed to defeat terrorism?

3. What is the relationship between the 'war on terror' and events in Afghanistan and Iraq?

4. Why is the world oil market structured the way it is? How and where has the structure of the world oil market influenced North–South relations?

5. How far was OPEC successful in restructuring the market in 1973 and 1999?

6. How far does oil help explain current South–North tensions?

7. Is oil only a special case of the conflict between countries in the developing world over scarce resources?

8. The reasons given by President Bush for ordering the intervention in Panama are not all valid under international law – which are which?

PART III

Politics of the developing world

CHAPTER 7

State-building

Introduction

The basic interaction of world politics is the relations of nation states. Originally, the term nation state was employed to distinguish the modern **state** from earlier forms of political organisation covering relatively small areas, such as tribes or city states. It is true that in modern states the majority of inhabitants generally identify themselves with one another, by the possession of a common language, religion and/or culture. A people with this sense of identity is regarded as a **nation**. However, the term 'nation state' is a misleading one, for there is no exact correspondence between state and nation. There are states with more than one nation (Britain), nations with more than one state (ethnic Albanians, Hungarians, Serbs etc.), states with no definite national identity (Chad) and nations with no definite state (the Palestinian Arabs) (Seton-Watson 1977). The reason why the term is so popular is that in nineteenth-century Europe there emerged, with the concept of **nationalism** (see below), the belief that the only appropriate basis for a state was the nation. To this day, therefore, states which lack a sense of national identity try very hard to inculcate it, as for example did the United States (Lipset 1979).

As so often with composite terms, over time the newly coined expression comes to have its own meaning which is more than (or possibly less than, but certainly distinguishable from) the sum of the parts. We can compare the term 'Latin American', which refers to Guaraní-speaking Paraguayans, Welsh-speaking Argentines, German-speaking Chileans, Brazilians of African descent, etc., as well as Colombians from old Spanish families. Similarly nation state may be seen as simply designating a unit approximating to the ideals of statehood as described by Michael Smith: 'sovereign territoriality, authority and legitimacy, control of citizens and their actions' (Smith 1992; 256). These elements express the international as well as the national aspect of nation statehood. Indeed, at its simplest, full penetration of the national area and the capacity to act as a single unit on the world stage might be taken as a starting point for some kind of definition and/or classification. Even this, however, would be more rigorous than would be wise in certain instances. For example, Sri Lanka would probably fail the first of these two tests: for much of the last 25 years the instruments of the state have not had access to the whole island, having been excluded from the Jaffna Peninsula by the Tamil Tigers (*The Guardian*, 4 May 2000). Nevertheless Sri Lanka, despite its ethnic divisions, remained a nation state on any meaningful definition. The great danger in seeking precision in such terms as nation state is that so few countries would fit any reasonably parsimonious definition and a new term seems unlikely to be any more useful or, indeed, accurate.

The rather arbitrary creation of many developing states raises the issue of nation-building (cf. Kedourie 1971; Golbourne 1979). It is necessary to establish some sense of loyalty to the new state. In the developing world, state boundaries do not unite people of common descent, language and customs. This ethnic pluralism has been the source of conflict, the most glaring examples being in Africa. The Organization of African Unity (OAU) sensibly enough took the view that the colonial boundaries should remain, since tinkering with them would open up Pandora's Box, and this remains the official policy of the African Union. Hence Igbo independence from Nigeria found little favour and the would-be state of Biafra was not officially recognised by any other power. However, in the brief period before it was overwhelmed by the military force of the Federal Government, General de Gaulle expressed his political support for it and France and some African nations supplied it with arms. Libya's intervention in Chad (Decalo 1980) in turn brought an armed response from France and Zaire (now the Democratic Republic of the Congo), while under OAU auspices Nigeria, Senegal and Zaire supplied troops for a UN-sponsored peacekeeping force.

To build a state is to institutionalise the need for emotional/ideological penetration of **society.** Such a link between state and society makes possible the viability of regimes. If there is no dominant group, political institutionalisation cannot occur and 'society' remains 'stateless' as in the Lebanon in the 1970s and 1980s. In addition, some peoples have a sense of nation but are stateless, for example the Palestinians and the Kurds today; others feel imprisoned in existing states and seek to create independent states, for example, Sikhs in the Punjab and Muslims in Kashmir.

However, it is not necessary for secessionist movements to be active for the state to lack authority and efficacy. The reorganisation of Indian states on a linguistic basis in the 1950s has been criticised for intensifying the potential for ethnic violence. Certainly it weakened provincial loyalties, though there is no evidence that it made local politicians any less keen on obtaining the favour of central government.

In such an atmosphere, developing world constitutions often seem quite unrelated to reality. Some regard them as foreign impositions, hastily put together and presented to referendum in the hope of enhancing popular legitimacy. But in reality they are compromises, as are constitutions in any other part of the world, between the desire of the central government to exert its will and the determination of peripheral regions to resist it. Hence constitutions often stress democracy and centralism when the reality is of centrifugal forces such as tribalism in Africa (Dunn 1978) and political gangsterism in Asia and parts of Latin America. Subrata Kumar Mitra says of India generally:

> the resilience of the state in India can be attributed to its success in incorporating some of the key features of the Indian tradition while retaining the essential features of modernity. Primordial sentiments have been balanced with those of economic interest and ideology. The edge is taken off the potential for authoritarianism through the division of power and widespread participation. By co-opting traditional centres of power and creating new ones the modern state has found a niche for most interests and norms with a support base in society. (Mitra 1990: 91)

It has therefore also institutionalised conflict between executives and legislatures, particularly, but not exclusively, in presidential systems (systems with an **executive president** – see below. Service as a legislator remains an important rung on the political ladder to preferment and the importance to a would-be developing world politician of a strong local power base in the region/area/tribe can hardly be overstated. In return rewards are expected by the local community as a result of support for the government, even in a one-party state.

In Latin American states institutionalised conflict between presidents and legislatures is compounded by multi-party politics. Factional squabbling was used as an excuse for President Fujimori of Peru to close Congress in 1992 and to rule by decree (Wood 2000). On the other hand, the fall of both Carlos Andrés Pérez in Venezuela and Fernando Collor in Brazil was made *easier* by their lack of an effective congressional power base.

However, there are limits on the power of other developing world governments to legislate. This is most noticeable in Muslim countries, such as Bangladesh, Pakistan or Sudan, where there has been strong pressure to make the Koran the sole basis of all law and governments have sought to reintroduce punishments such as flogging, amputation and stoning to death, which had been abolished by the former colonial power. In 1995 the government of Benazir Bhutto in Pakistan refused to intervene in the case of a 14-year-old Christian boy sentenced to death under Islamic law for having allegedly daubed walls with anti-Islamic slogans two years earlier. Fortunately for him, on appeal to a higher court, the evidence against him was dismissed as concocted, despite well-organised demonstrations outside the courtroom calling for the sentence to be upheld. In the long run the thing that may cause the greatest problem for these governments is the Koranic prohibition against charging interest on the use of money, since if it too is implemented it means that domestic banking systems will not function in a way that meshes comfortably with the international financial system.

Who makes the law?

The symbolism of developing world governments combines traditional elements such as chieftainship, colonial elements derived from the imperial past and modern notions such as the executive presidency. Some rulers, such as Sir Dawda Jawara of The Gambia or Sir Eric Gairy of Grenada retained the knighthoods of colonial governors. The government of India continues to operate from New Delhi designed by Sir Edwin Lutyens to serve as the capital of the Raj, and Indian regiments use bugles, bagpipes and the regimental silver as symbols of continuity. Pakistan is the world's largest manufacturer of bagpipes as well as of cricket bats. Yet the wheel of Asoka on the Indian flag, like the Sinhalese lion of Sri Lanka or the trigrams of Korea, speaks of a much older inheritance. The shield and spears of the flag of Kenya are traditional symbols of military and so of political power, but the fly whisk carried by Jomo Kenyatta (and other East African leaders) was also a symbol of chieftainship, even if the office he held was a modern, constitutional one.

By putting his own head on the coins of Ghana, Nkrumah not only demonstrated in the clearest possible way that power had passed to an African but, as earlier rulers had done, confirmed his leadership in enduring form (Clapham 1982: 62). In Kenya, Kenyatta's style was that of an African monarch:

> When Kenyatta moved between State House in Nairobi and his homes in Gatundu, Mombasa and Nakuru, it was less the seat of government that moved, so much as an entire court. Kenyatta became the centre of governmental activity and thus access to him was the *sine qua non* of preferment for politicians, bureaucrats and businessmen alike. As discussed earlier, access to decision-makers is never unlimited and not always free in Africa. The court 'gatekeepers' of Kenya extracted sizeable entry fees and most visitors left with lighter wallets or thinner cheque books after having 'voluntarily' contributed to one of Kenyatta's favourite causes or schemes. (Williams 1987: 83)

What is clear is that in many developing states, whether as heir of the colonial governor or as heir of the traditional chieftain, the president rules as well as reigns. Indeed this is the form of government the citizens understand and (despite some of its obvious shortcomings) are comfortable with. The initiative in legislation lies, inevitably, with the government. Within the government, the adoption of the presidential system has placed great emphasis on the role of presidential leadership. 'Politics is not just a game, it is the ultimate game: a game played with real people and real things' (Calvert 2002: 39). Very few people want to give up political power, and where the restraints on power are weak, ambition has no limits.

The problem of the weak state

Many of the problems of the developing world, therefore, come down to what can be called the problem of the weak state. Populist campaigning and the emotional appeal of television are used to reinforce the illusion that choice of a single candidate or party will solve all (or at least some) of the personal difficulties of the voter.

Even if it was possible to fund the overnight improvement in the distribution of wealth envisaged (for example) at the time of the election of President Mandela of South Africa (Sampson 1999), it is hard to see how he (or any other leader in a similar position) could be in a position to deliver. And the fact is that the developing world leader is rarely in a position to ensure policies become practice, not only because he or she lacks the resources, but because he or she does not have the power to see that those resources are actually allocated to the purpose for which they are intended. Even in relatively sophisticated states like Iran in the last years of the Shah (1963–79), or Mexico under Gustavo López Portillo (1976–82) large sums were expended for work that was not carried out, government inspectors being bribed to ignore the obvious fact that the buildings and roads did not exist.

State-building is the most vital process in any newly independent developing world country. It is intimately linked to the development process because without an adequate perception of the country as its own state, the dynamism and ambitions of the population (and in particular the entrepreneurial elite) will not be directed constructively. An identity must be forged at the collective level, just as it must for individuals. Nationalism, religion, ethnicity can either strengthen or weaken state identity, depending on how they are used. Clientelism, corruption and military intervention all act to undermine both authority and legitimacy, and in extreme circumstances can contribute to the collapse of regimes and the disintegration of the economic order. For a modern government to survive, it must be supported by a healthy civil society (see Chapter 8), in which individuals and groups are able to exist openly and pursue their interests free from the fear of arbitrary power.

Constitutional government

Liberal democracies are states in which government is limited in its powers by a constitution, a system of law and/or an independent judiciary and is responsive to the popular will as expressed through elections.

For a country to be a liberal democracy its **constitution** does not have to be embodied in a single written document. However, if it is not, the constitution is vulnerable to the ambitions of unscrupulous politicians. All countries in the developing world have written constitutions, although they are not always observed and are frequently changed or replaced for partisan reasons. Venezuela, one of the first developing countries to achieve independence, has had more than 20 constitutions.

It is certainly doubtful if many of the constitutions of independence would have survived for long anyway. Their main problem was that they were drafted by lawyers with a lawyer's concern for the *output* of government. Hence the way in which democracy was to function was left to a series of assumptions about the uses of power which were not widely shared and not necessarily understood. The result was a democracy for the elite, at best; at worst a system in which smooth-tongued demagogues manipulated unsophisticated masses to give electoral support to an essentially authoritarian system.

Naturally, too, in different ways the various colonial powers sought to ensure as far as possible the continuing protection of their own interests. The documents therefore took little or no account of the *input* side, especially the relationship of business and financial interests to government. Business is often inimical to democracy in its need to strike bargains and gain advantages over rivals, especially when armed with the financial resources of TNCs. The precursors of independence were in a particularly strong position. They could use their historical position to negotiate with the former colonial power a settlement which left them in control of the key resources. Hence in many cases the new government was dominated by a single tribe or regional faction. As long as it had the necessary resources it was then in a position to generate political support through clientelism. Where such systems have survived, therefore, there seem to have been at least two preconditions: that the resources available should be sufficient and that they be spent in a way that enhanced social satisfaction and not be frittered away on the self-indulgence of those in power.

The struggle for power takes place throughout a political system and at a number of levels. The continued working of a liberal democracy depends on some kind of balance being maintained, between **executive** and legislature, between the chief executive and his or her colleagues and between the government and the people. There are two main compromises: **parliamentary systems** and **presidential systems.**

Yet in the former Communist states (and some others) parliamentary and presidential systems still existed in form but were made ineffective by being brought under the control of a ruling party organisation. Despite the impact of the so-called 'Third Wave' of democratisation, which began in 1975, a third or more of modern states continue to be under authoritarian rule, either of a traditional ruler or of a military dictator. Among developing states, China is the most striking example of centralised, authoritarian government.

Since 1978, an American think-tank, Freedom House, has published *Freedom in the World*, an annual comparative assessment of the state of political rights and civil liberties around the world. It is, as they claim, widely used by policy-makers and journalists, as well as by scholars, often as a convenient indicator of the state of democracy in a given country. But it is not a measure of democracy as such and it is important to treat it with some caution. Countries are marked on a scale from 1 (free) to 7 (not free) on two criteria: political rights and civil liberties, which are combined to give an overall measure. The methodology is subjective, and so there can be argument about individual cases.

In 2005 Freedom House rated 48 countries as 'not free' (see Table 7.1). Some of America's strongest allies, such as Saudi Arabia and Pakistan, come out badly. But states with left-wing governments, such as Sri Lanka and Venezuela, are rated only 'partly free', despite well-established democratic traditions and free elections over many years (Freedom House 2005).

There has been much criticism of the fact that few of the constitutions of the newly emerging developing states in Africa or Asia long survived independence. Much of this criticism, in English-speaking countries, was directed at the 'Westminster model' of parliamentary democracy. Yet the governments of

Table 7.1   Freedom House ratings, 2005

Free	• **Ranking**	• New Zealand	• **Ranking: 2**
	• Andorra	• Norway	• Antigua and Barbuda
	• Australia	• Palau	• Argentina
	• Austria	• Poland	• Benin
	• Bahamas	• Portugal	• Botswana
	• Barbados	• San Marino	• Croatia
	• Belgium	• Slovakia	• Dominican Republic
	• Canada	• Slovenia	• Ghana
	• Cape Verde	• Spain	• Guyana
	• Chile	• Sweden	• Israel
	• Costa Rica	• Switzerland	• Lithuania
	• Cyprus	• Tuvalu	• Mali
	• Czech Republic	• United Kingdom	• Mexico
	• Denmark	• United States	• Mongolia
	• Dominica	• Uruguay	• Samoa
	• Estonia	• **Ranking: 1.5**	• Sao Tome and
	• Finland	• Belize	Principe
	• France	• Bulgaria	• Vanuatu
	• Germany	• Greece	• **Ranking: 2.5**
	• Hungary	• Grenada	• Brazil
	• Iceland	• Japan	• El Salvador
	• Ireland	• Latvia	• India
	• Italy	• Monaco	• Jamaica
	• Kiribati	• Panama	• Lesotho
	• Liechtenstein	• St. Kitts and Nevis	• Namibia
	• Luxembourg	• St. Lucia	• Peru
	• Malta	• St. Vincent and	• Philippines
	• Marshall Islands	Grenadines	• Romania
	• Mauritius	• South Africa	• Senegal
	• Micronesia	• South Korea	• Serbia and
	• Nauru	• Suriname	Montenegro
	• Netherlands	• Taiwan	• Thailand

Table 7.1 *(continued)*

Partly free	• **Ranking: 3**	• Fiji	• Zambia
	• Albania	• Georgia	• **Ranking: 4.5**
	• Bolivia	• Indonesia	• Armenia
	• East Timor	• Moldova	• Burkina Faso
	• Ecuador	• Mozambique	• Congo, Rep. of
	• Honduras	• Sierra Leone	• Gabon
	• Kenya	• Tanzania	• Jordan
	• Macedonia	• Ukraine	• Kuwait
	• Madagascar	• Venezuela	• Liberia
	• Nicaragua	• **Ranking: 4**	• Morocco
	• Niger	• Bangladesh	• Singapore
	• Papua New Guinea	• Colombia	• Uganda
	• Paraguay	• Comoros	• **Ranking: 5**
	• Seychelles	• The Gambia	• Bahrain
	• Solomon Islands	• Guatemala	• Burundi
	• Sri Lanka	• Guinea-Bissau	• Djibouti
	• Trinidad and Tobago	• Malawi	• Ethiopia
	• Turkey	• Malaysia	• Nepal
	• **Ranking: 3.5**	• Nigeria	• Yemen
	• Bosnia and Herzegovina	• Tonga	
Not free	• **Ranking: 5.5**	• Qatar	• Eritrea
	• Afghanistan	• Russia	• Haiti
	• Algeria	• Rwanda	• Laos
	• Angola	• Tajikistan	• Somalia
	• Azerbaijan	• Togo	• Uzbekistan
	• Bhutan	• Tunisia	• Vietnam
	• Brunei	• **Ranking: 6**	• Zimbabwe
	• Cambodia	• Cameroon	• **Ranking: 7**
	• Central African Republic	• Congo, Dem. Rep. of	• Cuba
	• Chad	• Cote d'Ivoire	• Libya
	• Egypt	• Iran	• Myanmar (Burma)
	• Guinea	• Iraq	• North Korea
	• Kazakhstan	• Swaziland	• Saudi Arabia
	• Lebanon	• United Arab Emirates	• Sudan
	• Maldives	• **Ranking: 6.5**	• Syria
	• Mauritania	• Belarus	• Turkmenistan
	• Oman	• China	
	• Pakistan	• Equatorial Guinea	

Note: Countries are ranked according to political rights and civil liberties on a scale from 1.0 (most free) to 7.0 (least free).
Source: *Freedom in the World, 2005*, published by Freedom House.
www.freedomhouse.org/research/survey2005.htm

both Sri Lanka and Pakistan have considered reintroducing it, and even before 1975 parliamentary democracy was well established in a number of developing countries. Jamaica, Trinidad and Tobago, Botswana, Mauritius, India, Papua New Guinea and some smaller island states have all had stable democratic systems since 1948. We could add to those Sri Lanka, which has had constitutional government since 1948 but has been challenged by a substantial insurgent movement, and Malaysia which has had constitutional government since 1957. Both have been independent longer than Jamaica (Burnell and Calvert 1999).

Stable presidential states are much harder to find outside the AICs. Among developing countries, Costa Rica, a presidential democracy in Central America, has had stable government since 1948 (Pinkney 1993: 83). In Latin America, Mexico has also had a stable constitutional government continuously since 1948: in fact, since 1920, though from the 1960s onwards it failed to evolve into a fully democratic system.

On the other hand, though small island developing states (SIDS) are a better bet for democracy than their mainland counterparts there is no guarantee of this: the Comoros (1975, 1978) and the Seychelles (1977) in the Indian Ocean, Fiji (1987, 2000) in the Pacific and Grenada (1979, 1983) in the Caribbean have all suffered from armed intervention in the political process. In 1994 the government of Sir Dawda Jawara in The Gambia succumbed, at the second attempt, to a military coup; in 1999 Melchior Ndadaye, its first Hutu head of state, was killed in a coup in Burundi. The **Third Wave** of democratisation (Huntington 1993b) has had setbacks. However, the overall trend remains towards the spread and consolidation of democracy in the developing world, other than Eastern Europe and Central Asia (Haynes 2001; Vanhanen 1997).

Obviously, as the inclusion of Costa Rica makes clear, the absence of military forces, or, alternatively, their weakness, is a major factor in safeguarding democracy (see Chapter 8). Other reasons for the survival (or otherwise) of democracy can be grouped as political, economic and social. Among the political reasons are: the existence of a widely-accepted constitution for government, the ability of major interest groups to influence decision-making and the emergence of broadly-based and well-organised political parties.

Parliamentary systems

As noted above present-day examples of working parliamentary systems include not only developed countries such as Australia, Belgium, Canada, Germany and the United Kingdom, but also developing countries such as India, Malaysia, Sri Lanka and Trinidad and Tobago.

In a parliamentary system executive decisions are in practice vested in a committee of the **assembly**, consisting of ministers responsible to the assembly for their political actions. In countries such as Grenada or Jamaica, where the **head of state** is a hereditary monarch, the monarch's functions are ceremonial only. In a state with an elected head, which is the case in almost all other developing countries, the president (as he or she is rather confusingly called), may have rather more power, though once elected he or she is expected to stand above the political struggle. And in most states, the head of state has to sign documents giving effect to laws, and retains in this and the choice of a first or prime minister reserve powers which may be activated by some unexpected crisis.

The prime minister, as **head of government**, chooses the executive committee, or ministry. This must normally consist of elected members of the assembly (though not in The Netherlands or its former colonies). However, in all cases the government can only survive as long as it can command a majority in the assembly.

As traditional theorists would have predicted, the parliamentary system seems to have worked well in the main in the small island states which inherited it. Its problems, too, are those that an eighteenth-century writer would have found familiar. A charismatic leader can easily dominate a very small assembly such as the unicameral parliament of St Vincent and the Grenadines, since it consists of only 15 elected representatives and six appointed senators. On the other hand, if the leader loses its confidence the ruling party may all the more rapidly go down to defeat.

Presidential systems

The other favoured compromise is the presidential system. This differs fundamentally. The prototype is the 1787 Constitution of the United States. But not only has this been amended substantially over time (Neustadt 1964) but as a model it has only been taken up throughout the world since 1946 and in a form which differs substantially from the original intentions of the framers of the American Constitution.

It was perhaps natural that in the first three decades of the nineteenth century presidential systems should have been adopted by most of the newly independent states of the Americas, with the exception of part of Haiti and of Brazil, which remained a parliamentary monarchy until 1889 (Needler 1963). Only one other presidential state dates from this period: Liberia, a colony for freed American slaves, independent in 1847. After that there was a long gap, until the rising power of the United States created Hawaii (1892; annexed by the United States 1898) and Cuba (1901).

It was only after 1946 when the Philippines, under American tutelage from 1898 onwards, became independent, that the presidential system came to sweep the rest of the Third World, beginning with the Middle East and North Africa, and spreading throughout Africa South of the Sahara in the wake of the dissolution of the British, French and Portuguese colonial empires after 1960. So powerful was the urge to imitate it that even established parliamentary systems such as those of Pakistan and Sri Lanka were modified in the direction of presidentialism. But few of the systems that have resulted are true presidential systems in the constitutional sense.

In the prototype presidential system the assembly remains separate and distinct from the executive. Law-making remains the function of the assembly; but seeing laws are put into effect is entrusted to one person, the president, elected directly for a limited term, who appoints officials to assist him or her, commonly called a cabinet, though not politically responsible to the assembly. And in the United States the potential conflict of function between president and legislature is met by a variety of devices, but most distinctively by the creation of an independent judiciary with power to rule on the constitutionality of specific actions of either of the other two branches of government.

Since there is no focus of power, this system is dynamically unstable, and its invariable tendency has been for the president to destroy the compromise by assuming, often with the aid of force, control over all functions of government. To be a true presidential state, therefore, three conditions have all to be observed.

1. The president must be *elected by the people* according to agreed rules generally regarded as fair. The president must not be a hereditary ruler, be self-appointed, come to power by a military coup, or be nominated by the chiefs of a military regime, as has so often been the case in developing countries over the past 60 years.

2. He or she must be *elected for a definite term*. There is some difference between being elected for a series of definite terms and being in power indefinitely, but in practice one tends to lead to the other. Consequently constitutional provisions limiting presidential terms are normal, though they are often abused, if necessary by the systematic rewriting of constitutional provisions, as with Menem in Argentina or Fujimori in Peru in the 1990s. Assumption of the presidential office for life invites the corollary that the shorter the life, the shorter the term, and six of the seven presidents-for-life of Haiti have been murdered.

3. The president *must not be able to dissolve the assembly* (or suspend its powers) during its fixed term of office. In practice this is often done, in what is often called a 'self-coup' or *autogolpe*, by the leaders of military or military-backed regimes, as in Uruguay in 1973. They also make use, in most if not all cases, of emergency powers, which will be considered further later (Weinstein 1975: 132–3).

   If, in a presidential state, secretaries are given the power to sit and vote in the assembly they become to an extent responsible to it, and the result is a mixed system which is neither presidential nor truly parliamentary. The adoption of this system in France in 1958 again had an impact on other francophone countries. Semi-presidentialism is characterised by a dual executive, consisting of an elected president with a defined political role and a prime minister and cabinet responsible to the assembly. Already these semi-presidential systems are themselves being differentiated from one another.

Some forty per cent of the world's population live under some form of **federal** government, a form of liberal democracy characterised by the **division of powers** between a central government and a number of 'state' governments. These systems emerged from the linking together of a number of smaller units and afford citizens an enhanced ability to participate in politics at more than one level. A federal state such as India or Brazil has to have a written constitution, as the precise distribution of powers has to be spelt out clearly.

Interest groups

In liberal democracies typically demands are articulated by interest groups and aggregated by political parties. But the **interest group** differs from the political party, to which it is closely related, by not seeking political power for itself. It merely seeks, when it acts at all, to influence decisions taken by others. However, this model is by no means always applicable elsewhere and a great deal of research still needs to be done on how interests are translated into public policy.

Demands on the political system originate in the minds of individual citizens, often in a quite unformed state. They may well not be immediately recognised as political, and whether they are seen as such will depend on the nature of the society concerned. However, except in a very local sense, the voice of one individual in a modern society will normally carry little weight unless the demands which that individual articulates come from within the central elite and its decision-making body – what Easton (1957, 1965) calls 'withinputs' or 'intraputs' – or until those concerned get together with others who share a common interest and aggregate their demands into a programme for action. The demarcation of articulation and aggregation in liberal democracies is by no means always applicable elsewhere.

It is now recognised that interest groups – people sharing a common interest – exist in all societies, though usually in a latent rather than an active state, waiting to be activated by a relevant issue. Hence the preference for the term 'interest group' rather than 'pressure group'. In a sense they cover the entire field of political interest articulation other than that of the individual, for the family itself can be regarded as an interest group. Many groups, especially those with better formal organisation, aggregate interests also into a common action programme.

In developing countries many if not most forms of interest groups are distrusted by would-be leaders, and when they take the form of ethnic or community groups there is great fear that they endanger national unity. In India where a caste, ethnic group or region dominates the politics of a state, that group will benefit disproportionately in the allocation of appointments and contracts. Many government officials, as Weiner (1962) noted, tended initially to decry this as a violation of democratic principles. They had, he suggests, a rather idealistic picture in their minds, not of the way that the British system of democracy actually works, but of how it was supposed to work and nor were they well informed about the politics of the United States.

Most developing world states are still characterised by a predominance of **non-associational** interest groups (groups into which people are born) and a relative scarcity of formally organised **associational** groups (groups which people choose to join – Almond and Coleman 1960: 33ff.). Theorists of democracy have identified a number of factors which appear to facilitate the emergence and/or maintenance of democracy. Two relate to the expression of interests. On the one hand, a wealthy society is better able to fulfil the demands made upon it than a poor one. By definition, therefore, many developing world states, lacking such resources, will find it difficult to satisfy these demands. On the other, the development of powerful opposition coalitions is much less likely where interests are diverse in nature and base, creating cross-cutting cleavages within society, such that no one tribe or group is able to dominate the whole. The problem is how to secure this state of affairs.

The device of the separation of powers (or the division of powers between federal and state governments in a federal system) is only effective where enough interests pull in each direction.

Political parties and elections

A political party is a formal organisation of people seeking to achieve or to retain political power. Parties do not exist in a vacuum. They are defined by their relationship to other parts of the political system. This means, first, whether there are other political parties, since, if there are, they collectively form a party system, which is a subset of the political system as a whole. Parties do not necessarily compete with other parties within a system; there are also non-competitive systems and semi-competitive systems and in the developing world these are still quite common. When new systems came under scrutiny after decolonisation, the structural-functionalists distinguished 'Western' political parties which competed with other political parties, and so-called 'non-Western' political parties that did not (Almond and Coleman 1960: 9–10, 17). They correctly recognised that both performed the function of **interest articulation** as well as to a greater or lesser extent that of **interest aggregation**. But it is, of course, the differences that are significant, and this requires a much more rigorous reason for classification than mere geographical location. Better to term them 'competitive' and 'non-competitive' parties.

The most important distinctions are those between competitive systems, in which a number of parties compete for power, and non-competitive systems, where there is only one party. Where there is more than one party, parties shape not only themselves but one another. Hence the number of parties active is certainly significant, though unfortunately the precise number is very difficult to define.

Plate 13   Voters registration drive: Mexico

A 'non-competitive' party is in a sense a contradiction in terms, since the origin of party lies in competition. Non-competitive parties are those that have no effective competing parties, although they may be in competition with other internal formations, e.g. the armed forces, or, as in the case of nationalist parties, with some exterior force. In the life of any community, at some stage, there emerges a cause of dispute which causes people to take sides and form **factions**. A faction is an informal group of people seeking a common policy within a political party, or where there are no political parties. The key difference between factions and political parties is that factions have no permanent organisation or membership. Some writers on political parties find it hard to see many developing world political groupings as parties and regard them only as factions. While all political parties derive ultimately from factions, factions are temporary and their future always uncertain. Parties, on the other hand, are characterised by permanence of structure, a deliberate attempt to win recruits and regular procedures for recruitment of political leaders. Possession of these attributes can and does lead to the formal acceptance of their right to exist in law.

For this reason Sartori believes that personalist parties, which often have a very short life with little or no institutional continuity, do not really deserve the title of party at all (Sartori 1976: 254–5). Since such parties are inevitably rather common in new states, where, that is, they are allowed to exist, this presents something of a problem. It is certainly also possible for them to institutionalise over time. Such was the case with the Peronist (or, more properly, Justicialist) Party in Argentina though other equally institutionalised parties, such as those of Venezuela, have since disintegrated.

Competitive systems are the ideal of democratic theorists. However the public display of dissension which democracy requires comes as an unpleasant surprise to those brought up under the enforced stability of a colonial government or traditional regime. It is also true that in many democracies, perhaps the majority, elections are often accompanied by a high level of violence, and sadly more people may be killed in the quarrels that accompany an election than in the course of a military coup. Three-quarters of all military coups in Latin America in the past half-century have resulted in no casualties at all; though the coups in Africa, on the other hand, have cost lives.

The View from the Ground

By *Randeep Ramesh, South Asia correspondent,*
The Guardian, Wednesday, 21 April 2004

Killings Overshadow India's General Election

Violence cast a shadow over the first round of voting in India's general election yesterday with more than a dozen people killed in attacks by Kashmiri separatists and Maoist guerrillas.

More than a quarter of the electorate, about 176 million people, were eligible to vote and early exit polls indicated that the ruling Bharatiya Janata party and its allies would return to power with a slim majority in the 543-member parliament.

There was relative calm in the western state of Gujarat, where two years ago Hindu mobs killed more than 1,000 people, mostly Muslims, in a rampage which lasted weeks. The BJP is expected to sweep the state.

More than 670 million people can vote in four main phases staggered over three weeks partly to allow the deployment of 2 million security officers. During the last election in 1999, 100 people were killed in violence.

As voters went to the polls, militants in Kashmir were blamed for shooting dead a soldier guarding a polling station and for a laying a landmine which blew up when a car carrying journalists and peace activists passed over, killing two. The separatists have called for a boycott of the elections, saying that they legitimise India's occupation of the Himalayan state.

In the north-east, Maoist rebels targeted voters. Twelve people, including a magistrate and police officers, were killed in election-related violence in three north-eastern states.

Voter turnout in the first phase was estimated at 55%, a little less than the historical average. The election, the 14th since independence in 1947, is the first carried out on electronic voting machines in the hope of ending alleged fraud.

The BJP has campaigned on its handling of the economy which grew by 8% last year, and on its peace overtures to Pakistan. This, coupled with India's triumphant Test series in Pakistan, has generated a feel-good factor.

The main opposition party, the Congress party led by Sonia Gandhi, has tried to highlight the plight of the rural poor, who have failed to benefit from economic reforms. In the last six years, the top 20% of India's population has seen consumption rise by a third while farming incomes have remained stagnant.

"The Congress party has failed to develop a long-term political programme for the poor and minorities, which form its core support," said Achin Vanaik of Delhi University.

Both big parties have enlisted Bollywood stars to their campaigns but the most high-profile campaigners have been the young scions of the Gandhi family, Rahul, 34, and his younger sister, Priyanka.

The campaign has also seen the rise of slick media campaigns, especially by the BJP. It has a rapid response unit and has texted political slogans to voters.

The rising costs of elections have worried commentators. The average cost to win a parliamentary seat is estimated at £300,000, about 1,000 times India's per capita income. "The people who can give parties this sort of money will just end up controlling policy," said VP Singh, a former prime minister. "All you have done is mortgaged power before the government is formed."

100m vote, for a start

- India has 670m voters and 700,000 polling stations
- Voting is spread over five separate days, ending on May 10
- There are six national parties, the biggest being the Bharatiya Janata party and the Congress party. There is also a Communist party and one representing the Dalit, or untouchables
- The elections will be completely electronic for the first time, allowing illiterate voters to take part by selecting a party symbol
- This will also save 10,000 tonnes of ballot paper
- An estimated 400m votes will be counted in hours, and the result known on May 13.

Organisation of political parties

'Who says organisation says oligarchy', wrote Robert Michels in 1911, and his observations on the the German Social Democratic Party are equally applicable both to political parties today and to other bureaucratic organisations. Michels's thesis (the 'iron law of oligarchy') was that in any organisation the minority will come to dominate the majority. 'It is organisation which gives birth to the domination of the elected over the electors, of the mandataries over the mandators, of the delegates over the delegators' (Michels 1968: 5).

There are three main reasons for this: the size of the organisation, the value of specialist information and the distance between the leaders and the led. Once an organisation has grown beyond a certain size, a division of labour becomes necessary. This leads in turn to the delegation of power to specialists. As a result, these specialists take on the status of experts. Concentration of expertise leads to the concentration of both power and influence in their hands. The rank and file have not had the necessary training, are not specialists and therefore cannot participate. The size of the organisation also means that participation is limited by the sheer physical distance between the top and the rank and file.

Provisions for the leaders to remain in power include:

(a) superior knowledge because of specialisms, access to files, just being there when decisions are made. Knowledge gives the power to manipulate the organisation and win any debate.
(b) control of the organisational media (journals etc.): views approved by the top are transmitted, others not.
(c) time, which, as highly paid, full-time organisational workers, the leaders have (together with the incentive) to prepare debates, accumulate knowledge etc.
(d) political skill, needed by full-time organisational workers in order to attain power; once in power they develop this skill further and become full-time politicians (Michels 1968; cf. Panebianco 1988).

Rise and fall of the 'one-party state'

However strong the control of the rulers over their own party, they may of course have to face opposition from other, rival parties. Hence, especially in the years immediately following independence, many developing states sought to control internal rivalries by creating what is often loosely called a 'one-party state'. There are in fact three distinct types of 'one party states' or non-competitive party systems:

- no-party systems – systems where no party is allowed;
- single-party systems – systems where only one party is allowed; and
- one-party (dominant) systems – systems where other parties can in principle contest for power but only one wins all or a large majority of electoral contests.

It is arguable that each is clearly separable from competitive multi-party systems, but in very different ways. It is also true that many non-competitive systems were created with genuinely idealistic motives in mind. From the 1960s onwards the idea that only one state-sponsored party was sufficient and indeed desirable was repeatedly justified by developing world leaders on the grounds that it overcame divisions damaging to an emergent nation. Successful examples were Julius Nyerere and his model of Tanzanian socialism in Africa, or Major-General Park Chung Hee who is credited with being the successful moderniser of South Korea. But the fact is that the most popular variety, single-party systems, established essentially authoritarian rule, which in turn paved the way for military intervention, especially but not exclusively in Africa. And against the examples above, we also have to remember the incompetent rule of Milton Obote which led to the catastrophic rule of Idi Amin Dada in Uganda.

The one-party state may be seen as replacing tribal loyalties and identifications in holding together a fragmented society such as that of Zaire (now the Democratic Republic of the Congo). However coalition-building is always vital even under single-party rule or military dictatorship. Opposition elements, such as newspapers or trades unions, may be and frequently are co-opted by government by a not very subtle combination of inducement and threat.

The weakness of authoritarian government is that it rarely meets the aspirations of the population at large. It is true that in both Brazil in South America and South Korea in Asia rapid economic growth was experienced under military government. However, in the former case this growth was accompanied by a widening of the gap between a rich elite and the poor masses, and there are very many cases in which authoritarian rule has wrecked the economy and precipitated crisis – Argentina between 1976 and 1982 and Iran before 1979 are both good examples.

The development boom of the 1970s was accompanied by the growth of grassroots organisations. These were often seen as subversive by developing world governments, and every effort was made to limit their effectiveness. The reason was that they might form the basis for an organised opposition and eventually threaten the power structure itself. However, there were some organisations that could not be eliminated in this way. Under authoritarian rule in Brazil, the Catholic Church came to some extent to fulfil the role of an official opposition. The number and importance of the 'base communities' sponsored by the Church helped legitimate a growing opposition which eventually successfully demanded direct elections for the political authorities.

In modern times political parties are so widespread that it is usually only under a military dictatorship, when they are forbidden to organise, that they are entirely absent. Notorious examples include Chile under General Augusto Pinochet Ugarte after 1973 and Myanmar (Burma) under the SLORC. However, there have been other cases. A noteworthy example was that of Afghanistan after the introduction by the then king of parliamentary government in 1964. Since there were no political parties, candidates ran as individuals and very few eligible voters bothered to turn out. With no basis for organisation, the parliament's proceedings were chaotic. This, as was possibly intended, enabled the king and the court clique to continue to run the country without effective interference, but in the end it helped create the conditions for the Soviet-backed military coup which overthrew the king and his parliament in 1973 (for conditions for coup see Weinbaum 1972).

By contrast, the Shah of Iran in 1963 had sponsored the organisation of one 'official' party, the Rastakhiz (New Iran) Party. Other parties were not banned, but strong pressure was brought to bear on members of the elite to show their loyalty to throne and country by becoming active members of the new organisation (Bill 1972: 44–51). Protected at least to some extent by the complex network of family influence, many did not do so, but initially the new party seemed to be very successful; it was only later that it was shown how far its introduction had broken up the traditional structure of loyalties and so helped focus opposition on to the regime and on the Shah personally.

A variant of the **one-party system** is to be found in Morocco, where officially there are a number of political parties, but it is known which one at any one time enjoys the favour of the king, without which nothing can be done.

The military government of Brazil which seized power in 1964 at first banned political parties altogether; then, rather more subtly, allowed the formation of two, one to govern and the other to act as the official opposition. Disconcertingly, the public realised what was going on and took the obvious course of voting for the opposition instead, forcing concessions from the government.

The ruling party in such cases serves merely to identify the political elite and to enable them to continue to control the political process behind a façade of democracy. The pretence is the more convincing if the government does not formally create a one-party state, and encourages the emergence of an official opposition which it can continue to control. Such states create an illusion of democratic participation while ensuring as far as possible that it does not become a reality. S.E. Finer termed them 'façade democracies' (Finer 1970: 56–7). As shown above, the mere existence of elections and parties does not guarantee that a system will give genuine and effective participation. It is essential to look closely enough to determine how the system works in practice, and especially what other political or social structures exist to control nominally 'democratic' activity.

Between one-party (or one-party dominant) systems and single-party systems the difference in theory is great but in practice there is a 'grey area'. In some states one party can obtain overwhelming dominance of the political system without restraints being placed on opposition parties. Once in power it then becomes very difficult to dislodge.

A striking example, as the opposition has found in recent years, is Mexico. When the Mexican Party of the National Revolution (from 1946 to be known as the Institutional Revolutionary Party – PRI) was founded in 1929, no one was in doubt about its 'official' status. All key interests were required to form part of it and it was financed by a levy on the salaries of state employees. However, other parties did function and in the period after the Second World War there seemed a genuine possibility that the system would evolve into a two-party system such as that of Colombia or Venezuela. But after 1964 it became increasingly clear that every step in that evolution would be strenuously and, on the whole, successfully resisted. It was widely believed that the election of President Carlos Salinas (1988–94) had been procured by fraud and under him the opposition found it virtually impossible to succeed, even at state level. In fact, it was not until May 1995 that an opposition party succeeded in winning the governorship of a key state, Guanajuato. His successor, however, realised that Mexico could no longer afford to ignore the 'Third Wave' of democratisation, and allowed the opposition to win more and more contests, until their candidate, Vicente Fox, won the presidency itself in 2000 with 43.43 per cent of the votes cast. By 2006, the PRI presidential candidate won only 21 per cent of the vote.

India in the years immediately following independence is another obvious example. The Indian National Congress enjoyed its initial hegemony owing both to its leadership of the struggle for Indian independence and the presence of Pakistan as a target for organisational and individual hostility. Nehru himself strengthened this position through the international goodwill and attention India obtained as the result of advocating, on behalf of smaller and less influential countries, a theory of their place in the world which they found congenial. But at home the supremacy of the Congress Party was maintained as the result of its success in monopolising patronage and being able to 'deliver' on its political promises. When excluded groups decided that they were not going to obtain access to patronage through the system, they were able through the democratic process to mount successful regional and ultimately national challenges. Their suspicions were confirmed by the autocratic style of Indira Gandhi and her willingness to use any means, including force, to maintain her leadership of a divided Congress. Still with the assistance of her land reform campaign, the dominant faction, Congress (I), retained sufficient credibility to recover from the disaster of the State of Emergency and its defeat at the polls in 1977. Though the party's hegemony has since been broken following the breach in its dynastic leadership by the assassination of Rajiv Gandhi in 1991, while campaigning for re-election, the example of the Congress Party in India seems to illustrate both the strength of one-party politics, and its most obvious limitations. However in the 2004 elections a Congress-led alliance again became the largest party in Lok Sabha and formed the government under the leadership of Manmohan Singh.

Such one-party systems, on the other hand, are quite different in principle from **single-party systems**, where opposition parties are either banned or persuaded by a variety of means, including if necessary force, to disband themselves. A number of countries in Asia and Africa adopted the single-party model after decolonisation. The nature and structure of the party system in these single-party states cannot be explained by internal factors alone, but must be sought in the wider context of world politics. Their proponents, including Kenyatta in Kenya, Nyerere in Tanzania and, more recently, Mugabe in Zimbabwe, argued that in the aftermath of colonisation the emerging state simply could not 'afford' the 'luxury' of competitive politics, because total control of the economic system was essential for the planning of future development. The trouble was, as events showed, that the silencing of the opposition, far from enhancing efficiency, allowed corruption to become rampant. In an extreme case, Sierra Leone, the existing economic base of the country was virtually destroyed without any compensating advantage for the bulk of the population.

In single-party systems elections are held. In the modern world there is no other universally accepted way of showing that a government is legitimate. But such elections (really plebiscites) merely act to confirm the continuity of a regime. There is no real chance of changing the office-holders. The problem is, of course, that this situation is unstable. The creation of a single party does not end competition for power or office; it merely creates a pretence that it does not exist, while at the same time allowing resentment to build up against the existing office-holders.

Two (and more) party systems do not guarantee rotation in office, but they do make it possible. Theorists of democracy regard the ability of the voters to change their rulers as one of the most important advantages of the system. The amount of harm they can do is limited to their elected term and rival groups are given a turn in managing the affairs of the state. Of course there is a cost. Holding elections is expensive and competitive politics leads to a great deal of money being spent to win votes (though the history of the **spoils system** in the United States and Japan suggests that clientelism in itself is not a barrier to economic or political development). The short time-span of an elected government may nevertheless also operate against long-term development planning. However, opposition builds up over time and giving up political power is better than facing the firing squad.

By comparison, in former Communist states a common feature was that the 'catch-all' opposition parties originally formed to oppose Communism, which formed the first non-Communist government, disintegrated by the second post-Communist election. Under Tudjman Croatia was an exception, and in 2001 had an eccentric arrangement in which the ruling party, with a minority in parliament, had the support of the opposition Conservative Liberals. But with four or five parties the norm, and the ideological distance low, most East European states had developed modified pluralism with coalition government the norm. A complicating factor was that in some cases (Romania, Moldova, etc.) the process liberated ethnic conflicts which have involved significant levels of violence (Kitschelt 1999).

In the developing areas of the Caucasus and Central Asia the former Communist parties, having made sure to retain control of the resources they managed before the transition, were able to restructure themselves into powerful competitive parties and either to hold onto or to regain power (Ishiyama 1999; see also Rose 1998). The term '**nomenklatura** democracies' is now often applied to these systems, the 'nomenklatura' being the term used for the Soviet-era elite.

Was Michels right, therefore? Is it impossible to democratise parties? Clearly Ware was right to argue that establishing procedures which formally cede power to members is insufficient to guarantee that members will be able to influence the selection of leaders and policies (Ware 1987: 173–4).

Primaries, previously almost unknown outside the United States, have also spread to Argentina and Mexico. But although in the United States the effect seems to have been to make it easier for 'outsiders' like Jimmy Carter (1976) and Bill Clinton (1992) to be nominated, it does not of course follow that they will find it easier to win. As for the choice of policies, the Greens in Germany have tried a variety of devices: mandating their representatives, rotating them every two years, forbidding multiple office-holding, encouraging the nomination of women and requiring all elected representatives to pay a proportion of their salary to the party (Ware 1987: 179–82). But rotating representatives and forbidding multiple representation prevented candidates building up a reputation and although such policies gave democratic control to members it was at the cost of making it harder for the party to compete successfully in elections. Parties in developing countries are generally so weak that to weaken them further would deny them any chance of achieving political power. However, as noted above, there are a significant number of countries with semi-competitive party systems in which opposition parties exist but stand little or no chance of gaining power.

Populism and democracy

Populism refers to the way in which leaders generate support by claiming to speak in the name of those who follow them. The term arises from its use by the People's Party of the United States, which achieved some electoral success in the early 1890s for its Omaha Platform, but was eventually swallowed up in the Democratic Party (Hicks 1961). Slightly earlier, a group of intellectuals in Russia had called themselves the *narodniki* – a term usually translated as 'populist'. They, like their very different American counterparts, believed in the proposition that 'virtue resides in the simple people, who are the overwhelming majority, and in their collective traditions' (Wiles 1969: 166).

Populist movements have received particular attention in the Latin American context, where they are associated with the early stages of industrialisation. There a populist movement has been defined as:

> A political movement which enjoys the support of the mass of the working class and/or peasantry, but which does not result from the autonomous organizational power of either of these two sectors. It is also supported by non-working class sectors upholding an anti-status quo ideology. (Di Tella 1965)

Dix (1985) has argued that there are two distinct forms of populism: authoritarian and democratic. For him, the authoritarian form is characterised by leadership from the military, the upper middle class, landowners and industry, support from a 'disposable mass' of urban/unskilled workers, and a short-term, diffuse, nationalist, status-quo-oriented ideological base. The democratic

form is led by professionals and intellectuals, its support comes from organised labour and/or peasants, and its ideological base is more concrete and
reformist, with its nationalism more articulate. Yet in practice populist movements are both democratic and authoritarian in differing degrees.

In Latin American at least, therefore, populism is 'urban, multiclass, electoral, expansive, "popular," and led by charismatic figures' (Conniff 1982:
13). However, as di Tella implies, it is stretching matters even there to suggest
that populism is urban rather than rural, and in practice the term has come to
refer to any movement characterised by three things:

(a) an assertion that the people are always right;
(b) a broad, non-ideological coalition of support;
(c) a charismatic leader, often lacking any specific ideological commitment.

As such it can be found in countries throughout the developing world, such
that Canovan derives from actual examples a typology of no less than seven
types of populism. These, too, are 'ideal types', and actual movements may
well overlap more than one of her categories (Canovan 1981: 13). The importance of them is precisely how clearly they demonstrate both how widespread
populism is and how its main characteristic is its *fluidity*. It was this that provided a vehicle for leaders such as Gamal Abdel Nasser of Egypt, Saddam
Hussein of Iraq and Robert Mugabe of Zimbabwe to mobilise the masses in
support of their governments. The key to their success is the way in which they
identify issues that call forth the maximum response from their chosen con-
stituency (Canovan 1981).

The populist leader, however, speaks on behalf of the masses and seeks to
control them for his or her own purposes. He or she finds out what they want
only to be able to offer it to them. To that extent, therefore, the successful
populist leader takes responsibility off the shoulders of the people, whereas if
they are to participate in a fully democratic society they have to avoid the
temptation to abandon the cares of responsibility to others.

Causes of insurgency

There is a considerable agreement on the main causes of insurgency. There is
much less agreement on which of them is the most important, and opinions
are inevitably polarised between those who think the insurgency is right and
those who believe that it is wrong.

That said, the immediate cause of insurgency is almost invariably a sense
of injustice. From the American and French Revolutions, down to relatively
minor military coups, the key actors seem to have the ability to detect this
sense of injustice and to exploit it. Poverty, which many people would also cite

as a cause of insurgency (see *inter alia* Myrdal 1968; Hayter 1983; Kane 2005) is a cause in that it leads to **relative deprivation**. As Evita Perón said, she was not concerned about being poor until she realised that there were also people who were rich.

There are three important influences which both fuel a sense of injustice and channel resentment into a political form. They are nationalism, religion and ethnicity. Poverty and ignorance open the way for leaders to exploit these issues. Poverty is important because of itself it deprives a person of opportunities, marginalises them in society and often denies them access to education. So poverty fosters ignorance, making available to the populist leader a 'disposable mass' of willing followers. Corruption, nepotism, abuse of power and violations of human rights by governments give the insurgent leader a target on which to focus their resentment.

Nationalism

Nationalism is loyalty and devotion to a 'nation' or ethnic group which places the interests or values of that group above all others and holds that it should rightfully be represented by a state of its own. National sovereignty has become the core value of international relations, as witness the moral indignation which was generated in response to Iraq's conquest of Kuwait in 1990. It is also the main obstacle to the solution of international problems. Yet in a sense at the national level nationalism looks increasingly obsolete, in the face of the developing importance of local action on the one hand and international interaction on the other. Nation-building involves generating a sense of common will and purpose, which in turn leads to a sense of community, identity, solidarity, loyalty etc. Without some kind of common political culture the modern nation state is difficult to sustain. Political culture is part of national identity. Yet it is often fragmented in the developing world because of the way in which people feel a lack of legitimacy after independence. There is a certain moral legitimacy to be obtained from the concept of national security, but the fact that there are no accepted rules is a powerful spur to corruption.

The social upheaval connected with independence can be countered with an open appeal to the historic past, especially if, as in the case of Egypt, Iraq, Ghana or Zimbabwe, that past is more glorious than the present (and perhaps the future). An emotional appeal to shared historical experience becomes a means both to acquire legitimacy and to delegitimise the opposition who become subversive. However, states can also suffer harmful effects from an appeal to territorial nationalism, such as the high cost of arms to defend borders often against non-existent threats. This cost has to be seen both in terms of what other things cannot be bought, such as schools or hospitals, but also the 'lock-in' effect that purchases of modern arms entail in terms of the need to maintain weapons systems, to replace ammunition and to buy spare parts from the foreign suppliers.

The colonial practice of 'indirect rule' left a dual legacy. This practice of indirect rule is often thought to be peculiarly British. It is associated particularly with Lord Lugard, the first Governor of Nigeria in 1914, and was given a theoretical justification by him in his *The Dual Mandate in Tropical Africa* (1922). It was also used by Britain in East Africa, in Malaya and other places. However, it was also employed by the French in Morocco and Indo-China and to an extent by the most successful colonising powers. Its effect was to leave the local elites responsible for the collection of taxes and the maintenance of law and order on a day-to-day basis. This maintained to an extent their standing in their own societies. But in the nature of things it also made them potentially very unpopular (see Crow et al. 1988: 28). Generally, indirect rule seems to have been very effective in undermining any general sense of national identity, by reinforcing a specific sense of identity in separate tribal areas.

Religion and ethnicity

Like nationalism, religion penetrates fragmented societies, binds disparate elements, overlooks present problems and establishes future – and past – orientation. Often it is invoked, as in Iran, to present an ideology opposed to that of the West which would suggest a glorious future when compared with so-called decadent advanced societies in decline.

Religion can be a political tool as a mobiliser of masses, a controller of mass action and an excuse for repression. On the other hand, religion can also form the ideological basis for dissent. Thus in the Catholic Church in Brazil and Central America 'liberation theology' was a response to repression, and its suppression by the Vatican has left room for the extensive penetration of both Brazilian and Central American society by Protestant evangelicals.

Ethnic politics is a powerful force challenging the cohesion of states, and in the developing world the challenge is occurring before the state has stabilised. There are four times as many self-defined ethnic groups as states in the world. As a result, ethnic nationalism is responsible for a variety of national and international tensions, such as the revival of communal tension in India.

Ethnicity is often a form of political identity and where it does not coincide with state boundaries a source of division. Such a coincidence is much less likely to occur in new states established by external intervention. Indeed, as in Nigeria, the establishment of the state itself may threaten ethnicity, and lead to insurgency or even secession.

Ethnicity is not, however, an exclusively developing world problem. There are ethnic divisions in older states too, and as the history of Europe in the twentieth century has shown, at least as much trouble can arise from trying to eliminate ethnic differences as from having to live with them. Everywhere the problem is compounded by the fact that the nation state is under increasingly strong attack both from without (international organisations, TNCs, regional economic groupings, satellite communications, global environmental concerns) and from within (ethnic nationalism).

Common ancestry is one possible basis for ethnic identity. But the anthropological evidence suggests that from earliest times people have used the notion of common ancestry as a convenient legal fiction, and certainly in the huge multi-ethnic states of today it is in the highest degree unlikely that cultural differences reflect real differences. For example, the Tutsi and Hutu of Rwanda and Burundi believe themselves to be different ethnic groups. But there is real doubt now whether their differences simply reflect a class structure in which the Tutsi have traditionally dominated the Hutu (a dominance encouraged by Belgium, the former colonial power). Some other factor or factors, most importantly a common language, often a different religion, perceived economic and/or political grievances, usually come into play to differentiate one 'ethnic' group from another. On the basis of such cultural distinctions is a collective ethnic consciousness then made the trigger for a belief in self-determination which may in turn lead to secessionist demands. The aspects of cultural distinctness emphasised may change according to their utility. Religion divides Sinhalese and Tamils as much as language, but it is language that is stressed by the LTTE in Sri Lanka, reflecting the fact that it was the attempt of Sinhalese politicians to deny Tamils the use of their language that triggered the continuing division between the two peoples. It also enabled the LTTE to claim majority status in some areas, including in their 'ethnic' headcounts Tamil-speaking Muslims, who are generally opposed to the LTTE.

Islamic societies are an exception, as there the principal bond is that of the *ummah*. *Ummah* means community, but specifically the community of believers in Islam. Thus the whole Islamic world is seen as a 'nation', and some Islamists go so far as to interpret this as including non-Muslim minorities (or majorities) in any country that at any time has been ruled by an Islamic government. The tendency to define identity in terms of religion alone has led the Turks in particular to deny the very existence of Kurds as a separate ethnic group, since they, too, are Muslims. Hence they have long resisted a special status for Kurds in neighbouring states, notably Iraq.

Religion is for Muslims the chief source of ethnicity, the means both to mobilise and to contain societies. The consensus on religion stems from the tendency for aspects of Islamic society to be mutually self-supporting. The popular level actions by fundamentalist groups such as the Muslim Brotherhood echo the official level (dogma and law). Moreover, there is an important international dimension to Islamic thought and organisation. There are more than 40 Muslim governments, whose agencies are supportive of Islam, wherever it exists. Muslim leaders have a political role by definition, since Islamic thought makes no distinction between the sacred and the secular.

Case study 7.1   **Sri Lanka**

Three-quarters of Sri Lanka's 17 million population are Sinhalese; about 2 million are Tamils. Tamils place great emphasis on education and seek professional jobs in the public services especially in law and medicine. Independence in 1948 'marked no great watershed in Sri Lankan politics' (Moore 1990) and Sri Lanka remained insulated from world politics for nearly three decades. However, in the meanwhile the disappearance of colonial rule unleashed Tamil success at obtaining jobs and at the same time promoted the rise of Sinhalese resentment and consequent chauvinism. In 1956 Tamil riots followed the decision of S.W.R.D. Bandaranaike's government to make Sinhala the sole national language in place of English. No allowance was made for Tamil, which would have been a problem anyway, but the exclusion of English as well made it difficult for the Tamils to continue to get jobs in the public sector. By the mid-1970s, with Mrs Sirimavo Bandaranaike as prime minister, the Tamils felt the government was deliberately loading the dice against them, especially since at the same time they were continuing with the policy begun by the British in the 1930s of resettling Sinhalese peasants from the south and centre in the north and east.

This was increasing ethnic tensions among Tamils, who were beginning to view all Sinhalese in Tamil-dominated areas, whether incomers or not, as intruders. The result was to encourage demands for a separate Tamil state. The LTTE was formed in 1976. In 1977 an electoral landslide overturned the Bandaranaike government and installed one led by J.R. Jayawardene, who took advantage of his victory to introduce a new constitution with himself as executive President.

In 1983 in a Sinhalese backlash a mob rampaged through the Pettah, the market district of Colombo, and fanned out into the suburbs. They killed more than 2,000 Tamils and more than 200,000 were made homeless. Within a year a dramatic escalation took place in the number of incidents ascribed to the LTTE, and soon the north and east were in a state of open insurgency. The Indian prime minister, Rajiv Gandhi, feared the spread of separatist demands to the south Indian state of Tamil Nadu. In 1987 he and the Sri Lankan government signed an accord which offered some autonomy to Tamils in the north and east in return for a ceasefire. An Indian Peace-Keeping Force (IPKF) was sent to police the agreement.

Two months later the LTTE broke the ceasefire. The Indian presence unleashed the problem of Sinhalese nationalism and Sinhalese left-wing extremists, the JVP, began a campaign of violence intended to stop any concession to the Tamils. The new Sri Lankan president, Ranasinghe Premadasa, negotiated a new ceasefire with the LTTE on condition that the IPKF withdrew and gave the Indian government notice to go. This they did in 1990 (Saravanamuttu 1990). However, 1990 saw also the beginnings of armed attacks on the small minority of Muslims. The LTTE claimed the attacks on the Muslims were a government ploy to blacken the name of the LTTE. The Muslims believed they were the victims of LTTE violence and began retaliatory attacks against Tamil villages.

Then on 21 May 1991 Rajiv Gandhi was assassinated by a suicide bomber at an election rally in Tamil Nadu, one of a series of rallies that had appeared to herald his return to power. The LTTE denied responsibility but the method was absolutely characteristic of the suicide squads of the LTTE known as the 'Black Tigers' and there is much evidence that the bomber was a member of such a squad. The LTTE

Case study 7.1 continued

had virtual control of Batticaloa for a while before the government launched an offensive to recapture it. However in early 2000 in a major offensive the LTTE defeated government forces, captured many heavy weapons and gained control of Elephant Pass, the key to the Jaffna Peninsula, which they clearly aimed to recapture (*The Guardian*, 4 May 2000), although at high cost in casualties the government was able to repel this attack and restore an uneasy stalemate.

Ethnic nationalism is likely to increase in certain specific circumstances: for example where a previously authoritarian state democratises or a formerly democratic one becomes more authoritarian. It is likely to find a sympathetic response given increased international concern for human rights. When it seems likely to work in their favour, emerging regional powers like India may seek to establish cross-border connections between ethnic groups. As Rajiv did not live to find out, they may pay a heavy price for doing so. On the other hand, regimes may manipulate ethnicity to their own ends. Where a leader's ethnic base is larger than that of the opposition he or she may strengthen relations with it when threatened. This is exactly what Premadasa did in Sri Lanka. This served to exacerbate ethnic tensions beyond the capacity of the system to manage them and in 1993 it cost him his life in a suicide bomb attack in Colombo. Unfortunately such passions once aroused are not easy to control.

President Chandrika Kumaratunga, who was elected president in 1994 on a platform of negotiated peace, was unable to achieve it, and though re-elected in 1999 only narrowly escaped death when a woman suicide bomber blew herself up as the president left a mass rally. The attack killed 21 people and injured 110; among the injured was the president herself, who lost the sight of one eye from a shrapnel wound. The LTTE's battle for an independent Tamil state – which no Sri Lankan government could ever concede – was then estimated to have cost 60,000 lives since 1983 (*Keesing's* 43311). A ceasefire was finally agreed in February 2002 and since then negotiations on a possible settlement have continued, but in 2006, following a fresh outbreak of violence, these had broken down.

Personalism

Personalism is a means to bridge the gap between state and society. In practice there is always a tendency for personalistic relations to coexist with a rational-legal framework; Clapham (1982: 48) terms this condition 'neo-patrimonialism'. It is a feature particularly of Latin American polities, but is also found elsewhere. Personalism, therefore, is not just the most spectacular form of charismatic authority. It is closely linked to three related phenomena: patrimonialism, populism and clientelism.

Patrimonialism is the most enduring legacy for new states of the pre-colonial society and comes back into its own at independence. Patrimonialism (or neo-patrimonialism) refers to the use of patronage networks to control a political system involving a lack of distinction between the private possessions of rulers and the states they control. Many would argue that Pakistan, which is a most important example of this phenomenon, came close to becoming the personal fiefdom of the Bhutto family and that politics had degenerated into factional infighting among family members. Certainly much of its social structure remains essentially feudal. Two-thirds of the people still live in rural areas where feudal justice is often arbitrarily dispensed by the local landed aristocracy. Eighty per cent of the country's politicians come from aristocratic families like the Bhuttos themselves and they rely first and foremost on the support of the local people to whom they are patrons.

In Africa indirect rule meant that traditional chiefs were maintained, forming a useful interface between colonial rule and the peasantry. However, they were not maintained unaltered. The colonial government frequently merged, promoted or suppressed chiefdoms. Moreover, they were not cheap to maintain, although since the costs of 'native administration' were borne by the people they helped administer, the full extent of them was not obvious at the time. In Sierra Leone in 1949, for example, no less than 46 per cent of the total cost of administration went in payments to hereditary rulers. Comparative figures for Tanganyika, Northern Nigeria and Western Nigeria show a very similar picture, and in Kano in Northern Nigeria the salary of the Emir alone accounted for 13 per cent of expenditure in 1936–37 (Kilson 1966: 31–32).

Max Weber (Weber 1964: 132, 324ff.) believed that the authority of government originally stemmed from what he termed charisma: that is to say, authority depended on the outstanding personality or personal qualities of an individual. In more developed societies, charisma was 'routinised', or subjected to legal forms and controls. It could be either traditional – accepted because it had always been accepted – or legal-rational, authority resting in an office not the individual who occupies it for a finite period of time. Weber therefore distinguished these three types of authority, charismatic, traditional and legal-rational, from one another, while treating them as 'ideal types' which were not found in pure form.

Charisma refers to the possession by the leader of outstanding personal qualities recognised as such by others and charismatic leadership has often accompanied the emergence of new regimes in the developing world. Thus Mao Zedong was hailed as a prophet, Mustafa Kemal as 'Father of the Turks' (Atatürk), Ho Chi Minh as 'Father of the Indo-Chinese People', Nkrumah as 'the Saviour, Redeemer and Messiah', Ayatollah Khomeini as Imam. Charisma has been sought by those who lack it. Imelda Marcos, wife of the president of the Philippines, likened herself to Eva Perón (Evita) of Argentina, but the real parallel lay in the use of economic rewards for mass political support as an alternative to the generally much more costly use of force (Bresnan 1986).

The idea that political office brings with it the duty, as well as the opportunity, to use patronage on behalf of one's family, friends or tribe, which is termed **clientelism**, is often seen as being the distinctive feature of developing world politics, and is often found in connection with the illegal making of personal gain out of one's office (Clapham 1982). Clientelism can be defined as 'the *exchange between politicians and voters of material private goods for* *votes*. Under clientelism, electoral support is the sole criterion on which politicians give goods to voters' (Brusco et al. 2002). Clientelism depends on establishing a reciprocal relationship between patron and client. Though patronage exists in a mild form in all political systems, here it is fully developed as a means to sustain one's political support base during the time in which the rallying force of nationalism declines and classes have not yet developed to provide the bases for political parties. It may be based on ethnicity, as in the tribal society of West African states, where national leaders may go in for 'pyramid buying', by buying up local leaders who can deliver the necessary support at election times. Its strength depends on the fact that the patron–client bond derives from the notion of responsibility to one's family characteristic of traditional society and so is immediately understood by all parties to a transaction. Its dangers lie in the way in which it lacks the traditional restraints on the individual and as a private relationship is not open to scrutiny by modern state structures. The key features of the patron–client relationship have been defined by John Duncan Powell (1970) as follows:

> First, the patron–client tie develops between two parties unequal in status, wealth, and influence . . . Second, the formation and maintenance of the relationship depends on reciprocity in the exchange of goods and services . . . Third, the development and maintenance of a patron–client relationship rests heavily on face-to-face contact between the two parties.

Because of its unequal nature the patron–client relationship is inherently unstable but in the context of traditional village life the fairly simple network of mutual relationships is well known and fully understood. This tendency to instability increases rapidly in the context of urban immigrants, whose desire for jobs makes them vulnerable to recruitment into a much more complex network where any sense of reciprocal obligation is easily lost. At a national level the network is wide open to exploitation by wealthy landowners and entrepreneurs and by foreign interests. Bill (1972) documents how under the Shah's so-called 'White Revolution' the professional middle class of Iran expanded uncontrollably, generating increasing criticism of the failure of the regime to allow it to grow even faster.

The role of the state in clientelism is also important, if not indeed crucial, for the patron in effect pays off his or her clients with their own money. The state tends to be the largest employer in developing world countries. Hence salaries are generally the state's largest expense. This is most marked in large federal states, such as Brazil, India or Nigeria, where the lower level of regional bureaucracy also has to be maintained. The use of patronage, in the form of appointments to sinecures and posts with **parastatals** (semi-autonomous, quasi-governmental, state-owned enterprises) such as Petrobras in Brazil, forms the means by which the state is enabled to intervene in both urban and rural sectors. But there is nothing in this situation which leads us to believe that the government has any interest in reversing it, nor is there any obvious reason why those who benefit from it in the provinces should wish to do so either.

The View from the Ground

By *Murray Armstrong*, *The Guardian*, Wednesday, 8 June 2005

Window on the World

On July 1 the youngest country in the world, Timor-Leste (what we used to call East Timor) will score a significant first goal in the fight against corruption. That Friday will see its petroleum laws, being finalised this month, come into effect. They will control exploration, development and exploitation of resources and, crucially, the distribution of revenues. That requires transparency. Put simply, everything that is paid is published.

Mari Alkatiri, the country's prime minister, said at a recent meeting in London: "We want to avoid the curse as it has affected many developing nations." The "resource curse" as it has come to be known, is the social decay, the political dictatorship, the financial dishonesty, and the conflict and instability that has visited many poor nations that are rich in raw materials.

"In our three short years since independence," said Alkatiri, "we have developed a reputation for transparency." Consultations on the petroleum laws, which the prime minister envisaged as "a tool that can contribute to the wise management of Timor-Leste's petroleum resources, to the benefit of current and future generations", took place in public and were broadcast on radio and television. The teams visited remote parts of the country and talked to village leaders.

All gas and oil revenue will now go into a fund dedicated to social and economic development. This wealth, according to Alkatiri, is "for human development and the elimination of poverty". That development is defined by law, and government withdrawals from the fund can only be made with the permission of parliament. Revenues and taxes coming from major corporations will be an open book and a code of conduct for public officials has been established with legal powers to examine unexplained personal assets.

Transparency in Timor-Leste came about partly because of an organisation put together by the British government. While its name does not easily roll off the tongue, the Extractive Industries Transparency Initiative (EITI) has achieved some significant successes since it was launched by Tony Blair at the 2002 Johannesburg earth summit.

Ten countries are now at different stages in implementing the principles and methods devised by the body and another 11 have endorsed the programme and are preparing to adopt the criteria.

The government of Azerbaijan signed a memo of understanding with energy companies and local non-governmental organisations last November, and in March published an independent auditor's report detailing payments made by oil companies and receipts by the government.

Kyrgyzstan was the first country to publish information in the form recommended by EITI when it detailed revenue from the gold mining industry in October last year.

In Nigeria, for years near the top of the world corruption league, President Olusegun Obasanjo has directed all government departments and oil companies operating in the country to give full cooperation with the transparency auditors and, to show he means business, has provided security guards for the team. Their first task is to reconstruct a picture of all payments paid and received in the last five years and to report monthly to a working group composed of government, industry and NGOs.

Nasir Ahmad El-Rufai, federal minister in the Nigerian government, said at the London conference hosted by Hilary Benn, minister for international development, that the audits taking place will be physical as well as financial, to identify and tackle theft of crude oil from pipelines and illegal bunkering. "The poor governance of our relatively substantial cumulative earnings from oil – about $300 bn (£165 bn) – in the last four decades has had the most devastating impact on our national growth, development, and therefore quality of life of our large population of about 150 million," he said.

But he warned that the "oyster of the corrupt" is still flourishing and pointed to the "glaringly worrying silence" about the "large scale thievery from public treasuries" by previous government officials who still have "comfortable housing within the territories of several G8 countries, all of whom are subscribers to the EITI principles." Repatriation of these monies, he said, "should be an important aspect [of policy] by the government of the UK in its current leadership of both the G8, the EU and its specific Commission for Africa initiative".

These moves have been welcomed by NGOs such as Transparency International (TI), whose chairman Peter Eigen said: "It would be good if developed nations were to set an example in all of this instead of merely requiring it of poorer countries. Moreover, TI would like to see the principles and process reinforced and further empowered by a UN General Assembly resolution."

This is echoed by the Publish What You Pay Coalition, a group of 270 worldwide NGOs, which has called on the Gleneagles summit to "send out a clear political message supporting revenue transparency efforts around the world". Mike

Aaronson, director general of Save the Children, also sees Gleneagles as being the place where the G8 countries could set the standard for global reporting. "It would help if it was a mandatory requirement in the rich countries to oblige companies to disclose all payments," he says.

The tragedies of corruption are continuing. A recent report from Global Witness showed $1.1 bn missing from Kazakhstan, with an American merchant banker, James Giffen, still awaiting trial in New York, accused of taking kickbacks worth $78 m; missing money in the Republic of Congo is currently running at about $250 m a year; $1.7 bn has been salted away somewhere by officials in Angola; Equatorial Guinea's treasury is missing $500 m; and in the tiny island of Nauru, halfway between Hawaii and Australia, the entire Nauru Phosphate Royalties Trust, worth more than $1.4 bn, is unaccounted for.

"Every time that Nigeria spends eight times the amount it spends on health annually to service its huge external debt," said El-Rufai, "the world fails that poor child in rural Nigeria, rather than our powerful elite and their international partners, who borrowed, stole or wasted the money in the first place."

On side

Countries implementing some or all of the EITI guidelines:
Azerbaijan, Republic of Congo, Ghana, Kyrgyz Republic, Nigeria, Sao Tome and Principe, Timor-Leste, Trinidad & Tobago

Countries that have endorsed the principles:
Angola, Bolivia, Cameroon, Chad, Democratic Republic of Congo, Equatorial Guinea, Gabon, Guinea, Niger, Peru, Sierra Leone

Corruption

Corruption is the misuse of public office for private gain. Gathering accurate information on corruption is, of course, an impossible task. Even the definition of corruption is problematic. However, the boundary is crossed when payment or reward is made directly to government officials to secure a service of some kind. A distinction can be made between payment to expedite a service to which one is entitled anyway, and payment to secure a service to which one is not entitled. But in practice both are properly regarded as corrupt. As Williams points out, there is a moral, as well as a political meaning to the term corruption. It is 'used . . . to describe a morally repugnant state of affairs and implicit in its use is the desire to eliminate it' (Williams 1987: 13; see also Wraith and Simpkins 1965; Heidenheimer 1970).

The most widely used definition of corruption in public office, that of Joseph Nye, describes it as:

> behavior which deviates from the formal duties of a public role, because of private-regarding (personal, close family, private clique) pecuniary or status gains; or violates rules against the exercise of certain types of private-regarding influence. This includes such behavior as bribery (use of a reward to pervert the judgement of a person in a position of trust); nepotism (bestowal of patronage by reason of ascriptive relationship rather than merit); and misappropriation (illegal appropriation of public resources for private-regarding uses). (Nye 1967: 419)

The dangers of corruption are highest where the divisions between public and private are blurred. 'The morally corrupt society is one where moral life has, so to speak, been privatised' (Dobel 1978). The persistence of traditional culture, where the structure of government is based on reciprocal gift-giving, may contribute to a culture of corruption. Similarly nepotism, the employment of or granting of favours to relatives, is often the logical extension of extended kinship networks. The low salaries paid in the lower echelons of bloated bureaucracies of states such as India, Nigeria and Mexico, and the fact that in all societies status is measured by the conspicuous display of wealth, contribute too.

It is impossible to tell just how much corruption costs developing world countries. However, estimates suggest that corruption in Italy accounts for some 15 per cent of gross national product, and it is likely that the rates for developing world states are much higher (see Table 7.2).

Certainly it is inevitable that under a clientelistic system there will be no hard and fast distinction between public and private and corruption will be endemic. What seems clear is that the effects of clientelism are much more serious in authoritarian or one-party states than they are in competitive systems. Although it is probably impossible to eliminate corruption entirely, the threat of public scrutiny establishes an effective brake on the more outrageous forms. Small-scale corruption may be relatively harmless, indeed it may be redistributive. But on a large scale it can literally undermine the foundations of society. A hospital and other modern buildings collapsed during the Mexican earthquake of 1986 when traditional buildings dating back to the colonial period survived. The ruins disclosed the extent to which the theft of cement and reinforcing bars during construction had compromised the stability of the modern buildings.

Accusations of corruption have long been standard practice in Latin American elections, but in recent years governments have started to take legal action against particularly flagrant examples. In Venezuela, the second term of Carlos Andrés Pérez was brought to a close by his impeachment, followed by his trial on corruption charges. More recently, President Collor of Brazil, on the eve of presiding over the Earth Summit at Rio, was accused of corruption by his own brother and subsequently resigned in December 1992 under the imminent threat of impeachment. In December 1994, however, he was cleared by the nation's Supreme Court, though not without criticism of the authorities for having failed to prepare their case properly. And in 1996 Colombia's Chamber of Deputies, many members of which themselves faced corruption charges, voted by 111 votes to 43 to acquit President Ernesto Samper of all changes of knowingly accepting funds from drug traffickers. This decision not only ended impeachment proceedings but ensured that the charges could not be reopened.

In Africa, long spells of military rule have made Nigeria notorious – possibly unfairly – for the depth and breadth of public corruption. 'By the mid-1970s, the corruption associated with the Gowon regime, if not with General Gowon himself, had reached amazing proportions and events like the Cement Scandal . . . confirmed popular impressions that the riches of the oil economy were being siphoned off by a parasitic elite at an alarming rate' (Williams 1987: 98). The problem was that it did not end with the return of civilian government and the end of the oil boom. Corruption was a feature of both the 1979 and 1983 elections, and within weeks of the latter the military were back in power, alleging that the main reason for them ignoring the result and seizing power was the corruption of the Shagari government.

However, there have also been important efforts to curb corruption made both in Nigeria and in other West African states, starting with the Forster Commission in Sierra Leone in 1968 (Sierra Leone National Reformation Council 1968). For the external dimension cannot be overlooked. The ready availability of unimaginably large sums of money, whether from drug traffickers or from foreign corporations, has undoubtedly been a major factor in promoting corruption among the ruling elites of the developing world (Adams 1991).

Table 7.2   World's most corrupt countries, 2005

Rank	Country
1.	Bangladesh
2.	Chad
3.	Haiti
4.	Myanmar
5.	Turkmenistan
6.	Côte d'Ivoire
7.	Equatorial Guinea
8.	Nigeria
9.	Angola
10.	Democratic Republic of the Congo

Note: The Transparency International Corruption Perceptions Index defines corruption as the abuse of public office for private gain, and measures the degree to which corruption is perceived to exist among a country's public officials and politicians
Source: Transparency International, 2005, www.transparency.org

Conclusion

An additional problem of administration in many developing countries is the scale of the bureaucracy and the extent to which it diverges from the 'ideal type' described by Weber and embodied in legislative form by the Northcote-Trevelyan reforms to the civil service in the UK. In a clientelistic system it is unlikely that personnel will be recruited on merit alone, and pay and promotion alike are dependent on the favour of the ruling elite. Few civil servants have been able to separate themselves convincingly from the political arena. Paradoxically, this situation has been worsened by the attempts of military regimes in countries such as Pakistan and Nigeria to use civil servants in the formation of allegedly 'non-political' governments. In addition, the contempt that military officers tend to have for the police reduces their status and pay, favouring a pervasive culture of low-level corruption in the enforcement of law and order, while in Mexico, as in many other developing world countries, the traffic police enhance their standard of living by arbitrary use of their power to obtain bribes from well-off motorists (*The Guardian*, 22 May 1995).

Certainly the nature and structure of the party system in the single-party states of Africa, Asia and Latin America after 1960 cannot be explained by internal factors alone, but must be sought in the wider context of world politics.

A developing state's external connections also feed corruption through the demonstration effect, through the payment of bribes by foreign companies or their agents and through their support of regimes known to be corrupt.

Key terms

assembly – representative body which makes laws (rules) in a political system

associational – interest groups formed by voluntary association

clientelism – asymmetric relationship that links patrons and clients together in a system in which jobs, favours and protection are exchanged for work, loyalty and political support

constitution – a document setting out the basic rules of government

corruption – the misuse of public office for private gain

division of powers – in federal states, the allocation of powers to the states and to the central government respectively

ethnicity – socially perceived differences in national origin, language, and/or religion

executive – branch of government responsible for making decisions

executive presidency – president who is both head of state and head of government (chief executive officer)

faction – clique within larger body seeking to influence it from within; lacking permanent form and membership

federal government – a form of liberal democracy characterised by the division of powers between a central government and a number of 'state' governments

head of government – chief executive officer of a state, exercising political power

head of state – individual who represents the state symbolically but does not necessarily hold political power

interest aggregation – combination of political demands into policy initiatives

interest articulation – formulation of political demands

interest group – group within society whose members have a number of interests in common

liberal democracies – states in which government is limited in its powers by a written constitution, a system of law and/or an independent judiciary and is responsive to the popular will as expressed through elections

nation – people united by possession of a common language, religion and/or culture

nationalism – devotion to a 'nation' or ethnic group which places the interests or values of that group above all others and holds that it should rightfully be represented by a state of its own

nomenklatura – term used for the Soviet-era elite in Eastern Europe and Central Asia

non-associational – interest groups resulting from hereditary divisions

one-party system – system in which, though other parties are not banned, one party monopolises all resources

parastatal – semi-autonomous, quasi-governmental, state-owned company

parliamentary systems – systems characterised by the accountability of the executive to the assembly

patrimonialism – the use of patronage networks to control a political system involving a lack of distinction between the private possessions of rulers and the states they control

personalism – the dominance of a charismatic personality in the political life of a state encouraged as a means of controlling it

populism – the way in which leaders generate support by claiming to speak in the name of those they follow; for Di Tella a political movement which enjoys the support of the mass of the working class and/or peasantry, but which does not result from the autonomous organisational power of either of those two sectors

presidential system – system in which there is a separation of powers between executive and legislature, the executive power being vested in a president elected for a fixed term

public policy – whatever a government chooses to do, including actions and inaction, decisions and non-decisions

relative deprivation – feelings or measures of economic or social deprivation as compared with the well-to-do

single-party systems – where opposition parties are either banned or persuaded to disband themselves

society – a group of human beings distinguishable from other groups by mutual interests, characteristic relationships, shared institutions and a common culture

spoils system – the practice of rewarding loyal supporters of the winning party by appointing them to public offices – 'to the victors belong the spoils' (US Senator William L. Marcy)

state – an organised political community occupying a definite territory, having an organized government, and possessing internal and external sovereignty

Third Wave – of democratsation: term given by Samuel P. Huntington to the democratisation of states throughout the world since 1975

Questions

1. What do we mean by 'the problem of the weak state'?

2. Account for the persistence of personalism, patrimonialism and corruption in developing countries.

3. What are the links between insurgency/intervention and relative economic disadvantage?

4. What has been the impact of 'Third Wave' democratisation in the developing world? What special problems has it encountered?

5. What are the causes of nationalism? Is it just a natural response to globalisation?

CHAPTER 8

Dictatorship and democratisation

Introduction

The absence of military forces, or, alternatively, their weakness, is a major factor in safeguarding democracy, so we can expect this also to be a requirement for forming democratic government in the first place. Other reasons for the survival (or otherwise) of democracy can be grouped as political, economic and social. Among the political reasons are: the existence of a widely-accepted constitution for government, the ability of major interest groups to influence decision-making and the emergence of broadly-based and well-organised political parties. Among the social reasons are ethnic harmony, a reasonably equitable distribution of economic resources and a sufficient level of prosperity for interest groups to feel that they have more to gain from democratic debate than from the use of force.

There are nearly 200 countries in the world but only three (Costa Rica, Iceland and Luxembourg) have no military forces. In general, where there are military forces there will be military intervention, though usually of a limited kind. Even in the AICs, where armed military intervention is a rarity, the armed forces are a major spending department of government and with the advantage of inside knowledge constitute a most formidable lobby in defence of their privileges and their budget, although this is not usually regarded as intervention. For that the armed forces have to show that they are ready and willing to make use of their unique resource, the ability to use force (Finer 1975; see also Luckham 1971b).

And in developing states armies are of very great importance indeed. During the 1980s they not only assumed and/or retained political power throughout the developing world, they spent at the same time an ever-increasing proportion of their countries' wealth on arms. The consequence was arrested development and (in some places) accelerated environmental degradation. Spending on arms in the developing world has again begun to increase in the early years of the twenty-first century.

Authoritarianism

As with corruption, the prevalence of authoritarianism is greater where legitimacy is less well developed. **Authoritarianism** is the belief in the principle of authority as opposed to that of individual freedom. In its most developed form this becomes advocacy of orderly government under military or other dictatorship. Although quite independent of it, it is therefore closely related to **militarism** – excessive pride in the glory, honour, power and prestige of the military forces.

With the rapid decolonisation of the 1960s came disillusion with the allegedly slow processes of democracy, and this in turn led to a wave of military coups in Africa and Asia. In a key study Linz identified the new authoritarian states as:

> political systems with limited, not responsible, political pluralism; without elaborate and guiding ideology (but with distinctive mentalities); without intensive nor extensive political mobilization (except at some point in their development); and in which a leader (or occasionally a small group) exercises power within formally ill-defined limits but actually quite predictable ones. (Linz 1970: 255)

On the basis of Linz's definition it is possible to distinguish as he does between new and old authoritarian regimes. The longer established an authoritarian regime is, the less it needs to rely on the overt use of force and the more it tends to develop new forms of legitimacy. However, for Linz authoritarian government is always a transitional state, either towards democracy or towards totalitarianism.

In addition, Sahlin (1977) suggests, it is also useful to distinguish between protective authoritarianism and **promotional authoritarianism**. Protective authoritarianism is the argument of those who intervene by force simply to protect the status quo and the position of those who benefit from it. After a traditional military coup, which has only the limited aim of displacing the existing government, a period of emergency rule normally follows in which the armed forces emphasise the power available to them, their limited ambitions in making use of it, and their intention to return the country to civilian rule as soon as possible. Some regimes of this type, for example that of Stroessner's Paraguay, do survive for a long period and, Sahlin notes, become 'old' authoritarian regimes in Linz's terms, gaining a degree of legitimacy through force of habit, and, generally, needing to depend less on the overt use of force. However, their principal aims remain the same: the depoliticisation of issues and the demobilisation of the masses.

Promotional authoritarianism, by contrast, is characterised by a desire to promote change, by supplanting the existing government and establishing one which will stay in power for a period of years to pursue certain stated aims. Chief among these aims is economic development, the desire for which is in itself rooted in a nationalistic belief in the value of a strong state. But this requires a certain degree of mobilisation of the masses in the interests of productivity and this can most safely be achieved by appealing to nationalism. However, even this does not resolve, but only postpones, a fundamental conflict between the desire for economic mobilisation and the fear of political mobilisation (Calvert 1994).

Coercive structures

The tendency towards authoritarianism is promoted by the crisis of legitimacy that follows independence or any other serious challenge to the continuity of the state. However, it is often in part able to rely on the tradition of paternalism. The masses, generally lacking education, especially in comparison with the elite, are not seen as being really fit for self-government. Any tendency to revolt is merely seen as confirmation that this judgement is correct. At the same time in the aftermath of a major crisis, such as independence invariably entails, the **fear of freedom** (Fromm 1942) drives many members of the public to seek refuge in the leadership of a single supposedly wise figure who represents both authority and stability. Where the leader is democratically elected with exceptional powers the result is what has been called 'delegative democracy' (O'Donnell 1994).

Long-serving autocrats with tame military support are noticeably less common now than they were 20 years ago and the move away from military government which began in Latin America in the late-1970s (O'Brien and Cammack 1985) gathered pace and has now affected almost every part of the world from Haiti to China. Twenty years ago most developing world states were characterised by military governments, personalist dictatorships or one-party rule – or a combination of these. In Asia in 2006 Thailand, South Korea, Bangladesh and Indonesia no longer have personalist or military governments. Mongolia and some of the Central Asian Republics of the former USSR have adopted democratic forms.

However authoritarian rule does remain in Myanmar (Burma) where Aung San Suu Kyi in 2005 remained under house arrest for the tenth consecutive year, despite the fact that as leader of the opposition she successfully won a democratic election organised by the military regime which is still holding her captive. Also, in October 1999 General Pervaiz Musharraf, seemingly reluctantly, assumed power in Pakistan when the Nawaz Sharif government collapsed. In 2001 he appointed himself president, a title confirmed by referendum in 2002, which gave him 97.97 per cent of the votes cast. King Gyanendra of Nepal suspended constitutional government and claimed to be winning the long-running war against Maoist rebels, but in 2006 has been forced to back down and yield his powers in the face of widespread popular anger.

China itself may look increasingly capitalist, but remains authoritarian, as are most of the states in the Middle East, notably Libya, Syria and Saudi Arabia. In Africa 25 out of 41 states have held competitive elections in the five years 2000–05, and all Latin American and Caribbean states have governments chosen by competitive election, though in Cuba's case the competition is severely restricted.

In liberal democracies, violence in society is controlled through the use of the **legal system**, but even there behind the legitimate authority of the government lies a very wide range of powers to control and to coerce, all backed by the sanction of force (see *inter alia* Hewitt 1992; Hillyard and Percy-Smith 1988). In the developing world, as in the AICs, most governments have at their disposal a substantial army, an extensive police system, and some kind of paramilitary reserve or militia that can be called upon in emergencies. However, since they tend to identify their own survival with that of the state they rule, they are much more likely to make open use of them.

The maintenance of a stable government is the fundamental assurance of the political control of a ruling elite. Losing control of government means at the least that their power will be severely curtailed, at most that it will be lost for good. But maintenance of a government is only part of political control, since it can only operate effectively if the system of relationships around it is maintained also, which is done by the use of both rewards and punishments. Rewards are available both for members and would-be members of the elite, and no less significantly for potentially useful people who might otherwise be political opponents, who may be co-opted into the system. As well as **co-optation (co-option)**, rewards include promotion, pensions and honours. Punishments include demotion, dismissal, fines, banishment, imprisonment and even execution. In Ghana, Jerry Rawlings had three of his predecessors – Generals Afrifa, Acheampong and Akuffo – shot during his first brief term in office, but even military-based governments seldom go quite so far.

Authority is never absolute or unlimited. To have authority is to have the accepted right to give orders or make decisions and to be obeyed. Authority can be and is routinely delegated, divided or shared; otherwise complex governments could not work. Hence a government in all but the very smallest states has to depend on the willingness of others to implement its orders. The fact that they do so depends less on a specific act of recognition or legitimacy than on the fact that, on their own, few people regard themselves as having any alternative but to obey. All Max Weber's forms of authority, therefore, result in the same thing, obedience (Weber 1965: 324–5). The collective habit of obedience gives a tendency to inertia in social systems; once established, they will tend to continue unaltered until a cultural shift occurs and society has forgotten any need for them. By extension, the longer a social institution continues in existence, the longer it is likely to continue.

Conquest formed the basis of colonial rule. In post-colonial states, paradoxically, despite their rejection of colonialism, governments claim their authority by virtue of being successors to the colonial power, notably in Nigeria and Ghana, where force has been used again and again since independence to install a series of military governments. In consequence, for many people in the developing world **internal colonisation** has simply replaced the traditional external variety. 'Internal colonisation' is a term that has been used occasionally by Marxist writers but not with a very consistent meaning. Here it is used in a very specific sense, to draw attention to the fact that large parts of many developing world states are still in effect colonised by their own ruling elite (Calvert 2001; see also below).

This process has serious consequences, since this elite is generally one of town-dwellers who tend both to fear and dislike the countryside and to seek their entertainment in what passes for an urban environment, or abroad in Paris or Las Vegas. The view from the capital involves the colonisation of the countryside by the town. The logical extension of the desire to control is the urbanisation of the countryside, reducing it to orderly controllable form. The effect of this is the rapid destruction of rural habitat and ecosystems, which has reached an extreme as in the area surrounding Manila in the Philippines. Hence it is this urban perspective which contributes to the environmental crisis of the developing world (see Chapter 9).

Military intervention

Despite the spread of democracy, many developing countries still possess armed forces which have both the disposition and the opportunity to intervene in politics. The armed forces possess many advantages relative to civilians and their potential for assuming political power should not be overlooked. Finer (1975) regards military intervention, in the more active sense usually implied by the term, as being the product of both the ability and the disposition to intervene. Virtually all armies, however, have the ability to intervene; the question is why and how they choose to do so.

Military intervention in politics in developing states results both from push factors (propensity/disposition to intervene) and pull factors (stimulation/provocation). Both may be needed to trigger an actual intervention, as for example when the breakdown of legitimate civilian government is accompanied by changes in the military institution.

Push factors for military intervention include the ambitions of individual officers, factional disaffection and institutional activity said or believed to be in the 'national interest'. Pull factors include the association of the armed forces with military victories, a general perception of a lack of cohesion, discipline or stability in society, and a specific perception by the armed forces of threats to the military institution or to the officer class, or to the dignity or security of the nation.

The ambitions of individual officers undoubtedly do play a part in military coups. However, their idiosyncratic nature makes it plain that they cannot of themselves be regarded as a general cause of coups. Some individual leaders, such as General Sani Abacha in Nigeria in 1993, have seized power in their own names. But, on the other hand, some coups have resulted in the choice as leader of personnel who did not take part at all in the coup itself. Examples from Africa are the choice by his fellow officers of Captain Valentine Strasser as head of state of Sierra Leone in April 1992 and the release of Major Johnny Paul Koroma from prison to head the junta which seized power in Sierra Leone in May 1997 (*Annual Register*, 1992, 1997; see also Wiking 1983: 134–5).

Factional disaffection is a serious problem when poorer developing world states are unable or unwilling to reward their armed forces at the level they have come to expect. The former was clearly the case in the mutiny of ordinary soldiers led by Master Sgt. Doe which overthrew and killed the President of Liberia in 1980, and the latter in the fall of Busia in Ghana in 1972. Both are exemplified by the episode in January 1994 in Lesotho when the capital Maseru was shelled by opposing army factions ostensibly seeking OAU mediation of a pay dispute. Behind this claim, however, lay the fear of both factions that they would lose both power and perquisites following the landslide defeat in Lesotho's first free elections of the military-supported Basotho National Party, which had ruled since 1966. On the other hand in an army mutiny in June 1998, President Viera of Guinea-Bissau received support from both Senegal and Guinea.

Institutional activity, the most important of these factors, rests on military ethos, socialisation of officers, the social standing of the military in developing world states and the organisational strengths of the military relative to other institutions. The armed forces intervened in Ghana in 1966 to put an end to the government of President Nkrumah which they regarded as 'interfering' with the army (Austin 1978: 51; Afrifa 1966).

The contagion theory of military intervention, that coups in neighbouring states contribute to the will to intervene, and the habituation theory, that coups are fostered by the tradition of past coups by the same military institution, are also aspects of military explanations. However though neither is necessarily simply military, and the latter in particular obviously reflects the weak legitimacy accorded to civilian institutions, both are supported by statistics which show clearly that coups tend to be particularly common in certain countries and do seem to be imitated within regions (Brier and Calvert 1975).

In a number of military takeovers external influence and encouragement can be inferred, though rarely proved. As Ruth First pointed out, even if foreign influence did play a part in African coups in the 1960s, internal factors were also at work and were at least equally important (First 1972: 17; see also Decalo 1976).

However, despite the argument of Samuel P. Huntington that military aid and assistance has no political effect (Huntington 1968: 192) the wave of military coups that occurred in Africa in the 1960s did receive significant foreign encouragement both before and after the event by the way in which foreign powers, especially the United States and France, provided support for military governments, military aid and training missions. Britain, too, welcomed the fall of Milton Obote, whose aircraft had been unaccountably delayed in returning to Uganda, enabling Idi Amin to seize power in his absence (Wiking 1983: 28). At the same time, post-1961 counter-insurgency training by the United States both in the United States itself and in the School of the Americas in Panama promoted the development of a virulent anti-Communism and the 'national security ideology' among the armed forces of Latin America. The latter was later summed up by the Argentine General (later President) Leopoldo Galtieri in the phrase, 'The Third World War is one of ideology against ideology', and it was to lead in that country to the atrocities of the 'dirty war'.

Civilian explanations rest on pull factors such as the weakness of civilian institutions, participation overload, lack of political legitimacy and economic instability.

The first three of these undoubtedly played a part in shaping the military assumptions of power in both Africa and Latin America during the 1960s. However, Jenkins and Kposowa (1992) found that the African military coups they studied had their roots in military centrality and ethnic competition not in participation overload or economic dependency causing social unrest. In Latin America, following encouragement from the Carter Administration in the United States, civilian institutions successfully reasserted themselves during the 1980s.

The economic failure of a civilian government affects the armed forces both directly, by leaving less money for them, and indirectly, by alienating popular support for the government (Nordlinger 1977). The impact of economic instability on the social groups of which officers are members, rather than on the military institution itself, may be important in encouraging them to take action. True, economic failure is seldom cited as a major reason for a military coup, and more often than not it has been given as a reason for the replacement of one military government by another (Wiking 1983: 116). However, the fall of Jamail Mahuad Witt in Ecuador in January 2000 did follow many months of unrest and rioting at the economic failure of his government.

Sometimes the military assumption of power results from a civilian government shooting itself, metaphorically speaking, in the foot. The *autogolpe*, or 'self-coup', led by an elected leader against his own government, continues to be a problem in Latin America. Even President Fujimori of Peru referred to his illegal assumption of additional powers in 1992 as an *autogolpe*. President Itamar Franco was still being urged to close Brazil's Congress in January 1994, but he wisely resisted the temptation to try to do so and the presidential elections scheduled for later in the year went ahead as planned.

The 'war on terror' has given a once-in-a lifetime opportunity to would-be dictators and leaders of the armed forces in the developing world to re-establish their dominant position in their native countries with the aid of the United States.

Structure and roles of armed forces

Obviously the military role in the politics of any given country does depend crucially on the nature and origins of the armed forces themselves, and their relationship to the society in which they serve. In Nigeria, for example, the military takeover of 1966 owed much to the persistence of tribal consciousness in the army, among the northerners who felt excluded by the commercially active and politically dominant Igbo (Ibo). The first coup, in January 1966, was directed not only against the civilian government but also the military leadership of Maj. Gen. Ironsi. The killing of senior officers that accompanied it significantly altered the composition of the officer corps, leaving Ibo officers holding nearly every senior position. The second coup, in April 1966, led to a massacre of both Ibo soldiers and civilians (Luckham 1971a: 76).

The coup which killed President William R. Tolbert in Liberia in 1980 was born of resentment. The dominant tribe of the interior, the Vai, resented their exclusion from power by the True Whig Party and Americanised settlers on the coast. Tolbert's predecessor, William V.S. Tubman (1944–71), had encouraged economic modernisation and enfranchised both male and female native Liberians. But he retained control through fraud and Master Sgt. Samuel Doe, who led the coup against Tolbert, came from a minority rural tribe in the interior, the Krahn. Many of Tolbert's government were summarily killed and a military dictatorship established, which received the active support of the Reagan Administration in the United States. Doe's favouritism to the Krahn led in 1990 to his downfall and to his execution at the hands of the insurgents.

However, it does not follow that the military act only as the armed wing of a tribe, or indeed of a class. Even weak developing world armies are highly organised and hierarchically-structured organisations, and the profound importance of the army as an institution to soldiers should never be underestimated. This is compounded by the fact that the majority of armies are dominated by a relatively small, professionally-trained officer corps (Howard 1957). Its recruits are in terms of their respective societies largely middle class. Though in a number of African states they tend overwhelmingly to be drawn from a single tribe or region this is not always the case, and in any case once recruited and trained they are bound together by important institutional ties. It is through the service as an institution, moreover, that they obtain their access to a system of substantial personal privileges, such as pensions, mortgages, credit, cheap goods, clubs and free medical attention. Most importantly, it is membership of the institution that guarantees at one and the same time a high standard of living relative to that of the societies they are supposed to serve, and also the opportunity through promotion to gain access to much greater rewards in various government positions.

Military intervention in politics is guaranteed by the need to maintain this institutional structure in the face of competing civilian interests. Its persistence is due to the complex interrelationship between the three levels of the social, institutional and personal interest of the intervenors, such that no one of them can be singled out as the cause, nor wholly disentangled from the others (Calvert 1990a: 42–4).

Competing roles of armed forces: military, social, political

The principal role of the armed forces is, of course, to fight the armed forces of other countries. However, for a variety of reasons this role is relatively unlikely to be dominant in many developing world states. In Latin America distance, formidable natural barriers and relatively small armies have helped prevent all but a handful of major conflicts. In Africa at decolonisation armies were often no more than token forces. The decision of the OAU to respect colonial boundaries meant that despite a very considerable build-up of potential trouble, actual conflicts have been few. In both cases the majority of armed forces are too small and too dependent on supplies from abroad to present serious resistance to the armed forces of a major power. However, as noted above, the 1980s saw a very rapid arms build-up in developing world states, especially in SSA.

In South Asia, on the other hand, the long-standing feud between India and Pakistan has resulted in four wars since 1947, and the loss by Pakistan, not only of parts of Kashmir but, more seriously, the whole of Pakistan's former eastern part, now Bangladesh. The Soviet Union invaded Afghanistan in 1979 but was unable to defeat its ill-organised, tribal armies. China's army has mounted a punitive expedition against Vietnam and its navy disputes with both Vietnam and the Philippines the sovereignty of the Spratly Islands. Significantly in each of these cases the armed forces seem for the most part to be highly professional and to have been brought in recent years under civilian control. Only in south-west Asia do large fighting forces operate under the command of authoritarian military governments, notably those of Syria and (until recently) Iraq.

Governments may also be challenged from within, by insurgent movements. In Latin America, such challenges have been a major reason (some would say excuse) why armies have intervened in politics. The wave of military coups that began in 1961 initially formed a limited response to the Cuban Revolution and to local circumstances (Lieuwen 1964). By 1965 the challenge of guerrilla-type movements had been effectively contained, and the attempt by some movements to switch their tactics into what was loosely and incorrectly termed 'urban guerrilla warfare' was to prove equally unsuccessful. Part of the reason was the intrinsic weakness of the movements themselves, criticised by Gérard Chaliand:

> A certain number of other sociological traits common to most Latin American societies also need to be mentioned. While these would be secondary in a major war, with the revolution held together by a central revolutionary ideology, these traits weigh against successful action in other circumstances: verbal inflation,

accompanied by a slight ability to keep secrets; lack of group cohesiveness, worsened by an obsession with authority (what Latin American in charge of a dozen others resists proclaiming himself *comandante*?); machismo and fascination with death (largely products of the Hispanic tradition). (Chaliand 1977: 48–9)

However, it was perhaps inevitable that Latin American armies, encouraged by fresh supplies of arms from the United States, should have taken the credit for defeating subversion. Hence, during the transition from the first to the second phase of the insurgency, in the mid-1960s the doctrine took root that the only way to cope with armed insurgency was through military government, beginning in 1964 with Brazil (Philip 1984, 1985; Black 1976; O'Brien and Cammack 1985). The training in counter-insurgency provided by the United States undoubtedly helped strengthen the Latin American military's perception of themselves as defenders of the nation against internal subversion.

With the return to civilian government over most of the Americas, the two major states in Latin America in which combating guerrillas remain a major task for the armed forces are Colombia and Peru, the former under civilian government, the latter at least nominally so. However, in other parts of the developing world governments are also faced with widespread insurgency. In Asia, combating insurgency is the excuse the government of Myanmar (Burma) has used for repressing all opposition to its dictatorial rule and despite the nominal victory of pro-Western forces in Afghanistan, in 2006 much of the country remained effectively outside the control of the government in Kabul.

In Africa, fearing the pro-Soviet government which had come to power in Mozambique after the Portuguese Revolution, the settler regime in Rhodesia (now Zimbabwe) established, and apartheid South Africa supported with arms, an anti-government guerrilla group, the Mozambican National Resistance (RENAMO), which soon gained control of much of the centre of the country. In 1992 a peace settlement brokered by the UN between the government of Mozambique and RENAMO left the latter in control of most of the core of the country, drawing their support (as did the government) from specific ethnic groups, and within three years more than 4 million internal refugees had returned home.

Military training may, however, even in broadly civilian societies be a valuable path to social preferment. In Latin America compulsory military training was introduced towards the end of the nineteenth century, enabling the armed forces to promote themselves as one of the major pillars of the national identity.

Historically, soldiers have played a major role in geographical surveying and the establishment of communications in remote regions. In developing world states these tasks too are still of considerable significance in the development of, *inter alia*, north-west India and modern Pakistan, Iraq and Egypt. In Amazonia the Brazilian army maintains communications, surveys geographical formations, watches for infiltrators, and teaches civics classes. In the remoter regions of Bolivia, Colombia, Ecuador and Peru, the army has often been the sole agency of government which is actually effective over large areas (see Bourricaud 1970: 313–15).

Military developmentalism

Not surprisingly, armies that have assumed such tasks are easily persuaded that they have a wider mission to bring about the development of their countries. In Latin America in the 'developmentalist' era of the 1960s a new phenomenon emerged, starting with Brazil in 1964, by which the armed forces seized power with the open intention of staying in power for an indefinite period, long enough to bring about the forced development of their societies. This phenomenon is often termed **bureaucratic authoritarianism**, a term originally invented by the Argentine Guillermo O'Donnell (1988), whose views derive from Marxism and more particularly from dependency theory (see Chapter 1: 38–9).

O'Donnell's theory envisages three stages of development of political systems. In the oligarchic stage the popular sector is not yet politicised, and so is neither mobilised nor incorporated in the state structure. In the populist stage, the popular sector is mobilised and incorporated. In the bureaucratic-authoritarian state it is then demobilised and excluded. For O'Donnell the bureaucratic-authoritarian state 'guarantees and organizes the domination exercised through a class structure subordinated to the upper fractions of a highly oligopolized and transnationalized bourgeoisie' (O'Donnell 1988: 31). Within the state structure two groups have decisive weight: specialists in coercion (the armed forces), whose job it is to exclude the 'popular sector' from power, and finance capitalists, whose role is to obtain the 'normalisation' of the economy, which performs the dual purpose of excluding the popular sector from economic power and promoting the interests of large oligopolistic interests. As part of the exclusion policy, social issues are depoliticised by being treated as a matter of narrow economic rationality, and direct access to government is limited to the armed forces, the state bureaucracy and leading industrialists and financiers.

However, the term 'bureaucratic authoritarianism' seems rather to be designed to distract from its key feature, the fact that the process was directed by the army and gained its distinctive features from the army's ability to make use of force. For this reason the broader term **military developmentalism** is preferred here because it stresses analogies with the military regimes of Egypt under Nasser, Pakistan under Zia ul-Haq or even Thailand, where a succession of military leaders have held office within a strongly formalised system of public administration deriving legitimacy from the charismatic and traditional authority of the monarchy.

Why do the military intervene? One answer is because civilians, as well as the armed forces themselves, easily succumb to **militarism**. We can, therefore, speak of two types of militarism: 'military' militarism – militarism among the military personnel themselves, and 'civilian' militarism – militarism among the civilian population (Vagts 1959).

Military militarism is a caste pride, a pride in the glory, honour, power and prestige of the military forces. This type of militarism, however, goes well beyond the normal pride of belonging to a well-organised force, resulting in extreme cases in an exaggerated sense of remoteness and of superiority over the outside world in all aspects, so that those functions which the military does not undertake are considered to be not worthwhile for society as a whole. Military militarism, then, tends to arise in one of two sets of circumstances.

The first is when, for whatever reason, the whole end, existence and pride of the state is seen by them to be the concern of the army and the army alone. In modern developing states this condition in its extreme form is fortunately rather rare, if only because few developing world armies can convincingly see themselves as an effective fighting force against all possible opponents. However, the Chinese army, which re-emerged as a distinct political force during the chaos that followed the Great Proletarian Cultural Revolution, showed in its handling of the Tiananmen Square demonstrations that in the last analysis it is prepared to intervene to safeguard the state structure that it has established. There is also some evidence of military militarism as a factor in North Korea.

However, a lower level of military militarism is widespread in developing world states. The forces in such countries – whether in Asia, Latin America or Africa – have a pride in their prowess which does not necessarily derive from recent combat, as in many cases, for geographical or other extraneous reasons, the opportunity has not arisen. Until recently, however, the fact of independence implied an important historic role for the forces. They had the role of guardians of the state thrust upon them, in their opinion, because they saw themselves as the ones who had given birth to it. Secondly, the forces in those countries are relatively well educated compared with their fellow citizens and in addition have a significant capacity for the use of force.

The alternative situation is when the military feel that they have been betrayed by their own civilians. The most striking developing world example may well still be Egypt after the humiliation of 1948, when the government of King Farouk accepted the Anglo-Egyptian Treaty. The fact that Egyptian forces were so conspicuously outclassed by the apparently amateur Israeli army (Naguib 1955) led to a process of military politicisation and ultimately to the Revolution of 1952. Throughout the Middle East, the military have continued to see the confrontation with Israel as justification for their continued rule, a situation deftly exploited by leaders such as Muammar Qaddafi in Libya and, in his time, Saddam Hussein in Iraq.

Civilian militarism is the other side of the same coin. It may afflict either the elite or the mass of the society, or in extreme cases both. It is a feeling among civilians that the army should be rewarded with the unconditional support of the population on whose behalf it fights. In extreme cases it then becomes a nationalist pride in crude power and can lead to 'self-immolation on the altar of violence' (Vagts 1959: 22). In weak states, relying for the effective use of force on inadequately trained and equipped armies, this can lead to catastrophe.

Thus the intervention by West African states in the civil war in Liberia did not succeed in arresting the slide of that country into chaos, but it did succeed in destabilising neighbouring Sierra Leone. Military rule is often seen as an efficient and therefore acceptable substitute for weak and divided civilian government. Unfortunately the reality is often very different.

Case study 8.1   **Democratisation in Argentina**

In 1929 Argentina appeared to be a wealthy and stable developing country, the first in South America to achieve sustainable development. But 1930 saw the first of the military coups which afflicted Argentine politics in the 20th century and which cut short its evolution into a fully democratic country. In 1930 it was the seventh richest country in the world; by 1980 it had fallen to seventy-seventh. In 1943 a small group within the armed forces seized power, fearing that Argentina would be drawn into the Second World War. But a few days before the end of the war the military government joined the Allies in order to become one of the founding members of the United Nations.

Meanwhile, one of the members of the military group, Colonel Juan Domingo Perón, secured the support of the powerful trade unions, and in 1946 was elected president. When he lost the confidence of the armed forces in 1955, they bombed the presidential palace, the Casa Rosada, and drove him into exile. But within months General Aramburu, a fierce opponent of Perón, became impatient that his influence was not being removed fast enough, mounted another coup and sought to demobilise the Peronist and non-Peronist left. Two years later he in turn was deposed. Ironically, under his rule the Peronists became the most powerful party in Argentina, displacing the Radicals as the natural party of government.

Fresh elections were held at which the Peronists were banned from standing. A Radical civilian leader was chosen, and embarked on a programme of economic development which accelerated inflation and drove the country to the brink of bankruptcy. But when he proposed to allow Perón to return, the army stepped in again. The new civilian government was unable to cope with mounting chaos and in 1966 the commander of the army made himself president. This time the armed forces made it quite clear that they intended to stay in power long enough to bring about an 'Argentine Revolution' which would lead to real economic development.

In 1969 an outbreak of insurgency in Argentina's second city, Córdoba, showed that they had failed. The armed forces were unable to find another leader among themselves and in 1973, with the country confronting an armed left-wing insurgency, reluctantly agreed to allow first the Peronists and then Perón himself to return. But the aging leader was already a sick man and when he died in 1974 he was succeeded by his vice-president, his wife María Estela Martínez de Perón, who lacked both his experience and his ability. By 1976 the country was in a virtual state of civil war and a military junta led by General Jorge Videla took power. There followed the so-called 'dirty war' (*guerra sucia*) in which between 9,000 and 15,000 alleged or suspected 'dissidents' were rounded up, tortured, murdered and their bodies disposed of in a variety of ingenious ways.

The first cracks in the military façade appeared in 1980 when the Mothers of the Plaza de Mayo (relatives of the 'disappeared') began to demonstrate openly in

▶

Case study 8.1 continued

the heart of the capital. Democratisation had already begun in other neighbouring countries when the junta tried to seize the Falkland Islands from the UK in 1982 and were unexpectedly defeated. The armed forces had failed at their primary purpose and had shown that they were not invincible. Yet though discredited a provisional military government was able to hold on to power for another year to try to hide the evidence of their misdeeds and salvage what they could. There was some liberalisation, in that a free press had re-emerged, but the return to democracy did not really begin until elections were held and a Radical lawyer who had openly defied the junta, Raúl Alfonsín, was chosen as president.

Under his government young people, who had suffered most at the hands of the armed forces, were targeted. Compulsory courses on Argentine history and social science were introduced in schools to teach civic responsibility. Higher education was massively expanded, with huge numbers of students taught by closed-circuit TV in disused warehouses in Buenos Aires. A new positive national pride was encouraged by cinema documentaries on the wonders of the national territory and the importance of the country's Amerindian heritage – something quite new for much of largely European, urban Argentina. A National Commission investigated the disappearances and published its report, *Nunca Más* ('*Never again!*'), in 1984, which listed the detailed testimony of witnesses (CONADEP 1984). This was the first such report and it not only played an important role in the transition to democracy in Argentina itself, but paved the way for similar inquiries and reports, such as that of the Truth and Reconciliation Commission in South Africa. There were the usual difficulties in bringing those responsible to justice, but before the Full Stop Law (*Punto Final*) put a stop to prosecutions in 1989 at least some of the military junta had been tried and placed under house arrest. Uruguay and Brazil both held free elections and the US government started to claim credit for the new state of affairs.

At Easter 1987 a rising of junior officers unhappy with the reduced status and responsibilities of the forces was countered by vast, well-organised public demonstrations in favour of democracy. Trade unions provided free transport into the capital. Congress and the Casa Rosada were surrounded by people carrying banners and flags. The soldiers retreated to their barracks and Alfonsín declared the crisis to be over.

Civilian government had become a hegemonic value for most Argentines by Easter 1987. Despite continuing economic crises, the Peronist Carlos Menem was elected president in free elections in 1989 and took over power in a peaceful transition, the first of its kind in Argentine history; in 1999 he transferred power in turn peacefully to a Radical. In the meantime he had succeeded in giving the armed forces new tasks and new responsibilities abroad, sending a ship to the Gulf and troops to patrol the 'green line' in Cyprus. In 2006, Argentina has not succeeded in breaking out of its past pattern of boom and slump, nor in realising the full potential of its vast natural resources. And, just as General Pinochet in Chile has succeeded in keeping himself out of prison, so have most of those who oversaw the 'dirty war'. However, the country has now had more than 20 years of democratic transfers of power despite a series of economic crises which in the past would have triggered military intervention, the democratic regime has been consolidated and on 25 March 2006 Argentina established a public holiday to remember the victims of the 'dirty war'.

Arms procurement

Independence was often accompanied, as we have already noted, by a rise in nationalism which in turn promoted enhanced arms expenditure. Since then the costs have escalated, and in most cases faster than income, but the expenditure is perceived as essential to national survival. The quest for 'security' has three aspects for both politicians and military. The importance of each kind varies between these two groups, but also within them too. The three aspects are:

1. defence of territory from invasion/occupation;
2. defence of raw materials and markets;
3. defence of political and social values.

The fact that military budgets are remarkably constant over time as a percentage of GNP suggests they are not responsive to actual threats but reflect aspects of the national political culture, such as how much the people will endure, the degree of paranoia or the salience of the presumed threat. Likewise, in the rare cases in which developing states have significant navies or air forces, the allocations of resources between the services seem to be more a consequence of their lobbying power than of a real estimate of a strategic or tactical threat.

Vested interests include not just military establishments and the arms industry, but also scientists and engineers, diplomats and other civil servants who administer the defence establishments of their countries. Though this is more obvious in the weapons producing countries it is no less true of those which are buying. Thus the perception of national 'security' contributes to economic and environmental insecurity. As Brundtland says in *Our Common Future*: 'Competitive arms races breed insecurity among nations through spirals of reciprocal fears. Nations need to muster resources to combat environmental degradation and poverty. By misdirecting scarce resources, arms races contribute further to insecurity' (WCED 1987). This was echoed in 1989 by Paul Shaw, a UN adviser on population and development: 'No amount of deforestation in Brazil, desertification in the Sahel, or water pollution in the Nile can compare with the cumulative effects of war' (Shaw 1992: 14).

It is hardly surprising that heterogeneous new states experience internal conflicts, sometimes even civil wars. These have during the Cold War period sometimes been exacerbated by great power intervention. When this takes place on opposite sides the risk of escalation increases dramatically.

Since 1945 there have been over 120 international and civil conflicts in the developing world. More than 20 million people have died as a consequence. There have been hundreds of attempted **coups**, some much bloodier than others. There are countless refugees from conflict both directly because of fear and indirectly from the environmental degradation it causes and the consequent loss of livelihood.

However, at the same time developed countries have lost no opportunity to promote profitable arms sales to the South. Four out of five of the largest arms dealers: the United States, the United Kingdom, France and Russia, are in the North and all are members of the UN Security (sic) Council. Credits for such purchases are generally easy to get and it is left to future generations to pay the bill. Even as it is, the military expenditure of developing countries is some 25 per cent of the world total, and in 1999 increased by 3 per cent to a record $245 billion. Of course the developing world's contribution to the arms trade specifically is proportionately much greater, accounting for some 60 per cent of the $21 billion trade by 1990 and for 75 per cent of the $976 billion world trade in arms in 2003 (Shah 2006). These figures represent a colossal transfer of funds from the South to the North and are estimated to have added some 40 per cent to the developing world debt burden.

In the developing world military expenditure is highly concentrated in a few countries but even so it is rarely proportionate to the potential threat or to the resources available. Developing countries spend more as proportions of their budgets on military activity than developed countries. Their spending on arms for example is three times as much as would be needed to provide healthcare, sanitation and clean water to all their populations. One of the most glaring examples of this obsession is Ethiopia where under the Derg, the armed forces consumed some 10 per cent of the country's GNP, while only some 1.5 per cent was spent on health. Moreover the diversion of resources to arms is only the direct cost to development. There are also indirect costs associated with the distortion of the political culture, including the decline of democracy and participation, the growth of corruption and popular alienation from the government and society. In the late 1990s the government of President Mugabe of Zimbabwe spent so much on military intervention in the Democratic Republic of Congo that it destabilised the Zimbabwean economy and resulted in the defeat of his proposals for constitutional reform (*Financial Times*, 9–10 April 2000).

In the developing world arms production also exists and is in fact becoming an increasingly significant, although a far from desirable South–South linkage! There is already generally a redistribution of funds within the developing world from the poorer to the richer and more powerful states. China stands out as the leading arms manufacturer and exporter in the developing world, with more than a million people employed in arms production. In 2004 China was the largest developing country arms exporter, ranking seventh in the world after the USA, Russia, France, the UK, Germany and Canada, and ahead of Israel, Libya, Brazil and Ukraine (Campaign Against Arms Trade 2006).

Regional powers

The role of **regional powers** in Asia has been much complicated by the fragmentation of the former Soviet Union. However, one thing remains certain: in East Asia the massive size of China outweighs all others, although in many ways it is still very much a developing world state with a developing world army.

In South Asia India has naturally assumed the regional role which its size and population seemed to indicate. Despite a string of successes in the early years following independence, however, it received a severe setback when Chinese forces entered Ladakh in 1962; even if the actual loss of territory was insignificant the blow to its security and even more to its morale was considerable. Its confidence revived to a great extent after its successful intervention in former East Pakistan in 1971, which resulted in the independence of Bangladesh. At the end of the 1980s, however, the mission of the Indian Peace Keeping Force (IPKF) in Sri Lanka was not accepted either by the insurgents or by the Sri Lankan government, which took the first convenient opportunity to invite it to withdraw. In return, in 2000, the Indian government refused to come to the aid of the Sri Lankan army when they were faced with a major offensive in Jaffna (*The Guardian*, 5 May 2000).

In South-east Asia, Vietnam has been unable to avoid involvement in its neighbouring countries since the end of war in 1975. The brief Third Indo-China War resulted from Chinese concern about its growing military strength, and tension remains between the two countries over control of the Spratly Islands, which are also claimed by Malaysia and the Philippines. Vietnamese intervention expelled the Khmer Rouge from Cambodia in 1979, but cut short the opening to the West begun in 1976 and halted its economic recovery. It was followed by a ruthless campaign to force Vietnamese withdrawal.

In 1962 the creation of Malaysia by the incorporation of Sabah (former British North Borneo) and Sarawak led to 'confrontation' (*konfrontasi*) with Sukarno's Indonesia. The effects of Indonesian incursions into East Malaysia were sufficiently serious to require a substantial deployment of British troops and resulted in the loss of 114 British servicemen before the abortive coup of October 1965. This led to the death of up to half a million Indonesians, the ending of confrontation and eventually the deposition of Sukarno himself (Hughes 1968). With the collapse of the Portuguese Empire in 1974 General Suharto ordered the seizure of East Timor, where tens of thousands of Timorese have since died resisting the new colonialism of Djakarta. The annexation was not recognised by the rest of the world, but the Western powers, fearful as they were of Communist influence gaining a foothold, were not prepared in the Cold War days to do anything about it and it was only after the fall of Suharto that East Timor achieved independence.

In the Middle East the most active regional powers have been Israel, a military power, and Iran, an oil-rich state with substantial economic resources. Iran in 2006 perceives itself as both a regional power and a leader of Islam against the rest of the world. Certainly many have perceived a desire to export the revolution to the secular states of Central Asia which have Muslim majorities. Iran's geographical position, controlling access to the Persian Gulf and therefore to half of the world's known oil reserves is at once a strength and a weakness, in that it makes Iran vulnerable. The eight-year Iran–Iraq War (1980–88) cost Iran a generation.

In Africa the most important regional role has been played by South Africa (an economic and military power). Nigeria (which gains its standing both from its size and from its considerable oil revenues) has also shown by its actions that it aspires to a significant regional role. In their different ways so too have Egypt, Guinea, Senegal and Tanzania.

As a regional power South Africa intervened in Mozambique after it had become independent from Portugal in 1975. Civil strife continued at some level for three decades. Of the rival guerrilla groups one, the National Revolutionary Movement (MNR) had South African backing. The MNR deliberately disrupted food production causing the 1983 famine in which more than 100,000 people died; they also poisoned wells and burned villages. Together these measures contributed to the displacement of more than half the rural population of the country, after the infrastructure on which they relied, including health clinics and schools, had been callously destroyed.

The ability of the apartheid regime to exercise regional power was considerably enhanced by its control of Namibia (then called South-West Africa), originally allocated to the South African government under a League of Nations Mandate. The apartheid government refused to recognise the authority of the United Nations and treated Namibia as a de facto territory of South Africa. This extended the reach of that government to the borders of Angola and, angered at the support given by the Angolan government to the South West Africa People's Organisation (SWAPO), the armed Namibian liberation movement, they had no hesitation in forming and supporting UNITA, a guerrilla force dedicated to overthrowing the government in Angola.

Unfortunately in recent years the South African government under Thabo Mbeki refused to use its regional leverage to try to rein in the increasingly dictatorial regime of President Mugabe of Zimbabwe. It is understandable that a South African government would not necessarily disapprove of a policy of taking land away from the white settlers who have continued to dominate its export economy in order to distribute it more fairly. Unfortunately, although that is what Mugabe has claimed to be doing, it is not what has actually happened. The land has instead gone to cronies, many of them with links to the 'war veterans' whom Mugabe uses to crush local opposition. Most of them have known nothing about farming, and in consequence whole tracts of fertile countryside lie idle. The result has been catastrophic for the Zimbabwean economy. What was in many respects the most successful economy in southern Africa is no longer able to fulfil the role of breadbasket to the region. But in November 2005 South Africa and Zimbabwe signed an agreement to strengthen defence ties and exchange intelligence at a ceremony at which the South African Intelligence Minister, Ronnie Kasrils, praised Zimbabwe's 'advances and successes' in the 25 years since its independence from Britain. He said the two countries shared a 'common world view' and would 'march forward shoulder to shoulder', thus emphasising the solidarity between the two neighbours (CNN, 17 November 2005).

In Latin America the dominance of the United States has tended to over-shadow that of all other regional powers, including that of the world's most populous Spanish-speaking country, Mexico. Brazil, however, can be considered a regional power in South America, as since at least the 1920s it has been seen as an ally by the United States and the United States has been prepared to let it act as a surrogate.

Developing states, therefore, have taken an increasingly active role in regional, if not in world politics. This activity extends to armed confrontation and in a number of specific cases of armed conflict. Taking into account also civil wars and insurgencies, at any one time in the 1990s there have been at least 30 wars in progress, and of those the overwhelming majority have involved developing states. In 2005 there were less than 30, which represented some kind of progress (*Christian Science Monitor* 2005).

Though fewer developing countries are now under formal military government, the tendency for armed forces to exercise a political role has been much enhanced since the beginning of the 1980s by the militarisation of the developing world. Developing countries have been the major target of the arms salespeople from the AICs. In many cases, notably in Britain, France and the United States, these efforts have had the vigorous support of government. However, the evidence is that arms sales of this kind, though they create a certain sense of dependence and lock the recipient country into a continuing sales drive, have won few friends, and those that are gained in this way are all too liable to turn on their former supporters if the political situation should change. This has certainly proved to be the case since the first Gulf War of 1991 and presents a major challenge to the belief that armed intervention by US-led forces in Afghanistan is serving the cause of democratisation.

What is a matter of real concern, however, is that regional powers rarely, if ever, seem to put the promotion of democracy before the need to make and to maintain alliances. In competing for influence, their interventions serve simply to strengthen autocratic regimes.

The View from the Ground

By *Jonathan Watts* in Beijing, *The Guardian*, Friday, 21 October 2005

Chinese Communists Dash Hopes of Democratic Reform

Hopes for political reform in China have suffered a setback with the publication of the government's first white paper on democracy – a document that despite its name reaffirmed the Communist party's determination to cling to power and postpone the introduction of elections.

The white paper was issued by the cabinet amid rising tensions in the countryside and calls from western leaders for

Beijing to adjust its archaic system of governance so that it keeps pace with the spectacular changes in the economy.

But initial optimism that President Hu Jintao and the prime minister, Wen Jiabao, might be any more willing than their predecessors to implement political reform were dashed by the 12–part document, which defined China as a "democratic dictatorship" in which the Communist party had been chosen by history to play a leading role.

The paper acknowledged that the system is "not yet perfect", highlighting the problems of corruption and the failure sometimes to implement laws and punish lawbreakers.

But it offered no specific policy proposals nor a timetable for change. There was no mention of media freedom, despite the increasingly apparent need for democratic checks and balances on abuse of authority.

Electoral reform was also pushed into the background. Last month Mr Wen told Tony Blair that China was moving to permit township-level elections, which would for the first time allow voters to choose policymakers responsible for budget issues such as education. But there was nothing in the paper to suggest that this would happen soon.

"This is simply a rehash of previous policy statements," said a western political analyst in Beijing, who asked to remain nameless. "It's a declaration that the Communist party intends to stay very firmly in control."

Political and legal reforms have slowed even as the economy surges ahead. New figures yesterday showed that China's gross domestic product grew by 9.4% between January and September.

Rising lifestyle expectations, better public understanding of human rights and the spread of internet and mobile phone technology have fuelled a grass-roots movement for bureaucrats to be more accountable for their decisions.

But the Communist party has made social stability its overriding concern, conscious of the chaos that followed political reform in Russia. Critical newspaper editors have been arrested, dissidents are frequently put under house arrest and censorship of the internet has been stepped up.

Local governments, who often face challenges from their residents, appear to have been given a free hand to use extra-legal means to put down disputes.

In one of the highest profile cases an impeachment campaign by residents in Taishi village, Guangdong province, was broken up by hired thugs, who have beaten up residents, civil rights campaigners and journalists. According to a new report on the attacks by the *South China Morning Post*, one member of almost every household in Taishi was arrested and told they would be imprisoned for at least three years until their families gave up the challenge against the village chief.

The newspaper said the central government had declared Taishi an "important political incident" – making it the same level of concern as the Sars outbreak and the Falun Gong movement.

Chinese policymakers argue that stability is the basis for gradual reform. "We need time," said Wu Jianmin, president of the Foreign Affairs University and a former ambassador. "At some point, things will move on."

Requirements for liberal democracy

The overwhelming majority of modern states claim to be 'democracies'. We call this form of democracy liberal democracy. On the one hand, liberal democracy is representative, distinguished from the older classical notion of 'direct' democracy in that, under it, citizens do not govern themselves directly but choose representatives to govern. On the other, it is limited – the government is restricted in what it can do. Liberal democracies are states in which government is limited in its powers by a written constitution, a system of law and/or an independent judiciary and is responsive to the popular will as expressed through free and fair elections. Under such a government certain basic freedoms (often termed **civil rights**) will be guaranteed to the individual (Holden 1993). In the political sense, liberalisation means extending the range of rights and freedoms available to the citizen, and it is important to distinguish between this usage and the so-called liberalisation of an economy by removing constraints on investment and trade. **Democratisation** refers to both the process by which other forms of government evolve (or are transformed) into democracies and the process by which existing democracies become more democratic, as by improvements in electoral representation or the defence of civil rights.

However, democracy is an **'essentially-contested'** concept, that is to say, a concept on which *by definition* agreement is not possible. Democracy is about a contest for power and the outcome of that struggle colours people's perception of it. Hence it is not possible to determine *with certainty* which states are liberal democracies and which are not. There are broadly three working possibilities:

(a) An *inclusive* definition allows the label to all governments which call themselves democratic and can claim to have been chosen by the people. Lincoln spoke of 'government of the people, by the people, for the people' (*Gettysburg Address*, 1863) but the United States of 1863 would not be accepted as a liberal democracy today. Schmitter and Karl hold that democracy does not reside in a single specific set of institutions. 'There are many types of democracy, and their diverse practices produce a similarly varied set of effects' (Schmitter and Karl 1993: 40).

(b) A *procedural* definition focuses on the way in which this process of choice is achieved. 'The democratic method is that institutional arrangement for arriving at political decisions in which individuals acquire the power to decide by means of a competitive struggle for the people's vote' (Schumpeter 1943: 269). It is easy enough to tell whether or not an election has been held, but it is another matter to tell whether it has been 'free and fair' (see Chapter 7). A criticism of this approach is that it can lead to low standards being applied and the acceptance of 'low intensity democracy' (Gills et al. 1993) as an adequate substitute for the real thing. But for most people, the basic minimum for a country to be considered a democracy is that its government should have been chosen in a free and fair election.

(c) An *exclusive* definition concentrates on determining whether or not features exist that are incompatible with free popular choice: there must be no military intervention, no armed repression of the opposition or of minorities, no secret police, no limits on candidature at elections and no ballot rigging. In addition some claim that there must be a vibrant civil society/civic culture. The point is that consent in itself does not make a government democratic (Partridge 1971; Ginsburg 1982). Consent can be coerced, or manufactured (elections can be fixed) and citizens may see no alternative to giving their passive consent to oligarchy or dictatorship. Practical difficulties as well as political ones make it difficult to hold free and fair elections in developing countries, even when, as in Afghanistan, the will is there (see below, 'The View from the Ground').

An election is a complex process and for an election to be free and fair in practice a large number of conditions have to be met, before, during and after the poll itself. Beforehand, a legal framework and a timetable have to be established and generally agreed; polling districts have to be delimited and arrangements made for voters to register so that each voter has one vote and only one vote. In the run-up to the election itself individuals and parties have to be free both to be nominated and to campaign. During the election, voters have to be able to get to the polling stations, to vote freely and in secret when they get there, and to be able to understand the nature of the choice they are to make, which means a fairly designed ballot paper or equivalent. Afterwards, the main thing is that the votes have to be fairly counted, without undue delay and in the presence of properly accredited observers on behalf of the candidates or political parties. However, there also have to be ways in which fraud can be reported and disputes settled and resolved. But defects in any or all of these stages do not necessarily mean that the election is unfree or unfair (Eklit and Reynolds 2005; see also Eklit and Reynolds 2002).

The View from the Ground

Declan Walsh, Kabul, The Guardian, Friday, 16 September 2005

Donkeys and Camels Hired to Aid Afghan Poll

Afghan election officials have hired 1,200 donkeys, 24 camels, 300 horses and nine helicopters to deliver ballot boxes to the most remote parts of the country's rugged terrain ahead of Sunday's election.

A deluge of candidates – 5,800 for the 249-seat lower house of parliament and 34 provincial councils – will see voters grappling with some of the world's largest ballot papers.

Voters in Kabul must wade through 14 broadsheet pages containing photographs and symbols of more than 700 candidates, choosing just two.

Voting is scheduled to take ten hours but could extend into the night, the chief electoral officer, Peter Erben, said. Officials are also worried about the "assassination clause" – a rule that provides for a second-placed candidate to be elected in the event of the winner's death. In a country still awash with private militias and weapons, that could be seen as an invitation for losing candidates to overturn defeat by murdering their victorious opponents.

Counting Sunday's vote will take at least three weeks and it is expected to be at least six months before the fractious parliament starts work. "It's going to be pretty chaotic", admitted a senior government official.

Gunmen in the conservative Nuristan province yesterday shot a female candidate several times. She was airlifted to Bagram military base north of Kabul. A US spokeswoman described her condition as "stable".

In Kabul intelligence officials warned of the likelihood [of] a spectacular Taliban attack against a western target to derail the historic poll.

Democratisation in the developing world

The prevailing 'three stage' model of democratisation reflects historical events in Europe and Latin America since 1975. It does not necessarily reflect the course of events in the developing world either at the time or in the future, if only because the starting point is different.

1. In the first stage, an established authoritarian regime comes under pressure and responds by making limited concessions to previously excluded groups or interests. These concessions may be political or economic, and it does not follow that any that are made form part of a coherent strategy. But at some point, it is possible to say that the regime has embarked on a systematic programme of liberalisation. In political terms, this implies some major changes: permitting opposition parties to organise, restraining the police and security agencies, extending the scope of free speech and expression and permitting the emergence (or re-emergence) of **civil society**.

2. With the deposition or resignation of the previous government, the stage of transition can be said to have been reached. However, as Burnell warns us: 'The term democratic transition should not blind us to the reality that "transition from" the previous regime type may not actually usher in a successful transition to democracy' (Burnell 2000: 23). Ideally, the next stage would be a free and fair election, leading to the installation of a government chosen by the people, but in the circumstances the choice of a post-transition government may be somewhat less than ideal. The requirements for an electoral choice that is truly free and fair are complex. As we have

seen, they involve events both before, during and after the polls themselves. However, assuming a reasonable degree of freedom, with the installation of the new government possibilities open up for a more radical programme of legislation that will raise standard of choice. As Thomas Jefferson realised, democratisation is not a 'one-off' event, but a process which has to be maintained if a country can be said to be democratic.

3. In the third stage, consolidation, the procedures of democratic government have to become customary and unchallenged. This takes time and there is no real end to it, though conventionally many accept that it can be assumed to have succeeded after power has changed hands twice through democratic elections: the 'two-turnover' test (Huntington 1993b: 267).

Democratisation in the developing world has certainly been encouraged by the fall of Communism in Eastern Europe. However, the pressure for democratisation already existed in the developing world before 1989. By 1989 most of the countries in Latin America had already returned to constitutional government, and more than half the countries in Africa had held competitive multi-party elections. But the end of the Cold War was not all good news, as now there is no superpower interest in restraining their former client states when local conflicts threaten to get out of hand. In a bipolar world, in a sense every conflict matters to the two camps as victory for one is defeat for the other. In an era of multipolarity (or US hegemony), most southern conflicts will not matter to the AICs at all. These conflicts will, of course, blight lives not only through acts of war, but through the social dislocation which is a byproduct. In 2006, virtually all the world's poorest countries are countries that have been devastated by civil wars which the international community has found great difficulty in stopping.

Democratisation movements have in the recent past been seriously hampered by their identification with anti-state activity, and in many cases concessions have been made which on closer examination often turn out to be more apparent than real. Hence the mere existence of multi-party elections does not guarantee that truly competitive politics will operate.

Singapore illustrates some of the ambiguities of the democratisation process. Before 1991 the ruling People's Action Party held all the seats in parliament. In 1991 four opposition members were elected to the 81-member parliament but by 1997 they had been reduced to only two directly elected. Since then the constitution has allowed them one extra seat, though with only three members in the 82-member parliament elected in 2001 this hardly adds up to an effective opposition, even if they were not also subject to constant harassment. In June 2006 Chee Soon Juan, secretary-general of the opposition Singapore Democratic Party, who had previously been bankrupted for allegedly libelling the former prime minister, was charged with speaking in public without a permit (Small 2006). Although he had had the support of the vast majority of his people since he came to power in 1959 with a programme of social reform/economic development which has been very successful for most of the population, Singapore's first Prime Minister, Lee Kuan Yew, who led the country into independence from Malaysia in 1965, had been in effect an autocrat for more than 30 years when he decided to retire. He continues to watch over his creation, a remarkably disciplined city-state, from the post of Senior Minister in the Prime Minister's office.

In consequence the impulse to democratisation may produce a system where democracy is defined in very limited terms (Arat 1991). For example, equal political rights may exist on paper but social and economic inequality may be protected from political interference. Developing world democracies often have quite restrictive politics with considerable coercive power, for example India and Kenya. The more adept regimes arrange for a public display of the trappings of democracy and may allow semi-official opposition parties to participate in doctored elections, as in Mexico.

A third possibility is illustrated by Brazil, where a mass electorate is influenced by the enormous power and highly questionable role in the developing world context of the media. Some 18 million people in Brazil get their news from the O Globo television station each evening and O Globo sees part of its role as manufacturing presidential candidates. But for Brazil as for some other developing world countries the replacement of formal military government with formal 'democratic' government conceals the continuing (and possibly enhanced) importance of some groups in society, including (and perhaps especially) the military establishment. If the military have ceased to intervene, it can be because they really do not need to do so. In 1994 President Cardoso, elected with the support of O Globo, sent troops into the *favelas* (shanty-towns) of Rio de Janeiro in search of drug dealers. Ever since these depressed neighbourhoods have echoed to the sound of gunfire, but the drug problem gets no better since the methods that are being used to counter it are entirely inappropriate.

Finally, where an authoritarian government enjoys access to sufficient financial resources, it not only has a strong incentive to retain power, but the means to ensure that it does so. That is why so many oil states have authoritarian governments. The wealth from oil enables their rulers both to buy off political opposition and to ensure that they retain the backing of the armed forces. In the last analysis, the security forces have a strong incentive to keep things as they are. Worse still, the oil majors and governments both East and West have repeatedly shown that they prefer to deal with existing autocracies rather than risk the unpredictable consequences of change (Karl 1997; Ross 2001)

Even if the formal structures of government are already in place, Schmitter and Karl warn us not to expect too much. Democracies are not necessarily more efficient economically than other forms of government, they argue. They are not necessarily more efficient administratively, either, and they are not likely 'to appear more orderly, consensual, stable, or governable than the autocracies they replace'. Lastly, 'democracies will have more open societies and polities than the autocracies they replace, but not necessarily more open economies'. What they will have, however, is a much better chance of delivering, in the end, a stable, peaceful and prosperous society (Schmitter and Karl 1993: 49–51). As Larry Diamond points out, three tensions or paradoxes are inherent in the very nature of democracy; conflict/consensus, representativeness/governability, consent/effectiveness (Diamond 1993; cf. Beetham 1992). Given the forces involved, and the inevitability of conflict between them, a certain degree of turbulence must be seen as normal.

Representative government was achieved before it became general practice to allow all citizens to vote, displacing the older idea that only the well-to-do had a stake in society. Liberal democracy originated, however, in a well-established concept of representation; the idea that the people's representatives must agree to taxes if they are to be expected to pay them. Hence there is general agreement that the appearance of democracy is associated with a certain minimum level of economic development. Here, however, agreement ends.

Again there are, broadly speaking, three alternative views of the relationship between economic development and the change to democracy. Those who take the *modernisation approach* believe that at a certain stage of economic development democracy becomes possible, and that, in the words of Seymour Martin Lipset, 'the more well-to-do a nation, the greater the chances that it will sustain democracy' (Lipset 1960: 75). The reasoning is clear: since the seventeenth century it has been recognised that sufficient economic resources to bring a certain sense of security are needed for people to take part in politics, and the better educated they are the more likely they are to be able to do so successfully. The emergence of an educated middle class has therefore been seen as a precondition for the emergence of liberal democracy. It works both ways, too. 'Low participation and social inequity are so bound up with each other that a more equitable and humane society requires a more participatory political system' (Macpherson 1977: 94).

Those who take a *structural approach* see the nature of structures of class and power as central. The accumulation of wealth gives rise to a middle class. But at a certain point in time it is the class as a whole that challenges the old elites for a share in political power, if necessary by force. Or, as Barrington Moore put it, 'no bourgeoisie, no democracy' (Moore 1969). This would imply that liberal democracy was in practice an instrument of class rule and that its institutions function to maintain the rule of middle-class elites and to disempower ordinary citizens. However, the structural approach is helpful in understanding the early stages of 'Third Wave' democratisation in Latin America (O'Donnell et al. 1986).

The *transition approach* sees the agreement to democratise less starkly, as a matter of elite choice, bargaining and negotiation, the impetus for which comes from the historical conflict over scarce resources. 'A people who are not in conflict about some rather fundamental matters would have little need to devise democracy's elaborate rules for conflict resolution' (Rustow 1970: 362) Again the question is, why do these conflicts arise, and how far do the mechanisms that purport to resolve them actually work to do so?

The evidence suggests that where, as in Chile, a **pacted transition** takes place between dictatorship and democracy, the democratic regime stands a much better chance of survival, though at the cost of concessions which may be keenly resented by those who have suffered under the dictatorship (Sanchez 2003). This would seem to confirm Rustow's view.

Liberal democracy is well established in Western Europe, North America, Japan and other AICs, and in only a small number as yet of the many developing countries. However, economic development is not a prerequisite for people to want democracy, as is demonstrated by the persistent reappearance of the liberal tradition in Latin America over the past century and a half, and some striking examples from South Asia, the Middle East and the Caribbean. Liberal democracy has proved adaptable and responsive to the pressures of survival in a competitive world, and with the collapse of the rival Soviet model, it currently has no effective competitor. This does not mean that all liberal democracies are the same. All states, even liberal democracies, exist in an evolutionary context and may well have diverged considerably from the ideal types they profess to represent (cf. Macpherson 1977). Moreover, on many occasions rulers have already argued that for reasons of national security, or otherwise, they have found it 'necessary' to suspend or dispense with any or all of the notions of individual rights, limitation of government power or the right to a fair trial.

Empowerment and the growth of civil society

Since the nineteenth century, it has been a widespread assumption, particularly in English-speaking countries, that stable democratic systems required a high level of social consensus. Where this was achieved, political stability was enhanced and society unified. Where it was not, there was a tendency for political order to break down and democracy to collapse. For some time it has been accepted that the key determinant of political stability is the number and nature of **social cleavages** in society (Lipset and Rokkan 1967; Rae and Taylor 1970; Lane and Ersson 1991). There are many factors dividing groups in all societies. If the dividing lines between these groups do *not* coincide with each other, competitive democratic politics can and does take place without endangering the whole structure. The problem comes when they do coincide with one another and a major split opens up.

However, there are several states which are among the most democratic in Europe in which, on the contrary, a high level of agreement is obtained in divided societies. Hence special interest attaches to what is now termed **consociational democracy**, a term originally formulated by Arend Lijphart, as a result of comparative studies by political scientists from Austria, Belgium, the Netherlands and Switzerland (Lijphart 1969, 1974, 1977; Lembruch 1967;

Steiner 1972, 1974). This involves a formal agreement to share power, and, as such, has been of great interest to those who have sought to broker peace between contending parties in the developing world.

Consociational democracy, Lijphart argued, exists in societies which are clearly and apparently permanently divided vertically into a number of communities, whether ethnic, religious or linguistic. These communities, after Dutch practice, are often referred to as 'pillars' and their division as 'pillarisation' (*verzuiling*). Consociational democracy is characterised by an elaborate process of *negotiation* between the elites of the different 'pillars' leading to *accommodation* and *compromise*. Four basic principles are used to diffuse and to resolve conflict:

1. Executive power-sharing. The executive is not vested exclusively in one group; all pro-system groups are represented in the government.
2. Autonomy. Each group has a right to regulate its own affairs in certain respects.
3. Proportionality. Jobs are shared in proportion to representation in parliament or congress.
4. The minority have a right to veto any proposal which they regard as violating their basic interests.

In fact, as Table 8.1 shows, Lijphart's argument is that it is the behaviour of the elite that makes this system possible. What is of particular interest is whether the strategy of seeking agreement is really successful, or whether its apparent success in the Netherlands was simply the necessary product of coalition government in a highly fragmented party system. It is true that it has not served to maintain a unitary state in the highly unpromising circumstances of

Table 8.1 Three waves of democratisation

Period	Type
1828–1926	**First long wave**: USA, Britain, France, Italy, Argentina, Canada, Australia, New Zealand*
1922–1942	**First reverse wave**: Italy, Germany, Argentina
1943–1962	**Second short wave**: India, Israel, West Germany, Italy, Japan
1958–1975	**Second reverse wave**: Brazil, Argentina, Chile
1974–?	**Third wave**: Portugal, Spain, and many southern states in Latin America, Asia, Africa, as well as Eastern Europe and part of the former Soviet Union. Impact on South, therefore, essentially only since 1979, when Ecuador began transition back to democracy in Latin America. But was already well established before 1989.

* *Note*: It has been argued that there were in fact three waves during the 'first long wave' and that they can be linked to the trends in the economic cycle (see Fraser 2001)
Source: Samuel P. Huntington, *The Third Wave: Democratization in the Late Twentieth Century*, 1993b

Belgium, where ethnic, linguistic and religious cleavages between Flemings and Walloons coincide with a clear-cut geographical split. It is also true that with depillarisation in the Netherlands it seems to have come to an end (van Mierlo 1986). But it seems to have worked well both there (see Gladdish 1991) and in Austria (Gerlich 1987) over a substantial period.

There is also evidence from developing states that where the same strategy has been adopted – Malaysia in South-east Asia – it has achieved a much higher degree of political stability than might otherwise have been expected. Conversely its abandonment in Cyprus, and in Colombia, Lebanon and Nigeria, among developing countries, has led to political instability, unrest and even civil war.

Power-sharing has worked because it leads to the empowerment of individuals and groups who would otherwise be excluded from the political process. Another way of putting this is that they have 'social capital' and can make use of it (Newton 1997). It enables them actually to make their own decisions and to take part in shaping their own future. This is not a new idea in the developing world. It lies at the root of the *panchayat* system in India and in the island states of Oceania the tradition is so strong that decisions concerning the whole community are made collectively by a Council of Elders. But empowerment, if it is to mean anything, means that people must be able to participate effectively in the making of decisions affecting them. In other words, it is not enough for them to be told what the government is going to do for them. They have to be able to initiate policies and to shape the development of policies initiated by others.

This means having the ability to participate in decision-making at all relevant levels and through a variety of channels. In most states significant decisions are made on at least two levels: local and national; in federal states, at least three. It is also true that certain important decisions relating to the national and local economy of developing world states are taken abroad, outside the state boundaries, whether by banks, aid agencies, TNCs or otherwise. Nevertheless, the first step in empowerment is learning how things work on the local level. External influences are only effective when they work with local interests.

Hence, rather than address the structures of government in the first instance, many people believe that democracy is best promoted by encouraging the development of civil society, which the British political philosopher John Locke argued was formed by the mutual agreement of citizens to resign their individual freedom to act to a collective agency. This is not, however, quite what is generally understood by the term today, which does not seem to have a generally agreed meaning.

'Civil society' is defined by Rueschemeyer et al. (1992: 49) as: 'The totality of social institutions and associations, both formal and informal, that are not strictly production-related nor governmental nor familial in character'. This is a very restricted definition. It is quite hard to think of any organisations that are likely to qualify. Walzer (1995) uses a slightly wider definition: 'The space of uncoerced human association and also the set of relational networks – formed for the sake of family, faith, interests and ideology – that fill this space'. The problem is that this space cannot exist unless civil and political rights are effective and organisations formed by individuals and groups enjoy associational autonomy. But of course a dictatorship is not likely to allow anything of the sort, though traditional rights may in a developing country allow some room for traditional structures, e.g. clubs and secret societies, to exist.

Modernisation and transition theorists argue that a 'vibrant' civil society is essential to successful democratisation, because:

1. it is an essential bulwark against the power of the state, concentrating people into groups and increasing interaction between them so that a protest against authoritarian rule is more likely (Diamond et al. 1997);
2. it mobilises previously excluded classes (Rueschmeyer et al. 1992);
3. it enables a political culture favourable to democracy to emerge and to become consolidated (Almond and Verba 1963, 1980; Dahl 1989).

It is the role of an emerging civil society in the consolidation of democratic regimes that naturally attracts the most interest (Gill 2000). A country such as South Korea, which has successfully made the transition from authoritarian rule to democracy, and where democracy can now be said to have become consolidated, also has a vigorous civil society (Armstrong 2002).

Democracy and development

In considering the political and social structures in developing states, we have to take account of the legacy of history, elites and authoritarianism, as well as the concept of good governance, participation and democracy.

Much of the period since 1960 has been dominated by the Cold War. Though almost all the new states that emerged during this time paid at least lip-service to the ideal of democracy, in practice most if not all were dominated to a greater or lesser extent by an oligarchy. The elite to which power was transferred at the moment of independence, or which seized power by force soon afterwards, was able to maintain itself by its control of recruitment. If it was challenged successfully by opposition pressure, the new government was distrusted by both the superpowers for different reasons: the United States, because it feared the loss of political support, and the Soviet Union, because it was uncertain about the real political intentions of the regimes which professed adherence to socialism.

But neither of the superpowers at that stage seriously questioned the overriding importance of development. The new governments therefore found themselves able to pursue developmentalist policies largely free of internal or external pressures to move to greater participation and democracy.

In some cases quite the opposite move occurred as the wave of military coups spread across Africa and Latin America in the 1960s and by the end of the decade most of the states in each region were under military rule.

Where the military assume power, they lack the ostensible legitimacy of governments founded on voting. Despite lacking legitimacy, they have tended to be very sure of their own abilities to rule, and have had every intention of continuing to rule in some guise or another. By assuming the mantle of developmentalism, they have been able to cloak their usurpation in nationalist rhetoric.

Despite their evident limitations, it may be important in encouraging them to take action. Economic failure is seldom cited as a major reason for a military coup, and more often than not it has been given as a reason for the replacement of one military government by another (Wiking 1983: 116). However, despite their evident limitations, military rulers are easily persuaded that they have a wider mission to bring about the development of their countries. The problem when the time comes to get rid of them is that by that time they have greatly strengthened their links to the sources of wealth and power, both within their countries and abroad. Demilitarisation, therefore, is a vital stage in democratisation.

The allies of the military when in power or out are the urban elites (and, all too often, the sole superpower, the USA) and the development process has extended and enhanced their acquisition of social, economic and political power. The urbanisation of the countryside and the expansion of towns is part of this process. The industrial revolution was preceded, and made possible, by an agricultural revolution which increased the product of a given amount of land dramatically. In some cases the process of conquest and colonisation was used to take productive land away from country-dwellers and to create large estates; the control of the state then kept it there. In turn the industrial revolution gave rise to transport systems which made possible the further conquest of the countryside. As this control was extended in the late twentieth century, it resulted in the industrialisation of agriculture (agribusiness).

The replacement of traditional subsistence agriculture by large farms or plantations managed for export and/or commercial sale of a single product or limited range of products remains one of the foremost problems for the states of the developing world today.

Decolonisation, paradoxically, accelerated this process. *The Ecologist* noted under the heading 'From colonialism to colonialism' how Nehru and his successors had rejected the Gandhian dream of agrarian self-sufficiency. They set out to industrialise India by export-oriented growth and other new states in the course of time sought to do the same:

A process of internal colonization, as devastating to the commons as anything that had gone before it, was thus set in motion. Using the slogans of 'nation-building' and 'development' to justify their actions, Third World governments have employed the full panoply of powers established under colonial rule to further dismantle the commons. Millions have lost their homelands – or the land they made their home – to make way for dams, industrial plants, mines, military security zones, waste dumps, plantations, tourist resorts, motorways, urban redevelopment and other schemes designed to transform the South into an appendage of the North. (*The Ecologist* 1993: 39)

Power, of course, was the key, and in this process TNCs, banks and lending agencies had at all times the willing collaboration of local commercial interests whose counterparts in other elites also depended in a variety of ways on the establishment and/or maintenance of international trading patterns. (Of course one could argue that these elements constitute fractions of an identifiable ruling class.)

In particular, the maintenance and indeed extension of plantation agriculture owes much of its vigour to the very special role of land as a badge of social distinction, an insurance and a hedge against inflation. Such landholding of course goes hand in hand with the growth of cash crops for export. The rulers of the South, therefore, are not often seeking any alteration in the terms of trade.

Resistance to this process was met by force. As weak civilian governments were displaced or supplanted by the armed forces, military governments set about conquering their own countries. Southern armies typically saw the economic situation confronting them as a military emergency, imperilling their ability to defend the state against its enemies. Their militarism, whether in Asia, Latin America or Africa, had a pride in their prowess which did not necessarily derive from recent combat, as, in many cases, for geographical or other extraneous reasons, the opportunity had not arisen, but it has proved much easier to get the armed forces into politics than to get them out again, and Nigeria, which has repeatedly succumbed to further military intervention, is also now rated one of the most corrupt governmental systems in the world. It is also much less prosperous than it should be, given its large and relatively well-educated population and its substantial natural resources.

Fortunately for the developing countries, democratisation is clearly on the global agenda. There is little room in the international financial institutions (IFIs) and other international agencies for action which does not at least pay lip-service to this ideal. As Pinkney pointed out:

A book on democracy in the Third World would have been a very short book if it had been written 20 years ago. Competitive elections and civil liberties had survived since the achievement of independence in India, the Gambia, Botswana, Mauritius and some of the West Indian islands and, since the ending of the civil war, in Costa Rica, but these were oases in a desert dominated by military governments, one-party regimes and personal dictatorships. Today all the governments of Latin America have been chosen by competitive election. In Asia, South Korea, Bangladesh, Thailand and Nepal have all emerged from military or personal rule, and in Africa 25 of the 41 nations have held contested elections within the past five years, or expect to do so in the near future. (Pinkney 1993: 1)

In independent Africa there were 198 leadership transitions between 1960 and 2002. Coup, war or invasion accounted for 104 of these. But there has been a steep decline in these since the end of the Cold War. Even coup leaders no longer hold a perfunctory plebiscite to legitimise their rule but as in Niger, Guinea-Bissau and Côte d'Ivoire have felt it necessary to organise internationally-acceptable elections, and in 17 cases (21 per cent) governments have actually lost power as a result of an election; something that was previously rare (Goldsmith 2004).

Pinkney considered this transformation over a relatively short period of time to be remarkable, and he was right. But, having said that, he goes on to show that democracy can have different meanings and different prospects in the wide range of countries which comprise what he calls the Third World. There is a real question as to whether democracy in most developing countries is more formal than substantive. Authoritarianism still predominated in the developing world as late as 1992 (Kamrava 1993: 1). Fortunately ten years on, though it is likely to take many years yet for it to become fully established, liberal democracy is now the norm, other than in Central Asia and the Middle East (United Nations University 2003).

Admittedly, even where there are reasonably long-standing democracies, such as India and Kenya, politics remains highly restrictive. Centrifugal forces such as tribalism confront national political structures including those which purport to be democratic. What meaning does democracy have to those with the formal right to vote in such circumstances? And how does the right to vote enhance the lives of people surviving on the margin? In situations of economic scarcity are individual, civil and political rights such as the right to vote in competitive elections anything more than a smokescreen for inequality? At least under a democratic system, with open competition for the people's vote, we have the opportunity to find out.

Democracy promotion

Democracy promotion, or democracy assistance (Burnell 1997, 2000), was virtually unheard-of before 1989. The concept only really emerged in the immediate aftermath of the Cold War when there was great enthusiasm in Western Europe and the United States for encouraging the spread of democracy in Eastern Europe and the former Soviet Union. One of the reasons for this was the myth of the so-called 'democratic peace' – the idea that two democratic countries would not go to war against one another (see Chapter 6). However, supporters argue that it is a good thing in itself that more people should be able to decide their own futures, and there is a good case for charitable foundations and other non-governmental organisations funding educational programmes in the mechanics of democratic choice. By extension these facilities were naturally seen as applicable also to developing countries generally.

Democracy assistance can, therefore, be defined as the provision of advice, training and technical support for elections, political parties and pressure groups in countries unused to democracy.

The German foundations (*Stiftungen*), each developed to give general support for a political party in Germany, namely the Konrad-Adenauer-Stiftung (CDU/CSU), Friedrich-Ebert-Stiftung (SDP) and Friedrich–Naumann-Stiftung (FDP), were already active in the field of democracy assistance before 1983 (Mair 2000). Since then the largest provider in this field has been USAID and the best known the National Endowment for Democracy (NED), based in Washington, DC, but many other organisations have also been active, some NGOs, such as the Soros Foundation in Eastern Europe, others semi-official, such as the NED itself and the British Westminster Foundation for Democracy (Burnell and Calvert 2005).

One area in which assistance can undoubtedly be valuable is that of election management (Norris 2004). As shown above, an election is a complex process, which if it is to be free and fair requires certain conditions to be fulfilled before, during and after the poll itself. Training for responsible officials can reasonably be seen as legitimate.

Support for opposition political parties may be equally necessary, but understandably the governments of the target countries may well be very suspicious of such programmes, and in consequence the early enthusiasm in the United States for the spread of democracy has had to be modified (Carothers 1999). Political parties are complex organisations, and international assistance is available to help them improve their organisational capacities, enable them more effectively to participate in elections and the legislature, and to enhance internal democracy within them, particularly the participation of women. Hence USAID has placed limits on the amount available to any one party and funded almost all parties presenting themselves in Bosnia, Mozambique and Nicaragua (Kumar 2005), the last being a particularly sensitive case given the well-known hostility of the US government to the opposition Sandinistas (who did not win). In the case of the so-called 'Orange Revolution' in Ukraine, each side accused the other of narrowly political motives, and the supporters of the opposition candidate and his party were accused of being in the pay of foreign powers. The same accusation has been used to bolster the authoritarian regime in neighbouring Belarus.

The position is different again in the post-conflict situations often found in developing countries. International assistance in eight post-conflict countries: Cambodia, Ethiopia, Rwanda, Uganda, Mozambique, Sierra Leone, El Salvador and Guatemala has had disappointing results, being effective in setting up new organisations but relatively unsuccessful in consolidating effective democratic institutions. Partly this seems to be the result of focusing on the short term, on the holding of elections, rather than on the long-term issues of political control and regulation (de Zeeuw 2005).

One legacy of the Cold War is the widespread distribution of arms throughout the developing world and the use of them by armed forces against their own people and vice versa. The other is the belief that democracy can be promoted by military intervention. US intervention in Iraq, as in Afghanistan, was repeatedly claimed by the Administration to be a struggle against dictatorship and in favour of democracy. Instead it has mobilised a formidable, if divided opposition, in which once more Islamic fundamentalism appears as the prime motivating force.

Case study 8.2   **Democratisation in Ghana**

Ghana was the first country in colonial Africa to achieve independence in 1957. However the rule of its first leader, Kwame Nkrumah, became increasingly authoritarian, laying him open to a military coup that overthrew him in 1966. Since then democratisation has been

(a) slow to come;
(b) very gradual; and
(c) until 2001, uncertain of being carried through to consolidation.

In 1966, after Nkrumah had been overthrown by the army and police, a National Liberation Council (NLC) was established under Colonel A.A. Afrifa. The main task of this Council was to dismantle the ruling apparatus; it also moved away from Nkrumah's ill-organised 'African socialism' with some market-oriented reforms.

In 1969 civilian government was restored under Dr Kofi Busia. However, it was not long before the Army was making the two standard complaints soldiers have against civilian rule, that it was inefficient and corrupt, and in 1972 a second coup led by Colonel I.K. Acheampong restored military rule under a National Redemption Council. Three years later, in 1975, General I.K. Acheampong abandoned the illusion of collective leadership (or redemption) and established a military dictatorship, only to be overthrown in turn in 1978 by Lt. Gen. F.W.K. Akuffo and a Supreme Military Council (SMC) which was nominally preparing return to civilian rule.

The following year, junior ranks led by the charismatic Flt. Lt. Jerry Rawlings rose in revolt against the military establishment. The Armed Forces Ruling Council (AFRC) purged the government, and Rawlings ordered the execution of no less than three former Heads of State (Afrifa, Acheampong and Akuffo), who were condemned for crimes committed under their rule and shot on the beach at Accra. Five other generals were also executed, as was the entire Supreme Court, though Rawlings himself was later not to be held responsible for that. After four months he retired in favour of a civilian, but in 1981 intervened a second time to depose the new government. A Provisional National Defence Council (PNDC) was formed, composed of both civilian and military members, but there was no doubt for the next 20 years that Rawlings, its Chairman, was boss.

The Rawlings era can be divided into four periods. The first, 1981–83, was a period of radical populism, in which the PNDC created local organisations on a Cuban or Libyan model; using them to impose price etc. controls, and to carry out a self-reliant socialist development strategy.

▶

Case study 8.2 continued

Between 1983 and 1989 there was a period of pragmatic authoritarianism. Government remained separate from the military establishment, but it controlled the armed forces though popular committees. In 1983 economic crisis made it turn to the IMF for support. Its Economic Recovery Programme was an orthodox stabilisation package. Introduced in April 1983 it appeared to halt economic decline but at heavy cost. Between 1987 and 89 further structural reforms followed. Banks resumed investment; state monopolies were finally phased out. The result was that cocoa farmers gained but the condition of the poor worsened. Increasing unrest and discontent brought about the election of district assemblies and a move back to democracy.

Political liberalisation, however, did not really get under way until 1989. Extension of popular participation occurred in stages leading up to a referendum on a new multi-party constitution in April 1992. Not surprisingly this resulted in a landslide win for Rawlings's National Democratic Congress (NDC) and the election as President of Rawlings himself. The divided opposition, realising that they were unlikely to win, unwisely decided to boycott the elections. But outside observers certified them as fair.

With no effective opposition, therefore the eight years 1993–2001, which began with the inauguration of the so-called Fourth Republic, were years of limited democracy. Rawlings remained commander-in-chief of the Army and the military security apparatus remained in place. However, when the opposition accepted the institutional arrangements, there was a revival of the independent judiciary, and in 1996 Rawlings was re-elected. President with 57.2 per cent of votes cast to 39.8 per cent for John Kufuor, whose New Patriotic Party (NPP) won one-third of seats in Parliament. Finally in 2001 Ghana re-emerged as a fully consolidated democracy when John Kufuor was elected President, with a peaceful and orderly transition of government to the opposition party.

The case study is compatible, therefore, with the 'three-stage' model of democratisation. However, it makes clear just how indefinite the boundaries and how protracted the timescale of each stage may be in practice. This blurring of boundaries is at least partly the result of the extent to which, even under an authoritarian regime, the assumptions of democracy continue to survive, ready to be revitalised when opportunity permits. As with many other developing countries, Ghana attained independence as a democratic country and that makes its experience very different from the Eastern European and Central Asian countries that have more recently emerged from the break-up of the former Russian Empire. In the latter case both the nature of the preceding regime and the way in which the transition occurred have combined to frustrate the possibility of genuine consolidation (Glenn 2003).

The Ghanaian case also shows that democracy is not without its costs. As Lindberg has confirmed, neo-patrimonialism has actually been on the increase in Ghana since the resumption of elections, and elections are seen as a reciprocal transaction which will lead to immediate personal benefits for the voter. Although he recognizes that this is consistent with the traditional culture of gift-giving in Ghana, he sees it as potentially dangerous for the consolidation of parliamentary institutions (Lindberg 2003).

Conclusion

With the fall of Communism in Eastern Europe there was after 1989 a new interest among international funding and lending agencies in promoting 'good government' in developing countries. Much of this, inevitably, was focused on Eastern Europe, but Africa and Asia were not overlooked. The implication of the drive for 'good governance' is that political conditions are attached to loans. These conditions may encourage formal democratic procedures rather than substantive democratic gains for the majority in the recipient countries, but obviously the hope has been that the process would become self-sustaining.

Certainly many more developing countries enjoy ostensibly democratic structures today than was the case, say, 20 years ago. However, there are factors which militate against real participation whatever the theoretical arrangements. First, democracy cannot be imposed from above, and it takes time to establish itself even in the most favourable circumstances. Secondly, democracy, like the market, functions less effectively in conditions of poverty, and where, for example, it means simply the freedom to sell your vote to a corrupt local politician it has little substance. Thirdly, even for many genuinely newly democratised countries, much energy has first to be consumed in trying to come to terms with an undemocratic past.

For the increasingly secular societies of the non-Islamic world, there is no other basis for legitimate authority than some form of democracy. How then can national history be satisfactorily explained? Democracy is no longer a decorative ideological overlay on a functional authoritarian base, it is the essence of that functioning. As the Brundtland Report so rightly pointed out, without participation, development will not happen and the environment that is the inheritance of all of us will be destroyed.

Key terms

authority – the accepted right to give orders or make decisions

bureaucratic authoritarianism – belief in the principle of authority as opposed to that of individual freedom

civil rights – rights claimed by or accorded to individuals as citizens of a specific country

civil society – all interest groups, networks and voluntary associations, excluding governmental agencies and profit-making organisations (businesses)

consociational democracy – for Lijphart, power-sharing government, characterised by an elaborate process of negotiation between the elites of the different 'pillars' of society leading to accommodation and compromise

co-optation (or co-option) – choice from within government of people to hold political office

coup – a sudden and decisive change of government illegally or by force at the hands of the armed forces

democracy assistance – the provision of advice, training and technical support for elections, political parties and pressure groups in countries unused to democracy

democratisation – (a) the process by which other forms of government evolve (or are transformed) into democracies; (b) the process by which existing democracies become more democratic, as e.g. by improvements in electoral representation or the defence of civil rights

'essentially-contested' concept – concept on which *by definition* agreement is not possible

fear of freedom – for Fromm, the urge to seek refuge in the leadership of a single supposedly wise figure who represents both authority and stability

internal colonisation – the effective colonisation of large parts of a country by its own ruling elite

legal system – orderly system of civilian courts to administer law, whether independently of government or not

militarism – excessive pride in the glory, honour, power and prestige of the military forces

military developmentalism – belief in the mission of the armed forces to seize power and retain it in order to bring about economic development

pacted transition – agreement for the transition from authoritarian to democratic government

promotional authoritarianism – a desire to promote change, especially economic development, by supplanting the existing government

regional powers – state with sufficient size and force capability to be recognised as a leader within a region

representative government – any form of government in which a representative assembly has to consent to taxation

social cleavages – permanent or long-lasting divisions between social groups

Questions

1. What is democracy and why is it desirable that developing states be democratically governed?

2. Do political and social structures in new states preclude democracy?

3. Does domination by elites inevitably imply authoritarianism?

4. What is the three-stage model of democratisation?

5. What is ideology and how does it relate to politics in the developing world?

6. What role does civil society play in democratisation?

7. Can developed states encourage the emergence of democracy in developing countries? Should they do so?

8. How far can or should non-governmental agencies (IFIs, NGOs) try to encourage democratisation in developing countries?

PART IV

Policy issues

CHAPTER 9

Policy issues

Introduction

This chapter deals with four major policy issues, aid, trade, tourism and the environment. Each is important in its own right, and, indeed, essential to a proper understanding of the relationship between the AICs and the developing countries. However, each also illustrates the special problems of policy-making in new states which lack the resources to explore the range of policy choices available to an AIC. First, therefore, we have to review the special problems of decision-making in the developing country environment.

(a) All decision-making tends to be concentrated at the top level of government. Structures exist for the **deconcentration** of power but it is always worthwhile to appeal against their decisions to the highest authority.
Examples: presidential states in Latin America (all), Africa, e.g. Nigeria, Asia, e.g. Philippines

(b) In foreign affairs, the diplomatic service established at independence lacks resources to maintain effective information systems. For both reasons it lacks continuity in policy-making and is presented with problems from the colonial era which it lacks the ability to resolve on its own.
Examples: boundary disputes in Africa (Western Sahara), Asia (Thailand-Cambodia) and Latin America (Guyana-Venezuela)

(c) The armed forces are not strong enough to fight an effective campaign against another southern state or even against local insurgents. They are strong enough to displace or even to supplant their own governments and so are in a position to exercise a 'veto power' on key decisions.
Examples: Africa (Liberia, DRC), Asia (Pakistan), Latin America (Colombia, Venezuela)

(d) Financially, the country is heavily dependent on the export of primary raw materials. It also has a very weak currency, the value of which is disproportionately affected by changes in the world environment and especially by changes in the world oil price. The finance/economy ministry is constantly under attack for the prevailing poverty. But on the other hand it has little or no alternative but to do what it is told by the IMF, World Bank, foreign banks etc. If they do, however, there will be riots in the streets and the government may fall.

Examples: Africa (Angola, DRC), Latin America (Argentina, Bolivia)

(e)   Any attempt to improve (or even maintain) fair returns from trade can be quashed by the refusal of large foreign corporations to accept it.

Examples: Caribbean (St Lucia, St Vincent, Dominica), Central America (Honduras)

Aid

The politics of aid

Foreign aid is a very new concept. It was virtually unknown before 1945. The use of economic aid as a tool of superpower competition in the Cold War established the practice, but it took much longer than that for the concept that rich countries had a duty to help poor ones to become accepted.

Plate 14   Street scene, Sierra Leone

Table 9.1   OECD countries, net ODA in 2004 as percentage of GNI

Norway	0.87
Denmark	0.85
Luxembourg	0.83
Sweden	0.78
Netherlands	0.73
UN target	*0.70*
Portugal	0.63
France	0.41
Switzerland	0.41
Belgium	0.41
Ireland	0.39
UK	0.36
Finland	0.35
Germany	0.28
Canada	0.27
OECD	*0.26*
Australia	0.25
Spain	0.24
New Zealand	0.23
Austria	0.23
Greece	0.23
Japan	0.19
USA	0.17
Italy	0.15

Source: OECD (2006), 'Net ODA in 2004 as percentage of GNI',
www.oecd.org/dataoecd/0/41/35842562.pdf

With the ending of the Cold War much of the self-interest which generated aid flows between 1950 and 1980 came to an end. The developing world is likely to be the main victim of the change. Already there is in human terms far too little economic aid, and despite their professions of good intentions at the Rio Summit and elsewhere, the budgets the AICs devote to aid are minimal (see Table 9.1). To put the figures in perspective, the EU uses two-thirds of its budget to subsidise European farmers through the Common Agricultural Policy (CAP) and spends only about 3 per cent of its budget on food aid.

Much excellent work is done, especially in emergency situations such as famine and earthquake, by NGOs such as Oxfam and Save the Children. But it is state action which is vital, the role of individuals and NGOs being minimal in comparison. For a variety of reasons government aid is, however, often of very little value for development purposes.

It is very difficult to decide where aid stops and other forms of financial transactions take place, but broadly aid refers to a transfer of resources at non-commercial rates. It may be official, that is collected from taxpayers and transferred by governments themselves or international agencies, or it may be voluntary; that is, raised and administered by NGOs. But this distinction is becoming more blurred as NGOs are increasingly being used to administer official funds. Likewise aid varies in purpose, but what is usually meant by the term foreign aid is official development assistance (ODA). It is possible to make the case that aid has a much broader generic meaning and that non-ODA transfers may in some circumstances carry far greater entitlement to the term.

The term ODA comes from the 1969 redefinition of aid by the Development Assistance Committee of the OECD. This redefinition was a recognition that the term should exclude money collected and administered by NGOs, should exclude assistance not intended for developmental purposes such as military aid and should exclude loans available only at commercial rates which conferred no concessions on the recipients (White and Woestman 1994).

But as Burnell notes, many authors suggest a broader definition of aid reflecting more strongly the donor intentions. To qualify for the name 'aid', transfers should not be self-interested: 'Foreign aid can be construed as inter-societal transfers of resources that are intended by all relevant parties, especially the provider, to serve first and foremost the recipients' needs, interests or wants' (Burnell 1997: 3). But many would see this definition as too tight. Transfers given for non-charitable reasons may have more benefit for the recipients than those given with good intentions which have adverse unintended consequences. There is also a question surrounding the coherence of the 'needs, interests or wants' of the recipient. These are not necessarily the same, and will certainly not be identically experienced by all within a recipient state. Aid varies according to recipients, donors, purposes and forms, or alternatively who it is given to, who gives it, what it is given for and whether it consists of money, material benefits, advice etc. Beneficiaries are specifically targeted, but by whom and why?

The Development Assistance Committee (DAC) of the 29 wealthy and mainly Western members of the OECD has produced a widely accepted definition of ODA as

> resources transferred on concessional financial terms with the promotion of the economic development and welfare of developing countries as the main declared objective. (Burnell 1997: 4)

This definition has strength in embracing both the older idea of humanitarian aid and development project aid. Of course, as Burnell (1997) points out, the two overlap. Without development aid, there may arise greater need for emergency relief, and emergency relief usually includes some element of development aid. For the DAC concessional is the key to what constitutes aid. It suggests that at least a quarter of any loan must effectively be a grant if that transfer is to be considered as assistance. There are resource flows which fund development which are not sufficiently concessional to meet these criteria and which therefore, according to the DAC definition, are not aid.

A financial transfer or some such similar arrangement is not only a means to enhance status because it suggests generosity, it may also happen for more practical and devious reasons. Sometimes there are attempts to swing items onto the aid budget, for example. This, according to Burnell, includes expenditure on the maintenance of refugees in the 'donor' country.

Even if such obvious abuses of the term can be identified and excluded, this still leaves some grey areas. The International Finance Corporation (IFC) is a private sector organisation affiliated to the World Bank which lends at market rates, but it is seen as a leading aid agency because it does so for developmental projects and is non-profit-making. Likewise the Islamic Development Bank established in 1973, in accordance with the edicts of Islam, makes all its loans interest-free.

There is a strong connection between aid and trade in many instances as is illustrated by the interconnections between the work of the British Overseas Development Agency and the Department of Trade and Industry, whereby the giving of aid and the winning of contracts for British companies are frequently dealt with in conjunction with one another.

Such close connections are part of the generalised problem of conditionality with regard to aid. Aid may be given to secure contracts, to boost exports through tying it to what it may be spent on or, as indicated above, to exert an ideological influence in favour of democratisation, human rights, environmental considerations or economic liberalisation (see also the discussion of structural adjustment). Even where such influence may be considered desirable, questions of cultural imperialism have been raised.

The developmental intentions of a transfer are not sufficient in themselves to measure what is or is not aid. More aid for infrastructural development could simply mean more domestic funds available in the recipient country for military expenditure or to reduce taxes on the wealthy who can then buy luxury items. Good intentions may have malign effects. Humanitarian supplies may be hijacked by the military and/or sold to buy arms. Development may not be the end in itself, but rather a step on the road to greater political/social stability in the recipient country and/or the donor state. Whose stability was aid to Russia in 1998 supposed to encourage?

Definitional problems reflect the variety of forms aid takes. Aid in its broadest sense is contributed by intergovernmental organisations (IGOs) such as the International Development Agency (IDA), a specialised section of the World Bank established in 1960, and UNICEF, as well as by states and their governmental organisations, charities and private individuals. Aid from international organisations is termed multilateral, compared with aid from one specific donor country which is called bilateral aid. These two kinds of aid differ in why they are given and in what they are given for.

Aid then is increasingly multinational and is increasingly channelled through international organisations (IOs) and international NGOs. Aid is given to states, to would-be states, to governments and to oppositional elements. An example of this latter kind of aid is the funding given by the World Council of Churches to liberation movements in Southern Africa in the 1970s.

Why is aid given?

Aid is at its most high profile and least contentious when it is a response to an emergency. Crisis aid may take the form of humanitarian aid from UN agencies or private disaster relief organised by pre-existing charities, such as Oxfam, or specially-convened organisations such as Bandaid.

Some countries give aid for idealistic reasons. These are mainly small countries, including Scandinavia, Belgium and the Netherlands, but also Canada, which take the view that the present level of global inequality is unjustified and ought to be rectified. But there is of course a less charitable view of the good intentions of donors in that aid may be seen as a legitimation of the very inequality it purports to address. Further, there may be, as some authors suggest, a First World collective interest here: 'If the international economic system is incapable of providing the wherewithal for an effective reduction of inequality within the community of nations, the developing countries will feel justified in their attempts to destroy the political and economic system which perpetuates international inequalities' (Singer and Ansari 1992: 139).

But the big aid-givers take a much more nationally self-interested and pragmatic line which can at times make aid seem to be little more than another branch of foreign policy. In the 1980s a Bureau for Private Enterprise was established within the US Agency for International Development (USAID) and this reflected the shift away from projects towards supporting private enterprise and restructuring economies. Also during the 1980s US aid was increasingly channelled through the Economic Support Fund (ESF) to areas where the United States perceived a threat to economic and political stability. ESF funds are whole-country subsidies and not targeted on the poor, thus they can be used to free up funds for military purposes.

It is not entirely clear where aid stops and loans or trade begin. Much that is not really aid is termed so to make it sound better and to confer status on the donor(s). Aid is often seen as being 'given' by the international financial institutions (IFIs), that is by the IMF, the main body of the World Bank, and the regional development banks, but in reality these organisations for the most part make loans at not particularly favourable rates and it is therefore difficult to perceive this funding (to which the recipients contribute) as aid. The same can be said of some loans from national institutions.

As Burnell points out, when the UN General Assembly Special Session (UNGASS) adopted in 1960 the target of 1 per cent GNP for net flows from developed to developing countries, it remained unclear whether this figure was to include corporate and/or private investment. Further, it was also unclear whether this figure was to exclude debt service repayments, profit repatriation and dividend remittances. This uncertainty led UNGASS to adopt a proposal from its Commission on International Development, usually known as the Pearson Commission, that there should be a specific and separate target of 0.7 per cent GNP for ODA.

What is it given for?

Despite all these uncertainties, there are clear trends in the patterns of aid. Food aid for example has diminished a good deal, and is now only around 10 per cent of ODA. Technical assistance and cooperation is a growing part of aid. Programme aid is growing, as is debt relief.

Military aid remains one of the biggest items on the aid agenda despite the ending of the Cold War. It includes programmes of military education and training as in the notorious School of the Americas in Panama, where the United States trained many Latin American officers in counter-insurgency techniques and thus equipped them to coup more effectively. It still functions at Fort Benning, Georgia, where anti-narcotics trade aid is expended on training personnel from developing countries (www.soaw.org). It also includes transfers of arms to developing countries, which lock them in to expensive maintenance contracts, benefiting primarily a highly specialised workforce in the donor country. Elaborate weapons systems saddle developing countries not only with the high cost of ammunition and supplies, but of the communications and logistics equipment needed to support a modern style of warfare.

The military aid nominally received by the developing countries in the late 1980s was in excess of the combined health and education budgets in one-fifth of cases. During President Reagan's second term (1984–88), direct military aid comprised more than one-third of all US aid and almost two-thirds of all US aid was military-related. Such aid was given for ideological reasons not only by the wealthy Western nations but also by developing countries themselves; for example, Saudi Arabia and Iran both supplied arms to the Bosnian Muslims in the 1994–95 fighting in the former Yugoslavia.

The most obvious failure of aid to address recipient country 'needs' in any real sense is military aid. It is possible to argue that all aid ultimately ends up as military expenditure because it frees up other funds for military purposes. But more directly there are notorious examples of the tying of aid to military purchases, for example British support for the Pergau Dam in the late 1980s 'coincided' with Malaysia's proposed purchase of Tornado interceptors.

With the end of the Cold War and the collapse of the USSR, Eastern Bloc aid, which was often military aid as can be seen by its concentration on recipients such as Vietnam and Cuba, effectively ended. Certainly this has led to a decline in conflict in some areas, for example Central America. Also it has helped donor agencies such as the IMF/World Bank to employ a policy of considering a recipient's military spending when deciding whether to make a loan. There have been massive decreases in arms imports to Africa, but this just reflects the dire economic situation in the region.

The decline of military aid, relative to its 1980s' highpoint, has been accompanied by a growth of political aid. As we have already noted, good governance, political pluralism and democratic consolidation are actively sought by donors to recipient countries in transition (Burnell 1997: 8). These are aims rather than specific objectives. British ODA has emphasised seven specific priority objectives:

- to promote economic liberalisation;
- to promote enhanced productive capacity;
- to promote good government;
- to reduce poverty;
- to promote human development, especially education and health;
- to enhance the position of women;
- to assist in tackling environmental problems (Eyben 1995).

As can readily be observed, these priorities may not sit comfortably together and in any case such a list does not address the question of what aid is directly given for. Apart from short-term disaster relief, what aid actually funds can be divided into particular projects and generalised development programmes.

In what form is aid given?

This is not just a question of whether aid is given in the form of money or some other form, it is also about the form that the transfer of funds takes. Grants are generally seen as more likely to comprise aid than loans, but loans have their supporters too. Loans are thought to encourage self-reliance rather than dependence. Start-up costs are preferred to aid to meet ongoing maintenance costs. This is better publicity for the donor nation, but it frequently means that projects get started but then fail through lack of continuing support.

Alternatively, as noted above, recipient countries get lumbered with very high maintenance costs, because they are locked in to the purchase of expensive replacement parts from the donor country. This is as true of hydroelectric and thermal generating plants, agricultural equipment, transport, computers and their consumables, as it is of military equipment.

As Cassen points out, the precise degree of effectiveness of aid is essentially 'unknowable', but it is vital that it is considered from the point of view of donors but also in order to enhance aid management (Cassen 1994: 1–6). Clearly the form in which aid is given will impinge on its effectiveness and the fact that donors and recipients will see aid differently contributes to the difficulty of assessing its effectiveness. There is an unusual degree of consensus between left-wing and conservative economists on the negative effects of aid for the recipient country. Both perceive domestic economic policy as becoming politicised in the search for aid to the detriment of developmental activity. Though it tends to be conservative economists who emphasise the growing culture of dependence in aid recipients, both sides acknowledge the capacity of aid to feed the consumption patterns of elites and promote a culture of corruption rather than meet the needs of the poor for economic growth and development. It is mainly radical economists who point to the distortion of local production patterns and markets as a consequence of aid.

A particularly glaring example of how aid can work for donors, but distort recipient economies is tied aid, which requires recipients to spend the funds received directly on the products of the donor country or alternatively to agree to projects which for some reason can only be undertaken by donor country companies. Tied aid is increasing and may now constitute more than two-thirds of bilateral aid. It is essentially a protectionist measure for northern industry against which the WTO cannot act. For example, most US aid is given for the purchase of US goods and services. The tying of aid means that aid recipients are not free to take advantage of global competition, to buy really appropriate products and to support local production.

Multilateral aid is much less likely to be self-interested and is therefore increasingly preferred by developing countries and it has now reached more than one-third of all aid transfers. Multilateral aid is also much more likely to go to the poorest countries because it is related more to need than other considerations and it does not create the same direct obligation on the part of the recipient. It can also offer some degree of coordination for the myriad different projects under way in some developing nations. However, it is also true that not all members are equal partners in multilateral agencies and that 'aid' from the Bretton Woods institutions has been highly conditional, inflexible and has produced extensive environmental damage.

Donors are generally the wealthiest nations so they have a vested interest in stabilising the existing global economy and that is precisely what the Bretton Woods system was set up to do. Perceptions of how this stability may be achieved have changed with time and the demise of the former Eastern Bloc. The 'first generation' conditionalities of the 1980s, fiscal stabilisation and macroeconomic liberalisation, have given way to the 'second generation' conditionalities of the 1990s, good governance, democratisation and human rights.

Too frequently, therefore, aid is given to further the aims (whether these be national economic or ideological aims) of the donor rather than to address the needs of the recipient. Flexibility is required for an aid programme to be effective; aid must have the capacity to respond to local conditions. Where it is donor needs that are being met by aid this is not the case; aid is for the most part tied to specific projects and worse still donor country inputs often must be used. Much food aid is not a response to local needs at all, but rather dumping of surplus production by the 'donor' countries as part of domestic price-support programmes which help to maintain global prices. Food aid has some peculiar problems all its own and is particularly controversial, partly for the reasons outlined by Sen (1981), that in a well-organised and less selfish world it should not be necessary, but also for other reasons. Food aid may avert disaster in the short term in the particular local area where it is distributed if it is targeted to those in need, but it does nothing to change the conditions which gave rise to the problem in the first place. It quite simply does not meet local needs beyond the very short term; in fact, it may even contribute to them by depressing local prices and thus reducing incentives to increase local food production. There have been glaring examples of food aid being used as a political weapon, for example by the United States during the 1974 famine in Bangladesh refusing to release food aid due to political disagreements with the recipient government.

Aid as an asymmetrical power relationship frequently reflects historical connections with donor nations rather than need on the part of recipients. This skewing of the aid process means that most aid does not go to the poorest countries where need is greatest. It may be given for strategic reasons or because the ex-colonial powers prefer to support their remaining colonies and to swing this support onto their aid budgets. Donors become trapped in the aid relationship too because they have so much invested in the recipients of their aid. The aid relationship is not a static one and recipients may well wish to enhance their power relative to the donor(s) of their aid by reducing their dependence, possibly by building up trade relationships with non-donor countries or by increasing self-sufficiency.

Aid requiring structural adjustment has been charged with not only environmental degradation, but also negative impact on human rights and especially on women. The adjustment may be a temporary process as optimists suggest, but much of what would be termed 'development', that is the better quality of life for the majority of the population, is being lost. Aid is being used to reverse development in any meaningful sense of the word. The very existence of an external creditor/donor applying unpopular conditions may be destabilising, promoting a nationalist backlash or popular unrest as in Peru's drastic stabilisation programme under President Fujimori ('Fujishock').

Perhaps the most devastating critique of aid is that, in an increasingly globalised world, economic aid is not only very small beer but is actually declining. US aid was 2 per cent GNP during the years of the Marshall Plan but is now only one-eighth of that. Jan Hogendorn (1996) writes: 'total aid from all sources is equal to less than 18 days' worth of military expenditure or two months' worth of rich-country alcohol and tobacco consumption'. From the donor countries' points of view aid is usually fairly minimal but even that may be difficult to get past an increasingly unequal and hostile tax base at home. For the recipients, net inflows from aid do not compensate for net outflows as debt service charges. Wayne Ellwood argues that in 1998 developing countries received $30 billion of official aid, but repaid $250 billion in debt. The anomaly is most striking where aid is most needed. In 1996 south of the Sahara Africa paid $2.5 billion more in debt service charges than it received as new loans and credits. The IMF alone has taken more than $3 billion out of Africa since the mid-1980s.

NGOs and aid

NGOs have been increasingly active as development agencies working in the distribution and administration of aid, both voluntary and official. The funds available to northern NGOs increased massively in the 1980s through media portrayal of their role in crises such as the 1984–85 famine in the Horn of Africa. This level of funding further ensured that such NGOs were taken seriously by IGOs such as the World Bank and UN agencies (UNDP, UNHCR, WHO, UNICEF).

Official aid such as that of the EU is increasingly channelled through NGOs for practical reasons. Inappropriate aid-funded development projects have frequently failed completely or at least failed to serve the intended beneficiaries. The outcome for aid has been negative as such failures have sapped the goodwill of First World taxpayers who suffer from 'aid (or donor) fatigue'. Aid is seen as having failed especially in the case of Africa where crises are more frequent, but also in other places such as India where inequality is increasing.

The recognition that an aid establishment exists which talks to developing world elites and keeps them sweet has led to the development of a new anti-aid movement as well as a more pragmatic recognition of the need to use aid to bolster grassroots, local, municipal and provincial involvement in development projects. NGOs are seen as having the capacity to target the poor and use local expertise via local fieldworkers in ways that official agencies cannot. Also they are seen as being less wasteful, having relatively lower administration costs. The costs related to aid greatly reduce its value. These include administration for all types of aid and transport costs for aid such as food which necessitates distribution.

But even if aid is administered and distributed through NGOs, there are logistical problems. Large northern NGOs have been less successful than had been hoped. They tend to be bureaucratic and, in some cases, are indulging in their own turf wars. They may even be seen as having been co-opted into the aid establishment. Southern NGOs are burgeoning. They often have the real grassroots expertise, though their importance in international relief work is often overlooked by the media. They are often fragmentary and difficult to coordinate, with different interests and approaches compared with the northern groups which aim to harness their energies.

It is hard to discern how effective NGOs are in their role as disseminators of aid. Processes of accountability are missing from the activities of most NGOs and there is very little information available. Resources are not expended on evaluations and where evaluations of projects have been done, the results are often not published except in an edited form designed to win further funding from the public. What little evidence there is suggests that they are not very cost-effective and their services often miss the poorest and also fail to extend participation to women. Provision is reactive and therefore tends to be patchy.

The importance of aid

As Bob Hammond has pointed out, the problems of aid are not necessarily inherent in the process itself, but may be the results of the ways in which it has been operated (Hammond 1994: 210–21). This does not just refer to the way it is perceived by donors, but also to the obstacles to success in the recipient countries. Cassen (1994: 7) writes that 'the relief of poverty depends both on aid and the policies of the recipient countries – a collaboration in which aid is definitely the junior partner.'

Perhaps this weakness reflects the fact that aid involves very small sums in comparison with direct investment and trade, but nevertheless these sums can be vital in moments of real crisis and are important to the very poorest states, which do not receive private investment anyway. For such countries aid is a major capital inflow. Aid can address problems which private investment cannot or will not address. It may provide the boost to infrastructural development which leads to a country being perceived as viable and thus to private foreign investment. In other words aid may be a sprat to catch a mackerel, it may be a catalyst for development by private enterprise. Further it may finance projects where the pay-off is not tangible, such as health and education schemes, or is too long term to interest private investors, such as agricultural research. Aid can be and has been a spur to growth in specific cases, Korea obviously, Brazil, Colombia and Thailand (Cassen 1994: 10). There have been real benefits as a result of official aid:

1. An increase in developing world food production, without which the crisis of global hunger would be much more widespread.
2. Extension of primary health care and support for UN agency health programmes.
3. Scholarships for study in the First World and other educational programmes through institutions such as the British Council. (Hammond 1994: 216–17)

Further there has been over the past 20 years a conscious effort on the part of aid-givers to target the least developed countries, to give them aid as grants (grants now comprise two-thirds of all ODA) rather than loans and to write off their debts at intervals. Even where, as in the Sahel, there has been no obvious economic achievement, in that aid has failed to stimulate growth or reduce poverty, it has certainly contributed to tangible social improvements which have been achieved against a barrage of obstacles, not least the massive increase in population. Food security has increased, as has educational provision (Naudet and Pradelle 1997).

The future of aid

Many have questioned whether aid has a future given the power of the criticisms levelled against it. As Burnell (1997: 232) has put it, 'as people look increasingly to the next millennium, aid is being talked about more and more as a transitory phenomenon of the twentieth century'. However, there is much evidence that the growing role of the UN in the post-Cold War world will more and more involve the administration of aid. This role is increasingly to address complex emergencies involving humanitarian issues, such as peace-keeping, the protection and resettlement of refugees through the UNHCR, and the distribution of food aid, the majority of which is now a UN responsibility. In fact, much ODA is now channelled through the UN and 45 per cent of it is spent on emergencies.

It is uncertain whether aid donors can expect any clear leadership from anywhere other than the UN as the United States as an aid-giver is in decline, Japan is recovering from a severe economic crisis and the EU is more con-cerned with the the problems of the euro and its territorial expansion. But the UN is not perceived as a total success in its international role (see the role of the UN in Rwanda, Chapter 2). The World Bank might have wished to pro-vide leadership in the sphere of aid, but its role is increasingly being questioned from within and without and it lacks the political leadership to coordinate the diverse agencies involved. The emergence of regional banks and the growing importance of private capital flows, which sit more comfortably with the dom-inant neo-liberal discourse, have reduced its role.

Trade

The role of trade

Trade is critical to the welfare of developing countries, because:

1. Trade (other than in arms, where normal rules do not apply) should not add to indebtedness and may actually generate a significant surplus.
2. No conditions normally attach to trade, although some trade expansion may be built on political and economic concessions, and political ideologies are normally not an issue.
3. Expanding and diversifying trade enhances security, although very new markets may be seen as insecure and terms of trade can change drastically.
4. Trade encourages self-reliance and yet is fully consistent with the dominant neo-liberal discourse and the Washington consensus.

However, the balance of trade is almost always tilted towards the developed countries. Developing countries depend on markets, but developed countries can choose between suppliers and so drive down commodity prices. And, as successive Rounds of trade negotiations have shown, despite their verbal com-mitment to free trade developed countries continue in key areas to maintain their own tariff barriers against the free entry of products from the developing world. The successful resistance of US sugar producers to an agreement with the Caribbean countries which would have lowered tariffs on imported sugar is a case in point.

Less obvious are the barriers of hidden protectionism. The EU, for example, imposes a variety of restrictions on the import of goods for reasons of health (banning meat from countries which have an outbreak of foot-and-mouth disease) or quality (prohibiting toys that do not meet certain safety standards and so might present a risk to small children). Such restrictions are not protectionist in intent but may be in practice if, for example, foot-and-mouth is endemic in the country in question. Other restrictions may be quite deliberately protectionist: requiring products to have special labelling for the country concerned, insisting on elaborate form-filling for each consignment, and so forth. However, if a country sells goods abroad below the cost of manufacture this is known as dumping and even under WTO rules countries have a right to protect their home markets against this sort of unfair competition.

The problem for developing countries is that goods produced in them may not in themselves be entirely fit for purpose, or are made or assembled by women or children who are paid so little and/or work such long hours in conditions of such dire poverty that a developing country may reasonably see this as unfair competition. But on the other hand insistence on higher standards may mean that the developing country is unable to sell any of its products and its people starve. For all these reasons, trade between developing countries (or South–South trade, as it is often termed) has great advantages, potentially.

South–South trade

South–South cooperation can provide important new opportunities for development based on geographical proximity, on similarities in demand and tastes, on relevance of respective development experience, know-how, and skills, and on availability of complementary natural and financial skills. . . . South–South cooperation offers developing countries a strategic means for pursuing relatively autonomous paths to development suited to the needs and aspirations of their people. (South Commission 1990: 16)

The assumption behind the stress on South–South trade is that, if widespread, South–South trade relations would break the stranglehold of dependency. Dependency on the North would be ended if the North could no longer control the terms of trade. However, some would argue that there is an infrastructure of northern domination, that the global institutions and the monetary system and the transport system are dominated by the North, and that in consequence dependency would not come to an end with the ending of the conditions that gave rise to it in the first place.

As well as enhancing the South's bargaining power against that of the North, South–South cooperation would possibly enable the South to benefit from economies of scale. Complementary and supportive neighbours would enhance the possibilities of development. However, working against the development of South–South linkages is the existing preoccupation of the developing countries with North–South negotiations. The greater the concern with relations with the North, the greater the tendency to place South–South co-operation on the back-burner. A second cluster of causes is to be found in the disagreements, hostilities and sometimes even wars which reduce cooperation between developing world states. These become much more likely where very similar economies see themselves as being in competition; single or very limited product economies force their members to be constantly aware of their dependency on the goodwill of their northern customers.

The diversity of the South at once militates against South–South cooperation and makes for economic complementarity with the North. Some developing countries have capital (Brunei, Saudi Arabia, the United Arab Emirates) and/or energy surpluses. Indeed, these and other OPEC members such as Kuwait have made development loans available at preferential rates to less fortunate developing world states. Others, such as Mexico and Brazil, are technologically advanced relative to their neighbours and their technology may be more accessible and more appropriate to other developing countries than that of the North.

Some countries rich in capital but lacking technical skills have made good this deficit by importing developing country nationals. Examples are Iraq and Kuwait. China has numerous technical and scientific exchange programmes with a variety of countries all over the world and has undertaken thousands of development projects in developing countries. Some countries, for example India, have enormous manufacturing capability, others, such as the Democratic Republic of Congo or Namibia, are rich in various natural resources. Collectively they have the components for a bright future if only the many political difficulties that stand in the way of cooperation can be overcome.

In the 20 years between 1955 and 1975 trade among developed countries grew faster than either trade amongst developing countries or between developed countries and developing countries. But developing countries' exports to developed countries increased much faster than developed countries' exports to developing countries, suggesting that interdependence has been enhanced. Yet it remains true that the main developed-country market is other developed countries and that they also provide the main market for developing-country products. The character of developed-country imports from developing countries is more vital than in the reverse case. They are either mainly non-renewable or developed countries cannot produce them due to the nature of their climate etc. This gives developing countries strength in the long term through import-substitution industrialisation. Japan and the EU are more dependent on developing-country imports than is the United States, which is the most self-sufficient of all developed countries, but projections suggest US import dependence will increase with time.

Another possibility, already tried in some cases, is cartelisation. To create a producer cartel in some products is possible, but the very poverty of developing world nations and their need for funds to tide them over in the short term works against success. Oil is the best-known case. But oil was an exception in that it is the essence of modern production, it would cost a great deal to substitute and a high proportion of supplies were held by OPEC members who had surplus resources which strengthened their position. There are few if any other products that would qualify under all these headings. And, indeed, since the beginning of the 1980s many of the best-known producer cartels have collapsed, not least the International Tin Agreement (ITA) (Crabtree 1987). OPEC itself no longer controls the greatest share of traded oil and is nothing like as powerful as it was in the 1970s, although as it showed at the end of 1999 it still had the capacity to raise oil prices if its members were prepared to act in concert.

Trade policies and the developing world

No one in their senses would want to stop the development of the developing world, nor could anyone make a moral case for people elsewhere in the world being denied the material things First World peoples take for granted. But the pattern of development that has been established over the years is not sustainable and has certain very obvious disadvantages. The problem of rapidly expanding populations has been met by encouraging uncontrolled and unplanned development. Those countries that have been successful in making the breakthrough into long-term growth have made industrialisation a prime target and invested heavily in education to provide a skilled workforce. Unfortunately at the same time they have degraded the environment and made their societies over-reliant on the continued expansion of production. Where plantation agriculture exists, and it is widespread, it has had serious effects on the capacity of a country to feed its own people. This mode of development, therefore, is not sustainable in its present form (Jackson 1990).

Foreign investment and the growth of TNCs are features of development in the developing world about which there is considerable controversy. To the proponents of the free market, they have been largely beneficial. To their critics, they have at the least produced significant negative effects, and there is reason to suspect that both act to widen the gap between rich and poor countries, and between rich and poor in any one country.

Tourism

Tourism is, of course, a form of trade. In 1950 about 25 million people travelled abroad as tourists, by the mid-1990s this figure had risen to 550 million and by 2000 to 698 million. These millions spent an estimated $575 billion, including their costs of transport. As Urry (1990) has it, tourism is a vital part of a 'modern' lifestyle. Its international form reflects time–space compression and other aspects of globalisation. It is also a part of that process or, more accurately, set of processes. Since it is necessary to be able to afford a 'modern' lifestyle to be a tourist, most of these tourists travel from developed countries. Most also prefer to experience that 'modernity' while on holiday and they travel to other developed countries, but there is a growing interest in travelling to the developing countries. Tourism employs one-ninth of the world's population. It is the fastest-growing industry in the world and according to the World Tourism Organisation it will soon be the largest. It is labour intensive and a massive source of employment. Further as a potential foreign currency earner it is obviously an attractive aspect of a development strategy for southern states which are touristically well endowed or just heavily indebted.

The mass tourism which developed after the Second World War was originally between North America and Western Europe, but by the mid-1970s 8 per cent of tourists were North Americans and West Europeans travelling to the developing world. By the mid-1980s, this figure had risen to 17 per cent and by 1998 it had reached 30 per cent. Over 50 million people travel from industrialised to developing countries every year. Tourism has replaced sugar as the Dominican Republic's main foreign exchange earner, and bauxite as that of Jamaica. In Jamaica more than one-third of the workforce were employed in tourism in 2005, and tourism and related services brought in an income of US$1.33 billion annually. In Barbados, tourism accounted for 12 per cent of GDP in 2002, gave employment to some 25,000 of the 141,000 workforce and was the main supplier of foreign exchange. Among the smaller Caribbean island states, St Lucia stood out with an economy almost entirely dependent on tourism. But this could suggest that a new dependency has developed, as Cynthia Enloe (1989: 32) put it: 'Countries such as Puerto Rico, Haiti, Nepal, Gambia and Mexico have put their development eggs in one basket, spending millions of dollars from public funds to build the sorts of facilities that foreign tourists demand.'

Although tourism implies a redistribution of resources, the tourist relationship is essentially one of purchaser and servant (some have gone further and suggested master and slave: see Patullo 1996: 63–5). It is an essentially unequal one in a way and to a degree that other trading relationships do not have to be. But on the other hand it puts First World people into the developing world, inducing cultural contact in a way that other industries do not.

Many would see tourism as a means to development, indeed, it was recognised as such by the 1963 UN Conference on Tourism and International Travel. Tourism generates employment, and money flowing into a tourist area is at least partly re-spent there creating further indirect developmental effects. The West Indian Commission established by the Caribbean Community (Caricom) in the early 1990s recognised this in their 1992 Report *Time for Action* (p. 106, cited in Patullo 1996: 6):

> Out of the tourist industry radiate stimuli for a wide range of industries producing goods and services; this is the concept of tourism as an axial product. Viewed in this light, the tourism sector can play an important role in the diversification and transformation of the region.

It is at once a modernising and conserving process. Preservation of the environment is a key aspect of tourism in a way it is not of other industries precisely because a damaged environment would be less saleable. Further, tourists provide new markets for traditional and threatened activities. Infrastructure developments benefit tourists and locals alike. Not only is it a means whereby First World wealth can be transmitted to the developing world, but also a means by which modern values can be diffused. This process would imply, for example, integration and empowerment of women, whose status and standard of living is expected to be enhanced. (See Levy and Lerch 1991 for a powerful critique of this position.) However, the clash of modernity and tradition is unresolved in the tourist relationship with developing countries. As Lanfant et al. recognise,

> A fundamental contradiction is that from the inside, from the native point of view, tourism is a route to economic development; but from the outside view, the natives are a traditional object of desire. From the inside, tourism means modernity and change; but from the outside, the tourist object is seen as exotic, primitive and immutable. The locals are called upon to preserve a purity that never existed. (Lanfant et al. 1995: ix, Preface)

Critics of tourism as development have argued that it does not produce the benefits claimed for it, indeed it may promote an essentially unbalanced development. It tends to confirm existing local class/gender relations along with existing international economic and power relations. It can be actively harmful, increasing vulnerability. The social, cultural and environmental costs are seen as outweighing any benefits. These costs include:

- Most of the benefit of tourism goes to the TNCs involved in global tourism. Less than 25 per cent of the cost of a package holiday, for example, reaches the host country. This situation has worsened in the Caribbean following the introduction in the late 1990s of 'all-inclusive' packages.
- Enclave development of tourist facilities means damage to local economies and social dislocation caused by people leaving their homes and families to work in tourist enclaves. The best sites are taken for hotel complexes and the price of land in such areas rises beyond the means of locals.
- Money spent on infrastructure is geared to tourism and tourist areas, not to the needs of local people for example in terms of health, education and housing.
- The need to import consumables for the tourists means some islands have to import vast quantities of water and in the most extreme case tourism constitutes a cost, not a gain.
- Local culture gets preserved as a spectacle, local people as a sort of human zoo. It may even be reconstructed or mythologised to suit tourist tastes. However, at the same time tourism is one source of a 'demonstration effect' which disenchants locals with their own condition and instils alien values such as materialism which damage local cultures (Harrison 1993).

Those who explain the problems of developing nations in terms of core/periphery would tend to argue the high costs of tourism as a development strategy. Like all such strategies it is doomed to failure because the inherent power imbalance between the core and the periphery ensures the continuance and increase of that inequality. Tourists from the core visit peripheral countries, but they do so through travel companies located in and repatriating profits to the core. Enclaves with First World advantages develop within the peripheral countries which receive these tourists. These outposts of the core draw resources, human and otherwise, from the surrounding areas.

Despite expecting many of the comforts of home, the long-haul traveller is looking for a different experience, otherwise there is no point in the expense and inconvenience of long-distance travel. Thus some of the most vulnerable societies, located in the developing countries, are targets for tourist attention. In the case of the most fragile such areas the 'carrying capacity' is already strained without the added impact of tourists. In most places this is not a particular problem and a well-managed tourist industry could enhance the conditions of local people. Unfortunately, these places often lack precisely that administrative and managerial expertise which could make tourism beneficial to the local community. Moreover, the relative strength of foreign stakeholders in the tourist industry ensures that they, not local interests, benefit. Local people often lack an effectively organised voice and are unable to assert their interests against those of foreign hotel chains and travel companies along with the national governmental interests they have persuaded to take their part.

Case studies on tourism

Case study 9.1   **Goa**

Goa is a small state on the West Coast of India with about 1.2 million people. It is a relatively healthy place compared with some parts of India, and culturally interesting. It was a colony of Portugal 1510–1961 but the Portuguese influence is mainly limited to coastal areas and it is to these areas that European visitors go. International tourism started to take off in the 1960s with young people from the First World who rejected Western materialism seeking enlightenment. In the mid-1980s, the Indian government drew up a tourist development plan designating Goa a national centre of tourism along with the beaches of Kerala and Orissa.

The Goan tourist industry is not popular with all sections of the local community. There has developed an opposition mainly informal but exemplified by the Goan Foundation. Concern is that development has been too large-scale and too rapid. Problems have developed which threaten the livelihoods and lifestyles of locals. These include the pollution of the coastline, visually damaged by high-rise hotels, through discharges of sewage from the hotels, pesticide/fertiliser run-off from the gardens and golf-courses surrounding those hotels and by pleasure boating in the inshore fishing grounds. There is much resentment of the profligate use of water for the tourist industry when locals often lack domestic running water. Further there is the perception that much of the financial benefit of the development has accrued to foreign stakeholders, the rest to national interests and very little to Goans.

Case study 9.2   **Belize**

There is much debate about precisely what 'ecotourism' is, but here it will be taken to imply tourism primarily aimed at experiencing aspects of the natural and social environments without necessarily implying the sustainability of this tourism. There is, it is argued, a built-in tendency to sustainability in such tourism because its attraction will cease if it develops into a mass tourist industry and thus spoils its purpose. Belize is a perfect place for ecotourism with dense forests in the interior and a barrier reef along its coast. Independence was so late because Belizeans were not particularly bothered to achieve it as they were subject to an unwelcome territorial claim by Guatemala to the southern fifth of their territory. It only became amicably independent from Britain in 1981. Only a small proportion of its land area is cultivated. It is clearly a country looking for ways of increasing its foreign exchange earnings.

Tourism is growing in importance and the tourism strategy is official government policy. It recognises Belize's unique attractions and has devised government actions to take account of the nature of ecotourism. Certain potential tourist groups are directly targeted and indigenous problems which might put off such tourists are addressed. The tourist potential is thought to be balanced against the needs of Belizean society present and future in a strategy of conservation and wise use. Belize is very anxious to avoid the problems associated with mass tourism, overdevelopment of tourist areas, pollution and damage to the natural environment. Just as it has a major market nearby in the United States so it is also located very close to some of the busiest tourist areas, for example Cozumel and Cancun in Mexico. And tourist numbers are growing at an accelerating pace, targeting two-centre tourists wanting to combine the mass package resorts with a week in Belize.

Tourism is hitting the developmental activities of Belizeans, though it is possible to argue this is not necessarily a bad thing. Over 30 per cent of the national area has been set aside as reserves in which no traditional slash-and-burn cultivation is permitted and traditional subsistence farmers are re-routed into tourist-related activities. Some ecological damage is inevitable and some has already occurred. For example, some mangrove swamps have been cleared for hotel development in the north, a loss in terms of breeding grounds for fish and as a protection against coastal erosion.

Case study 9.3   **Costa Rica**

Another haven of relative calm in Latin America also noted for the rapid development of ecotourism is Costa Rica. Costa Rica's government recognised its rich potential and planned its marketing of the country as a product and foreign exchange earnings from tourism have overtaken those from banana production. Although there is greater diversity in Costa Rican tourism with only a minority of tourists attracted primarily by the rich flora and fauna, others by the more usual sun and sea, most want to visit the extensive areas of national park. There is clearly a tension between the original protected status of the national parks and the recognition of their attractions to visitors evident in the National Tourist Board's large-scale tourism strategy. (Weaver 1999: 85–98)

Case study 9.4   **The Caribbean Islands**

Other parts of the Caribbean have also experienced the growth of large-scale tourism. This is an obvious strategy for an area caught between the emergent trading blocs of the EU and NAFTA, which has sought to protect Latin American producers at a cost to the EU's traditional Caribbean suppliers. This remains a small percentage of global tourism, but it is far greater than that experienced in other parts of the developing world. The number of visitors to the Caribbean each year is in excess of the total population of the region. This anomaly is most marked in the cases of the longer-standing tourist destinations, the Bahamas and Bermuda, but other islands are catching up. By the 1990s the Dominican Republic was the most popular destination in the Caribbean with 1.9 million stopover visitors in 1994 and, according to the UN, 3.4 million visitors in 2003, earning the country US$3.1 billion. In a region where unemployment is a key problem, tourism is a major source of jobs on many of the islands. The most extreme case is the Bahamas where more than a third of the official labour force are directly employed in the tourist industry. Direct employment of locals is for the most part low paid, unskilled and seasonal. Many more work in the informal sector in activities connected with tourism such as providing transport or selling souvenirs.

Development in the islands is primarily by foreign stakeholders, such as the British company Airtours and the Dutch airline KLM, and relatively little of the benefits accrue to the locals. This is especially true where the all-inclusive package is being developed to ensure that tourist expenditure remains in the enclave resort facilities.

The dependency and vulnerability of the Caribbean economies is being perpetuated in these new external linkages. George Monbiot's attacks in 1998 on the Dominican Republic's tourist industry (see below) were not directed primarily at the ignorance of the visitors, but at the damage that the tourist trade did to the host country. Tourist development, because its purpose was not primarily developmental and it was not therefore planned, is also very uneven. In some parts of the region there is just too much supply and too little demand. The number of visitors is limited by the relatively high costs of provision in the region, especially the costs of imports of goods and services which hits foreign currency earnings very hard. There are also other ongoing costs which fall not to the tourist industry itself but to the governments of the islands. Maintaining international airports is probably the greatest such cost in financial terms. For locals, tourist consumption of scarce water supplies could be still more important (Patullo 1996).

The View from the Ground

By *George Monbiot, The Guardian,* 25 April 1998

Whingeing Poms

"How do you know," the Australians used to ask, "when a planeload of Poms has arrived at Sydney Airport? Because", the answer went, "the whining doesn't stop when the engines are cut." The people of the Dominican Republic may well be telling the same gag.

Last month, three major tour companies either closed down or curtailed their business in the republic after hundreds of British tourists complained of upset stomachs. Though the far greater numbers of Germans and Canadians who visit the island had registered few complaints, British visitors were said to be falling like flies. "It's become a nightmare," Brenda Wall of Holiday Travelwatch moaned. "For the very first time a third world country has become a number one travel destination and the infrastructure can't keep up with it." Even the *Guardian* carried a lengthy sob story about a couple who had fallen ill on their holiday of a lifetime.

It's time we woke up and smelt the sewers. Every year, thousands of Dominican children die of gastric diseases, and not a murmur of protest comes from the *Guardian* or anywhere else. A bunch of British tourists turns up in one of the most impoverished places on earth to drink cocktails and soak up the sun, gets the runs, and it's reported as if the sky had fallen on our heads.

Tourists visit places like the Dominican Republic because they're exotic, then complain when they turn out to be just that. The tropics, as everyone knows, are blessed with fecundity and biodiversity, and we don't need David Attenborough to tell us that this exuberant fauna includes a fascinating range of pathological organisms, which love the high-fat, high-protein, meat-rich diet that visitors

to the republic, but not its inhabitants, enjoy. The tour companies conspired in the problems they later lamented: while enthusing tourists with promises that this would be a holiday unlike any other, in a place unlike anywhere they had ever been before, they simultaneously assured them that their break on the island would be no more challenging than holidays anywhere else; that the whole physical and cultural paraphernalia of British tourism could be transplanted unadjusted into the republic, regardless of what or whom lived there already.

But adjusting is precisely what you don't expect to do when you take a holiday abroad. Tourists are the aristocrats of the New World Order. They are pampered and protected wherever they go, they are treated with deference and never corrected. Tour companies do their best to provide what the tourists expect, rather than educating tourists to expect what the country can reasonably provide.

We may all become lords and ladies when we travel to the Third World, but we don't leave much of our fabulous wealth behind. Children in the slums of Santo Domingo continue to die of diarrhoea because the money visitors spend on their holidays doesn't reach them. Indeed, thousands are living in the most fetid conditions not despite the tourist industry but because of it: their homes on the coast were bulldozed and their parents' livelihoods destroyed to make way for hotels and engineer the unspoilt paradise the tourists expect to discover. Some of the dispossessed have found work in the industry: the luckier ones become servants in the big hotels. The less fortunate scrape a marginal living selling flipflops and coconuts on the beach, or offering the sort of services which, for many British men, are the primary, often the sole, reason for travelling abroad.

Nearly all the money you lay down for a package holiday on the island either stays in Britain or finds its way into the hands of the dispossessors, who use it to eradicate yet more coastal villages and drive their inhabitants into the slums. And yet we continue to convince ourselves that bringing our delicate stomachs, our pub crawls and our insatiable demands to impoverished parts of the world is to confer upon them the most munificent favour: ask any travel agent and she or he will tell you, without a scrap of supporting evidence, that tourism brings wealth to local people.

Moreover, as many of those who HAD found jobs in the republic's tourist industry now know to their cost, tourism is among the most volatile businesses on earth. A resort might be heaving one year and deserted the next, often through no fault of the local industry. During and after the Gulf War, Americans refused to travel to Europe or even Africa, in case Saddam Hussein shot their planes down. When the tourists disappear, the big operators can simply disinvest and reinvest elsewhere; local people are left with a ruined economy and a wrecked environment. More than five hundred years after Columbus brought his curse to the island, the new conquistadores continue to wreak the havoc he began.

Source: Http://www.monbiot.com/archives/1998/04/25/whingeing-poms/

Case study 9.5 **Kenya**

Africa south of the Sahara as a region has relatively little international tourism, largely due to the perception of Africa as poor, unsafe and unhealthy.

Sea and sun tourism has been concentrated in Kenya, The Gambia and South Africa; wildlife tourism in Kenya and Southern Africa. An ability to offer a combination of these two kinds of tourist activity in a two-centre package has been a great advantage to Kenya. Wildlife tourism in Kenya is an obvious development given the rich biodiversity of the game parks of the Kenyan interior. Its known mammal and bird species (what most wildlife tourists want to see) are outnumbered only by the Congo, a much less pleasant place for the northern tourist. The recognition of the actual and potential importance of this diverse fauna led to the creation in 1991 of the Kenya Wildlife Service.

The sheer quantity of tourist activity in Kenya constitutes a distortion of development and a vulnerability to changes of circumstances in the tourist-sending countries as well as in the host country itself (cf. Monbiot 1998). Tourism is Kenya's largest foreign currency earner and had contributed as much as 11 per cent of GNP before domestic problems in the mid-1990s caused a falling off in tourist numbers. However, by 2005 Kenya's services sector, which accounted for 63 per cent of GDP, was dominated by tourism (lcweb2.loc.gov./frd/cs/profiles/Kenya.pdf). Government policy has encouraged foreign investment in the tourist industry and the majority of Kenyan hotels are foreign-owned. They are also concentrated in the coastal area, around Nairobi and near the game parks. Development in these areas has not been planned and tourist numbers have not been controlled. This concentration can present problems in protected areas simultaneously charged with the preservation of biodiversity and the accommodation of tourists. Very little of the funds raised through tourism is spent on conserving the protected areas (Weaver 1999: 109–25).

Case study 9.6   **The Gambia**

The Gambia's problems resulting from its tourist industry are not so much the problems of conserving its natural resources as coping with its distorted development. The tourist industry has been developed with the support of UNDP and the International Development Agency (IDA) since the late 1960s. Most tourists are from Northern Europe and some two-thirds are British. This makes The Gambia highly dependent on the UK and tourism contributes more than 10 per cent The Gambia's GNP.

Further, the Gambian tourist industry is dominated by international hotel chains. This foreign investment was encouraged by a government policy of tax breaks and preferential land allocations. Although for The Gambia tourist industry receipts are vital, most of the profit generated accrues to foreign interests. Tourists book their seats on foreign-owned airlines, through foreign tour operators and stay in foreign-owned hotels, built with imported foreign materials, and during their stay they consume imported products because there is relatively little local production which could meet their needs. Clearly tourism provides an important source of both direct and tourist-related employment, but The Gambia is at the top end of the range for the seasonal component of employment in the tourist industry (Weaver 1999: 55). Two-thirds of those employed in the tourist industry are laid off in the low season from April to October. It is also highly localised, being concentrated in the area around Banjul. Thus tourism may be seen as exacerbating inequalities within The Gambia.

Case study 9.7   **Southern Africa**

Much of Southern Africa is experiencing the rapid development of ecotourism. Again it is the diverse fauna which attracts visitors. Wildlife tourism is a major source of income for Africa. In 1995 the chairman of the National Parks Board of South Africa estimated that within only a few years tourism would earn enough to fund the entire National Programme of Reconstruction and Development. 1996 was declared 'The Year of Eco-Tourism'. The game reserves are booked up months in advance and there are too few flights to meet demand. International and local hotel groups have cornered the market at present and most provision is in the top price bracket. There is a need for smaller scale, lower-priced provision if South Africa is to open up a mass market in order to integrate the wider local community in accordance with the expressed intentions of the National Programme of Reconstruction and Development which aims to boost jobs and welfare in rural areas. Zimbabwe earns more than $200 million a year from tourism.

But there is a conflict between what tourists want to see and the aspirations of the poor. In Zimbabwe conservation areas for endangered wildlife threatened by poachers are perceived as a means for large landowners to avoid the post-colonial redistribution of land. Further, in some areas, the traditional ways of life are being pushed aside for the tourist industry. The establishment of national parks in some parts of Africa has been damaging for the hunting or nomadic lifestyles of the local populations. George Monbiot points out that the Khwe Bushmen of Botswana have been pushed out of their traditional homelands which now form part of the Central Kalahari Game Reserve despite being supported by international human rights groups. They are considered a threat to the wildlife which tourists travel to see (Monbiot 1998).

Sex tourism

As Enloe (1989: 36) notes: 'To succeed, sex tourism requires Third World women to be economically desperate enough to enter prostitution; having done so it is difficult to leave.' Although there are newer centres such as Cuba and the Dominican Republic, sex tourism has developed often as an extension of the 'Rest and Recreation' facilities expected by US troops in the past. It is no accident therefore that some of the centres are former R&R locations, Thailand, South Korea and the Philippines; others, such as Indonesia and Sri Lanka are relatively nearby. Having said that, historical/cultural factors also contribute to the degree of acceptance of this exploitation. In Thailand, for example, prostitution expanded in the nineteenth century and child prostitution pre-dates the arrival of foreign troops in 1962 and the growth of the mass tourist industry (Kent 1995: 55; Lee 1991: 79).

But the connection of economic inequality and child prostitution in countries like India, Brazil and Thailand is no coincidence. The UN estimates that there are 700,000 female prostitutes in Thailand alone, most of whom are aged 17–24. Young girls are drawn to the cities such as Bangkok looking for work and are then unable to find formal employment. Male tourists outnumber female visitors to Bangkok by 3:1. Thailand has an increasing problem with AIDS cases and more than half a million Thais (of 59 million) are HIV positive. The Thai government deliberately moderated its restrictions on prostitution in the Entertainment Places Act of 1966 and thus encouraged the development of the sex tourist industry. It was only the emerging evidence of the extent of HIV infection which led to a change of policy in the late 1980s. Laws against prostitution elsewhere in South Asia may long have been stricter in theory, but they were and are often not imposed by police and tourist officials who turn a blind eye. This is true in Goa, one of the newer sex tourist areas.

Sex tourism is often the means to satisfy unusual sexual preferences because most people would not pay to travel somewhere far away to get something available at home. As Julia O'Connell Davidson points out (1996), those with these preferences include paedophiles, men who want multiple anonymous encounters with teenagers and those who have racialised fantasies. Different places cater for different preferences. Cuba, for example, does not cater for paedophiles: the main market is for men from Italy, Canada and Germany who seek teenage girls.

A unique set of historical circumstances has led to the development of the sex tourist industry in Cuba. The continuing US blockade and the collapse of Soviet support have meant a desperate need for foreign exchange and hence the development of tourism generally. For ordinary Cubans the blockade means food rationing and shortages of basics such as clothing, soap, cooking oil and painkillers. Tourists obviously expect better, hence the development of tourist enclaves. The Cuban government has sought to keep the tourist economy separate but this has been unsuccessful and a thriving black market in currency and goods meant for tourists has developed. Cubans are anxious to get hold of dollars to buy the basics which are only available for hard currency on the black market. Cuban girls and women are therefore more than willing to sell sexual favours to tourists for dollars (Davidson 1996).

It is not just the growing awareness of HIV/AIDS which is leading to demands for curbs on sex tourism from the supply side in parts of the developing world. A moral backlash from Islamic fundamentalist groups has grown, but so too has opposition from developing world nationalists and from feminists throughout the world.

Environment

Development and the environment

All our basic needs have sources in the natural world. The natural world, however, is finite. Human beings are, therefore, now faced with a two-pronged crisis. On the one hand in the near future more and more resources that we now take for granted are going to start to run out. On the other our environment is becoming increasingly contaminated by the waste we produce (Thomas 1992).

The combined pressures of the increasing awareness of coming scarcity and the build up of toxicity has increased the salience of the environment as an issue. Even more, it has given rise to **ecopolitics**, defined by Guimarães (1991) as 'the study of political systems from an ecological perspective'. Social, cultural and political understanding are as important as natural science when considering ecosystems and their capacities.

The late 1980s saw the change from the environment as a local and regional issue to a global one (Tolba 1988; Hurrell and Kingsbury 1992). Initially this formed part of the globalisation of security concerns. Security had historically always been defined primarily in military terms.

Jessica Tuchman Matthews (1993) says: 'Global environmental trends shift the balance [of power] . . . No more basic threat to national security exists.' However though interest coalitions straddle the North–South divide on some environmental issues the politics of the environment still mainly reflects a North versus South division. It is, sadly, not the spectacle of human misery as much as potential threats to global stability consequent on resource scarcity which invokes the concern of the First World. At the same time national economic advantage gets in the way of a coherent world policy. Agreements tend to be compromises between vested interests. They are not intended to save the world and they will not do so (Calvert and Calvert 1999).

The 1972 Stockholm Intergovernmental Conference on the Human Environment established that the problems of the environment were urgent and sought to identify those which were global problems. The work of the

Plate 15 Green and other politics, Uruguay

conference resulted in two documents: the Stockholm Declaration of basic environmental principles that should govern policy and a detailed Action Plan. This in turn led to the creation of the United Nations Environment Programme (UNEP), whose director, Maurice F. Strong of Canada, who had been Secretary General of the Stockholm Conference, was in due course to become Secretary General of the United Nations Conference on Environment and Development (UNCED), which met at Rio de Janeiro in 1992.

The message that the environment was too big and too important to be dealt with by national governments was unwelcome to many of those governments, and in the ten years that followed the majority of them were very slow to accept that it had any relevance. However, some progress was made. In 1972 the Convention on International Trade in Endangered Species of Wild Fauna and Flora (CITES) was concluded and a World Heritage Convention was held. But a potential setback to the cause of the environment came in 1974 with the adoption by the General Assembly of the otherwise welcome Charter of Economic Rights and Duties of States (CERDS). It laid heavy emphasis on the 'rights' of states to development but lacked any reference to environmental criteria. This was paralleled in the late 1970s and early 1980s by increased emphasis on free market 'solutions' in the AICs, accompanied by their abdication of responsibility for the outcomes of economic processes. At this stage the trend was away from international consensus.

The crucial turning point came in 1983 when the Secretary General of the UN asked the Prime Minister of Norway, Gro Harlem Brundtland, to form a commission to investigate how a planet with a rapidly accelerating population growth could continue to meet basic needs. The Brundtland Commission (properly the World Commission on Environment and Development – WCED) was charged with formulating realistic proposals linking development issues to the care and conservation of the environment and raising the level of public awareness of the issues involved. With the publication in 1987 of its report, *Our Common Future*, the concept of **sustainable development** became central to future thinking. It was the realisation of the extent to which matters had worsened since 1973 that was to lead directly to the Earth Summit.

The biggest shock to world public opinion had come from the discovery of the 'ozone hole' over Antarctica, which led in 1987 to the conclusion of the Montreal Protocol to the Vienna Convention on the Protection of the Ozone Layer, with the aim of regulating the use and release of ozone-depleting substances such as chlorofluorocarbons (CFCs) and halons. The belated realisation both that ozone depletion was accelerating and that it was also taking place, though at a slower rate, in the Arctic, where it posed a much greater threat to major concentrations of the world's population, led to urgent measures to extend the Montreal Protocol. As a result, the problem of the ozone layer was not directly addressed at Rio, though it was very much a matter of concern to delegates from the southern hemisphere.

Many other developments, however, did contribute to the agenda for the Earth Summit. In 1987 UNEP called attention to the alarming rate of

extinction of species. It was estimated that if the current rate of extinction continued, up to one-third of all species could be lost for good within 40 years. The international nature of the trade that was leading to extinction called for an international convention on biological diversity (biodiversity), and in 1988 the UN General Assembly established an ad hoc working group on biodiversity. In 1990 the Committee of Experts became the Intergovernmental Negotiating Committee (INC) on Biological Diversity.

In 1988 the Intergovernmental Panel on Climate Change (IPCC), which had been set up by the World Meterological Association and UNEP, reported that if nothing was done to arrest the rising level of **greenhouse gases** in the atmosphere the global mean temperature would continue to rise by about 0.3°C per decade. A global temperature rise of 1°C by 2025 would place serious strains on the capacity of agriculture to modify its procedures and risk flooding by the melting of the polar icecaps of low-lying areas and small islands. At the Second World Climate Conference General Assembly in 1990, 137 countries called for negotiations for a framework convention on climate change and by Resolution 43/53 the General Assembly established an INC on Climate Change to prepare a draft.

Both climate change and biodiversity were linked to a third major area of concern, the accelerating rate of destruction of forests. Forests act both as 'carbon sinks', returning to the earth the carbon dioxide liberated by the burning of **fossil fuels** (Leggett 1990) and so acting naturally to arrest global warming, and as a rich habitat for a diversity of species. Their destruction, on the other hand, releases significant additional volumes of carbon dioxide. In addition their sustainable management could in time prove to be of immense and increasing value to the rising populations of the developing states. Sadly, their governments have been unable or unwilling to act to prevent their hasty destruction for short-term gain or ground clearance. In the 1990s some 8.9 million ha were lost every year. In 2006 it was estimated that some 7.3 million ha were still being lost annually; some 31 million ha had been lost in 2001–05 (Mygatt 2006).

Several other areas of concern were side-tracked along the way. Notably, the poorer African states of the Sahel had been calling for global action on **desertification**. Desertification is the progressive destruction or degradation of existing vegetative cover to form desert. Common causes in the developing world are overgrazing, deforestation, drought, and the uncontrolled burning of forest and ground cover for land colonisation. When an area begins to undergo desertification, the new conditions typically include a significantly lowered water table, a reduced supply of surface water, increased salinity in natural waters and soils, progressive destruction of native vegetation, and an accelerated rate of erosion, which together make it very difficult if not impossible to restore its vitality. There was no doubt about the importance of desertification to Africa: television had beamed pictures of starving children in Ethiopia, Sudan and Somalia on to television screens throughout the developed world. What was at issue was its urgency as a global question. The UN

Plan of Action to Combat Desertification (PACD) instituted by UNEP and approved by the General Assembly in 1977 had never been effectively implemented, largely because of the lack of effective resources. However, reluctance to support it had recently been reinforced by new satellite pictures which seemed to prove conclusively that although poor quality lands were becoming more degraded, the general advance of deserts, though widely accepted, was a myth (Pearce 1992). But the question is still open, if only because so much land is still being degraded.

Sustainable development

The suggestion that there is a choice between environment or development is, like many political arguments, a false alternative. It is no longer possible (if it ever was) to have one without the other. The world is a closed system and everything affects everything else. In short, what is needed is sustainable development.

The Brundtland Report defined sustainable development as: '. . . development that meets the needs of the present without compromising the ability of future generations to meet their own needs' (WCED 1987: 43). Sustainable development does not use non-renewable resources faster than substitutes can be found, nor renewable resources faster than they can be replaced, nor does it emit pollutants faster than natural processes can render them harmless.

It was the World Commission who first popularised the term sustainable development. They defined it in terms of two criteria: intra- and **intergenerational equity**. The next generation must be left a stock of quality assets, and not simply left to scrabble among the scraps. It was hardly surprising, given the numerical majority of the developing world states in the UN, that when the World Commission was established, with commissioners from 21 countries, most of them were from the developing world. In the words of Gro Harlem Brundtland: 'the "environment" is where we all live; and "development" is what we all do in attempting to improve our lot within that abode' (WCED 1987: xi).

At the moment, however, unbalanced development is a major cause of the destruction of the environment. The poor can hardly be blamed for exploiting their environment in a way that destroys its long-term potential when the rich, including TNCs, are doing the same thing on a much more massive and destructive scale. Deteriorating terms of trade and the burden of debt on the developing world states increase pressure for exploitation by making short-term returns the most urgent consideration. The implication is that in any plan for sustainable development, the future development needs of the South must be allowed for. Development cannot be sacrificed for environment any more than the other way round. The North–South gap cannot be perpetuated if the world is to remain stable. Therefore, sustainable development must meet the economic, social and environmental needs of all the world's peoples.

Brundtland's call for sustainable development is now an article of faith in the developed countries but too often it has been seen as open to a much more limited interpretation, that of growth as usual but slower. The Brundtland report itself is a compromise. It is weak on the subject of population growth and does not really suggest a solution to the problem of rich world resource consumption. At present the depreciation of natural resources is not taken into account in calculating GNP etc. Economists have already been able to demonstrate 'the physical dependency of economic activity on the sustainability of crucial natural-resource systems and ecological functions, and to indicate the economic costs, or trade-offs, resulting from the failure to preserve sustainability and environmental quality' (Barbier 1989: xiv). If new measures were to be devised it would be easier to see where sustainability was attainable and where not.

Following the Earth Summit in 1992, the UN created a new Commission on Sustainable Development in December 1992 to oversee implementation of its most radical document, Agenda 21, a plan for the twenty-first century. Introducing the proposal to the General Assembly, the Secretary General, Boutros Boutros-Ghali, said in November 1992: 'The challenge after Rio is to maintain the momentum to sustainable development, to transform it into policies and practice, and to give it effective and coordinated organisational support . . . The UN must put its development objectives on a par with its political and social commitments.'

The Prince of Wales (1993) argues that the developing world needs the following for sustainable development to be possible:

- developed countries to put their own houses in order on pollution;
- a reversal of the flow of funds from South to North;
- different terms of trade that allow the South to sell more expensive goods to the North;
- the end of subsidies on agriculture etc. which make developing world products uncompetitive; and
- shared technology.

The technology that will most benefit the developing world (and the First) need not be complicated – in fact, the simpler and more trouble-free the better. The Prince, for example, recommends the use of photovoltaic cell technology as a non-polluting source of electricity to run 'the five great liberators of development':

- cookers (which conserve fuelwood resources)
- refrigerators (which keep food from spoiling)
- water pumps (which avoid diseases associated with scarce surface water supplies and save so much female time)
- radios (which provide cheap links to the outside world)
- lights.

Michael Grubb (1992) says: 'With the continuing pressure of public opinion and steady penetration of environmental concerns into governmental thinking sustainable development is on the agenda to stay.' However the inertia shown by First World governments since that time suggest that his optimism was rather premature (see also Grubb 2000; Carroll 1990).

Global warming

During the last glaciation, which ended only some 12,000 years ago, the average temperature was only 4°C lower than it is today. An increase of 2.5–5.5°C. on the present figure it was believed would raise sea levels initially only due to the expansion of water at higher temperatures. Although the temperature increase from global warming is expected to be greatest at the poles the vast ice sheets of Antarctica would take a long while to melt. However, recent studies have shown that the Arctic icecap is melting much faster than had previously been thought likely.

The main 'greenhouse gases', the increased emissions of which cause this rise in temperature, are:

1. Carbon dioxide from burning fossil fuels and burning off of the world's forest cover, especially in the tropics. Some 8.2 billion tons of CO_2 is being given off into the atmosphere each year. This is thought to contribute more than half of the global warming effect.
2. Methane from the decomposition of organic matter. Rice (paddy) fields are a major source. So too are cattle, so the conversion of tropical rainforest to poor quality ranching land, as in Costa Rica, has a double effect. Cattle, being ruminants, generate far more methane than goats, pigs – or human beings. A great deal of methane is held in suspension in the permafrost and the sea bed and is likely to be liberated if global warming takes place, thus accelerating the effect.

   Other gases which create major environmental hazards and need to be controlled, in developing as well as developed countries, are:
3. Nitrous oxide, especially from motor vehicles but also from the overuse of chemical fertilisers.
4. Low-level ozone mainly from the reaction of sunlight and pollution from motor vehicles (high-level ozone molecules, in the outer atmosphere, form an essential shield against radiation and are therefore crucial to our survival).
5. Chlorofluorocarbons (CFCs) synthesised by human endeavour. Although 'thoroughly' tested when discovered in the 1930s, nobody dreamt then that they would contribute disproportionately to the earth's warming, let alone that they would have damaging effects on the upper atmosphere. China is now the only remaining major source of these.

One hundred and fifty-seven governments signed the Climate Convention at Rio. Of these one country, the United States, is responsible for no less than

23 per cent of global CO_2 emissions. Other major contributors are the former USSR (19 per cent) and Europe (15 per cent). Their responses have been particularly disappointing, and it is not just political neurosis that has led some developing world countries to feel that they are being required to conserve their rainforest (Guimarães 1991; Hall 1991) to allow the rich countries to go on burning fossil fuels.

For the fact is that more than two-thirds of the global production of greenhouse gases is due to burning of fossil fuels. Only six countries agreed to cuts in their emissions of CO_2. The maximum was Germany's target of a reduction of 25–30 per cent by 2005, which would be partly met in any case by phasing out inefficient plant in the former East, but in practice was not achieved. For the United States, similar cuts in CO_2 would have meant cuts in GNP of the order of 3 per cent a year – less than the military budget. However the United States did not agree to sign the Framework Convention until it had succeeded in weakening it to the point of meaninglessness. Not surprisingly, US emissions had by 2005 significantly increased. In fact, as early as the Berlin Conference of 1995 it was clear that even the relatively weak targets established by the major states would not be achieved, except where (as in the case of the UK) economic recession fortuitously cut back emissions.

But the developed countries are not the only source of carbon emissions and the trouble with the developing countries is that their activities are much more difficult to control. Controlled burning, as in cooking and domestic heating, is only part of the problem. A major part of their contributions comes from the uncontrolled burning of forest and peat-bog for ground clearance. Not only is this a serious waste of natural resources but it has serious detrimental side effects for the environment.

The View from the Ground

By *Charles Clover, Environment Editor, The Daily Telegraph,*
Saturday, 3 September 2005

Peat Bog Burning Blamed for Much of Global Warming

Burning peat bogs set alight by rainforest clearance in Indonesia are releasing up to a seventh of the world's total fossil fuel emissions in a single year, the geographers' conference heard yesterday.

Tropical peatlands are one of the largest stores of carbon on the Earth's surface and setting them alight is contributing massively to global warming, said Dr Susan Page, senior lecturer in geography at Leicester University.

The carbon stored in the peat, formed by trees growing over 26,000 years ago, is 10 times greater than the carbon stored in the forest growing on top, making it a priority for the international community to stop them burning.

The peatlands burn each year during the dry season as farmers clear land, and once lit are hard to extinguish.

An area the size of Belgium has been cleared and burned in eight years, according to Dr Page.

At the current rate of burning the peatlands could be destroyed before 2040, she told the Royal Geographical Society's annual international conference in London.

Peatlands were burned on the orders of the former Indonesian dictator Suharto in an attempt to create one of the world's largest rice plantations. It has since been found that the acid soils are unsuitable for growing rice, making the Mega Rice Project one of the world's greatest environmental disasters and one that has led to air pollution as far away as peninsular Malaysia and Thailand.

See also: Page et al. (2002)

As things stand, a sea level rise of only *c*.20 cm is expected to take place by 2030. However, floods and storms can be confidently expected to make matters worse. The Maldives, to take an extreme case, have no land above 2 m above sea level. A 1 m rise in sea level would cost the Maldives $10,000 per person to defend against. Even their situation, however, could be better than that of the populations of the world's great river deltas in the South which are home to and rich food production areas for millions of people in the developing world. They will not have the means to defend their land against even small rises. Some 95 per cent of Bangladesh is already at risk from flooding. Monsoon shifts may be catastrophic for it as for some other tropical areas, although they are unlikely to experience much temperature increase.

An awkward problem is that environmental degradation will not affect all countries equally. Global warming will actually positively benefit some in the short term, since rainfall increases will not be uniform. Yet climatic zonal shift will be devastating for many animal and plant species owing to the lag between climatic change and species evolution. Even the most conservative estimates of the likely effects of global warming imply a rate of change that would be at the limits of what species have hitherto found it possible to accept. But because of these regional differences, it is very difficult to secure international agreement to take the necessary measures to arrest the warming process, still less reverse it.

Deforestation

In India 1.3 million ha are lost each year to commercial plantations, river valley and mining projects. Each year 7 million ha disappear worldwide and losses sustained at this level would mean total destruction of the rainforest well before 2050. Globally ten trees are cut down for every one planted.

Central America and Amazonia are losing more than 2.5 million ha of forest each year to cattle-ranching (even without small-scale slash-and-burn which may clear an even greater area). The fact that Brazil is the largest developing world debtor and one of the fastest-growing economies in the world has been a dangerous combination for its rainforest. Successive Brazilian governments have not sought to protect Brazil's forests. They have been much more concerned with Northern markets – the Amazon has been seen as a huge resource available to large-scale enterprise and extraction has accelerated. It has also been viewed as somewhere to relocate millions of displaced people who then slash and burn the forest to gain two or three years of crops. Sadly the red laterite soils of Southern Brazil, Northern Argentina, Paraguay and West Africa on which some of richest forest resource grows are very thin and particularly vulnerable. Once uncovered, they soon bake hard and, where not washed away into the rivers first, become impervious to rain. Soon the disappointed settlers begin the trek back to the big cities that they were heading for in the first place.

The loss of trees results in:

- loss of soil nutrients;
- loss of biodiversity – some 50 per cent of species live in the rainforest;
- fuelwood shortages;
- soil erosion and thus river silting, which results in flooding and droughts, and damage to dams, HEP installations etc.

Deforestation and consequent soil damage add every year to the numbers of refugees on the move, for example, from Haiti. Its most dramatic consequence is drought. The moisture given off by forests actually helps precipitate rain clouds.

Drought is not new to countries like Sudan and Ethiopia, but massive recurring famine in their newly treeless wastes is. Every year 12 million ha of land becomes desert.

Forest is frequently the most accessible aspect of the environment to debt-equity swaps. The World Wide Fund for Nature buys up developing world debt which is then paid to WWF in local currency and the funds used on local environmental schemes such as those in Ecuador. The activities of NGOs must, however, overcome nationalistic and selfish First World responses. For example, Japan protects its own rainforest while importing hardwoods from South-east Asia where their support for uncontrolled logging has already destroyed much of the valuable rainforest (Sizer 2005).

Biodiversity

The problem of biological diversity (Wilson 1988) affects all of us on three levels:

- there are different types of ecosystem;
- there are a multitude of different species;
- there is a great deal of genetic variation of individuals within species.

With extinction running at between 1,000 and 10,000 times the 'natural' rate, species losses are estimated at somewhere around 50,000 a year. Certainly more than 100 species a day, or four an hour, are being lost forever. There is no return from extinction – and ultimately that applies as much to human beings as to any other living creatures.

Though these are 'conservative' guesses, it is quite clear that extinction rates are not constant but are actually accelerating. The loss of between 2 per cent and 8 per cent of currently existing species can be expected over the next 25 years. Much of what is lost in this time will never have been 'discovered' by human beings and most of these species are in the developing world. Their loss, therefore, will be a loss to the developing world.

Biological diversity is not an optional extra but a matter of sheer self-interest. Biodiversity is an essential feature of the natural world, which enables species to respond to challenge. It is biodiversity, ironically enough, that enables the malaria parasite to survive the onslaught of the so-called 'wonder drugs'. At the same time the variety of the natural world offers us all sorts of medicinal and biochemical possibilities to combat disease. Quinine, still an effective drug against some kinds of malaria, was first introduced to Europeans by the Jesuits in the tropical rainforest of Paraguay.

For similar reasons, we need to conserve the wild relatives of major food crops, such as wheat or maize, in case, as happened with the potato in Europe in the years 1845–48, our few cultivated varieties should suddenly succumb to an attack from a new pest or disease.

These varieties are to be found mainly in what is now the developing world. But biodiversity is big business for the TNCs based in the developed countries. At the Earth Summit President Bush of the United States failed to sign the Convention on the Conservation of Biological Diversity (which President Clinton later signed but the US Senate refused to ratify) arguing that there was no agreement on what biodiversity was or how its benefits should be shared. The United States took the view that anything enhanced by human endeavour should be patentable and indeed the WTO appears to make it so. The states of the South disagreed, believing that the countries where new discoveries are made have a right to the lion's share of the rewards of development. But though they have the biodiversity, many of them have neither the will nor the strength to conserve it, with the result that some at least of it will be lost to the whole world.

Democracy and the environment

The Brundtland Report rightly saw democracy and participation as integral parts of sustainable development. Without the active participation of every member of the community, sustainability cannot be achieved. Rio was a reminder that the environment cannot be safeguarded without development and justice for the South. The relationship between the three can be represented by a triangle, each influencing the other two (see figure 9.1).

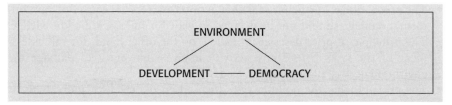

Figure 9.1   Environment, development and democracy

Democracy, often taken for granted in the industrialised countries, has in the developing world both a local and a global meaning.

The Mexican novelist, Carlos Fuentes, has pointed to the Zapatista insurrection in Chiapas as indicative of what could be expected without full participation and democratic rights (*The Guardian*, 15 January 1994). Base communities need incentives to improve their local environments and security of land tenure gives the peasantry a necessary stake in the long-term future.

The UN and the environment

The 'Earth Summit' or 'Eco 92', the UN Conference on Environment and Development (UNCED), held in Rio de Janeiro from 3 to 14 June 1992, was the largest high-level conference ever staged. Over 120 heads of state and heads of government took part in the 'summit segment' presided over personally for much of the time by President Fernando Collor de Mello, and some 20,000 people in all were involved in the preparation, planning and administration of the event. Its purpose was of appropriate importance: to concert measures to save the planet for future generations.

The publicity surrounding the Earth Summit aroused unrealistic expectations. Being an international conference it could not and did not fulfil the hopes of those – probably the majority of the world public – who expected it to produce concrete results. It is hard for the general public not to believe that, given that many of the world's leaders are powerful separately, they will be even more powerful together. But the Earth Summit was not an 'Earth Senate'. Both the constitutional position of international decision-making and the way in which decisions are arrived at are significantly different from the way in which things are done in a national context. The very fact that the Summit took place was itself significant. Beyond that, anything that could be achieved in the way of agreement was positive.

It was in 1989 that the UN General Assembly, in resolution 44/228, had decided to convene UNCED, and urged the nations of the world to send representation at head of state or head of government level. However, it is a well-established principle of international conferences that as little as possible must be left to chance and the Declaration of Rio would be a key statement of intent. The European Community favoured the idea of an Earth Charter, a relatively brief statement of principles. Four in particular were suggested.

- The precautionary principle was that action to arrest the causes of environmental damage should not be delayed to wait for full scientific knowledge.
- The principle of prior assessment called, on the other hand, for full assessment of the risks before any activity likely significantly to damage the environment was allowed to proceed.
- The principle that the polluter pays focused on the need for individuals or companies polluting the environment to meet the public costs of cleaning it up.
- The principle of non-discriminatory public participation called for all people to be fully informed about potential interference with their environment and to have a right to have their views taken into account in the making of policy.

Decision-making within the UN system, however, is characterised by three factors which make the attainment of these goals exceedingly difficult, if not impossible:

- The juridical equality of sovereign states. Each state has to be treated exactly the same as each other state. Hence each delegate who speaks is thanked for his or her 'important' statement, even if, as in at least one case at Rio, the delegate concerned simply reads out a civil service brief on the history of environmental politics since 1972.
- One state one vote. Decisions of all bodies other than the Security Council, where the five permanent members continue to exercise the veto, reflect the desires and wishes of the developing South rather than the developed North.
- Voluntary consensus. However wide the consensus, no decision (other than of the Security Council) is mandatory, unless the states concerned freely enter into a treaty obligation by signing and ratifying a convention or other agreement.

In practice, therefore, the politics of UNCED reflected the basic world divisions between North and South. Some optimism was generated by agreement on the Rio Declaration and on the formidable list of further problems to be investigated, termed 'Agenda 21'. Both represented a massive step forward in public awareness of the underlying problems. Both, however, were above all the product of compromise. Even the two formal treaties that survived the preliminary discussions, the Framework Convention on Climate Change and the Convention on Biological Diversity, though formally binding, lacked specific deadlines and so fell far short of what might have been hoped.

Worse still, the United States signed the Framework Convention on Climate Change only because it had first been watered down and all binding commitments removed. Malaysia refused to sign it, asserting its right to 'exploit' (i.e. destroy) its remaining tropical rainforest if it chose. Hence there was no agreement on a forestry convention which would check the destruction in time to forestall irrevocable loss on a massive scale. Instead, there was a vague

Statement on Forest Principles and a call for governments to meet again to iron out the remaining difficulties.

The 'Group of 77' developing countries (whose numbers had by 1992 reached 128) wanted a public recognition of their specific concerns, especially

> their sovereign right to development, acknowledgment that the industrialised countries were primarily responsible for current environmental problems, and the need for new financing and technology to enable developing countries to avoid taking the same polluting route to development as did the developing (sic) countries. (United Nations 1992)

President Collor had of course taken the opportunity to tell the world just how much Brazil (and by implication its president) was doing about the environment (Collor 1992). However his own 'green' credentials were rather dubious. Although no longer official policy, the destruction of the Amazon rainforest at the hands of would-be settlers continued, while the *garimpeiros* (gold prospectors) invaded Indian lands, carrying with them disease and other problems. The spectacle of the burning of the rainforest diverted attention from some very uncomfortable arithmetic. It was the 23 per cent of the world's population that consumed 77 per cent of the world's energy resources that had created and was continuing to accelerate the problem of global warming. Left to themselves, the world's own ecosystems could have coped with emissions of greenhouse gases from the countries of the South. However if these countries were, in the coming 30 years, to maintain a reasonable standard of living for their populations, it was all but certain that they would have to do so by burning fossil fuels. Even if they were to do so, however, they would not attain the limits recommended by the IPCC for the maintenance of climatic stability. Hence there was nothing that the developing countries could do, or not do, on their own to prevent the onset of catastrophic instability. Only by a substantial reduction in greenhouse emissions from the developed North could that risk be postponed and/or averted.

There were two obvious weaknesses in the position of the developing countries at Rio, neither of which has yet been solved. First, there was a wide range of special interests to be served among the very large number of states that might (or might not) be counted in that category. Secondly, the strong tendency in the UN for states to caucus by region was replicated at UNCED. For example, only a few of the island states of the Caribbean voiced the fears of their Pacific and Indian Ocean counterparts, that within a generation the rising sea level caused by global warming could threaten their livelihoods if not their actual existence as states. The president of the Republic of the Maldives, Maumoon Abdul Gayoom, said that he expected his country to be seriously damaged by 2030 and to cease to exist altogether by 2100. However, Michael Manley of Jamaica had been succeeded in March by his former deputy, Percival Patterson, thus depriving the Commonwealth Caribbean of their most experienced radical voice, and their contribution to the public debate was muted. Patterson, who had been forced out of Manley's cabinet for alleged corruption as recently as December 1991, made a good plea for the implementation of the Law of the Sea Convention, but predictably placed the responsibility for global warming on the developed countries. The prime minister of Barbados, Erskine Sandiford, treated the assembled delegates to an ode in honour of the occasion composed entirely by himself.

Africa South of the Sahara was universally recognised as the world's most seriously deprived region. As noted above, its main preoccupation, drought and the issue of desertification, was sidelined at UNCED, despite being the subject of Chapter 12 of Agenda 21, 'Management of Fragile Ecosystems: Combating Desertification and Drought'. A Convention to Combat Desertification was finally concluded in June 1994 and received the necessary 50 ratifications by 1997. However a Convention which is limited to the world's poorest countries and lacks adequate means of financial support is unlikely to be any more effective than its predecessor and so it has proved (Manu 1993).

The Earth Summit can fairly be evaluated not as an event in itself but as a beginning of a much longer process of global self-education. One of its most important results was the provision by each country of a report on the state of its own environment. Often these were the first reports of their kind and so of immense value in establishing the dimensions of the problem. Its importance, however, will in the end have to be measured in terms of the willingness or otherwise of the world's powers to recognise their own problems and to implement the programme so clearly set out for them. The first signs have been far from encouraging.

No one at Rio, least of all the authors of the numerous drafts of Agenda 21, thought that the 'major shift in priorities' it called for would be either easy or quick; involving as it did 'the full integration of the environmental dimension into economic and sectoral policies, decision-making in every sphere of economic and environmental activity and a major redeployment of human and financial resources at both national and international level' (Strong 1992: 19).

Critics argue that no real action resulted. Basic policy differences were highlighted, especially those between the United States and the developing world, but they were not resolved. The same patterns of production and consumption continue and in any case commitments made were not in proportion to the size and severity of the problems we face. Up to $2.5 billion in additional finance to begin funding the $400–600 billion estimated price of Agenda 21 may have been pledged as a result of Rio, but a minimum of $10 billion extra would have been needed to reckon it a success. The debate over how to fund it was, as we have seen, split along North–South lines with developing world countries seeking, but not getting, assurances that ODA funding would not simply be diverted for the purpose. As UNCED Secretary General Maurice Strong said of the possibilities of implementing Agenda 21: 'The real question is political will.'

Agenda 21 is above all a social programme. Social programmes take time and money to implement.

The priority actions of Agenda 21 are grouped within the context of principal substantive social themes, including a prospering (revitalization of Growth with Sustainability), a just (Sustainable Living for All) and a habitable (Human Settlements Development) world. They entail promotion of a fertile (Efficient Resource Use), a shared (Global and Regional Resources) and clean (Managing Chemicals and Waste) world, through wide and responsible participation at local, national and global levels. (Strong 1992: 19)

To deal with the obvious question first, the new and additional cost of implementing Agenda 21, if all activities had begun at once and were fully implemented between 1993 and 2000, was estimated at an average annual figure of $125 billion. Although this looks a large amount, in relation to the current expenditure of the developed countries it would have been minimal – less than 1 per cent of GNP (Strong 1992: 17).

Unfortunately it was already clear before the delegates left Rio that the developed countries, led by the United States, were simply not prepared to pay up. Worse still, the economic ideas which they were advocating were only likely to make things worse. Advocacy of the 'free market' was in practice accompanied by a clear tendency to try to define the parameters of the market in a way that sacrificed long-term stability to short-term returns.

The problem for developing world countries was not so much that the so-called 'free market', that they had embraced so enthusiastically, would not work, but that it would work all too well. Specifically, the beneficiaries were likely to be the larger, low-cost producers; the losers, the smaller, weaker economies. The result would be the further erosion of their already dubious ability to resist short-term demand for environmental degradation. Secondly, the action of the market promised to be much too slow to prevent irrevocable damage to the environment – the extinction of species, in particular, could not be averted once their numbers had declined below a critical level, and until that level was reached, there was insufficient motivation, under the unchecked market system, to halt the decline. In the last year before the formal implementation of CITES, South Korea imported 300 tonnes of tiger bones, representing the death of half of all the known Siberian tigers left in the wild. In March 1994 the UN Food and Agriculture Organization (FAO) reported that 'severe' political and economic consequences could be expected to follow the potentially catastrophic decline of species in nine of the world's 17 main fishing grounds. Given the importance of fish, both fresh and dried, in developing world diets, this warning came not a moment too soon. However, in 2002 it was estimated that there were still twice as many fishing vessels at sea as there were fish cargoes for them to catch, that 30 per cent of all fishing worldwide was illegal, and that 40 per cent of the catch of legal fisheries was wasted (Rischard 2002).

Some hope remained for the Commission on Sustainable Development proposed to monitor the implementation of Agenda 21. This was established by the UN Economic and Social Council (ECOSOC) on 12 February 1993. It

Plate 16   Earth Summit, 1992

consists of 53 members and meets annually for 2–3 weeks. The first session was held in New York in June 1993. The 14th session, chaired by Mr. Aleksi Aleksishvili, of Georgia, took place on 1–12 May 2006 and focused on energy, industrial development, air pollution and global warming (www.un.org/esa/sustdev/csc/htm).

Key terms

'carbon sinks' – agencies returning to the earth the carbon dioxide liberated by the burning of fossil fuels

deconcentration – of power: process by which decisions are devolved downwards to lower levels of decision-making

desertification – for the FAO, land degradation in arid, semi-arid and dry sub-humid areas resulting from various factors, including climate variations and human activities

ecopolitics – the study of political systems from an ecological perspective

extinction – the irreversible loss of a species when the last surviving members of it have died out or been deliberately killed by human beings

fossil fuels – fuels formed in the ground over a long period of time by heat and pressure acting on the remains of dead plants and animals: specifically peat, coal, oil and natural gas

greenhouse gases – gases such as carbon dioxide and methane, rising levels of which in the atmosphere increase the 'greenhouse effect' and help bring about global warming

intergenerational equity – the principle in environmental science that the next generations must be left resources in as good a condition as the previous generation inherited them

'ozone hole' – area over the South and North Poles where the layer of ozone in the upper atmosphere has been depleted owing to interaction with man-made chemicals

sustainable development – the rate of development that can be maintained for the indefinite future

Questions

1. What is the best way for the developed world to help developing countries?

2. How far do (i) free trade, and (ii) hidden protectionism help explain the present position of developing countries?

3. What are the economic advantages and disadvantages of tourism as a development strategy in southern states?

4. How far does tourism improve knowledge about conditions in developing countries for visitors from the AICs?

5. What is the impact of tourism on developing countries? How important is it?

6. What are the main environmental challenges facing developing countries?

7. Why is it so difficult to find funding for environmental protection?

CHAPTER 10

Conclusion

The first edition of this book was published in 1996 and the second in 2001. Since then, sadly, three of the trends we emphasised have become more evident. Despite a great deal of talk about relieving the debts of the poorer countries, little has been done. After a long argument, the debts of some of the world's poorest countries were written off but the debts of many of the rest continue to drain their resources. In fact, those resources have been depleted by the terms imposed by their creditors and especially the international financial institutions: devaluation, privatisation and the opening up of their economies to foreign competition. Meanwhile continuing pressure from migrants desperate for jobs has been met by the AICs constructing both legal and physical barriers to try simply to keep them out.

The old order is changing and there are some grounds for optimism. There have been massive gains in East Asia and some gains in South Asia, especially in India. China has emerged on the world scene as a major economic player. However although now accepted as the one of the largest economies in the world, it is still very much a developing country. In these countries (and in others) manufacturers are increasing their share of the developed world's markets, although the great irony is that China's success has largely been purchased at the expense of the manufacturers and workers in other developing countries, such as the Philippines, Sri Lanka and Bangladesh.

But there has been some loss of development in some parts of Latin America, and near total disaster for many countries of Africa South of the Sahara. So overall the developing world is not catching up with the developed world, and there is increasing concern that the resources simply may not be available to enable many countries to do so. In Africa, for example, Botswana has one of the fastest growth rates in the world while much of the rest of the region falls into the 'least developed' category and has stagnant or declining economies. There are also striking variations within countries; for example, in Indonesia Java is still rich, and Sumatra poor (and in Aceh alone more than 130,000 people were killed by the 2005 tsunami). Despite such variations, countries throughout the developing world are experiencing substantial gains in health and longevity, in education and opportunities for women, though the social gap, whether in life expectancy/health, education/literacy or otherwise, is increasing within the developing world. International Labour Organization (ILO) figures show that global economic growth is failing to translate into the new and better jobs that lead to a reduction of poverty in the developing world.

The 'pulling apart' of the developing world has therefore continued, so that since 2001 the gap between rich and poor has become wider, both between and within individual countries. In 1994 the GNP per capita of Switzerland, then the richest country in the world, was $36,080 per year. This was 13 times that of Brazil but 601 times that of Mozambique. The economy of Brazil was growing rapidly, so that by 1997 the GNP per capita of Switzerland ($43,060) was only nine times that of Brazil ($4,790). However, it was still 307 times that of Mozambique ($140). In 2004 Switzerland, now third in the world behind Luxembourg and Norway, had a GNI per capita of $48,230. This was 15 times that of Brazil ($3,090) and 172 times that of Mozambique ($250). So Mozambique seems to have little hope of catching up even with Brazil, let alone Switzerland (UNDP 1994, 1997, 2004 figures). The irony is that the best growth rates are to be found in the richest developing countries and in all the major regions of the world there are the same huge variations.

As many feared, the changes in Eastern Europe and North Asia have tended to reinforce, not reduce, the yawning gap between the rich countries and the poor ones. Some of the East Central European countries have already found their common European home within the European Union: the Baltic states, Poland, the Czech Republic, Hungary, Slovakia and Slovenia joined in 2004. Bulgaria, Croatia and Romania are still candidates. However, outside the boundaries of the former Austro-Hungarian Empire the picture is rather of a precipitate decline into the poverty-stricken existence that the poorest country in Europe, Albania, already held. In fact the sarcastic description of the former Soviet Union as 'Upper Volta with rockets', sometimes attributed to former US Secretary of State Henry Kissinger, now seems to have been uncomfortably close to the truth, and within the territories of the former Soviet Union and its satellites, we seem already to be witnessing the same process of 'pulling apart' that is characteristic of the developing world. The same economic and social problems are also already developing. So, despite some encouraging signs, are the political ones: the most conspicuous failure of democratisation has been in the Caucasus and Central Asia.

Modernisation in Asia

As we have seen, the emergence of the NICs (or NIEs) is an Asian phenomenon, based on a very special combination of local circumstances, and not easily replicable elsewhere. Far-reaching land reform in the 1950s in Taiwan and South Korea created a loyal class of small farmers and at the same time a substantial pool of industrial labour. Autocratic government, a large public sector controlling key industries and a command economy directing heavy subsidies into the manufacture of goods for export are distinctive features of the Asian NICs. So too are long working hours at low rates of pay for millions of workers and heavy costs borne both by individuals and by the local environment. Among reporting countries, Indonesia has the highest rate of industrial accidents in the world (43.7 per 100,000), although most industrial accidents there, and in Thailand (19.2) and South Korea (34.0) among rapidly industrialising countries, occur in agriculture (Takkala 2006).

India, Malaysia, Pakistan, Thailand and the Philippines in their different ways have all encouraged the emergence of a low wage, export-oriented economy. As we have seen, where there is a reasonably equal distribution of wealth, the society as a whole does benefit and the general standard of living improves. It is quite possible that in the twenty-first century Asia will again become what it once was, the most advanced region of the world in economic terms. However, much depends on the continued progress of India, soon to become the largest nation in the world in terms of population.

With the emergence of the United States as a world superpower in 1945 Americans recalled the old belief that the major centre of world civilisation tends to move in a westerly direction. At the beginning of the 1990s this interesting, but fallacious, historical notion received a new twist with the emergence of the concept of the Pacific Rim as the new centre of world economic activity.

It is true that the United States, Japan, China and the NICs are all situated on the edge of the Pacific. So too are Mexico and Chile, which have both at different times been tipped for future NIC status. Given the size of the Pacific, a great many of the world's countries are bound to be found on its shores. However, it is not the fact that they are on the edge of the Pacific that is the common factor among the most rapidly developing of these states, but the fact that they attached closely to the mainland of Asia.

The radicalisation of the Middle East

The launch of the US 'war on terror' has had catastrophic consequences for South-West Asia, and hence for the Middle East and North Africa (MENA). North of the Sahara, Islamic fundamentalism had been threatening economic progress in Egypt and Algeria throughout the 1990s. Five years ago we said: 'It is possible that this could result in improved conditions for some of the poorest sectors, but so far it looks more likely to mean a retreat to insularity and isolationism which damages whole societies. Any attempt at bloc-building by Muslim countries would undoubtedly provoke similar responses elsewhere. It would certainly provide a convenient excuse to pander to the increasingly

inward-oriented perspective of key sectors in the United States, for example.'
That was before '9/11'.

US intervention in Afghanistan has succeeded in its main objective, the fall
of the Taliban, and social conditions, especially for women, have improved.
However, it has also led to the return of the opium culture which the Taliban
had forbidden. In addition, the United States has sought new allies in the
region, with the result that any democratisation that Uzbekistan, for example,
might have experienced has now been put on hold.

In the Middle East the first casualty of US intervention has been Iraq itself.
It is not developing, it is not democratic and it has sustained such severe environmental damage that the consequences are likely to be felt for many years.
The second casualty has been any hope of finding an equitable settlement of
the Palestine issue, which today more than ever poisons relations between the
developed and the developing world.

Both successes and failures in the Middle East have been dependent on the
region's most desired commodity: oil. Qatar, which is expected to run out of
oil in the next ten years, has already planned to switch the basis of its relatively
affluent economy to tourism. However, the most dramatic effect of continuing
uncertainty in the region has been the soaring price of oil, which in real terms
has almost reached its 1979 peak. The result has been a sudden realisation not
only that the world peak in oil production has already passed but that earlier
estimates of the amount of oil still to come were over-optimistic, as was the
belief that as oil began to run out the world could continue to operate a high-
energy economy. The energy gap between the rich countries and the poor ones
is vast.

The decline of Africa

In Africa the situation is bleak and has deteriorated significantly in the past
ten years.

South of the Sahara the HIV/AIDS epidemic continues to spread and
there has been no significant economic advance over the last ten years. War
and insurrection have blighted the hopes of some of the poorest nations on
earth. An uneasy peace now exists between Ethiopia and Eritrea, but Ethiopia
is still spending heavily on arms. People are just now beginning to return to
the war-ravaged north of Uganda, an unstable coexistence prevails in Congo
and Niger, and fighting continues in Burundi, DRC, Somalia and Sudan.

One bright spot is in the far south, where the independence of Namibia and
the relative stability of South Africa offers that possibility of cooperative economic development which had for so long been denied by political considerations. However, the hopes that Zimbabwe, formerly one of the richest nations
in Africa, might once more produce enough grain to feed the hungry have been

dashed. Lands formerly owned by white settlers were seized but not distributed to those who could work them, and the result has been that many of the 400,000 who previously worked on the estates are now out of work, there are chronic food and fuel shortages and the economy has collapsed with inflation, even on official figures, topping 133 per cent in 2004 and 545 per cent in 2005. Botswana has placed electric fences along its border to stop refugees fleeing into its territory to escape poverty and political persecution. South Africa has achieved the same result with military patrols.

The de–industrialisation of Europe

The problem with the assumption that export-led growth is the route to economic development is that there has to be a market big enough to absorb the products. In the nineteenth century Britain prospered on free trade. When other industrialised countries put up tariff barriers, the markets of the Empire were big enough to allow trade to continue, at least for a time. The United States created a single internal market as early as 1791 and from that time on until 1930 was able to develop behind the shelter of tariff protection.

However, the industrialisation of the developing world in recent years has been accompanied by the de-industrialisation of Europe. As TNCs have moved production out into developing world countries, to profit from their low wages, unemployment in Europe has risen to levels which have not been sustained for so long a period in recent times. At the same time wages have become depressed, to the point at which Timex watches were for a long time assembled in Scotland and not in a developing world country, because the workforce was skilled enough to make sure that the work was done to a sufficient standard. When labour costs were no longer low enough to make the operation profitable production moved to China, India and the Philippines.

Such developments hardly suggest that Europe will be able to offer a big enough market for all the new goods that the developing world plans to put on sale. In fact, the markets of the developed world seem to have become saturated for some products already. People only need so many washing machines, refrigerators, vacuum cleaners, cars and television sets. Already the market for personal computers is getting very crowded. Prices are falling, quality and reliability has gone up to very acceptable levels, and after the first flush of enthusiasm for new electronic gadgetry it is clear that customers are becoming much more choosy. Hence NICs face the unpalatable truth that if they are going to succeed they are going to have to sell their goods to the developing world itself. Whether they can succeed in doing so does not merely depend on their own efforts, but on the creation of markets for those goods consequent upon development on a scale probably immensely damaging to the global environment we all have to share.

The future of the poorest countries

Finally we have to recall that the poorer countries of the developing world are slipping behind, not catching up. The 'pulling apart' of the developing world is continuing. Yet the boundary between richer and poorer sectors does not run between countries. Almost always it forms a series of invisible barriers between the rich and the poor of a single country, or of a group of countries.

Those of us who have the good fortune to live in the developed world have to some extent relied on the disparate and in many cases powerless nature of countries of the developing world. The reality of encroaching environmental problems if not catastrophe changes this situation. It is no longer possible to remain unconcerned about the plight of other people because their existence does not really impinge on ours. The futures of their children and of ours are now clearly recognisably bound together.

It is of course true that many people in the industrialised countries have more pressing problems than the apparently rather remote dilemmas which surround our relationships with other parts of the world. They have in many cases, compared with the wealthy of their own countries, too little to be expected to make any significant contribution to a more equal world by giving up material possessions. Nevertheless, the quality of all our lives ultimately depends on our recognising our interdependence. Above all, the developed world must acknowledge the special responsibility it now has for helping the developing world to achieve a quality of life appropriate for all human beings. We are very privileged to be living in the twenty-first century; it is up to us to make use of those privileges.

References

Adams, Nassau (1993), *Worlds Apart: the North–South divide and the evolution of the international economic system*, London, Zed Press.

Adams, Patricia (1991), *Odious Debts: loose lending, corruption, and the Third World's environmental legacy*, London, Earthscan.

Afrifa, Col. A.A. (1966), *The Ghana Coup, 24th February 1966*, London, Frank Cass.

Almond, Gabriel A. and Coleman, James S. (1960), *The Politics of the Developing Areas*, Princeton, Princeton University Press.

Almond, Gabriel A. and Verba, Sidney (1963), *The Civic Culture*, Princeton, Princeton University Press.

Almond, Gabriel A. and Verba, Sidney (1980), *The Civic Culture revisited*, Princeton, Princeton University Press.

Amin, Samir (1990a), *Delinking: towards a polycentric world*, London, Zed Press.

Amin, Samir (1990b), *Maldevelopment: anatomy of a global failure*, London, Zed Press.

Andreski, Stanislav (1968), *The African Predicament: a study in the pathology of modernisation*, London, Michael Joseph.

Anwar Ibrahim (1993), Speech to The International Seminar on Indigenous People, Kuala Lumpur, 29 November 1993, http://ikdasar.tripod.com/anwar/93-19.htm

Arat, Zehra F. (1991), *Democracy and Human Rights in Developing Countries*, Boulder, CO, Rienner.

Armstrong, Charles K. (2002), *Korean Society: civil society, democracy and the state*, London, Routledge.

Austin, Dennis (1978), *Politics in Africa*, Manchester, Manchester University Press.

Australian Broadcasting Company (1998), 'Oil production begins in Timor Gap', 21 July.

Avert (2006), World HIV and AIDS Statistics, September 2005, http://www.avert.org/worldstats.htm

Baran, Paul A. (1957), *The Political Economy of Growth*, New York, Monthly Review Press.

Barber, Benjamin R. (1992), 'Jihad vs. McWorld', *Atlantic Monthly*, March 1992, **269** (3).

Barbier, Edward B. (1989), *Economics, Natural-resource Scarcity and Development: conventional and alternative views*, London, Earthscan.

Beer, Christopher E.F. and Williams, Gavin (1975), 'The politics of the Ibadan peasantry', *The African Review*, 5 (3), 235–56.

Beetham, David (1992), 'Liberal democracy and the limits of democratization', *Political Studies*, 40, reprinted in David Held, ed. (1993), *Prospects for Democracy*, Cambridge, Polity Press.

Bernstein, Henry, ed. (1973), *Underdevelopment and Development: the Third World today*, Harmondsworth, Penguin Books.

Bernstein, Henry, Crow, Ben, Mackintosh, Maureen and Martin, Charlotte, eds (1990), *The Food Question: profits versus people?*, London, Earthscan.

Bernstein, Henry, Crow, Ben and Johnson, Hazel, eds (1992), *Rural Livelihoods: crises and responses*, Oxford, Oxford University Press and the Open University.

Bill, James Alban (1972), *The Politics of Iran: groups, classes, and modernization*, Columbus, OH, Merrill.

Billington, Rosamund, Strawbridge, Sheelagh, Greensides, Lenore and Fitzsimons, Annette (1991), *Culture and Society: a sociology of culture*, Basingstoke, Macmillan Education.

Black, Cyril E. (1976), *Comparative Modernization: a reader*, New York, The Free Press.

Black, Jan Knippers (1999), *Inequity in the Global Village: recycled rhetoric and disposable people*, West Hartfort, CT, Kumarian Press.

Bonilla, Frank, and Girling, Robert, eds (1973), *The Structures of Dependency*, Stanford, CA, Institute of Political Studies.

Boserup, Ester (1981), *Population and Technology*, Oxford, Basil Blackwell.

Boserup, Ester (1989), *Woman's Role in Economic Development*, New edn, London, Earthscan.

Bourricaud, François (1970), *Power and Society in Contemporary Peru*, New York, Praeger.

Bowden, Mark (2001), *Black Hawk Down: a story of modern war*, Harmondsworth, Penguin.

Bradley, P.N. (1986), 'Food production and distribution – and hunger' in R.J. Johnston and P.J. Taylor, eds, *A World in Crisis? Geographical perspectives*, Oxford, Basil Blackwell, pp. 89–106.

Brandt, Willy (1980), *North–South: a programme for survival. The report of the Independent Commission on International Development Issues under the Chairmanship of Willy Brandt*, London, Pan.

Brammer, H. (1990), 'Floods in Bangladesh: geographical background to the 1987 and 1988 floods', *Geographical Journal*, 156 (1), 12–22.

Bresnan, John, ed. (1986), *Crisis in the Philippines: the Marcos era and beyond*, Princeton, Princeton University Press.

Bretton, Henry L. (1973), *Power and politics in Africa*, London, Longman.

Brier, Alan and Calvert, Peter (1975), 'Revolution in the 1960s', *Political Studies*, **32** (1), 1–11.

Brown, G. Gordon (1957), 'Some problems of culture contact with illustrations from East Africa and Samoa', *Human Organization*, **16** (3), 11–14.

Brusco, Valeria, Nazareno, Marcelo and Stokes, Susan C., 'Clientelism and democracy: evidence from Argentina'. Paper prepared for presentation at the conference on Political Parties and Legislative Organization in Parliamentary and Presidential Regimes, Yale University, March 2002: http://www.yale.edu/las/conference/papers/Brusco.pdf

Bull, Hedley (1977), *The Anarchical Society*, London, Macmillan.

Burnell, Peter (1997), *Foreign Aid in a Changing World*, Milton Keynes, Open University Press.

Burnell, Peter, ed. (2000), *Democracy Assistance: international co-operation for democratization*, London, Frank Cass.

Burnell, Peter, and Calvert, Peter, eds (1999), *The Resilience of Democracy: persistent practice, durable idea*, London, Frank Cass.

Burnell, Peter, and Calvert, Peter, eds (2005), *Democratization*, **12** (4), August, Special Issue: *Promoting Democracy Abroad*.

Burnell, Peter and Randall, Vicky, eds (2005), *Politics in the Developing World*, Oxford, Oxford University Press.

Cairncross, Alec (1994), 'Forget Bretton Woods – recovery was born in the USA', *The Guardian*, 22 July 1994.

Calvert, Peter (1985), *Guatemala: a nation in turmoil*, Boulder, CO, Westview.

Calvert, Peter, ed. (1988), *The Central American Security System: North/South or East/West?* Cambridge, Cambridge University Press.

Calvert, Peter (1990a), *Revolution and Counter-Revolution*, Milton Keynes, Open University Press.

Calvert, Peter (1990b), 'The US intervention in Panama', *Small Wars and Insurgencies*, **1**, December, 307–14.

Calvert, Peter (1994), *The International Politics of Latin America*, Manchester, Manchester University Press.

Calvert, Peter (2001), 'Internal colonization, development and environment', *Third World Quarterly*, **22** (1), 51–63.

Calvert, Peter (2002), *Comparative Politics: an introduction*, Harlow, Longman.

Calvert, Peter, ed. (2004), *Border and Territorial Disputes of the World*, 4th edn, London, John Harper Publishing.

Calvert, Peter (2005a), 'Argentina: decline and revival', in Jan Knippers Black, ed., *Latin America, Its Problems and Its Promise: a multidisciplinary introduction*, 4th edn, Boulder, CO, Westview Press.

Calvert, Peter (2005b), 'Changing notions of development: bringing the state back in', in Jeffrey Haynes, ed., *Development Studies*, Basingstoke, Palgrave, pp. 47–64.

Calvert, Peter and Calvert, Susan (1999), *The South, the North and the Environment*, London, Cassell/Pinter.

Canovan, Margaret (1981), *Populism*, London, Junction Books.

Cardoso, Fernando Henrique (1972), 'Dependency and development in Latin America', *New Left Review*, 74, 83–95.

Cardoso, Fernando Henrique and Faletto, Enzo (1979), '*Dependency and Development in Latin America*', Berkeley, University of California Press.

Cardoso, Fernando Henrique with Brian Winter (2006), *The Accidental President of Brazil: a memoir*, New York, Public Affairs Books.

Carothers, Thomas (1999), *Aiding Democracy Abroad: the learning curve*, Washington, DC, The Brookings Institution for Carnegie Endownment for International Peace.

Carroll, John E. (1990), *International Enviromental Diplomacy: the management and resolution of transfrontier environmental problems*, Cambridge, Cambridge University Press.

Cassen, Robert (1994), *Does Aid Work? Report to an intergovernmental task force*, Oxford, Clarendon Press.

Chaliand, Gérard (1977), *Revolution in the Third World: myths and prospects*, Hassocks, Harvester Press.

Chilcote, Ronald H. (1978), 'A question of dependency', *Latin American Research Review*, 12 (2), 55–68.

Chilcote, Ronald H. and Edelstein, Joel C., eds (1974), *Latin America: The Struggle with Dependency and Beyond*, Cambridge, MA, Schenkman.

Chossudovsky, Michel (1995), 'IMF–World Bank policies and the Rwandan holocaust', *Third World Resurgence*, 52, 27–31, also http://www.hartford-hwp.com/archives/35/033.html

Clapham, Christopher, ed. (1982), *Private Patronage and Public Power: political clientelism in the modern state*, London, Frances Pinter.

Clapham, Christopher (1985), *Third World Politics: an introduction*, London, Routledge.

Clarke, Arthur C. (1945), 'Extra-terrestrial relays', *Wireless World*, October 1945, 305–8.

Colburn, Forrest D. (1994), *The Vogue of Revolution in Poor Countries*, Princeton, Princeton University Press.

Collor, Fernando (1992), *Agenda for Consensus: a social-liberal proposal*, Brasília, Governo do Brasil.

Colquhoun, Keith (1993), 'North Korea, the dangerous outsider', *World Today*, November, 210.

Comisión Nacional sobre la Desaparición de Personas (CONADEP) (1984), *Nunca Más*, Buenos Aires, EUDEBA.

Conniff, Michael L., ed. (1982), *Latin American Populism in Comparative Perspective*, Albuquerque, NM, University of New Mexico Press.

Crabtree, John (1987), *The Great Tin Crash: Bolivia and the world tin market*, London, Latin American Bureau.

Crow, Ben, Thorpe, Mary et al. (1988), *Survival and Change in the Third World*, Cambridge, Polity Press.

Crowder, Michael (1967), *Senegal*, London, Methuen.

Dahl, Robert A. (1989), *Democracy and its Critics*, New Haven, Yale University Press.

DANIDA – Danish Ministry of Foreign Affairs (1989), *Environmental Issues and Human Health*, Copenhagen, Department of International Development Cooperation.

Davidson, Julia O'Connell (1996), 'Sex tourism in Cuba', *Race and Class*, 38 (1), 39–48.

Decalo, Samuel (1976), *Coups and Army Rule in Africa*, New Haven, Yale University Press.

Decalo, Samuel (1980), 'Regionalism, political decay, and civil strife in Chad', *Journal of Modern African Studies*, 18 (1), 23–56.

De Zeeuw, Jeroen (2005), 'Projects do not create institutions: the record of democracy assistance in post-conflict societies', *Democratization*, 12 (4), August, Special Issue: *Promoting Democracy Abroad*, 481–504.

Diamond, Jared (1998), *Guns, Germs, and Steel: a short history of everybody for the last 13,000 years*, London, Vintage.

Diamond, Larry (1993), 'Three paradoxes of democracy' in Larry Diamond and Marc F. Plattner, eds, *The Global Resurgence of Democracy*, Baltimore, The Johns Hopkins University Press, pp. 95–107.

Diamond, Larry (1999), *Developing Democracy: towards consolidation*, Baltimore, MD, The Johns Hopkins University Press.

Diamond, Larry, Plattner, Marc F., Yun-han and Hung-mao Tien, eds (1997), *Consolidating the Third Wave democracies: themes and perspectives*, Baltimore, The Johns Hopkins University Press.

Dicken, Peter (1986), *Global Shift: industrial change in a turbulent world*, London, Harper & Row.

Dickenson, J.P., Clarke, C.G., Gould, W.T.S., Prothero, R.M., Siddle, D.J., Smith, C.T., Thomas-Hope, E.M. and Hodgkiss, A.G. (1983), *A Geography of the Third World*, London, Methuen.

Di Tella, Guido and Rodríguez Braun, Carlos, eds (1990), *Argentina, 1946–83: the economic ministers speak*, London, Macmillan with St Antony's College, Oxford.

Di Tella, Torcuato (1965), 'Populism and Reform in Latin America', in Claudio Véliz, ed., *Obstacles to Change in Latin America*, London, Oxford University Press, pp. 48–51.

Dix, Robert (1985), 'Populism: authoritarian and democratic', *Latin American Research Review*, 20 (2), 29–52.

Dobel, J. (1978), 'The corruption of a state', *American Political Science Review*, 72 (3), 958–73.

Dobyns, Henry F., Doughty, Paul L. and Lasswell, Harold D. (1971), *Peasants, Power, and Applied Social Change: Vicos as a model*, London, Sage Publications.

Dorman, Sara Rich (2000), 'Change now?' *The World Today*, 56 (4), April, 25–7.

Dos Santos, Theotonio (1969), 'The crisis of development theory and the problem of dependence in Latin America', in Henry Bernstein, ed., *Underdevelopment and Development: the Third World today*, Harmondsworth, Penguin, 1973, pp. 55–60.

Dos Santos, Theotonio (1970), 'The structure of dependence', *American Economic Review*, **60**, May, 291–336.

Dreze, Jean and Sen, Amartya (1989), *Hunger and Public Action*, Oxford, Clarendon Press.

Duncan, Tim, and Fogarty, John (1986), *Australia and Argentina: on parallel paths*, Carlton, Victoria, Melbourne University Press.

Dunn, John, ed. (1978), *West African States: failure and promise; a study in comparative politics*, Cambridge, Cambridge University Press.

Earth Policy Institute (2004), 'Resources on Population and Health', http://www.earth-policy.org/Indicators/Pop/2004.htm

Easton, David (1957), 'An approach to the analysis of political systems', *World Politics*, **10**, 383–400.

Easton, David (1965), *A Systems Analysis of Political Life*, New York, John Wiley.

Eklit, Jørgen, and Reynolds, Andrew (2002), 'The impact of election administration on the legitimacy of emerging democracies: a new comparative politics research agenda', *Commonwealth and Comparative Studies*, **40** (2), 86–119.

Eklit, Jørgen, and Reynolds, Andrew (2005), 'A framework for the systematic study of election quality', *Democratization*, **12** (2), April, 147–62.

Eliasson, Jan, and Blumenthal, Susan (2005), 'Dying for a Drink of Clean Water', *Washington Post*, 20 September.

Enloe, Cynthia (1989), *Making Feminist Sense of International Politics*, London, Pandora Press.

Eyben, Rosalind (1995), 'What can aid do for social development?' *Development in Practice*, **5** (1), 45–9.

Fanon, Frantz (1967), *The Wretched of the Earth*, Harmondsworth, Penguin.

Farhi, Farideh (2005), 'The contending discourses on women in Iran', Third World Network, http://www.twnside.org.sg/title/iran-cn.htm

Finer, Samuel (1970), *Comparative Government*, Harmondsworth, Penguin.

Finer, Samuel (1975), *The Man on Horseback: the role of the military in politics*, 2nd edn, Harmondsworth, Penguin.

First, Ruth (1972), *The Barrel of a Gun*. Harmondsworth, Penguin African Library.

Foray, Cyril (1977), *Historical Dictionary of Sierra Leone*, Metuchen, Scarecrow Press.

Foster, Geroge M. (1967), *Tzintzuntzan: Mexican peasants in a changing world*, Boston, MA, Little Brown.

Foster, George M. (1973), *Traditional Societies and Technological Change*, New York, Harper & Row.

Foster, George M. (1976), *Traditional Societies and Technological Change*, 2nd edn, New York, Harper & Row.

Francis, David J. (2001), *The Politics of Economic Regionalism: Sierra Leone in ECOWAS*, Aldershot, Ashgate.

Francis, David J. (2006), *Unifying Africa: Building Regional Peace and Security Systems*, Aldershot, Ashgate.

Frank, André Gunder (1966), 'The development of underdevelopment', *Monthly Review*, **18** (4), 17–31.

Frank, André Gunder (1967), *Capitalism and underdevelopment in Latin America*, Harmondsworth, Penguin.

Frank, André Gunder (1969), *Lumpenbourgeoisie: lumpendevelopment, dependence, class, and politics in Latin America*, New York, Monthly Review Press.

Frank, André Gunder (1970), *Latin America: underdevelopment or revolution*, New York, Monthly Review Press.

Frank, André Gunder (1974), 'Dependence is dead, long live dependence and the class struggle: a reply to critiques', *Latin American Perspectives*, **1** (1), 87–106.

Frank, André Gunder (1981), *Crisis in the Third World*, London, Heinemann.

Fraser, Duncan (2001), 'Long waves in economics – waves of democracy', *Democratization*, **8** (4), Winter, 41–64.

Freedman, Lawrence and Karsh, Efraim (1993), *The Gulf Conflict 1990–1991: diplomacy and war in the New World Order*, Princeton, Princeton University Press.

Freedom House (2005), *Freedom in the world*, www.freedomhouse.org/uploads/pdf/charts2006.pdf

Friedman, Milton (1962), *Capitalism and Freedom*, Chicago, University of Chicago Press.

Froebel, Friedrich, Henricks, Jurgen and Kreye, Otto (1980), *The New International Division of Labour*, Cambridge, Cambridge University Press.

Fromm, Erich (1942), *The Fear of Freedom*, London, Routledge & Kegan Paul.

Fukuyama, Francis (1992), *The End of History and the Last Man*, London, Hamish Hamilton.

Furtado, Celso (1970), *The Economic Development of Latin America: a survey from colonial times to the Cuban Revolution*, Cambridge, Cambridge University Press.

Gamer, Robert E. (1976), *The Developing Nations: a comparative perspective*, Boston, Allyn & Bacon.

George, Susan (1993), 'The Debt Boomerang', *New Internationalist*, May.

Gerlich, Peter (1987), 'Consociationalism to competition: the Austrian party system since 1945', in Hans Daalder, ed. (1987), *Party Systems in Denmark, Austria, Switzerland, the Netherlands and Belgium*, London, Frances Pinter.

Gerschenkron, Alexander (1962), *Continuity in History and Other Essays*, Cambridge, MA, Belknap Press.

Ghosh, J., and Bharadwaj, K. (1992), 'Poverty and employment in India', in Henry Bernstein, Ben Crow and Hazel Johnson, eds (1992), *Rural livelihoods: crises and responses*, Oxford, Oxford University Press and the Open University.

Giddens, Anthony (1990), *The Consequences of Modernity*, Cambridge, Polity Press.

Gill, Graeme (2000), *The Dynamics of Democratization: elites, civil society and the transition process*, London, Palgrave Macmillan.

Gills, Barry, Rocamora, Joel and Wilson, Richard (1993), 'Low intensity democracy' in Barry Gills, Joel Rocamora and Richard Wilson, eds, *Low Intensity Democracy: political power in the new world order*, London, Pluto Press, pp. 3–34.

Ginsberg,, B. (1982), *The Consequences of Consent*, Reading, MA, Addison Wesley.

Gladdish, Ken (1991), *Governing from the Centre: politics and policy-making in the Netherlands*, London, Hurst & Co.

Glade, William (1991), 'The contexts of privatization', in William Glade, ed., *Privatization of Public Enterprises in Latin America*, San Francisco, CA, International Center for Economic Growth, Institute of the Americas and Center for US-Mexican Studies.

Glenn, John (2003), 'The Economic Transition in Central Asia: Implications for Democracy', *Democratization*, 10 (3), Autumn, 124–47.

Global Reach (2006), Online Language Populations, http://global-reach.biz/globstats/evol.html

Golbourne, Harry, ed. (1979), *Politics and State in the Third World*, London, Macmillan.

Goldsmith, Arthur A. (2004), 'Predatory versus Developmental Rule in Africa', *Democratization*, 11 (3), June, 88–110.

Goldthorpe, John (1975), *The Sociology of the Third World: disparity and involvement*, Cambridge University Press.

Goode, W.J. (1970), *World Revolution and Family Patterns*, Glencoe, IL, The Free Press.

Grubb, Michael (1992), *The Greenhouse Effect; negotiating targets*, 2nd edn, London, Royal Institute of International Affairs.

Grubb, Michael (1992), *The World Today*, 48 (8/9), 140–2.

Grubb, Michael (2000), 'Protecting the planet', *The World Today*, 56 (5), 8–11.

Grugel, Jean (1995), *Politics and Development in the Caribbean Basin: Central America and the Caribbean in the New World Order*, Basingstoke, Macmillan.

Guimarães, R. (1991), *The Ecopolitics of Development in the Third World: politics and environment in Brazil*, London, Rienner.

Ha Joon Chang (2005), *Why developing countries need tariffs. How WTO NAMA negotiations could deny developing countries right to a future*, South Perspective Series, South Centre and Oxfam International, November 2005, www.southcentre.org/publications/SouthPerspectiveSeries/WhyDevCountriesNeedTariffsNew.pdf

Hall, Anthony L. (1991), *Developing Amazonia: deforestation and social conflict in Brazil's Carajás programme*, Manchester, Manchester University Press.

Hall, Stuart, and Jefferson, Tony, eds (1976), *Resistance through Rituals: youth subcultures in post-war Britain*, London, Hutchinson in association with the Centre for Contemporary Cultural Studies, University of Birmingham.

Halliday, Fred (1994), *Rethinking International Relations*, Basingstoke: Macmillan.

Halliday, Fred (2001), *Two Hours That Shook the World: September 11, 2001 – Causes and Consequences*, London, Saqi Books.

Hammond, Bob (1994), 'A Geography of overseas aid', *Geography*, **79** (3), 174: 210–21.

Hardoy, Jorge E., Mitlin, Diana, and Satterthwaite, David (1992), *Environmental Problems in Third World Cities*, London, Earthscan.

Harley, C.K. (1991), 'Substitution for Prerequisites: Endogenous Institutions and Comparative Economic History', in R. Sylla and G. Toniolo (eds), *Patterns of European Industrialization*, London: Routledge, 29–44.

Harris, Nigel (1986), *The End of the Third World? Newly industrialising countries and the decline of an ideology*, London, I.B. Tauris.

Harrison, Paul (1993), *The Third Revolution: population, environment and a sustainable world*, Harmondsworth, Penguin.

Hayek, Friedrich August (1960), *The Constitution of Liberty*, London, Routledge & Kegan Paul.

Haynes, J. (2001), *Democracy in the Developing World: Africa, Asia, Latin America and the Middle East*, Cambridge, Polity.

Hayter, Teresa (1983), *The Creation of World Poverty: an alternative view to the Brandt Report*, London, Pluto Press.

Heidenheimer, A.J. (1970), *Political Corruption*, New York, Holt Rinehart.

Held, David, ed. (1993), *Prospects for Democracy*, Cambridge, Polity Press.

Hewitt, Vernon Marston (1992), *The International Politics of South Asia*. Manchester, Manchester University Press.

Hicks, John D. (1961), *The Populist Revolt*, Lincoln, NB, University of Nebraska Press.

Higgins, Graham, et al. (1982), *Potential Population Supporting Capacities of Lands in the Developing World*, Rome, FAO.

Hilling, David (1978), 'The infrastructure gap', in Alan B. Mountjoy, ed., *The Third World, Problems and Perspectives*, London, Macmillan.

Hillyard, Paddy and Percy-Smith, Janie (1988), *The Coercive State*, London, Pinter.

Hirst, Paul, and Thompson, Grahame (1999), *Globalization in Question*, 2nd revd edn, Cambridge, Polity Press.

Hogendorn, Jan S. (1996), *Economic Development*, London, Longman.

Holden, Barry (1993), *Understanding Liberal Democracy*, 2nd edn, Hemel Hempstead, Harvester-Wheatsheaf.

Holmberg, Allan R. (1971), 'Experimental intervention in the field', in Henry F. Dobyns, Paul L. Doughty and Harold D. Lasswell, eds, *Peasants, Power, and Applied Social Change: Vicos as a model*, London, Sage Publications, pp. 21–32.

Hoogvelt, Ankie (1978), *The Sociology of Developing Societies*, London, Macmillan.

Horowitz, Donald L. (1971), 'Three dimensions of ethnic politics', *World Politics*, **23** (2), 232.

Howard, Michael, ed. (1957), *Soldiers and Governments*, London, Eyre & Spottiswode.

Hughes, John (1968), *The End of Sukarno: a coup that misfired: a purge that ran wild*, London, Angus & Robertson.

Huntington, Samuel (1968), *Political Order in Changing Societies*, New Haven, Yale University Press.

Huntington, Samuel (1976), 'The change to change: modernization, development, and politics', in Cyril E. Black, ed., *Comparative Modernization: a reader*, New York, The Free Press.

Huntington, Samuel (1993a), 'The clash of civilizations', *Foreign Affairs*, 72 (3), Summer, 22–8.

Huntington, Samuel (1993b), *The Third Wave: democratization in the late twentieth century*, Norman, OK, University of Oklahoma Press.

Huntington, Samuel (1997), *The Clash of Civilizations and the Remaking of World Order*, New York, Simon & Schuster.

Huntington, Samuel P. (1999), 'The lonely superpower', *Foreign Affairs*, 78 (2), March/April, 35–49.

Hurrell, Andrew, and Kingsbury, Benedict, eds (1992), *The International Politics of the Environment*, Oxford, Clarendon Press.

Ianni, Otávio (1975), *A formaçao do estado populista na América Latina*, Rio de Janeiro, Civilizaçao Brasiliera.

India, Government of (2006), Calorie needs to lose/gain weight, http://www.webindia123.com/health/diet/calorie/gain.htm

International Cocoa Organization (ICCO) (2005), Facts about the International Cocoa Organization, www.icco.org/facts.htm

Inter-Parliamentary Union (2006), *Women in National Parliaments: situation as of 28 February 2006*, www.ipu.org/wmn-e/world.htm

Ionescu, Ghita and Gellner, Ernest, eds (1969), *Populism: its meaning and national characteristics*, New York, Macmillan.

IDRC/CRDI (2006), *Environmental Trends: The State of World Population 2001*, The International Development Research Centre, http://web.idrc.ca/en/ev-34477-201-1-DO_TOPIC.html

Ishiyama, John (1999), 'Sickles into roses: the successor parties and democratic consolidation in post-communist politics', *Democratization*, 6 (4), Winter, 52–73.

Jackson, Ben (1990), *Poverty and the Planet: a question of survival*, Harmondsworth, Penguin.

Jaguaribe, Helio (1967), *Problems do desenvolvimiento Latino-Americano*, Rio de Janeiro, Civilizaçao Brasiliera.

Jenkins, J. Craig and Kposowa, Augustine J. (1992), 'Political origins of African military coups: ethnic competition, military centrality and the struggle over the postcolonialist state', *International Studies Quarterly*, 36 (3), 271–91.

Joffé, George (1993), 'The issue of water in the Middle East and North Africa', in Caroline Thomas and Darryl Howlett, eds, *Resource Politics: freshwater and regional relations*, Buckingham, Open University Press, pp. 65–85.

Johnson, John J. (1964), *The Military and Society in Latin America*, Stanford, CA, Stanford University Press.

Johnston, R.J. and Taylor, P.J., eds (1986), *A World in Crisis? Geographical perspectives*, Oxford, Basil Blackwell.

Kamrava, Mehran (1992), *Revolutionary Politics*, London, Pinter.

Kamrava, Mehran (1993), *Politics and Society in the Third World*, London, Routledge.

Kandiyoti, Deniz, ed. (1991), *Women, Islam and the State*, Philadelphia, Temple University Press.

Kane, David (2005), 'Land Reform and Poverty Alleviation Project (Cedula da Terra)', in NEWS FROM BRAZIL supplied by SEJUP (Serviço Brasileiro de Justiça e Paz). No. 355, 18 June 1999, www.oneworld.org/sejup/ and www. converge.org.nz/lac/articles/news990623d.htm

Kang, Ouyang and Yong, Li (1998), 'Management and utilization of water resources in the People's Republic of China', in Dhirendra Vajpeyi, ed., *Water Resource Management: a comparative perspective*, Westport, CT, Praeger, pp. 33–50.

Karl, Terry Lynn (1997), *The Paradox of Plenty: Oil Booms and Petro-States*, Berkeley, CA, University of California Press.

Kedourie, Elie (1971), *Nationalism in Asia and Africa*, London, Heinemann.

Keesing's Contemporary Archives, 1931–86, London, Longman, 1981–86; *Keesing's Record of World Events*, Harlow, Longman, 1987–96; since 1997, Keesing's Worldwide, Bethesda, MD.

Kent, George (1995), *Children in the International Political Economy*, Basingstoke, Macmillan.

Keohane, Robert O. and Nye, Joseph S. (1977), *Power and Interdependence: world politics in transition*, Boston, MA, Little Brown.

Kerr, Clark, et al. (1960), *Industrialism and Industrial Man: the problems of labor and management in economic growth*, London, Heinemann.

Kilson, Martin (1966), *Political Change in a West African State: a study of the modernization process in Sierra Leone*, Cambridge, MA, Harvard University Press.

Kitching, G. (1982), *Development and Underdevelopment in Historical Perspective: populism, nationalism and industrialization*, London, Methuen.

Kitschelt, Herbert (1999), *Post-Communist Party Systems: competition, representation and inter-party cooperation*, Cambridge, Cambridge University Press.

Kleveman, Lutz (2005), 'Street-fighting boys', *Telegraph Magazine*, 17 September, 30.

Krugman, Paul (1995), 'Dutch tulips and emerging markets', *Foreign Affairs*, **74**, 28–9.

Kumar, Krishna (2005), 'Reflections on international political party assistance', *Democratization*, **12** (4), August, Special Issue: *Promoting Democracy Abroad*, 505–27.

Kuperman, Alan J. (2001), *The Limits of Humanitarian Intervention: genocide in Rwanda*, Washington, DC, The Brookings Institution.

Laclau, Ernesto (1977), *Politics and Ideology in Marxist Theory: Capitalism–Fascism–Populism*, London, NLB.

Lane, Jan-Erik and Ersson, Svante O. (1991), *Politics and Society in Western Europe*, London, Sage.

Lanfant, Marie-Françoise, Allcock, John B. and Bruner, Edward M., eds (1995), *International Tourism, Identity and Change*, London, Sage for International Sociological Association.

Lasswell, Harold D. and Holmberg, Allan R. (1966), 'Toward a general theory of directed value accumulation and institutional development', in H.W. Peter, ed., *Comparative Theories of Social Change*, Ann Arbor, MI, Foundation for Research on Human Behavior.

Lasswell, Harold D. and Kaplan, A. (1950), *Power and Society: a framework for political inquiry*, New Haven, CT, Yale University Press.

Lee, Wendy (1991), 'Prostitution and tourism in South-East Asia', in Nanneke Redclift and M. Thea Sinclair, eds, *Working Women: international perspectives on labour and gender Ideology*, London, Routledge.

Leggett, Jeremy, ed. (1990), *Global Warming: the Greenpeace report*, Oxford, Oxford University Press.

Lembruch, Gerhard (1967), *Proporzdemokratie: politisches System und politische Kultur in der Schweiz und in Österreich*, Tübingen, Mohr.

Levy, Diane E. and Lerch, Patricia B. (1991), 'Tourism as a factor in development: implications for gender and work in Barbados', *Gender and Society*, 5 (1), 67–85.

Lewis, Oscar (1962), *The Children of Sánchez: autobiography of a Mexican family*, London, Secker & Warburg.

Lieuwen, Edwin (1964), *Generals versus Presidents: neomilitarism in Latin America*, London, Pall Mall.

Lijphart, Arend (1969), 'Typologies of democratic systems', in Arend Lijphart, ed., *Politics in Europe: comparisons and interpretations*, Englewood Cliffs, NJ, Prentice Hall.

Lijphart, Arend (1974), *The Politics of Accommodation: pluralism and democracy in the Netherlands*, 2nd edn, Berkeley, CA, University of California Press.

Lijphart, Arend (1977), *Democracy in Plural Societies: a comparative exploration*, New Haven, CT, Yale University Press.

Lindberg, Staffan I. (2003), ' "It's our time to 'chop' ": Do elections in Africa feed neo-patrimonialism rather than counteract it', *Democratization*, 10 (2), Summer, 121–40.

Linz, Juan J. (1970), 'An authoritarian regime: Spain', in E. Allardt and S. Rokkan, eds, *Mass Politics: studies in political sociology*, New York, The Free Press, pp. 251–83, 374–81.

Lipset, Seymour Martin (1960, repr. 1983), *Political Man*, New York, Basic Books.

Lipset, Seymour Martin (1979), *The First New Nation: the United States in historical and comparative perspective*, New York, W.W. Norton.

Lipset, Seymour Martin, and Rokkan, Stein, eds (1967), *Party Systems and Voter Alignments: cross-national perspectives*, New York, Collier-Macmillan.

Lipton, M. (1977), *Why Poor People Stay Poor: urban bias in world development*, London, Temple Smith.

Little, K. (1965), *West African Urbanisation*, Cambridge, Cambridge University Press.

Little, Richard (1975), *Intervention: external involvement in civil wars*, London, Martin Robertson.

Lloyd, Peter C. (1971), *Classes, Crises and Coups: themes in the sociology of developing countries*, London, Paladin.

Luckham, Robin (1971a), *The Nigerian Military 1960–67*, Cambridge, Cambridge University Press.

Luckham, Robin (1971b), 'Comparative typology of civil-military relations', *Government and Opposition*, 6, 5–35.

Lugard, Sir Frederick D. (1922), *The Dual Mandate in British Tropical Africa*, Edinburgh, William Blackwood & Sons.

McAfee, Kathy (1991), *Storm Signals: structural adjustment and development alternatives in the Caribbean*, Boston, South End Press in association with Oxfam America.

McGrew, Anthony G. and Lewis, Paul G. et al. (1992), *Global Politics: globalization and the nation-state*, Cambridge, Polity Press.

McKean, Liz (2000), 'Women 2000: the struggle for their rights persists', *Amnesty*, 100, March/April, 12–13.

Macpherson, C.B. (1977), *The Life and Times of Liberal Democracy*, Oxford, Oxford University Press.

Mair, Stefan (2000), 'Germany's Stiftungen and democracy assistance: comparative advantages, new challenges', in Peter Burnell, ed., *Democracy Assistance: international co-operation for democratization*, London, Frank Cass, pp. 128–49.

Malinowski, B. (1961), *The Dynamics of Culture Change*, New Haven, Yale University Press.

Mannion, A.M. (1992), *Global Environmental Change*, Harlow, Longman.

Manu, Christopher (1993), 'The road to the Desertification Convention', *Resources*, 4 (2), 7–10.

Matthews, Jessica Tuchman (1993), 'Nations and nature. A new view on security', in Glyn Prins, ed., *Threats Without Enemies: facing environmental insecurity*, London, Earthscan, pp. 25–37.

Mayall, James (2000), 'The Concept of Humanitarian Intervention Revisited', in Albrecht Schnabel and Rames Thakur, eds, *Kosovo and the Challenge of Humanitarian Intervention: selective indignation, collective intervention, and international citizenship*, Peace and Governance Programme, The United Nations University, www.unu.edu/p&g/kosovo_full.htm#20

Mead, Margaret (1956), *New Lives for Old*, New York, New American Library.

Mehta, Gita (1990), *Raj*, London, Mandarin.

Michels, Robert (1968, first publ. 1915), *Political Parties: a sociological study of the oligarchical tendencies of modern democracy*, New York, Dover Publications.

Mitra, Subrata Kumar, ed. (1990), *The Post-colonial State in Asia: dialectics of politics and culture*, New York, Harvester-Wheatsheaf.

Monbiot, George (1998), 'Whose wildlife is it anyway?', *The Guardian*, 20 June.

Moore, Barrington, Jr. (1969), *Social Origins of Dictatorship and Democracy: lord and peasant in the making of the modern world*, Harmondsworth, Penguin.

Moore, Mick (1990), 'Sri Lanka: the contradictions of the social democratic state', in Subrata Kumar Mitra, ed., *The Post-colonial State in Asia: dialectics of politics and culture*, New York, Harvester-Wheatsheaf, pp. 155–91.

Mygatt, Elizabeth (2006), 'World's Forest continue to Shrink', Earth Policy Institute, 4 April 2006, http://www.earth-policy.org/Indicators/Forest/2006.htm

Myrdal, Gunnar (1968), *Asian Drama: an enquiry into the poverty of nations*, Harmondsworth, Penguin.

Naguib (Neguib), Muhammad (1955), *Egypt's destiny*, Garden City, NY, Doubleday.

National Council for Science and the Environment (2000), *Sustaining water: population and the future of renewable water supplies*, Washington, DC, Population Action International, www.cnie.org/pop/pai/water-14.html

Naudet, David and Pradelle, Jean-Marc (1997), 'A verdict on aid to the Sahel', *The OECD Observer*, No. 205, April/May, 15–18.

Needler, Martin C. (1963), *Latin American Power in Perspective*, Princeton, Van Nostrand.

Neustadt, Richard E. (1964), *Presidential Power*, New York, Signet.

Newton, Ken (1997), 'Social capital and democracy', *American Behavioral Scientist*, 40 (5), 575–86.

Nordlinger, Eric A. (1977), *Soldiers in Politics: military coups and governments*, Englewood Cliffs, NJ, Prentice Hall.

Noreng, Oystein (2002), *Crude Power: politics and the oil market*, London, Tauris.

Norris, Pippa (2004), *Electoral Engineering: voting rules and political behaviour*, Cambridge, Cambridge University Press.

Nye, Joseph S. (1967), *Pan-Africanism and East African Integration*, Cambridge, MA, Harvard University Press.

Nye, J.S. and Keohane, R.O. (1971), *Transnational Relations and World Politics*, Cambridge, Cambridge University Press.

O'Brien, Donal B. (1971), *The Mourides of Senegal*, Oxford, Oxford University Press.

O'Brien, Donal B. Cruise (1978), 'Senegal', in John Dunn, ed., *West African States: failure and promise; a study in comparative politics*, Cambridge, Cambridge University Press, pp. 173–88.

O'Brien, Philip, and Cammack, Paul, eds (1985), *Generals in Retreat: the crisis of military rule in Latin America*, Manchester, Manchester University Press.

O'Donnell, Guillermo (1988), *Bureaucratic authoritarianism: Argentina, 1966–1973, in comparative perspective*, Berkeley, University of California Press.

O'Donnell, Guillermo (1994), 'Delegative democracy', *Journal of Democracy*, 7 (2), 151–9.

O'Donnell, Guillermo, Schmitter, Philippe and Whitehead, Lawrence (1986), *Transitions from Authoritarian Rule*, Baltimore, The Johns Hopkins University Press.

Ohmae, K. (1990), *The Borderless World*, London, Collins.

Oneworld (1998), www.oneworld.org/ips2/oct98/21_32_090.html

Page, S.E., Siegert, F., Rieley, J.O., Boehm, H-D.V., Jaya, Adi and Limin, Suwido (2002), 'The amount of carbon released from peat and forest fires in Indonesia in 1997', *Nature*, 420, 61–5.

Palmer, David Scott, ed. (1992), *Shining Path of Peru*, London, Hurst.

Panebianco, Angelo (1988), *Political Parties: organisation and power*, Cambridge, Cambridge University Press.

Parsons, Talcott (1964), *Essays in Sociological Theory*, New York, The Free Press.

Partridge, P.H. (1971), *Consent and Consensus*, London, Pall Mall.

Patullo, Polly (1996), *Last Resorts: the cost of tourism in the Caribbean*, London, Cassell with Latin American Bureau.

Pearce, Fred (1992), 'Last chance to save the planet?', *New Scientist*, 30 May, 24–8.

Percival, Debra (1996), 'The changing face of trade unionism in Africa', *The Courier ACP-EU*, No. 156, March–April, 76–77, www.oneworld.org/euforic/courier/156e_pet.htm

Petersen, Kurt (1992), *The Maquiladora Revolution in Guatemala*, Occasional Paper Series 2, Orville H. Schell, Jr., Center for International Human Rights at Yale Law School.

Philip, George (1984), 'Military-Authoritarianism in South America: Brazil, Chile, Uruguay and Argentina', *Political Studies*, **32** (1), 1–20.

Philip, George (1985), *The Military and South American Politics*, London, Croom Helm.

Pinkney, Robert (1993), *Democracy in the Third World*, Buckingham, Open University Press.

Poku, Nana, ed. (2006), *International Affairs*, **82** (2), March 2006, HIV/AIDS, special issue.

Poole, Deborah and Rénique, Gerardo (1991), 'The new chroniclers of Peru: US scholars and the "shining path" of peasant rebellion', *Bulletin of Latin American Research*, **10** (2), 133–91.

Poole, Deborah and Rénique, Gerardo (1992), *Peru: time of fear*, London, Latin American Bureau.

Population Reference Bureau (PRB) (2005), www.prb.org/pdf05/05WorldDataSheet_Eng.pdf

Postel, Sandra (1989), *Water for Agriculture*, Washington, DC, Worldwatch Institute, Worldwatch Paper 93.

Potter, David, Goldblatt, David, Kiloh, Margaret and Lewis, Paul, eds (1997), *Democratization*, Oxford, Polity Press.

Powell, John Duncan (1970), 'Peasant society and clientelist politics', *American Political Science Review*, **64**, 411–25.

Prebisch, Raúl (1950), *Economic Development of Latin America and Its Principal Problems*, New York, United Nations Department of Economic Affairs, ECLA document E/CN 12/89/Rev.1.

Prescott, J.R.V. (1965), *The Geography of Frontiers and Boundaries*, London, Hutchinson.

Prince of Wales (1993), 'Introduction', in Gwyn Prins, ed., *Threats Without Enemies: facing environmental insecurity*, London, Earthscan.

Prins, Gwyn (2000), 'Water, water, everywhere . . .', *The World Today*, **56** (4), 4–6.

Prusher, Ilene R. (2000), Kuwaiti women seek right to vote, *Christian Science Monitor*, 8 August, http://www.csmonitor.com/atcsmonitor/specials/women/rights/rights080800.html

Rae, Douglas W. and Taylor, Michael (1970), *The Analysis of Political Cleavages*, New Haven, CT, Yale University Press.

Randall, V. and Theobald, R. (1985), *Political Change and Underdevelopment*, London, Macmillan.

Rappaport, Roy A. (1968), *Pigs for the Ancestors: ritual in the ecology of a New Guinea people*, New Haven, Yale University Press.

Redclift, Michael (1984), *Development and the Environmental Crisis: red or green alternatives?*, London, Methuen.

Rischard, Jean-François (2002), *High Noon: twenty global problems, twenty years to solve them*, New York, Basic Books.

Robbins, Richard H. (1999), *Global Problems and the Culture of Capitalism*, New York, Allyn & Bacon.

Roett, Riordan (1985), 'Latin America's response to the debt crisis', *Third World Quarterly*, 7 (2), April.

Rose, Richard (1998), *Democracy and Its Alternatives: understanding post-communist societies*, Cambridge, Polity Press.

Ross, Michael L. (2001), 'Does Oil Hinder Democracy?', *World Politics*, 53, April, 325–61.

Rostow, W.W. (1960), *The Stages of Economic Growth*, Cambridge, MA, Harvard University Press.

Rostow, W.W. (1971), *Politics and the Stages of Growth*, Cambridge, Cambridge University Press.

Roxborough, Ian (1979), *Theories of Underdevelopment*, London, Macmillan.

Rueschemeyer, Dietrich, Stephens, Evelyne Huber and Stephens, John D. (1992), *Capitalist Development and Democracy*, Cambridge, Polity Press.

Rustow, Dankwart (1970), 'Transitions to democracy: toward a dynamic model', *Comparative Politics* 2 (2), April, 337–66.

Sahlin, Michael (1977), *Neo-authoritarianism and the Problem of Legitimacy: a general study and a Nigerian example*, Stockholm, Reben & Sjögren.

Sampson, Anthony (1975), *The Seven Sisters: the great oil companies and the world they made*, London, Coronet.

Sampson, Anthony (1999), *Mandela, the Authorised Biography*, London, HarperCollins.

Sanchez, Omar (2003), 'Beyond pacted transitions in Spain and Chile: Elite and Institutional Differences', *Democratization*, 10 (2), Summer, 65–86.

Santiso, Carlos (2004), 'The contentious Washington Consensus; reforming the reforms in emerging markets', *Review of International Political Economy*, 11 (4).

Saravanamuttu, Paikiasothy (1990), 'Instability in Sri Lanka', *Survival*, 32 (5), 455–68.

Saravanamuttu, Paikiasothy (1993), 'South Asia: the Ganges and the Brahmaputra', in Caroline Thomas and Darryl Howlett, eds, *Resource Politics:*

freshwater and regional relations, Burkingham, Open University Press, pp. 110–28.

Sartori, Giovanni (1976), *Parties and Party Systems: a framework for analysis*, Cambridge, Cambridge University Press.

Schmandt, Jurgen (1994), 'Water and development in semi-arid regions' paper presented to the XVI World Congress of the International Political Science Association, Berlin, Germany, 21–25 August.

Schmitter, Phillippe, ed. (1979), *Trends Towards Corporatist Intermediation*, Beverly Hills, CA, Sage.

Schmitter, Philippe and Karl, Terry Lynn (1993), 'What democracy is . . . and is not', in Larry Diamond and Marc F. Plattner, eds, *The Global Resurgence of Democracy*, Baltimore, MD, The Johns Hopkins University Press, pp. 33–52.

Schor, J.B. (1998), *The Overspent American: upscaling, downshifting and the new consumer*, New York, HarperCollins.

Schumpeter, Joseph A. (1943), *Capitalism, Socialism and Democracy*, London, Allen & Unwin.

Scott, J.C. (1976), *The Moral Economy of the Peasant: rebellion and subsistence in Southeast Asia*, New Haven, Yale University Press.

Scutz, Barry M. and O'Slater, Robert, eds (1990), *Revolution and Political Change in the Third World*, London, Adamantine.

Sen, Amartya (1981), *Poverty and Famines: an essay on entitlement and deprivation*, Oxford, Clarendon Press.

Seton-Watson, Hugh (1977), *Nations and States: an inquiry into the origins of nations and the politics of nationalism*, London, Methuen.

Shah, Anup (2006), 'High military spending in some places', www.globalissues.org/Geopolitics/ArmsTrade/Spending.asp#WorldMilitarySpending

Shaw, Paul (1992), quoted in *New Internationalist*, September 1992, 14.

Shearer, David (2000), 'Sanctions straitjacket', *The World Today*, 56 (5), May, 12–13.

Shiva, Vandana (1988), *Staying Alive. Women, ecology and development in India*, London, Zed Books.

Sierra Leone National Reformation Council (1968), *Report of the Forster Commission of Inquiry on Assets of Ex-Ministers and Ex-Deputy Ministers*, Freetown, Government Printer.

Singer, H.W. and Ansari, Javed A. (1992), *Rich and Poor Countries*, 4th edn, London, Routledge.

Sinha, R. (1976), *Food and Poverty*. London, Croom Helm.

Sizer, Nigel (2005), 'Halting the theft of Asia's Forests', *Far Eastern Economic Review*, May, 50–3.

Sklair, Leslie (1994), *Capitalism and Development*, London, Routledge.

Small, Vernon (2006), 'Singapore PM brands his opponent liar and cheat', *The Dominion Post* (New Zealand), 20 June.

Smith, Michael (1992), 'Modernization, globalization and the nation-state', in Anthony McGrew, Paul G. Lewis et al. (1992), *Global Politics*, Cambridge, Polity Press.

Smith, Tony (1979), 'The underdevelopment of development literature: the case of dependency theory', *World Politics*, **31** (2), 247–88.

Somjee, A.H. (1991), *Development Theory: critiques and explorations*, Basingstoke, Macmillan.

South Commission (1990), *The Challenge to the South: the report of the South Commission*, London, Oxford University Press.

Staley, Eugene (1954), *Political Implications of Economic Development*, New York, Harper.

Stanislaw, Joseph and Yergin, Daniel (2002), *The Commanding Heights: battle for the world economy*, New York, Touchstone.

Steiner, Jürg (1972), *Politics in Austria*, Boston, MA, Little Brown.

Steiner, Jürg (1974), *Amicable Agreement Versus Majority Rule: conflict resolution in Switzerland*, Chapel Hill, NC, University of North Carolina Press.

Stepan, Alfred, ed. (1973), *Authoritarian Brazil*, New Haven, Yale University Press.

Stepan, Alfred (1978), *The State and Society: Peru in comparative perspective*, Princeton, NJ, Princeton University Press.

Strong, Maurice F. (1992), 'Foreword', *The Global Partnership for Environment and Development: a guide to Agenda 21*, Geneva, UNCED.

Sunkel, Osvaldo (1969), 'National development policy and external dependence in Latin America', *Journal of Development Studies*, **6** (1), 23–48.

Suzman, Helen (1993), *In No Uncertain Terms: memoirs*, London, Sinclair-Stevenson.

Sylla, Richard and Toniolo, Gianni, eds (1991), *Patterns of European Industrialization: the nineteenth century*, London, Routledge.

Takkala, Jukka (2006), Global estimates of fatal occupational accidents, http://www.who.int/quantifying_ehimpacts/methods/en/takala.pdf

Tangri, Roger (1985), *Politics in Sub-Saharan Africa*, London, James Currey.

Taylor, Lewis (1987), 'Agrarian unrest and political conflict in Puno, 1985–87', *Bulletin of Latin American Research*, **6** (2), 135–62.

Taylor, Lewis (1998), 'Counter-insurgency strategy, the PCP-Sendero Luminoso and the civil war in Peru, 1980–1996', *Bulletin of Latin American Research*, **17** (1), 35–58.

The Annual Register (etc), 1758–1953; *The Annual Register of World Events*, 1954–1994, London, Longmans; 1995–96 Catermills; since 1997, Keesing's Worldwide, Bethesda, MD.

The Ecologist (1993), 'Whose common future? Reclaiming the commons'.

Thomas, Caroline (1985), *New States, Sovereignty and Intervention*, Aldershot, Gower.

Thomas, Caroline (1987), *In Search of Security: the Third World in International Relations*, Boulder, CO, Rienner.

Thomas, Caroline (1992), *The Environment in International Relations*, London, The Royal Institute of International Affairs.

Thomas, Caroline (1999), 'Where is the Third World now?', *Review of International Studies*, **25** (4), 225–44.

Thomas, Caroline and Howlett, Darryl (1992), *Resource Politics: freshwater and regional relations*, Buckingham, Open University Press.

Thrift, Nigel (1986), 'The geography of international economic disorder', in R.J. Johnston and P.J. Taylor, eds, *A World in Crisis: geographical perspectives*, Oxford, Basil Blackwell, pp. 16–78.

Timberlake, L. (1985), *Africa in Crisis*, London, Earthscan.

Todaro, Michael (1994), *Economic Development*, London, Longman.

Toffler, Alvin (1970), *Future Shock*. London, The Bodley Head.

Tolba, Mostafa, ed. (1988), *Evolving Environmental Perceptions: from Stockholm to Nairobi*, London, Butterworth.

Toma, Hideko (1999), Displaced persons and international human rights with reference to Rwanda and Cambodia. Unpublished PhD thesis, University of Southampton.

Tylor, E. (1891), 'Culture defined', in L.A. Coser and B. Rosenberg, eds (1964), *Sociological Theory: a book of readings*, London, Collier-Macmillan, pp. 125–31.

United Nations (1992), *Earth Summit: Press Summaries*, New York, United Nations.

United Nations Development Programme (UNDP) (1994a), *World Urbanization Prospects: the 1994 revision*. United Nations Population Division, gopher://gopher.undp.org:70/00/ungophers/popin/wdtrends/urban

United Nations Development Programme (UNDP) (1994b), *Human Development Report, 1994*, New York, Oxford University Press.

United Nations Development Programme (UNDP) (1995), *Human Development Report, 1995*, New York, Oxford University Press.

United Nations Development Programme (UNDP) (1998), *World Population 1998*. UN Department of Economic and Social Affairs, www.undp.org/popin/wdtrends/p98/fp98toc.htm

United Nations Development Programme (UNDP) (1999), *Human Development Report, 1999*, New York, Oxford University Press.

United Nations Development Programme (UNDP) (2000), *Population Distribution, Urbanization and Internal/Migration*, United Nations Population Information Network, www.undp.org/popin/icpd/prepcomm/official/rap/RAP8.html

United Nations Food and Agriculture Organization (UNFAO) (1999), *The State of Food Insecurity in the World 1999*, www.fao.org/FOCUS?E?SOFI?Count-e.htm

United Nations Food and Agriculture Organization (UNFAO) (2004), *Rice and Water: a long and diversified story*, www.fao.org/rice2004/en/f-sheet/factsheet1.pdf

United Nations Food and Agriculture Organization (UNFAO) (2005), *Serious Concern About Food Situation in Southern Africa*, www.fao.org/newsroom/en/news/2005/1000189/index.html

UNICEF (1990), *State of the World's Children*, London, Oxford University Press.

United Nations Fund for Population Activities (UNFPA) (1992), *The State of World Population, 1992*, New York, United Nations.

United Nations University (2003), *Democratization in the Middle East: experiences, struggles, challenges*, Washington, DC, The Brookings Institution.

Urry, John (1990), *The Tourist Gaze: leisure and travel in contemporary societies*, London, Sage.

US Office of National Drug Control Policy (2004), press release, 19 November www.whitehousedrugpolicy.gov/news/press04/111904.html

US Office of National Drug Control Policy (2005), press release, 25 March www.whitehousedrugpolicy.gov/news/press05/032505.html

Vagts, Alfred (1959), *A History of Militarism, Civilian and Military*, London, Hollis and Carter.

Vajpeyi, Dhirendra (1994), 'To dam or not to dam? Social, economic and political impact of large hydro-electric projects: case studies of China, India and Brazil', paper presented to the XVI World Congress of the International Political Science Association, Berlin, Germany, 21–25 August 1994.

Vajpeyi, Dhirendra, ed. (1998), *Water Resource Management: a comparative perspective*, Westport, CT, Praeger.

Vanhanen, Tatu (1997), *Prospects of Democracy: a study of 172 countries*, London, Routledge.

Van Mierlo, H.J.G.A. (1986), 'Depillarisation and the decline of consociationalism in the Netherlands, 1970–85', *West European Politics*, 9 (1), 97–119.

Various (2000), 'Solving insolvency', *New Internationalist*, January/February: 32–33.

Vogt, Evon Z. (1969), *Zinacantan. A Maya community in the highlands of Chiapas*, Cambridge, MA, The Belknap Press.

Wallerstein, Immanuel (1974), *The Modern World System*, New York, Academic Press.

Walzer, Michael, ed. (1995), *Toward a Global Civil Society*, Providence, RI, Berghahn.

Ware, Alan (1987), *Citizens, Parties and the State: a Reappraisal*, Cambridge, Polity Press.

Warren, Bill (1977), *Inflation and Wages in Underdeveloped Countries: India, Peru and Turkey, 1939–1960*, London, Frank Cass.

Weaver, D.B. (1999), *Ecotourism in the Less Developed World*, Wallingford, CAB International.

Weber, Max (1964), *The Theory of Social and Economic Organisation*, New York, The Free Press, trans. by A.M. Henderson and Talcott Parsons.

Weinbaum, Marvin G. (1972), 'Afghanistan: Nonparty parliamentary democracy', *Journal of Developing Areas*, 7 (1), 57–64.

Weiner, Myron (1962), *The Politics of Scarcity: public pressure and political response in India*. Chicago, University of Chicago Press.

Weinstein, Martin (1975), *Uruguay: the politics of failure*, Westport, CN, Greenwood Press.

Weymar, F.H. (1968), *The Dynamics of the World Cocoa Market*, Cambridge, MA, MIT Press.

White, Howard and Woestman, Lois (1994), 'The quality of aid: measuring trends in donor performance', *Development and Change*, 25, 527–54.

Whitehead, Ann (1990), 'Food crisis and gender conflict in the African countryside', in Henry Bernstein, Ben Crow, Maureen Mackintosh and Charlotte

Martin, eds, *The Food Question: profits versus people?*, London, Earthscan Publications, 54–68.

Wijkman, Anders and Timberlake, Lloyd (1984), *Natural Disasters: acts of God or acts of Man?*, London, Earthscan.

Wiking, Staffan (1983), *Military Coups in Sub-Saharan Africa: how to justify illegal assumptions of power*, Uppsala, Scandinavian Institute of African Studies.

Wiles, Peter (1969), 'A syndrome, not a doctrine: some elementary theses on populism', in Ghita Ionescu and Ernest Gellner, eds, *Populism: its meaning and national characteristics*, New York, Macmillan.

Williams, Gavin and Turner, Terisa (1978), 'Nigeria', in John Dunn, ed., *West African States: failure and promise; a study in comparative politics*, Cambridge, Cambridge University Press.

Williams, Robert (1987), *Political Corruption in Africa*, Aldershot, Gower.

Williamson, J. (1999), 'What Should the World Bank Think About the Washington Consensus', Institute for International Economics, Washington, D.C., July 1999, http://www.iie.com/papers/williamson0799.htm. Published subsequently in the *World Bank Research Observer*, 2000.

Wilson, E.O., ed. (1988), *Biodiversity*, Washington, National Academy Press.

Wolf, E.R. (1969), *Peasant Wars of the Twentieth Century*, New York, Harper & Row.

Wood, David (2000), 'The Peruvian press under recent authoritarian regimes, with special reference to the *autogolpe* of President Fujimori', *Bulletin of Latin American Research*, **19** (1), 17–32.

World Bank (1992), *World Development Report 1992*, Oxford, Oxford University Press.

World Bank (1994), *World Development Report 1994*, Oxford, Oxford University Press.

World Bank (1997), *World Development Report 1997*, Oxford, Oxford University Press.

World Bank (1999), *World Development Report 1999*, Oxford, Oxford University Press.

World Bank (2005), *World Development Report 2005*, Oxford, Oxford University Press.

World Commission on Environment and Development (WCED) (1987), *Our Common Future (The Brundtland Report)*, Oxford, Oxford University Press.

World Health Organisation (WHO) (1993), *World Health Statistics Annual 1993*.

World Health Organisation (1999), *World Health Statistics Annual 1999*.

Worsley, Peter (1967), *The Third World*, 2nd edn, London, Weidenfeld & Nicolson.

Wraith, Ronald and Simpkins, Edgar (1965), *Corruption in Developing Countries*, London, Allen & Unwin.

Wuthnow, Robert, Hunter, James Davison, Bergesen, Albert and Kurzweil, Edith (1984), *Cultural Analysis: the work of Peter L. Berger, Mary Douglas, Michel Foucault and Jürgen Habermas*, London, Routledge & Kegan Paul.

Index

9/11 82, 250, 254

Abu Dhabi 283
achieved status 219
advanced industrialised countries (AICs)
    4, 20, 40, 41, 44, 46, 62, 145
Afghanistan 4, 59, 79, 122, 124, 162,
    251, 259, 268, 316, 358–9, 425
Africa, globalisation and marginalisation
    of 152
African Economic Union 271
African Union (AU) 270, 300
    see also Organisation of African Unity
Agenda 21 197, 409, 416, 418–19
AGENDA FOR GREATER
    ECONOMIC INTEGRATION
    187
agribusiness 116
agricultural revolution 154
agriculture 82–6, 367
aid
    economic 388
    food 117–18, 387–8
    foreign 164
    form of 386
    future 390–1
    importance 390
    military 385
    multilateral 387
    NGOs and 389–90
    politics of 380–3
    programme 385
    reason for 384
    tied 387
air transport 101–2

Algeria 12, 14, 54, 235, 241, 283
al-Qaeda 81, 240, 250, 251, 252, 254,
    276
aluminium 86, 87
Andean Community 187–8
Andean Pact 187, 188
Andean System of Integration 187
Andorra 124
Angola 75, 122, 209, 258, 258, 264,
    268, 271
Antigua and Barbuda 189
anti-poverty approach to development 25
Arab League 272–3
Arab Maghreb Union (UMA) 271
Argentina 6, 8, 18, 28, 44, 66, 90,
    149–51, 155, 156, 165, 174–5,
    180, 188, 201, 210, 214, 217,
    267, 268, 313, 316, 320, 349–50
Argentine Revolution 37
armed forces 344–7
Armenia 11
arms procurement 351–2
art 243
Arusha Declaration 177
ascribed status 219
Asian Tigers 31, 62, 165, 107, 165, 182,
    195
Asian tsunami (2004) 69, 70–2
assembly 307
Association of Caribbean States (ACS)
    189
Association of South-east Asian Nations
    (ASEAN) 186–7, 273
associational interest groups 311
Atlantic Charter 241

austerity measures 178
Australia 6, 90, 210, 307
authoritarianism 338–9, 347
authority 340
autogolpe 309, 343
average income 29
axis of evil 252
Azerbaijan 11

Bahamas 189, 201
Bahrain 62
balance of power 249
bananas 184–6
Bandung Afro-Asian Solidarity
    Conference (1955) 5
Bangladesh 19, 20, 22, 26, 90, 96, 115,
    124, 126, 200, 201, 206, 210, 226,
    227, 229, 292, 301, 345, 412
banks 38
Barbados 189, 395
basic needs 25, 109–10
bauxite production 86–7, 88
Belarus 11
Belgium 18, 233, 307
Belize 189, 270, 398
Benin 75, 217
Bhopal disaster 56
Biafra 300
bilateral treaties 251
billiard ball model 172
biodiversity 413–14
biomass 197
bird flu 132–4
Bolivia 44, 54, 93, 107, 162, 179, 187,
    201, 217, 220–1, 222
Bosnia 261
Botswana 75, 258, 306, 426
boundary disputes 75–9
    Ethiopia–Eritrea 76–7
BP-Amoco 54
Brandt Commission 50
Brandt Report 6, 38
Brazil 6, 9, 18, 28, 42, 44, 51, 53, 54,
    55, 61, 63, 83, 86, 90, 98, 104–5,
    114, 154, 155, 165, 179, 182,
    188, 202, 205, 208, 214, 228,
    234, 238, 266, 267, 308, 316,
    317, 361, 423
    poverty alleviation project 118–19

Bretton Woods system 61, 175–6, 180,
    387
BRIC 34
bride price 194
British Council 390
broadcasting 235–6
Brundtland Commission 406
Brundtland Report 51, 198, 373, 408–9,
    415
Brunei Darussalam 187
Bunge y Born 53
bureaucracy 212–13
bureaucratic-authoritarianism 44
Burkina (Faso) 217
Burma see Myanmar
Burundi 155, 209, 425
Bush, George W. 250–2, 253, 261, 265,
    284, 414
    administration (1989–93) 273–4
business class 213–14

Cambodia 187, 264, 265
Cameroon 154
Canada 65, 86, 90, 210, 270, 284, 307
Cape Verde 258
carbon sinks 407
Caribbean Basin Initiative (CBI) 52
Caribbean islands 399
Caricom 189
cartelisation 394
cash crops 154–5
Cayman Islands 73
Chad 209, 216, 217, 268, 272, 300
charisma 327
Charter of Economic Rights and Duties
    of States (CERDS) 50, 406
chemical weapons 267–8
Chevron 54
Chile 27, 28, 44, 51, 57, 88, 93, 175,
    187, 201, 205, 217, 259, 268, 316
China 6, 13, 26, 27, 32–4, 35–6, 48, 59,
    61, 66, 68, 86, 88–9, 90, 111–13,
    116, 138, 161, 168, 169, 179,
    195, 196–7, 198, 201, 218, 268,
    274–5, 304, 355–6
cholera 120
Ciskei 211
cities 97–9, 225–6
civil rights 357

civil society 359, 363–6
civilian militarism 348–9
civilisations 230–1
clash of civilizations thesis 230
clientelism 327–8
climate change, human-induced 74
climate zones 66–8
coca 162
Coca-Cola 57
Coca-colonisation 56
cocoa 154
coercive structures 339–41
Cold War 5, 13, 36, 47, 61, 180, 186,
    249, 257, 261, 366, 371, 380
collectivisation 93, 94
Colombia 68, 162, 187, 212, 215, 228,
    250, 255, 317
colonisation 13, 233
Common Agricultural Policy (CAP) 60,
    381
Common Market for Eastern and
    Southern Africa (COMESA) 271
Commonwealth, the 273
Commonwealth of Independent States
    (CIS) 272
communications 58, 101–5, 236–8
Comoros 307
comparative advantage 40
conditionality 177, 179
conflicts 264–5
conglomerates 167
Congo, Democratic Republic 4, 5, 27, 425
    see also Zaire
Congo-Brazzaville 217
consociational democracy 363
constitution 303
constitutional government 303–7
Convention on International Trade in
    Endangered Species of Wild
    Fauna and Flora (CITES) 406,
    419
Convention on the Conservation of
    Biological Diversity 414, 416
co-optation (co-option) 340
copper 88
Cornell Peru project 214
corruption 322, 331–3
Costa Rica 159, 215, 307, 337, 398
Cote d'Ivoire 27, 53, 154, 211, 369

Cotonou Agreement 182
coups 351
Cuba 5, 17, 51, 57, 62, 73, 93, 94, 123,
    163, 208, 238, 255, 257, 264,
    265, 268, 403–4
cultural imperialism 234
culture
    concept of 231–3
    high 242–6
culture shock 234
Curacao 201

Dahomey 217
dams 75, 113, 224, 291
debt 155–60, 161
    as percentage of GNP 157
debt boomerang 161
debt crisis 155
debt service 155
debtors' cartel 156
decolonisation 367–8
decommissioning of weapons 280
deconcentration of power 279
deforestation 412–13
Del Monte 43
delegative democracy 339
democracy 320–1, 366–9
    delegative 339
    promotion 369–72
democracy assistance 370
democratic peace 249
democratisation 357, 359–63
Department of Trade and Industry (DTI,
    UK) 383
dependency 39–43
deregulation 147
desertification 407–8
developing countries, definition 4–5
Development Assistance Committee
    (DAC) 382
development, definition 3–4
development in the free market 51
development of underdevelopment 39, 41
developmentalism 38
diseases 120–1, 126–7, 132
    see also HIV/AIDS
Disney Corporation 58
division of powers 309
Doha 183

Dominica 189, 201
Dominican Republic 73, 93, 154, 249, 395, 403
drainage 72–5
drugs, narcotic, war on 161–3
dumping 392
dyadic exchange 218

Earth Summit 136, 332, 406, 409, 414, 415, 417, 418
earthquakes 72
East Asian crisis (1997) 48, 62, 164–5, 169–71, 224
East Timor (Timor Leste) 80–1, 329–30
ECOMOG 280
Economic Commission for Latin America (ECLA) 46
Economic Community of Central African States (EECAS/CEEAC) 271
Economic Community of West African States (ECOWAS) 265, 271
economic indicators 29
economic migrants 173
economic policy 146–9
Economic Processing Zones (EPZs) 195–6
Economic Support Fund (ESF) 384
economy 34
ecopolitics 404
Ecuador 154, 187, 188, 201, 214, 215, 222
education 29, 30, 134–5, 194, 206–7, 234, 241
Egypt 11, 14, 53, 179, 229, 238, 241, 322, 348
El Nino 74
El Salvador 90, 113, 254, 255, 259, 277
empowerment 25, 214, 227–8, 363–6
entrepreneurial class 213–14
environment
  development and 404–8
  democracy and 414–15
  UN and 415–20
Eritrea 249, 425
essentially-contested concept 357
Estonia 11
Ethiopia 13, 155, 209, 242, 249, 265, 258, 264, 268, 425
ethnic cleansing 277

ethnic cleavages 207–9
ethnic nationalism 323
ethnicity 228, 323–4
Europe, de-industrialisation of 426
European Community 415
European Union (EU) 181, 251, 261
exclusive definition 358
executive president 301
exploitation 193
export-oriented industrialisation (EOI) 46, 47
extended family 218, 219
Exxon 53
Exxon-Mobil 54

factions 312
family 218–20
famine 116–17, 242
fear of freedom 339
federal government 309
female circumcision (infibulation) 20
Fiji 208, 273, 307
films 239–40
First World 5, 11, 38, 56, 182, 210, 394, 396, 397, 413
five stages of development 36
food 113–18
Food and Agriculture Organization (FAO) 84, 419
Ford Foundation 37
fossil fuels 407
Four Little Tigers 47
Framework Convention on Climate Change 410, 411, 416
France 14, 46, 48, 152, 233, 300, 309
free market 419
Freedom House ratings 304–6

Gabon 154, 217
Gambia, The 75, 155, 272, 402
gender
  roles of women and men 19
  and society 193–4
  stratification by 193
  see also women
General Agreement on Tariffs and Trade (GATT) 180–3
General Agreement on Trade in Services (GATS) 181

General Electric 53
General Motors 53
geographical features 66–9
geological fault lines 72
Georgia 11
Germany 32, 38, 307
Ghana 4, 15, 53, 75, 152–3, 154, 155,
    179, 194–5, 211, 212, 217, 218,
    302, 322, 340, 371–2
Gini index 82, 92
global income tax 50
global network 235–6
global warming 74–5, 410–13, 417
globalisation 57–9, 61, 171–2, 233
Goa 397
Gold Coast 18, 152
    see also Ghana
Green Revolution 83, 115–16, 145
greenhouse gases 407, 410, 417
Grenada 163, 189, 255, 257, 307
Gross Domestic Product (GDP) see
    Gross National Income
Gross National Income (GNI) 3, 27, 28,
    29, 181
Gross National Product (GNP) 7, 10,
    53, 423
Group of Seven (G7) 158, 269
Group of Eight (G8) 38, 51
Guatemala 88, 110, 113, 216, 222, 254,
    268, 277
Guinea-Bissau 258, 369
Gulf War (1991) 229, 275–7, 282
Guyana 86, 189, 201, 208–9, 270

Haiti 73, 308
Hawaii 308
head of government 308
head of state 307
health 120–1
    see also diseases
Health for All (WHO) 121
Heavily Indebted Poorer Countries
    (HIPCs) Initiative 159, 164
hegemony 51, 60, 61, 233
    cultural 244
HIV/AIDS 20, 104, 111, 129, 130, 131,
    403, 404, 425
Honduras 249, 255
Hong Kong 47, 58, 90, 165, 168, 169

housing 131–2
Human Development Index (HDI) 29, 30
Human Development Report 29
human rights 25, 48, 49
human settlement 88–92
hydroelectric power (HEP) 111, 112
hyperinflation 175
Hyundai 46

IBM 53, 57
Iceland 337
import-substitution industrialisation (ISI)
    40, 46
inclusive definition 357
Independence and the legacy of war and
    militarism 17–19
India 5, 18, 19, 22, 27, 37, 51, 57, 92,
    116, 166, 172, 179, 182, 198–9,
    201, 202, 210, 218, 228, 229,
    241, 263–4, 266, 267, 268, 306,
    307, 313–14, 318, 345
indigenous peoples 221–5
Indonesia 6, 27, 32, 53, 88, 90, 164,
    165, 166, 168, 169, 187, 209,
    223, 229, 236, 403, 424
industrial accidents 424
infant mortality rate (IMR) 29, 122
infanticide 199
insurgency, causes of 321–3
Inter-American Commission on Human
    Rights 274
Inter-American Treaty of Reciprocal
    Assistance (Rio Pact) 270
interest aggregation 311
interest articulation 311
interest groups 310–11
intergenerational equity 408
Intergovernmental Negotiating
    Committee (INC) on Biological
    Diversity 407
intergovernmental organisations (IGOs)
    383
Intergovernmental Panel on Climate
    Change (IPCC) 407
internal colonisation 341
internal transfers 110
International Bank for Reconstruction
    and Development (IBRD) see
    World Bank

International Cocoa Organization (ICCO) 154
International Court of Justice (ICJ) 77
International Development Agency (IDA) 383
International Development Association (IDA) 179
International Finance Corporation (IFC) 383
international financial institutions (IFIs) 368, 384
International Monetary Fund (IMF) 4, 18, 52, 54, 60, 61, 146, 156, 159, 169, 175, 176–9, 180, 183, 204, 205, 210, 256, 384, 385
Compensatory Financial Facility (CFF) 177
international organisations (IOs) 172, 269, 383
international peacemaking/peacekeeping 280
International Tin Agreement (ITA) 394
International Trade Organization 180
International Whaling Commission 58
International Women's Year (1975) 25
internet 236, 238
intervention 256–60
cultural 257
diplomatic (psychological) 257
economic 256–7
foreign 249
humanitarian 249, 254, 274–5
military 256, 341–3
Iran 13, 20, 62, 222, 230, 249, 268, 281, 284, 303, 316, 328
Iran-Contra Scandal 259
Iraq 21, 54, 59, 62, 238, 252, 281, 282, 284, 289, 322
Iraq war 252–3
Ireland 27, 28
irrigation 113
Islamic Conference 273
Islamic fundamentalism 241
Israel 27, 28, 63

Jamaica 53, 73, 86, 87, 110, 164, 189, 306, 307, 395

Japan 6, 33, 38, 42, 47, 51, 53, 62, 63, 86, 90, 124, 168, 218, 227, 319
Jordan 229

Kashmir 77–9, 82
Kazakhstan 11, 66
Kenya 155, 208, 210, 211, 213, 215, 216, 257, 258, 272, 302, 401
Kiribati 62, 218
Korea 5, 63
Kuwait 107, 202–4, 238, 261, 281, 282, 283
KwaZulu 211
Kyoto protocol 251
Kyrgyz Republic 11

labour 56
land reform 92–4, 118–19
Land Reform and Poverty Alleviation Project (Brazil) 118–19
language 238
Laos 187, 209
Latin America, debt in 155–60
Latvia 11
Law of the Sea Convention 417–18
League of Arab States 272–3
Lebanon 229, 249
legal system 340
Lesotho 211
liberal democracies 36, 37, 303, 357–8
liberalisation 46
Liberation Tigers of Tamil Eelam (LTTE) 209
Liberia 4, 88, 170–1, 179, 201, 264, 265, 272, 280, 308, 349
Libya 54, 268, 272, 284, 287–8, 300
life expectancy 29, 30, 121–4
literacy 207, 227, 228
adult 29, 30
literature 244, 245–6
Lithuania 11
Lomé Convention 182
Lusaka Declaration (1970) 271
Luxembourg 337

magical realism 245
malaria 127–9
Malawi 271

Malaysia 14, 31, 53, 55, 62, 88, 154, 164, 165, 168, 169, 187, 209, 213, 223, 306, 307, 353
tsunami aid 70–2
Maldives 62, 412
Mali 217
malnutrition 114–15
mammy lorry 103
Marxism 43
Mauritania 208, 272
Mauritius 165, 209, 306
medical services 125–7
Mercator's map projection 65
Mercosur 188
Mexico 6, 8, 18, 30, 43, 54, 68, 90, 93, 114, 155, 156, 165, 195, 201, 210, 215, 222, 223, 225, 255, 307, 312, 317, 318, 320
peso crisis 170, 173
migration 97–8, 100–1, 227
refugees 80, 173
militarism 338, 347–8
military developmentalism 44, 347–9
military intervention 37, 256, 341–3
military expenditure 155
military militarism 348
mining 86–8
MINUGUA 280
mission civilisatrice 232
modernisation theory 36, 37, 362
Moldova 11, 319
Mongolia 66
Monroe Doctrine 254
monsoon 73, 74
Montreal Protocol 406
Montserrat 189
Morocco 14, 53, 77, 271, 272, 317, 323
mortality
infant 121–4
maternal 198
mountains 73
Mozambique 17, 27, 125, 258, 271, 346, 423
music 243
Myanmar (Burma) 187, 201, 209, 268, 316, 339

Namibia 4, 258, 425
nation state 299

National Endowment for Democracy (NED) 370
nationalism 299, 322–3
nation-building 300
négritude 244
neo-liberalism 37, 59–62, 110
neo-Marxism 43
neo-structuralism 61
Nepal 218
nepotism 322
Nestlé 53
Netherlands 18, 19, 96, 233, 364, 365
New Guinea 6, 223, 234
New International Economic Order (NIEO) 50
New Zealand 6, 90, 210
newly industrialised countries (NICs) 4, 42, 43, 44, 47, 48, 52, 165, 166–9, 423
newly industrialised economies (NIEs) 4, 47
news management 241–2
Nicaragua 51, 201, 249, 255, 259
nickel 88
Niger 217, 369, 425
Nigeria 14, 18, 53, 75, 90, 91, 123, 152, 154, 155, 179, 182, 205, 209, 211, 212, 217, 238, 300, 332, 368
Nkrumah, Kwame 18
nomenklatura 319
Non-Aligned Movement (NAM) 5, 260–1, 269
non-associational interest groups 311
non-discriminatory public participation principle 416
non-governmental organisations (NGOs) 172, 381–2, 389–90
Non-Proliferation Treaty 266
North American Free Trade Agreement (NAFTA) 189, 223
North Atlantic Trade Organisation (NATO) 251, 277
North Korea 267
North-South divide 38, 65, 66
nutmeg 163

official development assistance (ODA) 382, 390, 391

oil 49, 54, 281–5, 394, 425
  crises 50, 145
  Cuba 285–6
  first oil shock (1973) 282–3
  history 281–2
  Iraq 286
  Iraq and Kuwait 284–5
  Libya 286–8
  OPEC and Israel 286
  Rhodesia/Zimbabwe 285
  second oil shock (1979) 283–4
  in South–North relations 288–90
  Sudan 289–90
oligarchy 211–12
one-party state' 315–20
one-party system 317–19
OPEC 51, 288
opinion formers 240–1
opium 162–3
Organisation for Security and
    Cooperation in Europe (OSCE)
    202
Organisation of African Unity (OAU)
    270, 271, 272
Organization for Economic Cooperation
    and Development (OECD) 168–9,
    181, 382
Organization of African Unity (OAU)
    77, 186, 300
Organization of American States (OAS)
    186, 270, 288
Osama bin Laden 250
Oslo Accords (1992) 285
Ottawa Convention 251
outsourcing 37
Overseas Development Agency (UK) 383
Oxfam 381, 384
ozone hole 406

pacted transition 363
Pakistan 5, 20, 23, 90, 92, 162, 172,
    201, 210, 218, 229, 266, 267,
    268, 277, 301, 302, 305, 306,
    308, 345
pan-Africanism 244
Panama 201, 255, 273–4
Papua New Guinea 154, 194, 306
Paraguay 188, 223
parastatals 328

parliamentary systems 304, 307–8
Parsonian social theory 36
patrimonialism 326–7
patron-client relationship 328
peace dividend 251
Pearson Commission 384
peasantry 214–17
personalism 326–8
Peru 54, 88, 156, 179, 187, 188, 206,
    210, 212, 214–15, 216, 217, 222,
    268
Peters Projection 65
Philippines 6, 17, 116, 165, 187, 201,
    209, 229, 236, 308, 403
physical location 65–6
pluralism 36
political indicators 29
political parties
    elections and 311–13
    organisation of 314–15
political system analysis 36
polluter pays principle 416
population 88–91, 107, 135–8
populism 320–1
Portugal 14, 233, 258
poverty 3, 25, 30, 91, 107, 109–10, 166,
    120, 226, 321–2
Poverty Reduction Strategy Initiative 178
Poverty Reduction Strategy Papers
    (PRSPs) 178
precautionary principle 416
presidential systems 304, 308–10
primate cities 97
prior assessment principle 416
Prisoners' Dilemma 156
privatisation 147, 164, 174–5
procedural definition 357–8
promotional authoritarianism 338
protectionism 180, 181, 392
protectorates 14
public policy 310
Puerto Rico 73
Purchasing Power Parity (PPP) 28, 29

Qatar 283, 425

radio 235, 238
railways 102–3
Reagan Doctrine 259

Reaganomics 60
Reagan, Ronald 254
recession 145
Red Line Agreements 281
refugees 80, 173
regional powers 352–5
relative deprivation 322
relative economic backwardness (REB)
    38
relief 72–5
religion 194, 228–30, 323–4
representative government 362
research in the developing world 26–7
Rhodesia 258
    see also Zimbabwe
right to development 48
river basins 73
rivers 73–5, 290–3
road transport 103–5
Romania 54, 319
Royal Dutch-Shell 54
rural settlement 91–2
Russia 11, 38, 65, 233
rutile 88
Rwanda 27, 91, 154, 209, 210, 277–9

Saharan Arab Democratic Republic
    (SADR) 77
Sahrawi Republic 271
sanitation 120–1
SAPs 204, 205
Sarawak 224
satellite television 59
satellites 236
Saudi Arabia 62, 229, 283, 285, 305
Save the Children 381
sea levels, rising 417–18
Second World 5, 6, 10, 33
self-coup 309, 343
Senegal 3, 210, 211, 217
sex tourism 403–4
Seychelles 307
shanty towns 98
Sierra Leone 4, 15, 27, 75, 88, 117, 122,
    123, 124, 179, 193, 195, 200,
    213, 238, 272, 280, 319, 327,
    332, 349
Singapore 47, 51, 62, 164, 165, 168,
    171, 187, 209, 213, 360–1

Sky TV 59
slash-and-burn agriculture 83–4, 223
slavery 14, 208
Slovenia 27, 28
small island developing states (SIDS)
    105–6, 307
social cleavages 363
social exclusion 229
Social Indicators 27, 29
social provision 226–8
social services 227–8
society 300
Somalia 118, 179, 242, 258, 264, 272,
    275, 425
Soros Foundation 370
South Africa 16, 27, 28, 53, 61, 86, 210,
    211, 219, 234, 266, 268, 272,
    354, 425
South Asia 30
South Asian Association for Regional
    Cooperation (SAARC) 273
South Korea 37, 46, 47, 51, 62, 164,
    165, 166–7, 168, 169, 196, 316,
    403, 424
    New Community Movement 47
South Pacific Commission (SPC) 273
South Pacific Forum (SPF) 273
South, the 5
Southern African Development
    Community (SADC) 271
sovereignty 257
Soviet Union 5, 6, 10, 11, 27, 54, 86
    see also Russia
Spain 14, 18, 233
Spencer, Herbert 36
Sri Lanka 19, 24, 27, 68, 83, 110, 125,
    135, 201, 209, 210, 229, 238,
    280, 300, 302, 305, 306, 307,
    308, 325–6, 403
St Kitts and Nevis 189
St Lucia 62, 189, 395
St Vincent and the Grenadines 62, 189,
    308
state-building 303
strategies of industrialisation 44–8
strikes 217–18
Structural Adjustment Programmes
    (SAPs) 88, 177, 178
structural approach 362

structural differentiation 219
structural heterogeneity 41
structural-functionalism 36
substitutes for prerequisites 38
Sudan 114, 118, 229, 301, 425
sugar 54, 110
superexploitation 41
superpowers 249
supranational organisations 269
Suriname 86, 189, 270
sustainable development 406, 408–10
Swaziland 123, 201, 211
Switzerland 87, 423
Syria 229, 238

Taiwan 47, 51, 62, 165, 166, 167–8,
     423
Tajikstan 11
take-off model of development 152–3
Taliban 124, 250, 251, 425
Tamil Tigers 280, 300
Tanzania 94, 110, 207, 211, 218, 257,
     258
tariffs 174–5
Tate & Lyle 54
taxation 174–5
television 236, 239, 240
tequila crisis (1994) 62
terrorism 81–2, 162, 250, 253–4
Texaco 54
Thailand 13, 31, 164, 165, 168, 169,
     173, 187, 209, 268, 403
Thatcher, Margaret 60, 174, 273, 284
Third Wave of democratisation 304, 307
Third World 5, 13
Tibet 59
tin 107
Togo 154, 217
Tokyo Round 181
tourism 173, 394–7, 400–1
  sex 403–4
trade
  developing world and 394
  role of 391–2
  South-South 392–4
transfer pricing 174
transition approach 362
transnational corporations (TNCs) 43, 44,
     52, 53, 145, 182, 394, 396, 414
transnational links 172–3

transport 101–2
Treaty of Westphalia 172
Trinidad and Tobago 154, 189, 306, 307
tuberculosis 131
Turkey 168, 169
Turkmenistan 11

Uganda 57, 75, 208, 211, 213, 257, 316,
     425
Ukraine 11, 370
United Arab Emirates (UAE) 4, 62
United Kingdom (UK) 145, 149, 164,
     284, 288, 307
United Nations (UN) 50, 257, 268–70,
     274, 275
  Cancun Conference (1981) 51
  environment and 415–20
  Fourth World Conference on Women
     25
United Nations Commission on
     International Development 384
United Nations Commission on
     Sustainable Development 409,
     419
United Nations Conference on
     Environment and Development
     (UNCED) see Earth Summit
United Nations Conference on Tourism
     and International Travel 395
United Nations Conference on Trade
     and Development (UNCTAD) 50,
     158, 270
United Nations Conferences on Food
     and Population 25
United Nations Decade for the
     Advancement of Women 25
United Nations Decade of Development
     49
United Nations Development
     Programmes (UNDP) 389
United Nations Economic and Social
     Council (ECOSOC) 419
United Nations Economic Commission
     for Latin America (ECLA) 39
United Nations Economic Commission
     for Latin America and the
     Caribbean (ECLAC) 39
United Nations Economic, Scientific and
     Cultural Organization (UNESCO)
     51

United Nations Environment Programme (UNEP) 406–7
United Nations Food and Agriculture Organization (FAO) 113–14
United Nations General Assembly Special Session (UNGASS) 384
United Nations High Commission on Refugees (UNHCR) 389
United Nations International Children's Emergency Fund (UNICEF) 123, 127, 205, 383, 389
United Nations Mission for the Referendum in Western Sahara (MINURSO) 77
United Nations Plan of Action to Combat Desertification (PACD) 408
United Nations Working Group on Indigenous Populations 221
United States Agency for International Development (USAID) 52, 370, 384
United States of America (USA) 5, 17, 33, 36, 38, 42, 48, 51, 53, 57, 58, 65, 157, 210, 233, 285–8, 309, 319
    see also Bush, George W.
universal banking 38
Universal Declaration of Human Rights 49
Upper Volta 217
urban workers 217–18
urbanisation 95–9, 225, 226, 292
Uruguay 53, 178, 188, 205, 210, 309
Uruguay Round 62, 169, 174, 180, 181, 182
Uzbekistan 11

Venezuela 54, 107, 154, 155, 179, 187, 250, 255, 283, 304, 305, 313, 317
Vienna Declaration 49
Vietnam 5, 14, 168, 187, 197, 206, 209, 249, 264, 268, 353
Virgin Islands 73
vulcanism 73

war on terror 251, 343, 424
Washington consensus 60

water 68–9, 111–13
    international politics of 290–3
weak states 303
weapons of mass destruction (WMDs) 21, 252, 266–8
Weber, Max 36
West Indian Commission 395
Western Sahara 77
Westminster Foundation for Democracy 370
women
    and children 198–200
    and development 24–6
    education 194
    orthodoxy of development 204–5
    and political power 200–2
    religion, politics and 228–30
    rights 48
    voting rights 202–4
    work and 194–8
World Bank 4, 26, 27, 33, 52, 53, 60, 61, 146, 159, 166, 168, 169, 170, 175–6, 177, 178, 179–80, 205, 383, 384, 385, 389, 391
    classification of income 66, 67
World Commission on Environment and Development (WCED) 406, 408
World Conference on Human Rights (June 1993) 25, 48, 49
World Council of Churches 383
World Health Organization (WHO) 125, 127, 389
World Heritage Convention 406
World Systems analysis 42
World Trade Organisation (WTO) 57, 61, 62, 169, 174, 180–3, 387, 392, 395, 414
World Wide Fund for Nature (WWF) 413

Yemen 229
Yugoslavia 277

Zaire 57, 88, 212, 217, 258, 300, 316
Zambia 51, 55, 57, 75, 88, 122, 125, 179, 212, 258
Zanzibar 213
Zimbabwe 93, 94–5, 115, 122, 155, 210, 216, 272, 322, 354, 425